In the thirteenth century, Raymond Lull defied mission to the Muslims of North Africa and Eu of love and intellectual understanding of Islam. Arabic to debate and write many books in their own heart language. Fast forward to the early twentieth century when Dr Zwemer declared in a mission conference in Zurich that doors are wide open to reach Muslims if we hold the right key in our hands: that of love and deep understanding of the religion of Islam. Fast forward again to the twenty-first century, Martin Accad and Jonathan Andrews bring to us a new, yet proven approach to communicating the gospel of Jesus Christ with love and deep intellectual understanding of Islam. Together with a host of theologians and practitioners, they bring us a wealth of knowledge and biblical truths on the best approach to reaching adherents of other religions.

Henri Aoun
Strategic Outreach Projects Leader,
LifeAgape International

This book is a fantastic and unique accomplishment! Its comprehensive, multi-dimensional approach to Islam, its scholarly content which is also sensitive to real life testimonies, its respect for Muslims who are made in the image of God, and its call for preaching the good news of Christ, make this work an indispensable resource for any Christian interested in Christian-Muslim relations.

Sasan Tavassoli, PhD
Co-Founder, Pars Theological Center

This is the fruit of a unique kind of collaboration between Christians who are engaging with Muslims and Islam in the Middle East and several other contexts. Martin Accad has brought together a remarkable group of people with expertise in several disciplines – including traditional Islamic studies, biblical studies, sociology, anthropology and missiology – who actually interact with each other; and in every chapter there are significant contributions from believers from Muslim backgrounds. This is not a recycling of material readily available elsewhere, but new and original research and reflection which push the boundaries in many different directions and should force Christians to think carefully about every aspect of their relations with Muslims.

Colin Chapman
Former Lecturer in Islamic Studies,
Near East School of Theology, Beirut, Lebanon
Visiting Lecturer, Arab Baptist Theological Seminary, Beirut, Lebanon

For many years Martin Accad and the Institute of Middle East Studies (IMES) have been at the forefront of pioneering appropriate engagement between Christians and Muslims, asking questions, within their context, of how authentic Christian witness of Christian truths may be made while building sincere relationships between the faiths. The development of Accad's kerygmatic approach within his SEKAP spectrum of Christian approaches to other faiths has given much clarity for all Christian believers in our approach to sharing the good news of Jesus. This edited volume entitled *The Religious Other: A Biblical Understanding of Islam, the Qur'an and Muhammad*, gives an account of the ground-breaking annual Middle Eastern Consultations (MEC) in 2018 and 2019, the second of which I attended, finding it to be one of the most stimulating events that I have had the privilege to attend. The proceedings of the consultations, jointly edited by Accad and Jonathan Andrews, are creatively presented, interspersed with testimonies, stories and poetry. I commend this publication and indeed the consultations if opportunity presents itself to attend.

Phil Rawlings, PhD
Co-Director,
Manchester Centre for the Study of Christianity and Islam,
Nazarene Theological College, Didsbury, Manchester, UK

The religion practiced by Muslims worldwide is not monochrome – it is a broad continuum. There is not a single "Islam" – there are many Islams, just as there is a wide variation in the beliefs and practices among Muslims. This book acknowledges that variety by venturing into such issues as textual integrity, historical analysis and spiritual discernment. The book offers a broad and multi-faceted approach to Islam from a range of authors with different perspectives, based on their own backgrounds and experiences. Needless to say, there is not complete agreement on every issue by the different writers, and this is to be expected. This is also healthy – a single viewpoint would not do justice to the complexity of the topic. What they are all agreed on, however, is the necessity of dispelling the ignorance and fear held by many when Islam and Muslims are discussed. The strength of this book lies in its rigorous academic methodology, combined with a gentle love of Muslims and a humble commitment to Jesus and his gospel.

Bernie Power, ThD
Lecturer in Islamic Studies,
Melbourne School of Theology, Australia

The Religious Other is truly a gold mine created out of the Middle East Consultations (MEC) 2018 and 2019. It is well worth digging deep into this expansive range of thought, values and experience, in order to mine the true gold which will provide a valuable currency and corrective framework for us as we envisage stepping into a new era of embracing the religious other and unveiling Jesus to them.

Gordon Hickson
Co-founder,
Mahabba Network International

Institute of Middle East Studies

The Religious Other

Langham
GLOBAL LIBRARY

The Religious Other

*A Biblical Understanding of Islam,
the Qur'an and Muhammad*

General Editors

Martin Accad and Jonathan Andrews

To Angus and Sheila

With thanks for your prayerfulness for God's children and your encouragement throughout the creation of this book.

Jonathan

June 2021

Langham
GLOBAL LIBRARY

© 2020 The Arab Baptist Theological Seminary (ABTS)

Published 2020 by Langham Global Library
An imprint of Langham Publishing
www.langhampublishing.org

Langham Publishing and its imprints are a ministry of Langham Partnership

Langham Partnership
PO Box 296, Carlisle, Cumbria, CA3 9WZ, UK
www.langham.org

ISBNs:
978-1-78368-790-9 Print
978-1-83973-444-1 ePub
978-1-83973-445-8 Mobi
978-1-83973-446-5 PDF

Martin Accad and Jonathan Andrews hereby assert to the Publishers and the Publishers' assignees, licensees and successors in title their moral right to be identified as the Author of the General Editor's part in the Work in accordance with sections 77 and 78 of the Copyright, Designs and Patents Act 1988.

All rights reserved. No part of this publication may be reproduced, stored in a retrieval system or transmitted, in any form or by any means, electronic, mechanical, photocopying, recording or otherwise, without the prior written permission of the publisher or the Copyright Licensing Agency.

Requests to reuse content from Langham Publishing are processed through PLSclear. Please visit www.plsclear.com to complete your request.

All Scripture quotations, unless otherwise indicated, are taken from the Holy Bible, New International Version®, NIV®. Copyright ©1973, 1978, 1984, 2011 by Biblica, Inc.™ Used by permission of Zondervan.

Most qur'anic citations, except where explicitly stated, are taken from Safi Kaskas, trans., *The Qur'an: A Contemporary Understanding* (Fairfax: Bridges of Reconciliation, 2015). Used by permission from the author.

British Library Cataloguing-in-Publication Data
A catalogue record for this book is available from the British Library.

ISBN: 978-1-78368-790-9

Cover & Book Design: projectluz.com

Langham Partnership actively supports theological dialogue and an author's right to publish but does not necessarily endorse the views and opinions set forth here or in works referenced within this publication, nor can we guarantee technical and grammatical correctness. Langham Partnership does not accept any responsibility or liability to persons or property as a consequence of the reading, use or interpretation of its published content.

This book is dedicated to

. . . past generations of Christians who have engaged with Islam and Muslims (courageously and sometimes at great personal cost); current generations who are living in uniquely troubled times; and future generations for whom we hope this book will be an insightful gift and a tool that contributes toward peaceful relations with their Muslim neighbors.

. . . followers of Jesus who were born in the Christian tradition, in the Muslim tradition, in other faith traditions, and in no faith tradition at all.

. . . the global church. Developing a biblical and theological understanding of Islam is a long overdue task for the church globally.

May this book be an offering of peace and truth which contributes to the common good and to the emergence of more peaceful societies for the glory of God.

Contents

Preface xv

Acknowledgements xix

Introduction: Engaging Kerygmatically in a Multifaith World 1

Abbreviations 7

Part I: Considering the Religious Other

1   The Challenge of Religious Diversity 11
    1.1 Jonah: An Encounter with God in the School of Creation   11
    1.2 Something New, Something Old: The Challenge of
        Religious Diversity   13
    1.3 Susan's Story: Visit and Love the Other   20
    1.4 View of Islam: Between Demonization and Idealization   22
    1.5 Muhammad's Story: Dialogue with Sheikhs and Lay Muslims   28
    1.6 Beyond the Religious Divide: Development in a Multicultural
        Society   31
    1.7 The Tender Samaritan   34
    Concluding Reflections and Questions for Discussion   36

2   Toward a Biblical Understanding. 37
    2.1 Naaman the Syrian: Four Responses to the Religious Other   37
    2.2 Do You See What I See: The Story of Hagar   42
    2.3 Paul in Athens (Acts 17:16–34): A Babbler or an Evangelistic
        Scholar of Religion?   52
    2.4 There Is No Difference: A Pauline Anthropology of the
        Religious Other   61
    2.5 The Questions: Scripture and the Religious Other   66
    2.6 Christian Zionism and Mission: How Does Our Understanding of
        Christianity Impact Our Witness in the World?   74
    2.7 A Conversation among Friends: On the Abrahamic Family, Old
        Testament Law, Zionism and Sin, Punishment and Grace   81
    Concluding Reflections and Questions for Discussion   86

3   Looking at Religion and Society 87
    3.1 Christianity, Islam and the Secular: Learning from and through
        the Social Sciences   87
    3.2 Religion in a Shared Society: Finding Peace in a Fractured Society   96
    3.3 Beyond Comparative Literature: Beyond the Sacred Page –
        Academic Engagement with the Religious Other   98
    3.4 One Question: Where Is the Shekinah?   106
    3.5 Adaptive Missiological Engagement with Islamic Contexts   108
    3.6 Beyond Cognitive Approaches to Christian Witness: Orthopathy
        and the Affective in Multifaith Contexts   117
    Concluding Reflections and Questions for Discussion   120

Part II: Thinking Biblically about Islam, the Qur'an, Muhammad and Muslims

4   Introduction to Part II...................................... 123
    Poetry by Anna Turner   123
    4.1 Developing a Biblical Theology of Islam: A Practical
        Missiology Based on Thoughtful Theology, Moving Beyond
        Pragmatic Intuition   124
    4.2 A Conversation among Friends: Jesus Christ and the
        Religious Other   133
    4.3 Opening Reflection: Jesus Is Better   134

5   Exploring Islamic Origins..................................... 141
    Poetry by Teresa Sfeir   141
    5.1 Early Christian Views of Muslims, Muhammad and the Qur'an   143
    5.2 What We Don't Know about Islamic Origins   173
    5.3 Hermeneutical Hinges: How Different Views of Religion and
        Culture Impact Interpretations of Islam   189
    5.4 Testimony 1: Hanane on Following Jesus in Morocco   203
    5.5 A Conversation among Friends: Exploring Missiological
        Implications   205

6   Thinking Biblically about the Qur'an 211
    Poetry by Anna Turner   211
    6.1 Opening Reflection: Is Intellectual Conviction Enough?   212
    6.2 Qur'an Case Study: Questions the Church Asks   213
    6.3 Testimony 2: Amal Gendi on Ministry to Muslims in the West   215
    6.4 The Honorable Qur'an: From Revelation to the Book   217

6.5 The Reception of the Character of Jonah in the Qur'an: Toward a Better Understanding of the Qur'an and Practical Implications for the Church	240
6.6 Where Do Scriptures Come From?	257
6.7 Testimony 3: Senem Ekener on Following Jesus in Turkey	273
6.8 A Conversation among Friends: Exploring Missiological Implications	276

7 Thinking Biblically about Muhammad 281

Poetry by Yasser (translated by Martin Accad)	281
7.1 Opening Reflection: Who Is This Man?	282
7.2 Muhammad Case Study: Questions the Church Asks	284
7.3 The Quest for the Historical Muhammad	285
7.4 The Seal of the Prophets: Reflections on John the Baptist and Muhammad	308
7.5 The Messengers and the Message: A Biblical Perspective on Qur'anic Prophethood	323
7.6 A Conversation among Friends: Exploring Missiological Implications	330

8 Thinking Biblically about Muslims and Salvation 335

Poetry by Anna Turner	335
8.1 Opening Reflection: From Shame to Honor	336
8.2 Salvation Case Study: Questions the Church Asks	337
8.3 Testimony 4: Shirin Bahrami on Following Jesus in Iran	338
8.4 Who Is the Other? Reconsidering "Salvation" through Classical Islamic Thought	341
8.5 Salvation Made Plain: How Some New Fellowships from Muslim Background Create Community	356
8.6 Is There a Place for Islam in God's Salvation History?	367
8.7 Testimony 5: Gamal Zaki on Following Jesus in Egypt	384
8.8 A Conversation among Friends: Exploring Missiological Implications	386

9 Thinking Biblically about Islam, Muslims and the Spirit World 393

Poetry by Teresa Sfeir	393
9.1 Opening Reflection: When Human Resources Are Inadequate	395
9.2 Testimony 6: Michel and Janane Mattar on Following Jesus among Refugee Communities in Lebanon	397

    9.3 The Powerful Helper: A Narrative Study of the Holy Spirit in Mark   400
    9.4 Christian and Muslim Perspectives on African Traditional
        Practices: A Case of Luo Funerals in Kendu Bay, Kenya   414
    9.5 Discerning Spiritual Realities in Islamic Contexts: Missional
        Reflections of a Boring Charismatic   430

Conclusion 443
    Poetry by Yasser (translated by Martin Accad)   443
    Closing Reflections and Practical Applications: A Conversation
        among Some Contributors   444
    Summary and Conclusions: Toward a Biblical Theology of Islam,
        the Qur'an, Muhammad and Muslims – An Attempt at Answering
        the Church's Questions   449

Appendix 1: Transliteration of Qur'anic Sūra Names 469

Appendix 2: Arabic Transliteration Alphabet 471

Glossary. 473

Bibliography 483

List of Contributors 505

Subject Index 513

Bible Index 525

Qur'an Index. 529

Preface

Martin Accad and Jonathan Andrews

How we, Christians, view the "religious other" affects our attitudes toward them, which will be reflected in how we interact with them, which in turn will affect how they perceive the God whom we worship and seek to serve. This applies whether the other is Muslim, Hindu, an adherent of Judaism, a hedonistic secular consumerist, or a follower of any other belief system.

What we think of the other is shaped by our theology, either consciously or otherwise. Human beings naturally and relatively instinctively develop notions of those who are different from them based on social collective memory and personal experience. Yet a faith community that relates to the teaching and model of Jesus cannot stop there. The New Testament challenges those common notions and entreats us to develop our understanding of the "other" in a far more intentional manner. Where this concept is best reflected is in Jesus's teaching that his followers should love their enemies. There is nothing in general wisdom or social convention that requires normal citizens to love their enemy. Such a heart-level value has to be embraced very intentionally before it can affect our attitudes and relational approaches. At some point, Jesus's instruction will need to be carefully explored and theologized. Its implications in practice and its impact on our personal life – both positive and negative – will need to be considered and quite intentionally embraced. There is nothing intuitive about this injunction. It truly is a "theological" demand.

Within much of the Middle East we therefore need to be aware that our "theology of Islam" impacts our attitude, approach and ultimately the outcome of our witness. What is our theology of Islam – or indeed, of any other non-Christian belief system? We each have one, even if we are unaware of it. The premise underpinning this book is that proactively exploring our presumptions and developing a conscious awareness of our understanding will improve the quality and effectiveness of our engagement as Christians with other people. It aids us in fulfilling both the great commission to make disciples and the great commandment to love others. It is crucial to being effective salt and light.

One essential element as we begin our exploration is to recognize that Christianity and Islam embrace a variety of theological understandings and religious practices. Consequently, we must avoid painting Islam as one entity and presuming that all Muslims are the same. The same can be said for many religions and belief systems, including Christianity.

This book is based on two consultations organized by the Institute of Middle East Studies and held at the Arab Baptist Theological Seminary in Beirut in June 2018 and June 2019. The first of these had the title "Jesus Christ and the Religious Other"; the second, "Thinking Biblically about Muslims, Muhammad and the Qur'an: Practical Implications for the Church Today." This book's title is derived from these.

The first consultation provided the contents for Part I where we look at the place of religion in society and acknowledge that the Bible was written in a multi-religious context. This part introduces a number of themes.

One theme is what we see or observe in scripture, in society and in the interactions of adherents of different religious beliefs. What is it that we see, and how carefully do we look? A second and related theme is what are the right questions to be asking? The right questions will aid our observing. A third theme is being willing to learn from those who are different from ourselves. It is by design that the contributors to this book come from a variety of geographic backgrounds, including four continents as well as the Middle East.

One participant reminded us – the audience then and readers now – of the childhood experience of being in a room full of mirrors, each of which distorted one's view of oneself. In 1 Corinthians 13:12 Paul reminds us that we have a partial view of God; a full, clear view is not possible in this world. Just as we strive to see God more clearly, to understand him more fully, so we acknowledge that others are likewise striving for a clearer view of God. If we can see more clearly, then that is because of God's grace toward us. Similarly, let us seek God's help in striving to get a clearer view of "the religious other" and how we might better relate to them.

The second consultation had five themes, which form the titles of chapters 5 to 9. At the core of each theme were three keynote presentations. We framed each of these with a blend of poetry, devotional reflections on scriptures, case studies, interviews with practitioners and panel discussions between imaginary friends. These panels, each entitled "a Conversation among Friends," bring three disciples of Jesus together – from Jewish, Christian and Muslim religious backgrounds. They engage in a moderated discussion that seeks to draw the material of the chapter together in a more palatable way and to explore its practical implications. We also inserted one of these at the end of chapter 2 of part I (2.7), where our three imaginary friends engaged in conversation on some sensitive topics. All the various pieces around the core keynotes are derived from the two consultations, but they are weaved together with a good deal of creative license in the hope of making the book accessible to the broadest possible audience.

Needless to say that, as editors, we do not have to agree or be entirely comfortable with everything that was said in order to include it in this volume. Some presuppositions, exegetical and theological nuances, or stretching of boundaries we were not always comfortable with. A position on Islam may have felt overly conservative to us here, a view of salvation overly progressive or bold there. But we felt it important, nevertheless, that a sufficiently broad scope of Christian voices be represented. The point is to get us moving "toward a biblical understanding of Islam, the Qur'an and Muhammad," recognizing that the path to new territory requires human courage but also divine grace and mercy.

Two central doctrines of Christianity are the incarnation and the triune nature of the one true God. These are problematic to Muslims and yet also profoundly significant in witness amongst them. A central tenet is that God is missional, actively seeking a relationship with every human being. Yet many Christians have some degree of reluctance to reach out with the good news of Jesus to those who are different from themselves. One term used by some for this phenomenon is the Jonah Syndrome.

The motivation of this book is to encourage us to be more intentional in our thinking about "the other" – non-Christians – so that the triune God is seen in every encounter with them, be that casual human interaction in the course of daily life or intentional Christian engagement. Our goal is greater clarity in making Jesus accessible to all.

Acknowledgements

Our thanks to all those who spoke at the consultations in June 2018 and June 2019 upon which this book is based. Our thanks as well to the organizers, particularly Jesse Wheeler, who managed both of those events, but also to the entire team of the Institute of Middle East Studies and the Arab Baptist Theological Seminary for their outstanding work of bringing these important events together for the service of the church. We especially appreciated the work of the listeners group as they sought to summarize each day's presentations. In 2018, this group was ably chaired by Chaden Hani with assistance from Ali Khalil; in 2019, it was astutely overseen by Carla Nelson.

A number of people provided helpful comments and suggestions after reviewing drafts of various sections of this book, including many of the contributors as well as Malcom Catto, David Hunt, Gordon Grüneberg and Alison Pascoe. We are grateful to each of you.

We would like to express our thanks to Dr Safi Kaskas, who graciously and generously allowed us to use his translation of the Qur'an for most of the citations in this volume. The flowing contemporary English style of his translation adds necessary readability to the qur'anic text for a readership that may not be familiar with the Muslim scripture. For ease of reference, we have decided to include both the transliteration of the Arabic name of the sūra (the usual preference of a Muslim familiar with the text), as well as the sūra number (for the less initiated), followed by the verse number for all qur'anic citations. A list of sūras with transliterated names and numbers can be found in appendix 1.

The reader will also note that we have omitted the use of honorifics for the Qur'an and Muhammad, except in Issa Diab's contribution (6.4) and a few other places where usage reflects the personal choice of authors, as well as for Jesus and other prophets. This omission should not in any way convey disrespect or inappropriate familiarity toward the subjects discussed. It is merely a pragmatic decision for the sake of better flow in the text.

As far as possible, we have tried to minimize the technical transliteration of Arabic words. Where we assumed a word was familiar enough to the reader, such as Hadith or Hijra, we have omitted diacritical points. Where words are more technical, such as *asbāb an-nuzūl* or *isnād*, we have included them. As such things vary from one reader to the next, we have provided a comprehensive list of these terms in the glossary. Words in the book that are bold can be found in the glossary. To note as well is that only Arabic words have been translated with diacritical points. Syriac words, when occurring, have been rendered without them, with the assumption that most of our readers would be less familiar with Syriac.

Our concern throughout the process of collecting this volume was to make it readable and useful for a general audience, but also of interest to the more technical reader. We hope to have succeeded.

Martin Accad and Jonathan Andrews
July 2020

Introduction

Engaging Kerygmatically in a Multifaith World

Martin Accad

Human relationships are complex and multidimensional. They are rarely driven by a single purpose. As suggested briefly in the preface, this book will argue that the way we think and feel about people who are religiously different from us – the "religious other" – has a deep impact on our attitude and behavior toward them. In section 1.4 of chapter 1, readers will be presented with my **SEKAP spectrum** – albeit briefly since they will be referred to other sources where they can read about it in greater detail. Amidst a cacophony of perspectives on Islam in the world today, each leading to various attitudes, behaviors and approaches, we must sadly recognize that the church is not seeing more clearly than the world. If anything, because the church tends to develop – whether we like it or not – a "theology" of things, the amount of negative information that we have often disseminated about Islam has led within the church to more prejudice, and sometimes even more discrimination toward Muslims, than in the broader population. Surely this is not acceptable. In section 1.4, I will examine the relationship of belief to behavior across the breadth of possibilities, including the middle position that I call the "**kerygmatic approach**." In this introduction, I want to focus on this median position, establishing a few of the theological milestones that will remain attached to it throughout this book.

There is an enlightening passage in Paul's second letter to his disciple Timothy, which Paul addressed to him from prison as he awaited execution in Rome. I find this passage particularly enlightening because Paul speaks of his opportunity to present his "first defense" before the Roman court system (2 Tim 4:16). This occasion represented a precious opportunity for a prisoner to offer an *apologia*, in other words to defend himself. If he succeeded, he might have been able to clear his case, save his own life and return to freedom. But there is a detail here that we often miss. Paul in fact does no such thing. What we learn from verse 17 is that, rather than use his rhetorical training and skill to build a defense for himself, Paul used this occasion instead to proclaim the gospel fully, so that "all the Gentiles might hear it":

> At my first defense (*apologia*), no one came to my support, but everyone deserted me. May it not be held against them. But the Lord stood at my side and gave me strength, so that through me the message (*to kerygma*) might be fully proclaimed and all the Gentiles might hear it. And I was delivered from the lion's mouth. (2 Tim 4:16–17)

So rather than embracing his right to self-defense, Paul gave it up for the sake of the gospel, and instead embraced the *kerygma*, Greek for "proclamation," of the gospel. He was still "delivered from the lion's mouth" for a time, but he was under no illusion for the long term. He simply knew that eventually the Lord would "bring me safely to his heavenly kingdom" (2 Tim 4:18). This conscious choice, modeled by Paul, instructs us that we are in the business of "proclaiming" the gospel rather than defending ourselves and our ideology. What, then, is the posture and content of this kerygma?

The kerygmatic approach understands that the heart of the gospel is the proclamation of the values, character and teaching modeled in the person of Jesus Christ. As such, it is supra-religious and centered on Christ; it is respectful and loving toward Muslims; and it is prophetic and scientifically honest. I will expand on these six components in pairs to lay out the kerygmatic foundation of this book.

Supra-Religious and Christ-Centered

The Christ-centeredness of the kerygmatic approach represents a challenge to institutional religion. To say that it is Christ-centered means that it is not Christianity centered. This statement still needs interpretation, for it is not simply a reaction to institutionalism. In some societies, when you say that you are a Christian, you are actually making a statement of faith. You are saying that you have a personal commitment and loyalty to Christ and that you belong to a community of faith with Christ at its core. In other words, you are saying that you are "of Christ," which is the actual meaning of the Greek *Xristianos* and the original meaning of "Christian," and you are affirming that you are "in Christ," *en Xristo* in Greek, which is the Apostle Paul's take on being "reborn" into Christ.[1] If you live in such a society, then by all means continue to preach Christ by inviting people to "become Christian."

In other societies, however, when you say that you are a Christian, you are making a political and sociological statement. You are affirming your loyalty to a specific social or ethnic group, with a few options for political allegiance. This is the case in Lebanon. If I say that I am a Christian in Lebanon, my interlocutor is likely to ask next whether I am an Orthodox or a Maronite, a Protestant, an Armenian, or a Syriac. Then they will be curious to know whether my political allegiance tends toward Aoun, Geagea, Frangieh or the Kataeb – all of whom represent traditional Maronite political factions, which even possessed at a time each their militia and fought Palestinians, Muslims and often one another through the **Lebanese civil war** (1975–1991). Given these realities, I am quite keen on preaching Christ, rather than – or even in *contrast* to – Christianity.

Things become even more serious if you were not born into a Christian family but decide at one point in your life that you want to become a follower and disciple of Jesus. It is not difficult to imagine, in light of the description above, how your family would view your conversion as treason if you suddenly announced to them that you have become "a Christian!" This is a question of "translation." Your intention is to communicate spiritual redirection and loyalty to Christ, yet your words are understood as treason and a shift in socio-political loyalties. If the latter is not the biblical meaning of discipleship, then the kerygmatic approach will always seek to advance a supra-religious program and a Christ-centered message.

Respectful and Loving

Missionary religions, such as Christianity and Islam, often win converts each at the expense of the other. By painting Islam negatively, I affirm the superiority of Christianity. By demonstrating the absurdity of Christian doctrine, a Muslim proclaims the triumph of Islam. The problem with this approach is that it does justice neither to the diversity that exists within each religion, nor to the complexity and inner integrity of each faith system as a whole. By painting a travesty of the other, we disrespect each other deeply, and at least

---

1. I undertook a more detailed exegesis of this Pauline expression and its relationship to the Johannine concept of "new birth" in Martin Accad, "Mission at the Intersection of Religion and Empire," *International Journal of Frontier Missiology* 28, no. 4 (Winter 2011): esp. 184–185.

for those who claim allegiance to Christ, surely disrespect is not a manifestation of love – Jesus's most central command.

Love begins with the hard task of knowing genuinely and honestly. When we love someone, we avoid stereotyping them. If I tell my son, "you are always messy," or my wife, "you are always late," I am not doing justice to certain circumstances that may have led to a specific behavior. It may be, for example, that my son's room is messy because he has not yet learned how to fold his clothes and has no patience for them at his age, but that he is quite well organized when it comes to placing his football stickers in the right place in his sticker book. And if I learned to give equal attention to pleasant situations as to unpleasant ones and to be more grateful, I am quite sure that I would find that my wife is on time at least as often as she is late. Stereotyping locks my loved ones into clichés that slowly poison our relationship. It essentializes their behavior into a single type. It denies the diversity of my experience with them.

In the same way, if I say that "Islam is a religion of violence," or if a Muslim says that "all Christians are immoral" because of what they see broadcast on Western television, then we are stereotyping each other and denying the diversity that exists in our communities. My experience growing up and currently living on the Muslim-majority side of Beirut tells me that most Muslims are in fact peaceful and loving neighbors, brimming with hospitality and kindness. Muslims, too, know better about Christian morality, otherwise evangelical schools in Lebanon would not be so densely populated with Muslim children, whom their parents send there precisely because of their good moral reputation. Of course there are violent people, born Muslim, who claim to be acting in the name of Islam, as we know from the recent experience of many in the Middle East. Equally, there are immoral people, born Christians, who manifest immoral behavior with a cross dangling from their necks. Christians and Muslims show respect to each other when they acknowledge that there is diversity, both within their religions and among their adherents.

Close to diversity is complexity, a concept primarily relevant to the world of ideas. If I say that Islam is essentially violent because the Qur'an permits or even encourages the use of warfare against non-Muslims, I am oversimplifying Islam and ignoring the depth and complexity of qur'anic hermeneutics. I am refusing to read the Qur'an except in its most superficial and literal sense, an approach rejected by most Christians when it comes to their Bible. In the same way, if a Muslim insists on accusing Christians of polytheism, they are ignoring the fact that the doctrine of the Trinity emerged precisely in sharp opposition to Hellenistic polytheism, seeking biblical faithfulness through a complex expression of God's nature, in tension between radical Jewish monotheism and Greek paganism.

Christians and Muslims truly demonstrate love and respect toward each other when they acknowledge the manifest diversity among their adherents and the complexity of each other's scriptural interpretation and theological ideas. For followers of Jesus, love and respect for fellow human beings are fundamental. And I know it is the case as well for faithful Muslims. These two values are core elements of the kerygmatic approach.

Prophetic and Scientifically Honest

To complement and balance the section on respect and love in our understanding of the kerygmatic approach, we must speak about scientific honesty and the prophetic stance. Respect and love are two values that belong primarily to the affective domain, whereas the prophetic voice and scientific honesty are primarily behavioral and cognitive. The diversity and complexity discussed in the previous section lead to two double-sided implications. Acknowledging diversity in Islam affirms the peaceful nature of most Muslims, but by the same token it recognizes the existence of violent individuals who claim to be the most authentic of Muslims. Acknowledging Islam's complex dimensions recognizes the legitimacy of some Muslim scholars' dismissal of the universal value of violent passages in the Qur'an. But by the same token, it accepts as legitimate as well the affirmation of most classical scholars, as well as contemporary **Islamist** scholars, that the violent verses take primacy in defining Islam by abrogating the more moderate and peaceful passages. Scientific honesty requires that we should not essentialize Islam, either for the purpose of demonizing or for the purpose of idealizing it. I have tried to demonstrate scientific honesty, with love and respect and to the best of my ability, when contrasting the Muhammad of history with the Muhammad of faith (section 7.3).

As for the prophetic, it is the stance that should permeate our engagement with Islam and Muslims. It would be easy to keep engaging with Islam and Muslims either at the intellectual level or at the emotional or pragmatic levels. The prophetic approach frames our kerygmatic engagement with Islam within a more holistic and transformational vision. It is the prophetic approach that motivates us to challenge the general status quo that dominates the church's stance vis-à-vis Islam – as proposed for example in the preceding section. So, crucially, the prophetic stance of the kerygmatic approach is self-critical and willing to push the traditional boundaries, as a starting point. Second, the prophetic stance dares to imagine an alternative future for Christian-Muslim relations. Where the dominant view is that we are condemned to a permanent clash of Christian and Muslim, or East–West, "civilizations," the prophetic view advances an alternative vision with new possibilities. With a perceptive biblical lens, we identify new trends in this global culture that make the present different from the past. And if the present is different, then we need not remain prisoners of past opinions, practices, patterns and relational dynamics.

What I am proposing as a framework for our attitudinal, intellectual and practical approach to the religious other, particularly Islam and Muslims, is the kerygmatic. When our stance is Christ-centered and supra-religious, practices love and respect toward all, within a scientific and prophetic approach, it may be possible to challenge the status quo and begin to imagine new possibilities for our world and for our future. It is within such a framework that we invite you to read the rich, varied and creative chapters in this book.

Abbreviations

ABTS	Arab Baptist Theological Seminary, located in Mansourieh, Lebanon
ATR	African Traditional Religions
CBD	Christian background disciple
CMCS	Centre for Muslim-Christian Studies, located in Oxford, UK
IJFM	International Journal of Frontier Missiology
IM	Insider Movement
IMES	Institute of Middle East Studies, located at ABTS
ISIS	Islamic State in Iraq and Syria, also known as ISIL, Islamic State in Iraq and the Levant
JBD	Jewish background disciple
KJV	King James Version
MBB	Muslim background believer, meaning someone who was a Muslim who now follows Jesus Christ
MBD	Muslim background disciple
MENA	Middle East and North Africa
NGO	non-governmental organization
SEKAP	syncretistic, existential, kerygmatic, apologetic and polemical spectrum
USA	United States of America
UK	United Kingdom

Part I

Considering the Religious Other

1

The Challenge of Religious Diversity

*The sections of this chapter have a **chiastic** structure. The first and seventh (or last) sections are biblical stories about God's people interacting with those of different religious beliefs. The second and sixth are sociological analyses, the former taking a global perspective and the latter looking at a very religiously diverse context, namely Ghana. The central three sections bring us a focus on Islam, with two testimonies of those raised in Muslim communities who became followers of Christ placed either side of a central analysis of why our view of the religious other is essential to Christian living.*

1.1 Jonah: An Encounter with God in the School of Creation

Emad Botros

Jonah chapter 4 addresses our theme. In speaking with Jonah, God also speaks to us. Jonah fled to avoid a commission from God to speak with the religious other. We must accept God's conversation and challenge to us, which requires that we examine our thoughts about how we see the religious other.

The book of Jonah is a fast-paced story. In chapter 1, God calls Jonah to go and preach in the city of Nineveh. Jonah knew this to be an important city in the world of his day. However, he does not want to go. Instead of just sitting still at home, he chooses to travel in the opposite direction, taking a ship to a distant place. God sends a storm that causes serious distress and loss to Jonah and his fellow travelers. Jonah is cast into the sea and rescued by a large fish. He then accepts God's call and commission: he travels to Nineveh where he preaches a message of God's pending judgment. Chapter 3 ends with good news as the people of Nineveh respond to Jonah's message with repentance.

Jonah remarks that he knew God to be merciful which is why his first response was to reject God's call. We can commend Jonah for knowing God's character, that he is "slow to anger and abounding in love" (Jonah 4:2). However, it is crucial that we realize that how we perceive the religious other and what we desire to see God do for them profoundly affects how we relate to them. So, our mission and all we do must begin with how we perceive the religious other and how we understand God. We need to see the other in the same way that God does, namely as a person made in his image, loved by him, and with whom he desires to have a close relationship. We should note when our view is the opposite of God's, as Jonah's was.

So, Jonah knew God well, yet his knowing the doctrine did not enable him to act well, at least prior to his time at sea. Is this true of us? Do we live out our faith well? Jonah wanted to see punishment; God wanted to see repentance. Justice rightly leads to punishment, but God's higher purpose is to seek repentance and for individuals and communities to change their ways. Jonah was challenged to complete and live out his theology: to be compassionate toward the other and allow them the opportunity to respond to God's love for them.

We see the God of creation throughout the story of Jonah in the storm, the ship, the big fish and the vine. Jonah testified to the sailors (Jonah 1:9) which again shows that he knew God's authority over creation. Ironically, Jonah accepted God's mercy toward himself but not toward the people of Nineveh, the religious other. Likewise, how do we react when we see God's mercy extended toward the other?

The hero of this story is not Jonah but the grace of God that embraces us all. God contrasts Jonah's reaction to the plant and the city (Jonah 4:6–11): Jonah felt pity for the plant but not for the people. God's desire is not to judge and destroy but to be merciful. God describes some of the Ninevites as "people who cannot tell their right hand from their left" (Jonah 4:11). It is a call to Jonah and us to an evaluation from God's perspective: in this story, the religious other is not the source of the problem; their ignorance is the problem with consequences for their behavior. Let us look deeply into the reasons why others behave as they do. The New Testament includes imagery that we are not fighting human beings but sin and ignorance (e.g. Eph 6:12).

We observe the presence of anger within Jonah. We see too that God addresses Jonah's theology, thoughts and feelings. God evaluates Jonah's knowledge and inner thoughts; Jonah needs God to show his anger to him and address it. There is a challenge here for us: to address our inner feelings and attitudes and to perceive the other as God does. Be aware that our perspective will shape, even define, our mission. We must shun caring only for our own. God taught Jonah to have mercy for the other, to care for the other.

We must live and act in the light of God's care, love and mercy for all, allowing God to shape all our attitudes. We should seek the Spirit's guidance toward this.

The term "Jonah Syndrome" is used by some to refer to the reluctance of some Christians to engage with the other. Do we want to see God's blessings spread to others?

1.2 Something New, Something Old: The Challenge of Religious Diversity

Richard McCallum

By training I am a sociologist of religion, but really I am a "jack of all trades." I spent ten years teaching English in Tunis and then seven years leading a large evangelical church in England before doing a PhD and moving to Oxford. Since 2013, I have been based at the Centre for Muslim-Christian Studies in Oxford where our vision is "wisdom and hope in Christian–Muslim relations through transformed minds" – part of what this book is about. We are a Christian center which offers hospitality to both Christian and Muslim scholars to come and research Muslim–Christian engagement with academic rigor, so we offer in microcosm a picture of what religious diversity could look like.

This section is about the global context in which we discuss religious diversity and the questions it raises for us as Christians. As a sociologist, I want to paint a broad-stroke picture of the different factors that we would do well to bear in mind. Our contexts vary, adding to the complexity of the whole. For example, religious diversity in the West usually means ethnic and cultural diversity with all its implications for language and so on. In contrast, religious diversity in the Middle East region is not always ethnic diversity, and although there are definitely cultural differences between communities, there may well be a shared language and history. Nonetheless the factors I want to consider are global factors that I believe we cannot ignore in our considerations.

The title of this section concerns "religious diversity," not "religious pluralism." We are not advocating a pluralism informed by relativism and universalism. Rather, we are addressing an observable fact: our communities wherever we live are increasingly diverse in many ways, including religiously.

There are theological factors and historical factors. Our different narratives, both of the founding of our faiths and the subsequent behavior of followers of those faiths, is of huge importance as we consider our encounter with those of other religions. We cannot entirely dismiss and disown our histories – much as we may wish to do so. As Christians, we may have to account for the Crusades, Bosnia, Afghanistan and the Gulf Wars,[1] as much as Muslims have to deal with the early imperial expansion of Islam and **ISIS**.

Yet as we look around the world, there are new things happening. We live in momentous times. We only have to think of some of the demographic statistics in our world to know that the world is rapidly moving into troubled waters. According to a 2015 UN report, the then global population of 7.3 billion was expected to rise to 9.7 billion by 2050 and, depending on what happens to the birth rate, may reach 11.2 billion by 2100.[2]

Further, this growing population is increasingly young looking. In 2019, it was estimated that over 41 percent of human beings were under age twenty-five.[3] Age and generational factors not only have huge implications for future population, they also mean that as we discuss religious diversity, it is imperative to know what generational shifts are taking place. A few years from now our religious communities will have very different age profiles to what they have today. How is the younger generation practicing their religion? How do they view diversity? Reported disenchantment among Western young Christians is not necessarily shared by the younger generation in other religious communities who are finding new meaning in their religious identity. Further, these young people are on the move. The ageing population in Europe and the need for workers creates a strong pull factor alongside the push factors of poor economies, lack of prospects and hunger even before we think about war.[4]

---

1. These are all historical events in which some perceive that those claiming to be or perceived to be Christians acted with physical force against those of another faith. Here Gulf Wars refers to the Iran–Iraq war (1980–1988), the reversal of Iraq's invasion of Kuwait (1991) and the US-led invasion of Iraq (2003).

2. United Nations, Department of Economic and Social Affairs, "World Population Projected to Reach 9.7 Million by 2050," 29 July 2015, www.un.org/en/development/desa/news/population/2015-report.html.

3. "World Demographics Profile 2019," Index Mundi, 7 December 2019, www.indexmundi.com/world/demographics_profile.html.

4. *Note from the editors: One way to analyse patterns of migration is push and pull factors, meaning what prompts people to think of leaving their present location and what attracts them to their preferred destination. See Jonathan Andrews,* Last Resort *(Malton: Gilead Books, 2017).*

These population changes are straining the earth's resources, with huge environmental consequences including ever expanding cities, food shortages and water scarcity. We have already seen some of the effects on the MENA region, such as Turkey's dams on the Euphrates and Tigris and Israel's control of water supplies in the West Bank. There will be increasing competition for resources, and this competition may well at times have a religious aspect to it. Will this lead to conflict and war, or collaboration and service of our neighbors?

One thing appears certain: environmental factors will continue to fuel migration. The UN's International Migration Report 2017 estimated that there were "258 million people [or 3.4 percent of the world's population] living in a country other than their country of birth – an increase of 49 percent since 2000." They were living disproportionately in high-income countries: why else would you make a perilous journey half-way across the world?[5] The majority of these people are economic migrants.

In June 2018 the UNHCR stated that there were 68.5 million people around the world who have been forced from their homes. Of these, 40 million were internally displaced within their own country and 28.5 million were abroad as refugees or asylum seekers, with more than half of these people being under eighteen. Shockingly, worldwide more than twenty people were forcibly displaced every minute during 2017, with 57 percent coming from Syria, Afghanistan and South Sudan. Further, over half of them were still in the Middle East and Africa, placing great strains on neighboring countries.[6]

All forms of migration have fueled diversity around the world. We are familiar with the major religious blocs – Christian, Muslim, Hindu and others including the irreligious. A report from the Pew Forum[7] in 2017 suggested that Islam is the fastest-growing religion in the world and that it will be the largest bloc by the end of the twenty-first century.[8] Globally, Muslims had a birth rate of 2.9 compared with the global average of 2.2, and their median age was seven years below the worldwide average. In Europe, the birth rate was

---

5. United Nations, Department of Economic and Social Affairs, "The International Migration Report 2017 (Highlights)," 18 December 2017, www.un.org/development/desa/publications/international-migration-report-2017.html.

6. Note that this page is updated annually, usually in June; www.unhcr.org/uk/figures-at-a-glance.html.

7. An organisation doing research on religion and public life; www.pewforum.org.

8. Michael Lipka, "Muslims and Islam: Key Findings in the U.S. and Around the World," Pew Research Center, FactTank, 9 August 2017, www.pewresearch.org/fact-tank/2017/08/09/muslims-and-islam-key-findings-in-the-u-s-and-around-the-world/. The Pew Research Center is an organisation doing research on religion and public life: www.pewforum.org.

only 1.6, although despite alarmist YouTube videos, the Muslim birth rate in Europe was 2.1 – the replacement rate.[9] However, nation states by and large are looking increasingly diverse – and not only in the West. Pew's Religious Diversity Index ranked Singapore, Taiwan and Vietnam as the top three most religiously diverse nations. African countries which include Muslim populations such as Guinea Bissau, Togo and Ivory Coast were ranked sixth, seventh and eighth. China at number ten is hugely religiously diverse.[10]

The top three most diverse countries in the MENA region are Qatar in thirty-third place, Lebanon in forty-first and Bahrain in forty-second. The Gulf states host huge numbers of guest workers from very diverse cultures. Lebanon has been diverse for many years, and its **Sunni** and **Shi'a** dynamics remind us that intra-religious diversity can be just as challenging if not more so than inter-religious diversity.

Such migration and diversity have been made possible by a host of technological factors. Modern travel has transformed the world by enabling many people to migrate. Communication and the internet have made religious diversity obvious and relevant for all: we know more about each other than ever. Young people (and old too!) are chatting with people from different continents, cultures and religions all the time. There are no frontiers and borders on the internet. The gospel speaks into this multi-voiced context in which people are wrestling with the huge ethical issues raised by science and secularization.

Modern communication means that more than at any other time, people are aware of the differences and inequalities that exist among our civilizations. In January 2016 it was reported that the wealth of the richest 1 percent of the world's population equaled that of the other 99 percent.[11] We might add that this wealth is disproportionately owned by America and Western Europe. This can only feed the resentment of people who see these places as "Christian countries." This Western wealth has huge implications for our presentation of the gospel. This is not a new phenomenon, but we have to continually bear it in mind. Sadly, that wealth does not translate into Christian financial giving for the cause of the gospel. Many of our Muslim neighbors seem to be rather better funded than we are, and Islamic funding of **da'wa** is an economic factor we need to consider.

---

9. Lipka, "Muslims and Islam."

10. "Table: Religious Diversity Index Scores by Country," Pew Research Center, 4 April 2014, www.pewforum.org/2014/04/04/religious-diversity-index-scores-by-country/.

11. "Oxfam Says Wealth of Richest 1% Equal to Other 99%," BBC News, Business, 18 January 2019, www.bbc.com/news/business-35339475.

Ironically in the context of economic inequality, it is often the elite and middle classes that have more in common with each other across the religious divide than among co-religionists of a different economic profile. I was talking to a second-generation Bangladeshi in London who sounded a lot like some right-wing politicians as he told me that they tell their family and friends in Bangladesh, "Do not come! We do not want you! There are too many already."

While you might expect solidarity among the poor because of their struggle against injustice and poverty, often the competition for scarce resources works against the possibility of collaboration and that competition breeds hatred, resentment and eventually conflict. So, wealth often reduces tension in religious diversity whereas poverty may well increase inter-religious tension – a fact which we may want to correlate with receptivity to the gospel among different socioeconomic groups.

These economic factors remind us of some of the political realities that provide the backdrop for present religious diversity. We live in a world that still bears the marks of colonialism in previous eras. While Western empires brought much good to the world and were not always hated, there was undoubtedly huge injustice and exploitation. Some of us still face the fallout and carry the baggage of those failings. At the same time, we live in a world shaped by Arab and Islamic imperialism from a previous age. Empires have always come and gone, and we are living in a transitional period with only one current superpower but with another competitor, China, rising, not to mention the lingering influence of Russia. The fact that America is seen and even describes itself as a Christian power is another unavoidable factor in our conversation with other faiths.

How do we explain the behavior and attitudes of some who publicly call themselves Christian and yet may be an embarrassment to us? The West may be becoming more secular, but some of its leaders are often not: Barack Obama, George W. Bush, Tony Blair, David Cameron and Theresa May all identify themselves as Christian, as also does Vladimir Putin.

Partly because of the policies these politicians and their governments have pursued, a significant percentage of Muslims around the world define themselves in opposition to all things Western – secularism, democracy, capitalism and Christianity. *(We will return to this in section 3.1.)* One result of this opposition is that radicalization among Muslim young people, often fueled by cash from the Gulf, remains a significant issue that is putting a huge strain not just on security services around the world but on Muslim relations with other faith groups, particularly Christians. *(We will return to this topic in section 1.4.)*

So, while religious and cultural diversity in many countries is increasing, that does not mean it is necessarily popular. In our considerations, we must not forget our brothers and sisters who suffer persecution and discrimination because of their faith under Muslim majorities or under authoritarian and cultural domination including aggressive secularism or non-religious regimes.[12] Sadly their plight is often made worse by the association between their Christian faith and Western foreign policy and interventionism. Along with this, as much as generous-hearted liberals on the social left may want to throw the doors wide open to immigration and multiculturalism, we have seen a rise around the world in right-leaning nationalist populism that wants to build walls to keep migrants, and hence diversity, out.[13]

This reaction has led to new tensions between religion and law, which has always been problematic in the Islamic context – especially where Sharī'a coincides with national laws. However, it is also increasingly problematic in places where governments are trying to restrict immigration, combat extremism and apply stricter ideas of secularism. *(We shall return to this topic in chapter 3.)*

Matthew Kaemingk's excellent book wrestles with these polarized approaches and suggests that a nation – or in his metaphor a house – needs both walls and open doors.[14] What is missing is a table at which all can sit down to eat, talk and feel comfortable. In a sense, it is that conversation that is the subject of this book. How do Christians take part in that religiously diverse, multicultural conversation about how to build a home or create a society together? How do we have that conversation not only individually with Muslims but with a community as a whole – especially when alongside seeking the common good we also believe that we have a particular message of good news to share? We hold this conversation in the presence of many belief systems, including Islam and the secular.

Much of all this current situation is unprecedented. It is indeed something new for us. We are living in a dramatically changing world. Yet Christianity has been living with religious pluralism and diversity from the very beginning, and the church has been wrestling with these questions since its founding. How

---

12. *Note from the editors: See for example Gordon Showell-Rogers, "Victims or Heroes in the Search for Meaning?" in* The Church in Disorienting Times, *ed. Jonathan Andrews (Carlisle: Langham Global Library, 2018), 26–30.*

13. *Note from the editors: See for example Tim Marshall,* Divided: Why We're Living in an Age of Walls *(London: Elliot & Thompson, 2018).*

14. Matthew Kaemingk, *Christian Hospitality and Muslim Immigration in an Age of Fear* (Grand Rapids: Eerdmans, 2018).

did Christians live as a minority under a majority of religious Jews? How did they live in diaspora at a time of migration such as the movements of people around the Roman Empire after the destruction of the temple in Jerusalem in AD 70? How did Christians live as a minority within a pluralist religious society with multiple gods such as the Greeks concocted? How did they live under the despotic rule of religious dictators like the Roman emperors including megalomaniacs such as Nero? There is little that is entirely new in today's context, albeit greatly amplified through population growth, globalization, competition for resources and superpower politics.

Our discussion will necessarily be theological. Who are we? Who is God? What about other religions? Who are "they?" Who do "they" think God is? Other religions and religious diversity clearly pose serious questions to our theological accounts. What is truth? How do you know *your* truth is *the* truth? How exclusive or inclusive is your theology? What is history? Whose version of history is the true history?

So, we must deal with questions of **soteriology**, **missiology** and **ecclesiology**. Soteriology is about how people can be reconciled with God. How can "they" be reconciled to God? What must "they" do to be saved? This leads us into missiology, the study of mission. Who are "we" and "they" in encounter? How do we communicate? What is the gospel in their context? Can those who choose to follow Jesus remain inside their context, or do they have to leave their social network? This leads us into ecclesiology: what is the church? Are our churches fit for purpose? What does it look like when "they" want to join "us"? And also when they prefer not to do so?

We also need to keep in mind the broader context of the world in which we live. So, we need to be challenged in our political theology, meaning the theology of how we live together and organize ourselves in society while at the same time holding out a distinctive hope.

What are the political implications of our mission? Are we merely to "save" people out of society, out of the world? Or are we to transform society, to make people better citizens? How important is it that we live together in peace? Many evangelicals are talking today about peacemaking and reconciliation and starting agencies to those ends – including reconciliation with Muslims.[15] What does that even mean? Is that a distraction from our "main

---

15. See for example Salim Munayer with Samah Fakhreldein and Jesse Wheeler, "Peacebuilding in the Mission of God," in *The Missiology behind the Story*, ed. Jonathan Andrews (Carlisle: Langham Global Library, 2019), 91–105.

purpose," or is it in fact central to that mission? How do we continue to share the good news with people while also trying to live at peace?

Furthermore, what is our political theology in relation to other religions? If our societies are to be plural, what will those societies look like? As Christians, what about when we are the minority or when we are at least culturally apparently the majority? How should Christians live under a non-Christian religious majority? Especially a Muslim majority? What then of social action, law, justice and government? All huge questions.

I want to conclude with the most important factor: God. He is at work in the world through his Spirit. The wind of God is blowing everywhere – including through the House of Islam.[16] There has never been a wind or a gale like it. It is hugely encouraging and yet hugely challenging. God is doing something new. However, what do we do when we find it difficult to agree on how God is working and what exactly he is doing? We might even find it difficult to discern exactly what he is doing in different situations. How do we join in with the flow of what he wants to do through us wherever we encounter religious diversity?

So as we start this journey, we must strive for balance. We are thinking about religious diversity and the religious other while keeping Jesus Christ and his example firmly at the center: not just his historical example but also his presence and work in the world today through the Holy Spirit. He is building his church. Nothing – no religious system, not Islamism, secularism, not any amount of religious diversity, not even hell itself – can stand in his way (Matt 16:18).

1.3 Susan's Story: Visit and Love the Other

interview by Martin Accad

We come to the first of our testimonies, which leads into an analysis of how we regard Muslims. Susan Azzam is Lebanese by nationality, ethnically **Druze** *and by faith a follower of Christ. She is married and has two grown sons.*

Martin: Please describe your faith journey.

Susan: At age thirteen, I was exploring who I am, and at that time I knew nothing about Christ. My explorations continued over a period of years. Eventually,

---

16. See for example David Garrison, *A Wind in the House of Islam* (Monument: WIGTake Resources, 2014).

I came to see that God is love, and this Christian teaching drew me to accept Christ. I converted shortly before my husband. The language of love, of giving and accepting love, spoke deeply to him, as did the humility he saw in Christ. Our two sons subsequently chose to follow Christ as they saw the difference that our new faith had on our lives.

Martin: What pressures has your family faced as a consequence of this change?

Susan: Like many fellow Druze believers in Jesus, we faced a dilemma. It looked hard to remain in our community, and it looked hard to leave it. The latter would mean losing some aspects of who we are. We chose to remain, seeking to live Christ-like lives within a Druze community. At that time, there was no recognized church with a building that we could attend. So, we met with other Christ followers regularly, becoming bound together in worship by mutual relationships, not by regularity of being together in the same physical space. We noticed that people were being attracted to join by love and were introduced to the Bible. The fellowship was very biblically based.

Martin: So in your context, you can be fully Druze and a faithful disciple of Jesus.

Susan: Correct. In the Druze context, believers can remain Druze, seeing this as cultural and ethnic, but not religious. My identity card states that I am Druze, but I see this as ethnic and social, no longer as religious. Druze for me is knowing God through Jesus. The near sacrifice of Abraham's son was a starting point for my journey to Christ. We live according to the Bible, including reaching out to fellow Druze. I accept that God has put me in this situation.

Martin: Please explain how you witness to fellow Druze.

Susan: I want all Druze to see that I am one of their community. I am aware of the pressure from some Christians that I and others leave; they question the authenticity of the faith of people like me who convert and remain in their community. They seem to think that a clean break with everything is essential. Yet, it cannot be a strong testimony if someone comes to faith in Christ and immediately flees the community; we must remain and be witnesses. There is no need to be extracted from the community. My desire is that we apply and live out our faith among family and community, showing the distinctive difference that Christ makes. It is not, "I am right and you are wrong," which would alienate me from the community. I want all Druze to review their history and culture to see how much of it is actually derived from the Bible.

Martin: What are your hopes for your sons?

Susan: I desire that they marry followers of Christ; whether they are Druze or not is secondary to this. Further, that they marry in a Christian way. I have very mixed emotions with traditional Druze rites. I am encouraged when I observe changes within Druze communities.

Martin: What advice would you give to others?

Susan: Visit and love the religious other; reach into the hardest places.

1.4 View of Islam: Between Demonization and Idealization

Martin Accad

One of our central themes is that how we view the religious other will be reflected in our attitude toward them. This in turn shapes and affects how we relate to them, which influences the outcome of such encounters. Do we view religious others as people loved by God, whom he longs to bless so that they might know the fullness of his love and care? Or do we see them as deserving his judgment? The latter is where Jonah started.

A central assumption I hold is that how we view or think about Islam affects how we approach, relate to and engage with Muslims. In turn this influences the outcome and fruit of our interaction with them. What we think about Islam is significant, but so is how we feel about them – something that we will return to in chapter 3.

We live surrounded by conflicting messages about Islam. Some of these are demonizing, others idealizing. On the demonizing side, the media focus on violence, on terrorism, on events such as **9/11** and the more recent rise of **ISIS/Daesh**, or on the Muslim world's seemingly juvenile reaction to the Danish cartoons as a sign of religious intolerance.[17] Within Christian circles, some focus on **dhimmitude** and **jizya** as evidence of intolerance and the long-standing suppression and **minoritization** of Christians. Other Christians go so far as to regard Islam as a scheme of the devil that emerged with the

---

17. This was a set of cartoons depicting Islam's prophet, Muhammad, first published in Denmark on 30 September 2005. They attracted little attention when first published, but widespread protests (some of which turned violent) erupted when they were reprinted by a Norwegian paper in January 2006 and subsequently by other Western publications. These events prompted debate over freedom of expression including satire and what constitutes blasphemy.

sole purpose of defying Christian doctrines. This can lead to the wholesale demonization of the entire Muslim community.

In contrast, there is also a strong idealizing voice in the media, among politicians, and of course within the Muslim community. In apologetic and defensive reaction to violence perpetrated in the name of Islam, its depiction as a religion of peace and tolerance has become fashionable in some circles. The linguistic linking of the word "Islam" with *salam* ("peace" in Arabic) is now common, even though a competent Arabic linguist will consider the two words as cognates, deriving from the same verbal root but not exact equivalent. Interestingly, I have not encountered this argument a single time in six centuries of classical literature (eighth to fourteenth) that I have surveyed. Presumably Muslim scholars never felt the need to make this argument in the pre-modern world, where religion was rarely viewed as belonging to a different domain from politics. In rejection of violence perpetrated in the name of religion, a contemporary Muslim will easily argue that Islam is the best version of Jesus's message but that it is blemished by extremists. They might argue that Jews historically received better treatment under Muslim rule than under Christian,[18] offering the situation in medieval Andalusian Spain as a model of hospitable coexistence. In the first affirmation they might not be totally wrong; though on the model of Andalusia, other scholars have painted a different picture – one study refers to the "myth of the Andalusian paradise."[19]

The conflicting messaging about Islam, between demonization and idealization, forces us to reflect over what we believe. For it is better to do so consciously and intentionally rather than simply fall prey to social beliefs and norms that infiltrate our subconscious particularly through the media and public discourse. This is all the more important when we are convinced that our ministry and fruitfulness in advancing the values of God's kingdom are largely shaped by our attitudes toward the religious other.

In my introduction to part II, section 4.1, I will explore in greater detail three areas of Christian ministry that have become controversial among evangelicals today: the issue of the so-called "**Insider Movement**" (IM), the controversy surrounding the translation of "familial terms" such as Father and Son in so-called "Muslim-friendly" Arabic translations of the Bible, and the

---

18. See Colin Chapman, *Whose Holy City?* (Oxford: Lion Hudson, 2004), 104.

19. See Darío Fernández-Morera, *The Myth of the Andalusian Paradise: Muslims, Christians, and Jews under Islamic Rule in Medieval Spain* (Wilmington: Intercollegiate Studies Institute Books, 2016). Even though Fernández-Morera's tone often verges on polemics, he nevertheless presents sufficient evidence at least to question that the behavior of Muslim rulers in Andalusia was much more humane than that of non-Muslim rulers.

question of the legitimacy of **dialogue** in evangelical missions. Rather than expanding on these controversies in this section, I will simply advance my observation that our position on these issues is affected significantly by our view of Islam. What I believe about Islam and actually feel toward Muslims will largely determine my position on these three questions. This observation will serve as the basis of my argument for part II of this book, where I will advance that theology is to be developed intentionally and thoughtfully, rather than intuitively and in a reactionary way. Here, I simply want to advance that these three issues, though not novel in themselves, have become acutely controversial since the attacks of 11 September 2001 that brought the reality of Islam in the West from a subject of study among the intelligentsia to an object of popular opinion among the great majority of people. Sadly, more often than not these controversies are accompanied by verbally violent and unusually personal attacks between people holding different positions within the evangelical camp.

Thus, for those familiar with the IM controversy – on the extent to which it is legitimate for Muslims who come to faith in Christ to remain within their community of birth – it is not difficult to understand why someone with a demonizing view of Islam would feel quite uncomfortable with the model. Conversely, if one views Islam as a complex of interconnected layers of cultural practices and social norms and structures, as well as of spiritual beliefs, and with a long and often tumultuous history with Christianity to boot, it is normal that they would support the idea of developing a Bible translation that is sensitive to those realities and that avoids cultural and semantic pitfalls that might prevent it from communicating clearly within a Muslim worldview. Finally, unless you believe that Islam is so evil that engaging with it at the basic human level might expose you to the demonic, there is no reason why one should object to dialogical engagement with Muslims – a concept so fundamental to the incarnation and the gospel.

Over recent years, as I kept meeting with resistance within the evangelical world to the very possibility of positive engagement with Muslims and Islam, I began to develop and promote what I now call the SEKAP spectrum of Christian–Muslim interaction. It describes five positions on a spectrum of ways in which Christians engage with Muslims. SEKAP is an acronym formed from the initials of these five approaches: namely, syncretistic, existential, kerygmatic, apologetic and polemical. I have expanded on the kerygmatic approach in my introduction to this book, arguing for the adoption of a **kerygmatic** theology in our approach to the religious other. The kerygmatic is the median level (D3) on the spectrum. I have also explained this framework extensively elsewhere, and therefore need not expand on it here. But a brief description will nevertheless be helpful for our purposes.[20] We will use a chiastic structure, starting from the two ends and moving to the center.

The first of these (D1), syncretistic, presumes that all religions have some parts of the truth and that everyone may pick the elements that they wish. This approach denies the exclusive truth claims made by most major religions. Consequently, it lacks the theological depth that takes any religious tradition seriously. Therefore, although using this approach does occur in practice, it is not useful in interfaith conversation.

Moving to the other end of the spectrum (D5), the polemical approach seeks to undermine the tenets of Islam based on its sacred texts, primarily the Qur'an and **Hadith**. This approach is innately argumentative and requires detailed knowledge of narratives from Islamic sources that reflect ideas and behaviors that are frowned upon in our contemporary worldview. The polemical approach tends to paint Islam with a monochromatic, demonizing brush, failing to do justice to its inherent diversity.

The existential approach (D2) focuses on finding common ground with those of other faiths, often in the ethical outworking of religious belief in society. We might say that, as a consequence of highlighting the positive, it downplays or overlooks theological differences in order to work together on practical matters.

The apologetic approach (D4) seeks to defend Christian belief whenever challenged. It addresses the questions being asked by religious others, seeking to show the truth, relevance and application of Christian teaching. The apologetic approach generally distinguishes itself from the polemical approach, and though in its best manifestations it can be quite gracious and loving, it remains rather dogmatic in its promotion of Christianity as the superior religion.

The kerygmatic approach (D3) is rooted in the proclamation – the Greek word *kerygma* means to proclaim – of the values, character and model of Jesus Christ as the heart of the gospel. In this approach, the kerygma is not Christianity but Christ. As expounded in my introduction, the kerygmatic approach is respectful and loving toward Muslims, and it is prophetic,

---

20. See my seminal chapter, "Christian Attitudes toward Islam and Muslims: A *Kerygmatic* Approach," in *Toward Respectful Understanding and Witness among Muslims*, eds. Evelyne A. Reisacher et al. (Pasadena: William Carey Library, 2012), 29–47. Shorter presentations of the framework, used with applications in fields of current affairs, missiology and hermeneutics, can be found in Jonathan Andrews, ed., *The Church in Disorienting Times*, 94–96 and 117–120; and in Martin Accad, *Sacred Misinterpretation: Reaching across the Christian–Muslim Divide* (Grand Rapids: Eerdmans, 2019), esp. 1–33.

scientifically honest, supra-religious and centered on Christ. The conflicting messages about Islam that we get through the media, through our politicians, through our preachers and through our writers can all be located at different places along this D1–D5 spectrum of Christian–Muslim interaction. But this is not simply a horizontal classification system. It also has a vertical dimension that consists of many variables which together constitute a frame of mind, a worldview or a plausibility structure.

As I observe the world and reflect on various approaches to Islam, I see six areas – or variables – that are relevant to the nature of our engagement with the religious other. The first variable is one's religious worldview. Do I see myself as a member of one among many religions constantly engaged in conflict with one another? Though most systems of faith would fit adequately in a definition of religion as institution, where theology and practice sit comfortably with a legal and social system, Christianity in my view should resist such a description in its essence. Before coming together with the Roman empire in AD 313, being a Christian meant simply being "in Christ." But as Christianity got recognized, first as a legitimate religion of the empire, and later as the only religion recognized by the empire, Christianity became fused with Christendom. But if we are to remain faithful to the message of Christ and his gospel of the kingdom, then I believe that Christianity needs to be seen by its adherents once more as a movement inaugurated by Christ which can penetrate and permeate all spheres of life, including those typically thought of as Islamic. Jesus described this as the kingdom of God.

The second variable is one's understanding of the Islamic phenomenon, which in my view consists primarily of one's understanding of four areas: of Islam's emergence, of the Qur'an, of Muhammad and of the destiny of Muslims. As noted above, depending on where you stand along the dialogical spectrum, your view of the Islamic phenomenon might vary widely, from viewing it as a scheme of the devil to simply a natural phenomenon with no spiritual undergirding. These four areas constituting the "Islamic phenomenon" concept, along with the spiritual dimension of Islam, will form the basic framework for the five-chapter structure of Part II of this book.

The third variable addresses the purpose of the engagement of Christians with Islam and Muslims. Once again, depending on one's position along the dialogical spectrum, one might engage with Islam with the aim of discrediting and destroying it, or one's primary purpose might be to proclaim the good news of Jesus.

Furthermore, from my purpose derives the means or approach to ministry – the fourth variable. Does my understanding of Islam motivate me to engage with Muslims primarily aggressively, or through a ministry of deliverance from bondage, because I view Islam as a set of occult practices,[21] or through evangelism for the purpose of conversion, or through dialogue and peace building? Where one stands along the dialogical spectrum often determines the approach that one is willing to adopt for this interfaith interaction.

The fifth variable derives from Jesus's principle that one reaps what one sows. This variable directly ensues from the fourth. Where aggression is sown, quite often one will reap conflict. Where peace is sown, harmony and the common good are more likely to grow.

Finally, the sixth variable is our level of knowledge of Islam. To what extent are a deep knowledge and balanced understanding of Islam necessary in order to engage with Muslims authentically? Here again, whatever your position on the dialogical spectrum, a certain type and level of knowledge of Islam will ensue. You may be able to engage in syncretistic or existential interaction with little knowledge beyond Islam's broad lines. Knowledge of Islam's most negative aspects and historical moments may be sufficient to serve a polemical or even an apologetic agenda. But in order to engage with Islam kerygmatically, I would argue that you will need to have an understanding of Islam's vast diversity, supported by what I call a "legitimate" understanding of Islam's methodologies and inner functioning.[22] As a student of Islam who stands outside the faith tradition, to what extent will I want to reveal the worst or seek the best in the religion?

In closing, it is appropriate to ask about the practical applications of the SEKAP spectrum. In practice, I vary my approach depending on the situation, setting and audience. I avoid both syncretism and polemics and always seek to lean toward the kerygmatic. However, in public settings I find myself using a combination of the existential and the kerygmatic. When I am invited to take part in a public dialogue or a discussion on seeking our societies' common good, I respect the purpose of the invitation and engage with the topic at hand by adhering to the rules of dialogue, which usually requires an approach somewhere between D2 and D3 as well. If I am engaged in a peacebuilding initiative, I do not take advantage of the situation in order to launch on an evangelistic spree. When I am engaged in conversation with a leader from another religion, I am not constantly trying to proselytize him. Conversely,

---

21. See for example the approach of Mark Durie, *Liberty to the Captives: Freedom from Islam and Dhimmitude through the Cross*, 2nd ed. (Melbourne: Deror Books, 2013).

22. As an example of this, I discuss the difference between biblical and qur'anic hermeneutics in chapter 2 of my book, *Sacred Misinterpretation*, 34–74.

when engaged in private conversations with Muslims – leaders or otherwise – and they ask me a question about the Christian faith, I seek to answer in a way that reflects the teaching of the Epistle of 1 Peter, who encourages us always to "be prepared to give an answer to everyone who asks you to give the reason for the hope that you have." And in line with the Epistle's further injunction, as far as I am able I "do this with gentleness and respect" (1 Pet 3:15). So in most settings and with most people, I tend to adopt an attitude and approach that combines sometimes the existential and the kerygmatic and other times the kerygmatic and the apologetic. In all situations, I seek to highlight the values and model of Jesus. Yet in every situation I am also careful to respect the "rules of the game" to which I have been invited, all to the glory of God, for the sake of peace and reconciliation, and in the hope that I might contribute to the common good and the restoration of individuals and communities.

1.5 Muhammad's Story: Dialogue with Sheikhs and Lay Muslims

interview by Martin Accad

Our second testimony is from an Egyptian raised within a devout Muslim family who chose to become a believer in Christ. What followed was a journey of exploration as to how to express his religious beliefs appropriately. As with our first testimony, his includes staying within his community of origin as a witness to Christ and notes the need for different approaches for different audiences, in this case Islamic clerics and "ordinary" Muslims.

Martin: Welcome. Please describe your social, cultural and religious heritage.

Muhammad Al Arabi: Most of my family were members of the **Muslim Brotherhood**; they were very devout but were not extremists. I was not raised on values of hate for the religious other but very much with the safe conviction that Islam is the solution. This limited my contact with religious others. I saw myself as a *dā'iya*, an evangelist for Islam, using polemical approaches primarily. These remain my roots after I became a follower of Christ. Of note is that I remain zealous about my religious beliefs and keen to express them to others. I have fellowship with many followers of Jesus, some raised in Christian families, others from Muslim backgrounds like myself. The language we use about religion has a profound effect on others. In my case, it affected how I was accepted within churches in the initial period following my conversion: I was perceived as being deceitful, of being an infiltrator. This led to my fleeing from Egypt.

Martin: You moved to Jordan in 2013 with the objective of emigrating to the West. That did not happen. Instead, you moved to Lebanon and studied at ABTS. After graduation you returned to Egypt and your family. Please explain how your time at ABTS proved pivotal to how you approach the religious other.

Muhammad: When I arrived, you, Martin, recognized that I was an evangelist by nature. In discussion with you, I modified my approach, moving from being very polemical toward a more kerygmatic approach. Of note is that I describe myself as "a believer in Christ" not as "a Christian," a subtle but significant distinction that opens conversations. I regard the term "Muslim" as a social identifier, not as a theology or belief system, since this is how it is frequently used in society.[23] How I engage with Muslims has changed. Immediately after my conversion, my goal was saving them from hell. After my first year of study, I visited Egypt during the summer recess. I asked an imam if I could speak in a mosque. He agreed and I talked about Christ. Subsequently, I have been invited to speak on several occasions. I have also met with a sheikh and am pleased that he now offers lifts to Christians in his car. The mosque leaders do not expect me to adhere to the Muslim times of prayer. They recognize that I have studied Christianity, and they ask me about what I have learned. We have a relationship that allows us to address our differences.

Martin: So, how do you view Islam?

Muhammad: It is an idea, neither heavenly nor satanic, that has taken many people to a new place. At its historic origin in Arabia, it called people to worship the one God and was one of many ideas to do this. Islam has endured. In my discussions with the sheikh, if I said that "Islam is satanic," then the conversation would end. I endeavor to think like a Muslim, sensitive to their questions about their own faith and aware of what they think about Jesus. My

---

23. *Note from the editors: This use of the religious terms – Muslim and Christian – as social labels is prevalent across the Middle East. Such a label is assigned to everyone at birth and is recorded on birth certificates, identity cards (in many countries), and government computer systems. It determines which religiously based court system is applicable for Personal Status Law matters such as marriage, religious education of children, divorce, custody, burial and inheritance. A critique of this issue is given in Jonathan Andrews,* Identity Crisis *(Malton: Gilead Books, 2016). This book argues that this system has profound significance for the whole of society.*

goal in dialogue is to slowly broaden their understanding of who Jesus truly is. Doing this must include speaking well of Muslims, though I do not dwell on Islam. To repeat, if I were to view Islam as satanic, then I would have only one goal, namely that the other leaves Islam, and this would inevitably involve a combative approach. I think this would be ineffective. Instead, I take a more dialogical approach.

Martin: How do you handle having to interact with both Christians and Muslims?

Muhammad: I am well aware that I operate in two very different spheres: when I am with Muslims and when I am with followers of Christ. Further, I need to vary my approach with different Muslims. My approach with the sheikh is different from that with "lay" Muslims. As a former evangelist for Islam, I know how those wanting to challenge me will begin. For some, they simply say their speech and the conversation ends. However, others move on to engagement, and I can begin to address the obstacles they see in our faith, including the divinity of Christ, the crucifixion and the alleged corruption of the Bible. So, as well as broadening their view of Jesus, I seek to change their view of the Bible. I can see the context changing; for example, the sheikh is modifying his attitude toward Christians. This is creating more opportunities for dialogue with the religious other.

Martin: How do Christians respond to your engagement with Muslims?

Muhammad: Alas, some doubt the authenticity of my being a follower of Christ. Susan made a similar remark *(see 1.3 above)*.

Martin: Please tell us about your family.

Muhammad: My wife has stood with me throughout, though she is not yet a believer in Christ: she has stayed with the "other." She has, though, told a friend that "he has changed, and I have changed." We have four children. Will my daughters marry Muslims or Christians? I endeavor to think biblically and intend to look at whether their suitors are honorable men. When the youngest was born, some urged me to choose a name that would work in both Christian and Muslim communities. I resisted this: why treat people according to their name? We must challenge assumptions about people based on names: we should engage with people based on their actual beliefs. When my third child started school, she was placed in the Christian class based on her name. Subsequently, the school realized that she should be in the Muslim class because that was what was on her birth certificate. My desire is that she lives well, which is much more than according to some simplistic Muslim–Christian duality.

Martin: What advice would you give to others about relating to the religious other?

Muhammad: I have visited a Druze church and seen that these brothers and sisters are authentically Druze and devout followers of Christ. They live within their communities without compromising their faith in Christ or biblical principles. Their example complemented my theological studies. I used to interact with religious others by arguing; now I seek to be a well-discipled believer that people enjoy interacting with, whatever their religious beliefs.

1.6 Beyond the Religious Divide: Development in a Multicultural Society

Rose Mary Amenga-Etego

Like many human beings, I grew up wondering who I am. Similarly, listening to the discussions in this consultation on "Jesus Christ and the Religious Other," I have asked the same question again: Where do I fit in this world? Am I included, or am I being left out?

I was born into a Catholic family, which is one reason for being called Mary. At least, I say a Catholic family because my father was. Having lost my mother early, my maternal grandmother helped to nurture me, though she continued to follow the traditional religious practices. Other relatives were adherents of Islam. Yet, we lived as family. My grandmother told family members to worship according to their beliefs. So I grew up in a very religiously diverse setting. It is in this context that I understand the term "religion" as being the search for a loving relationship with the seen and the unseen. Such an endeavor contains many embedded elements including environmental, sociocultural, political, linguistic, community, clan, family and ancestral histories. Many of these elements are corporate or collective in cultural study terms, yet this religious search is very personal, and individual experiences are deeply significant.

My country, Ghana, is significant in this context. It is a secular nation, and its people are of various ethnicities. Many of these ethnicities can be viewed as theocratic communities, even as small states within the nation. The three major religions are Christianity, Islam and indigenous belief systems.[24] There are also small groups of adherents of Baha'i, Judaism, Buddhism and Hinduism.

Historically, Islam and Christianity came to Ghana (then Gold Coast) in the twelfth, thirteenth (especially in Dagbon) and fifteenth centuries respectively. Both faiths used the term "pagan" to describe the indigenous people and their religious practices, even though both were welcomed and understood as "another religious viewpoint." So, as exemplified in the indigenous greetings and welcoming of guests, they were welcomed and told, "Come in, be part of the mix. We want to learn from you, and we expect you to listen to us."

This situation creates a huge struggle for some Muslims and Christians. People outside of this context cannot understand this form of plurality, the blending of religious practices as we have in Ghanaian marriage and funeral rites. They call for what they regard as the pure expressions of their faiths, devoid of so-called syncretistic practices. This amounts to the importation of a foreign expression of the other (religion) in question, devoid of its current context. We must however recognize the mutual transformation of all religions within a society, which in turn affects the expressions of the religions involved.

In Ghana, Christianity and Islam are practiced in ways that may not be seen elsewhere because both have been modified by the context in unique ways. For example, before I joined academia, I worked as gender and development coordinator in the Navrongo-Bolgatanga Diocese of the Catholic Church in Ghana. The project was funded by Cordaid in the Netherlands. Though the implementing context was the Catholic Church in Ghana, and the funding body a Catholic organization, the same cannot be said about the source of the funds. Yet that did not prevent the desire for and shared need of development. Again, at the community level, although the meeting places of this project were always on Catholic Church grounds, beneficiaries were not limited to church members or Catholics. Just as the communities in the Upper East Region of Ghana are made up of Christians, Muslims and Traditionalists, beneficiaries brought in other family members and community women who were neither Catholics nor Christians. Even so, these other women did not have to convert to become beneficiaries, but their inclusion espouses the very nature of this topic.

This presentation is not to create an impression that all is well; the situation has created several struggles, including the disregard for some indigenous religio-cultural practices like the Ga Homowo festive ban on drumming and

---

24. *Note from the editors: These are referred to as African Traditional Religions by some, including in chapter 9.*

noise making, and the unguarded use of some derogatory religious and cultural terms in specific contexts. Consequently, these are potential areas for intra- and inter-religious conflicts which have the propensity to destroy property and lives. *(We will return to this topic in chapter 3.)*

It is within this context that we ask whether multi-religious societies are divided. Further, should religious differences destroy existing relationships and societies? What about our desire for development? Whose concept of development are we dealing with? Whose agenda?

Economic growth, material development, travel and connections reshape society, producing complex relationships: religious, social, cultural, political, etc. Within these complex dynamics of contemporary society, many have strived to retain family, especially the extended family ties as their source of identity. This desire can be seen clearly concerning burial rites, with many wanting to die or be buried "back home" with familiar rituals to bring closure. So in this context, it is crucial for "development" to include some provision for family and tradition.

We must live in the knowledge that contemporary society cannot be reversed. That is, the past is gone with whatever nostalgia some people may have. So also, we need to acknowledge that a multi-religious context can be dangerous in contemporary society, especially if there is a lack of knowledge about the religious other and an unwavering attachment to traditional systems and ways of life.

So, we need to review our concept of progress and reconceptualize development to ensure that they are holistic. Development must expand beyond economics and infrastructure to encompass the socio-cultural and spiritual health of the community, taking into account the collective worldviews and values of the people. That is, religion must be taken into account, irrespective of its diverse manifestations.

I long to see such an approach implemented in northern Ghana, which is underdeveloped when compared to the rest of the country. Much of what is being done in that region is being implemented by Catholic groups. I am pleased that they are doing so, and note that they are acting in ways that are inclusive of the religious other.

1.7 The Tender Samaritan

Abed Zieneldien

In Luke 10:25–37, we read about the interaction between Jesus and an expert in Jewish law. We are invited to join the audience in watching this encounter unfold. The story begins when the expert asks Jesus a question about the law and salvation. Jesus responds by asking a question in return. The expert gives Jesus an answer, which Jesus affirms. This pattern is repeated as the expert asks a second question, this time about neighborliness, an aspect of the ethical outworking of religious belief and observance. He is expecting the answer that his neighbors are fellow Jews, as was taught by most rabbis of that period. He, together with the watching audience, are stunned that Jesus extends neighborliness to include the religious other. Jesus follows the story by asking the expert a question. As with his first question, Jesus affirms the expert's answer and challenges him to, "Go and do likewise" (Luke 10:37).

The expert appears to be attempting to justify himself, to affirm his lifestyle and theology. Respect for the teacher was important in the culture of Jesus's era. The interaction begins and ends with the law. In the Judaism of the time, law keeping was linked to salvation. It was also very closely linked to the survival of the Jewish people as a distinct ethnic group living in and around Jerusalem. *(This topic will be picked up in section 3.4.)* It would seem likely that Jesus and his audience had Leviticus chapter 11 in view as the background to this incident.

A New Testament view would critique this linkage concerning salvation. As Karl Barth expressed it, "only through mercy can one acquire eternal life." Nobody can keep the law sufficiently well. (We will explore this topic further in section 2.4.) Jesus brings a radical transformation of neighborliness which challenges the social barriers in society. Who is the enemy, the outsider, the religious other? Can these people be saved?

Jesus's story in Luke 10:30–35 has seven scenes. In the first, we meet the traveler who becomes the victim of thieves. The traveler is dispossessed of everything he has with him including all his clothes. He is left alone, unconscious on the road.

In the second scene, a priest comes upon the traveler. The priest must decide whether to help the victim or not; is this a neighbor? His usual means of deciding would be based on the traveler's accent and his clothes. Neither of these work in this situation; the victim is unconscious and naked. The priest decides to continue on his way. Kenneth Bailey notes that we can safely assume that the priest is riding, since he is a businessman on a journey.

Further, to intervene entailed a serious degree of risk: he risks defiling his ritual cleanliness, which would require a seven-day purification period during which he could not work as a priest, thereby reducing his income and potentially his ability to provide for his household. Jesus's audience would have applauded the priest's decision to pass by.[25]

The third scene is a Levite coming upon the man. He might have seen the priest pass by or at least been aware that a priest was on the road ahead of him. He had an example to follow.

The fourth scene is the arrival of a Samaritan. This is a religious other to the expert and the attentive audience. The stereotype of the time would have dismissed all such people as "no good," "cannot be trusted" or "only mean to harm us." Yet this Samaritan does not go past. He stops. He expends time and effort. He ignores any risk that he might be the thieves' next victim.

The fifth scene is the Samaritan's tender actions – he cleans and binds the victim's wounds. In mind here is the picture in Isaiah 53 of the God who cleans and binds wounds, and the God who says, "I desire mercy, not sacrifice" (Hos 6:6). There is a prophetic voice here.

The sixth scene is the journey to the inn. The Samaritan puts the traveler on his donkey. In this action, he reverses the decision made by the priest. Does he have a second donkey, or is he obliged to walk the rest of the way to Jericho? On arrival, he makes a commitment to the innkeeper.

The seventh and final scene is the Samaritan giving money to the innkeeper for the traveler's care. In doing this, he reverses the actions of the thieves in scene one; he gives money rather than takes it and leaves the traveler in the inn, not alone on the road.

The challenge to the expert is to reconsider who is his neighbor, or who does God expect him to act tenderly toward. Likewise, how do we view the religious other? How does this view affect our interaction with those who are different?

Here in Lebanon, I have noticed a major shift since 2011. The historic context mitigated against us as Christians working among others, especially Syrians. This was a legacy of the **Lebanese civil war** (often dated 1975–1990) and the intervention of the Syrian army. The arrival of many Syrians from 2011 onward, displaced by conflict in their country, forced many of us to evaluate our attitude toward them. Was it one of, "Oh good, now they can feel what it is like," or was it one of compassion toward those in need? Over time, I

---

25. Kenneth E. Bailey, *Jesus through Middle Eastern Eyes* (London: SPCK, 2008), 292.

have witnessed many fellow Lebanese realizing the need and opportunity to serve others. As this has grown, so some Syrians have come to faith in Jesus.

Who can be saved, and on what basis?

Concluding Reflections and Questions for Discussion

This chapter has introduced a number of themes within our focus on our theology, attitudes and engagement with religious others. The people in our two interviews both experienced suspicion of the authenticity of their heart conversion because of their continuing engagement with the community that they were raised within. In theological terms, what is our soteriology, or who can be saved? What is our mission; can we break the Jonah Syndrome? And what is our ecclesiology; can the religious other who chooses to follow Jesus join a recognized church, or are they obliged to form new churches?

This chapter began and finished in the biblical text. In chapter 2, we focus on our scriptures. One theme is what do we see.

Questions for Discussion

1. How do we create open houses with open doors and an open table for discussions with religious others?

2. Religious belief and practice are both individual and collective: how do we find an appropriate balance?

3. How widespread is the Jonah Syndrome? How compassionate are we toward the religious other?

4. What will we risk in order to act tenderly toward the religious other? Do we desire to see them blessed by God?

2

Toward a Biblical Understanding

In this chapter, we look more deeply at our scriptures, examining a selection of specific passages together with some broad sweeps of biblical themes. We begin with the story of Naaman the Syrian. We then take a detailed look at Hagar, an Egyptian in Abraham's household, which explores the issues surrounding who is and is not of the household of faith or the people of God.

We move next to the New Testament, looking first at Paul's visit to Athens as recorded by Luke in Acts where we note Paul's contextual approach. We follow this example of Paul's practice with a survey of his theology as revealed in the Pauline epistles. There we see how he is scathing of anything and anybody outside of Christ. We look at the opening chapters of the Bible before addressing what can be a controversial topic, namely the contemporary understanding of Israel-Palestine, focusing on its effects on local Christian communities, be they ethnically Jewish, Palestinian or other. We conclude with a conversation which draws these different contributions together.

One theme in this chapter is that of seeing; how well do we read the Bible? Do we see what the authors intended? Throughout we are urged to choose carefully, wisely and compassionately how we respond to the religious other.

2.1 Naaman the Syrian: Four Responses to the Religious Other

Karen Shaw

You couldn't get much more "other" than Naaman whom we meet in 2 Kings chapter 5. Religiously, he called on the territorial gods. Politically, he was an Aramean, a Syrian, Israel's enemy. Militarily, he was head of the army, having conducted raids on Israel and enslaved captives, including children. God's people had every reason to fear and hate the man.

So it comes as a surprise when the Bible introduces Naaman in glowing terms: a great person in the eyes of the Aramean king, having a fine reputation, made victorious by God and a valiant soldier (2 Kgs 5:1). God was blessing this unclean idol-worshipper, this enemy, this terrorist – at the expense of his own covenant people.

But Naaman was also a person of great need. He had leprosy (2 Kgs 5:1), a disease that would likely cost him his friends, his status in society, his job and eventually his life. In the Old Testament, leprosy is sometimes seen as a punishment from God for rebellion – think of Miriam and King Uzziah (Num 12:10–11; 2 Chr 26:20). Any Israelite who heard about Naaman's leprosy might well have rejoiced and thought, "At last! He's getting what he deserves!" I wonder how I would respond if I heard that a senior military leader of some Islamic terrorist organization was terminally ill. You can find videos on YouTube by Christians gloating over Ahmed Deedat as he dies of cancer of the throat. How *should* we respond to someone like Naaman?

Our passage gives four strikingly different examples of how God's covenant people responded to the need of the religious other. Let's have a look at all four and consider what we might learn from them. The first is a young migrant domestic worker, kidnapped in a military skirmish, trafficked and used as cheap labor. She is only a girl. Her encounter with the religious other has already cost her family, her homeland, her liberty and her future. We don't know whether she was raped – it certainly was a common practice to rape captive virgins. Now, she spends her days serving the wife of the man responsible for the catastrophic devastation of her life.

Yet when she learns of her master's illness, her first thought is to want him well and to wish aloud that Naaman could find healing. She says two simple sentences that express faith and hope as well as love. "If only my master would see the prophet who is in Samaria! He would cure him of his leprosy" (2 Kgs 5:3). Here we find a simple, loving witness from below. Though simple, it arouses hope. It comes from one of the weakest and lowliest, and it is for one of the most powerful and highest-ranking. Yet her two sentences move to action her mistress, the commander of Aram's armies, the Aramean king and God's prophet.

I serve in a church attended by many migrant workers from Africa and Asia. Believers like these are often ignored by churches, pitied, or seen as not capable of significant mission. Yet they have access to the intimate daily lives of hundreds of thousands in this region who will never experience the love and hope of Christ any other way. Their power, as Paul puts it, is in their weakness.

Despite my years of theological education (or perhaps because of them), I am not a great evangelist. But this uneducated slave girl knows just what to say: two sentences which don't even mention God directly, but which start the seemingly unapproachable religious other on his journey of spiritual discovery. Two simple sentences said in love.

The second of God's covenant people in this story, King Jehoram, responds to the religious other with suspicion and anger.[1] It's not hard to understand why. The fate of the slave girl had nearly been his own. Naaman comes with a letter from Ben-Hedad II, the son of King Ben-Hedad I to whom Jehoram's father, Ahab, had been a vassal. When Ahab was sick of being humiliated and over-taxed, he had looked for another patron, and in retaliation, Ben-Hedad I threatened to wipe out Samaria unless Ahab allowed his palace to be looted and his wives and children given as property to the Aramean king. Ahab had been forced to agree to these terms, and only God's intervention prevented Jehoram and his family from facing brutal humiliation and captivity, and his mother and sisters from rape. Now Jehoram must answer to Ben-Hedad II. What is he to think of the letter Ben-Hedad sends him, instructing him to cure of leprosy the general who has invaded his land, killing, kidnapping and pillaging his people?

Jehoram might well be right that the Aramean king is looking for a reason to exploit and humiliate him further. After all, what does Ben-Hedad have to lose? If Naaman is cured, great! He'll have his commander back and be able to go on harassing Israel. If not, he can blame Jehoram and use it as an excuse for punishing him. Either way, he wins and Jehoram loses. So Jehoram tears his robes in dismay (2 Kgs 5:7).

Those of us who come from Christian homes can sympathize with Jehoram. Most of us have grown up on the stories of Muslim violence against Christians. We have been raised hearing the echoes of the Islamic conquests, Salah el-Din, the advance of Islam through Europe to the very gates of Vienna, centuries of **dhimmitude** and, in our lifetimes, numerous acts of terrorism and barbarism in the name of Islam. We have come to expect Muslims to be treacherous. We treat any communication from them with a hermeneutic of suspicion.

---

1. *Note from the editors: The biblical text does not name the king, and commentators vary in their identification. Some agree with Jehoram as here (sometimes shortened to Joram); others place the incident toward the end of Elisha's ministry which would be after Jehoram's reign. The point being made here about the king's reaction remains.*

And like Jehoram, we know that we are not God. We cannot perform miracles. We are weak and vulnerable in the face of Muslim aggression. But the Bible makes it clear that God was not pleased with Jehoram's response to the religious other. "When Elisha the man of God heard that the king of Israel had torn his robes, he sent him this message: 'Why have you torn your robes? Have the man come to me and he will know that there is a prophet in Israel'" (2 Kgs 5:8). We may not *be* God, but God is in our midst doing wonders, keeping his covenant, and making us a kingdom of priests for the world. If we don't act on this truth, we are practical unbelievers. Jehoram knows that there is a prophet in Israel (2 Kgs 3:10–11), but he neither wants Naaman healed, nor does he long to see God glorified by showing kindness to an enemy (a little bit like Jonah). The people of Nazareth had something of the spirit of Jehoram on the day when Jesus preached his first sermon there. They loved his preaching until he mentioned God's grace and preferential favor to a Lebanese woman and Naaman, a Syrian man, neither believers in God alone when God blessed them. At that point in the sermon, the people of Nazareth tried to kill Jesus (Luke 4:20–29).

Most of us are here because we care about religious others and long to see the grace and glory of God extended to them. Most days. But I would be surprised if there were *anyone* here who did not have a Jehoram lurking in their heart, poking his head up every now and again, saying, "See? That's what they're like. They're out to get us. Poor us. But what can we do? Nothing!" Like all of Ahab's line, that Jehoram needs to die.

The third of God's covenant people whom Naaman encounters is Elisha, the man of God, who recognizes what God is doing in Naaman's life and cooperates. I admit, I'm uncomfortable with the prophet's approach. Part of me says he should have gone out to meet Naaman and show him hospitality and respect. Didn't Elisha attend missionary training school?! He should have explained why the Jordan and not some other river, rather than leaving it to Naaman's idolatrous aides to convince him. He should have exploited Naaman's openness and gratitude after his healing in order to gain publicity for God and give the general much-needed instruction about his newfound faith. And surely Elisha should have corrected Naaman's wonky theology and practice. Taking *dirt* back to Damascus?! Really? The Lord is the only God, but I ask forgiveness in advance because I intend to fake worship to a false god in order to keep my job?!! Is anyone else uneasy with Elisha's silence? The inspired writer of scripture doesn't seem fazed at all. The Aramean commander, God's servant to punish Israel, has been healed *and* has acknowledged, at least in private, that Yahweh alone is God. Elisha is grateful for the double miracle. It is enough.

In May 2018, Prince Harry married Meghan Markle. After this royal wedding, I was amused to read some of my clergy friends' Facebook postings, critiquing Bishop Michael Curry's sermon "The Power of Love." They said, "He missed his chance to present the full gospel." And added, "He didn't define love." Or, "He failed to make personal application to the couple." All fair critiques. By contrast, secular commentators, dignitaries and celebrities sat entranced during the homily and afterwards critiqued Curry mostly for outshining even the bride. They made comments like, "If that's what sermons are like today, I might have to start going to church again." If someone had predicted *before* the wedding that the sermon would have been the highlight, he or she would have been laughed at. God does something extraordinary, witnessed by millions, and some of God's people respond by saying, "Not good enough."

Is it possible that we have such high and rigid expectations of what *ought* to happen in the life of the religious other that we fail to appreciate what God *is* doing, his power at work? The Hebrew prophet simply says to the Aramean man of war, "Go in peace" (2 Kgs 5:19)! Sometimes it is right to pronounce peace on the incomplete.

Finally, Naaman meets Gehazi, Elisha's servant. Gehazi exploits the religious other for his own benefit. How easy to rationalize it! Naaman's wealth comes, at least in part, from looting Israel. Naaman owns vast wealth and doesn't need the money, while Elisha and his servant live off charity. Elisha has *earned* the money by healing the man, and good health is worth an awful lot. Naaman offered, even urged. Gehazi is probably the servant who had brought Elisha's message out to Naaman, so he deserves something, too. Gehazi sneaks and lies to get what he thinks is rightfully his: a share of the benefits of ministry. What's a pair of suits when the general has come with at least a dozen camels and mules laden with precious metals? If this rich Aramean is going to benefit from Israel's God, Israel should get *something* in return, right?

Elisha will have nothing of it. "Is this the time to take money or to accept clothes?" he asks, sounding a tad like Jesus (2 Kgs 5:26). Elisha has got all that he wanted out of the day: God's power made known, and Naaman healed and sent off in peace. That is all we want in the religious other: God's glory, and their salvation and peace, isn't it? Or maybe not.

A friend once told me how she and her husband lost the friendship of a Muslim they had led to Christ. They had sent a picture of their friend's baptism to a supporting church in New York with the usual warning not to publish or post. But a few years later, someone in the church had put the old picture on a corkboard next to an appeal for people to support the couple. It happened that their friend travelled to New York at the time, attended that very church, and saw the corkboard. He was furious. He told them, "You were making money off of me all this time, and you didn't share any of it with me."

It would be so easy to say that this former friend didn't understand how these things work, but perhaps he understood better than we care to admit. Most MBBs know that their testimonies bring in many times more publicity and funds than the testimony of someone from a secular or Christian background, not to mention their usefulness as weapons or trophies in the propaganda war between Christianity and Islam. Easily our enthusiasm for people's salvation morphs into a fixation with keeping the needed support flowing in our direction, and Muslims become a means to convincing others and even ourselves that we are successful and a good investment of the church's money. God is at work as never before among the largest and most gospel-resistant religious other. This is not the time to manipulate the signs of God's lovingkindness to enhance our image or to gain financial security. Gehazi's leprosy tells us so.

Naaman, the ultimate religious other, encounters four of God's people:

- His maid, with her simple words of love
- King Jehoram, full of suspicion and anger
- Elisha, a non-judgmental channel of God's blessing
- Gehazi, scheming how to exploit.

Which would you most like to be? God grant that we choose our answers well.

2.2 Do You See What I See: The Story of Hagar

Havilah Dharamraj[2]

In this section we test how well we can see. We look at the intermeshing stories of Abraham, Sarah and Hagar which are told in two panels, Genesis 16 and

---

2. After presenting this section and her contribution in the next chapter in Beirut in June 2018, Havilah combined them into a single presentation given at the ATA Theological Consultation held in Manila during August 2018, which was subsequently published in the *Journal of Asian Evangelical Theology*. Havilah Dharamraj, "The Curious Case of Hagar:

Genesis 21. It may be that we will surprise ourselves by detecting in these stories a motif that somehow our eyes have failed to pick up.

Hagar in Hagar's Story

Hagar is introduced as a member of the household of faith – yet we cannot help noticing the **liminality** of that membership. She is Egyptian, she is a slave and she is a woman. Further, she is introduced into the story against the fact of Sarah's continued barrenness; Hagar is less a person and more a solution to a longstanding problem.[3] In the conversations that follow between Sarah and Abraham, she is nameless, a possession – "my slave/your slave" (Gen 16:2, 5, 6). She is given to Abraham "to be his wife" (Gen 16:3) but in the very next verse we learn that the status quo has not changed. Sarah continues as her mistress (Gen 16:4b). We understand that Hagar is a wife only in function, not in status. She will "build a family" for Sarah (Gen 16:2) but can never be what Sarah is. Hagar lives on the edges of being "us."

The trouble starts when Hagar takes tentative steps away from the edges and toward the core of "us-ness," of belonging. She treats Sarah lightly, as a fertile woman would a barren co-wife. In a later period of history, Peninnah gets away with provoking the barren Hannah, year after year until Hannah, red-eyed with weeping, plunges into "deep anguish" (1 Sam 1:1–10). Even the disgruntled Rachel can only envy her co-wife Leah's fecundity (Gen 30:1) and try to increase her chances of child-bearing with aphrodisiac mandrakes (Gen 30:14). However, in contrast to Peninnah and Leah, Hagar has no immunity. She is an outsider who has arrogated to herself the place of an insider. We understand now how completely devoid of privilege is her position as Abraham's wife. Hagar understands it too: she sees that Abraham absolves himself of any obligation toward her when Sarah turns on her. Thus, in her conversation with the angel of the Lord, Hagar describes her place in the household with no illusions. She refers to Sarah as her "mistress" (Gen 16:8). Hagar has returned to her place on the edges of belonging.

Understanding her place on the periphery of belonging, Hagar now moves in the other direction, away. "I'm running away," she explains to the angel of

---

Biblical Studies and the Interdisciplinary Approach of Comparative Literature," *Journal of Asian Evangelical Theology* 23, no. 2 (2019): 49–71.

3. On whether slave surrogacy was an ancient West Asian practice or not, see J. Cheryl Exum, "The Accusing Look: The Abjection of Hagar in Art," *Religion and the Arts* 11 (2007): 143–171, here, 156 fn 34; and Victor Hamilton, *The Book of Genesis: Chapters 1–17*, NICOT (Grand Rapids: Eerdmans, 1990), 444–445.

the Lord (Gen 16:8). Where to, she does not say. However, her southerly route is suggestive: she is heading to Egypt, her home country. As an Egyptian slave in a Hebrew household, Hagar has been living, we now see, as an "other" to two communities: to the Egyptians, she would be seen as the slave-concubine of a Hebrew; to the Hebrew household, she is a slave-concubine from Egypt. When movement toward belonging is blocked on the Hebrew side, she moves toward Egypt. The "other" persistently seeks a place where they can belong. When Hagar returns to Abraham's household on the command of the angel, it is clearly as the "other," for she returns to her "mistress" and to a life of submission to that mistress (Gen 16:9).[4]

Fourteen years pass. Abraham's family now has two sons, Hagar's Ishmael and Sarah's Isaac. Between the stories of their birth is the account of the covenant of circumcision, established as the primary identifier of the unique relationship between the Lord and Abraham and his descendants. Thrice in this account, we are told that Abraham circumcised "his son Ishmael" (Gen 17:23–26). In fact, "on that very day" Abraham and his son Ishmael were both circumcised (Gen 17:26). Dozeman sees in this how "Ishmael represents an expansion of election beyond the boundaries of Israel, and as such Ishmael models the proselyte who undergoes circumcision."[5] Yet despite the divine initiative to embrace Ishmael, how easily Sarah tosses aside Ishmael's identity as an insider! Circumcised or not, he is to her the son of "that slave woman" (Gen 21:10) and as such is easily stripped of his birth-right and quickly disqualified from being (at least) one of Abraham's heirs (Gen 21:10). Ishmael's offensive action is a word-play on Isaac's name (יִצְחָק); Ishmael is (מְצַחֵק) "Isaac-ing," somehow in competition with Isaac, "threatening to take Isaac's position as the legitimate heir."[6] The outsider is immediately shown his place – literally outside the household.

Exum preferentially uses the psychological term "abjection" to describe the expulsion of Hagar. Abjection is "an ongoing process in the development of subjectivity, begun when the infant starts to develop a sense of self whose borders it seeks to establish by abjecting or rejecting that which seems to be a part of itself but which it also perceives as threatening the fragile boundaries

---

4. Toba Spitzer notes that the command to "submit" is in the *hitpael* (i.e. reflexive) verb form thereby making Hagar the agent of her submission. "'Where Do You Come From, and Where Are You Going?': Hagar and Sarah Encounter God," *Reconstructionist* 8 (1998): 10.

5. Thomas B. Dozeman, "The Wilderness and Salvation History in the Hagar Story," *JBL* 117, no. 1 (1998): 42.

6. Exum, "Accusing Look," 149 fn 117.

of itself."[7] She explains that one of the central concerns of the patriarchal stories is the issue of Israel's identity: who belongs to the "chosen people" and who does not? "Israel alone receives the special promises of God, while its relatives – the Ishmaelites, the Edomites, the Ammonites, the Moabites, the Midianites, the Arameans – are excluded. Throughout Genesis, Israel is continually defining itself over against its neighbors, whose relation to Israel is described in terms of complex family relationships."[8] In Genesis 19, Israel will separate itself from the Moabites and Ammonites through the story of Lot and his daughters (Gen 19:30–38). On either side of that story, in Genesis 16 and 21, Israel tells the history of how it separated itself from the Ishmaelites. Lot is only a nephew to Abraham, but Ishmael is his own son. Ishmael is perceived as the greater threat to the boundaries of Israel's selfhood and, as such, must be expelled with proportionately greater force.[9] Thus, while the Moabites and Ammonites are expelled through the story of incest in a faraway mountainous cave, Israel establishes the other-ness of the Ishmaelites by recording that their eponymous ancestor was physically and forcibly evicted from the household of Abraham.

To graphically demonstrate the strength of the abjection, or expulsion, Exum uses a painting by the Italian artist Guercino.[10] The family is neatly divided by placing the two mothers on opposite sides. Sarah has completed the act of expulsion – her back is already turned away. She clearly wishes Hagar dismissed in aggressive manumission – the act of freeing a slave. So safely is her son Isaac distanced from the threat of Ishmael that he is not even in the

---

7. Exum, 144 fn 3.

8. Exum, 144–145. The identification of Ishmael's descendants with (pre-Islamic) Arabs goes back at least to Josephus: *Antiquities* 1.220–221. It could even pre-date him by a further 150 years. See Erich Gruen, *Rethinking the Other in Antiquity* (Princeton: Princeton University Press, 2011), 300–301. From around the same period, Jubilees 20:12–13 makes a similar identification. See a quick and helpful etiological and historical overview in Christopher Heard, "On the Road to Paran: Toward a Christian Perspective on Hagar and Ishmael," *Interpretation* 68, no. 3 (2014): 270–285, esp. 274–279. Pre-Islamic rabbinic sources made the association, but less critically before the arrival of Islam in the seventh century. See Deeana Klepper, "Historicizing Allegory: The Jew as Hagar in Medieval Christian Text and Image," *Church History* 82, no. 2 (2015): 308–344, esp. 313–315. Medieval Christian interpretation, especially in Byzantine lands, carried through the Josephus tradition. For example, John of Damascus (d. 743) offered an etymology that linked the current Islamic threat with biblical data: the Arab invaders "were called Hagarenes because they were born of Hagar, cf. Gen 25:13–15, Jetur and Naphish, tribes descended from Ishmael, who are linked with Hagrites; 1 Chr 5:10, 19–21; 27:31; Ps 83:6; they were called Ishmaelites because they were descended from Ishmael; they were called Saracens because Sarah sent them away without an inheritance." Klepper, "Historicizing Allegory," 318.

9. Exum, "Accusing Look," 145.

10. Exum, 161–163. To see the painting, go to www.artbible.info/art/large/82.html.

picture. At the two-thirds position, which is the focal point of a well-composed picture, is Abraham in the very act of abjection. Does the furrowed brow speak of the distress he has suffered the night before, or of his determination to enact his divorce from his firstborn? While he and Sarah stand shoulder-to-shoulder, his hands come between him and Hagar – one hand appears to block her off from his home (or is it a feeble attempt at blessing?), and the other points the way out into the wilderness. Exum sees that "the pure line of Israel's descent through Isaac is vigilantly guarded, with Abraham making a double gesture of dismissal."[11] We observe that even though Abraham stands at the focal point of the painting, the artist draws the viewer's gaze to Hagar and her son by the use of light. As Hagar stands on Abraham's threshold, she hovers between home and desert, between security and danger, neither insider nor outsider – as always, liminal. Exum points out that Sarah and Ishmael both have faces hidden, the latter the cause of the former's action.[12] We know that next time scripture records Ishmael raising his head to look on Abraham's face, it is as an adult son burying his dead father.

Though Abraham had once wished before God that Ishmael might be the son of the promise (Gen 17:18), and though Abraham has agonized the night before he sends Ishmael away (Gen 21:11), he awakes with the capacity to dismiss the mother and son with no more than "some food and a skin of water" (Gen 21:14). Ishmael, who the previous night was "his son" (Gen 21:11) becomes next morning "the boy" (Gen 21:14). Of course, Abraham had received the divine assurance that God will take care of Ishmael. Yet, it takes dissonance at the deepest psychological level for Abraham to "refuse to recognize the 'self' in the other."[13] Martin Luther asks in bewilderment, "Who would believe this had Moses not recorded it?"[14]

---

11. Exum, 161.

12. Exum, 163.

13. Exum, "Accusing Look," 168. Exum (150–152) sees the narrator mitigating the Hebrew couple's culpability by foregrounding the divine assurances in both stories and this "permits the reader to give no more thought to their welfare" (150–152). Other examples of such reading are Meir Sternberg, *The Poetics of Biblical Narrative: Ideological Literature and the Drama of Reading* (Bloomington: Indiana University Press, 1985), 494; and Danna Nolan Fewell, "Changing the Subject: Retelling the Story of Hagar the Egyptian," in *Genesis: A Feminist Companion to the Bible*, ed. Athalya Brenner, Second Series (Sheffield: Sheffield Academic Press, 1998), 194.

14. Martin Luther, *Comm. Gen.* 21:15–16 (WA 43.164; LW 4.40–41) in John L. Thompson, "Hagar, Victim or Villain?: Three Sixteenth-Century Views," *Catholic Biblical Quarterly* 59 (1997): 226.

The question to ask at this point is this: what is the narrator telling the reader through this recounting of Israel's earliest history? Is he, as Exum proposes, detachedly setting out the process by which Israel actualized its selfhood, by a series of careful, and even violent, exclusions starting with the Ishmaelites? Or worse, is he on the side of Israel, interested in nothing else but the formation and elevation of its "self"?

To arrive at a decision on that, we need to look more closely at how the narrator has arranged his collection of Abraham stories. That should help us pick out the quiet but persistent pattern that he hopes our eyes will catch.

Hagar's Story within Abraham's Story

The Abraham cycle largely runs from Genesis chapters 12 to 23. In chapter 12, Abraham emigrates from his native **Mesopotamia**; in chapter 23, he buries Sarah in Canaan. In between, the stories alternate Abraham's status – and self-identity – in these lands west of Mesopotamia. In chapter 12, he is a foreigner who sojourns (the verb *gûr*) briefly in Egypt; in chapters 13 to 19, he is a resident of Canaan. In chapter 20, he is a foreigner in Gerar (again, the verb *gûr*); in chapters 21 and 22, he is again a resident of Canaan. In chapter 23, we are taken aback by the fact that, even after all these years in Canaan, Abraham sees himself not as a resident but as an alien: "I am a foreigner (*gēr*) and stranger among you," he says to the Hittites of Hebron (Gen 23:4). In the legal canon, *haggēr* (or *haggār* in participial form) refers to "the resident alien," the "class of people who occupy the intermediate position between the native and the complete foreigner."[15] The Egyptian slave and the Mesopotamian chieftain are "resident aliens" in Canaan, aurally linked: one's name is "Hagar"; the other describes himself as *haggār*.

In these stories, the expected black and white moral categories dissolve: are the natives bad and the resident aliens good? Not necessarily. Abraham and Lot welcome strangers while Sodom looks to abuse them, dismissing Lot as a foreigner (Gen 19:9). In Gerar, "Abraham assumes [Sarah] will be an object of sexual appropriation [and Abraham] the target of murder. In the event he is entirely wrong: Abimelech is a decent, even noble man, and the category of 'sodom' is not to be projected onto everything that is not the seed

---

15. Paul Edward Hughes, "Seeing Hagar Seeing God: Leitwort and Petite Narrative in Genesis 16:1–16," *Didaskalia Spring* (1997): 50.

of Abraham."[16] Rather, it is Abraham's deceit that foregrounds Abimelech's righteousness. What is more, as Leveen points out, the story of Hagar's departure in chapter 21 is framed by two stories of Abimelech's peace treaties with Abraham (Gen 20:15; 21:23). Abimelech warmly accepts Abraham, a *gēr* dependent on him. When it comes to his turn, Abraham expels Hagar, a gēr dependent on him.[17] It would appear, then, that "the redactor has created a sustained and serious biblical reflection on 'the other.' What does it [take] for different peoples to live alongside one another, either sharing borders or even tents?"[18] It takes a discerning eye. If only Abraham had been able to see himself in Abimelech – a man receptive of and responsive to God's instructions. If only Sarah had been able to see in Hagar a fellow foreigner. Apparently, the characters in the stories do not have the required discernment. With a sigh, the narrator turns to us readers.

A careful reader will find it hard to miss that Genesis 21, the expulsion of Hagar, and Genesis 22, the binding of Isaac on Moriah, run like two parallel panels of a tapestried story. In both, Abraham receives communication from God, apparently at night since, in both cases, the action begins "early the next morning" (Gen 21:14; see the same phrase in 22:3). Abraham speechlessly makes provisions for the journeys: for Hagar food and water; for himself in the next story, he loads the donkey with wood.

Hagar heads toward Egypt via the desert of Beersheba (Gen 21:14). A mother and son are in the wilderness, just as father and son will be by themselves, climbing up into the wild mountains of Moriah. If Hagar lays Ishmael under a bush, Abraham lays on Isaac's back a bundle of wood. Hagar sits down resigned to her belief that Ishmael will die; Abraham moves forward trusting that Isaac will somehow survive (Heb 11:17–19). Hagar sobs (Gen 21:16) while Abraham speaks in faith that God will provide (Gen 22:8).

God provides for both the boys. The angel of God halts Ishmael's death cries (Gen 21:17), while "the angel of the LORD" (Gen 22:11) intervenes to save the unresisting Isaac. Both references are to the same being, a divine messenger. The angel calls Hagar by name just as he called Abraham by name. "Both times, the angels call from the heavens, as if the urgency to comply with the sacrifice – Abraham's volition and Hagar's despair – did not leave time for

---

16. Robert Alter, *Genesis: Translation and Commentary* (New York: W. W. Norton, 1997), 94.
17. Adrianne Leveen, "Reading the Seams," *JSOT* 29, no. 3 (2005): 259–287.
18. Leveen, "Reading the Seams," 280.

a terrestrial visit to undo the harshness of the decree."[19] Both Ishmael and Isaac are guaranteed a blessing each to his own measure (Gen 21:18; 22:17–18). Both Hagar and Abraham saw alternatives by which to save their sons' lives (Gen 21:19; 22:13): God showed Hagar a well that she had not noticed so far; similarly, Abraham saw a ram for the sacrifice. Just as Ishmael received a life-giving drink, Isaac was literally released from death. Ishmael receives the promise that he will become a nation. Isaac receives the promise that his descendants will be as numerous as the sand and stars.

The readership of Genesis has not disappointed the narrator – they have been sensitive to his twinning of stories and characters. So, for example, in recognition of the look-alike stories, Genesis 21 and 22 are read on successive days in synagogues at Rosh Hashanah, the Jewish new year.

The reader is led to draw the startling conclusion that Hagar is Abraham and Abraham, Hagar; that Ishmael is Isaac and Isaac, Ishmael. They are each other by life circumstances; they are each other in human condition; they are each other as recipients of God's favor.

If we are not persuaded, consider how the Hagar story ends. We are told that God was with Ishmael as he grew up. Abraham had long renounced his responsibility as father, but God took charge as his guardian. In anticipation of the nation that Ishmael would become (Gen 21:13), the story ends by telling us that his mother found him a wife from her people – just as Abraham will do for Isaac in the years to come (Gen 24). God does not own Abraham's expulsion of Hagar. Rather, by compensating for it he neutralizes it. Guercino gets it right in his painting. Even though Abraham stands at the classic two-thirds position focal point, the light falls on the helpless slave mother and her son, one's face hidden and the other's face wounded by the betrayal. Both biblical storyteller and Italian artist succeed in thumping the rejection into the pit of our stomach.

Abraham's story continues, but the careful reader will not fail to hear the echoes of Hagar and her son in it. At Hagar's well – Beer Lahai Ro'i (Gen 24:62; 25:11) – is where Isaac lives at a later time, sustained by water that first quenched his half-brother's thirst. At Abraham's death, the expelled Ishmael will return to honor the burial of a father who did dishonorably by him (Gen 25:9). In the tabling of Abraham's descendants, rightfully, Ishmael's genealogy is rehearsed first (Gen 25:12–18) – twelve nations, living in fierce independence as promised, "in hostility" toward competing kin. Esau will come to take

---

19. Aryeh Cohen, "Hagar and Ishmael: A Commentary," *Interpretation* 68, no. 3 (2014): 254.

himself a wife from his uncle Ishmael, whom the narrator identifies as a "son of Abraham" (Gen 28:9).

Though abjected by Abraham, "Ishmael hovers on the borders of the self that is Israel . . . haunting its edges (Gen 16:12; 25:18; 37:25–28, 36; Judg 8:24; Ps 83:6)"[20] with otherly names and places. The narrator is insistent that Ishmael should not be disremembered, that Abraham's amputation of what Abraham saw as non-self should not achieve what the surgery intended.

Hagar's Story alongside Israel's Story

If we had the time to move on to narrative on a grander scale, we would note more than a dozen parallels between the story of Hagar and Ishmael and the story of Israel's Egyptian bondage, including the setting free from slavery, the wandering in the desert, the water source in the wilderness and the promise to be made into a nation.[21] Here, the subversive twist is that the narrator feeds the reader enough clues for the reader to see that "Sarah does to a child of Egypt . . . what the Egyptians would later do to the children of Sarah."[22] As Jewish theologian Frymer-Kensky observes, "The unsettling nature of the [exodus] story is that Sarah is our mother, but Hagar is us."[23] In the larger story of Israel's history, Israel reprises the experience of Hagar.

Toward a Conclusion

Are we beginning to see what the narrator intends us to see? Hagar looks uncannily like Abraham; Ishmael and Isaac sport an unmistakable family resemblance; Israel's story is strangely similar to that of the first ancestors of the Ishmaelites.

That is not to say that the narrator is on Hagar's side and against Abraham: God does not take sides, but humans may. Hagar did. In the encounter with the angel, Hagar discerned who God was so clearly that she could name

---

20. Exum, "Accusing Look," 169.

21. D. Daube, "The Exodus Pattern in the Bible," *All Souls Studies* 2 (London: Faber & Faber, 1963), 23–38; Yair Zakovitch, *"And You Shall Tell Your Son . . .": The Concept of the Exodus in the Bible* (Jerusalem: Magnes, 1991), 26–30. Dozeman, "Wilderness and Salvation History," 23–43, sets up parallels between Hagar and Moses, especially 29–32.

22. M. Tsevat, "Hagar and the Birth of Ishmael," in *The Meaning of the Book of Job and Other Biblical Studies: Essays on the Literature and Religion of the Hebrew Bible* (New York: Ktav, 1980), 69–70.

23. Tikvah Frymer-Kensky interviewed in Brett Schaeffer, "Five Scripture Scholars Pick Their Golden Oldies," *US Catholic* 61, no. 11 (Nov. 1996): 21–26.

him, something not even the patriarch Jacob managed. As Spitzer insightfully observes, unlike Jacob, Hagar does not need "to wrest a name away from the angel – she has provided it on her own."[24] Neither does she "displace this act of recognition/naming onto an intermediate symbol, as does Jacob in naming a place . . . Hagar names this deity face to face: You are El Ro'i. Hagar has not limped away. Her words indicate that she is still in the presence of the divine even as she calls its name."[25] Hagar gratefully takes the side of God by her obedience to the divine command.

The reward is a dramatic reversal. Spitzer points out that where Hagar had suffered "beneath the hand of" Sarah, the angel promises that Ishmael's hand will be against his brothers in independence. While Hagar had to flee "before" her mistress, Ishmael will eventually dwell "before" his brothers. "Her flight is turned into his defiance."[26] When she weeps in the desert, it is Ishmael's cries that come before God.[27] Hagar puts Abraham to shame, for when she fills the flask from the miracle well, she "sustains her child where Abraham could not."[28] In due time, Hagar moves from being a "victimized and endangered slave woman" to becoming the "autonomous matriarch of a nascent people."[29] More than a millennium later, the records will impartially set out the genealogy of Abraham as follows: the "sons of Abraham: Isaac and Ishmael" (1 Chr 1:28).

Later Judaism, in its inimitably creative manner, provided two backstories for Hagar – both routes for Hagar's entry into the household of Abraham. Genesis Rabbah maintains the tradition that Hagar was no less than the daughter of Pharaoh, and given to Abraham as a gift from Pharaoh (Gen 12:10–20).[30] After the death of Sarah, tradition brings Hagar back into the family as Keturah (Gen 25:1), whom Abraham marries. Genesis Rabbah 61.4 describes her with fulsome praise, linking the name Keturah (קְטוּרָה) with the fragrant noun קְטֹרֶת, meaning "incense" – "since she was fragrant with [obedience to the] commandments and [with] good deeds." In the Jewish tradition, the wrong is righted, and Hagar the "other" is established as "us."

---

24. Spitzer, "Where Do You Come From?," 12.
25. Spitzer, 11.
26. Spitzer, 11.
27. Spitzer, 13–14.
28. Spitzer, 14.
29. Spitzer, 14.
30. Genesis Rabbah, XLV 1.5:A.

Cooper sums up well what we are trying to get at: "In filiation lies the potential for reconciliation."[31] That is precisely what the narrator of Genesis is encouraging us to do. He is asking us to filiate, to recognize the brother in the human "other": like us, fallen and pitiable, yet willing to seek, and startlingly capable of apprehending the mysterious, truly "other" who is happy to wait in unlikely places in order to ambush us with hope.

Us and the other: same difference.

2.3 Paul in Athens (Acts 17:16–34): A Babbler or an Evangelistic Scholar of Religion?

Anton Deik

The book of Acts narrates numerous interactions between Christianity and other religions, perhaps more than any other New Testament book. It is a good place, therefore, to search for an answer to the following questions: How do followers of Christ make sense of and engage with other faiths? And how does our understanding of religion impact our witness in the world?

Luke includes no less than ten interactions between the followers of Christ and non-Jewish religions. He records, for example, the interactions of Philip and Paul with sorcery (Acts 8; 13; 19), a religious practice that was part of the Graeco-Roman world in spite of it being unorthodox. Luke describes some scenes of the official imperial cult that were prevalent in the Roman Empire since the days of Augustus Caesar (e.g. Acts 12:1–4, 21–22; 17:6–9) and also narrates episodes of Paul's interaction with the civic cults that were practiced in certain cities (e.g. Acts 14:8–21; 19:21–41).[32]

This section focuses on one of Paul's interactions with other beliefs: his encounter with the Athenian philosophers in Acts 17:16–34, an episode that lies at the climax of Paul's missionary work in the book of Acts.[33]

---

31. Alan Cooper, "Hagar In and Out of Context," *Union Seminary Quarterly Review* 55, no. 1–2 (200): 46.

32. For a more complete list of Christianity's interaction with other religions in the book of Acts, see David W. J. Gill and Bruce W. Winter, "Acts and Roman Religion," in *The Book of Acts in Its Graeco-Roman Setting*, eds. David W. J. Gill and Conrad Gempf (Carlisle: Paternoster; Grand Rapids: Eerdmans, 1994); Hans-Josef Klauck, *Magic and Paganism in Early Christianity: The World of the Acts of the Apostles* (Minneapolis: Fortress Press, 2003).

33. Howard Marshall, *Acts*, Tyndale New Testament Commentaries (Leicester: IVP; Grand Rapids: Eerdmans, 1980), 281. Ben Witherington III, *The Acts of the Apostles: A Socio-Rhetorical Commentary* (Grand Rapids: Eerdmans, 1998) considers this passage "in many regards one of the most important in all of Acts" (511).

The Context

Paul visits Athens in his second missionary journey (Acts 15:36–18:22). He embarks on the journey accompanied by Silas (15:40), and they are later joined by Timothy (16:1–4). Paul and his companions pass through the provinces of Asia Minor and then cross the Aegean Sea with Luke (16:10–11). Starting from the northern provinces of Macedonia (the northern part of modern Greece), they first visit Philippi and then move to Thessalonica and Berea. They encounter many difficulties. In Philippi, Paul and Silas are beaten by the rulers and thrown into prison (16:16–24), and in Thessalonica, they face great persecution by the Jews who incite the city against them (17:1–9). They escape to Berea but are then followed by the Jews of Thessalonica who stir some of the locals against Paul and his companions (17:10–13). In response, Paul is smuggled out of the city and escorted to Athens (17:14–15).

Being left alone in Athens after a period of intense persecution, the reader might expect Paul to take a break and enjoy the beautiful city. Instead, he goes to the agora (the marketplace) and starts "preaching the good news about Jesus and the resurrection" (Acts 17:18). There, he gets into a debate with the philosophers of Athens, the Stoics and the Epicureans. The Stoics, whose philosophy was one of the most popular in the first-century Graeco-Roman world, were pantheistic; they believed that God is the spirit of the world and that "all things, including God, [are] 'fragments of the divine force.'"[34] They also "spoke of the Logos that designed and governed the cosmos."[35] Regarding their ethics, they valued virtue, courage, moderation and self-control, and they considered lust and the pursuit of pleasure as evils. In contrast, the Epicureans, a minority among first-century philosophers, thought that the gods – if they existed at all – were distant, remote and did not interfere in the functioning of the universe. Consequently, there was no need for religious worship or fear of the gods. Their ethics contrasted sharply with the Stoics; they saw pleasure as the greatest good and pain as the greatest evil, although pleasure for them was not merely carnal as they were often portrayed by the Stoics. Today, we might describe them as agnostic secularists.[36]

---

34. Alan Cairns, *Dictionary of Theological Terms* (Greenville: Ambassador Emerald International, 2002), 436.

35. Craig S. Keener, *Acts: An Exegetical Commentary*, Vol. 3: 15:1–23:35 (Grand Rapids: Baker Academic, 2014), 2594.

36. For an excellent introduction to the Stoics and the Epicureans, see Keener, *Acts*, 2584–2595.

Paul at the Areopagus

Paul's debate with the Stoics and the Epicureans results in him being taken to the Areopagus; a council that historically met at a rocky hill with the same name (also known as Mars Hill) to settle disputes in religious, educational, political and philosophical matters.[37] The charge against him is twofold (Acts 17:18). First, that he is a *spermologos*; a popular insult, often translated as "babbler," which was applied in ancient Athens to those who, like birds picking up seeds, collected ideas, opinions, and words from other thinkers and used them in their own discourse to appear as seasoned philosophers.[38] The second charge is that Paul is "advocating foreign gods" (17:18). Most likely, Paul's accusers thought of Jesus (*Iesous*) and the resurrection (*anastasis*) as two separate foreign gods.[39]

As is often the case in his trial narratives, Luke outlines the accusations clearly and then provides a response through a speech. Examples include Stephen's trial before the Sanhedrin (Acts 6:8–7:60), Paul's arrest and defense before the Jewish crowd (21:27–22:21), and Paul's trial before Felix in Caesarea (24:1–23). In his Athens narrative, Luke does the same. He presents to the reader the accusations (17:18) and then provides a synopsis of Paul's speech in response (17:22–31).

So, how does Paul respond to the charges here, specifically the *spermologos* accusation? In a nutshell, Paul's response demonstrates that he is far from being a *spermologos* as alleged by his opponents. On the contrary, his Areopagus speech illustrates his deep understanding of the rhetoric, arguments, theology and texts of the other, placing him among the greatest philosophers of the ancient world. For example, Paul's speech contains some of the most important rhetorical devices in the ancient world which aim to convince, influence and convert the listeners. First, it follows the classical outline of Graeco-Roman rhetorical speeches.[40] It starts with *exordium* and *narratio* (Acts 17:22–23a) which serve as an introduction to capture the attention of

---

37. W. Bauer, F. W. Danker, W. F. Arndt, and F. W. Gingrich, *A Greek-English Lexicon of the New Testament and Other Early Christian Literature* (Chicago: University of Chicago Press, 2000), 129; C. Kavin Rowe, *World Upside Down: Reading Acts in the Graeco-Roman Age* (Oxford: Oxford University Press, 2009), 29–31; Keener, *Acts*, 2600–2603; Witherington, *Acts of the Apostles*, 515.

38. Bauer, Danker, Arndt, and Gingrich, *Greek-English Lexicon*, 937; Keener, *Acts*, 2595–2596.

39. John Chrysostom was the first to make this comment: John Chrysostom, *Homily XXXVIII*, 233, as cited in John Stott, *The Message of Acts*, The Bible Speaks Today (Leicester; Downers Grove: IVP, 1994), 282.

40. Witherington, *Acts of the Apostles*, 518.

the listeners. It is followed by the *propositio* (v. 23b), or the main thesis of the speech, which in Paul's case is the proclamation of the unknown God revealed in Christ. The *propositio* is then followed by the *probatio* (vv. 24–29), the argument that defends and establishes the thesis. The speech concludes with a *peroratio* (vv. 30–31) which Paul, as good Graeco-Roman rhetoricians did, reserves for his most controversial proclamations – repentance, judgment day and Jesus's resurrection.[41]

Second, Paul's speech fulfills the three rhetorical requirements that Aristotle stressed, namely, *ethos*, *logos* and *pathos*.[42] *Ethos* (Acts 17:22–23) is where the speaker establishes his credentials. *Logos* is the logical argument (vv. 24–29). *Pathos* (vv. 30–31) is where the speaker utilizes emotional appeals to encourage the listeners to engage with the argument and respond to the questions posed and the challenges set. In a nutshell, from a rhetorical point of view, Paul's speech puts him on par with the high-caliber philosophers of the ancient world.

Moreover, the outline of Paul's argument (the *probatio*, Acts 17:24–29) is strikingly similar to the structure of the Stoic argument that was used to prove the existence of the gods and their nature.[43] The argument typically begins with the existence of the gods (cf. v. 24a). It then moves to specifying their character (cf. vv. 24b–25) and then to illustrating that they rule the world (cf. v. 26). The argument ends with a demonstration of how the gods take care of humans and their needs (cf. vv. 27–29). This demonstrates that Paul is not only versed in the rhetorical devices of his time, but also with the arguments of the other.

Paul's speech is also packed with Hellenistic ideas to the degree that liberal scholars have argued that the Areopagus speech cannot be Paul's, as it reflects someone deeply steeped in Hellenistic thinking and religious life.[44] I personally give Luke the benefit of the doubt and therefore believe that the text is his faithful summary of Paul's speech on the Areopagus.[45]

---

41. Keener, *Acts*, 2667.

42. Witherington, *Acts of the Apostles*, 518.

43. Keener, *Acts*, 2595.

44. See for example Martin Dibelius, *The Book of Acts: Form Style and Theology*, ed. K. C. Hanson, trans. Mary Ling and Paul Schubert (Minneapolis: Fortress Press, 2004), 114–120. Dibelius also references other scholars who have argued that Paul's Areopagus speech is a later insertion to the book of Acts (95).

45. There is no convincing reason for me to believe that Paul of Tarsus was not versed in Hellenistic thinking as well as biblical thinking. Furthermore, methodologically speaking, the diachronic approaches to exegesis typically used in arguments over authorship can be highly speculative.

However, the scholarly work done on Paul's Areopagus speech helps us to better appreciate the depth of understanding that Paul had of other faiths. A cursory comparison of Paul's speech with Graeco-Roman religious thinking reveals that Paul is far from being a *spermologos*, as accused by his opponents. On the contrary, he is someone deeply versed in other faiths and as a result is able to articulate a highly contextual proclamation of the gospel. For example, Paul speaks of "God who made the world and everything in it . . . the Lord of heaven and earth" and the one who "does not live in temples built by human hands" (Acts 17:24) in a way that resonates profoundly with Stoic religious thinking. Epictetus, a Stoic contemporary of Paul, argues that the one who looks at nature and yet denies a creator's existence is stupid. Horace's *Odes* portrays "the sire on high" as the one "who rules the sea, the earth, the sky" (Horace, *Carmina*, 1.12.15). Zeno, the founder of Stoicism, is against the use of temples. For him, nothing offered by human builders is worthy of the gods. Furthermore, Paul's assertion that God "gives everyone life and breath and everything else" (v. 25b) is similar to the belief expressed by Dio Chrysostom, a first-century Greek philosopher, that God is "the Giver of . . . life and of all our blessings, the common Father and Savior and Guardian of mankind" (Dio Chrysostom, *De dei cognitione [Or. 12]*, 74). Also, Paul's statement in Acts 17:26 that "from one man [God] made all the nations" resonates with the thinking of Stoic philosopher Seneca the Younger that "all men, if traced back to their original source, spring from the gods" (Seneca the Younger, *Epistles morales* 44.2).[46]

Furthermore, Paul's speech at the Areopagus reveals his mastery of the texts of the other. The speech contains two quotations from Greek poets, both in Acts 17:28. The first quotation ("in him we live and move and have our being") has been attributed to the poet Epimenides of Crete who said of Zeus that "thou art not dead for ever; thou art alive and risen; for in thee we live and move, and have our being."[47] The second quotation ("for we are his offspring") is found in the writings of two Greek poets, Cleanthes and Aratus, although the version found in the latter is closer to the wording of Paul:[48] "For

---

46. For these comparisons with Graeco-Roman thinking, I am in debt to the meticulous work of Keener, *Acts*, esp. 2637, 2639, 2644, 2648.

47. This quote from Epimenides was originally found in a Syriac commentary on the book of Acts by ninth century Isho'dad of Merv, Bishop of Hadatha (the city of Haditha in Al-Anbar Governorate of modern-day Iraq). Isho'dad's commentary is the earliest extant source which indicates that Paul was quoting Epimenides here. See Dibelius, *Book of Acts*, 109, and Keener, *Acts*, 2657.

48. Keener, 2657, 2659–2660; Dibelius, *Book of Acts*, 110–111.

we are also his offspring; and he in his kindness unto men giveth favorable signs and wakeneth the people to work" (Aratus, *Phaenomena* 4–6). What is striking about Paul's use of Aratus is not only this quote, but also the common themes in the two texts: "[human's] origin in God, and the relationship that results, the mention of the earth and the seasons as proof of God's existence."[49] This knowledge shows that Paul is far from a *spermologos*. Rather, as rightly argued by German scholar Martin Dibelius, he "really [knows] Aratus's poem and not only this one-half verse taken from it."[50]

Finally, the majority of scholars agree that Luke's account of Paul's activity and trial in Athens intentionally alludes to that of Socrates.[51] First, Paul's discussions with people and philosophers in the agora (Acts 17:17–18) is similar to that of Socrates. Second, the charge against Paul that he "seems to be advocating foreign gods" (17:18; cf. 17:19b–20) echoes the charges against Socrates that he "corrupted youth and rejected the gods accepted by the *polis* and brought in strange new deities."[52] Third, the manner in which "they took [Paul]" (17:19; Greek *epilabomenoi autou*, here meaning they took hold of him by force, caught him and arrested him; cf. Acts 16:19; 18:17; 21:30, 33) is analogous to the way Socrates was taken to trial.[53] Finally, both the trials of Paul and Socrates were before the Areopagus.[54] All this indicates that the allusion to Socrates is purposeful. That is, Luke intended to make this allusion, thereby placing Paul on a par with one of the greatest minds of the ancient world.[55] Additionally, it is very likely that the Socrates allusion resonated with both audiences of the narrative world (i.e. the Athenian philosophers as well as Luke's original readership), for the story of Socrates was especially famous among Stoics and was widespread in Graeco-Roman literature between the fourth century BC and the fourth century AD.[56]

---

49. Dibelius, 110.

50. Dibelius.

51. Rowe, *World Upside Down*, 31–32; Keener, *Acts*, 2603–2605; Witherington, *Acts of the Apostles*, 515–516. Keener, *Acts*, 2604–3043 includes an exhaustive list of scholars who support this interpretation.

52. As cited in Keener, *Acts*, 2604.

53. See Witherington, *Acts of the Apostles*, 515; Keener, *Acts*, 2604. For a convincing argument on the meaning of *epilabomenoi autou* here, see Rowe, *World Upside Down*, 29.

54. Keener, *Acts*, 2600.

55. Many in the ancient world actually referred to Socrates as "the wisest of all men" (Keener, 2605).

56. Keener, 2607.

So, how does Paul make sense of and engage with other religions? Definitely not as a *spermologos* collecting scraps of thought from here and there. But rather as a "new Socrates" who deeply understands the rhetoric, arguments, theology and texts of the other.[57] Today, we might consider him a scholar of religion, one with depth of understanding of other faiths. And how does Paul's understanding of religion impact his witness? His profound understanding of the other enables him to articulate a highly contextual proclamation of the gospel that resonates deeply with the rhetoric, arguments, theology and texts of the other.

Paul as a Passionate Preacher of the Gospel

To complete our analysis of how Paul viewed and engaged with other faiths in Athens, we need to go back to the beginning of the story. John Stott notices two main things that happened to Paul upon his arrival to Athens.[58] First, he *saw* that the city was "full of idols" (Acts 17:16). The word in Greek used to describe how Paul saw the city, *kateidōlos*, actually means "utterly idolatrous – wholly given to idolatry";[59] that is, "the city was 'under' [idols]. We might say that it was 'smothered with idols' or 'swamped' by them."[60] One Roman comedian actually said of Athens that "it was easier to find a god there than a man."[61] Paul probably started seeing the idols of Athens even before arriving there. As he approached the city by sea, he perhaps saw the statue of the goddess Athena (also known as Athena Promachos) which was standing at a high point on the Acropolis of Athens.[62] In the agora and its surrounding area, he probably saw numerous idols and street temples dedicated to Themis (Justice); Eueteria (Prosperity); Apollo Agyieus, "the god of streets and gates"; Hekate, "the goddess of junctions"; and Hermes, "the great god of the roads."[63] At the Acropolis, not far from the agora, Paul was perhaps "struck by the way that the temples of the main civic sanctuary . . . dominated the city."[64] While all

---

57. Witherington, *Acts of the Apostles*, 514; Keener, *Acts*, 2603.

58. Stott, *Message of Acts*, 276–280.

59. James Strong, *A Concise Dictionary of the Words in the Greek Testament and The Hebrew Bible* (Bellingham: Logos Bible Software, 2009), 41.

60. Stott, *Message of Acts*, 277.

61. As cited in Stott.

62. Gill and Winter, "Acts and Roman Religion," 85.

63. Eckhard J. Schnabel, *Early Christian Mission*, Vol. 2: Paul and the Early Church (Leicester: Apollos; Downers Grove: IVP, 2004), 1175.

64. Gill and Winter, "Acts and Roman Religion," 85.

these sights would have amazed the average Roman visitor to the city,[65] Paul instead saw a city that was *kateidōlos* – utterly idolatrous.

The second thing that happened to Paul upon his arrival is that he became "greatly distressed" by what he saw in the city (Acts 17:16); the idolatry of Athens created a strong emotion in his heart. The Greek word used to describe Paul's distress is *paroxynō*, and it occurs only twice in the New Testament: here and in 1 Corinthians 13:5 ("[love] is not easily angered"). Paul's admonition in 1 Corinthians 13 is a warning against being easily angered by people. Here, however, Paul's anger is directed against idolatry. In fact, the same Greek word is repeated fifty-three times in the Septuagint translation of the Old Testament, which Paul and Luke would have read and studied. In most instances, it refers to the wrath of God toward idolatry. As John Stott rightly concluded, "the pain or 'paroxysm' which Paul felt in Athens was due neither to bad temper, not to pity for the Athenians' ignorance, nor even to fear for their eternal salvation. It was due rather to his abhorrence of idolatry, which aroused within him deep stirrings of jealousy for the Name of God."[66]

What Paul saw and how he felt caused him to go out into the streets of Athens to preach the gospel:[67] "So (Greek *men oun*) he reasoned in the synagogue with both Jews and God-fearing Greeks, as well as in the marketplace day by day with those who happened to be there" (Acts 17:17). He did not go to the marketplace to fight with people and attack their temples, but he went as a high-caliber philosopher, as a "new Socrates," to "reason/discuss" (Greek *dielegeto*) with those whom he met. Nevertheless, Paul's discussions should not be mistaken as mere intellectual exercises. On the contrary, through his debates, "Paul was preaching the good news (Greek *euēngelizeto*) about Jesus and the resurrection" (17:18). This is also evident from the conclusion of his Areopagus speech (the *peroratio*, vv. 30–31), which he reserves for the most controversial elements: his call for repentance and his proclamations of the day of judgment and Jesus's resurrection. Although Paul preached the gospel in a highly contextual way, he did not shy away from preaching the full gospel, even when it contrasted sharply with the beliefs of the other. For the ancient Greeks, "once a person has died . . . there is no return to life

---

65. Gill and Winter, 85–86.
66. Stott, *Message of Acts*, 279.
67. Stott, 280.

[*anastasis*, resurrection]."[68] However, this belief did not prevent Paul from preaching the resurrection of Jesus Christ.

Conclusions and Implications for Today

This analysis demonstrates that Paul does not view and engage with other religions as a *spermologos* who collects scraps of thought and uses them to polemically refute other faiths. Rather, he approaches other beliefs as a "new Socrates" who profoundly understands the rhetoric, arguments, theology and texts of the religious other. As a result, he is able to articulate a highly contextual proclamation of the Christian gospel in a way that resonates deeply with the other. Nevertheless, Paul should not be mistaken for a disengaged scholar who studies religion from a distance. Rather, Paul combines the mind of a scholar with the heart of a passionate evangelist who deeply longs to see God's name known and glorified. While his scholarly mind and depth of understanding give him the ability to contextualize the gospel, his passionate evangelistic heart guards him against preaching a watered-down version of the gospel. When his gospel proclamation contrasts with the faith of the other, Paul does not shy away from preaching a full, Christ-centered gospel. Paul does this, however, in a highly contextual way rooted in a profound understanding of the other.

Like Christians in the first century, today's Christian communities in the Middle East are trying to witness in a context of religious diversity. In our attempt to witness to our Muslim brothers and sisters, in particular, many of us use polemic approaches. Unfortunately, in most cases, such approaches are based on shallow arguments that aim to refute the faith of the other. These arguments usually do not come from a deep understanding of Islam, but rather from a *spermologos*-like approach toward the religious other. The text of Acts 17 challenges this popular approach to evangelism in the Muslim world. Instead, it encourages us to nurture a heart that longs to deeply understand the faith of the other, including their rhetoric, arguments, theology and texts. Only then, the book of Acts tells us, can we effectively witness to the religious other, proclaiming a highly contextual articulation of the gospel. This contextual proclamation does not mean that our message would be a diluted gospel. On the contrary, if we combine our evangelistic fervor with a scholarly approach

---

68. Athenian poet Aeschylus, *Eumenides* 647–648, as cited in Keener, *Acts*, 2673. See also Witherington, *Acts of the Apostles*, 532.

2.4 There Is No Difference: A Pauline Anthropology of the Religious Other
Karen Shaw

When I started listing the ways Paul describes those who are not "in Christ," I did not like what I was finding, and I doubt that you will. For example, "dead in your transgressions and sins" (Eph 2:1), "followed the ways of this world and of the ruler of the kingdom of the air" (Eph 2:2), "disobedient" (Rom 11:30), "deserving of wrath" (Eph 2:3), "without hope and without God in the world" (Eph 2:12), "the god of this age has blinded the minds of unbelievers" (2 Cor 4:4), "God's enemies" and "enemies for your sake" (Rom 5:10; 11:28) and "foolish, disobedient, deceived and enslaved" (Titus 3:3).

That all sounds awfully close to demonizing people. It is not flattering. No religious other wants to be spoken of in such a way. Yet these are the apostle's words in the sacred scriptures.

Paul does modify his critique depending on the group, making some distinctions in the way he talks about idolaters, philosophers and Jews outside of Christ. But the group that is for Paul most "other" is the pagans. Here Paul is effusive in his critique, claiming that the pagans are guilty of godlessness, wickedness, suppressing the truth, not glorifying God, ingratitude, idolatry, sexual impurity and degradation, changing truth into lies, more idolatry, more sexual perversity, devaluing the knowledge of God, having depraved minds, and being filled with every kind of wickedness and evil including greed, depravity, envy, murder, strife, deceit, malice, gossip, slander, hatred of God, insolence, arrogance and boasting, sinister creativity, disobedience to parents, senselessness, faithlessness, heartlessness and ruthlessness – and they deserve to die. This list is all taken from Romans chapter 1. There is plenty more elsewhere.

Paul distinguishes between the ordinary pagans and the philosophers, whether pagan, Jewish, or gnostic, but his view of the learned is no higher. They also are ignorant (Acts 17:30). Their philosophies are hollow and deceptive, and their humility is false (Col 2:8, 18). God considers their wisdom to be foolishness, and he will bring their wisdom to nothing (1 Cor 1:19–20). So much for the philosophers!

Having blasted pagans in Romans chapter 1, Paul turns to ordinary Jews in chapter 2 and says that they are just the same, even though they think of themselves as morally superior (Rom 2:1, 17–20). They have stubborn and unrepentant hearts and are stockpiling wrath for themselves for judgment day. They are lawbreakers, stealing and committing adultery and sacrilege (Rom 2:21–27). This is true of Jews, whether or not they try to keep the law of Moses (Rom 3:18–20). They are enemies of the gospel (Rom 11:28). In 1 Thessalonians, Paul accuses the Jews of conducting persecutions, of killing "the Lord Jesus and the prophets," and of preventing apostolic ministries. They are hostile to everyone, Paul claims, and God's wrath is upon them (1 Thess 2:14–16).

So, while sometimes Paul tailors his criticisms to fit the worldview and lifestyle of a particular religious other, he holds all types up for severe censure. I told you that you would not like it!

Yet Paul's behavior is not always the hostile stance that we would expect from someone who holds such a negative view of the other. Sometimes he intentionally provokes people, and controversy seems to follow him. However, Acts and the Epistles describe another side to Paul. He defends intently the right of new Gentile believers to keep their culture as he has "become all things to all people" (1 Cor 9:22) and reminds the Thessalonians that he has behaved toward them "just as a nursing mother" (1 Thess 2:7). When the Ephesian metalsmiths stir up a riot against Paul and his companions, the city clerk silences the mob by saying, "You have brought these men here, though they have neither robbed temples nor blasphemed our goddess" (Acts 19:37). Paul suffers extreme danger and cruelty to express the love of God to the religious other, whether Gentile or Jew (2 Cor 11:23–27). He wishes himself accursed if it would save the very Jews who are persecuting him from city to city (Rom 9:1–3). He has compassion for the life of the Philippian jailor, who has illegally whipped and imprisoned him and Silas. And he writes 1 Corinthians 13. How do we reconcile the outspoken but loving Paul with his degrading descriptions of the religious other?

The key to reconciling these apparently contradictory "Pauls" is his phrase, "There is no difference" (Rom 3:22; 10:12; cf. Rom 2:11; Gal 3:28; Col 3:11). There is no difference because all are sinners. "Jews and Gentiles alike are all under the power of sin. As it is written: 'There is no one righteous, not even one'" (Rom 3:9–10). "For all have sinned and fall short of the glory of God" (Rom 3:23). "God has bound everyone over to disobedience" (Rom 11:32). Paul links all humanity to the first sin and its consequences: sin and trespass reign among all through Adam (Rom 5:16–17) and "as in Adam all die" (1 Cor 15:22).

Paul tells the Ephesians, "you were dead in your transgressions and sins" (Eph 2:1), and then continues, "All of us also lived among them at one time, gratifying the cravings of our flesh and following its desires and thoughts. Like the rest, we were by nature deserving of wrath" (Eph 2:3; cf. Titus 3:3). Commonly, when people of one religious group talk about another, we compare which is better. Paul says we all start at zero.

Paul even says it about himself. After listing all the ways in which he may have seen himself as having a religious head start over others, he admits that all of this is now of no value to him (Phil 3:7–8). If anything, he sees himself as worse than others: "of whom I am the worst" (1 Tim 1:15; cf. 1:13); whereas before he met Jesus, he clearly thought he was better. Paul, despite all the terrible things he says about the religious other, is also humble, respectful and loving toward them because he knows he is made of exactly the same stuff. "There is no difference" (Rom 3:22; cf. 10:22): we have all been wretched sinners, bound for the wrath of God.

What does all of this mean in practice? To begin with, we need to appreciate the horribleness of sin. Theirs, ours, mine, yours. I admit I have, many times, talked about Muslim, Druze and secular friends outside Christ as "good people." I have talked that way about Christians who are doing good deeds in their own strength. Paul will have none of this. There is not any goodness apart from Christ. When I see others' religious devotion, honesty and generosity and compare it to my own iffy behavior, I label them good. The truth is, most of us, most of the time, think of ourselves as good people and are impressed with people who appear to be even better. As soon as we start thinking this way, we have lost the gospel. Apart from Christ, there is nothing good in me, in Christians, or in anyone else. Sin makes us enemies of God, children of disobedience, cut off from him, spiritually dead. The minute I start thinking of some people as being worthier of salvation than others, I begin to preach a false gospel (Gal 1:6–9).

We also need to appreciate the greatness of God's grace shown in Christ. There is nothing we can do to earn God's love. We have all heard it a thousand times, but how little we believe it! In most of us there is a little child trying desperately to gain God's approval. It was only because Paul experienced the kindness of Jesus on the Damascus road that he was able to let go of persecuting the religious other and devote the rest of his life to living among and sharing the precious gospel with people he would previously have refused to eat with, or even touch, if he could avoid it. Paul's secret to humility in inter-religious situations is not praising the good in the practices of others, but comprehending the profound nature of one's own depravity and the greatness of God's mercy. As John Newton, slave trader turned abolitionist, puts it in the film *Amazing Grace*, "Although my memory's fading, I remember two things very clearly: I am a great sinner and Christ is a great Savior."

And no boasting! "For it is by grace you have been saved, through faith – and this is not from yourselves, it is the gift of God – not by works, so that no one can boast" (Eph 2:8–9). "Not even those who are circumcised keep the law, yet they want you to be circumcised that they may boast about your circumcision in the flesh. May I never boast except in the cross of our Lord Jesus Christ" (Gal 6:13–14). "If some of the branches have been broken off, and you, though a wild olive shoot, have been grafted in among the others and now share in the nourishing sap from the olive root, do not consider yourself to be superior to those other branches" (Rom 11:17–18). "God chose the lowly things of this world and the despised things – and the things that are not – to nullify the things that are, so that no one may boast before him" (1 Cor 1:28–29). This prohibition on boasting is frequently repeated in Paul's writings, but it seems to get thrown right out the window when we compare ourselves with the religious other. "We're cleaner, more loving, treat our women better, give more, raise our children better" – you name it! Unfortunately, Christianity has a reputation among many "others" for arrogance and self-righteousness, and to some degree, we deserve it. "Where, then, is [our] boasting?" Paul asks, then answers himself, "It is excluded" (Rom 3:27). If Abraham had nothing to boast about before God, neither do we. We have nothing which is not a gift of pure grace. Christ is our only boast.

There is another way in which we are all alike. There is no difference because, in every situation, God has left everyone a witness to himself. Not only are we all guilty of sin, but we are culpable, liable to judgment, because we have willfully suppressed the truth we have. There is the witness of creation, available to all (Rom 1:20), and the witness of our consciences (Rom 2:14–15). To the pagans of Lystra, Paul points out God's witness in rain and abundant, joyful harvests (Acts 14:17). In the previous section, Anton Deik pointed out that in Athens Paul found witnesses to the truth of God in the geographical distribution of the world's peoples and in the writings of pagan philosophers and poets (Acts 17:28). Jews have an advantage in many ways because of the witness of the Hebrew scriptures, the covenants and the prophets and because the Christ was born among them, but these advantages do them no good apart from faith in Jesus (Rom 3:1–2, 9; 10:4–5). All of this evidence simply furthers their guilt.

So, we look for God's witness among religious others. For all Paul's devastating descriptions in the epistles of sin and its consequences among the religious other, that is not where Paul begins when he speaks with them. Instead, Paul begins by finding evidence of God revealing himself among them, something they themselves acknowledge. Although he actively discourages idolatry, his focus is to preach Christ from the evidence at hand rather than to belittle or criticize their beliefs. Paul finds God revealing himself in many ways, including pagan literature; we should seek, not shun, signposts pointing to God in the sacred texts of other religions. Quoting them does not put these texts on the same level with the Bible but does demonstrate an alertness to the keys God has already placed at our disposal for opening for others the door of salvation. By finding God's means of self-disclosure, we affirm God's love to a group of people in their own environment and culture.

There is no difference because we are all sinners and because we have all chosen to ignore the evidence God has given us. There is one more way in which there is no difference: in Jesus Christ, God is longing to show mercy to all without distinction. Paul writes, God "wants all people to be saved and to come to a knowledge of the truth. For there is one God and one mediator between God and mankind, the man Christ Jesus, who gave himself as a ransom for all people" (1 Tim 2:4–6). "For the grace of God has appeared that offers salvation to all people" (Titus 2:11). "For there is no difference between Jew and Gentile – the same Lord is Lord of all and richly blesses all who call on him" (Rom 10:12). "For God has bound everyone over to disobedience so that he may have mercy on them all" (Rom 11:32). Paul goes to great lengths to show that this mercy results not from racial or religious discrimination, nor any human goodness or distinction, but purely from God's choice to shower kindness on the undeserving.

God's kind intent to sinners of every religious and ethnic background goes a long way to explain the apparent contradiction in Paul, that he could say those horrible things about people of other religious affiliations while living, suffering and being willing to die for them. About the unsaved among his kinfolk, the Jews, Paul sees them both as "enemies of the gospel" and "beloved" by God. The gentile "children of wrath," and "without God" as the apostle describes them in Ephesians 2 are also "God's offspring," and so in God they live and move and have their being in the Athens sermon (Acts 17:27–29). Paul sees all people in two ways at once: what they are without Christ and what they can be through God's mercy. Even with believers (and himself!) Paul never stops reminding them of what they were so that they can better appreciate the grace of God lavished on them.

Putting Paul's example into practice means, first, that we should do good to everyone (Gal 6:10; Titus 3:1–2) because of God's universal desire to save. Believing that God desires the common good of society (1 Tim 2:1–4), and that governments are God's means for good (Rom 13:1–7), Paul urges obedience to and prayer for rulers, even pagan rulers. He tells believers to do all in their power to live at peace with others and echoes Jesus's teaching of practical, humble love of enemies (Rom 12:17–21) and gracious speech to everyone (Col 4:6). God's kindness to us becomes a model of our behavior toward others.

Second, we should live to serve others. Paul famously writes, "I have become all things to all people so that by all possible means I might save some" (1 Cor 9:22). Willing to suffer damnation if it would save the Jews and to suffer chronic brutality for the sake of the Gentiles, Paul demonstrates what he teaches, leaving us a daunting model of determined love for the other.

Third, we welcome believers of all backgrounds, fully, unstintingly, relishing the differences in tradition and culture and our unity in the Holy Spirit. Like us, they were sinners with nothing to commend them to God. Like us, they are beloved for Christ's sake, fellow heirs and fellow workers. Muslim and Christian, Jew and Gentile, Hindu and materialist, all belong fully, because in Christ, there is no difference.

Fourth, we live "in Christ." What we have to offer is not an idea but the life of God in us. This is what gave Paul his energy to persevere and his spiritual power. Our goal is not that others see us, but that they see Jesus in us, a treasure in a clay jar, strength in weakness (2 Cor 4:7; 12:9).

There is no difference but Christ – but what a difference Christ makes! The difference between our own righteousness, which is never good enough, and being dressed in God's own righteousness through the faithfulness of Christ. The difference between alienation and reconciliation, between death and life, between judgment and honor. Not in our sinfulness, not in our culpability, and not in the saving mercy God longs to show. The only difference is whether a person is apart from Christ or in Christ. If we are truly in Christ, the religious other will see in us the saving kindness of our God.

2.5 The Questions: Scripture and the Religious Other

Ida Glaser

I often tell my students that 90 percent of genius is asking the right questions, and a further 9 percent is determining what the questions mean. One theme of this section is determining what questions we need to be addressing about our world, our scriptures and the religious other.

In 1998, I was asked to write a book on Theology of Religions. In exploring this request, I concluded that a better question would be how we read the Bible in the light of religious diversity.[69] We need a biblical understanding of human beings and an inclusive anthropology which recognizes that all people are religious.

Genesis chapters 1 to 11 introduce the Bible. It is significant that they do so through an account of the whole of humanity, from whom and for whom the special people of Israel will be called. These chapters are, therefore, the place to which we will turn for a foundational understanding of humans as religious beings. Chapter 1 describes God bringing order from chaos, a process that has historical, environmental, political, legal, secular and theological dimensions. Chapters 2 and 3 portray the first human beings in God's good world and describe how things went wrong. I shall read chapters 4 to 11, then, as an analysis of the "fallen" world in which humans have lived ever since. It is, as we shall see, a religious world; and its analysis gives us a basic framework for thinking about religious humankind.[70]

But first, how do we read the biblical text? How do we approach hermeneutics? I describe hermeneutics as relating three worlds or contexts: behind the text, of the text, and in front of the text. By "behind the text," I mean the context and setting in which it was written: we need to ask what questions the author(s) and editor(s) were seeking to address. Second, the world "of the text" is the text itself: we require a careful analysis of its structure and genre and of what it actually says. Finally, the world "in front of the text" is our own context as readers: we ask where we might see ourselves and our world, as it were, in the mirror of the text.

Typical readings of the Bible move step by step through these three worlds. We ask who wrote the text, when and why. We then study the text and move on to applying it in our world. The problem is that it is not really possible to work in this way. Whether or not we acknowledge it, we come to our study of the text and its context with the assumptions and questions of our own time and place.

---

69. The resulting book is *The Bible and Other Faiths: What Does the Lord Require of Us?* (Carlisle: Langham; Leicester: IVP, 2012), which develops the hermeneutic used here.

70. See my "Towards a Biblical Framework for Christian Discipleship in a Plural World," in *Pursuing the Friendship of Strangers*, ed. H. Boulter (Oxford: Oxford Diocesan Committee for Inter-Faith Concerns, 2009); and *Thinking Biblically About Islam: Genesis, Transfiguration and Transformation* (Carlisle: Langham Global Library, 2016), ch. 1.

My approach is explicitly to ask how the "world behind the text" is similar to and different from the "world in front of the text." Seeing similarities enables us to hear how the text speaks into our world as it spoke into the ancient world. Seeing differences helps us to avoid inappropriate applications of the text. In the particular context of today's religious world, we need to explore the religious world of the biblical authors. And it was indeed a religious world in which every person had a faith with gods and rituals and stories. However, we cannot always jump from that religious world to today's religions. For example, the many gods of ancient Canaan cannot easily be paralleled with the monotheism of Islam, so it is not appropriate to read denouncements of Canaanite polytheism as denouncements of Islam.

For reading Genesis 1 to 11, there are many relevant religious texts about origins from the nations surrounding Israel. While much of the material in these chapters originates in very early times, there are also many allusions to Babylon and its legends, so it seems likely that these chapters reached their present form during the exile. We can imagine people exploring why they were in exile, away from their own land, and looking around the city and seeing the massive temples, statues of deities and symbols of power.

So for Genesis 1 to 11, our consideration of the world behind the text needs to include what Babylonians thought about creation and the origins of their people. Our sources would review their writings, especially those which include parallels to the Genesis stories. We would also look at what history, archaeology and other disciplines can tell us about the Babylonians' culture and beliefs. From such studies we know that they had many gods and stories of creation and flood, sacrifices and rituals. They spoke about gods and nature, gods and people, and gods and kings. They had epic accounts of the warring between gods which led to the creation of the world through the division of the slain goddess of the seas into the heavens and the earth and of a great flood from which just one man was saved through building a boat.

This transforms our reading of Genesis. Chapters 1 to 11 include hardly any reference to spiritual powers other than the one creator God. There are only the cherubim of 3:24 and perhaps the mysterious "sons of God" and Nephilim of 6:2–4. Even the tempter is only a created animal. So a reading of the text alone would suggest that it has no relevance to the many faiths of today's world. When we read these chapters in the context of the ancient world, however, we realize that this text is in fact speaking into a world which had similar questions to our own. The Israelites in exile would have been asking, "Who are we? Who is our God? Who is their god or gods? Why are we here? What about them, the Babylonians? And how do we understand power?"

Today we are asking, "Who are we in relation to Hindus, Muslims, Sikhs and Druze? How does our God relate to their gods? Why do we live in a multi-religious world, in our particular places of power or weakness? What should be our attitudes to people of other faiths? And how should we understand the links between religion and power in our world?"

Having considered the worlds behind and in front of the text, we are ready to reread Genesis 1 to 11 with our questions in mind. It is important that we take into account the overall structure of the text as well as the details of its particular sections. I shall not take the space here to consider how Genesis 1 to 3 and 6 to 9 reshape the Babylonian creation and flood stories. Suffice it to say that they replace the warring pagan deities with the One Creator God, demonstrating that all the entities that have been seen as divine are actually part of creation. Further, they establish that One God as good and holy and as the one who supplies all that his world needs. For example, they turn the Babylonian stories upside down by showing that he feeds us and does not require us to feed him.[71]

There is much to be learned from this, not least from how the scriptures relate to and use pagan imagery, but I want here to move on to the less frequently considered portrayal of the post-Eden world in Genesis 4 to 11. The major thesis of this contribution is that these chapters portray a fallen *religious* world. They may not mention "religions," but when we read these chapters with the world behind the text in mind, we can see that the humanity to which they refer is, throughout, multi-religious humanity. I stress this point because so much of our Bible reading assumes that the norm from which everything else deviates is Christianity, or Judaism and Christianity, or maybe secularism. In fact, the Bible was written into a world where the norm is many expressions of religion, and God's work among the Jews and in Christ is the exception. I would suggest that this religious view is also how we should regard today's world! Hence, the Bible's anthropology is the inclusive anthropology which I have said that we need.

I analyze the structure of Genesis chapters 4 to 11 in chiastic form. Diagrammatically, it looks as follows:

---

71. For a thorough treatment, see Gordon Wenham, *Genesis 1–15*, Word Biblical Commentaries (Nashville: Thomas Nelson, 1995); and his *Rethinking Genesis 1–11: Gateway to the Bible* (Oregon: Cascade Books, 2015).

A		Cain and Abel (Gen 4)
B		Genealogy of death (Gen 5)
C		Story of Noah (Gen 6:1–9:29)
B'		Genealogy of life (Gen 10)
A'		Tower of Babel (Gen 11:1–9)

When we bring our questions about the religious worlds behind and in front of the text to this structure, we realize that A and A' are dealing specifically with aspects of *religious* humanity. As in any chiasm, the center, C, will give us the heart of the message. The intervening sections, B and B', show us how the whole text fits together.

Looking at it in detail, first, the story of Cain and Abel portrays individual religion. The very first narrative of humans born outside Eden is of people seeking to please God by acting religiously. We learn that offering sacrifice is something that can be expected from all human beings. However, we also learn that some sacrifices are acceptable, and some are not, and it can be hard to tell the difference or to explain why. It is interesting that most people want to know why Cain was rejected without realizing what good news it is that Abel was accepted. Even outside Eden, it is possible to relate to God! In this story, we are not told what makes Abel's sacrifice acceptable, so we cannot use it to discern which religious acts in today's world are acceptable to God and which are not. Rather, we must be content with the observation that God can see the human heart and we cannot.

Not only are religious acts normal to the post-Eden human condition, so is religious violence. It is the rejection of his sacrifice which leads to anger and violence within Cain. People often ask why others are violent, and especially whether particular religions are violent. Genesis 4 teaches us that violence and religious violence are to be expected in our fallen world: the key question is, "What prevents some human beings from being violent?"

There are more challenges for us here. Following the violence, we observe God dealing with the rejected one, having not acted to protect or save the accepted one. This illustrates, right at the start of the Bible story, God's concern for the rejected, in contrast to the qur'anic account which has Abel speaking to Cain while God is silent (*al-Māʾida* 5:27–31). This Genesis narrative is about God and Cain rather than about Cain and Abel. It is about God dealing with a sinner.

Second, the tower of Babel (Gen 11:1–9) portrays imperial religion: religion being used to build what I have called the "dangerous triangle" of people, power and land.[72] The residents of Babel speak of their place where they want to remain and to make a powerful name for themselves (11:4). This is a distortion of the created order in which humankind is told to spread into all the world, in the image of God but acknowledging their dependence on him (1:28). So dangerous is this to God's creation that he puts a stop to it.

The story clearly reflects the Babylonian story of the building of the temple to Marduk, the finale of the Babylonian creation story which leads to the coming of the gods to live in the temple where they will be served and fed by the humans. As a reflection inverts its object, so Genesis inverts the Babylonian story. The tower is not the apex of civilization: it is mocked. Far from reaching God, he has to come down in order to see it (Gen 11:5). He does not come to get food from humans: Genesis has already told us that he is the one who feeds them (1:29; 2:17; 9:3). He does not come because he needs a home: he comes to stop the building. The message to the believers looking at the Babylonian empire rings out: there really is One God, and he will deal will all the apparent power of other gods.

The Babel story tells us that the frightening links we see between religion and power in today's world are not surprising. Rather, they are a reflection of human nature, and we can expect to find them among Christians as well as among all other peoples. The good news is that God limits their project. He completely stops the tower building and limits all future human collaboration (Gen 11:6–8). He will not let dangerous religion go further than he chooses.

Third, B and B' are major genealogical passages. Genesis is a book of genealogy,[73] and it is not coincidental that the Bible often does history through genealogy (e.g. 1 Chr 1–9; Matt 1:1–17). In the context of the ancient world, Genesis 5 and 10 together emphasize the common origin of all peoples. The different peoples were not created by different gods: one God created all. Neither did he create different peoples in different categories: all trace their roots to the same ancestors. Chapter 5 emphasizes the continuity of individuals, and chapter 10 emphasizes the continuity of peoples.

Further, all the peoples of all religions share in both the creation blessings and the results of the "fall." In Genesis 5, we see the blessing of multiplication continuing in the long lives outside Eden, but the effects of the fall are emphasized as all but Enoch die. In chapter 10, we see the blessings not only

---

72. See my later contribution, section 8.6.

73. Evidenced not only by the genealogical lists but also by the marking of sections by the *toledoth* formula, "these are the generations of," rendered as "this is the account/family line of" by the NIV (Gen 2:4; 5:1; 6:9; 11:10; 11:27; 25:12; 25:19; 36:1; 36:9; 37:2).

of multiplication but also of the allocation of land and the development of languages, but this chapter is immediately followed by the Babel story which shows the darker side of people, land and language.

Today as in ancient times, this genealogical framework is the necessary context for understanding both the individual religious practices of Cain and Abel and the communal religion of Babel and for understanding both the violence arising from the former and the power abuse represented by the latter. In short, we are all in this together!

Fourth, in the center of the chiastic structure is the story of Noah and the flood. Violence and power abuse: we are all in this together. The Noah story, at the heart of Genesis's diagnosis of this religious world, is about how God himself responds to these terrible aspects of the world which he created. The story begins with an enigmatic description of sexual exploitation and descent into violence (Gen 6:1–5) and moves into God's declaration of his commitment to human beings in the still-fallen world which has emerged from the cleansing judgment of the flood (9:1–17). The latter is a fresh, clean picture of the One True Creator God in relationship with his creatures – if you like, of true religion. The former is the opposite. It is, as I have said, an enigmatic picture, and there are many opinions on the identities of the "sons of God," the "daughters of men" and the "Nephilim." It is very likely that they are allusions to stories in the religious world behind the text, but as elsewhere in Genesis 1 to 11, the religious dimensions are not made explicit. Rather among all the religions, what concerns God is the sin that damages the good world he has made – this is evidenced in 6:2, where the women are described as the daughters of *adam* who are *tov* (the word also used for good in Gen 1:4, etc.). The flood story is, then, about how God deals with the evil which keeps on erupting in our religious world.

The story of Noah and the flood in Genesis 6:5–8:22 is chiastic in structure. Diagrammatically, it looks like this:

    A   The heart of God and the human heart (6:5–6)
      B   Decision to destroy (6:7)
        C   The unmaking of the world (6:8–7:24)
          D   God remembers Noah (8:1)
        C'   The remaking of the world (8:2–20)
      B'   Decision to preserve (8:21)
    A'   The heart of God and the human heart (8:21–22)

Central at D is Genesis 8:1 where God remembers Noah. The extensive details of the flood in C reverse the order of the emergent creation of Genesis 1 as the flood waters engulf the earth: in C' when God "remembers," the flood recedes and the creation re-emerges. At B, we have God's decision to judge and destroy (Gen 6:7) which contrasts with his later decision to preserve in B' (Gen 8:21–22).

What, we may wonder, is the difference in the worlds before and after the flood? Why does God decide to preserve rather than to destroy? A and A' are our clues: both give glimpses into the human heart and into the heart of God. It is the evil of the human heart to which the divine heart (the seat of decision-making rather than the seat of emotion) responds in judgment, out of grief, pain and anguish (Gen 6:5–6). Will the waters of the flood cleanse the human heart? Will the next generations of "Cains" master the sin which crouches at their doors (Gen 4:7)? NO! In Genesis 8:21, the human heart is still evil. But, somehow, the heart of God responds to Noah's sacrifice with a commitment never again to destroy most of mankind. Yet Genesis gives even less explanation of why Noah's sacrifice was accepted than it gave for why Abel's sacrifice was accepted.

In the context of the flood stories of the ancient religious world, Genesis presents one God rather than many. It presents the reason for the flood as destructive human wickedness rather than as humans annoying the gods. Noah is not the favorite of one of the many gods, but a righteous person chosen by the one true God. We may have to wait to find out why any sacrifice is acceptable to God, but this simple story contrasts sharply with the Babylonian tale of the gods being hungry after the flood and swarming toward Noah's cooking to be fed.

In the context of today's religious world, we learn that the one true God is thoroughly aware of the problems of religious violence and power and sacrifice, and is well able to deal with them. In fact, the world was remade in recognition of such problems. Today, God could bring judgment at any time, yet he has chosen to deal with sin through the mystery of sacrifice. Neither the flood of judgment nor the sacrifices of Abel and Noah were adequate for dealing with human wickedness, but New Testament believers understand that judgment and sacrifice have come together in Jesus's death on the cross.

I offer this Genesis 4 to 11 analysis as a helpful framework for looking at religion elsewhere in the Bible and in today's world. First, we normalize religions: it is a recent Western phenomenon to regard "religion" as a problematic category. Normalization implies seeing all religious people as sharing the same human origins, with similar sinfulness and mortality, and with similar longings for God and for belonging to a people, a culture and a land. Next, we distinguish between individuals seeking for God on the one hand and groups seeking for power on the other hand. For example, it is interesting to take this distinction into our reading of the Gospels and also to see how Jesus deals with these two aspects of religion and their intersections. Finally, we recognize the underlying problems of human wickedness, the tensions between judgment and covenant, and God's priority of salvation.

Religions are, then, normal and diverse, and all, including Christianity, can become dangerous. Likewise, religious people are normal and so should not be regarded as other. Like us, they are likely to be seeking God; like us, they are definitely sinful; like us, they want a place for their own people; like us, they will die; and like us, they are under the rainbow covenant.

Perhaps most importantly, God's priorities for them are the same as his priorities for us. The Noah story is at the center of Genesis 4 to 11, and it is about God's concern for his whole creation. At the center of this central story is "God remembered Noah," the person from whom all the nations of the world would be spread out. The cross which brings together the judgment of the flood and the acceptable sacrifice is the culmination of God's remembrance of sinful humanity. His concern for the "Cains" has at last triumphed! Like us, people of all religions and of none are loved by God.

2.6 Christian Zionism and Mission: How Does Our Understanding of Christianity Impact Our Witness in the World?

Anton Deik

"Why is the number of people coming to Christ significantly less in Palestine than in other Arab countries?" a high-profile evangelist asked during a meeting of Palestinian Christian leaders. The answer came back sharp and clear from a Muslim background believer: Christian **Zionism**.

While one of the main themes of this book is the relation between our understanding of *other* religions and our Christian witness, in Palestine, there is an equally important concern that this section touches upon: namely, the relation between our understanding of *our own* religion (i.e. Christianity) and our Christian witness. More specifically, *how does Christian **Zionism** impact our witness?*

What Is Christian Zionism?

In the words of Colin Chapman, Christian Zionism is simply the "Christian support of Zionism that is based on theological reasons."[74] What fuels this support is the conviction that God has a special relationship with the Jewish people which continues today regardless of Christ. As a result, the promises of land do not apply to Jesus and his followers but to modern Jews. Therefore, according to Christian Zionists, the Jews have a "divine right" to the land of Palestine.

This theology legitimizes the ongoing Palestinian *Nakba*, or what Israeli historian Ilan Pappe rightly calls "the ethnic cleansing of Palestine." For many Christian Zionists, the establishment of the State of Israel in 1948 and its expansion in 1967 are "acts of God." For the Palestinians, however, they are *Nakba* (catastrophe) and *Naksa* (setback) respectively. The establishment of Israel in 1948 was accompanied by the expulsion of 750,000 Palestinians (among them 50,000–60,000 Palestinian Christians), the depopulation of more than five hundred Palestinian towns and villages, and no less than twenty-four massacres of Palestinian people.[75] In 1967, Israel occupied what remained of historical Palestine: the West Bank, the Gaza Strip and East Jerusalem, referred to as the Occupied Palestinian Territories. Today, life in these areas is marked by Israeli military checkpoints, an apartheid wall, confiscation of land, economic blockage, continuous expansion of settlements, forced separation of families, illegal military detention, and water and electricity shortages, to name a few of the challenges to daily living.[76]

Sadly, these atrocities and human rights violations are unnoticed by many evangelicals. Some actually go as far as justifying them, describing them as "miracles of God." I will never forget the first time I heard this from a brother I was serving with in East Asia as part of a mission organization. I was asked to share about life in Palestine with a community of around four hundred fellow missionaries. When I finished, a group of friends surrounded me and started questioning what I shared. After two hours or so of heated discussion, one brother encouraged me to open my eyes and see the "miracles" that God did in establishing and sustaining the State of Israel. As a new believer back

---

74. Colin Chapman, *Whose Promised Land?* (Oxford: Lion Hudson, 2015), 369.

75. For more about the Palestinian *Nakba* of 1948, see Ilan Pappe, *The Ethnic Cleansing of Palestine* (London: Oneworld Publications, 2007); and Nur Masalha, *The Palestine Nakba: Decolonising History, Narrating the Subaltern, Reclaiming Memory* (London: Zed Books, 2012).

76. For an introduction on the situation in the West Bank, East Jerusalem and the Gaza Strip since 1967, see Ben White, *Israeli Apartheid: A Beginner's Guide* (London: Pluto, 2014).

then, this came to me as a big shock: how can wars, ethnic cleansing and massacres be described as "miracles of God," and by someone who is a genuine follower of Jesus?!

If you ask the average Palestinian Christian about Christian Zionism, they will probably tell you that it is a cult somewhere in the West – in the USA – similar to Jehovah's Witnesses. This is what I thought before becoming an evangelical Christian. For me, Christian Zionism was something at the periphery of Christianity which did not represent genuine Christian faith. However, when I committed my life to Christ and decided to become evangelical, I found out that Christian Zionism is actually a default belief of evangelical churches in many parts of the world. In the USA, for example, between 25 and 30 million evangelicals are Zionists, along with no less than 80,000 pastors, 1,000 Christian radio stations and 100 Christian TV stations holding and proclaiming Christian Zionist teachings.[77]

With the widespread presence and work of Western missionaries, Christian Zionism was exported to other parts of the world. Today, Christian Zionist organizations have far-reaching branches and representations across the globe. For example, the ultra-Zionist International Christian Embassy Jerusalem (ICEJ) claims to have networks in eighty-six countries around the world, reaching as far as Latin America and Asia.[78] It is not an exaggeration to say that wherever evangelical Christianity spreads, so does Christian Zionism. Personally, everywhere I have met fellow evangelicals, I have also encountered Christian Zionism. In Hong Kong, my prayer booth was closed down because I wanted to share about Palestine. In Germany, I heard prayers for the protection of Israel and its military against the enemy (i.e. us, Palestinians). In the Philippines, I met a pastor who made his Filipino congregation kneel down in repentance of the Holocaust. In Bolivia, I saw Israeli flags in prayer houses and churches where no cross was present. In the UK, a fellow student at Bible college used the book of Joshua to justify the slaughter of children and women in Gaza. And the list goes on and on.

---

77. Stephen Sizer, *Christian Zionism: Road-Map to Armageddon?* (Leicester: IVP, 2004), 23–24.

78. The International Christian Embassy Jerusalem (ICEJ), "Worldwide Branches: The ICEJ's Presence around the Globe," https://int.icej.org/about/worldwide-branches.

What Impact Does This Have on Our Christian Witness?

I was born and raised in a Roman Catholic family in Bethlehem, Palestine. Although as a child I did have a living relationship with the Lord, as I grew into adolescence, I gradually left the faith. By the time I was at university, I had become an agnostic, almost an atheist. In the spring of 2010, however, I had a profound spiritual experience where I saw a vision of the cross. That incident turned my life upside down. A few months later, while reading the Gospel of John, I decided to commit my life fully to Christ. Although meeting Jesus was the most significant event of my life, it also brought many challenges. In the early months as a new believer, I became attracted to the evangelical faith, particularly its focus on Jesus and the Bible. However, as I started investigating and reading more about my newfound faith, I entered into a major crisis when I discovered that Zionism is the default belief of many evangelicals. Had it not been for the encouragement of Palestinian believers and the writings and witness of evangelical theologians, I would have probably left the Christian faith altogether.[79]

My story is not an isolated case. Sadly, many Palestinian Christians, especially among the youth, are leaving the evangelical church, and others are stumbling in their faith because of Christian Zionism. Although Palestinian evangelicals have been fighting against Christian Zionism for years, we still have a strong stigma in our community of being Zionists by mere association. This is one of the main reasons it took evangelicals more than two decades to be officially recognized by the Palestinian National Authority.[80]

What makes matters worse are the activities and beliefs of many missionaries and Christian workers in the Holy Land. For example, a few years ago a Christian organization held a big conference in Jerusalem which brought together Jewish and Arab believers. During one of the conference sessions, a missionary was asked to share a word with fellow believers. She read from the story of Hagar in Genesis 16, and after she finished, she commented saying

---

79. Among the evangelical theologians who helped me hold to my faith despite Christian Zionism were Palestinian evangelical scholar Yohanna Katanacho, especially *The Land of Christ: A Palestinian Cry* (Eugene: Pickwick, 2013); British Anglican priest Stephen Sizer, especially *Christian Zionism: Road-Map to Armageddon?* (Leicester: IVP, 2004) and *Zion's Christian Soldiers? The Bible, Israel and the Church* (Leicester: IVP, 2007); and American New Testament scholar Gary Burge, especially *Jesus and the Land: The New Testament Challenge to "Holy Land" Theology* (Grand Rapids: Baker Academic; London: SPCK, 2010).

80. The Council of Local Evangelical Churches in the Holy Land, which represents evangelical churches in the Occupied Palestinian Territories, only received Palestinian government recognition in 2019, around twenty-five years after the establishment of the Palestinian National Authority in 1994.

that it is time for the Arab church to take its place as a servant of the Jewish people, in the same way Hagar was a servant of Sarah.[81]

This story is not uncommon in Palestine-Israel. Unfortunately, a significant number of Christian missionaries and ministers who are active in evangelism in the Holy Land hold a Christian Zionist theology that marginalizes the Palestinians and justifies the continued settler-colonial occupation of their land. Their proclamation of the gospel is often intertwined with strong religio-political convictions such as "the Jews are God's chosen people," "they are the apple of God's eye," "God gave the land to Israel," "the establishment of Israel is fulfillment of prophecy," and so on. As a result, when the gospel is proclaimed to the Palestinians, we hear on the one hand "Jesus loves you" but on the other, "he gave your home to the Jews because they are special."

Sadly, this interweaving of mission and Christian Zionism is influencing Arab evangelists. Certain Arab Christian TV stations that are active in evangelism are hosting Zionist speakers, some of whom are not even Christians. These speakers are not invited to dialogue or even to share their views. Rather, they are invited on their own without any dialogue partner holding a different perspective and are given hours of airtime to passionately proclaim their radical Zionist views to Arab seekers and believers. What damages the Christian witness the most is that these Zionist teachings are broadcast on the same programs that aim to proclaim the gospel to the Arab world.

Such intertwining of evangelism and Christian Zionism is a major stumbling block to the gospel, as it jeopardizes the Holy Name of God, the Bible and the good news of the gospel. First, whether intentionally or not, this theology portrays God as a god of favoritism, one who prefers the Jews and discriminates against the Arabs on the basis of bloodline. It also depicts God as a warlord who is behind the *Nakba* and *Naksa* of the Palestinians, and who endorses colonialism, war and ethnic cleansing. In the words of Palestinian Christian theologian Naim Ateek, "what is at stake today in the political conflict over the land . . . is nothing less than the way we understand the nature of God."[82] Second, Christian Zionism distorts the Bible. Instead of using the scriptures to bring life and healing to the Palestinians, Christian Zionism uses the Bible to justify the Zionist project at the expense of the Palestinian community. The word of God that is supposed to be "a source of life and not of death"

---

81. *Note from the editors: see section 2.2 which counters such an interpretation of the Genesis text.*

82. Naim Ateek, *Justice, and Only Justice: A Palestinian Theology of Liberation* (Maryknoll: Orbis, 1989), 111.

is used "to threaten our existence as Christian and Muslim Palestinians."[83] Finally, Christian Zionism distorts the gospel of Christ. Instead of proclaiming the good news of the kingdom of righteousness and peace where a just God reigns, Christian Zionism brings news of discrimination, war and death. In the words of the Kairos Palestine document, "The 'good news' in the gospel itself has become 'a harbinger of death' for us."[84]

A Way Out

The early church in first-century Palestine grappled with something comparable to Christian Zionism. As Jewish believers, early Christians were impacted by the strong nationalist theology of Second Temple Judaism. Like other Jewish sects of their time (e.g. see Matt 3:7–9), they thought of themselves as special because of their ethnicity; they believed that God treated them differently than other nations. Therefore, at the beginning, they did not fully understand that the gospel included Gentiles.

This is why in the first nine chapters of the book of Acts we do not see the gospel reaching the Gentiles. The first evangelistic sermon to the Gentiles does not occur before chapter 10, in the house of a Roman centurion by the name of Cornelius. This story, commonly known as the "conversion of Cornelius," tells us also of another conversion, Peter's.[85] While Cornelius and his house were being converted to Christ, the Holy Spirit was transforming the theology of Peter and the early church. This theological transformation happened *before* the preaching of the gospel to Cornelius and his household, and *not after*.

In the first part of Acts 10, Luke records a vision that Peter sees while praying on the roof of Simon the tanner's house in Joppa (10:9–16). In this vision, Peter sees a big sheet coming down from heaven with all kinds of unclean animals in it. A voice tells him, "Get up, Peter. Kill and eat." Peter answers, "Surely not, Lord! I have never eaten anything impure or unclean." At that point the voice tells him, "Do not call anything impure that God has made clean." This happens three times before the sheet is taken up to heaven.

Peter does not understand the meaning of this vision until he reaches the house of Cornelius in Caesarea. There he is given the interpretation of the

---

83. Rifat Kassis et al., "Kairos Document – A Moment of Truth: A Word of Faith, Hope and Love from the Heart of Palestinian Suffering," Section 2.3.4, www.kairospalestine.ps/index.php/about-kairos/kairos-palestine-document.

84. Rifat Kassis et al., Section 2.3.3.

85. I am in debt to my PhD supervisor, Professor Steve Walton, who helpfully refers to this story as "the conversion of Peter."

vision through two distinct theological revelations. The first one happens at the moment he enters the house of Cornelius. Upon seeing the Gentiles that are gathered there, Peter tells them, "You are well aware that it is against our law for a Jew to associate with or visit a Gentile. But God has shown me that I should not call anyone impure or unclean" (Acts 10:28).

This first theological revelation is related to the way the early Jewish church viewed other nations. Although they were a genuine believing community and were filled by the Holy Spirit and spoke in tongues (the day of Pentecost), early Christians, like their contemporary Jewish sects, looked down upon Gentiles; they were outcasts that they were not to associate with. God had to change this mentality and theology of Peter and the early church before the gospel could reach the Gentiles: "God has shown me that I should not call anyone impure or unclean" (Acts 10:28).

After hearing the testimony of Cornelius and how he was directed by an angel of God (Acts 10:30–33), Peter says, "I now realize how true it is that God does not show favoritism but accepts from every nation the one who fears him and does what is right" (10:34–35). This profound theological statement is the opening line of his evangelistic sermon (Acts 10:34–43). Before Peter could even start to preach Christ, he needed to change his theology first and to clearly articulate his new understanding. While the first theological revelation was about how Peter and the early church viewed the other, this second theological revelation was about their understanding of God. As much as it might be striking, Peter's statement in Acts 10:34–35 indicates that the early church, up to that point, believed that God showed favoritism and partiality! This understanding of God needed to be transformed first before the gospel could be preached to the Gentiles. How could God's love be proclaimed while holding a false image of God as ethnocentric and discriminatory?

I cannot stress enough the importance of the events recorded in Acts 10 for the mission of the church. It is not an exaggeration to say that if it was not for this theological transformation of the early church, the gospel would probably not have reached the nations. Before the church could preach the gospel to the world, God had to cleanse his church from its false theology: how it looked at the other and the way it understood God. Only then was the church able to preach the gospel to the nations.

Today, the evangelical church is in utter need of this theological transformation. We simply cannot continue to preach the gospel while holding discriminatory and ethnocentric Christian Zionist theologies. Before preaching the gospel in the Arab world (or anywhere else), we need to go back to the basics: God shows no partiality, and no one has any privilege over another on the basis of race and ethnicity. "God does not show favoritism but accepts from every nation the one who fears him and does what is right." (Acts 10:34–35).

2.7 A Conversation among Friends: On the Abrahamic Family, Old Testament Law, Zionism and Sin, Punishment and Grace

"Conversation among Friends" sections in this volume represent semi-fictional reconstructions of various panels and group conversations that took place throughout the weeks of MEC 2018 and 2019. We tried to imagine how conversations between disciples of Jesus from Jewish (JBD), Christian (CBD) and Muslim (MBD) backgrounds around key themes of the book might pan out. They are meant to distill some of the key issues emerging from core chapters and to stimulate further thinking and conversations among readers or church study groups.

Abrahamic Family

Moderator: How do we understand the concept of the Abrahamic family? Is it useful in the elaboration of a common identity between Judaism, Christianity and Islam?

Christian-Background Disciple (CBD): In the Pauline writings, being a child of Abraham isn't primarily about genealogy. It's more a matter of faith than of bloodlines.

Muslim-Background Disciple (MBD): Well, Galatians chapter 3 speaks about the promises to Abraham being fulfilled through his seed. Is this not related to genealogy? Paul makes much of this seed being singular. Paul's argument is Christ-centric, though. In this CBD is right: all the promises are fulfilled in Christ. In Genesis, Abraham was called, chosen by God to be a route of blessing for others.

Jewish-Background Disciple (JBD): We all like to think that we are of the true faith of Abraham. To Jews, the children of Abraham are primarily Jews, although many like to include Christians and Muslims as belonging to the "Abrahamic religions." Similarly, to Christians, the true children of Abraham are Christian brothers and sisters, and for Muslims they are their fellow Muslims.

In the world in which Abraham was called, he was an obscure person in a small, obscure context. The Bible was written, revealed, in a very religious world, even if Genesis itself has few references to other gods: two are Rachel taking her father's household gods (Gen 31:19) and Joseph's wife being the daughter of an Egyptian priest (Gen 41:45). These acknowledge the existence of religious practices in the world. The focus is on belittling other gods and showing that everything comes together in the one true God.

Abraham is a problematic character when looking for harmony among Jews, Christians and Muslims. Only three stories are similar in the Qur'an and the Bible. There is material in the Qur'an that is not in the Bible, and little of the biblical material appears in the Qur'an. *(We will see an example of this in section 3.4.)* There is much more common ground with Moses, and some of us think that the character with the most commonality is actually Jesus.

Moderator: It is interesting, then, that though many like to speak of Abrahamic religions, this reference may not actually be very useful in interfaith engagement, since there seem to be more differences than commonalities in the Abrahamic narratives. Do religious adherents use Abraham more to emphasize what makes them unique rather than what unites them with the religious other?

CBD: In terms of engaging with others, I believe it is helpful to regard God as the only one who is truly other, and as we observed above *(see section 2.1)*, he waits in truly surprising places to ambush us with hope. God does not take sides. One illustration of this is when Joshua is preparing to attack Jericho. He asks "an angel" whose side he is on. The heavenly messenger responds "neither" (Josh 5:13–14). We have the option to take sides with God. So for Muslims, we should ask who is truly on God's side: it might be them, us, both or neither. The criterion ought to be acceptance of Jesus.

Old Testament Law and Its Relation to Grace

Moderator: What about Old Testament law? How does it relate to grace? Is that also a subject of division rather than unity?

MBD: Peter is an instructive character. In the Gospels, he fluctuates from profound insight and courage to denial of Christ (e.g. Matt 14:29; 16:16; 26:69–74). In the incident in Galatians (Gal 2:11–21), he is under intense social pressure from fellow Jews.

JBD: I think we can be too harsh on Peter! We must not underestimate the challenge that Paul and Peter faced. They were Jews, raised believing that the Jewish people were special. God's law had been given to them; it remained God-given law. What should they do with it? Pastorally and practically, they had Gentile and Jewish believers to consider. Some of them were mixing, others were being exclusive. Two deeply problematic questions were who could meet with whom, and could one meet with both? Similar situations occur in our era. Peter needed Paul's help to think it through.

Moderator: This moves us to how we understand grace today. In summary, the call of Jesus is why there is no difference between Jews and Gentiles: the only difference is whether or not one is in Christ.

CBD: All human beings share a common humanity and sinfulness. Jesus is the essence of our religion. Our faith is in him; it is not in ourselves. God sent Jesus for all: there cannot be any barriers among people. Some might reject Christ: that is their choice. Yet no barrier on ethnic or any other aspect of humanity should be erected by us.

JBD: Some reject us because they reject Christ. How do we cope when people reject us?

Moderator: Great question indeed, which I hope will be addressed later. But speaking of rejection, it is often preceded by a process of dehumanization, which leads us nicely into our next topic – Zionism.

Zionism

Moderator: Zionism has become a term that connotes conflict and oppression for many. But surely that could not have been its original intent. And many people today, both Jews and evangelical Christians, object to the negative use of the term. As a MBD, what can you tell us about this word? And how has it become a meaningful word at all within some church circles?

MBD: The term "Zionism" refers to the Jewish national movement founded by Theodor Herzl in 1897. At the core of Zionism is Herzl's notion of "the Jewish State," which is actually the title of a pamphlet that he published in 1896 – *Der Judenstaat*, a year before the First Zionist Congress in Basel, Switzerland. Central to Herzl's proposal is the idea of establishing a Jewish state, somewhere in the world, as a solution to Europe's antisemitism. When the choice of the Zionist movement fell upon Palestine, Herzl's preferred option, the Zionists faced a major problem. They wanted to establish an ethnically homogenous Jewish state, but Palestine was inhabited by other people – the Palestinians.[86]

It is important to note, however, that at least sixty years prior to Herzl's Jewish Zionist movement, Christians started paving the way for the Jewish colonization of Palestine, providing both theological justification and active support for the return of the Jews to Palestine.[87] For example, the infamous slogan used by the Zionists to colonize Palestine – "a land without a people for a people without a land" – was actually first coined by a Christian clergyman in 1843, long before the foundation of the Jewish Zionist movement.[88] This Christian support of Zionism took a more radical turn after the establishment of Israel in 1948, and especially after the 1967 six-day war, which is often remembered by Christians as a "miracle of God." Today, many Christians, especially among evangelicals, believe that Zionism and Jewish restoration to Palestine are simply part and parcel of Christianity. This, in my opinion, is a dangerous theology for many reasons.[89] How do you view this as a JBD?

JBD: In summary, Zionism today is, in practice, dehumanizing people. For the Palestinians, it pushes the Arab world toward instrumentalizing them: Palestinians are treated as pawns in a supposed long-running contest about the legitimacy of the State of Israel.[90] Christian Zionists tend to dehumanize Jewish people: typically, they do not care about Jews as individuals or their journey toward righteousness or criminality. I cannot understand how those who claim to follow Christ can be like this toward fellow human beings.

---

86. Israeli historian, Benny Morris, describes the dilemma by noting that the "obvious and most logical solution ... [was] moving or transferring all or most of the Arabs . . . And this, in fact, is what happened in 1948 [when Israel was established]." See Benny Morris, "Revisiting the Palestinian Exodus of 1948," in *The War for Palestine: Rewriting the History of 1948*, ed. Eugene L. Rogan and Avi Shlaim (Cambridge: Cambridge University Press, 2001), 40.

87. See Stephen Sizer, *Christian Zionism: Road-map to Armageddon?* (Leicester: IVP, 2004), 254. Sizer also notes that "without the initiative and commitment of some Christians (clergy, politicians and statesmen) during the nineteenth century, it is questionable whether the Jewish Zionist dream of a national homeland in Palestine would have been realised" (255).

88. For more on the history of this slogan, see: Diana Muir, "A Land without a People for a People without a Land," *Middle East Quarterly* 15.2 (Spring 2008), 55–62, https://www.meforum.org/1877/a-land-without-a-people-for-a-people-without.

89. The reader is referred back to the previous section (2.6) for further details on the negative impact of Christian Zionism on Christian witness.

90. *Note from the editors: See for example Marwan Muasher,* The Second Arab Awakening *(London: Yale University Press, 2014), 20–21. Muasher is a former deputy prime minister of Jordan.*

CBD: One resource that has helped me understand this is Colin Chapman, *Prophecy Fulfilled Today? Does Ezekiel Have Anything to Say about the Modern State of Israel?* (Cambridge: Grove Books, 2018). Chapman argues against Restorationism – the recreation of the State of Israel as the fulfillment of biblical prophecy; Restorationism underlies Christian Zionism. Chapman's argument is that Old Testament prophecy about Israel following exile in Babylon is rightly understood as being fulfilled in and through Christ.

Sin, Punishment and Grace

Moderator: So we touched upon the topics of Abraham, law and grace, and Zionism. All three topics seem to have come out as symbols of exclusion and difference, based on beliefs in election and exclusive right to land, rather than help us focus on inclusion and commonality. Is there anything at all that can bring people of different faiths together?

JBD: Your question, Mr Moderator, returns us to Abraham, where this conversation began, and continues the focus on grace. A "big picture" view of Genesis 3 to 12:3 is to regard it as a repeating pattern of sin, punishment and the grace of God. The first cycle is in chapter 3. The sin is that Adam and Eve ate the forbidden fruit. God responded by expelling them from the garden of Eden (Gen 3:23) and showed his grace by making garments to clothe them (Gen 3:21).

The second cycle is chapter 4 where the sin is murder (Gen 4:8), a more serious offense than eating a fruit. The punishment is further expulsion (Gen 4:11–12), and the grace of God is a mark of protection (Gen 4:15). The third cycle is the story of Noah. The sin is universal, affecting the whole earth, as does the flood as punishment. The sign of grace is the designation of the rainbow to mark the covenant of God not to destroy the earth a second time by flood (Gen 9:12–16).

The fourth cycle is the tower of Babel, in which the sin is arrogance and independence from God. There is a similarity here with Adam's sin. The punishment is scattering and confusion of language (Gen 11:7–8). The sign of God's grace is the genealogy to Abraham (Gen 11:10–32) and the promised blessing to all peoples (Gen 12:1–3). So, applying this to the biblical themes of election and land, we can see that God's grace covers the whole of humankind. Abraham is a conduit of God's grace for all and is a response to Babel.

Moderator: Fantastic! So perhaps there is hope in adopting Abraham as an inspiration for interfaith relations after all. Surprisingly, not in the way he is often put to use through the claim of "Abrahamic religions" or "Abrahamic family." Abraham, though a conduit of God's grace for all, is also a reminder of our common frailty and sinfulness. Perhaps it is universal sin that Jews, Christians and Muslims should adopt as their symbol of unity – what really unites them and should be the focus of their interfaith conversations. Nothing else! Thank you all very much for this delightful conversation.

Concluding Reflections and Questions for Discussion

The Bible was written in a multi-religious context. It is a recurring motif that the boundary between inclusion in and exclusion from God's people is blurred. What is clear in the New Testament is that one's response to Jesus is critical.

Our next chapter draws the themes of chapters 1 and 2 together as we explore the place of religion within society based on several geographic contexts.

Questions for Discussion

1. The Naaman story showed four different responses to a religious other in need: (a) simple words of loving care; (b) suspicion and anger; (c) a non-judgmental channel of blessing; and (d) scheming to exploit for selfish purposes. Which do we see in ourselves? And how consistently?
2. If the other constantly seeks a place of belonging, what welcome, acceptance and inclusion do we provide?
3. Why are some religious people, including some Christians, violent? What keeps more of us from turning to violent means?
4. Do we view and treat all people as loved by God?

3

Looking at Religion and Society

This chapter combines the findings of the previous two by examining the role of religion in society. We begin with the social sciences, asking what they teach us about our engagement with the religious other. This is followed by two examinations of different settings, seeing how the sacred and secular combine, often in subtle ways, to shape society. Our fourth contribution examines the presence of God and how this is understood in the sacred texts of Judaism, Christianity and Islam. This analysis moves us toward our focus on Islam which will consume us in part II.

We conclude with two perspectives on our approach to mission. The first picks up on social sciences in making a call for us to be very adaptive in our methods. The second perspective provides practical advice on how the religious other sees us. One recurring theme is the diversity within all major religions and the observation that people's practices often have multiple roots arising from culture and history as well as sacred texts. The themes of accurate perception and asking the right questions recur.

3.1 Christianity, Islam and the Secular: Learning from and through the Social Sciences

Richard McCallum

Many years ago when I was teaching at a university in Tunis, we were having a class discussion about whether it was possible to be Tunisian and Christian. Most of the class felt that this was impossible – except maybe for a few expatriate descendants born in the country. However, one group said that it was and they even knew someone who had become a Christian. I talked with this group afterward, and one of the girls admitted that she was the person. I asked her what had made her decide to become a Christian. She responded,

"I like the fashion and freedom." She clearly had no idea of Christian theology or who Jesus is; she just wanted freedom and a different set of clothes in her wardrobe. Alas, that is how many Muslims see Christianity: it is lawless. Its freedoms open the way to decadence and licentiousness, and it lacks the essentials of religion.

So in this section, I want to open up our conversation from our Christian consideration of Islam and other religious diversity to include the non-religious, or what we often refer to as the secular, and include the social sciences. Christians do not always see social scientists as natural allies, and many social scientists are suspicious of Christians, although they are sometimes interested in them as subjects to be studied.

I did my doctorate in the sociology department of a mainstream university with a wonderful Christian supervisor called Grace Davie. I was concerned that my faith position would be an obstacle, but as Grace pointed out, everyone has a position. So it proved: there were many people of faith in the department – Christian, Muslim and other – but also some convinced of no faith who were just as ideological and, if anything, more so.

What follows are broad brush strokes and pegs on which to hang our thinking, so details are necessarily lacking. I am aware that we must be discerning. We will need to "test the spirits," taking the good and rejecting that which is unhelpful. I have found that social science has some helpful ways of seeing things and poses some good questions. So I want us to consider: Why do religions exist? What role do they play in society? What is happening to religion in society and to society through religion? How do Christianity, Islam and secularism relate?

These questions are fundamental to a Christian understanding of other religions, and more importantly, to the psyche and lives of the followers of those religions. When a Christian invites a Muslim to follow Jesus, it is not a decision that can be seen in individual isolation. When a Muslim encounters Jesus, the earthquake affects not just the individual's life or just the life of their family but the whole of society. A second reason I want us to consider these questions is the prevalent Muslim accusation that Christianity is just the forerunner of secularization: they assert that it is Christianity in its Western form that has allowed secularism to dominate the state.

Why Do Religions Exist? Where Do They Come From?

For adherents, the answer to the question of where their religion comes from – certainly within the monotheistic traditions – is clear. Their religion has come by revelation: God has revealed it. It is the true faith whether revealed in written word, prophetic utterance or incarnate flesh. The question then arises as to where other religions have come from. This question is not so easy and attracts a range of answers. Maybe they also come from God and are all heading in the same direction. Maybe they started out being from God but have been distorted by human interference. Or maybe they simply came from the devil to deceive people and draw them away from the truth. All of these possibilities posit a supernatural explanation of origins.

Anthropologists have been acutely aware of this question and have proposed other answers. Indeed, many of the early missionaries were very careful observers of culture, and many leading anthropologists have been Christians, for example Edwin W. Smith and E. Evans-Pritchard. There are great resources within anthropology and **ethnography** that help those who are working cross-culturally and moving into new contexts.

Some of the answers that anthropologists have come up with to explain the origins of religions are interesting. The naturalistic school observes that people tend to want to know what causes things and so seek causal explanations of natural events. For instance, a thunder storm is interpreted as heavenly giants throwing rocks at one another, or illness is seen as caused by evil spirits. The animistic school feels that the inner world of thoughts and dreams is what led people to see a supernatural world. For the Christian, there are certainly echoes here of the biblical worldview. Some events are seen as having a supernatural cause, and we hear stories today of how dreams are affecting people, including Muslims, with visions of Jesus that are often very similar to his appearance in Revelation chapter 1.

Psychologists have also been very interested in religion. The way that religion meets emotional needs is a huge consideration in our understanding of and approach to people of other faiths. We need to be very careful that we are not manipulating people and taking advantage of them, particularly at times of vulnerability. Recently there has been much interest in the cognitive science of religion, looking at the degree to which religion is "hardwired" into people. A report from Oxford researchers suggests that Augustine might have been right: that the human soul is indeed "restless until it finds its rest in God."[1] The writer of Ecclesiastes might have got there before him (Eccl 3:11).

Whereas anthropologists and psychologists tend to start with the individual, sociologists start from the macro-societal level and are interested in the

---

1. Augustine quoted in Roger Trigg and Justin L. Barrett, *The Roots of Religion* (Farnham: Ashgate, 2014).

interactions among religion, people and society. One of the founding fathers of sociology was Max Weber who famously failed to provide a definition of religion. At the very beginning of his *Opus Magnus* on the sociology of religion, he wrote, "To define 'religion' to say what it is, is not possible at the start of a presentation such as this. Definition can be attempted, if at all, only at the conclusion of the study."[2]

Sadly, Weber died before he finished the book and never gave us a definition! However, he was the founder of what is called the ***Verstehen* movement** which is very interested in understanding what religion means for people and for society. This movement was a reaction to the positivist approach to science and involves putting yourself in the place of the people that you are considering – no bad place to be. Weber also developed the use of what is called the "ideal type." For instance, he discerned three types of authority – legal, traditional and charismatic – and we can identify these in 2018 as we look at different religious contexts. The ideal type is a useful method of categorizing things, although it is open to abuse and stereotyping.

What Role Do Religions Play in Society?

Beyond understanding what religion means to people, sociologists want to know what role religions play in society. Karl Marx showed an interest in religion and was convinced that it could not be understood apart from its context. He had a rather negative view of religion, seeing it as a way for economic elites to exploit people by numbing them to the pain of injustice; he viewed religion in terms of a class struggle. The role of religion in society remains an important question for us today. Religion is very much part of international conflict and struggle. What Marx failed to understand is that religion often becomes a tool of the oppressed in revolt against elites. In today's complex world, we see religion being used in many different ways. For example, in some cases it is used by powerful elites to maintain order. Yet it can be subversive of power both in violent forms and also in radical non-violent resistance seeking the common good.

Émile Durkheim, a contemporary of Max Weber, was particularly interested in the role of religion in structuring society. He saw religion as unifying a primitive society through its veneration of certain totems or sacred objects. He famously defined religion as a unified system of beliefs and practices relative to sacred things (meaning things which are set apart and forbidden)

---

2. Max Weber, *The Sociology of Religion* (London: Methuen, 1965), 1.

which unite into one single moral community (such as a church) all those who adhere to them.[3]

We still see religion binding societies together more or less through things such as religious law, for example *Sharī'a*, revered figures and leaders, or even through certain objects such as the flag in nationalistic "civil religion."[4]

However, if religion is important to the structure of a society, what happens when that religion is threatened? Peter Berger, one of the greatest contemporary sociologists of religion who died in 2017, coined the term "plausibility structure" to talk about the way that religion has traditionally provided a "sacred canopy" over a society bringing order and making sense of life. This canopy, or system of thought, provides cohesion for society and protection for the individual from what Durkheim termed the "**anomie**" of life, that is, the instability resulting from the breakdown of standards and lawlessness. Religion also provides a sense of group identity.

Religion has always been an important identity marker for the individual and groups. It provides a way of creating boundaries between "us" and "them." Just as surely as a tribe marks out its boundaries with stones and trees, so religions mark out their boundaries with clothing, buildings, food laws and marriage rules. Islam still provides a tremendously strong sense of identity through all of these visible markers. For instance, for many particularly young Muslims, their identity as a member of the worldwide ***umma*** has become formulated in opposition to the Western, secular, even "Christian" identity. Boundaries such as these are creating huge tensions in communities around the world and is a particular issue for converts to Christianity from a Muslim background who suddenly find that they have lost their sense of group belonging.

Tim Green's work on identity is particularly helpful in this respect. Drawing on social science theory along with his own empirical fieldwork, he looked at different levels of identity – the individual, the social and the collective. While new believers obviously find a new personal identity in Christ as sons and daughters of God, their struggle for social identity is more acute. In a sense they become victims again of anomie. They have lost their frame of reference and need new boundaries and relationships of belonging, which raises significant challenges for us in thinking what sort of new community we

---

3. Émile Durkheim, *The Elementary Forms of Religious Life* (Oxford: Oxford University Press, 2001). First published in French, 1912.

4. See for instance R. Bellah, "Civil Religion in America," in *Daedalus* 96, no. 1 (1967): 1–21.

are offering to converts in situations of religious diversity, but also the degree to which that new community can be contextualized within that diversity.[5]

In his early work, Peter Berger viewed the type of plurality and religious diversity that modernity brings as undermining and fatally weakening the "sacred canopy" or "plausibility structure" of a society. When people realize that there are other plausible explanations for the issues that they are thinking about, then the question arises as to whether any of the explanations are true. This became the accepted rule within social science: as societies modernize, they secularize, and one day religion will become irrelevant at least in its conservative, patriarchal forms. If Europe is in the vanguard of this secularization, then other countries are following suit including places like Turkey and Egypt. Yet over the last twenty to thirty years, this trend has looked less and less the case. America is still very religious, and Turkey appears to have gone into reverse, becoming more Islamic. In fact, if anything fundamentalism is on the increase, and conservative religion is thriving.[6]

Consequently in the 1990s, Berger had a radical rethink. He admitted that, "The assumption that we live in a secularized world is false. The world is as furiously religious as it ever was, and possibly more so . . . those who neglect religion in their analyses of contemporary affairs do so at great peril."[7] He also stated, "What I and most other sociologists of religion wrote in the 1960s about secularization was a mistake."[8]

So here is the challenge. In our consideration of religious diversity, we must take into account the role religion plays in binding society together. I think that Protestant Christianity is particularly weak here. The Catholic and Orthodox traditions have a different story, but Protestant Christianity has had less and less of a role in structuring societies in the Western world. In the MENA region, I am aware of notable exceptions in Egypt and elsewhere

---

5. See Tim Green, "Identity Issues for Ex-Muslim Christians, with Particular Reference to Marriage," *St Francis Magazine* 8, no. 4 (2012): 435–481. See also Tim Green's chapter in David Greenlee ed., *Longing for Community: Church, Ummah, or Somewhere in Between?* (Pasadena: William Carey Library, 2013). *Note from the editors: see also Jonathan Andrews,* Identity Crisis *(Malton: Gilead, 2016), 197–203.*

6. See Martin Marty and Scott Appleby, eds, *The Fundamentalism Project* (Chicago: University of Chicago Press, 1995).

7. Peter Berger, *A Far Glory: The Quest for Faith in an Age of Credulity* (New York: Free Press, 1992), 32. *Note from the editors: See also Madeleine Albright,* The Might and the Almighty *(London: Macmillan, 2006); and John Micklethwait and Adrian Wooldridge,* God Is Back *(London: Penguin, 2009).*

8. Peter Berger, "Epistemological Modesty: An Interview with Peter Berger," *The Christian Century* (29 October 1997): 972–978.

where evangelicals have been very active in society addressing issues of social justice, but I am sure that it is also true that Christian discipleship in Protestant thought is often presented as a privatized personal journey, an idea which the Orthodox and Catholic churches have found threatening. This perception has not been lost on Muslims who fear that Christianity is just an agent of secularization taking religion out of the public domain and privatizing it, enshrining it in the individual.

However, we need to pause and draw a few distinctions in the way that we use various terms surrounding what we call "secular." Originally the word in its Latin form merely differentiated the time of this life from the time of the age to come. In that sense, it referred to the present overlap of the ages as opposed to the fullness of the coming age or kingdom. In time, however, the term "secular" became associated with the separation of the religious and the non-religious, of the church and the state. This process of separation is what we call "secularization." It is an observable process that takes place and sometimes goes into reverse. José Casanova along with others has helpfully further subdivided this process.[9]

First, there is the differentiation of the spheres of power. In the West in the past, it was the church which provided health care and education and at times was even involved in government and the economy. However, a shift has taken place where it is now the state which takes responsibility for these things. In particular, the church no longer has governmental power. Rather, the secular state rules on behalf of all the diverse groups within society. This is sometimes called "procedural secularism." Abdullah Sahin has called this "inclusive secularity," which I prefer, and as a Muslim he welcomes it, as do many Christians.[10] He sees this type of secularization as protecting the rights of religious minorities in the West, and he bemoans the fact that such protections do not exist in many majority Muslim countries.

Second, Casanova observes that secularization is also used to refer to a decline in religious practice, such as church attendance, along with a decline in belief in God. Third, secularization is associated with the privatization of religion. In the West, religion has become a question for the individual, and it

---

9. José Casanova, *Public Religions in the Modern World* (Chicago: University of Chicago Press, 1994), 212.

10. Abdullah Sahin, "Islam, Secularity and the Culture of Critical Openness: A Muslim Theological Reflection," in *British Secularism and Religion: Islam, Society and the State*, ed. Yahya Birt, Dilwar Hussain, and Ataullah Siddiqui (Markfield: Kube, 2011), ch. 1.

has become less acceptable to talk about religion or use religious arguments in the public sphere.

It is the latter two aspects of secularization which particularly concern Muslims – as they should Christians. A decline in practice and belief has been observable in the West for many decades. There have always been public Christian voices, but they are increasingly marginalized. However, while secularization is the observable process of this happening and secularity may be a welcome bulwark between church and state, secularism is also an ideology associated with these processes. What concerns Christians and Muslims is an aggressive ideology that seeks to bring about the process of declining belief and practice and enforces the third process of expunging religion from public life. It is anti-religious, anti-clerical, and very vocal in some contexts.

The classic illustration of this phenomenon is perhaps the difference between American secularity with its wall of separation ensuring freedom of religion by protecting church and state from one another and the French concept of *laïcité* with its ban on religious symbols, insistence on assimilation, and phobia of all things religious in public life.[11]

Christians are rightly concerned about secularism. In 2011, the Pew Forum conducted a survey asking evangelicals what they saw as the greatest threat to Christianity. Secularism came out on top at 71 percent; Islam was fourth. Interestingly, that figure on secularism decreased among Christians in the Middle East to just 37 percent; still a significant number. Yet it is nowhere near how concerned Muslims would be if asked the same question.

Many Muslims fear secularization leading to secularism, and they see Christianity as an instrument of that process. For many Muslims, Christianity has allowed secularization to take place on its watch. Shabbir Akhtar talks of "Christian capitulation to secularism over the past three centuries when Western nations accommodated a politically truncated Christianity solely on secular terms."[12] Secularism's apparent lack of emphasis on law has opened the way for lawlessness, unchecked immorality, liberalization and unfettered freedom. For many, these things are what democracy is, and it is democracy that is seen to be the end goal of Christian civilization, the holy grail of Western foreign policy. Alas, promoting democracy is no longer seen to be

---

11. *Note from the editors: See Philip Halliday, "France's Evangelical Christian Community," in* The Church in Disorienting Times, *ed. Jonathan Andrews (Carlisle: Langham Global Library, 2018), 104–107.

12. Shabbir Akhtar, *Islam as Political Religion: The Future of an Imperial Faith* (Abingdon: Routledge, 2011), 9.

a pure motive. We all know that the Gulf Wars, Abu Ghraib, Guantanamo,[13] and protectionist policies have all convinced many Arabs that the "Christian" West is not interested in democracy and human rights. So secularization leads to democracy which is just the forerunner of capitalism and Western domination. Once religion has been marginalized, then greedy people have unfettered power.

Being dominated by others was the Arabs' experience of colonialism, and it has been their experience since. For Muslim countries, modernization and secularization – including democracy – in post-independence has meant injustice and authoritarianism under dictators supported by the "Christian" West. In many Muslim-majority countries, the secularist option often has links to the old regime, as in Tunisia where I used to live and work. Nader Hashemi neatly summarizes this West and non-West contrast: "In contrast to the West, therefore, where secularism has historically been a force for political and religious pluralism, in Muslim societies, secularism's legacy has been almost the exact opposite."[14]

I am not recommending starting Christian political parties or trying to seize control in an attempt to impose some Christian utopia. I recognize that in many places Christians do not have the right or opportunity to take part in government. However, I do want to remind us that religion always has political implications. Mahatma Gandhi is quoted as saying, "Those who thought that religion could be separate from politics understand neither religion, nor politics."

The challenge for us as Christians is twofold. First, to explain to Muslims and others that Christianity is not the bearer of secularization or worse, secularism. It is not lawless but rather has a higher law, the royal law of love for God and neighbor. It does not privatize faith and ignore social evils but has something to say to a whole society.

Second, we need to explain how we see our Christian faith shaping not just the individual but society as a whole. How do we see it as a force for good in our communities – even if we are numerically small? New believers need to know that there is a larger picture of hope. Sadly, Muslims do not

---

13. Abu Ghraib and Guantanamo refer to injustices perpetrated by a Western ("Christian") country. Abu Ghraib is an Iraqi prison in Baghdad which became infamous in April 2004 when photographs of US soldiers abusing Iraqis were made public. Guantanamo is a US military base on the island of Cuba used as a military prison to hold those suspected of being involved in violence motivated by extremism.

14. Nader Hashemi, *Islam, Secularism, and Liberal Democracy: Toward a Democratic Theory for Muslim Societies* (Oxford: Oxford University Press, 2009), 141.

see it that way. Shabbir Akhtar parodies the situation suggesting that while Christianity wrings its hands and says, "Things are so bad that nothing can be done about it," Islam counters with, "Things are so bad that something must be done about it."[15] We know that the kingdom of God is a force for good, but it is sometimes difficult for others to see this.

Thankfully there are some great examples of Christians getting involved in transforming society. Some examples include Musalaha's work in reconciliation in Israel-Palestine,[16] how Garbage City in Cairo was transformed by Christian hope,[17] and the Lighthouse project making films and documentaries for mainstream Arab television. All these types of projects encourage us – and Muslims – that Christianity still has a vital role to play in public life. Christians are not secularists, while at the same time believing that there is another king and an alternative kingdom (Acts 17:7).

3.2 Religion in a Shared Society: Finding Peace in a Fractured Society

Rose Mary Amenga-Etego

Ghana is a very mixed society. In terms of religious affiliation, over 70 percent are Christian, 17 percent Muslim, and the remaining 13 percent are shared among indigenous faiths and other religions.[18] Yet socially it is the indigenous religious beliefs and socio-cultural practices that govern daily life.

In this respect, Ghanaians live in and with multiple religious systems and identities. In another respect, Ghana is a religiously fragmented society. For example, there is the indigenous religio-cultural and communal system which undergirds the society, and the contemporary religions of Africa (Islam and Christianity) which are the socio-political and public religions. In this case, we now have a society that has been fragmented not only religiously but also culturally, socially and politically. The passing of my mother-in-law showed that some longstanding religio-cultural practices (the communal system) cannot be destroyed by the religious other. As the family gathered and participated in the burial rites, it was the family that mattered, not their individual religious

---

15. Akhtar, *Islam as Political Religion*, 240.

16. www.musalaha.org/.

17. The Garbage City area of Cairo has been transformed over a period of years by the faithful engagement of Christians; see Andrews, ed., *Church in Disorienting Times*, 74–76.

18. *Note from the editors: The term "African Traditional Religions" is used by some, including in chapter 9.*

inclinations. This point is instructive for the church in its dealings with the religious other.

In the African context, at least for sub-Saharan Africa, religious pluralism is the norm. From John Mbiti's text, it is often quoted that "Africa is notoriously religious." This is partly because indigenous societies believe in a plurality of spirits and the religio-cultural practices that are derived from them. There are multiple religions, even if in some groups people are defined by ethnicity and a shared religion like Akan Religion or Yoruba Religion. We accept diversity as a feature of God's creation. Globally and locally, the contemporary world is heterogenous in its religion. Consequently, there is a need to strive for unity amidst this diversity. I am all too aware that religious pluralism is often exploited by some to justify a variety of problems in society. Just as it has been used to justify problems arising from political, economic, environmental and socio-cultural backgrounds, so also is it applied to issues of exclusion, marginalization, oppression and exploitation.

Contemporary societies include both global and local aspects; ideally, the local is maintained within the global. This is especially important when considering one's sense of identity. We need to beware of the tendencies for homogenization, making everywhere appear the same, and isolationism, the rejection of external influences and ideas. We must reject both. One key area we can learn from is the contemporary patterns of courtship and approval for marriage rites in Ghana. How does the emerging generation balance global patterns with traditional practices? What role do they envisage for family elders in the local? We see this balance in the way the local is catered for by the customary marriage, which is in addition to any other form of marriage.

We need to understand what peace means. It is much more than the absence of conflict, including armed conflict and war. My interest in it has to do with its ability to produce or create wholeness even in the midst of diversity. In my society, peace is evidenced by the concept *sumasum*, coolness of or in the heart. It is believed that when one's heart is cool, not cold, it generates peace, goodness, kindness, happiness, joy, love, togetherness, unity, etc. In this case, it is generated from the inner being and is believed to occur only when one is in good relationship with one's spiritual entity/entities and family or community. In other words, peace has a religious and a communal source. Peace is about sharing responsibilities. It enables individuals to fulfill their roles, whether they are primarily religious, cultural, economic or political. Peace enables individuals to seek self-fulfillment, bringing both internal peace to oneself as well as sharing external peace with others. It underpins communal harmony which is dependent on our interpersonal relationships. Peace makes life worth living, and it is essential because it facilitates sharing.

In this context, there is the need to think and see peace holistically because it includes health and healing, especially in our traditional societies. Healing in this case is more than curing illness or disease. Health and wellbeing are more than physical illness, disease, dysfunctional relationships, destruction, environmental pollution, etc. Health includes the social, cultural, psychological and practice of religion, all of which are deeply significant.

We must realize that there are multiple levels of meaning to many symbols or symbolic expressions. Many aspects of symbols have deeper meanings that are significantly internal to individuals, even as they also have communal meanings. In my culture, our humanity is seen as both secular and sacred. In this sense, our very humanity is fractured, sometimes causing tensions, but it is also within this context that a shared relationship between the sacred and secular is needed to produce peace. It is also within this background that religious diversity thrives. It is therefore incumbent on each and all to find creative ways to accommodate competing views. As indicated in the funeral rites of my mother-in-law, the individual members of the family profess different religions, yet in our gathering as a family, we performed the different tasks demanded of us based on our status and roles. Performing those individual roles contributed immensely to the socio-cultural harmony, family bonding and healing of broken relationships, as well as the fostering of peace in our otherwise fractured religious life. At the same time, it provided an opportunity for dialogue and transformation through sharing, especially those times of music and dance. In conclusion, we must remember that the angels sang about peace on earth (Luke 2:13–14), and we should do likewise. We need to contribute toward peace for others, indeed for all.

3.3 Beyond Comparative Literature: Beyond the Sacred Page – Academic Engagement with the Religious Other

Havilah Dharamraj[19]

In India, the Christian canon has always had to compete with texts that also claim to be divine revelation(s). When the Bible first entered India through

---

19. As noted before, this contribution has been published elsewhere: Havilah Dharamraj, "The Curious Case of Hagar: Biblical Studies and the Interdisciplinary Approach of Comparative Literature," *Journal of Asian Evangelical Theology* 23, no. 2 (2019): 49–71.

the trading routes, perhaps in the first century, the sacred texts of Hinduism had already been around for a couple of millennia.[20] When the Bible came again, this time through the gateways of colonial rule and more forcefully than before,[21] it was preceded by another scripture: the Qur'an had been in India for almost a millennium as the sacred text of the Muslim rulers.[22] Perhaps there is no other environment as competitive for a sacred text as India. The canons of major world religions jostle for space, while acknowledging as demographically lesser rivals the Parsi *Zendavesta* and the sacred writings of the reform movements within Hinduism, namely Buddhism, Jainism and Sikhism.

In such religiously pluralistic environments, we regularly use **comparative literature** as a research method in seminaries. We routinely have our students comparing the biblical texts with textual or conceptual parallels in other sacred texts. Traditionally, comparative literature has been largely text-oriented. That is, the purpose of the comparatist was to establish a vector of influence pointing from an older work to a later one, to show how the production of the latter was shaped. This is what we might do in Islamic studies when we compare, say, the qur'anic account of the "son of the sacrifice" with Genesis 22, the account of Abraham's near sacrifice of Isaac. Here, the direction of influence (some call it "borrowing") is considered incontestable. The comparatist takes the Hebrew text as the norm against which to examine the continuities and discontinuities of the younger qur'anic version. Beyond this, the comparatist may wish to investigate the historical route of influence; and, being a theologian, they will be intrigued by the theological significance of the continuities and discontinuities.

In recent times, however, the secular discipline of comparative literature has shifted from being text-oriented to reader-oriented. Comparative literature now describes itself as "scientifically endorsing some of the intuitions we have as common readers."[23] For our purposes, the common reader[24] can be anyone

---

20. The entry of the Aryans into the Indian sub-continent may be dated between 1500 and 1300 BC. John Keay, *India: A History* (London: Harper, 2010), 27.

21. The first European Protestant missionaries were the Pietists Bartholomew Ziegenbalg and Heinrich Plütschau dated to 1706. The century following saw a tremendous burst of missionary activity in India as across the rest of the "pagan" world. See a global overview in Paul E. Pierson, "Why Did the 1800s Explode with Missions?," Christianity Today, www.christianitytoday.com/history/issues/issue-36/why-did-1800s-explode-with-missions.html.

22. Muslim entry into India began c. 663, e.g. Keay, *India*, 181.

23. César Domínguez, Haun Saussy, and Darío Villanueva, *Introducing Comparative Literature: New Trends and Applications* (Abingdon: Routledge, 2015), ix.

24. See the origin of the phrase from Samuel Johnson borrowed by Virginia Woolf, in Domínguez, Saussy, and Villanueva, *Introducing Comparative Literature*, xi.

we minister to: the people at our small group Bible study or the people with whom we wish to share our faith. Here are three things to learn about the common reader that might make our engagement with religious others more effective. First, what does the common reader read?

The Common Reader Reads Other Literature

Common readers have in their head a "mental encyclopedia" within which connections are made among literary works. Let me give you an example using the book *The Handmaid's Tale* written by Margaret Atwood, a Canadian, and first published in 1986. This is a futuristic novel set in a time when North America has been laid waste by environmental disasters which have affected human fertility. In this dystopian world, run by a Christian theocratic state, it is illegal for women to hold jobs, own property, handle money or read. They are controlled by a minority male elite which assigns them group identities. Some are married off by the State and are called Wives. Many are maintained as servants and called Marthas. The precious few who are fertile are forcibly assigned to barren Wives as concubines, designated Handmaids, and treated by the state as a "national resource." If we know our Genesis stories, we will spot that this is Atwood's re-creation of household structure in the patriarchal stories.

The government uses the Bible to keep its subjects in a perpetual state of terrified submission, each person with clearly defined roles. Here is how the protagonist of the story, a Handmaid, describes herself: "We are for breeding purposes: we aren't concubines, geisha girls, courtesans. On the contrary, everything possible has been done to remove us from that category. There is supposed to be nothing entertaining about us. . . . We are two-legged wombs, that's all."[25] The Handmaid temporarily lives with the Husband and his barren Wife in a repressive *ménage à trois* till such time as she conceives and bears a child. She is impregnated through a bizarre ceremony that literally enacts the words of Rachel to Jacob: "Behold my maid Bilhah, go in unto her; and she shall bear upon my knees, that I may also have children by her" (Gen 30:3 KJV).

The Handmaid's Tale has now reached the status of a contemporary classic and is hailed as insightful social commentary. The common reader who has read it comes to the Hagar stories "influenced" one way or another. Therefore,

---

25. Margaret Atwood, *The Handmaid's Tale* (New York: Houghton Mifflin Harcourt, 1986), 128.

let us say a student of mine wants to do an exercise in comparative literature to prepare her for youth ministry in an educated, urban Indian setting. Rather than asking the traditional question, "How does the qur'anic account of Hagar influence a Muslim background believer's reading of the biblical account of Hagar?" she could ask, "How does *The Handmaid's Tale* influence a new Christian's reading of the Hagar narrative in Genesis 16 and 21?"

In such a scenario, you see how the task of the comparatist is even more adventurous than before. We may move beyond comparing one sacred text with a parallel sacred text. We may get into the mind of the common reader, the religious other, to examine how their reading of the biblical text may be influenced by contemporary literature that has gained widespread standing.

The Common Reader "Reads" the Public Meaning(s) of Literature

As a literary work "moves through time and space it accrues meaning, sheds meaning, provokes meaning."[26] In historiography, this is the *longue durée* – the long stretches of time over which imperceptible changes can happen. In comparative literature, the *longue durée* of circulation and transmission of a text (perhaps including orality) creates what is called its "public meaning."[27]

For an example, I take a Hagar-like heroine from the sacred literature of Hinduism, from the ancient epic poem called the *Ramayana*. The female protagonist of the *Ramayana* is Sita, married to a legendary king named Rama. By a series of unfortunate events, the royal couple are forced into exile for fourteen years. In the course of their wanderings, Sita is abducted by Ravana, ruler of the island kingdom of Lanka, modern day Sri Lanka. Rama then journeys south at the head of a great army, invades Lanka, fights the abductor Ravana, and rescues his wife, Sita. However, as he prepares to meet his wife, he has to deal with the idea of living again with a wife who might now be damaged goods. So, he devises a way out. He requires Sita to undergo an ordeal by fire before she is taken back as his wife. If she burns to death, it means she has been ravished by her captor and is no longer worthy to be his queen. If she survives, the miracle affirms that she remained chaste

---

26. Michael Lucey, "A Literary Object's Contextual Life," in *A Companion to Comparative Literature*, ed. Ali Behdad and Dominic Thomas (Chichester: Wiley-Blackwell, 2011), 128. See Kumkum Sangari's treatment of this idea using Mughal art as an illustration. "Aesthetics of Circulation: Thinking between Regions," *Jadavpur Journal of Comparative Literature* 50 (2013–2014): 9–38.

27. Lucey, "Literary Object's Contextual Life," 121.

in captivity and should be reinstated as his wife. Sita acquiesces to the ordeal and miraculously emerges from the fire unharmed.

Rama and Sita live happily, but not ever after. She becomes pregnant, but despite having passed the test for purity, rumors persist that she conceived in captivity. Rama eventually gives in to public opinion and banishes Sita to the forest to save his reputation. There, she is taken into the hermitage of a sage and gives birth to twins. Years later, the sage brings the twin princes to the royal court to present them to their father. Rama is overjoyed at the sight of the little lads, grieves that he expelled his wife, and asks to see her. Sita comes forward but refuses to return to Rama. In the sight of Rama and his court, she prays to her divine mother, the earth-goddess, to receive her into her bosom. The ground opens and Sita is swallowed up, never to be seen again.

The *Ramayana* exists in dozens of versions across an arc of countries and cultures where Hinduism found a home. Besides the multiple Indian versions, there are Nepali, Thai, Myanmarese, Cambodian, Filipino, Malaysian and Indonesian retellings. As sacred literature in the form of narrative allegory, it is prescriptive for practitioners of Hinduism: so, for example, Rama is seen as the ideal husband; Sita is the ideal wife.

The stories of Sita and Hagar are not without parallels. One of my students may wish to employ the method of comparative literature to study these two sacred texts side by side. That is what the traditional comparatist would do, but now we think of the common reader, the one whom my student will serve in their ministry setting. So, before my students rush off to find a critical edition of the *Ramayana* to commence study on, I might point them to something more relevant to their future ministry. For example, the blog of Satya Chaitanya, a management consultant based in north India. This is what Chaitanya blogs about Sita:

> The popular image of Sita that so powerfully shapes the Indian womanhood is essentially that of a very docile person, someone who gives unbounded love but accepts injustice, cruelty, neglect, humiliation and banishment quietly, uncomplainingly. The ideal wife archetype is perceived as a martyr, willingly sacrificing herself for the purposes of her man, with no purposes of her own.[28]

---

28. Satya Chaitanya, "Reimagining Indian Womanhood: Sita as a Woman of Substance," Inner Traditions (July 2009), http://innertraditions.blogspot.com/2009/07/reimagining-indian-womanhood-sita-as.html.

Having set out this conception of Sita's characterization, Chaitanya labors at length over the original Sanskrit text to demonstrate that Sita's "popular image" is flawed. He wishes to show from the sacred text that Sita is a feisty woman with a keen sense of justice and who does not hesitate to stand up for herself.

You see what we mean by a text having "public meaning." The public meaning of a text often triumphs over the specifics of the text's stated meaning. Our common reader, the one we serve in our ministry setting, is often influenced by the public meaning of a text more than by what the text actually says. The implication is that the religious other brings to their reading "acquisitions that are not simply personal." These are acquisitions "that are related to that person's trajectory through a particular social universe, related to her or his interaction with that universe."[29]

So, let us say a student of mine wishes to do an exercise in comparative literature, comparing Sita in the *Ramayana* with Hagar in the Bible. I would encourage my student to compare the Hagar story with the Sita out there in the public domain, rather than with the Sita buried in the *Ramayana*. That is the way we engage with our common reader because they know the public Sita, not the one that must be exegeted out of Sanskrit text.

How do we get at the public meaning of a text? The public meaning of a text is usually to be encountered in the non-text forms of the text. Here is an example. I met a student who was writing an essay on how Hinduism views widows. Library research will probably take her to what the Hindu sacred texts say about widows, revealing that older texts are sympathetic to them while some later texts are not. Texts are a good starting point. However, the student should also watch the movie *Water* which was released in 2005 in the face of stiff opposition from Hindu extremists who thought it depicted Hinduism in a poor light. What the movie sets out is the ugly public voice of centuries of practice that has overpowered the gentle voices of the more sympathetic sacred texts. Here is a carefully researched movie that sets out the public face of Hinduism's perspective on, and treatment of, widows.

So, the question that secular comparative literature is asking is whether the method should confine itself to oral and written textual traditions or must it embrace the arts also? The answer is that comparative literature is the meeting point for the arts. Being the only word-based art, it is the sole verbalizer of the

---

29. Lucey, "A Literary Object's Contextual Life," 121.

comparative threads running across the plastic arts (e.g. painting, sculpture and film) and the performance arts (e.g. music, dance and theatre).[30]

For an illustrative example, we return again to the *Ramayana* to consider its multiple appearances in non-text forms: it is performed in various dance traditions; it is sung by local troubadours; and it is the subject of the folk art Madhubani style of paintings[31] which has received a geographical indication (GI) tag.[32] It was a successful television series that ran for seventy-eight episodes from 1987 to 1988 and entered the Limca Book of Records as the "world's most viewed mythological serial." Which other discipline could analyze and critique and synthesize this transduction across the arts but comparative literature? Think of how impoverished a study of the use and appropriation of the *Ramayana* would be if we limited it to extant textual traditions. More critically, think of how alarmingly inadequate would be our understanding of the common reader to whom all these various media provide the bits and pieces by which they construct the lenses with which they come to the biblical text.

The Common Reader Reads "Postliterature"

In an age beyond Gutenberg, our common reader has become a digital native. This demands a catch-up with new forms of literature created by "technologies of the word,"[33] for example the narrative art of augmented reality games like *Pokemon Go*.[34] Indeed, "digital Humanities" makes necessary "a fundamental rethinking of *how* knowledge is created, *what* knowledge looks (or sounds

---

30. Domínguez, Saussy, and Villanueva, *Introducing Comparative Literature*, 108.

31. Neha Das, "Recounting Ramayan through Madhubani Art," *Deccan Herald* (15 October 2014), www.deccanherald.com/content/435958/recounting-ramayana-through-madhubani-art.html.

32. A geographical indication (GI) is an identification given to certain products which correspond to a specific geographical location or origin (e.g. a town, region or country) in order to protect the product from being duplicated. Darjeeling tea was the first GI tagged product in India in 2004–2005.

33. J. Walter Ong, *Orality and Literacy: The Technologizing of the Word* (London: Routledge, 1982), cited in Domínguez, Saussy, and Villanueva, *Introducing Comparative Literature*, 130.

34. Niantic CEO John Hanke thinks that augmented reality (AR), compared to virtual reality that isolates the player, is "far more interesting and promising . . . for humanity" because "AR is designed to add, enhance the things you do as a human being: Being outside, socializing with other people, shopping, playing, having fun." Eric Johnson, "Full Transcript: Niantic CEO John Hanke Talks Pokémon Go on Recode Decode," Recode (4 October 2016), www.recode.net/2016/10/4/13166612/john-hanke-niantic-pokemon-go-recode-decode-podcast-transcript.

or feels or tastes) like, *who* gets to create knowledge, *when* it is 'done' or published, *how* it gets authorized and disseminated."[35]

What is more, the democratization of reading and writing has gathered speed to give rise to a landslide of those who write without having (sufficiently) read, creating an avalanche of work that might be called "postliterature."[36] It is an age in which "the boundaries between high and low culture, between advertising and art have been erased."[37]

So, yet another alternative for a student doing a comparative literature assignment on the Hagar story is "postliterature" in the form of the #MeToo movement. This is the hashtag that went viral on social media in October 2017 against sexual harassment and assault, especially in the workplace. I would relish reading an essay that thoughtfully and insightfully put the Hagar narrative into conversation with the Facebook posts and Twitter feeds of the #MeToo movement. Theology and theologizing have kept pace with each new expression of literature, and sooner or later, it will have to negotiate with the digital revolution.

Conclusion

We have described the new ground that lies before the theologian-comparatist. The task has moved on from text-related enquiry to reader-oriented investigation. The comparatist works from the point of view of the common reader. This is comparative literature from below, and it consists of three new elements. First, we consider the relevant contemporary literature that our common reader is reading. Second, we consider the public meaning of sacred texts as generated within the social universe of the common reader that they access largely through the plastic arts and the performing arts. Third, we consider digital "literature" which is a part of our common reader's daily life, some of which could be low-brow "postliterature."

For the sake of relevant theology, missional application and pastoral practice in an increasingly religiously plural world, seminaries should at least follow where secular comparative literature is going. It is going beyond sacred

---

35. Todd Presner, "Comparative Literature in the Age of Digital Humanities," in *A Companion to Comparative Literature*, ed. Ali Behdad and Dominic Thomas (Chichester: Wiley-Blackwell, 2011), 195, emphasis original.

36. Domínguez, Saussy, and Villanueva, *Introducing Comparative Literature*, 134.

37. Efraín Kristal, "Art and Literature in the Liquid Modern Age," in *Companion to Comparative Literature*, 118.

texts into contemporary literature, into the public theatres of the arts, and even into cyberspace!

3.4 One Question: Where Is the Shekinah?

Jonathan Andrews

This contribution moves toward our focus on Islam and Muslims by examining the presence of God as described in the sacred texts of Judaism, Christianity and Islam. It is a brief summary of some aspects of a wide-ranging presentation given by Ida Glaser.

Where Is the Shekinah, the Presence of God with His People?

We will take snippets from the Torah, the rest of the Hebrew scriptures and two New Testament passages. Along the way, we will comment on corresponding passages in the Qur'an. We begin in the book of Exodus, which opens with a description of the Israelites oppressive bondage in Egypt. Their cries go up to God (Exod 2:23), who looks on them with concern (Exod 2:25). The exodus from Egypt happens, and there is rapid progress to Mount Sinai. Moses ascends the mountain several times. On the third day, the Lord comes down in sight of all the people with the mountain summit wrapped in smoke and fire (Exod 19:16). One theme of Exodus is going up and down. Moses goes up and receives the Ten Commandments on two stones. Alas, while he is absent the people fall into idolatry, creating the golden calf. Moses breaks the tablets, restores due order to the camp, and seeks God's forgiveness on behalf of the community. Later in the story, the tabernacle is constructed, and the glory of the Lord descends to fill the sacred space (Exod 40:34–38); shekinah has arrived. The book ends with God coming to dwell among his people, those whom he has called to be a blessing on the nations.

What do Muslims make of this account? The Qur'an includes similar material in *Sūrat al-A'rāf* (7), although there are crucial differences.[38] The Qur'an focuses on God taking Israel out of Egypt. The law is given, but the details are omitted since the Qur'an replaces previous revelations of God's law. The Qur'an also omits all reference to priesthood and tabernacle and has just one mention of the Jewish sacrificial system. In the qur'anic version of

---

38. The insights of comparative literature, especially direction of influence, discussed in the previous section would be applicable to study of these qur'anic passages.

events, God shows himself to the mountain which collapses (*al-A'rāf* 7:143). The actual presence of God is absent: God is up there, and we are down here.

Yet many Muslim people do not think like this; they seek God in prayer. **Sufis** in particular have a longing for the presence of God. As noted in the two preceding sections, people's religious practices can have multiple roots, including some outside of their sacred texts.

Returning to the story of the Israelites, they settle in the land promised to the patriarchs, inaugurate a kingship and build the temple. When commissioned, the presence of the Lord descends to fill the temple (2 Chr 7:1). Prior to the final exile in Babylon, the shekinah is seen to leave this temple (Ezek 10:18).

The exiles returned to the land, and the temple was rebuilt and dedicated (Ezra 6:16). Yet the overt presence of God was not perceived as returning. In this post-exile era, Ezra taught the law, and worship comprised reading and studying the law, Torah, a practice that continued in the first century.

This overview sets the context for the incarnation of Jesus and the life of the early church. Followers of Judaism were aware that they had the law and that breaking the law had led to the Israelites being exiled. Consequently, they had an intense focus on keeping the law; the Pharisees are a prime example. The shekinah would return with the Messiah; its loss was crucial.

We will look at one incident in the life of Christ and one of Paul's epistles. The transfiguration of Jesus (Matt 17:1–13; Mark 9:2–13; Luke 9:28–36) occurred on the top of a mountain. Moses, the recipient of the law and leader of the people, and Elijah, who was zealous for the law, spoke with Jesus about his forthcoming exodus in Jerusalem. The disciples present were left with Jesus and the instruction to listen to him. The incident is a clear expression of the glory of God and of shekinah, God's presence with us, his dwelling with us.

The Qur'an presents the transfiguration differently. Ida Glaser presents a detailed analysis of this presentation in her book *Thinking Biblically about Islam: Genesis, Transfiguration and Transformation*.[39] Simplistically, the Qur'an records the instruction to listen to Jesus but includes no indication of what was said or discussed. Jesus is given a similar status to Moses and Elijah. Muhammad is presented in the Qur'an as similar to Moses, the recipient of revealed law and leader of God's people. Muhammad is also presented as zealous for law like Elijah was. In a sense, Islam combines Moses and Elijah into Muhammad. Much in Islam is continuous with Christianity, yet there is

---

39. For a fuller treatment of this, see Ida Glaser, *Thinking Biblically about Islam: Genesis, Transfiguration and Transformation* (Carlisle: Langham Global Library, 2016).

the devastating removal of the heart of the gospel, notably the cross, Jesus's exodus, and the presence of God with his people: shekinah is neither present nor expected.

Finally, we will take a snapshot from one of Paul's epistles. One theme of Galatians is that we are all one in Jesus; there is neither Jew nor Gentile (Gal 3:26–28). In the middle of Galatians, Paul poses a question: "Did you receive the Spirit by the works of the law, or by believing what you heard?" (Gal 3:2). The first readers knew that the shekinah had not returned despite all the efforts at law-keeping. These readers knew the answer. Paul's argument is that faith in Christ is the route to the Spirit and hence the presence of God. This casts out keeping the law as the means of acquiring the shekinah.

To conclude, where is the shekinah? For Judaism, awaited with the Messiah; for Islam (as described in the Qur'an), not available to human beings in this world; but for Christianity, available to those who follow Jesus. The Holy Spirit was given widely at Pentecost, with a flame touching each recipient. The shekinah has come in a new way.

3.5 Adaptive Missiological Engagement with Islamic Contexts

Warrick Farah[40]

Developing appropriate missiology in a Muslim context takes wisdom, patience and skill. So how can we, as practitioners who love Muslims, deal with the diversity of approaches to the religious other in the New Testament and the diversity of approaches to Muslims seen across the church?[41] Why does God seem to be blessing so many drastically different approaches to working with Muslims today, sometimes even in the same context? I propose an "adaptive" approach to mission: in a world full of multifaceted challenges, mission must adapt to the issues it faces in each context. This follows the example of how Jesus and his disciples engaged with complex situations in the New Testament. Adaptive missiology is a reflective process that enables us

---

40. A fuller version of this contribution appears in Warrick Farah, "Adaptive Missiological Engagement with Islamic Contexts," *International Journal of Frontier Missiology* 35, no. 4 (2018): 171–178. Some referencing has been omitted here. www.ijfm.org/PDFs_IJFM/35_4_PDFs/IJFM_35_4-Farah.pdf.

41. See for instance Warrick Farah and Kyle Meeker, "The 'W' Spectrum: 'Worker' Paradigms in Muslim Contexts," *Evangelical Missions Quarterly* 51 (2015).

to deal with complexity as we discern gospel-centered responses appropriate for specific contexts.

Changing Understandings of Muslim Contexts

Significant shifts in recent decades have influenced how we conceptualize Muslim contexts and make the gospel accessible in such communities. Reactions against colonialism and the influence of postmodernism led to changes in anthropology and religious studies which have played a large and often unexamined role in how we, as Christians, understand our biblical calling to engage Muslims in Islamic contexts. I offer a brief survey of these influences.

In 1978, Edward Said published an influential critique of Western scholarship on Asia titled *Orientalism: Western Conceptions of the Orient* (revised in 1994).[42] Even if Said's arguments are at times polarizing (or if he, ironically, negatively stereotypes Western scholarship), he exposes the prejudicial and monolithic thinking of some Western scholars in their descriptions of the "orient" during the colonial period. Worth highlighting is his framing of the way some European and American scholars describe Arabs, and especially Muslims, in a generally pejorative construct. Such a narrative created a discourse in the West of a *civilized Western "us"* versus an *uncivilized Eastern "them,"* which was used to reinforce Western colonialism and imperialism over parts of Africa and Asia.

Some traditional missionary discourse was a form of orientalism. Muslims were often described in a way that dichotomized the world into two antagonistic and incompatible realms, Christian and non-Christian. "Like Orientalism, missionary discourse traditionally has been aggressive and derogatory in its treatment of Asians of other faiths, expressing attitudes that have frequently also included negative views of indigenous cultures."[43] Said's insights offer critical reflection upon our approaches to understanding Muslims, leading us to ask if we describe Islam in overly negative ways, failing to also see the problems in our own cultures (cf. Matt 7:5). When seeking to describe unknown and seemingly threatening contexts, do we resort to a simplistic

---

42. Edward W. Said, *Orientalism: Western Concepts of the Orient* (New York: Pantheon, 1978; Random House, 1994).

43. Herb Swanson, "Said's Orientalism and the Study of Christian Missions," *International Bulletin of Missionary Research* (2004): 109.

"textual attitude"[44] by cherry-picking our descriptions of Muslims from the worst texts found in the Qur'an and Hadith? Do we feel superior to Muslims, or do we approach them with humility and with the attitude of a learner? This kind of missiological reflection is an important antidote for biased and injurious theologies of mission.

Another common assumption challenged by postcolonial studies is the idea of a unified geopolitical entity called "The Muslim World." This idea does not come from the Islamic teaching of *umma* but instead emerged in the nineteenth century:

> Mistaken is the belief that Muslims were united until nationalist ideology and European colonialism tore them apart. This is precisely backward; in fact, Muslims did not imagine belonging to a global political unity *until* the peak of European hegemony in the late nineteenth century, when poor colonial conditions, European discourses of Muslim racial inferiority, and Muslims' theories of their own apparent decline nurtured the first arguments for pan-Islamic solidarity.[45]

"The Muslim World" construct is a racial product of the colonialist narrative and has been embraced by both Muslims and Westerners to homogenize "Muslims" and the "West" in (often antagonistic) political discourse. In mission, we can learn to recognize the phenomenon without being biased by this understanding of Muslims.

Colonialism and imperialism continue to be seen in the twenty-first century, often referred to as "neocolonialism." The influences of neocolonialism call us to reflect critically on our models of anthropology in understanding Muslim contexts. Just as everyone has a framework for understanding theological anthropology, everyone also assumes a cultural anthropology, whether consciously realized or not. One outdated understanding of mission assumes that the missiological task of communicating the gospel was a simple exercise: a messenger (evangelist) encodes a message (the gospel) to a receiver (a religious other), like sending a letter in an envelope. In this view, individuals within a culture are well-integrated and nearly identical to other members of their culture. Thus, one simply interprets the gospel for the "others" in a static process.

This modernist model of anthropology taught that cultures are homogeneous and that people in each culture were objectively understandable, basically

---

44. Swanson, "Said's Orientalism," 110.
45. Cemil Aydin, *The Idea of the Muslim World* (Cambridge: Harvard University Press, 2017), 3, emphasis original.

spoke only one language, and were virtually unaffected by peoples around them. However, "neither culture nor the missiological situation is like this anymore, and it seems questionable that it ever was."[46] We should realize that people in their contexts are much more complex and quite different from the simplistic way modernist anthropology often describes them.

Postmodern anthropology developed precisely to correct the errors of modern anthropology. However, it was an exercise in pendulum swinging and made many mistakes of its own: the objectivity and certainty of modernity was replaced by subjectivity and skepticism. If modernity is characterized by essentialism, then postmodernity is marked by relativism. Unfortunately, both modernity and postmodernity are insufficient for framing our understanding of mission. One way forward is for "a post-postmodern missiology"[47] which tries to handle the complexity of understanding contexts while rejecting the pluralist theology of religions. George Yip's proposal for a polythetic and progressive contextualization helps us deal with the variations that exist within religions even within the same context.[48]

Related to this postcolonial reframing of how we understand the other is the shift found in religious studies. The current consensus in this field is that there is no timeless, transcultural definition of "religion" that is not also a function of political power, and that the ability to frame a distinct category of religion within society has more to do with the **Enlightenment** and Protestant Reformation than with how people understand themselves.[49] The "religious" category also fails to adequately tie together dissimilar ritualistic practices in different faith traditions. Evangelicals often reduce religion to a system of beliefs. One of the major problems in this approach is that "social and psychological research shows that people tend to hold a collection of contradictory beliefs that cannot be put together into a coherent system. In addition, research shows that people's behavior is often based on something other than

---

46. Michael Rynkiewich, "A New Heaven and a New Earth? The Future of Missiological Anthropology," in *Paradigm Shifts in Christian Witness*, ed. Charles Van Engen, Darrell Whiteman, and Dudley Woodberry (Maryknoll: Orbis, 2008), 33.

47. George Yip, "The Contour of a Post-Postmodern Missiology," *Missiology* 42, no. 4 (2014): 399–411.

48. Polythetic means many in a category. For more on polythetic and progressive contextualization, see Warrick Farah, "Polythetic and Progressive Contextualization," circumpolar (29 June 2017), http://muslimministry.blogspot.com/2017/06/polythetic-and-progressive.html.

49. Brent Nongbri, *Before Religion* (New Haven: Yale University Press, 2013).

their beliefs."[50] Further, in Muslim contexts, beliefs often take a back seat to practices: "For Islam, orthopraxy is more important than orthodoxy."[51]

Islam as it is lived and practiced repeatedly transforms to match the realities of different contexts. Classifying all Muslims (or Hindus, Christians, etc.) into a single category in the "world religions" paradigm obscures many of their crucial defining characteristics specific to many contexts. Martin Accad proposes a way beyond this limitation:

> The "world religions" approach has a tendency to view people of faith as prisoners of theological systems, whose every move can be predicted by their communities' sacred scriptures. Whereas the "sociology of religions" approach offers a dynamic vision of mutually-influential forces between theology and the practice of religion. I would argue that the latter vision offers us a far richer field of inquiry, engagement and action than the former. From a missional perspective, therefore, it is far more useful, far more empowering and energizing; it invites us to new possibilities in terms of creative and constructive action required for the mission of God.[52]

Therefore, as Christians who long for Jesus to be embraced as Lord and Savior in Muslim contexts, we need to be alert to how we use the category "religion" in mission. These monumental changes in postcolonial theory, anthropology and religious studies demand that Christians reject one-size-fits-all strategies for working with religious others and be adaptable to their context.

A Call for Adaptive Missiology

So, how should the church attempt to understand what Muslims in their context believe, love and do? And how should that contextual understanding inform our missional impulse in view of God's mission in Christ to redeem all nations back to himself?

---

50. Craig Martin, *A Critical Introduction to the Study of Religion* (New York: Routledge, 2014), 7. See also sections 3.2 and 3.3 above.

51. Joseph van Ess, *The Flowering of Muslim Theology* (Cambridge: Harvard University Press, 2006), 16.

52. Martin Accad, "Mission in a World Gone Wild and Violent," *Global Reflections Blog*, 17 June 2016, https://sparks.fuller.edu/global-reflections/2016/06/17/mission-in-a-world-gone-wild-and-violent-challenging-the-monochromatic-view-of-islam-from-a-silent-majority-position/.

We must deal with the plurality of Islams and the diversity of Muslims around the world. In the personal-missional encounter, simply put, *Islam should be whatever our Muslim friend says it is*. This is not to deny that our friends could be further or nearer to what certain "mainstream" Muslims throughout history have decreed as authentic Islam. Neither do we deny that there exists something called Islam and that our friends might be somewhere on the margins of Islam. What this does mean is that we must primarily deal with how Muslims shape and use Islam in their context.

Furthermore, when using mass media or writing, it is important to be informed through cultural anthropology that there are great variations among individuals in cultures. Even when looking for the broad-based values in an ethnic group, it is still doubtful that one could determine an approach that is properly contextualized for the "Egyptian culture," for example. Any approach focusing on a large grouping of people will have to acknowledge such inherent limitations. This is especially important at a time when the understanding of ethnicity is evolving: some peoples are losing the sense of "groupness" in ethnic identity which undermines the concept of "people groups" common in evangelical missiology.[53] We need to be adaptive.

Consider the biblical support for adaptation according to context. Jesus engaged people in their situations. Moreover, mission historian Andrew Walls makes an important point concerning debating the true nature of Islam (or any other religious system) and quarrelling over whose understanding is the most accurate:

> Argument about which is correct, or the more correct, picture of "Hinduism" is beside the point in the light of Romans 1:18–32, for Paul's concern here is not with systems at all, but with men. It is people who hold down the truth of unrighteousness, who do not honor God, who are given up to dishonorable passions. It is upon men, who commit ungodly and wicked deeds, that the wrath of God is revealed.[54]

Walls continues that our message must not be a religious system, for it is "not Christianity that saves, but Christ."[55] If it is best to view "Islam" as

---

53. Brad Gill, "Global Cooperation and the Dynamic of Frontier Missiology," *International Journal of Frontier Missiology*," 31, no. 2 (2014): 90.

54. Andrew Walls, "Romans One and the Modern Missionary Movement," in *The Missionary Movement in Christian History: Studies in the Transmission of the Faith* (Maryknoll: Orbis, 1996), 66.

55. Walls, "Romans One," 66.

simply being what people who profess it actually believe and do, then we begin our engagement with every Muslim by understanding their worldview in the light of Romans 1:18–32. We should indeed be good students of Islam, but we should be even better students of Muslims.

To deal with the elastic concepts of religion previously discussed, one possible proposal is to be "supra-religious" in our engagement with religious others by attempting to rise above the fray of worldly religiosity.[56] This is not to say that religion is unimportant, but to ensure that we are gospel-centered in our approach instead of clouding mission with flexible concepts like religion. However, instead of bypassing religion in our missiological approaches, I propose that a more fruitful way of engaging Muslims is to deal with idolatry, which, depending on the context, may be a much more specific topic than Islam.

Any discussion of idolatry necessarily begins with the theology of God and worship:

> As God eternally outpours within his triune self, and as we are created in his image, it follows that we too are continuous outpourers, incurably so. The trouble with our outpouring is that it is fallen. It needs redeeming, else we spend our outpouring on false gods appearing to us in any number of guises. Salvation is the only way our continuous outpouring – our continuous worship – is set aright and urged into the fullness of Christ.[57]

In this understanding of idolaters as continuous and habitual worshipers in need of redemption, we find a missional hermeneutic which leads toward an adaptive approach to Muslims. In this sense, religion has no redemptive benefit. No matter what religious identity people claim, Christian, Muslim, pagan, atheist, etc., they are all lost apart from the gospel (Rom 3:22–23; *see section 2.4 above*) and are left clinging to various types of idols instead of Christ alone.

The central theological theme in the Bible is the refutation of idolatry,[58] yet expressions of it are quite diverse. In his seminal book *The Mission of God*, Christopher Wright teaches that biblical monotheism is necessarily missional, and biblical mission is necessarily monotheistic. The biblical concept that keeps people from honoring God as God is idolatry, not the wrong religion. Wright describes the motivations behind our idolatrous worship:

---

56. E.g. Martin Accad, "Christian Attitudes toward Islam and Muslims," in *Toward Respectful Understanding and Witness among Muslims*, ed. Evelyne Reisacher (Pasadena: William Carey, 2012), 29–47.

57. Harold Best, *Unceasing Worship: Biblical Perspectives on Worship and the Arts* (Downers Grove: IVP, 2003), 10.

58. Brian S. Rosner "The Concept of Idolatry," *Themelios* 24, no. 3 (1999): 21.

Having alienated ourselves from the living God our Creator, we have a tendency to worship whatever makes us tremble with awe as we feel our tiny insignificance in comparison with the great magnitudes that surround us. We seek to placate and ward off whatever makes us vulnerable and afraid. We then counter our fears by investing inordinate and idolatrous trust in whatever we think will give us the ultimate security we crave. And we struggle to manipulate and persuade whatever we believe will provide all our basic needs and enable us to prosper on the planet.[59]

Biblically speaking, idolatry is a broad concept that plays a large role in our engagement with religious others. This begs the question: what is the relationship between religion and idolatry?

The idea that religion can be separated from culture or simply reduced to a theological system is an assumption heavily influenced by the **Enlightenment**. Therefore, it is a mistake to assume that the totality of one's so-called "religious heritage" is something that must be "renounced" in all cases and times and contexts by those becoming disciples of Christ. This is akin to equating the ambivalent, modern concept of religion with the biblical category of idolatry. So instead of "Islam," what should be abandoned, biblically speaking, are idols.

I am not defending Islam nor being naïve to the powerful influence of Islamic ideologies. There are indeed times and contexts where Muslims who turn to Christ will need to reject the majority of their religious heritage. In that case, the supra-religious approach may be inappropriate, and religious change may be a clear way to deal with idolatry. An example of this is that salvation for many Muslims is a "**prophetological** concept," meaning "the logic of salvation has everything to do with one's relation to the Prophet Muhammad."[60] In this case, Muslims will indeed need to turn from Muhammad as an idol (as previously defined). *(This topic will be explored further in chapter 7.)*

Idolatry can take many forms. Potential idols in Muslim contexts (other than those discussed above) can include merit-seeking through good works to appease God, nationalism, pride, intercession of saints, materialism, prophetolatry, personal reputation, folk religious practices, strict adherence to ritual or any combination of these. (Christians are equally prey to such idols.) In the midst of context-specific encounters with Muslims, adaptive missiology

---

59. Christopher J. H. Wright, *The Mission of God: Unlocking the Bible's Grand Narrative* (Downers Grove: IVP Academic, 2006), 216–219.

60. Perry Pennington, "From Prophethood to the Gospel," *International Journal of Frontier Missiology* 31, no. 4 (2014): 198.

requires Christian workers to discern the form of idolatry in which they are entangled, then offer an appropriate gospel-centered response. Yet this is a dynamic process; we will frequently cycle between our response, the Bible and the context. "Combating idolatry can take many forms. The Bible itself prepares us to recognize that different approaches may be relevant in different contexts. Wisdom in mission calls us to be discerning and to recognize that what may be appropriate in one situation may not be so helpful in another."[61] Taking our cues from the previous discussion on postcolonialism and anthropology, and realizing there is more than one way to deal with idolatry, we recognize how unwise it would be to respond apart from relationships with those who know their own contexts far better than we do.

Adaptive missiology recognizes that all people everywhere who embrace the gospel experience both a continuity and a discontinuity with their past. Earlier approaches to contextualization taught that previous practices and beliefs can be either retained, rejected or repurposed.[62] This reflects how Paul saw his ministry of becoming all things to all people (1 Cor 9:19–23) while avoiding harmful syncretism (2 Cor 6:14–18). Yet there are clearly limits to the usefulness of contextualization when it is a one-sided exercise done by the worker for the local community. In such cases, the valuable ways in which indigenous people contribute to the process and the ways in which God is already at work may be overlooked, even before the unique and sufficient message of Christ is proclaimed (1 Cor 2:2).

Our focus should not be on envisioning what the church looks like in a context as an end result and then prescribing a static mission praxis from that assumption. Instead, we need continual missiological inquiry into the nature of the dynamic relationship among ourselves, Muslims and God revealed in Christ. Transformative relationships are key in this process and will require us to be vulnerable in a postcolonial spirit while walking in humble confidence in the authority of Jesus. It is, after all, God's mission, and we often get in the way. "The Bible shows that God's greatest problem is not just with the nations of the world, but with the people he has created and called to be the means of blessing the nations. And the biggest obstacle to fulfilling that mission is idolatry among God's people."[63]

---

61. Wright, *Mission of God*, 337–339.

62. Paul Hiebert, *Anthropological Insights for Missionaries* (Grand Rapids: Baker, 1986), 188.

63. The Lausanne Movement, *The Cape Town Commitment* (Peabody: Hendrickson, 2011), 145.

Adaptive missiology aims to get at the heart of how Jesus and the apostles approached "the other" in the New Testament. No two evangelistic addresses were identical; they always took the context into account in their witness. By understanding the New Testament itself as a missiological document, we can see Jesus and the apostles taking time to humbly reflect and give an appropriate consideration to their audience; they were continually adapting to the challenge of seeing lives and communities transformed by the power of God.

Conclusion: An Apostolic Challenge for Our Day

We need to be faithful to the apostolic spirit of Jesus and the apostles if we want to see our Lord receive the worship he alone deserves among Muslims. One way is to call the church to a renewed apostolic imagination. I use "apostolic" in two senses: *extending* the kingdom and *innovating* in mission praxis. The spirit of adaptive missiology is to take up residence among Muslims in humble relationship and seek to discern how they use Islam, what their idols are, and what a pioneering, Christ-centered engagement requires.

Adaptive missiology is a conversation and a communal exercise. We need each other since new contexts need innovative approaches, not quick fixes. As ministers of the gospel, we must adapt to people in the complexity of their contexts. Our job is to make disciples of Jesus, not to define Islam. We need to engage people *as they are* which requires embracing their complexity.

Islam is perhaps the greatest challenge the church has faced. Through seeking to extend and innovate, adaptive missiology calls the church, in prayerful dependence on the Holy Spirit, to help more Muslim communities discover God in Christ and to see Jesus glorified, even "to the ends of the earth" (Acts 1:8).

3.6 Beyond Cognitive Approaches to Christian Witness: Orthopathy and the Affective in Multifaith Contexts

Karen Shaw

Faces tell us a lot about the other person and about our relationship.

Each year, I teach one session at ABTS wearing a hijab. In 2018, as I was on my way up the stairs to class, I met a man I did not know coming the other way. I saw him before he saw me, and I knew the moment that he noticed me: there registered succeeding flashes of surprise, then disgust, then hatred in his expression. He quickly rearranged his features into a blank expression accompanied by a coldly polite "good morning" and passed by.

When we want to know what is in someone's heart, we search their face. The face is the window of the heart. In English, "affect" means face, and "affective" refers to a person's emotions and attitudes. In Arabic, we "whiten" or clean someone's face – that is, we save them from shame. Our eyes connect directly with our brains through the ocular nerve. A trained person can pick with a high degree of accuracy the true emotions of a person by that first unguarded reaction of the eyes. People who want to hide their attitudes and feelings wear sunglasses or turn their faces away.

The Bible begins with a face. In the second verse of Genesis, darkness covers the face of the deep like a veil, and the Spirit of God is fluttering over the surface of the water like a bird. God says, "Let there be light!" What happens? God sees his Spirit reflected back, however imperfectly, in the world he has made. God created men and women in the divine image and likeness (Gen 1:26–27) and created woman to be an *ezer knegdo*, a strong help who stands face to face with the man (Gen 2:23). We were created to see the image of the invisible in one another.

When there is enmity or shame in the Bible, people hide their faces from God or from one another. God's favor is in his smile, as the levitical benediction so beautifully words it (Num 6:25). When God is angry, he hides his face – turns away – or his frown is so devastating that people beg him to do so. God appeals to people everywhere to turn back to him – to repent. "Turn to me and be saved, all you ends of the earth" (Isa 45:22). We tend to think of repentance as a change of mind or a change of behavior, but it is also a change of heart. The last chapter of the Bible promises that God's servants will see his face (Rev 22:4).

In describing his ministry of reconciliation in 2 Corinthians chapters 3 to 6, Paul latches onto the imagery of Moses, who was so transfigured by seeing God's glory that he had to wear a veil, at the request of the Israelites, to hide the afterglow of God's reflection from them because they could not bear to look (Exod 34:33–35; cf. 2 Cor 3:13). Paul says, "And we all, who with unveiled faces contemplate the Lord's glory, are being transformed into his image with ever-increasing glory, which comes from the Lord, who is the Spirit. Therefore, since through God's mercy we have this ministry, we do not lose heart" (2 Cor 3:18–4:1). Because of the chapter break we might miss it: our ministry to those outside of Christ is to gaze at God's glory and be transformed. Paul goes on to say, "God, who said, 'Let light shine out of darkness,' made his light shine in our hearts to give us the light of the knowledge of God's glory displayed in the face of Christ. But we have this treasure in jars of clay to show that this all-surpassing power is from God and not from us" (2 Cor 4:6–7). Jesus is the icon, the image, the face of God to us; we in turn are the face of Christ to people estranged from him. I did not see the face of Christ in that person on the stairs.

Whatever is in our heart toward the religious other will appear on our faces. There are always students from Christian families who are visibly agitated when I wear the hijab in class, and I always hear a sigh of relief, and sometimes even applause, when I take it off. Yet, there are always one or two students from Muslim families who spend that session beaming at me. The question is, what expression is on God's face when he looks at a person or group of people? Have we been so transformed by Christ that people see God's heart in our faces, or merely our own very human reactions? What does this mean in practice? The following steps seek to develop sound orthopathic responses in all our interactions with the religious other.

First, gaze on God's face. We are so quick to give our opinions and our emotional reactions to others. Others will see God in us only if we are profoundly impacted by the way God feels about the people and circumstances we encounter. Spend time in intimate relationship with the Lord. Look for God's image everywhere it is revealed: in nature, in the Bible and, most importantly, in Jesus.

Second, learn about emotions and attitudes. There is a wealth of psychological scholarship that can help us understand both our own affective responses and the responses of others.

Third, look in the mirror. Often what passes for rationality is actually a collection of logical-sounding justifications for our gut reactions. Unless we are honest with ourselves about our feelings of disgust and anger, superiority and anxiety, the best we will show the other is a mask; it does not take long for most people to distinguish between a mask and a genuine face.

Fourth, train your emotions. We inherit prejudices from our parents and our community, but we do not have to keep them and pass them on to our children. Experiences like Khebz w Meileh (literally bread and salt) provide alternative ways of thinking and feeling about the other.[64] Anger can be contained and directed. Courage can replace fear of others or the need to please them. Love can be nurtured by prayer and action.

Fifth, look into the face of the other. We are sent by God with the gospel, not like the pizza delivery guy but as ambassadors of God with a mission

---

64. Khebz w Meileh, based in the Institute of Middle East Studies at ABTS, is an initiative that brings young Christians and Muslims together to eat and converse about faith.

of reconciliation. We search the face of the other to know their heart: their longings and how Jesus can be the fulfillment of those longings; their fears and how Jesus might vanquish them; their pain and how Jesus might heal. We seek to build trust so that people will have the courage to look into the face of Jesus and gaze without a veil at the glory of God.

The Spirit of God still hovers over the deep, dark face of people's hearts, waiting for the word to proclaim light to reflect the divine image. May that light shine in our hearts and from them into the hearts of the religious other so that we may see in one another the face of God.

Concluding Reflections and Questions for Discussion

Our overall theme is that one's view of the religious other informs one's attitudes toward them, which will be evident in one's interaction with them, which in turn affects the outcomes of such contact. This chapter has shown how religion is an integral aspect of culture even in places which endeavor to reduce or minimize the place of religion in the public square. Having looked at the religious other in broad terms here in part I, we now move to an in-depth focus on Islam, the Qur'an and Muhammad in part II.

Questions for Discussion

1. What roles does religion play in your context? In what ways are these roles seen, and in what aspects are they more subtle?
2. What prior reading and other influences are people bringing to their first encounters with the biblical text?
3. How might we adapt our missiological practices in relation to the religious other?
4. What view of Jesus do others perceive when they look in my eyes?

Part II

Thinking Biblically about Islam, the Qur'an, Muhammad and Muslims

4

Introduction to Part II

Poetry by Anna Turner
Rise Up

Rise up you peacemakers,
You forgers of the way.
Rise up you sayers
For those who have no say.
Let not the distance keep us,
Let not apathy meeken us,
Let our hearts beat within us
With kingdom bringing,
Freedom singing,
Wholeness filling
Peace.
Let's walk the peace out into
A world being rent in two
For people who are human too
Because we are the change.

Rise up you mourners,
You ones who ache and sway,
Rise up you grieving
With pain too deep to say,
For comfort is coming
To stand with you at the cross,
We are coming to hold up
Hands weighed down by loss.

So rise up you mourners,
For we will stand with you,
As you look to Jesus
Who knew this hollow horror too.

Rise up you who are thirsty
For all that which is right.
Stand up you who are starving
For justice bringing light.
Let's not be satisfied
With fullness that makes others empty,
With insufficient for most
Because a few have more than plenty.
Let us rail against,
Break down weep and protest,
Empty ourselves in the process
Of bringing righteousness and justice.

4.1 Developing a Biblical Theology of Islam: A Practical Missiology Based on Thoughtful Theology, Moving Beyond Pragmatic Intuition

Martin Accad

I argue by way of introduction to this second part of the book that one of the top priorities for the church today, when it comes to its relationship with Muslims, should be to develop a proper "theology of Islam." What I mean by this is that we need to develop a biblical way of thinking, reflected in our discourse, about the origins of Islam, its prophet, its holy book, the destiny of its people and its perception of the spirit world. Though this sounds somewhat theoretical, it is imminently practical. As shown in part I, there exist complex and multidirectional connections between our experiences and beliefs, on the one hand, and our practices on the other, and these essentially drive our relationships. If we generally have less control over our daily experiences, we could argue that we have more control over the cognitive processes that shape our thinking and beliefs. This premise is not only prescriptive, in the way that we have used it in the first part of the book, but it is also descriptive. For example, our particular theology of Islam may help explain three of the most enduring controversies about Islam that have been raging in the evangelical world over the past few years, namely, the questions of (1) the Insider Movement, (2) Muslim-friendly translations of the Bible, and (3) inter-faith dialogue. This is not the place to discuss these issues exhaustively. I will simply present their main features in a few paragraphs in order to show afterward that the stance we take on any of these questions largely derives from the way we think about Islam and Muslims.

When it comes to the Insider Movement, much ink has been spilled. The controversy began when Christian anthropologists and missionaries observed that groups of Muslims who became followers of Jesus were forming new spiritual fellowships akin to "messianic mosques." These fellowships, most common at that point in Southeast Asia, were initially described phenomenologically in anthropological surveys.[1] It was when such fellowships were eventually adopted by some missionaries as models for the development of methodologies and ideal practices to be applied in ministry among Muslims everywhere that the issue became controversial.[2] Even more controversial was when some missionaries took on a Muslim identity in order to be more effective in drawing out Muslims to become followers of Jesus.

On both sides of the controversy, scholars became either staunch supporters or staunch critics of what had begun as a descriptive study but eventually turned prescriptive.[3] One question became whether it was possible to provoke the emergence of movements of Muslim fellowships around Christ by applying certain ministry principles.[4] Another question was whether such fellowships would even be legitimate if their members had not completely denounced Islam as they embraced Christ. Full bibliographies on the issue can readily be found. For our present purpose, I mention four recent volumes that have

---

1. J. Dudley Woodberry, "Contextualization among Muslims: Reusing Common Pillars," in *The Word among Us: Contextualizing Theology for Mission Today*, ed. Dean S. Gilliland (Dallas: Word Publishing, 1989), 282–312. Reprinted with more complete footnotes in *International Journal of Frontier Missions* 13, no. 4 (Oct–Dec 1996): 171–186. www.ijfm.org/PDFs_IJFM/13_4_PDFs/03_Woodberry.pdf.

2. See for example the set of articles published together in 1998 in the *Evangelical Mission Quarterly* 34, no. 4 (1998): Philip L. Parshall, "Danger! New Directions in Contextualization," 404–406 and 409–410; John Travis, "The C1 to C6 Spectrum: A Practical Tool for Defining Six Types of 'Christ-Centered Communities' ('C') Found in the Muslim Context," 407–408; and John Travis, "Must All Muslims Leave 'Islam' to Follow Jesus?," 411–415.

3. For a good description of this shift from descriptive to prescriptive, where the author discusses various misunderstandings associated with the C1–C6 spectrum, see John Travis's reflection on his own journey in John Jay Travis, "The C1–C6 Spectrum after Fifteen Years," *Evangelical Missions Quarterly* 51, no. 4 (2015): 358–365.

4. See for example J. Dudley Woodberry, ed., *From Seed to Fruit: Global Trends, Fruitful Practices, and Emerging Issues among Muslims*, rev. ed. (Pasadena: William Carey Library, 2011).

brought together the writings both of supporters[5] and opponents[6] of the Insider Movement into helpful readers. In addition, sections 3.5, 5.3, 8.5, and 9.5 of the present volume are relevant to this issue.

The second controversy relates to the translation of the Bible. Theologians have debated for centuries different approaches to the task. Bible translations always end up somewhere on a broad spectrum between primary concern for the text and primary concern for the audience. On one end of the spectrum, some translations follow as literally as possible the original Hebrew and Greek texts, up to the very word order and original idiom. At the other end of the spectrum are translations of the Bible that are so paraphrastic and idiomatic in the receiving language that it can be hard to reconstruct the source text from which a verse has emerged. In the English language, one can think of the literal and linguistically sophisticated King James Version on one end of the spectrum, and a Bible in Cockney English on the other end.

The Arabic language is not new to this debate. The literal and somewhat artificial (in Arabic) style of the Smith-Van Dyck-Boustani translation was somewhat of a novelty in the Arab world when it first emerged, the product of Protestant efforts. Otherwise, throughout most of its history, the Arab church has been very conscious in its Bible translation work of the foremost need to make sense to a Muslim audience. Of course, Arab Christians have cared for accuracy with the original Hebrew and Greek as well. But they have always carried closest to their heart the great concern for transmitting the original into an Arabic idiom that made sense for their Muslim neighbor. The contrast between the King James Version and the Bible in Cockney in the English language can be paralleled with the contrast between the Smith-Van Dyck-Boustani and the True Meaning translations of the Bible in the Arabic language. Both the Cockney Bible and the True Meaning give priority to their readership over literality with the Hebrew and Greek. Why the issue is more controversial in Arabic than in English I believe relates to the reality of Islam.

Most English readers will probably smile at the Cockney Bible and, at worst, dismiss it as of no concern to them. But those who do not like the

---

5. Harley Talman and John J. Travis, eds., *Understanding Insider Movements: Disciples of Jesus within Diverse Religious Communities* (Pasadena: William Carey Library, 2015); and Gene Daniels and Warrick Farah, eds., *Margins of Islam: Ministry in Diverse Muslim Contexts* (Pasadena: William Carey Library, 2018).

6. Joshua Lingel, Jeff Morton, and Bill Nikides, eds., *Chrislam: How Missionaries Are Promoting an Islamized Gospel*, rev. ed. (Garden Grove: i2 Ministries Publishing, 2012); and Ayman S. Ibrahim and Ant Greenham, eds., *Muslim Conversions to Christ: A Critique of Insider Movements in Islamic Contexts* (New York: Peter Lang, 2018).

True Meaning translation do not smile at it. They have militantly opposed it. Good people, with a passion for the translation of God's word, have become staunch enemies because of their disagreement over translation philosophy. Disagreement is normal and acceptable, and debate over important issues is good. However, when respect for diversity of opinion is not maintained, and opinionated positions become platforms for launching personal attacks against those who disagree with us, the result is character assassination.

The typical display of the controversy can be observed in a brief recent article published on the Biblical Missiology website.[7] This common approach to the debate over Bible translation starts by listing the sins of these translations by reflecting – quite frankly – only one side of the story and making it sound like there is a conspiracy standing behind the project. This list is followed up with a postcolonial critique that claims that the translation is the work of foreign missionaries imposing their will on "the natives." The argument then follows that those who are doing this work are compromising the gospel simply in order to make discipleship less arduous and less prone to persecution. Span argues that "a reason that people do this is because they think that the essential problem that a Muslim faces is a lack of information," whereas, he would argue, what they need is "a whole new gift of sight," for Muslims are not, as Span puts it, "slightly myopic, slightly sick, or slightly misinformed."[8]

Personally, I would argue that this sort of perspective suffers from cultural blindness and double standard. One might ask why the consumerist, materialistic, human-worshiping culture of the West is an acceptable substratum for the gospel, whereas the God-fearing, generally piously devoted culture of Muslim societies has to be wiped out for the "true gospel" to take root. Is the Western person coming to faith in Christ less myopic to begin with than the Muslim person, so that the former can keep much of their baggage while the latter have to get rid of it all? It is sufficient to look at many churches in the West (and in the East too, of course) to realize that consumerism and materialism there are alive and well. But these salient sins of the Western world seem less troubling to critics of the Muslim-focused contextualized translations than the assumed "demonic" nature of the Muslim world.

---

7. John Span, "Are Bible Translators Trying to Bring Christianity and Islam Closer Together?" *Biblical Missiology*, 24 February 2020, https://biblicalmissiology.org/2020/02/24/are-bible-translators-trying-to-bring-christianity-and-islam-closer-together/.

8. Span, "Are Bible Translators Trying."

Of course, all of this anti-contextualized translation drumming is generally embedded – as it is in this article – in the wrapping of finances, enforcing the deeply problematic idea that if you control the money, you can control the agenda. Indeed, it is hard to read many such articles without wondering whether their primary motivation is not simply a fight over donors. The more those holding differing views from them are discredited, the more they themselves will be able to hoard donors for their cause.

We move to the third issue, which is what I consider an artificial dichotomy between evangelism and dialogue in the evangelical mindset on mission. Until fairly recently, the lines within the Protestant tradition between the *evangelistic* approach of the "conservatives" and the *dialogical* approach of the "liberals" could pretty much be assumed. Organizations like the World Council of Churches and the Middle East Council of Churches, primarily populated with those churches we usually refer to as "mainline" (Lutherans, Presbyterians, Anglicans), were engaged in dialogue with other religions. Whereas the more conservative evangelicals (Baptist, Church of God, Christian Missionary Alliance, Pentecostal), the "Bible-believing" churches, held on faithfully to evangelism and the necessity of personal salvation and conversion. But something happened in recent years that changed this traditional dichotomy – whether real or perceived – placing dialogue with Muslims at the center of evangelical thinking about mission.

On 13 October 2007, the Royal Aal al-Bayt Institute of Amman, Jordan, released publicly a letter entitled, "A **Common Word** between Us and You."[9] Initially launched with the support of 138 signatories of various Muslim creeds and traditions, the letter inviting Christians of all traditions all over the world into dialogue is as of today (15 May 2020) endorsed by 19,174 entities. The initiative from the beginning elicited a broad array of responses, no doubt the most significant of which – as far as the evangelical world is concerned – was the Yale Response entitled "Loving God and Neighbor Together: A Christian Response to *A Common Word between Us and You*."[10] The most official version

---

9. 13 October was the public release of the letter, and its symbolism was important to the authors, marking the one-year anniversary since the release, on 13 October 2006, of the response of Muslim scholars to Pope Benedict XVI's Regensburg address of 13 September 2006. As stated on their website in the introduction to the document, the final form of the letter was already presented at a conference of the Institute in Amman in September 2007. See www.acommonword.com for ongoing updates about the progress of the initiative.

10. The Yale Response was very prompt, first issued on 12 October 2007 (therefore before the "official" release of the "Initiative"; see preceding footnote). See "'A Common Word' Christian Response," https://faith.yale.edu/common-word/common-word-christian-response, for all information regarding the Yale Response.

of the Yale Response is the one that was published in the *New York Times* on 18 November 2007.[11]

What made the Yale Response significant was not so much that it came from a top USA academic institution, for several other respected universities around the world offered responses as well. What made the Yale Response a turning point is that it was known to bear the mark of two well-known evangelical figures: the renowned scholar Miroslav Volf and former missionary now scholar Joseph Cumming. No one could doubt the evangelical commitments to biblical faithfulness and missional passion of these two scholars. Their participation got the evangelical world's attention, and as a result, many other evangelical leaders – including myself – endorsed and signed the Yale Response.[12]

Yale University followed up on their initial response by organizing a workshop and conference on 24–31 July 2008. Most of the signatories of the original "A Common Word" document as well as of the Yale Response were invited to participate in the gatherings. A total of over 150 people were present, and a book ensued, where several of the public presentations, including my paper entitled "Loving Neighbor in Word and Deed: What Jesus Meant" were published.[13] From my reading as a historian of ideas, I see these events of 2007–2008 as marking a turning point in the history of evangelical involvement in interfaith dialogue. However, though I am personally enthusiastic about these developments that took place over a decade ago, I am not convinced that enough theological thinking has gone into the establishment of a foundation that would guide evangelicals in a sufficiently thoughtful engagement with Islam and Muslims. Many evangelical leaders with passion for mission became, in the aftermath of the Yale Response, passionate about interfaith dialogue. To avoid sounding judgmental, I will refrain from mentioning any names here. But I have observed some getting into dialogue as a substitute for evangelism and mission, seeing 2007 as a turning point in their own life's calling. Others have attempted to maintain balance between evangelism and dialogue, not always ending with a happy synthesis. Many

---

11. A PDF version can be found on the A Common Word website: www.acommonword.com/wp-content/uploads/2018/05/Response_300_leading_Christian_scholars.pdf.

12. See the list of signatories at the time at the end of the *New York Times* ad page (see preceding footnote).

13. Miroslav Volf, Prince Ghazi bin Muhammad, and Melissa Yarrington, eds., *A Common Word: Muslims and Christians on Loving God and Neighbor* (Grand Rapids: Eerdmans, 2009). My paper is found on pages 157–161.

other evangelicals have responded to the A Common Word initiative, as well as to the Yale Response, rather aggressively, accusing signatories of betrayal.[14]

What the reader exploring these three controversies will discover is that several matters have contributed to turning important phenomena – which we might argue reflect the diverse work of the Holy Spirit among Muslims – into controversies. First is the human tendency to generalize and exaggerate what can be observed in a certain context into an all-out theory and methodology, often turning description into prescription. This can be observed in the controversy over the Insider Movement. Another matter is the human proclivity to become passionate about a certain issue to the point that we want to champion it against another, often turning a theoretical question into a personal attack against those in disagreement with us. This is particularly pertinent to the controversy surrounding the Muslim-friendly translations of the Bible. Third, and here is the matter most relevant as the background for this book, the two camps that take position either for or against any of these three issues seem each to be aligned on all three. And I would argue that their alignment is quite often subconsciously theological, while claiming to be methodological and biblical. In other words, those who are against the Insider Movement (IM), against Muslim-friendly translations of the Bible and against interfaith dialogue – let's call them the "skeptical" movement – are united by a rather negative view of Islam; whereas those who are supportive of the IM phenomenon, enthusiastic about Muslim-friendly translations and engaged in interfaith dialogue – we will call them the "sympathetic" movement – are united by a view of Islam that consciously resists the wholesale dismissal of Islam as a negative phenomenon. The latter speak against "essentializing" Islam, while the former accuse them of compromise or of theological syncretism.

As has become clear in the preceding chapters, and as will become even clearer in this second part, the present book argues for a more nuanced approach to Islam than the one adopted by the "skeptical" movement. But I want here to build a foundation for further nuance within the "sympathetic" movement. It is not enough to be pragmatic about the need to reach out sympathetically to Muslims by adopting a more positivist position on Islam. Missiology sometimes errs on the side of pragmatism because of an obsession with results, and in doing so it is in danger of losing theological depth and biblical faithfulness. Since all three questions above belong to the field of missiology, our task of reframing therefore needs to be thoroughly theological

---

14. See for example the very title of Sam Solomon and E. Al Maqdisi, *The Common Word: The Undermining of the Church* (n.p.: Afton, VA: Advancing Native Missions, 2009).

and biblically faithful. Between the sympathetic Yale Response and the angry skeptical response, can we move beyond instinct and emotion? What this second part of the book does is lay the foundations for a credible "theology of Islam." It therefore behooves us to ask, what is a theology of Islam?

"Doing theology" implies the desire to think biblically on a topic, and I will break down the task into five further areas. First, doing theology is an exploration that seeks to be faithful to the biblical witness. We must not be too quick in questioning the motivations of those engaged in ministry to Islam and Muslims, but thoughtful and critical engagement across methodological positions must be encouraged. Second, doing theology is to think on a topic in a way that addresses the questions of context in every age and every place. Simply holding on to traditional positions in the name of biblical faithfulness amounts to a capitulation before the task of doing theology.

This thinking leads into the third area, which is that the very task of doing theology consists, by its very nature, in pushing boundaries in a way that connects with the present generation. Most theologians approach their task from within a certain theological tradition, hence they acknowledge and willingly embrace some boundaries. For most Christian theologians, the Nicene Creed has represented the minimal common denominator, outside of which the task of theology would be seen as departing from the "Christian" boundary. Evangelical theologians generally agree to a number of additional, self-imposed boundaries that have been defined by some of our most notable modern "church fathers" such as John Stott, J. I. Packer, Alister McGrath and D. W. Bebbington.[15]

Fourth, doing theology is at the service of the church and for the purpose of the church's mission and diverse ministries. This service is directly related to the third task and is an affirmation that legitimate theology is never done in a vacuum. And fifth, doing theology is a big responsibility, a dangerous task, and an imperative for the church; it is a community task. This fifth point is crucial, and, I believe, is not always understood and embraced by those engaged in ministry to Islam and among Muslims. It is the affirmation that theologians must be willing to take risks, make mistakes and stand corrected

---

15. In a 2011 article, I listed these boundaries as (1) the supremacy of holy scripture, (2) the majesty of Jesus Christ and his sacrificial death, (3) the lordship of the Holy Spirit, (4) the necessity of conversion, (5) the priority of evangelism, and (6) the importance of fellowship (from Stott, Packer, and McGrath), adding to this the importance of activism from Bebbington. See Martin Accad, "Mission at the Intersection of Religion and Empire," *International Journal of Frontier Mission* 28, no. 4 (2011): 185–186, with notes 12 and 13. www.ijfm.org/PDFs_IJFM/28_4_PDFs/IJFM_28_4-Accad.pdf.

within the community of faith. They are to stand at the forefront of scientific discovery and must be able to build upon the synthesis of their various theological disciplines with clarity of mind and courage of spirit. But this lucidity and courage are non-negotiables, and this is why developing a theology of Islam must remain a community task.

In sum, developing a theology of Islam consists in thinking biblically about Islam. The task requires a sustained and committed dialogue between biblical scholars and Christian **Islamicists**. With this goal in mind, the Middle East Consultation hosted in 2019 at the Arab Baptist Theological Seminary, from which the remainder of this book derives, invited the participation of some – not all of course, for all practical purposes – of the most notable and emerging voices on the Bible, missiology and Islam in the evangelical world today. The reader will discover a blend of Middle Eastern and Western voices, Arab and non-Arab, that manage to give this volume a rich, unusual and pioneering flavor.

The task of developing a Christian theology of Islam was divided into five themes represented in the next five chapters. Each chapter offers three voices that represent either variants on perspective, method and discipline, or variants on the angle of approach. Each offers a blend of poetry, devotional reflection on the scriptures, testimonies and forums rewritten as conversations among friends. The three core chapters on the Qur'an (ch. 6), Muhammad (ch. 7) and salvation (ch. 8) each begin with a case study that asks some key questions and sets the tone and urgency of the exercise. Chapter 5 takes on the task of exploring the often opaque period of the emergence of Islam and belongs to the complex discipline of historiography. Chapter 6 explores the nature of the Qur'an and the doctrine of divine revelation and inspiration, often engaging in intertextuality with the Bible. Chapter 7 blends biblical, theological and historical approaches to tackle the sensitive topic of prophethood in Islam, pushing the boundaries of what is normally admissible in the thinking of Muslim theologians about their prophet. It treads on the dangerous boundary between faith and history, a liminal space with which Christianity is well acquainted when it comes to the study of the historical Jesus versus the Christ of faith. Chapter 8 approaches the question of salvation. Some of this chapter may turn out to be the most controversial in this book, but it is no doubt an imminent need given the current place of global evangelical mission, at the intersection and balance between evangelism and dialogue. Soteriology, to my mind, is perhaps the most urgent task today, since evangelicals – at least as a group – entered the sandbox of dialogue just over a decade ago. Chapter 9 is perhaps most crucial to missiological method, approaching the difficult question of the spiritual realm biblically, anthropologically and from the perspective of practical ministry. This is a difficult task because the spirit world evades scientific inquiry for being so steeped in subjective experience. In the concluding chapter, I attempt a reflection on and evaluation of the plausibility of the task of developing a biblical theology of Islam, the Qur'an, Muhammad and Muslims. We present the remainder of this book as a labor of love, in all humility, and in real fear and trembling before the seriousness of the task.

4.2 A Conversation among Friends: Jesus Christ and the Religious Other

Moderator: Welcome and many thanks for joining me. Let's start by asking what the Bible allows in approaching religious others. Please summarize some of the lessons and approaches we have journeyed through in the first part of this book.

Muslim-Background Disciple (MBD): A crucial observation is that diversity is part of God's original plan for mankind. Our attitude toward the other will be seen by them: it is revealed on our faces, especially our eyes. We need to be aware that religion and community are interlinked; they cannot be separated, which has significant implications.

Christian-Background Disciple (CBD): There is both a theological challenge and an emotional one. Jonah, for example, displayed angry responses to God's mercy being shown to the other. All are created in God's image, even those who are not within his people. So, the other might appear as an enemy, but they do not deserve to be killed.

Jewish-Background Disciple (JBD): One thing that is sure is that the other is not "other" in terms of sinfulness: we all live under the effects of the fall. Some use religion to propagate power, an extreme example being territorial expansion. We have seen some valuable case studies about reaching out to the other which are a helpful balance to the anti-Islam rhetoric that we observe in this era, but we could have looked at more conflictual cases. For example, we looked at Naaman as a character but not at his place within the Israel-Syria context in general, a context that includes Elijah and the prophets of Baal as well as Naboth's vineyard (1 Kgs 18:16–45; 21:1–16).

Moderator: By focusing too much on grace and inclusion, can we go too far? Do we run the risk of falling into syncretism? How might we balance this?

JBD: We ought to be wary of having a dichotomy of approaches. It is always possible to choose case studies that suit our agenda and presuppositions.

Moderator: So, we need to be open to critique and alternative perspectives. What other categories have we observed?

CBD: We need to beware of "us" and "them" thinking. We are all sinners under judgment and need the grace that reaches out to all. Any thinking that uses just two categories can hide this biblical truth. We need to beware of judging others and of demonization. In the Bible, Jesus says, "Get behind me, Satan!" to Peter (Matt 16:23; Mark 8:33). There is a huge range of God's responses to the religious other and also to his own people.

MBD: I think that we need to be aware of our own biases. I am aware that we can invariably find evidence for our own view, including biblical examples. Islam is very diverse, so our approaches need to be diverse.

Moderator: We could conclude that the most legitimate way of relating includes love, joy, grace, peace, listening, truth and patience.

4.3 Opening Reflection: Jesus Is Better

Karen Shaw

Comparisons are dangerous. For example, "which of your children is more beautiful?" "Which student got a higher grade?" "Which country is better?" "Which religion is best?" Rarely do these questions lead to true enlightenment or healthy relationships.

Yet we live by comparisons: food, politics, cars, movies and books, sports, ethics. We are always alert to what is better, who is better – or worse. Comparisons help us decide. They bring to light what we value. Even when we do not say them aloud, our minds are full of them.

When Muslims and Christians talk to one another, always there are comparisons, spoken or unspoken. They are dangerous, opening the door to pride, disrespect and hostility. But deep inside, we need to compare. How do two missionary religions converse unless each feels it offers something better?

The Bible says nothing directly about Muhammad, the Qur'an and Muslims, but years ago, Colin Chapman pointed out to me a helpful comparison: The relationship between Muslims and Christians is like the relationship between Samaritans and Jews in Jesus's day. They shared geographic, religious and ethnic roots and were entrenched in conflicting theology and practices – augmented by ugly politics, prejudice and bitterness passed down through generations. They shared a history of mutual insults and aggressions and vitriolic debates about which sacred book was corrupted. In the high-tension situation described in John chapter 4, Jesus, the woman, the people of Sychar and John the Evangelist make their own comparisons. And their conclusion is unanimous: Jesus is better.

The comparisons start quickly. Who has access to the better, more profound source of life and refreshment? Which water is better quality and more sustaining? Jesus counters the woman's reluctance to give him a drink with an offer designed to point out the contrast between them: "If *you* knew . . . *you* would have asked *him* and *he* would have given *you living* water." She contrasts back: "*You* have nothing to draw with and the well is deep" and then ups the ante: "Are *you* greater than *our* father Jacob who gave us the well . . .?" (John 4:10–12, italics added here and below).

Jesus's answer is indirect but clear. To paraphrase, "Yes, I am greater. I am *the greater source*. Jacob's water is standing; mine is gushing. You need something to draw water, but my life is a spring. Your well sits deep in the earth, but my living water would flow out of your inmost being. Jacob's water satisfies temporarily. Mine not only satisfies you forever, but others through you" (John 4:13–14).

Jesus is sitting alone by a sacred site in enemy territory claiming he is better than the saint of the site and more vital than the product of the site. And within minutes, a woman whose identity is tied to that site, body and soul, is seeking the "more" Jesus has to offer. His comparison has not damaged the relationship as comparisons usually do. Why?

Jesus's assertion that he is better is for her benefit and not his own. Jesus does not want to compete with the woman: he wants to bless her. He does not say what he *could* have said: "Jacob is *our* father, too – not just yours! (More, since you're only a half-breed.)" He does not denigrate her heritage, Jacob's well, as less than one of many, far more impressive Jewish sites. Between the Mountain of Blessings and the Mountain of Cursings, Jesus chooses to bless. Jesus offers her the life of the same Spirit who lives in him. There must be something credible about the way Jesus says it, something about his expression that reassures her that this man is genuinely *for* her, and some spiritual force and sensitivity that convince her that she can take Jesus's outrageous promise to the bank, although she doesn't fully understand it.

As a follower of Jesus, I am convinced that he is better than anything Islam has to offer because he is the spring of life. But if we try to use that truth as a cudgel to beat and humiliate Muslims into admitting the inferiority of their religion to ours, if we use that truth to defend our religion against Muslims, we have substituted a religion for the Lord of Life, and Muslims will not see Jesus in us or be attracted to him. When Muslims meet us – when *anyone* meets us – do they experience the life-giving power and spiritual refreshment of Jesus? Too often others do not meet Jesus, but me: my beliefs and opinions, my discomfort, anxiety, tiredness, anger, or need to be right or successful. No life there! Jesus is the source that refreshes and transforms people.

The conversation has become quite intimate, with Jesus's appeal to the woman's deepest longings and her positive response. This is dangerous for a single man in his early thirties and a woman with a considerable sexual history. They are sitting beside a well, one of the few places in ancient Palestine where men and women could socialize and where romances often began. At a well Abraham's servant found Rebekah for Isaac; Jacob fell in love with Rachel; and Moses met his wife. Jesus not only establishes the purity of his intentions by asking the woman to bring her husband, but he also opens the way to demonstrate to her that he is the prophet of a truer worship. As in the story of Simon the Pharisee (Luke 7:36–50, *see section 8.1 below*), a prophet should know what sort of woman is attending him, and Jesus knows exactly what sort of woman this Samaritan is. He doesn't use this God-given knowledge to demean her, but to demonstrate that he has divine power to keep his promise of living water.

But how can a person of the wrong religion be a prophet? This time the woman starts the comparisons: "*Our ancestors* worshiped on *this* mountain." She points upward. The well is at the base of Mount Gerizim, the Mountain of Blessings topped with the ruins of the Samaritan temple which the Jews had destroyed a century and a half before. "*You Jews* claim that the place where we must worship is in Jerusalem" (John 4:20). The pain and accusation are obvious.

Less clear to us is the issue of ***taḥrīf*** (scriptural alteration), although it was surely plain to both Jesus and the woman. Which scripture is better? The Jewish Torah? Or the Samaritan Torah? The latter renders Exodus 20:17 as, "across the Jordan you shall raise these stones, which I command you today, *on Mount Gerizim*, and you build there the altar to the LORD your God."

For Samaritans, questions about prophecy, *taḥrīf* and correct *qibla* (direction of prayer) are all parts of one question: whose worship is the truer worship?

Jesus's answer comes in two parts. The lesser part is his assertion that Jews know more than Samaritans about God and are the source from which salvation springs. Jesus adds a further barb: "*You* Samaritans worship what you do *not* know; we worship what we do know" (John 4:22). This is a direct reference to 2 Kings 17:26, which is NOT in the Samaritan Bible: "It was reported to the king of Assyria: 'The people you deported and resettled in the towns of Samaria *do not know* what the god of that country requires. He has sent lions among them, which are killing them off, because the people *do not know* what he requires.'" A Jewish priest had to be sent back to Samaria to teach the people about correct worship and ethics. This part of Jesus's conversation is where the comparisons should have damaged the relationship and led Jesus and the woman back into the same rut of fruitless arguments which had plagued Jewish-Samaritan relations for a millennium.

However, there is a second, greater part to Jesus's answer. Again to paraphrase, "*I* know what the Father requires, and you will not find it either here or in Jerusalem. God is seeking worshipers who worship in Spirit and in truth," and he strongly implies to her, "You can be one of them" (John 4:23–24). Jesus declares himself to be the priest sent for the salvation of the Samaritans, the priest who knows what God wants.

The Samaritan remembers another verse from the Old Testament, a verse that is found in the Samaritan Torah and is well-known to many of our Muslim friends: "I [Yahweh] will raise up for them a prophet like you [Moses] from among their fellow Israelites, and I will put my words in his mouth. He will tell them everything I command him" (Deut 18:18; cf. Matt 28:20).

Unlike the Jewish leaders in John 1, the Samaritan immediately grasps that Jesus is the great prophet, Moses's real successor, who acts as the priest of true worship. He must also be the Messiah, God's promised King who would set everything right, including the place of worship. Jesus says, "I am he" (John 4:26). Kenneth Cragg stated that the church needed no sacred land, people or language: its great locative was, "in Christ."[16] The Samaritan believes in Jesus. She grasps what virtually no one else in the book of John gets: Jesus is prophet, priest and king, three-in-one. Greater than either Mount Gerizim or Zion and their temples, priests and rituals. Greater than either the Jewish

---

16. Kenneth Cragg, *The Arab Christian: A History in the Middle East* (Louisville: Westminster John Knox, 1991), 239.

Tanakh or the Samaritan Pentateuch. Greater than Moses, Samuel, David, Jeroboam or any other prophet or leader.

When the woman compares religion and religion, Jesus compares both with himself and finds them wanting. Jesus is not offering this woman his religion. He has been to the temple in Jerusalem and found it full of merchants and thieves. He has talked with Nicodemus, a teacher in Israel, and found him dim as the night in which he came. But in broad daylight Jesus, a tired, thirsty Jew, dazzles a Samaritan with his glory because he is full of grace and truth.

When Muslims meet us, do they meet a religion, or do they meet the unsurpassable Jesus?

At this critical moment in the conversation, as often happens when we witness to the truth, the conversation is interrupted by idiots. Twelve disciples come back and can only think of two things: not Spirit and truth, but propriety and food (John 4:27, 31). They are uncomfortable that the woman is there. They say nothing, but their non-verbals hiss at her. She leaves her jar and scurries back to the town (John 4:28). How many Muslims are on the brink of believing in Jesus, but then they meet Christians who imagine they are hiding their wish that Muslims would just go away?

But this is not an opportunity lost. Jesus will not eat the disciples' food. John does not mention Jesus's forty-day fast, but here Jesus is fasting and praying to the Lord of the harvest to send laborers into his harvest. Jesus's handpicked disciples are not yet those laborers. They go into town, and all they come back with are groceries. The woman comes back with a whole town of people ready to believe in him. The disciples go into town looking for something to eat and hardly noticed the people; Jesus sits at an empty well and sees fields white and ready for harvest. *Jesus has the better vision.* He looks beyond the woman's ungracious response to his request for water, beyond whatever has caused five men to reject her, beyond her wrong theology and misplaced loyalties. He sees both her thirst and her potential.

In these early pages of part II, I announce with John and the other writers of scripture that *Jesus is better.* Jesus is the divine source of life, through whom the world was made – he has the words of eternal life. Jesus is the One before whom every knee will bow in heaven and on earth and below the earth – *the* prophet, *the* Messiah and *the* great high priest of the new covenant written in his blood. And Jesus sees what God is up to.

Yet the knowledge that Jesus is better is as worthless to Christians today as were all the Jewish advantages in Jesus's day, unless the life-giving water of Jesus gushes from us, unless the people we encounter are dazzled by the Spirit, grace and truth of Jesus the prophet living in us. I confess I find this a challenge to me: far too often I am more like the disciples than like Jesus or even the Samaritan. If you feel the same way, Jesus's words are for you, as for me, the woman and the disciples: If you had asked, he would have given you living water (John 4:10). Jesus invites us to go back, not to our evangelical religious culture, but to him, the source of life.

He says, "I, the one speaking to you – I am he" (John 4:26)!

Then finally, "I tell you, open your eyes and look at the fields! They are ripe for harvest" (John 4:35). God is looking for true worshipers, and there are many out there thirsting for him. They will not find him in Jerusalem or Samaria, Mecca or Mansourieh.[17] No religion can own or contain him. It is only in Jesus that "all the fulness of the Deity lives in bodily form" (Col 2:9). What follows describes many comparisons between Islam and Christianity, but neither religion can compare with the incomparable Jesus: the source of ever-gushing life, the prophet, priest and king of truer worship.

Please, God, let Muslims see this Jesus in me!

---

17. Mansourieh is the suburb of Beirut where ABTS is located.

5

Exploring Islamic Origins

Poetry by Teresa Sfeir
With You
>Let the noises inward scatter.
>Hush the clanking and the clamor
>And the madmen's hopeless railing
>With their weary, woeful wailing.
>
>Hush the grinding that's been grating
>And the blaring horn's berating.
>Let the striking silence settle.
>Let your world be still and waiting.
>
>Hear then the quiet voice of God.
>I haven't much to take along,
>But here I am with all I am.
>I will walk with You.
>
>I've thrown my treasured store of dreams.
>Right off the cliff and down the stream.
>The road is long. Take me along.
>I will walk with you.
>
>Those stars that used to shine so bright
>Are dimmed in Your candescent light.
>And though to all I'll now be strange,
>I know my home will be in You.
>
>Kingdoms will rise; kingdoms will fall.

And all things are subject to change,
But as the world will run its course.
I will walk with You.
I will walk with You.

He bid me march to the forefront.
Of all the valiant men he chose
A timid soul who's to confront
Who'll stand before a crowd opposed.

Those faith champions – when I assess
Their polished version set in prose,
I stand with my redundant mess
Unsightly nooks and untrimmed flaws.

I did protest. I said, "Unfit."
"I, child, will move heaven's great force,"
He said, "only when you submit,
Just when a willing heart steps forth."

I march on with my trembling feet –
Too raw, too bare and too sincere.
In Him, I hid. I am complete.
He made me brave. I will not fear.

But if I ever grow too vain –
Too proud to ask Him to confront,
A spectacle to entertain,
I'll stand disarmed at battlefront.

I only brought my sling and stone.
My armor never was manmade.
I asked He'd make His glory shown.
He rose. I hid in His wings' shade.

5.1 Early Christian Views of Muslims, Muhammad and the Qur'an[1]

Ashoor Yousif

The Arab-Islamic conquests that swept the Middle East and North Africa in the seventh century started a new era that permanently redefined the regional reality. The Christian populations of the conquered Graeco-Roman and Persian Empires that had dominated the region for over a millennium were surprised by what had happened.[2] Initially, Christians reacted with minimal notice and only brief comments in their writings.[3] However, with time, they started reflecting upon what had occurred and proposing explanations and responses to the phenomenon of Islam.[4] This contribution turns to these incidental and deliberate Christian writings to survey their views of the conquests, Muslims, Muhammad, the Qur'an and Islam in the seventh to ninth centuries.[5] These views come from a range of literary genres – apocalypses and visions, apologies and disputations, chronicles and histories, and martyrologies – that were written in multiple languages, including Arabic, Armenian, Coptic, Greek, Latin and **Syriac**. We will not offer a comprehensive survey but rather a thematic summary with examples focusing primarily on the views that existed within the newly formed Islamic world.

The Conquests

The earliest Christian comments about the new phenomenon of Islam were triggered by the seventh-century conquests. At first, these conquests were mainly noted anecdotally, without significant religio-theological reaction or reflection. The earliest references noted the Arab conquests of the **Levant** and Persia, spoke of the defeats of the **Byzantines** and Persians, highlighted the

---

1. This contribution has a substantial number of footnotes, many of which contain detailed material primarily intended for academic readers.

2. For example, a gospel manuscript completed on 24 December AD 633 in a monastery outside Damascus testifies to the lack of awareness among Christians of the coming watershed moment of the conquests. See Sebastian P. Brock, "Syriac Views of Emergent Islam," in *Studies on the First Century of Islamic Society*, ed. G. H. A. Juynboll (Carbondale and Edwardsville: Southern Illinois University Press, 1982), 1.

3. Robert Hoyland, *Seeing Islam as Others Saw It: A Survey and Evaluation of Christian, Jewish and Zoroastrian Writings on Early Islam* (Princeton: Darwin Press, 1997), 53–236.

4. Hoyland, *Seeing Islam*, 257–522.

5. Michael Philip Penn, *When Christians First Met Muslims: A Sourcebook of the Earliest Syriac Writings on Islam* (Oakland: University of California Press, 2015), 9–17.

destruction of many towns and villages, and recounted the death of thousands of soldiers and civilians, including clergy and monks.[6] Such incidental and brief comments were common across the board, mainly documenting the swift and destructive nature of the conquests.

In these accounts, the conquests were viewed as a temporary event, either part of the common raids of the Arab nomads or part of the constant geopolitical shifts in the region due to the most recent Byzantine-**Sassanian** conflict of the early seventh century (602–628).[7] The latest (and last) Byzantine-Sassanian wars witnessed the alternating passing of territorial control of the Levant and Mesopotamia between the two superpowers and their local Arab allies. Hence, the Arab conquests might have been viewed as another chapter in such common experiences, which explains why the earliest Christian reactions were mainly concerned with noting the pain and suffering of the population, especially their Christian communities.

Soon, the Christians realized that the uncertainty of power shifts seemed to have ended and that a new power, the kingdom of the Arabs, had replaced the entire Sassanian Empire and claimed half of the Byzantine territories. Thus, by the mid- to late-seventh century, Christian thinkers shifted their focus from noting briefly and incidentally what had happened to questioning the reason for such events. They began contemplating why fortunate incidents happen to others, thinking and writing about why and how the Muslims were able to conquer, and why the Christians were left to suffer.[8] In their reflections, the Christians' reasoning for the conquests was purely Christian. They did not

---

6. Accounts are found in one of the earliest surviving references to the Islamic conquests, referred to as *Account of 637*, and by West-Syriac Thomas the Presbyter (ca. AD 640), who produced the so-called *Chronicle AD 640* a few years later. For these accounts, see Hoyland, *Seeing Islam*, 118–120; Penn, *When Christians First Met Muslims*, 21–28; Penn, *Envisioning Islam: Syriac Christians and the Early Muslim World* (Philadelphia: University of Pennsylvania Press, 2015), 19–21. The East-Syriac *Chronicle of Khuzistan* (ca. 660s) echoes with details a similar picture. See Hoyland, *Seeing Islam*, 182–189; Penn, *When Christians First Met Muslims*, 47–53; Penn, *Envisioning Islam*, 26–27; David R. Thomas and Barbara H. Roggema, eds., *Christian-Muslim Relations: A Bibliographical History, Volume 1 (600–900)* (Leiden; Boston: Brill, 2009), 130–132. Further, Fredegar, who wrote a Latin Frankish Chronicle (ca. 650s), presents a similar picture about the massive casualties among Byzantine soldiers; see Hoyland, *Seeing Islam*, 216–219; Thomas and Roggema, *Christian-Muslim Relations*, 137–138.

7. Alan M. Guenther, "The Christian Experience and Interpretation of the Early Muslim Conquest and Rule," *Islam and Christian–Muslim Relations* 10, no. 3 (1999): 363; Penn, *When Christians First Met Muslims*, xiii–xiv; Penn, *Envisioning Islam*, 7–8.

8. Penn, *Envisioning Islam*, 16–18.

consider the motives of the Arab conquerors or offer any reasons why they had embarked on this quest to take over the world.[9]

Christians interpreted the conquests from a point of view that understands historical events – especially political ones – as part of God's providence. They saw the conquests as part of God's will and action that could not be resisted, explaining their extraordinary nature and outcome as the result of divine intervention.[10] This divine intervention was the result of the conquered people's own doing rather than an act of the Arab Muslims. The conquerors were not God's special and privileged nation but his instrument to inflict punishment and chastisement on others, the sinful conquered people. To take one example out of many, the Chalcedonian Patriarch Sophronios of Jerusalem (d. ca. 639), who supposedly negotiated the capitulation of the city to the Muslim forces (638), writes that, "the Saracens [i.e. the Arabs], on account of our sins, have now risen up against us unexpectedly and ravage all with cruel and feral design, with impious and godless audacity."[11]

On 25 December 634, Sophronios preached in Jerusalem on the inability of Christians to visit Bethlehem due to Islamic occupation, offering this message: "We, however, because of our innumerable sins ... are prevented from entering Bethlehem.... We have only to repent, and we shall blunten the Ishmaelite sword ... and break the Hagarene bow, and see Bethlehem again."[12] Whose sin? Two views were common. The first view considered Christians collectively as sinners due to their deviation from true Christianity in terms of doctrines to their laxity in practice and morality.[13] Non-Chalcedonian

---

9. Robert G. Hoyland, "The Earliest Christian Writings on Muhammad: An Appraisal," in *The Biography of Muhammad: The Issue of the Sources*, ed. Harald Motzki (Leiden: Brill, 2000), 286.

10. This view is reflected in multiple works, such as the letter of Syriac Patriarch of The Church of the East, Isho'yahb III of Adiabene (d. 659), in his letter to Simeon the metropolitan bishop of Rev Ardashir, as well as in the *Chronicle of Khuzistan*, in John bar Penkaye's *Ktaba d-R'ish Melle (The Book of Main Points)*, in *Pseudo-Methodius*, and in Jacob of Edessa (d. 708). These are well documented in Brock, "Syriac Views," 15–18; Hoyland, *Seeing Islam*, 160–167, 174–189, 194–200, 263–267, 465–472, 524; Guenther, "Christian Experience and Interpretation," 367–368; Penn, *When Christians First Met Muslims*, 29–38, 47–53, 85–107, 160–187; Penn, *Envisioning Islam*, 21–23, 26–27, 34–39; and Thomas and Roggema, *Christian-Muslim Relations*, 133–136, 176–181, 226–233, 245–248, 268–273.

11. Sophronios quoted in Guenther, "Christian Experience and Interpretation," 366; Hoyland, *Seeing Islam*, 67–73.

12. Sophronios quoted in Brock, "Syriac Views *of Emergent Islam*," 9, no. 3; see also Hoyland, *Seeing Islam*, 67–73; Thomas and Roggema, *Christian-Muslim Relations*, 1–125.

13. This viewpoint is shared by the West-Syriac apocalyptic work *Pseudo-Methodius* and by Chalcedonian and East-Syriac works, which list examples of the ethical-moral sins God was punishing (Hoyland, *Seeing Islam*, 263–267; Penn, *Envisioning Islam*, 29–30; Penn, *When*

Miaphysites and East-Syriac Dyophysites blamed the confessional others – both Chalcedonian elites and communities – for the wrath of God through the Arabs.[14] Thus, inter-ecclesiastical issues and cross-confessional competition were the key lenses through which Christians read these conquests.

The second perspective blamed the religious and/or political elites for what happened. Occasionally, the Byzantine emperors were condemned for theological stands and/or moral sinfulness, while the Byzantine (Chalcedonian) ecclesiastical elites were blamed for their beliefs and policies, and the Zoroastrian Sassanians for their paganism. For example, such sectarian interpretations appeared in Egypt, which witnessed after the Persian-Byzantine war a vicious persecution of the Miaphysite community by Byzantine (Chalcedonian) authorities.[15] Similar views are found in West-Syriac writings in the Levant.[16] Sometimes the Chalcedonians also understood and explained the Arabs' victories through similar confessional sectarianism, linking Arab victories to specific political and religious conflicts from a Byzantine imperial perspective.[17] As for the problem of religio-ethical laxity as the key factor for the conquests, some Latin sources offered such views in the Latin West.[18] Finally, East-Syriac authors of the Mesopotamian world spoke about the conquests

---

Christians First Met Muslims, 108–138; Thomas and Roggema, *Christian-Muslim Relations,* 245–248). Patriarch Sophronios, Maximus the Confessor (d. 682), Jacob of Edessa, Ishoʻyahb III, and other anonymous works have similar attitudes (Brock, "Syriac Views," 15–17; Hoyland, *Seeing Islam,* 67–73, 76–78, 160–167, 174–182, 525; Penn, *Envisioning Islam,* 21–23, 26–27; Penn, *When Christians First Met Muslims,* 29–37, 62–68, 85–107, 160–187).

14. Brock, "Syriac Views," 10; Guenther, "Christians Experience and Interpretation," 365–366; Hoyland, *Seeing Islam,* 141, 524–525; Penn, *When Christians First Met Muslims,* xiv–xvi.

15. This view is reflected in the *Chronicle of John Bishop of Nikiu* (see Hoyland, *Seeing Islam,* 152–156, esp. 154; Thomas and Roggema, *Christian-Muslim Relations,* 209–218, esp. 214).

16. For example, the apocalyptic work *Pseudo-Ephrem* (late seventh century) and *The Chronicler of Dionysius of Tell-Mahre* (d. 845); Brock, "Syriac Views," 10–11; Hoyland, *Seeing Islam,* 260–263, 416–419; Penn, *Envisioning Islam,* 15, 23–24, 45–46; Thomas and Roggema, *Christian-Muslim Relations,* 622–626.

17. Thus the Chalcedonian work known as *Pseudo Anastasius,* attributed to Anastasius of Sinai (d. ca. 700) (Hoyland, *Seeing Islam,* 92–103; Thomas and Roggema, *Christian-Muslim Relations,* 193–202). Further, the Monothelete author of *A Syriac Life of Maximus the Confessor* links the conquests to the "error of Maximus," Dyotheletism (Penn, *When Christians First Met Muslims,* 63, 68; Penn, *Envisioning Islam,* 24).

18. For example, the Latin historian Fredegar views Heraclius's marriage to his niece Martina as the problem (Hoyland, *Seeing Islam,* 216–219).

as God's punishment of the Persians for their polytheism and the Byzantines for their doctrines.[19]

The Christian interpretations of the conquests and their reasons were guided by biblical-theological readings of history, which consider historical events as part of God's divine will and action. Influencing these Christian perspectives were biblical motifs and models of the past that heavily depended on the history of God's dealing with ancient Israel. Key to such views was the cyclical history of Israel in the book of Judges and in prophetic books (e.g. the book of Amos) which recount God's cycle of punishment and liberation of his people (the Israelites) caused by their sinfulness and repentance.[20] God's covenant with Israel contained the stipulation of their faithfulness to him and his law. When they deviated from it, whether in belief or in practice, God punished them through his instruments: the surrounding nations and peoples, such as the ancient Assyrians. Hence, history was repeating itself. Yet this time the Christians took Israel's place, and God's rod of punishment was the Muslims.[21]

A parallel line of thinking about the coming of the Muslims appeared in the seventh century in apocalyptic-eschatological works. In this view, Christians perceived the events as part of a linear history progressing to the eschaton, making the end of time near.[22] Such a viewpoint depended on a common Christian biblical understanding of political history based on the Danielistic model of the succession of kingdoms. For a long time, Christians read history through Daniel's vision of the four beasts, often viewing the Roman-Byzantine Empire as the fourth kingdom that would be followed by ten kingdoms, after which would come the messianic age. Prior to the messianic reign, there

---

19. Thus John bar Penkaye (Penn, *When Christians First Met Muslims*, 86; Penn, *Envisioning Islam*, 26–28). East-Syriac Patriarch Timothy I (d. 823) highlighted both issues in his theological debate with Caliph al-Mahdi (d. 785), which took place around 781 (Penn, *Envisioning Islam*, 45–46).

20. Hoyland, *Seeing Islam*, 525–526; Penn, *When Christians First Met Muslims*, 94, 105, 109–110; Penn, *Envisioning Islam*, 45–46.

21. Notably, similar readings of history continued among Christians and were applied to other events in Islamic history such as the Abbasid Revolution in the mid-eighth century. The late eighth century *Chronicle of Zuqnin* pulls back the biblical motif of God equating the Abbasids with the ancient Assyrians, depicting them as God's rod of punishment for the sins of his community (Amir Harrak, "Ah! The Assyrian Is the Rod of My Hand!: Syriac View of History after the Advent of Islam," in *Redefining Christian Identity: Cultural Interaction in the Middle East Since the Rise of Islam*, ed. Jan J. van Ginkel, Hendrika L. Murre-van den Berg, and Theo van Lint (Leuven: Peeters, 2005), 45–65; Penn, *Envisioning Islam*, 76).

22. Sidney H. Griffith, *Syriac Writers on Muslims and the Religious Challenge of Islam* (Kottayam: St. Ephrem Ecumenical Research Institute, 1995), 15; Penn, *Envisioning Islam*, 25–31.

would be the dominion of the antichrist, according to the Gospel of Matthew and to Paul's writings.[23]

Therefore, when Muslims appeared, defeating the Romans and crushing the Sassanians, they were seen as part of the end times and the rise of the antichrist before God's final act of bringing his heavenly kingdom.[24] In due course Muslims, like the previous nations that God had used providentially in ancient times, would be punished by God for their sinfulness. For now, they were used for chastising God's people. This expectation especially intensified during the seventh century at the time of the inter-caliphate civil wars which were seen as a sign of the impending end of Arab rule.[25] The seventh-century inter-Islamic civil conflicts witnessed revolts, wars and assassinations between competing groups and **caliphs**, hence ushering the expectation among Christians of the end of the Muslims' temporary dominion.[26]

These events paralleled the regrouping and counter-push of the Byzantines following their initial shock and defeats. The end would come at the hands of the Byzantines, limiting the dominion of Arabs to seventy years with the rise of Christian Byzantine kings.[27] Simply, God would bring back his dominion through a Christian emperor, a view that made use of Old Testament imagery in the Psalms.[28] Thus early Christians hoped that Arab domination would only be temporary, but first Christians needed to repent.[29] Notably, neither West-Syriac nor East-Syriac authors incorporated the Byzantines in their perspectives on the end of time. This view was mainly held among Greek Christians.

---

23. See Dan 7; 2 Thess 2; Matt 24 (Hoyland, *Seeing Islam*, 532; Penn, *Envisioning Islam*, 25–31).

24. See *Doctrina Jacobi* (AD 634), where the author fits the events into an apocalyptic scheme (Brock, "Syriac Views," 9; Hoyland, *Seeing Islam*, 55–61). Likewise, in Maximus the Confessor's letters dated to AD 634 and 640 (Hoyland, *Seeing Islam*, 76–78). And finally, the Armenian chronicler Sebeos (ca. 660s) who explains how Daniel foresaw the events of the seventh century (Hoyland, *Seeing Islam*, 124–132, 534–535).

25. For example, John bar Penkaye (Brock, "Syriac Views," 17–19; Hoyland, *Seeing Islam*, 533–534; Penn, *Envisioning Islam*, 26–28; Penn, *When Christians First Met Muslims*, 85–107).

26. Brock, "Syriac Views," 17; Hoyland, *Seeing Islam*, 533–534.

27. See *Pseudo-Methodius* (Brock, "Syriac Views," 18–19; Griffith, *Syriac Writers on Muslims*, 14–16; S. H. Griffith, "Muhammad and the Monk Baḥîrâ: Reflections on a Syriac and Arabic Text from Early Abbasid Times," *Oriens Christianus* 79 [1995]: 7–8; Penn, *Envisioning Islam*, 28–30; Penn, *When Christians First Met Muslims*, 108–129).

28. Ps 68:31 talks about Cush. *Pseudo-Methodius* links the Greek king via Alexander's Kushite mother, similarly to John of Damascus's prayer of deliverance at the hands of the Byzantines (Brock, "Syriac Views," 18).

29. Patriarch Sophronius called his people to such a repentance (Hoyland, *Seeing Islam*, 526).

However, when the inter-caliphate civil wars settled and it became clear that the Byzantines lacked the intention to reclaim previous territories, Christians started rethinking the Danielistic model and abandoning the eschatological hope that the end was near.[30] They now incorporated Muslims in their model. The Islamic caliphate moved from being viewed as an off-shoot of the fourth beast to being the fourth beast itself.[31] Now the four kingdoms of the vision of Daniel were seen as the Romans, Persians, Medes and Arabs.[32]

The Arab Muslims

The Christian readings of the seventh-century conquests shaped their views and images of the conquerors – the Muslim Arabs. The Arab conquerors were depicted as primitive and barbaric nomads of the desert who brought destruction and death to the conquered lands.[33] These low views of the conquerors were accompanied with expressions of surprise at how such primitive people were able to defeat the superpowers of their age.[34] So who were those people in the Christian views?

The Christian authors gave the new conquerors from the desert multiple names and identities. Ethno-culturally, they were called by the old names given to the residents of the Roman province of Arabia and North Arabian Peninsula, such as "Saracens" (Greek *sarakenoi*) and sometimes "Arabs"

---

30. The *Chronicle of 1234* highlights the Christian perspective that read the conquests prophetically as ushering a new era (Brock, "Syriac Views," 13).

31. See the Armenian chronicler, Sebeos, who identified the Ishmaelites with the fourth beast, dreadful with teeth of iron and claws of bronze (Brock, "Syriac Views," 9–10; Hoyland, *Seeing Islam*, 124–132, 534–535).

32. See *The Apocalypse of John the Little* (Brock, "Syriac Views," 19; Griffith, *Syriac Writers on Muslims*, 15–16; Hoyland, *Seeing Islam*, 267–270; Penn, *Envisioning Islam*, 31–33; Penn, *When Christians First Met Muslims*, 146–155).

33. Maximus the Confessor calls them a "barbaric people from the desert," reflecting the terminology of Sophronius, who also calls them barbarians (Brock, "Syriac Views," 9; Hoyland, *Seeing Islam,* 67–73, 76–78). *Pseudo-Methodius* echoes such labeling, calling them "barbarian tyrants" and characterizing them as "rebels, murderers, blood shedders and annihilators." They were "not men but children of devastation" (Hoyland, *Seeing Islam*, 295–297; Penn, *Envisioning Islam*, 15, 28–30; Penn, *When Christians First Met Muslims*, 108–129, esp. 119–124). Similarly, Patriarch Dionysius, who notes their rise from the South, describes them as the most "despised and insignificant of the peoples of the earth," calling them "the lowest of men" (Brock, "Syriac Views," 11; Penn, *Envisioning Islam*, 46–50, esp. 48).

34. John bar Penkaye wonders how "naked men, riding without armour or shield, were able to win" (Brock, "Syriac Views," 16; Hoyland, *Seeing Islam*, 194–200; Penn, *Envisioning Islam*, 26–28; Penn, *When Christians First Met Muslims*, 85–107, esp. 89).

(Greek *arabes*) in the Greek sources.[35] Eventually, the term "Saracens" also became synonymous with the term "Muslims" in Latin sources. Some Syriac sources used the Greek term in a Syriacized version (Syriac *Sarqaye*; singular *sarqaya*),[36] while the term "Arab" or "Arabian" (Syriac *'arabaya*) appears occasionally.[37]

Yet in Syriac sources, the term *tayyaye* (singular *tayyaya*), which is often translated "Arabs," was the most common name for the Arab conquerors. This use is evident in the earliest accounts of the conquests in the early seventh century[38] and as late as the twelfth century.[39] The term is derived from the Arab tribe of *al-Tayy* that dwelled in the northern desert of Arabia.[40] Traditionally, the term did not have religious classification and was used by Christians and pagans in the pre-Islamic period with reference to the nomadic dwellers of deserts.[41] For some time, there remained a lack of distinction after the conquests.[42]

---

35. See *Doctrina Jacobi* (634), the monk John Moschus (d. 634), Patriarch Sophronius (d. ca. 639), and Pope Martin I (d. 655). Hoyland, *Seeing Islam*, 53, 55–76.

36. The Maronite Chronicle (Penn, *When Christians First Met Muslims*, 19, 56–63, esp. 58).

37. In Jacob of Edessa and the apocalyptic-apologetic work known as *The Legend of Sergius Bahira* (Penn, *When Christians First Met Muslims*, 19, 183; Penn, *Envisioning Islam*, 87).

38. See *The Account of 637* (Penn, *Envisioning Islam*, 19–20, 59–60; Penn, *When Christians First Met Muslims*, 21–24).

39. Thomas the Presbyter (ca. 640) calls the new conquerors "the Arabs of Muhammad" (Syriac *tayyaye d-Mhmd*) in his *Chronicle AD 640*, which is used again much later by Dionysius bar Salibi (d. 1171) in his apologetic work entitled *Against the Tayyaye* (S. H. Griffith, "The Prophet Muhammad, His Scripture and His Message according to Christian Apologies in Arabic and Syriac from the First Abbasid Century," in *La vie du prophète Mahomet. Colloque de Strasbourg, Octobre 1980*, ed. Toufic Fahd [Paris: Presses Universitaires de France, 1983], 124; Griffith, *Syriac Writers on Muslims*, 22–23; Hoyland, "Earliest Christian Writings on Muhammad," 277–278; Hoyland, *Seeing Islam*, 118–120; Penn, *Envisioning Islam*, 20–21, 59–60; Penn, *When Christians First Met Muslims*, 19, 25–28).

40. Griffith, "Syriac Writers on Muslims," 8.

41. Judah B. Segal, "Arabs in Syriac Literature before the Rise of Islam," *Jerusalem Studies in Arabic and Islam* 4 (1984): 98–123; Penn, *Envisioning Islam*, 19–20, 56–58, 62; J. Spencer Trimingham, *Christianity among the Arabs in Pre-Islamic Times* (London: Longman, 1979), 312.

42. Such is the case of Patriarch Isho'yahb (Brock, "Syriac Views," 16; Hoyland, *Seeing Islam*, 174–182; Penn, *Envisioning Islam*, 60–61).

The Arab conquerors were also religiously identified.[43] Most often they were called "Ishmaelites" (Syriac *'Ishma'elaye*, Greek *Ismaelites*),[44] and "Sons of Ishmael" (Syriac *bnay* or *bar 'Ishma'el*).[45] For example, the early *Chronicle of Khuzistan* (ca. 660s) used "Sons of Ishmael." Sometimes they were called "Hagarenes" (Syriac *mhaggraye*,[46] singular *mhaggraya*, Greek. *Hagarenos* or *hoi hagarenoi*) and "Sons of Hagar" (Syriac *bnay* or *bar Hagar*).[47] These names were the most common labels of Muslims[48] in different genres,[49] and they were often used interchangeably.[50]

Biblical genealogy and theology, presumably, guided the Christian religious naming of the Arabs. The names were the product of a biblical reading of races that was shaped by the fourth-century Christian historian Eusebius. His classification saw the Arabs as the descendants of Ishmael, son of Abraham from Hagar. Notably, the Greek historian Sozomen (d. ca. 450) associated Arabs with Ishmael and Hagar pejoratively, claiming that the Arabs hid their identity as sons of Hagar by calling themselves sons of Ishmael.[51] Syriac

---

43. Brock, "Syriac Views," 15; Griffith, "The Qur'an in Arab Christian Texts: The Development of an Apologetical Argument: Abu Qurrah in the Maglis of al-Ma'mun," *Parole de l'Orient* 24 (1999): 207; Hoyland, *Seeing Islam*, 536, 549; Penn, *Envisioning Islam*, 61–62.

44. Hoyland, *Seeing Islam*, 53.

45. Many examples in Penn, *When Christians First Met Muslims*, 47, 52, 77, 78, 107, 109–10, 114, 116–117, 123–124, 130, 136, 146, 191–193.

46. Sometimes with the Syriac spelling *mhaggre* (Penn, *Envisioning Islam*, 61).

47. Examples in Penn, *When Christians First Met Muslims*, 37–38, 42, 86, 87, 90–92, 133–134.

48. See the writings of Patriarchs Isho'yahb III, John Sedra, and Dionysius of Tell-Mahre. David Bertaina, *Christian and Muslim Dialogues: The Religious Uses of a Literary Form in the Early Islamic Middle East* (Piscataway: Gorgias Press, 2011), 89; Sidney H. Griffith, "Disputes with Muslims in Syriac Christian Texts: From Patriarch John (d. 648) to Bar Hebraeus (d. 1286)," in *Religionsgespräche im Mittelalter*, eds. B. Lewis and F. Niewöhner (Wiesbaden: Otto Harrassowitz, 1992), 257–258.

49. The *Book of Main Points*, the *Chronicle of Khuzistan*, and the *Legend of Sergius Bahira* are a few examples of different Christian genres that used such terminologies (Brock, "Syriac Views," 15–16; Griffith, *Syriac Writers on Muslims*, 9–14; Griffith, "Prophet Muhammad," 122–124; Hoyland, *Seeing Islam*, 174–189, 194–200; Penn, *Envisioning Islam*, 58, 60–62; Penn, *When Christians First Met Muslims*, 29–36, 47–53, 85–107).

50. John bar Penkaye was the first to use the ethno-cultural title *tayyaye* and the religious titles Hagarenes and Ishmaelites interchangeably (Penn, *Envisioning Islam*, 65). Jacob of Edessa employs a derivative of the Syriac term *mhaggraya* (Syriac verb *ahgar* or *haggar*) to indicate conversion to Islam, giving the term a pure religious tone. He also speaks of Hagarene confession (Syriac *tawdita haggarayte*) (Griffith, *Syriac Writers on Muslims*, 11, 13; Penn, *Envisioning Islam*, 67–69).

51. John of Damascus is one post-conquest Greek author who made a similar connection between the Muslims and Abraham, Ishmael, and Hagar (Brock, "Syriac Views," 15; Griffith, "Prophet Muhammad," 124; Hoyland, *Seeing Islam*, 480–489, esp. 485–486).

sources also linked the Arabs with Abraham directly via the association with Ishmael and Hagar.[52]

The association of Arabs, Abraham, and his son Ishmael is also qur'anic (Sūrat *Ibrāhīm* 14:39), where Abraham and Ishmael are associated with building the ***Ka'ba*** in Mecca.[53] This connection was an Islamic theological reading of biblical genealogy to promote the Arab Muslim religious status among other monotheists (Jews and Christians). Thus, while Muslims sought through such religio-genealogical claims to advance their case, Christians employed the same connections to undermine them.

Alternatively, the Syriac term *mhaggraye* sounds like the Arabic title for the early followers of Muhammad, "the emigrants" (*muhajirun*), which might offer a parallel reason for the naming. This term was commonly used to refer to the earlier followers of Muhammad who fled with him from Mecca to Medina in the year 620. Many of those "emigrants" settled in the new conquered lands, such as the new garrison city of Kufa near the ancient Persian capital Seleucid-Ctesiphon in Iraq. Likewise, if the early Muslim followers of Muhammad were known as *muhajirun*, then the Syriac verb *ahgar* and the name *mhaggraye* carried the religious connotations of "becoming Muslim" and "Muslims," respectively.[54]

Setting aside the possible reasons behind the Islamic names, it is important to highlight the Christian theological ideologies that led to linking Muslims with Ishmael and Hagar. The Judeo-Christian readings of Genesis understood Israel as the heir of God's covenant with Abraham through Isaac – his son from the free-wife, Sarah – and excluded from such privilege the descendants of Ismael, the son of the slave Hagar. In Pauline theology, the apostle shifted the labels, creating a more exclusive sub-group of heirs, the followers of Christ. Christians are the heirs of the free Sarah and her son Isaac, while the unbelieving Jews are the theologically enslaved sons of Hagar and Ishmael (Gen 21:9–21; Gal 4:21–31). Almost six centuries after Paul, a new shift in

---

52. In fact, the Abrahamic link goes beyond the naming. The *Chronicle of Khuzistan*, John bar Penkaye, and Jacob of Edessa mention the "Dome of Abraham" as the site of the Arabs' worship and prayers, while the Greek author Anastasius of Sinai says it is a site of sacrifice (Hoyland, *Seeing Islam*, 92–103, 160–167, 182–189, 194–200, esp. 536, 549). A similar association is found in the *Legend of Sergius Bahira* and in the writings of the monk Abraham of Tiberias (Griffith, "Qur'an in Arab Christian Texts," 207; Samir Khalil Samir, "The Prophet Muhammad as Seen by Timothy I and Some Other Arab Christian Authors," in *Syrian Christians Under Islam: The First Thousand Years*, ed. David R. Thomas [Leiden: Brill, 2001], 77–81, esp. 78–79).

53. Griffith, *Syriac Writers on Muslims*, 9; Griffith, "Prophet Muhammad," 122.

54. Brock, "Syriac Views," 15; Griffith, *Syriac Writers on Muslims*, 12–13.

this biblical concept developed. Muslims became the new Jews, heirs of Hagar and Ishmael.[55] Thus, the Christian self-promoting theological agenda becomes clear, like that of the Muslims earlier, when these names were used.[56] Both sides reflected their theologies in the labels.

The double-entendre of naming also manifests itself in another Syriac title used for Muslims. Syriac authors often called the Muslims *hanpe* (singular *hanpa*), which could mean "pagans" (i.e. "Hellenes" in ancient Greek thought), or less pejoratively "non-Christians."[57] Furthermore, Syriac authors employed the verb form *ahnap* to mean "apostasy" from Christianity (i.e. to become *hanpa*) in the same way that they used the term *mhaggraya* to produce the verb *ahgar* or *haggar* to indicate conversion to Islam.[58]

Furthermore, the name might have Arab-Islamic connections, for it sounds like the Arab-Islamic term *ḥanīf*, which is often translated "monotheist" and refers either to a Muslim or a pre-Islamic monotheist such as Abraham (*Āl-'Imrān* 3:67). The famous relative of Muhammad's wife, Waraqa b. Nawfal, who recognized Muhammad's prophethood, according to the traditional biography, was called as such in Islamic sources.[59] Likewise, Syriac authors used the term *hanpe* to identify the Sabians in Harran, a city linked with Abraham, and later Muslims did the same, calling them *ḥunafā'*.[60] This agreement highlights how the term might be understood to define a type of monotheistic

---

55. Griffith, *Syriac Writers on Muslims*, 10–11; Griffith, "Prophet Muhammad," 122–123; Hoyland, *Seeing Islam*, 538–541; Penn, *Envisioning Islam*, 61–62.

56. Griffith, *Syriac Writers on Muslims*, 14.

57. The *Life of Maximus* is one of the early sources that used the term (Brock, "Syriac Views," 13; Griffith, *Syriac Writers on Muslims*, 11; Griffith, "Prophet Muhammad," 118–122; Penn, *When Christians First Met Muslims*, 62–68).

58. See as examples Jacob of Edessa, the author of the *Chronicle of Zuqnin*, the monk of Beth Hale, Theodore bar Koni, Timothy I and Nonnus of Nisibis (Griffith, *Syriac Writers on Muslims*, 8–9, 17–19; Griffith, "Prophet Muhammad," 118–122; Griffith, "Disputes with Muslims," 259–267). In his apologetic work titled *Scholion*, Theodore bar Koni speaks of the Muslim interlocutor as *hanpa*, while Nonnus of Nisibis calls the Muslims "present-day" or "recent" *hanpe*. He says, "The recent *hanpe* are more right minded than others," i.e. the Jews and Magians in their beliefs about Christ (Griffith, *Syriac Writers on Muslims*, 18–19; Griffith, "Prophet Muhammad," 121; Griffith, "Jews and Muslims in Christian Syriac and Arabic Texts of the Ninth Century," *Jewish History* 3, no. 1 [1988]: 72; Griffith, "Disputes with Muslims," 261–262, 265–266).

59. Griffith, "Prophet Muhammad," 119; Griffith, "Jews and Muslims," 72.

60. Griffith, "Prophet Muhammad," 119.

person. Yet the Islamic terminology was not hidden from Christian apologists who argued that Muslims misunderstood what the term *ḥanīf* meant.[61]

A third name that appeared in Christian writings was *mashlmane* (singular *mashlmana*), which is closest to the word "Muslims."[62] In some Syriac texts, the term *mashlmanuta* was used to refer to Islam or Muslimness, which was equated with *hanputa* (paganism). This terminology is late, not appearing in Syriac texts until the late eighth century, and although rare, it was still in use in the twelfth century.[63] Clearly, the term is very close if not identical to Muslims' self-identification, which is why Arabic-writing Christian authors used it frequently.[64]

Yet in this case also, Christians understood *hanputa* and used it differently from Muslims in some of their theological debates.[65] Those Christians argued that the name in its core meant "submission," as it does in the Islamic understanding. However, Christians used a particular qur'anic understanding of it to accuse Muslims of lack of faith. After all, the Qur'an seemed to differentiate between submission/submitted (*al-Islām/aslama*) and belief/believed (*al-īmān/āmana*). Christians claimed that they were the true qur'anic believers in God, while Muslims were only forceful submitters to him. Hence, again, though these sets of names might have pleased both groups (Christians and Muslims), they each heard what they considered to be the authentic label for Muslims from their own perspective.

Regardless of how the new conquerors' behavior was characterized and of their religio-cultural naming,[66] early Christian authors highlighted the religious tendencies of the new people, noting aspects of their religious beliefs, laws and

---

61. For example, Abraham of Tiberias (Griffith, "Prophet Muhammad," 120–121). Likewise, the author of the *al-Hashimi/al-Kindi Correspondence* utilized polemically the Islamic claim that Abraham was a *ḥanīf*, and he equated Islam with *al-ḥanīfiyya* to undermine it (Griffith, "Prophet Muhammad," 120).

62. See the *Chronicle of Zuqnin*, Patriarch Timothy I, and Theodore bar Koni. It comes from the idea, as Bar Koni notes, that Arabs were the receivers of a "tradition" (Syriac *mashlmanuta*). Griffith, "Prophet Muhammad," 125).

63. See the *Chronicle of Zuqnin* (Griffith, "Prophet Muhammad," 121; Griffith, "Disputes with Muslims," 270; Penn, *Envisioning Islam*, 56, 76–79).

64. Griffith, "Prophet Muhammad," 125.

65. See the works of the Chalcedonian Theodore Abu Qurrah (d. ca. 820s), Abraham of Tiberias, and the *al-Hashimi/al-Kindi Correspondence*, as well as the theological treatises of East-Syriac 'Ammar al-Basri (d. ca. 850) and West-Syriac Abu Ra'ita al-Takriti (d. ca. 830s). Griffith, "Prophet Muhammad," 125–127.

66. In the *Legend of Sergius Bahira*, all names were used interchangeably (Penn, *Envisioning Islam*, 87).

practices.[67] The key belief of the conquerors that Christian authors mention is their new monotheism.[68] Occasionally, Christian authors spoke of three types of monotheists: Christians, Jews and *tayyaye* (i.e. Arabs), which is an admission that Islam is a monotheistic faith.[69] Early sources frequently mentioned the conquerors' conversion to monotheism, noting that the Arabs were previously polytheists/pagans who worshiped idols. They specifically noted that these conversions were the result of Muhammad's efforts.[70] However, they claimed that the Muslim faith was an elementary form of monotheism which was more suitable for the intellectually deficient polytheist Arabs, compared to the more complex Christian view of God.[71]

Furthermore, Christian apologists highlighted the materialistic nature of the new monotheistic faith of the Arabs.[72] Based on such characterization, they argued that Islam was developed to appeal to Arab sensuality, either in matters of doctrine (e.g. doctrine of paradise) or practice (e.g. prayer, food/fasting, lack of celibacy and social laws).[73] At the same time, the Arabs' new

---

67. For example, the Frankish chronicler Fredegar (650s) highlighted that Muslims were circumcised (Hoyland, *Seeing Islam*, 216–219, esp. 218).

68. The monk of Zuqnin points this out in his *Chronicle* (Penn, *Envisioning Islam*, 77).

69. See Thomas of Marga (860s) in his monastic history *Ktaba d-Rishane* (*The Book of Governors*). Hoyland, *Seeing Islam*, 213–215; Penn, *Envisioning Islam*, 97).

70. John of Damascus says that Arabs were worshipers of the morning star and Aphrodite, but that they turned to a form of monotheistic heresy through the efforts of Muhammad, who was influenced by the Arian Christian monk Bahira. John also documents the Muslim views about Christ and Christians, as well as some of their religious rituals and practices, such as circumcision and alcohol prohibition (Bertaina, *Christian and Muslim Dialogues*, 126; Griffith, "Prophet Muhammad," 124; Griffith, "Qur'an in Arab Christian Texts," 207; Hoyland, *Seeing Islam*, 480–489, esp. 485–488). Other Christian apologetic works spoke of Muhammad's monotheism as well, such as *The Dispute of the Monk of Bet Hale* and *The Legend of Sergius-Bahira* (Bertaina, *Christian and Muslim Dialogues*, 141–142; Griffith, "Muhammad and the Monk Bahira," 24, 79–81; Griffith, "The Qur'an in Christian Arabic Literature: A Cursory Overview," in *Arab Christians and the Qur'an from the Origins of Islam to the Medieval Period*, ed. Mark Beaumont [Leiden: Brill, 2018], 15; Griffith, *Syriac Writers on Muslims*, 31–32; Hoyland, "Earliest Christian Writings," 287; Hoyland, *Seeing Islam*, 468, 537–538).

71. Patriarch Timothy I made this argument in his theological dialogue with Caliph al-Mahdi (d. 785). Bertaina, *Christian and Muslim Dialogues*, 151–152; Penn, *Envisioning Islam*, 110).

72. The author of the *Legend of Sergius-Bahira* made this point when depicting the way that Muhammad described his followers to the Christian monk. Muhammad is reported as saying, "my comrades are uncouth desert Arabs who are not accustomed to fasting and prayers, nor to anything which causes them trouble or bother." See Hoyland, "Earliest Christian Writings," 287; Hoyland, *Seeing Islam*, 537–538.

73. Bertaina, *Christian and Muslim Dialogues*, 127–128; Griffith, "Muhammad and the Monk Bahira," 20–21, 27–28; Griffith, "Qur'an in Christian Arabic Literature," 18; Griffith, *Syriac Writers on Muslims*, 31–32, 37–49; Hoyland, "Earliest Christian Writings," 287; Hoyland, *Seeing Islam*, 537–538; Penn, *Envisioning Islam*, 111.

monotheism was sometimes complimented and sometimes criticized for its beliefs and positions toward Christianity, especially when it came to Christ.[74] Notably, sometimes this assessment led to comparisons and contrasts with Judaism. Occasionally, Muslims were complemented for their beliefs about Christ, which were seen as more acceptable in comparison to the beliefs of the Jews.[75]

Yet the relation among the three monotheistic groups remained complex in Christian writings. Christian writers often compared and blended the beliefs of Muslims and Jews, distinguishing them from the Christian faith. For example, they pointed out that the Muslim rejection of key Christian doctrines and practices, such as the Trinity and Christ's divinity and the veneration of crosses and icons, was similar to the Jewish position.[76] In the Levant region, the common direction of prayer (*qibla*) toward the south that both Muslims and Jews used added further reason for this type of association. Syriac authors noted the Muslim reception of new religious traditions (Syriac *mashlmanuta*) and teachings (Syriac *malpanuta*) about the law and the prophets. They highlighted the Muslim acceptance of the Hebrew Bible and their rejection of the scriptural teachings about Christ.[77] Thus, they sometimes spoke about Muslims as the "new Jews."[78]

---

74. For example, Nonnus of Nisibis, who called Muslims "recent *hanpe*," highlighted their beliefs in the virgin birth and in Christ as the word and spirit of God, that he worked miracles, that he was the Creator who created a bird from clay just as he created Adam, and their confession that he ascended into heaven and would come into the world a second time. But Nonnus pointed out that, "being excessive in giving honor, they do not accept the fact that he was crucified and died" (Griffith, "Jews and Muslims," 72).

75. Like Nonnus of Nisibis, Jacob of Edessa also compared Jewish, Muslim and Christian beliefs about the Messiah (Griffith, "Jews and Muslims," 73). Likewise, Patriarch Timothy favored the beliefs of Muslims over those of the Jews. He pointed out that today Ishmaelites were "held in great honor and esteem by God and men, because they forsook idolatry and polytheism, and worshiped and honored one God; in this they deserve the love and praise of all" (Griffith, "Prophet Muhammad," 121).

76. See for example Anastasius of Sinai, Patriarch Germanus (d. 730), Abu Qurrah, and Abu Ra'ita (Griffith, "Jews and Muslims," 73–44, 76–80; Hoyland, *Seeing Islam*, 92–107, esp. 94, 105–106. For evidence in Latin authors, see Hoyland, *Seeing Islam*, 226–231, esp. 228, 230).

77. Theodore bar Koni comments to his Muslim interlocutor, "as I see it . . . you are believing as a Jew" (Griffith, "Prophet Muhammad," 122; Griffith, "Jews and Muslims," 65).

78. Patriarch Timothy I refers to Muslims in this way in his ecclesiastical letter to his bishop on his debate with al-Mahdi. He writes, "In the days of Herod, Pilate and the old Jews, there was both defeat and victory, and truth and falsehood. So also, now, in the days of the present princes, in our own time, and in the days of the new Jews among us, there is the same struggle and the same contest to distinguish falsehood and truth" (Griffith, "Jews and Muslims," 65; Griffith, "Prophet Muhammad," 122; Hoyland, *Seeing Islam*, 538–541).

Ritualistic and doctrinal similarities between Jews and Muslims, and their differences with Christian ones (such as the veneration of icons), guided the Christian apologetic response to Islam. Christian apologists defended their beliefs and practices as they did previously toward Jewish polemics against Christianity.[79] Further, in their apologies, Christian authors also criticized Muslim beliefs and rituals. They rejected, for example, the Muslim forms of prayer and fasting, claiming them to be false and invalid.[80] And in their defense of the Christian veneration of icons, they responded to Muslims' comments by criticizing their idolization of a "lifeless stone" with reference to the Black Stone in the *Ka'ba*.[81]

Furthermore, the link was emphasized between Muslims and Jews in earlier Christian reports of Muslims building a place of worship on the ground of the Jerusalem temple (i.e. Umar I's mosque).[82] Interestingly, some Christian accounts claimed it was Jews who built it, but that later Muslims claimed it and prohibited the Jews from using it.[83] Later Syriac authors echoed similar reports about the construction of a place of worship, the Jewish temple, reflecting a biblical-eschatological motif common among Christians concerning the end times.[84] Similar claims were found in Byzantine circles, where the relation between Muslims and Jews around the theme of the construction of a mosque was also connected with iconoclasm.[85]

---

79. Such is the case in Timothy I, Theodore Bar Koni, Abu Ra'ita, Abu Qurrah, and 'Ammar al-Basri, to mention a few (Griffith, "Jews and Muslims," 78–79).

80. See, for example, the *Homily on the Child Saints of Babylon* (c. 640s). Hoyland, *Seeing Islam*, 120–121).

81. See Germanus in particular (Hoyland, *Seeing Islam*, 100–101, 105–106).

82. Arculf, who visited Jerusalem in 683, described the construction of a mosque with its wonderful and grandiose characteristics, noting its size as a place that can accommodate 3000 worshipers (Hoyland, *Seeing Islam*, 218–223, esp. 221).

83. See Sebeos, in Hoyland, *Seeing Islam*, 124–132, esp. 127.

84. See for example the *Chronicle of Dionysius of Tell-Mahre*, in Brock, "Syriac Views," 12.

85. The *Chronicle of Theophanes* (d. 818) notes: "In that year 'Umar began to build the mosque in Jerusalem, and the structure did not stand, but kept falling down. The Jews told the person who was inquiring about the cause that, 'if the cross that is on top of the Mount of Olives is not taken down, the structure will not stand.' On account of this proposal, the cross was taken down from there and so their building held together. For this reason, the Christ-haters brought down many crosses" (Griffith, "Jews and Muslims," 77).

Muhammad

The Christian perception of Muslims and their conquests, in turn, shaped and were shaped by their various views of Muhammad, which ranged from socio-political to religious depictions. The earliest Christian historians recorded Muhammad's political career by focusing on the Arab conquests. After all, political history is essential in historical writings.[86] They portrayed him as a political leader who initiated the conquests and even led the earliest activities against the Romans in the Levant, referring to Muslims as followers of Muhammad.[87] Hence, Muhammad's leadership of the conquests was emphasized,[88] noting for example his motivational and practical roles.[89] Christians often labelled Muhammad with political designations.[90] Syriac authors called him "king" (*malka*), "leader" (*mdabbrana*), "commander" (*shallita* or *shallita rabba*) and "head" (*risha*) of the Muslims. They referred to Muslims as "the Arabs of Muhammad." In these cases, it was the conquests as political events that created the titles, depicting Muhammad as the ruler of a new kingdom (*malkuta*).[91]

---

86. Hoyland, "Earliest Christian Writings," 277–281; Penn, *Envisioning Islam*, 106–107.

87. Hoyland, "Earliest Christian Writings," 277–281; Hoyland, *Seeing Islam*, 535–536; Penn, *Envisioning Islam*, 106–107. *The Account of 637* and *The Chronicle AD 640* speak of battles between Byzantine forces and "the *tayyaye* of Muhammad" (Hoyland, "Earliest Christian Writings," 277–281; 118–120; Penn, *Envisioning Islam*, 106).

88. The *Chronicle of Khuzistan* confirms Muhammad's leadership role, noting that "God brought the Ishmaelites . . . their leader (Syr. *mdabbrana*) was Muhammad" (Hoyland, "Earliest Christian Writings," 278; Penn, *Envisioning Islam*, 106). Muhammad's leadership of the conquests is also emphasized in Syriac sources, such as the *Chronicle of Zuqnin*, the *Chronicle AD 819*, the *Chronicle AD 846*, the *Chronicle of Theophilus of Edessa*, the *Chronicle of Dionysius of Tell-Mahre*, and a Latin chronicle by a Spanish writer (Hoyland, "Earliest Christian Writings," 278–280; Penn, *Envisioning Islam*, 106).

89. Sebeos mentioned that Muhammad preached to the Arabs in battle. As for George, a companion of the patriarch of Alexandria, he recounts Muhammad's success in taking cities in the Levant, while the monk of Zuqnin speaks of Muslims defeating the Romans under Muhammad's leadership (Hoyland, "Earliest Christian Writings," 277–281).

90. For example, a Maronite chronicle mentions "Muhammad's throne," while Jacob of Edessa calls Muhammad "first king," which is also noted in the *Chronicle of Zuqnin*. Further, Abraham of Tiberias says that Muhammad was "a king approved by God" (Griffith, "Qur'an in Arab Christian Texts," 204, no. 1; Hoyland, "Earliest Christian Writings on Muhammad," 282; Samir, "Prophet Muhammad as Seen," 78). Certain Islamic-Arabic leadership terms, such as caliph and emir, appeared in Syriacized versions and were used with later Muslim caliphs, commanders and local governors, while others, like the East-Syriac patriarch Isho'yahb, used Syriac terms (e.g. *shallita rabba* and *risha*) (Brock, "Syriac Views," 14, 16, 20).

91. See the conversation between patriarch John of Sedra and a Muslim ruler around 644 (Brock, "Syriac Views," 13–14).

Notably, the conquests also influenced Christian depictions of Muhammad's early life, including his pre-conquest biography.[92] One key piece of biographical information that Christian authors mentioned was Muhammad's involvement in trade journeys to the Levant as a merchant.[93] They pointed out that such trade journeys might have inspired his later interests in raiding and conquering the Levant and adopting monotheism. They further noted his encounters with Jews and Christians on these journeys and on other occasions, claiming that these encounters influenced his religious and political agenda and actions.[94] Moreover, they advanced that Muhammad's success in his early raids motivated the Arabs to join him, given their natural habits and predispositions toward raiding. The efforts of Muhammad and his early companions brought wealth to them, which attracted others to join him and to continue with the raids, even after he had ceased to be personally in command of the campaigns. Christian authors explained that it was the practice of raiding and the early military successes that increased the interest of Arabs in pushing further into territories beyond Palestine.

Christian authors also linked these early encounters with the Jews to the construction of the mosque on the site of the Temple of Solomon.[95] Notably, the act of removing the cross from the Mount of Olives by early Muslims when building the mosque of 'Umar I was linked with Jewish advice. Likewise, the

---

92. See the dialogue of Abraham of Tiberias and that between al-Kindi and al-Hashimi on Muhammad's earlier life in the Hijaz (Griffith, "Prophet Muhammad," 132–134).

93. See Sebeos, Jacob of Edessa, Theophilus of Edessa, and Dionysius of Tell-Mahre for examples (Hoyland, *Seeing Islam*, 128–132, 403–404, 535–536; Hoyland, "Earliest Christian Writings," 280–281).

94. One example suffices from the *Chronicle of Dionysius of Tell-Mahre* who writes:

> This Muhammad, while in the age and stature of you, began to go up and down from his town of Yathrib to Palestine for the business of buying and selling. While so engaged in the country, he saw the belief in one God and it was pleasing to his eyes. When he went back down to his tribesmen, he set this belief before them and he convinced a few and they became his followers. In addition, he would extol the bountifulness of this land of Palestine, saying, "Because of the belief in one God, the like of this good and fertile land was given to them." And he would add: "If you listen to me, God will give to you, too, a land flowing with milk and honey." To corroborate his word, he led a band of them who were obedient to him and began to go up to the land of Palestine, plundering, enslaving and pillaging. He returned laden with booty and unharmed, and thus he had not fallen short of his promises to them" (Hoyland, "Earliest Christian Writings," 280).

95. Theophilus of Edessa and Dionysius of Tell-Mahre recount Caliph Abu Bakr's address to his four generals on the eve of their departure to Syria, which was motivated by Muhammad's earlier visits (Brock, "Syriac Views," 11–12; Hoyland, "Earliest Christian Writings," 280–281; Hoyland, *Seeing Islam*, 400–409).

Jews' rejoicing in the Arabs' victories against the Byzantines was seen as a sign of partnership between them. Some even pointed to the Jews' participation in the conquests and/or supporting Arab efforts as an example of this partnership.[96]

The Christian narratives of Muhammad's early career and encounters also allude to his religious identity in Christian sources, especially his role in converting the Arabs into a form of monotheism. They often spoke of Muhammad giving the Arabs religious laws and scriptural traditions, depicting him as their religious guide and legislator. Such images are very common in Christian sources, regardless of their author's confessional belonging.[97]

Christian authors highlight that Muhammad's religious teachings had biblical tendencies, in which he accepted the Torah (not the Prophets) and the gospels as divine revelation, but not all Christian doctrines (e.g. the Trinity and Christ's divinity).[98] As highlighted above, the similarities between Muslim and Jewish beliefs (e.g. their anti-Christian tendency) and some ritualistic practices were noted in the Christian sources. Further, they referred negatively to some of Muhammad's teaching about the afterlife and paradise, highlighting its carnal characteristics[99] and its materialistic nature.[100]

On the other hand, Christians spoke about Muhammad's divine purpose and favor, depicting him as a man of God who implemented his divine will and plan.[101] As noted, for some Muhammad was God's tool to chastise the Christians, while for others he was God's way to bring the Arabs into primitive but acceptable monotheism. In both cases, God used him to deal with two

---

96. See *Doctrina Jacobi*, Sebeos, Maximus the Confessor, and John of Nikiu (Hoyland, *Seeing Islam*, 55–61, 76–78, 152–156, 527–530, 538–539). Christian sources also viewed these trade journeys as the setting for the encounter between Muhammad and the monk Sergius Bahira, which will be examined further (Griffith, "Muhammad and the Monk Bahira," 5).

97. John bar Penkaye and the Armenian chronicler Sebeos echoed such sentiments (Hoyland, "Earliest Christian Writings," 283–286). The same is found in the Coptic work *History of Alexandrian Patriarchs*, as well as in the West-Syriac monk of Zuqnin in the Syro-Arabic *Chronicle of Seert*, in Sebeos, in John of Damascus, and in Dionysius (Hoyland, "Earliest Christian Writings," 283–285; Hoyland, *Seeing Islam*, 535–536, 549; Penn, *Envisioning Islam*, 107).

98. See for example Patriarch John of Sedra, Dionysius of Tell-Mahre, and the monk of Beth Hale (Brock, "Syriac Views," 12; Hoyland, *Seeing Islam*, 459–472; Bertaina, *Christian and Muslim Dialogues*, 126).

99. See Theophilus of Edessa in Hoyland, *Seeing Islam*, 400–409, 541–544.

100. Nonnus of Nisibis writes: "Rivers of fattening foods, along with time in bed that does not satiate; a new creation of women whose birth is not from Adam and Eve – things known and acknowledged to incite carnal people" (Griffith, "Disputes with Muslims," 266).

101. For example, see Abraham of Tiberias in Samir, "Prophet Muhammad as Seen," 78–79.

groups, bringing them from their ungodly ways into God's acceptable path.[102] Therefore, the awareness that Christian authors had of Muhammad's religious and spiritual leadership among the Arabs led to their speaking of him as a religious "guide" (Syriac *mhaddyana*) and "instructor" (*tar'a*) of the Muslims.[103] In their views, he was a monotheistic preacher and lawgiver (*sa'em namose*) who gave the Arabs religious "teaching" (*malpanuta*), "laws" (*namose*, singular *namosa*), "tradition" (*mashlmanuta*) and "covenant" (Arabic *'ahd*).

The compliments Muhammad received in Christian writings did not mean their authors endorsed the Islamic claims of his prophethood.[104] In fact, some explicitly rejected such claims, depicting him as a false prophet.[105] Christians rarely called Muhammad "prophet" (Syriac *nbiya*) or "messenger/apostle" (Syriac *rasula*), although the terms appeared in Syriac chronicles.[106] Even when they used them, Christian authors were not endorsing their validity.[107] However, some Syriac authors associated him with such religious roles more positively.[108] Even in such cases, however, Christian apologists were only speaking of the alignment of Muhammad's monotheistic and moral teachings with ancient biblical prophets of Israel, mainly saying that he followed their ways or walked in their paths. They argued that Muhammad could not be a prophet because he neither performed any miracles nor did biblical scripture foretell his coming.[109]

---

102. Brock, "Syriac Views," 10–11, 15–16; Hoyland, *Seeing Islam*, 525; Penn, *Envisioning Islam*, 108–109.

103. Hoyland, "Earliest Christian Writings," 284. Notably, in a late sixth-century text, the term *mhaddyana* is used of the initiator of a heresy (Brock, "Syriac Views," 14).

104. Griffith, "Prophet Muhammad," 132–143; Hoyland, "Earliest Christian Writings," 285–286; Penn, *Envisioning Islam*, 108–115.

105. The *Doctrina Jacobi* was one of the earliest sources to do so (Hoyland, *Seeing Islam*, 57).

106. See the *Chronicle of Zuqnin*, the *Chronicle of 1234*, the *Chronicle of Elias of Nisibis*, and the *Apocalypse of John the Less* (Brock, "Syriac Views," 14; Hoyland, "Earliest Christian Writings," 285; Hoyland, *Seeing Islam*, 413–414; Penn, *Envisioning Islam*, 104–105, 107).

107. The *Chronicle AD 724* utilized such terminology neutrally, calling him "the messenger of God," (Penn, *Envisioning Islam*, 105). The monk of Zuqnin, on the other hand, used the terms polemically (Hoyland, "Earliest Christian Writings," 285; Hoyland, *Seeing Islam*, 413).

108. Most notably, Patriarch Timothy I in his conversation with Caliph al-Mahdi systematically compares Muhammad with ancient biblical prophets (Bertaina, *Christian and Muslim Dialogues*, 153; Hoyland, "Earliest Christian Writings," 286; Penn, *Envisioning Islam*, 93–96, 108–110; Samir, "Prophet Muhammad as Seen," 93–96).

109. Patriarch Timothy even claimed that if such biblical testimonies had existed, he would have been the first to convert to Islam. The question of whether Muhammad had performed miracles or not became a major theme in Islamic circles as part of the proofs of his prophethood (Bertaina, *Christian and Muslim Dialogues*, 151; Griffith, "Prophet Muhammad," 138–143; Penn, *Envisioning Islam*, 109–110; Samir, "Prophet Muhammad as Seen," 96–98).

This comparison of Muhammad with biblical prophets – without endorsing his prophethood – had its theological and biblical reasons. Christian theologians were guided by the New Testament perspective that the age of prophets had ended with the incarnation of Christ, the full and final revelation of God. They claimed that Christ had brought about the perfection and culmination of the revelation; hence Christianity is the climax of revelation. Furthermore, they stated that Christ had warned his followers against anyone claiming prophethood, arguing that John the Baptist was the last of the biblical prophets.[110]

Muslims frequently attempted to prove Muhammad's divine mandate by referencing biblical passages which they claim contain testimonies about him (e.g. Deut 18:18; Isa 21:7; John 16:7). The Caliph al-Mahdi did so in his conversation with Timothy.[111] Yet Christians could not accept the Muslim interpretations of these verses (e.g. Moses's prophecy about the new prophet, Jesus's statement on the Paraclete, etc.), but argued otherwise.[112] For example, they emphasized the lack of miracles in Muhammad's career,[113] using qur'anic statements (such as *al-An'ām* 6:109 and *al-Isrā* 17:59) to prove their claims.[114] Others refuted the Muslim claims on the biblical testimonies, which the latter relied on to support Muhammad's prophethood.[115]

Rejecting Muhammad's divinely mandated prophethood left Christians with the task of explaining how Muhammad had become acquainted with monotheism and his motivation for preaching it. Christian apologists of the eighth and ninth centuries led both the internal discussion on the subject and the external debate with Muslim interlocutors. They argued that a Christian monk, often referred to as Sergius Bahira, had influenced Muhammad's

---

110. See Patriarch Timothy's conversation with Caliph al-Mahdi in Samir, "Prophet Muhammad as Seen," 99–104.

111. Hoyland, "Earliest Christian Writings," 287; Penn, *Envisioning Islam*, 109–110; and Sarah Stroumsa, "The Signs of Prophecy: The Emergence and Early Development of a Theme in Arabic Theological Literature," *The Harvard Theological Review* 78, no. 1–2 (Jan–Apr 1985): 101–114.

112. See Timothy's *Apology* in Griffith, "Prophet Muhammad," 138–143.

113. John of Damascus was the first author to do so. See Bertaina, *Christian and Muslim Dialogues*, 126; Hoyland, "Earliest Christian Writings," 287.

114. See 'Ammar al-Basri and the author of the *al-Hashimi/al-Kindi Dialogue* in Griffith, "Prophet Muhammad," 142.

115. For examples, see Abraham of Tiberias, 'Ammar al-Basri, Abu Qurrah, Abu Ra'itah, *al-Hashimi/al-Kindi Dialogue* and the *Legend of Sergius-Bahira* (Griffith, "Prophet Muhammad," 134–138; Griffith, "Muhammad and the Monk Bahira," 23; Samir, "Prophet Muhammad as Seen," 80–82).

religious consciousness and career. This argument came from multiple authors and sources.[116]

The association of Bahira with Muhammad is Islamic. According to the Islamic biographical tradition of Muhammad, Bahira was a Christian monk who recognized the young Muhammad during his trade journey with his uncle to the Levant, noticing a prophetic sign and predicting his great future.[117] Most likely, Christian authors knew this Islamic tradition. However in the Syriac tradition, Bahira is not a name but a title of honor for monks,[118] which is why Syriac Christians called this monk Sergius. If the Christian authors agreed on the name, they disagreed on his confessional affiliation. He was an Arian according to some, a Nestorian according to others, and a monk without a confessional identifier in other sources.[119]

In any case, Christians collectively argued that Sergius Bahira was behind Muhammad's call to the Arabs to turn to God.[120] Further, they noted that Bahira was the reason behind Muhammad's teaching and behavior, since he systematically taught him everything that he knew, ranging from Islamic doctrines to rituals and practices. Bahira helped the illiterate Muhammad to claim prophethood through the composition of the Qur'an and its presentation as a divinely inspired and sent revelation. This revelation is referred to as *Qur'an*, ***Furqān*** or *Sūrat al-Baqara*, depending on the preserved version of the story.[121]

---

116. See John of Damascus's *Fount of Knowledge*, the *Chronicle of Theophanes*, the *Dialogue of Patriarch John of Sedra with a Muslim Emir*, the *Dialogue of Monk of Beth Hale with an Arab Notable*, the *al-Hashimi/al-Kindi Correspondence* and the *Legend of Sergius-Bahira* (Griffith, "Muhammad and the Monk Bahira," 1–5, 9–11, 17–30; Griffith, "Prophet Muhammad," 134–138; Griffith, "Christians and the Arabic Qur'an: Prooftexting, Polemics, and Intertwined Scriptures," *Intellectual History of the Islamicate World* 2, no. 1–2 [2014]: 255–259; Griffith, "Qur'an in Arab Christian Texts," 206–214; Griffith, "Qur'an in Christian Arabic Literature," 14–18; Griffith, *Syriac Writers on Muslims*, 31–32, 37–49; Hoyland, *Seeing Islam*, 400–409, 459–472, 476–479; Penn, *Envisioning Islam*, 87–90, 110–112; Penn, *When Christians First Met Muslims*, 212–215).

117. Griffith, "Muhammad and the Monk Bahira," 3, 9, 10–11, 16; Griffith, "Qur'an in Christian Arabic Literature," 15; Penn, *Envisioning Islam*, 111.

118. Griffith, "Muhammad and the Monk Bahira," 3.

119. Bertaina, *Christian and Muslim Dialogues*, 126; Griffith, "Muhammad and the Monk Bahira," 9–11; Griffith, "Prophet Muhammad," 135; Griffith, "Qur'an in Arab Christian Texts," 207; Griffith, "Christians and the Arabic Qur'an," 255; Hoyland, *Seeing Islam*, 479.

120. The author of the *Legend of Sergius-Bahira* claims that the monk specified Muhammad's purpose "to turn people away from the worship of images to the worship of the one God" (Griffith, "Muhammad and the Monk Bahira," 18–19, 24).

121. They argued that Sergius Bahira wrote the Qur'an and sent it on the horn of a cow, thus the qur'anic Chapter of Cow (*Sūra al-Baqara*) would become the name of the text (Bertaina, *Christian and Muslim Dialogues*, 129; Griffith, "Muhammad and the Monk Bahira," 22, 28; Griffith, "Qur'an in Arab Christian Texts," 208–210; Griffith, "Christians and the Arabic

Christian apologists claimed that the monk first taught Muhammad Christianity with the intention of evangelizing Bedouin Arabs.[122] For example, Bahira taught Muhammad that Christ was the Word and Spirit of God (*an-Nisā* 4:171). He taught him about the Trinity, Christ's incarnation, resurrection, ascension, second coming and miracles. Bahira also taught Muhammad many of the other key passages in the Qur'an.[123] Yet the apologists argued that the complexity of Christian doctrines (e.g. the Trinity) was not fitting for Muhammad's audience. Hence a simpler, elementary form of monotheism was a more suitable and needed version of religion, which Muhammad could teach. And his polytheist followers would grasp and follow it without the risk of turning the trinitarian faith into a new polytheistic religion.[124]

Hence in Christian sources, Muhammad was not recognized as a prophet by Bahira but made into one. Muhammad was not a new prophet with a new religion, but he was a crypto-Christian reviver of Abrahamic monotheism who did not benefit entirely from Christianity's full revelation in Christ. His followers were only able to take one step toward the true religion, moving only from polytheism to a primitive monotheism, but without endorsing Christianity.[125]

Furthermore, in their apologetic efforts to defend Christianity and discredit Muhammad's prophethood, Christian apologists highlighted the factors that led to the spread of Islam. Beside the materialistic rewards, which the earlier followers were promised and given during the early raids, Christians argued that violence was also a factor. In other words, they claimed that Muhammad spread Islam by the power of the sword.[126]

In such arguments, they compared the spreading of Christianity with that of Islam, highlighting the peaceful nature of Christianity as compared to

---

Qur'an," 256–258; Griffith, "Qur'an in Christian Arabic Literature," 16–17; Hoyland, *Seeing Islam*, 478; Penn, *Envisioning Islam*, 111).

122. Griffith, "Muhammad and the Monk Bahira," 19–20, 24; Griffith, "Qur'an in Christian Arabic Literature," 15.

123. Griffith, "Muhammad and the Monk Bahira," 25–27.

124. The monk of Beth Hale makes this argument in his reply to his Muslim interlocutor's question about his views of Muhammad (Bertaina, *Christian and Muslim Dialogues*, 141–142; Griffith, "Qur'an in Christian Arabic Literature," 18; Griffith, "Christians and the Arabic Qur'an," 256–258; Griffith, *Syriac Writers on Muslims*, 31–32, 37–49; Hoyland, "Earliest Christian Writings," 286–287; Hoyland, *Seeing Islam*, 468, 537–538; Penn, *Envisioning Islam*, 110).

125. Griffith, "Muhammad and the Monk Bahira," 17–30.

126. The East-Syriac patriarch Hnanisho' (d. 693) tells Caliph 'Abd al-Malik (d. 715) that Islam is "a religion established by the sword and not a faith confirmed by miracles" (Hoyland, "Earliest Christian Writings," 288).

Islam.[127] Such comparisons were common in Christian-Muslim debates, which later apologists used and developed as a criterion to measure the truthfulness of a religion. In their apologetic works, they suggested several criteria to determine the truthfulness of a religion. If a religion promoted worldly desires, ambition, fear, personal whim and partisanship, then such practices led to the rejection of the religion's authenticity. Christian apologists claimed that Islam was guilty of encouraging such practices, which in turn discredited Muhammad's prophethood.

Despite the firm rejection of Muhammad's prophethood by Syriac and Syro-Arabic Christians within the caliphate, Muhammad was not vilified in their writings as he was in Western (Greek and Latin) sources.[128] As early as the eighth century, Greek authors developed negative views. They depicted Islam as a heresy, and Muhammad and the Qur'an as an inauthentic prophet and scripture. They often characterized Muhammad as a lustful and morally depraved man who loved debauchery, massacres and pillage. In other cases, he was depicted as a miserable epileptic, as a blasphemous and obscene man, as an idol-worshiper, a demon-possessed man, an enemy of God and an antichrist who was influenced in his teachings by the errors of Jews, Arians and Nestorians, as well as having received his teachings from demons.

The Qur'an

The Christian narratives of Muhammad's religious history, mission and followers defined their perceptions of the Qur'an. As noted earlier, Christians were aware that Muhammad had brought in religious teachings and traditions. They sometimes referred to the compilation of his teachings through different names, including the term "Qur'an."[129] Yet Christians who argued that Muhammad was not a divinely sent prophet but merely the disciple of a

---

127. A monk of Mar Sabas, named Michael, makes a similar argument in his reply to 'Abd al-Malik (Hoyland, "Earliest Christian Writings," 288).

128. John of Damascus was key in shaping the thinking of both Greeks and Latins (Griffith, "Prophet Muhammad," 131; Griffith, "Christians and the Arabic Qur'an," 244–245; Hoyland, *Seeing Islam*, 488; Hoyland, "Earliest Christian Writings," 276; Penn, *Envisioning Islam*, 112–113).

129. The earliest Christian writer to use the word "Qur'an" was the monk of Beth Hale (Griffith, "Muhammad and the Monk Bahira," 22, 28; Griffith, "Qur'an in Arab Christian Texts," 209; Griffith, "Christians and the Arabic Qur'an," 244; Griffith, "Qur'an in Christian Arabic Literature," 16–17; Hoyland, *Seeing Islam*, 471; Penn, *Envisioning Islam*, 111).

Christian monk refused to accept his teachings in the Qur'an as a new, divinely inspired revelation. They argued that it was composed by a human.[130]

The Christian pushback against the claim of Muhammad's prophethood, especially due to his lack of miracles, led Muslim apologists to argue that the Qur'an was his miracle. The argument had its basis in the Qur'an (*al-Baqara* 2:23; *al-Isrā* 17:88; *al-Ḥashr* 59:21).[131] This was the Muslim way of arguing that Muhammad received a divine revelation. Christian apologists counter-argued these claims. They emphasized that Muhammad was an illiterate man who had received no divine inspiration. The first claim was influenced by the qur'anic verses in Sūrat *al-Aʿrāf* 7:157–158. Muslims asserted that Muhammad's illiteracy proved the miracle of the Qur'an.[132] Christians disagreed,[133] explaining that his illiteracy had no bearing on him receiving a divine revelation.[134]

Once again, the biblical conviction that Christ is the ultimate and complete revelation of God nullified and prohibited the need for a new and additional revelation. In the past when claims of new divine revelation were made, they were interpreted as heresy, especially if they deviated from the common Christian beliefs and scriptures. Hence, some Christians saw Islam as a heresy, more specifically one influenced by Judaism.[135]

In their responses to Muslim questions about whether Christians viewed the Qur'an as divinely inspired, Christian apologists often argued against the Qur'an as revelation. They asserted that the lack of miracles in Muhammad's life, in contrast to those of ancient prophets and Christian apostles, was proof that the Qur'an was not divine. God's messengers performed miracles by God's power, but Muhammad did not. Thus, neither was the Qur'an a divine revelation, nor was Muhammad God's messenger. In other words, the biblical

---

130. John of Damascus argued that Muhammad "spread rumors that a scripture was brought down to him from heaven." He rejected Muhammad's claims, explaining that he "composed many idle tales, on each one of which he prefixed a title." He mentioned some of the sūra titles as examples (Griffith, "Christians and the Arabic Qur'an," 244–245; Hoyland, *Seeing Islam*, 488).

131. Griffith, "Prophet Muhammad," 143.

132. Stroumsa, "Signs of Prophecy," 106–109.

133. Notably, the author of the *al-Hashimi/al-Kindi Correspondence* and 'Ammar al-Basri used qur'anic statements such as those in *al-Anʿām* 6:109 and *al-Isrā* 17:59 to reject the claim that the Qur'an was Muhammad's miracle (Griffith, "Prophet Muhammad," 142–145; Griffith, "Qur'an in Arab Christian Texts," 211).

134. Griffith, "Prophet Muhammad," 143–144.

135. This view was reflected in John of Damascus, John bar Penkaye, Sergius the Stylite, Timothy I, and Theodore bar Koni (Griffith, "Prophet Muhammad," 122, 124; Hoyland, *Seeing Islam*, 540–541).

model that God's (oral and/or written) revelation was accompanied by God's power did not apply to the Qur'an.[136]

If the Qur'an was not a divinely inspired scripture in the early Christian view, what was it then? Early Christian apologists often spoke of the Qur'an as a fragmented, flawed scripture,[137] with multiple human-corrupted origins. They highlighted its fragmentation by noting and referencing multiple Islamic scriptures.[138] Such claims of separate scriptures might point to the absence of a codification of all of the qur'anic sūras into one book in the early stages.[139] Terms such as Qur'an, *Sūrat al-Baqara* and *al-Furqān*[140] were often used to speak of different scriptures.[141] By mentioning the later collection of the Qur'an by early Muslim caliphs, such as Abu Bakr and 'Ali b. Abi-Talib, they argued for an earlier text (*Urtext* of the Qur'an).[142]

---

136. See for example Timothy's answer to al-Mahdi on this question, in Griffith, "Prophet Muhammad," 145.

137. Griffith, "Qur'an in Arab Christian Texts," 214.

138. In his dialogue with a Muslim notable, the monk of Beth Hale mentioned that Muslims were learning from the Qur'an and from *Sūrat al-Baqara*, as well as from two more sources, G-y-g-y and T-w-r-h, which may be references to *Sūrat al-'Ankabūt* and *Sūrat at-Tawba*. The last two might also be references to the Gospel (*al-Injīl*) and the Torah (*at-Tawrātal-Tawrat*). Bertaina, *Christian and Muslim Dialogues*, 143; Griffith, "Qur'an in Arab Christian Texts," 205–206; Griffith, *Syriac Writers on Muslims*, 32–34; Hoyland, "Earliest Christian Writings," 286–287; Hoyland, *Seeing Islam*, 465–471; Sidney H. Griffith, "Disputing with Islam in Syriac: The Case of the Monk of Bêt Halê and a Muslim Emir," *Hugoye: Journal of Syriac Studies* 3, no. 1 (2000 [printed 2010], Section VII, paragraphs 29–30).

139. John of Damascus, who names each sūra a scripture, also references *Sūrat al-Baqara* as a separate work. Yet for him, the entire Qur'an, which he considers to have been compiled by Muhammad, was only "worthy of laughter" (Griffith, "Qur'an in Arab Christian Texts," 206; Griffith, *Syriac Writers on Muslims*, 34).

140. The author of the *Legend of Sergius-Bahira* says that Muhammad called the text *Furqān* because it was scattered (*mufarraq*), referring to one of the text's names in the Qur'an (*al-Baqara* 2:53, 185; *Āl-'Imrān* 3:4). Bertaina, *Christian and Muslim Dialogues*, 128).

141. The *Legend of Sergius-Bahira* explains why the scripture given to Muhammad was called *Sūrat al-Baqara*, claiming that Muhammad received the Qur'an from Bahira on the horn of a cow (*Baqara*):

> I shall write a book for you and I shall teach you. On a Friday, I will put it on the horn of a cow. You go and assemble the people in one place . . . and say, today the Lord will send you from heaven a great book, laws and statutes, by which you are to be guided all your life . . . say to them, this book has come down from heaven, from God. The earth was not worthy enough to receive it, so this cow received it on its horn. From that day on the book was called, *Sūra al-Baqara* (Griffith, "Qur'an in Arab Christian Texts," 208).

142. Griffith, "Muhammad and the Monk Bahira," 22, 28; Griffith, "Qur'an in Arab Christian Texts," 212–213; Griffith, "Christians and the Arabic Qur'an," 256–258; Griffith, "Qur'an in Christian Arabic Literature," 16–17; Hoyland, *Seeing Islam*, 478; Penn, *Envisioning Islam*, 111. Abraham of Tiberias mentions multiple authors (Samir, "Prophet Muhammed," 79).

As noted, Christian apologists attributed the human origins of the Qur'an to the teachings that the monk Sergius Bahira transmitted to Muhammad and which often reflected Christian beliefs.[143] They argued that Sergius Bahira's original intention was that Muhammad would teach Christianity to his people. Hence, the monk is depicted as teaching Muhammad about Christ as the Word and Spirit of God. Muhammad, who is left wondering how his people would accept his message as a prophet without having a scripture, is reassured by the monk who promises him that he will write such a scripture for him.[144]

In other words, the notion that the Qur'an was originally a Christian religious work designed for the Arabs was common.[145] Christian apologists often quoted sections and verses from the Qur'an, claiming that their origins resided with the Christian monk and required a Christian understanding and explanation. For example, they argued that it was the monk who introduced the qur'anic *basmala* (In the name of God, the Merciful, the Compassionate). The formula was interpreted as a trinitarian statement, where "the merciful" was the Son and "the compassionate" was the Holy Spirit.[146]

However, Islam diverged from Christianity at critical points, and key theological disagreements with Christian doctrines in the Qur'an could not be ignored.[147] Christian apologists explained these differences as the product of post-Bahira and post-Muhammad changes. They claimed that the disagreements were the product of Jewish influence on the Qur'an, which put it at odds with what the monk would have taught Muhammad in the first place. The divergences were the work of the Jews Ka'b al-Ahbar and Abdallah b. Salam.[148] This Jewish influence was also the reason for the closeness between

---

143. Griffith, "Christians and the Arabic Qur'an," 255–259.

144. Sergius Bahira says, according to some sources, "I will take it upon me to write for you what you need and to tell you about any given matter that they ask you about, be it reasonable or not" (Griffith, "Christians and the Arabic Qur'an," 256; Griffith, "Qur'an in Christian Arabic Literature," 16).

145. The *Legend of Sergius-Bahira* gives many examples of what the monk had written, putting it in the first person singular: "I wrote for him . . ." (Bertaina, *Christian and Muslim Dialogues*, 127–128; Griffith, "Christians and the Arabic Qur'an," 257–259; Griffith, "Qur'an in Christian Arabic Literature," 16–18; Griffith, "Qur'an in Arab Christian Texts," 209–210).

146. Griffith, "Christians and the Arabic Qur'an," 257; Griffith, "Qur'an in Christian Arabic Literature," 16.

147. A now lost *Refutation of the Qur'an* by East-Syriac Abu Nuh al-Anbari focused on these divergences (Griffith, "Qur'an in Christian Arabic Literature," 9; Griffith, "Qur'an in Arab Christian Texts," 205, no. 1).

148. See for example the *Legend of Sergius-Bahira* in Bertaina, *Christian and Muslim Dialogues*, 128; Griffith, "Prophet Muhammad," 137–138, 143–144; Griffith, "Muhammad and the Monk Bahira," 6, 22–23; Griffith, "Christians and the Arabic Qur'an," 256; Griffith,

Islam and Judaism in certain aspects of doctrine, ritual and material reality. The Christian-Muslim (biblical-qur'anic) differences were mostly a product of a later corruption of Muhammad's teachings, rather than original to Bahira's teachings. The Qur'an, then, was also "a crypto-Christian scripture"[149] which was later corrupted. The latter was a simple reciprocal argument against Islamic views of the Bible's corruption.[150] For these Christian apologists, it was not the Bible that was corrupted by later Christians – as Muslims claimed – rather it was the Qur'an that suffered corruption at the hands of Muhammad's Jewish followers.

However, the Qur'an was still viewed as preserving certain truths[151] because it was based on the Christian teachings of the enigmatic monk. There were many statements of truth (narratives and doctrines), either related to the history of God's teaching and actions in the Old Testament, or related to the New Testament revelation of Christ's identity, teaching and actions. This approach was needed, and it proved useful since Muslims, driven by the qur'anic model found in *al-Baqara* 2:111, demanded that others advance their proofs.[152]

Christians sought and found such proofs in the Qur'an, showing the power and authority of the Qur'an in the Islamic world of the Middle East. For example, they quoted from the Qur'an and used its vocabulary to argue for the Christian doctrine of God (the Trinity) and for Christ's divinity.[153] This sort of engagement with the Qur'an continued for centuries in Christian apologetics.[154] Thus although Christians saw the Qur'an as a flawed and corrupted scripture,

---

"Qur'an in Arab Christian Texts," 208, 212; Griffith, "Qur'an in Christian Arabic Literature," 15; Penn, *Envisioning Islam*, 112.

149. Griffith, "Christians and the Arabic Qur'an," 255; Griffith, "Qur'an in Christian Arabic Literature," 14.

150. Griffith, "Prophet Muhammad," 140–141.

151. Griffith, "Qur'an in Arab Christian Texts," 214–232; Griffith, "Christian and the Arabic Qur'an," 245–252; Griffith, "Qur'an in Christian Arabic Literature," 4–14.

152. Griffith, "Christians and the Arabic Qur'an," 244; Griffith, "Qur'an in Christian Arabic Literature," 4.

153. See the apologetic treatise *On the Triune Nature of God*, as well as Theodore Abu Qurrah's debate in the court of Caliph al-Ma'mun and Abraham of Tiberias's apology, in Griffith, "Christians and the Arabic Qur'an," 246–251; Griffith, "Qur'an in Arab Christian Texts," 214–232; Griffith, "Qur'an in Christian Arabic Literature," 5–10.

154. For example, see Elias of Nisibis's (d. 1046) *Kitab al-Majalis* and the later *Letter to a Muslim Friend* of Paul of Antioch (twelfth century) in Griffith, "Christians and the Arabic Qur'an," 252; Griffith, "Qur'an in Christian Arabic Literature," 10–12.

they used it in their apologetics as a sort of non-canonical or apocryphal quasi-scripture.[155]

Islam

The Christian perspectives on Muslims, Muhammad and the Qur'an were what constructed their views of Islam as a religion. If Muhammad's teachings (the Qur'an) were the product of a Christian teacher, then Islam was a type of religion. They often referred to Islam with such terms as "faith" (Syriac *haymanuta*), "confession" (Syriac *tawdita*), "religion" (Syriac *dehlta*) and "doctrine" (Syriac *re'yana*), but they refused to recognize Islam as new, divinely instituted religion.[156] It was a limited and distorted monotheistic faith that early Arabs could grasp and follow.[157] Hence, although Christian authors conveyed convoluted and mixed perspectives on Islam, they mostly agreed in seeing Islam as a form of primitive monotheistic faith that approximated Judaism and Christianity.[158]

Furthermore, since Jews were charged with influencing and changing the Qur'an, and there were reports of early encounters and collaboration between Muslims and Jews, Islam was sometimes seen as a Jewish sect, a new form of Judaism or at least a Jewish-inspired religion. This view was reinforced by the similarities in certain doctrines and practices between Islam and Judaism. Both religions agreed on God's oneness and rejected key Christian doctrines such as the Trinity and Christ's divinity as well as certain practices like the veneration of symbols and icons. Both religions also engaged in similar religious rituals and practices such as circumcision, dietary restrictions, prayer schedules and direction of prayer (*qibla*).[159]

---

155. Griffith, "Christians and the Arabic Qur'an," 259.

156. In the debate between the monk of Beth Hale and a Muslim notable, we find one of the earliest Syriac works that referred to Islam in religious terms, expressed, however, through the mouth of the Muslim interlocutor (Penn, *Envisioning Islam*, 73–144).

157. This is the view expressed in the thirteenth-century West-Syriac *Chronicle of Bar Hebraeus* (d. 1286): "They have indeed left darkness far behind, in that they reject the worship of idols and worship the One God, but at the same time they are deprived of the perfect light, in that they still fall short of complete illumination in the light of our Christian faith and orthodox confession" (Brock, "Syriac Views," 12–13; Hoyland, *Seeing Islam*, 537).

158. Such views were found in the Armenian chronicler Sebeos in the East-Syriac *Chronicle of Khuzistan*, in John bar Penkaye, the monk of Beth Hale, and Timothy I (Hoyland, *Seeing Islam*, 535–538).

159. The *Legend of Sergius Bahira* says that it was the monk who changed the direction of prayer from the Christian eastward (rising sun) to Mecca (Griffith, "Muhammad and the Monk Bahira," 27).

These suspicions were confirmed by reports of early encounters and cooperation between the two communities since the days of Muhammad. In fact as already noted, Christian reports highlighted that the conquests were the product of an earlier encounter between Muhammad and some Jews near the Holy Land. This encounter motivated him to adopt monotheism and initiate the conquest of the Levant, seeking the promised land of milk and honey and promising his followers such rewards. Christian authors perpetuated the same image later, emphasizing Muslim-Jewish cooperation during the conquests and afterward, especially in relation to the status of Jerusalem and the activities around it, like building the mosque of 'Umar I' on the site of the Temple of Solomon. It was there, Christian reports said, that Muslims removed the cross from the Mount of Olives after the suggestion of the Jews.[160] Moreover, as noted earlier, the motives and promises of material gain that Muhammad made to his followers, including the promise of a land filled with milk and honey, highlighted another Christian view of Islam as a materialistic ideology.[161]

Certain authors argued that Islam was a faith spread by the sword that only attracted followers by offering them pleasure and wealth.[162] Other Christians emphasized how the Islamic conquests were driven by material enticement, while similar arguments explained later conversions to Islam. Christian martyrological accounts[163] also highlighted that apostates to Islam were lured by materialistic means. Such sources emphasized the difference between Christianity and Islam by emphasizing the faithfulness of Christian martyrs who focused on the spiritual blessings of life and beyond.[164]

Thus in Christian views, Islam was not truly a divine religion. It was nothing more than a worldly religion whose followers only cared to live and enjoy worldly pleasures while hoping for further material rewards in the afterlife. Islam's main motives and manifestations were materialistic. It was concerned with earthly gains and pleasures; its practices focused on material aspects; and even its **eschatology** reflected a materialistic theology. Simply, heaven was an idealized version of earth with limitless access to physical and material pleasures. Surprisingly in some Christian apologies, it was the monk

---

160. Brock, "Syriac Views," 11–12; Hoyland, *Seeing Islam*, 538–541.

161. Hoyland, *Seeing Islam*, 541–544.

162. Griffith, "Prophet Muhammad," 134.

163. Other genres that made the same argument were either apologies (e.g. John of Damascus, Theodore Abu Qurra, and Abu Ra'ita) or chronicles (e.g. the *Chronicle of Zuqnin* and the *Chronicle of Dionysius*) (Hoyland, *Seeing Islam*, 409–414, 454–458, 485–489, 542–544; Hoyland, "Earliest Christian Writings," 280–281, 288).

164. *The Passion of Vahan* reflects this view (Hoyland, *Seeing Islam*, 541–542).

Sergius Bahira who created the materialistic views of eternal life, attempting to attract the Arabs' sensuality.[165]

This Christian attitude that viewed Islam as nothing more than a new Jewish heresy or sect shaped their terminology of the religion. Notably, while terms like Christianity, Judaism and Zoroastrianism were used among Christian authors, the abstract term "Islam" or "Muslimness" (Syriac *mashlmanuta*) did not appear in Christian texts until the late eighth century and was used again only in the twelfth century.[166] This observation reflects a Christian understanding that did not view the beliefs and practices of the new masters as a new religion that merited its own naming until the later period. Many continued to adopt this attitude even decades after living and interacting with Muslims within the Islamic milieu.

Conclusion

In conclusion, a few statements can be made to summarize early Christians' collective views of the new phenomenon of their age. First, Arab Muslims were not God's favored and privileged people bearing divine promises and blessings to conquer the world; but rather they were God's instrument to discipline and bring his beloved sinful Christian people, the heirs of the Abrahamic covenant, back to his fold. Muslims were the descendants of Ishmael, the child of a slave maiden of Abraham, whose limited intellectual ability and sensuality confined Muslim religiosity to an elementary form of monotheism and divine truth. Second, Muhammad was not God's new and final prophet, bearing divinely sanctioned teaching and scripture, but a monotheistic religio-political leader and teacher who was taught by a Christian "heretical" monk, influenced by Jews, and used by God to fulfill his plans to convert polytheist Arabs and discipline sinful Christians. Third, the Qur'an was not God's final and inspired revelation and scripture but a fragmented and flawed collection of Judeo-Christian teachings based on some biblical truth, but largely accommodating to Muhammad's audience of limited intellectual abilities and instinctive desires. It was not revealed from heaven but was written and delivered by a Christian monk and corrupted by later Jewish followers of

---

165. Penn, *Envisioning Islam*, 111.

166. The earliest use of the term appeared in the *Chronicle of Zuqnin* and in Theodore Bar Koni's *Scholion*. In these examples, the term mainly meant "tradition." By the twelfth century, Dionysius bar Salibi was clearly speaking about Islam in the abstract. Hence, Christians often spoke about Muslims (the people) rather than Islam (the religion). Griffith, "Disputes with Muslims," 270; Penn, *Envisioning Islam*, 56–57.

Muhammad. Fourth, Islam was not a new, divinely inspired and supreme religion that spread by God's will and was sought by people for its truthfulness. Rather, it was an elementary, humanly distorted, monotheistic religion with materialistic interests, practices and manifestations that accommodated its audience's limitations and wishes.

Many of these perceptions have lasted through centuries among Christians, while Western scholars have just recently taken note of them and started using them to challenge and revise the Islamic narratives and depictions of early Islam.[167] Yet in order to carefully understand and utilize the early Christian views, a few notes are needed in conclusion. First, it is evident that early Christian perspectives of Islam (i.e. Muslims, Muhammad, and the Qur'an) during the seventh to ninth centuries were diverse and far from monistic. Second, these views demonstrated how the historical/chronological changes in the religious and political context shaped and reshaped Christian readings and presentations of the events and people, casting themselves and others in different lights. Third, it is evident that early Christians were shaped in their understanding and presentations of Islam by theological convictions and biblical motifs which defined their narratives and depictions. Fourth, the Christian views show how Christian writers were concerned with themselves in their works, seeking to understand their context, to defend their faith, and to define their place in the new Islamic world.

5.2 What We Don't Know about Islamic Origins

Daniel Brown

In the last 150 years, beginning in earnest with Ignaz Goldziher, scholarly confidence in the traditional accounts of Islamic origins has been severely shaken. Yet Christians who think, write, or teach about Islam often still rely on these traditional accounts. Does it matter? That is, does it matter to the real world of day-to-day Christian-Muslim interaction? It is not immediately obvious that it does. I may find obscure debates about early Islamic history immensely absorbing, but it is hard to make the case that other Christians must share my eccentricity. What difference will it make, really, whether I accept traditional sources that place the rise of Islam in seventh-century Arabia, or whether, at the other extreme, I am convinced that traditional sources are back projections, and that the real origins of Islam should be looked for in

---

167. Penn, *Envisioning Islam*, 4–6, 8–10; Penn, *When Christians First Met Muslims*, 1–6.

Syria or Iraq a century or more later? Many ordinary, thoughtful Christians who interact on any regular basis with ordinary, thoughtful Muslim friends or colleagues will find that obscure discussions of the Hadith, the **Sira**, or John Wansbrough's approach to the Qur'an[168] are unlikely topics for fruitful conversation. What I think about these things is unlikely to interest most of my Muslim friends, and even less likely to change their minds. We might allow an exception for those who feel called to Jay-Smith-style polemical ministry.[169] For committed polemicists, our topic may indeed have obvious relevance. But many of us lack either the inclination or the conviction for such polemics.

There are more foundational, theological reasons for dismissing revisionist arguments as irrelevant, or at least peripheral, to how Christians think about Islam. A Christian's orientation to Islam should be shaped primarily by good theology, and a sound biblical theology should be able to account for whatever historical data it finds without needing to be modified when faced with the vagaries of history or the fashions of historians. Consequently, revisionist arguments about early Islam will not be of any special importance in establishing the foundations of our approach to Islam, which should already be set on more solid footings. Whether the Qur'an originated in seventh-century Arabia or was canonized a century or more later will have no fundamental impact on the foundations of Christian belief. The data about Islam that will be relevant to a Christian theological response to Islam is clear, uncontroversial and largely theological itself: Islam is a monotheistic system, claims revealed authority, and further claims to be in continuity with biblical revelation. But Muslim belief does not center on and does not even acknowledge the good news of God revealed in Christ. At a basic level, this is all we need to know. How one responds to this basic data will be a product of one's theological orientation, not vice versa. Historical scholarship doesn't make anyone a syncretist or a polemicist; bad theology does.

---

168. John Wansbrough, *Qur'anic Studies: Sources and Methods of Scriptural Interpretation* (Oxford: Oxford University Press, 1977) and *The Sectarian Milieu* (Oxford: Oxford University Press, 1978). Gerald R. Hawting, "John Wansbrough, Islam, and Monotheism," *Method & Theory in the Study of Religion* 9, no. 1 (1997): 23–38; Charles J. Adams, "Reflections on the Work of John Wansbrough," *Method & Theory in the Study of Religion* 9, no. 1 (1997): 75–90.

169. Jay Smith, "The Case for Polemics," in *Between Naivety and Hostility: Uncovering the Best Christian Responses to Islam in Britain*, eds. Steve Bell and Colin Chapman (Milton Keynes: Authentic, 2011), 241–247. Deann Alford, "Unapologetic Apologist: Jay Smith Confronts Muslim Fundamentalists with Fervor," *Christianity Today* (13 June 2008).

What We Do and Don't Know

If critical scholarship about Islamic origins is unlikely to help us communicate with Muslim friends, and if a Christian theology of Islam must be based on other foundations, do such questions have any importance for Christians as we think about Islam? I think they do, but in a way that may come as a surprise. To see why, we will begin with a quick tour of our sources for early Islamic history. As we survey these, I will ask a familiar sounding question in an unfamiliar way. Rather than cataloguing what we *know* about the origins of Islam, the usual approach, I will focus instead on documenting what we *don't* know, what the sources *do not* tell us, and what we *cannot* say with any confidence about the origins of Islam. It turns out to be quite a lot.

We begin with sources prior to 72 AH/AD 691 when the caliphate of 'Abd al-Malik b. Marwān begins to usher in major changes. These seventh-century sources fall into two rough categories, those independent of the Muslim literary tradition and those embedded in it.

Sources Independent of the Muslim Literary Tradition

Archaeology

Archaeological remains in the Arabian Peninsula include tombs, rock drawings, weapons, coins, dwellings, and other buildings. The most numerous and significant are concentrated in the south; the most important finds in the north are connected with Nabatean civilization. No archaeological work has been done in Mecca, Medina, or the **Hijaz** more generally. Consequently, archaeology contributes only indirectly to our understanding of the rise of Islam by providing limited data on the material culture of the Arabian Peninsula before Islam, and by occasionally confirming and occasionally bringing into question data gleaned from literary sources. Archaeological evidence outside of the Peninsula from the period of the conquests and after is also contested and limited in what it can tell us. For example, much has been made of possible evidence that the earliest Muslims prayed toward Jerusalem during the period of the conquests, but this evidence is mixed at best. The most we can say for sure is that direction of prayer seems to have been important, as it also was for Jews and Christians. The evidence does suggest, however, that the Islamic conquests were less disruptive to the economic, material, or religious life of the major populations of the Near East than traditional narratives might lead us to think.[170]

Epigraphy

We have abundant rock inscriptions and graffiti spanning pre-Islamic and early Islamic periods. Many such inscriptions are undatable. Those that can be dated give us our firmest evidence of the worldview of the earliest proto-Muslims.[171] By the 660s, inscriptions document a movement with a new calendar that begins in 622 that is led by a "commander of the believers" whose followers primarily speak Arabic and who use language and ritual invocations consistent with the phraseology of the Qur'an. Those followers worship the one God, the "Lord of the worlds," who has no partners and is compassionate and merciful.[172] Such inscriptions are sparse, and they are silent about many of the distinguishing features of Islam. They lack, for example, any mention of Muhammad. What we should conclude from this apparent silence is a matter of contention.

Non-Muslim Literary Sources

Non-Muslim accounts of early Islam have been discussed in depth in the previous contribution. As with epigraphic evidence, they confirm in a general way the emergence by the 640s of a new and significant Arab religious movement while leaving us mostly in the dark about its specific character.

To take stock at this point, here's what we cannot know with any certainty from these sources: We cannot know where or how Muslim religious ideas emerged. We have no certain knowledge of the identity, teaching, or motivations of the movement's founder(s). We don't know the specific content of religious belief or practice, or the relation of the movement to Christianity or Judaism (or to heterodox outgrowths of these). And we do not know at what point the community possessed a fixed, canonical scripture.

---

170. For an excellent, succinct overview and evaluation of the sources, see Ilkka Lindstedt, "Pre-Islamic Arabia and Early Islam," in *Routledge Handbook on Early Islam*, ed. Herbert Berg (Abingdon: Routledge, 2018), 159–161.

171. Robert Hoyland, *Seeing Islam as Others Saw It: A Survey and Evaluation of Christian, Jewish and Zoroastrian Writings on Early Islam* (Princeton: Darwin, 1997), Excursus F; Robert Hoyland, "New Documentary Texts and the Early Islamic State," *Bulletin of the School of Oriental and African Studies* 69 (2006): 396.

172. Hoyland, "New Documentary Texts," 396.

Early Sources Embedded within the Muslim Literary Tradition

The Constitution of Medina

There has been unusually wide agreement on the authenticity of a famous text, preserved within the Muslim literary tradition, which gives the terms of a pact between Muhammad and the Jewish tribes of Medina. The document suggests a close alliance between Jews and proto-Muslims and describes them as belonging to a single *umma*, while still retaining their own religion (*dīn*) and tribal organization and identity. It establishes Muhammad as the arbiter of this confederation. The *umma* is described as composed of the righteous and the God-fearing; beyond these generalities, the document tells us little about the content of religious belief or practice.

The Qur'an

A preponderance of evidence, especially radiocarbon dating of manuscript leaves, now suggests that consonantal texts of the Qur'an were circulating by the 650s. While this dating is consistent with traditional accounts of ʿUthmān's promulgation of a standard text, debates over the accuracy of radiocarbon dating continue, and debate over when the qur'anic text was fixed in its canonical form continues. Even if we accept the ʿUthmānic recension, we still know little about the formation of the text prior to the 650s, and we cannot entirely exclude the possibility of later interpolations.[173] These caveats aside, the Qur'an is undoubtedly our earliest substantial source for the content of Muslim belief and practice. It depicts a monotheist community that closely identifies with the prophets, history, scriptures and traditions of Judaism and Christianity, that is nevertheless in tension with at least some contemporary Jews and Christians (engaging for example in christological controversy), that evidences devotion through a variety of pious and ascetic rituals and activities, that lives in fear of God, and that expects imminent divine judgment. What the Qur'an does not tell us is equally significant: It offers us no significant data about Muhammad, offers only the vaguest hints about its geographical milieu, reveals little about the identities of its opponents or interlocutors, and leaves us guessing about the specific context of any particular passage and often about the origin or meaning of its vocabulary.

---

173. Fred Donner, "Early Muslims and Peoples of the Book," in *Routledge Handbook on Early Islam*, ed. Herbert Berg (New York; Abingdon: Routledge, 2018), 189. Donner suggests that strident anti-Trinitarian passages fit nicely with ʿAbd al-Malik's program.

Adding these literary sources, we now know a lot more. We can now assign a name to, and outline the general religious outlook of, the founder of Islam, and we can begin to get a rough and somewhat confused picture of relations with Christians and Jews. But huge gaps in our knowledge remain. It is still impossible to write a biography of Muhammad. We have no knowledge of even the bare outlines of his life. We do not know what influenced him, nor do we understand how the Qur'an came to be in its present form. We are unable to confidently establish the context of any particular qur'anic verse or passage, neither do we know with any certainty whether the qur'anic text had any pre-history before Islam or when and how it reached its final canonical form. We are left with a great many questions about the relationship of proto-Muslims to Christians or Jews, and our knowledge of the earliest Muslim beliefs and practices remains hazy at best. Based on these sources alone, the scope of what we don't know remains expansive.

Hadith and Sira

Move forward a century, roughly to the mid-700s, and this significant gap in our knowledge has been almost completely filled. From the late **Umayyad** period onward, in a trend that rapidly accelerates under the **Abbasids**, we are inundated with detailed literary sources describing Muhammad's life, the context of the Hijaz, pre-Islamic Arab tribal norms and religious life, Arab history and genealogy, pre-Islamic poetry, and specific contextual and linguistic background to the Qur'an. This data comes to us in many different literary genres; the two most relevant for our present purposes are biographies of Muhammad and collections of Hadith.

Sira Literature

Biographical literature on Muhammad is voluminous and detailed. Our earliest full **Sira** comes from Ibn Isḥāq (d. 767) in a version extensively redacted several decades later by Ibn Hishām (d. 808). Ibn Isḥāq establishes the basic chronology of Muhammad's life, and biographers after him all adopt the same basic chronological structure, though their knowledge of particular events sometimes significantly varies and often increases in detail. The Sira literature, supplemented by other literary products of the **Abbasid** era, fills in almost every possible gap in our knowledge of the origins of Islam. In the end there is very little left that we don't know.

But where did this detailed knowledge come from, and how was it transmitted during the century separating Ibn Isḥāq from Muhammad?

Hadith

The answer to this question of how Ibn Isḥāq and other early biographers and historians knew what they knew about Islamic origins is tied up with a second major literary genre, the Hadith literature.[174] According to its technical definition, the term "Hadith" refers to a report about something the Prophet Muhammad said or did, or about something that happened in his presence to which he silently consented. This technical definition betrays the major function of Hadith reports as a basis for normative behavior, *sunna*, and hence as a basis for Islamic law. Each Hadith report is composed of two parts, the *isnād*, which is an ordered list of transmitters of the Hadith, ideally ending with a Companion of the Prophet who serves as the primary witness, and the *matn*, the text of the Hadith report itself. Beginning around the same era as Ibn Isḥāq, Hadith specialists began systematically sifting, organizing and collecting Hadith reports. This activity culminated in the ninth century with the famous canonical collections of Hadith, most notably those of **Bukhārī** and Muslim. These collections preserved, sifted and organized thousands of discrete reports about Muhammad, each accompanied by a carefully scrutinized record of transmission back to the time of the Prophet.

The *isnād-matn* system for transmitting and documenting historical information was not limited to the technical activity of Hadith collection. Ibn Isḥāq was not a Hadith specialist, but he made use of the same system. Indeed, Hadith became the basic building block for all historical writing and thus the primary link to the past. When Ibn Isḥāq recorded information about Muhammad, he knew what he knew because it had been passed on to him by means of this system, providing an unbroken chain back to the time of the Prophet. While we are free to question this or that report, and Hadith specialists did, for example, severely criticize Ibn Isḥāq for insufficient rigor, the system as a whole inspired widespread confidence. Every major biography of Muhammad and almost everything we want to know or think we know about Islamic origins depends on this system. It is at this point in the story that critical scholarship becomes important.

---

174. For general introductions to the Hadith literature, see Jonathan Brown, *Hadith: Muhammad's Legacy in the Medieval and Modern World* (Oxford: Oneworld, 2009); and Daniel Brown, ed., *The Wiley Blackwell Concise Companion to the Hadith* (Chichester: Wiley, 2020).

Goldziher and Western Hadith Scholarship

Since the nineteenth century, historical scholarship has demolished our confidence in the reliability of Hadith as a source for the emergence of Islam.[175] The story is long and convoluted, beginning with the work of Aloys Sprenger and William Muir in India. Sprenger, an Austrian scholar, called attention to Hadith forgery on a large scale, arguing that forgery was endemic from the **Companions** of the Prophet onwards. In his seminal *Muslim Studies*, Goldziher extended Sprenger's conclusions to argue that, "The ḥadīth will not serve as a document for the history of the infancy of Islam, but rather as a reflection of the tendencies which appeared in the community during the more mature stages of its development."[176] And because "by far the greater part" of the Hadith is "the result of the religious, historical and social development of Islam during the first two centuries,"[177] a Hadith report is a primary source of documentation for the outlook of those who first attributed that report to the Prophet and circulated the tradition. "Every stream and counter-stream of thought in Islam," Goldziher argues, "has found its expression in the form of a ḥadīth, and there is no difference in this respect between the various contrasting opinions in whatever field."[178] No political or doctrinal controversy was left without numerous supporting Hadith reports, "all equipped with imposing *isnāds*."[179] Goldziher found the Hadith literature to be filled with anachronistic reports supporting particular dynasties or rulers, taking a position on theological controversies, praising particular localities or tribes, prophesying later conquests and rebellions, and supporting or contesting the legitimacy of Ali's descendants. He argues that such features of the Hadith literature cast doubt on the entire corpus. Forgery became so engrained in the system that Hadith reports were fabricated to combat forgery.[180] It was not long before other scholars began to amplify and extend Goldziher's skepticism.[181]

---

175. For a fuller account of Western Hadith scholarship, see Daniel Brown, "Western Hadith Studies," in *The Wiley Blackwell Concise Companion to the Hadith*, ed. Daniel Brown (Chichester: Wiley, 2020), 39–56.

176. Ignaz Goldziher, *Muslim Studies*, trans. C. M. Barber and S. M. Stern, 2nd ed. (London: Allen & Unwin, 1971), 2:19.

177. Goldziher, *Muslim Studies*, 2:19.

178. Goldziher, 2:126.

179. Goldziher, 2:44.

180. Goldziher, 2:127.

181. Whereas Goldziher's analysis was largely restricted to legal and theological Hadith, Lammens and Caetani extended his conclusions to the genres of Qur'an commentary, Sira literature and historical reports generally. Lammens argues, for example, that the biography of Muhammad was in large part the product of qur'anic exegesis. See Henri Lammens, "Qoran

Apart from a few noteworthy holdouts,[182] Goldziher's broad premise won the day: The vast bulk of the Hadith literature will be of little help as a source for seventh-century Arabia or the career of the Prophet. Rather, it will provide evidence about the beliefs of the Muslim community and the development of Islamic law and piety in the following centuries.

Fifty years later, Joseph Schacht's *The Origins of Muhammadan Jurisprudence* built on Goldziher but also launched Western Hadith studies in new directions. Schacht's conclusions are sweeping: "Every legal tradition from the Prophet, until the contrary is proved, must be taken ... as the fictitious expression of a legal doctrine formulated at a later date."[183] Where Schacht departed from Goldziher was in reclaiming the *isnād* as a source of usable data that might preserve clues to a tradition's provenance. He argues that *isnāds* tend to grow backwards in such a way that "traditions from Successors become traditions from Companions, and traditions from Companions become traditions from the Prophet."[184] This turns classical *isnād* criticism on its head: for Schacht, the earlier a tradition, the less likely it will be to have a complete *isnād*, and "the most perfect and complete *isnāds* are the latest."[185] Schacht argues that this process of backward projection left behind clues to the true originator of the Hadith.[186] Thus Schacht repurposed *isnād* criticism, no longer as a means of authenticating prophetic Hadith but as a tool for dating when

---

et tradition: comment fut composé la vie de Mahomet," *Recherches des Sciences Religieuses* 1 (1910): 27–51; Leone Caetani, *Annali dell'Islam* (Milan: Ulrico Hoepli, 1905–1907); and Gregor Schoeler, *The Biography of Muhammad: Nature and Authenticity*, ed. J. E. Montgomery, trans. U. Vagelpohl (New York: Routledge, 2011), 3.

182. Naturally, direct attempts to refute Goldziher have also been plentiful. One line of argument is especially associated with the Turkish scholar Fuat Sezgin and relies on a defense of the *isnād*. See Fuat Sezgin, *Geschichte des arabischen Schrifttums, Band I: Qur'ānwissenschaften, Hadith, Geschichte, Fiqh, Dogmatik, Mystik bis ca. 430 H* (Leiden: Brill, 1967), 53–233. Azami, Siddiqui and Abbott also argue that Hadith reports were scrupulously transmitted in writing from the generation of the Companions onwards. See Muhammad Zubayr Siddiqui, *Hadith Literature: Its Origin, Development and Special Features*, ed. Abdal Hakim Murad (Cambridge: Islamic Texts Society, 1993); Muhammad Mustafa Azmi, *Studies in Early Ḥadīth Literature*, 2nd ed. (Indianapolis: American Trust Publications, 1978; 1st ed. Beirut: Al-Maktab al-Islami, 1968); Muhammad Mustafa Azmi, *On Schacht's Origins of Jurisprudence* (Riyadh: King Saud University, 1985); Muhammad Mustafa Azmi, *Studies in Hadith Methodology and Literature* (Indianapolis: American Trust Publications, 1992); Nabia Abbott, *Studies in Arabic Literary Papyri II: Qur'ānic Commentary and Tradition* (Chicago: University of Chicago Press, 1967).

183. Joseph Schacht, *The Origins of Muhammadan Jurisprudence* (Oxford: Clarendon, 1950), 149.

184. Schacht, *Origins*, 156.

185. Schacht, 165.

186. Schacht, 163.

a tradition began to circulate, meaning, for him, when it was forged. These methods of dating then gave Schacht the tools to reconstruct the emergence and evolution of the Hadith literature in the context of the development of Islamic law.

Schacht's legacy has been taken in two directions. One trajectory underscores Schacht's negative conclusions, while at the same time dismantling his positive program for dating Hadith. Cook for example argues that Schacht's *isnād* analysis fails, and he thus brings into doubt any scheme which relies on the *isnād* to date Hadith. If we follow Cook, the vast bulk of the Hadith literature will tell us almost nothing about the first two Islamic centuries, and we will abandon any hope that *isnāds* can help us to fill this void. We see the most dramatic application of this extreme skepticism in the works of Patricia Crone.

But not all serious scholars of Hadith have embraced such radical skepticism. Efforts to establish that at least some Hadith reports can be confidently traced at least back to the late first century AH, sixty or seventy years after Muhammad's death, have been especially associated with the work of Harald Motzki, Gregor Schoeler and Andreas Görke. Motzki's approach would seem to significantly increase confidence that *isnāds* were in play by the end of the first Islamic century and that some Hadith reports can plausibly be traced to transmitter-compilers of the late first and early second century AH. This clearly undercuts Schacht, who discounted all ascriptions to first-century authorities. But although Motzki's source reconstruction takes us back to the late first/early eighth century, we are still left with a significant gap in knowledge. Another method promoted by Motzki, Schoeler and Görke claims to establish that traditions about certain key events in the life of Muhammad can be traced to within sixty or seventy years of Muhammad's later life.[187] Proponents of

---

187. Events studied in this way include the beginning of revelation to Muhammad, the scandal involving ʿĀʾisha, the murder of the Jewish satirical poet Ibn Abī l-Ḥuqayq, the treaty at al-Ḥudaybiya, traditions concerning the Hijra, and accounts of the battles of Badr, Uḥud, the Trench and the conquest of Mecca. See Schoeler, *Biography*; Harald Motzki, "The Murder of Ibn Abī l-Ḥuqayq: On the Origin and Reliability of some Maghazi-Reports," in *The Biography of Muhammad: The Issue of the Sources*, ed. Harald Motzki (Leiden: Brill, 2000), 170–239; Andreas Görke, "The Historical Tradition About al-Ḥudaybiya. A Study of ʿUrwa ibn al-Zubayr's Account," in Motzki, *Biography*, 240–275; Andreas Görke and Gregor Schoeler, "Reconstructing the Earliest *sīra* Texts: The Hiǧra in the Corpus of ʿUrwa ibn al-Zubayr," *Der Islam* 82 (2005): 209–220; and Andreas Görke and Gregor Schoeler, *Die Ältesten Berichte über Muhammads: Das Korpus ʿUrwa ibn az-Zubair* (Princeton: Darwin Press, 2008).

the method are convinced that the gap is sufficiently small that these earliest layers of tradition are "likely to reflect traces of the historical Muhammad."[188]

How much historical data do these methods leave us after later embellishments and accretions are stripped? Not much. The best that optimistic scholars can offer is a "proto-Sira" or "mini-history" that will fall far short of a full biography. Christopher Melchert concludes that the historical kernel recovered is "so small as to be virtually worthless."[189] Thus Goldziher's conclusion that Hadith cannot serve as a source for the origins of Islam has been widely accepted, and indeed strengthened and broadened. This is clearest for revisionists like Cook or Crone, but even more optimistic scholars have accepted Goldziher's basic premise: the Hadith literature can tell us about later development in Islam, but little to nothing about Muhammad.

What Options Do We Have?

Pre-Critical Traditionalist Approaches

What options does this leave us? First, we could simply ignore historical-critical scholarship altogether, continuing to approach the traditional story of the origins of Islam pre-critically. This may be the most common response among Christians. To be fair, this is also the path chosen by many biographers of Muhammad.[190] It is easy to empathize. It is frustrating to write a biography with no story to tell.[191] Thus many textbooks and popular books on Islam ignore or marginalize critical scholarship entirely. And to be fair, the relative inaccessibility of serious scholarship poses a formidable challenge; even those who read widely in Islamic studies may have difficulty understanding the intricacies of recent Hadith scholarship.

Two additional factors may incline Christians toward a pre-critical approach. The first is pragmatic. If I actually want to interact with Muslim friends, revisionist scholarship is unlikely to help my relationship building efforts. Is it not more charitable to engage, as much as possible, with what

---

188. Andreas Görke, Harald Motzki, and Gregor Schoeler, "First Century Sources for the Life of Muhammad? A Debate," *Der Islam* 89 (2012): 3.

189. Christopher Melchert, "The Early History of Islamic Law," in *Method and Theory in the Study of Islamic Origins*, ed. Herbert Berg (Leiden: Brill, 2003), 303.

190. Montgomery Watt, *Muhammad at Mecca* (Oxford: Clarendon, 1953); Watt, *Muhammad at Medina* (Oxford: Clarendon, 1956); Maxime Rodinson, *Mahomet*, 2nd ed. (Paris: Éditions du Seuils, 1968); Tilman Nagel, *Allahs Liebling: Ursprung und Erscheinungsformen des Mohammedglaubens* (Munich: Oldenbourg, 2008).

191. Michael Cook, *Muhammad* (Oxford: Oxford University Press, 1983).

my friend actually thinks about the origins of Islam rather than summarily dismissing it as myth? Second, having ourselves experienced the destructive impact of critical biblical scholarship, Christians may be prone to empathize with Muslims and to reverse the hermeneutic of suspicion, becoming more suspicious of the skeptics than of the sources. Any believer who has had to endure a hostile New Testament professor at a typical university religion department will understand this impulse.

Phenomenology

A more sophisticated excuse for ignoring historical-critical scholarship is to substitute **phenomenology** for historical method. Phenomenology of religion is not quite so complex as its purveyors sometimes make it seem, and I will use the term fairly loosely here. "The believer is always right" is sometimes used as a handy summary, although it might be more palatable to reframe the maxim as a tautology, "The believer is always right about what the believer believes." The point is that from the perspective of phenomenology, what matters for understanding religion is the experience, beliefs and practices of adherents and believing communities. These are endlessly varied and changeable so that "all religions are new every morning."[192] Consequently phenomenological approaches to religion tend to be ahistorical; the past is not determinative of how religion actually functions in human lives and communities. Religions just don't work that way. In fact, just the opposite; dominant religious paradigms tend to be projected back onto origins narratives so that the Jesus or the Muhammad "of history" is manifestly a product of the beliefs, prejudices and limitations of the particular historian. We have no trouble spotting this tendency in historical Jesus scholarship; modern views of Muhammad, Muslim or non-Muslim, are shaped in the same way.

Phenomenological approaches to religion overlap with and feed off anthropology. We see the intersection of the fields especially in the work, for example, of Clifford Geertz.[193] The two fields draw on the same data set, that is, human religious behaviors, structures and belief systems as they are actually lived. This overlap becomes important to understanding the impact of phenomenological thinking on missiology, which is a close sibling of anthropology.

---

192. Wilfred Cantwell Smith, "Comparative Religion: Whither and Why?" in *The History of Religions: Essays in Methodology* 34, ed. Mircea Eliade and Joseph M. Kitagawa (Chicago: University of Chicago Press, 1959).

193. Clifford Geertz, *Islam Observed: Religious Development in Morocco and Indonesia* (Chicago: University of Chicago Press, 1971).

Phenomenology of religion and anthropology also share a common tendency to reject value judgments in ways that put them in tension with missiology. Phenomenologists of religion tend to reject value judgments in two ways. First, the phenomenologist makes no value distinction among sources of data, "whether highly learned . . . or simple illiterate villagers."[194] This is because, "The study of a religion is the study of persons. . . . For religions do not exist up in the sky somewhere, elaborated, finished and static; they exist in men's hearts."[195] Thus one of Annemarie Schimmel's themes was the seamless continuity between the most ordinary and everyday religious phenomena and the loftiest religious thought. The world is saturated with the signs of God, and therefore saturated with *baraka*. Sacred objects, sacred words, and holy men and women are all signs marking the path to the one Divine Reality. Second, phenomenology brackets off theological and metaphysical truth claims. It is important what a Buddhist thinks about or experiences of Nirvana; it is irrelevant to our study of the religion whether what he or she believes depicts a transcendent reality. The object is to understand the religious experience itself, not the validity of that experience or the believer's truth claims.

These tendencies become important to understanding the impact of phenomenological thinking on missiology, and also the tensions between secular phenomenology and missiology. Among Christians, the tendency to focus on understanding Islam via actual Muslim practice goes back at least to Samuel Zwemer.[196] However, the current trend can be more usefully traced to the 1970s when many evangelical missiologists and missions programs began to de-emphasize the importance of a text-based understanding of Islam, focusing instead on "folk Islam" or "popular Islam" as key to both understanding and reaching Muslims.[197] Since that time, courses on folk Islam have become com-

---

194. Annemarie Schimmel, *Deciphering the Signs of God: A Phenomenological Approach to Islam* (Albany: State University of New York, 1994), vii.

195. Smith, "Comparative Religion," 34.

196. Samuel Zwemer, *The Influence of Animism on Islam: An Account of Popular Superstitions* (New York: Macmillan, 1920); Samuel Zwemer, *Studies in Popular Islam: A Collection of Papers Dealing with the Superstitions and Beliefs of the Common People* (London: Sheldon; New York: Macmillan, 1939).

197. For useful background on the emergence of this trend, see Colin Chapman, "Going Soft on Islam?," *Vox Evangelica* 19 (1989): 7–32; influential articles include Arthur F. Glasser, "Power Encounter in Conversion from Islam," in *The Gospel and Islam*, ed. Don McCurry (Monrovia: MARC, 1979): 129ff.; Bill Musk, "Popular Islam: The Hunger of the Heart," in *Gospel and Islam*, 208–224; Paul Hiebert, "Power Encounter and the Challenge of Folk Islam," paper submitted to the meeting of the Lausanne Committee for World Evangelization, Zeist, Netherlands, 27 June–4 July 1978.

mon in seminaries,[198] and books about Christian ministry to folk Muslims have proliferated.[199] A further impetus for this trend has been the increasing influence of charismatic ideas on mission thinking. Charismatic convictions about the reality of the unseen spirit world, and charismatic practices for confronting it, would seem to predispose their holders to take popular Muslim practices and beliefs seriously rather than dismissing them as mere superstition. Thus the notion of a "power encounter" is frequently paired with an emphasis on folk Islam.[200] Animistic and charismatic Christian views of spiritual reality are close enough to be mutually recognizable.

Such missiological trends draw on and are closely connected to academic phenomenology of religion, but they also part ways on key points. We can mention three: (1) we see a persistent tendency in missiological thinking to sharply distinguish between formal and folk Islam, a division which is rejected by most phenomenologists of religion; (2) missiology cannot completely bracket off metaphysical truth claims, or it will no longer be missiology; and (3) missiologists and mission practitioners often lack the empathy encouraged by phenomenologists, perhaps with good theological reason; the missiologist can hardly be expected to withhold judgment on the ultimate validity of religious experiences. Nevertheless, the connections and resemblances are also clear. It is easy to see why phenomenology of religion might find a hearing among both mission thinkers and practitioners. It seems like common sense to focus on understanding the actual beliefs and practices of the people with whom we seek to communicate rather than on an idealized and imagined belief system.

But a phenomenological approach to Islam is also vulnerable to serious critique, especially if we use it to escape the challenge of history. I can illustrate this weakness from hard experience. Many years ago in a job talk presentation, I suggested that phenomenology might provide a way around

---

198. Mark A. Hausfeld, "Folk Islam and Power Encounter," AGTS Evangel University, Summer 2018, http://agts.edu/wp-content/uploads/2018/05/Folk-Islam-AGTS-Syllabus-05.24.18.pdf; Warren Larson, "The Spirit World of Islam," Columbia International University, n.d., http://www.ciu.edu/sites/default/files/academics/S14%20-%20ICS%206013%20-%20Larson.pdf.

199. Bill Musk, *Touching the Soul of Islam: Sharing the Gospel with Muslim Cultures* (Crowborough: MARC, 1995); Bill Musk, *The Unseen Face of Islam* (E. Sussex: MARC, 2009); Rick Love, *Muslims, Magic and the Kingdom of God: Church Planting Among Folk Muslims* (Pasadena: William Carey Library, 2000); Philip L. Parshall, *Bridges to Islam: A Christian Perspective on Folk Islam* (Grand Rapids: Baker, 1983).

200. Vivienne Stacey, *Christ Supreme over Satan: Spiritual Warfare, Folk Religion and the Occult* (Lahore: Masihi Isha'at Khana, 1986).

the problems posed by revisionist views of early Islam. In response an argumentative faculty member asked, "But isn't Islam an historical religion? Doesn't the whole structure of Islam therefore rely on historical claims?" He proceeded to shred my argument, and he was right to do so. We can learn a great deal from phenomenology, but it will offer no escape from questions of history. Evangelicals might easily appreciate this by placing the shoe on the other foot. Were a Muslim to adopt a purely phenomenological approach to Christianity, arguing that historical questions about the life of Jesus, the crucifixion, the resurrection or the early church don't really matter to understanding Christianity, would we think he had grasped what is most important to our faith? Phenomenology may be an expedient foundation for missiological practice, but narrowly applied, it risks condescension.

Historical Agnosticism
Having worked hard to evade the challenge of critical historiography by retreating first to pre-critical approaches then to phenomenology, what might happen if we embrace historiography instead? The doubts I catalogued about how much our sources can tell us about the earliest history of Islam, the life of Muhammad and the context of the Qur'an are substantial. They are unlikely to dissipate any time soon. Will these doubts lead me inexorably (in spirit at least) to my soap box at Speakers' Corner[201] to hammer away at the historical foundations of Islam and the naïve confidence of my Muslim friends?

I don't think so. As a thought experiment, suppose I really do take revisionist ideas about Islamic origins seriously. I neither feel that historical questions can simply be ignored, nor am I comfortable just bracketing off historical questions for the sake of pragmatism. On the other hand, suppose that I am an equal opportunity skeptic. That is, I am equally shy of accepting the novel and sometimes far-fetched models that revisionists substitute for the traditional account. I take seriously the doubts and questions the revisionists raise about the sources, but I don't feel obligated to swallow their sometimes fantastic re-mythologizations. I conclude, in other words, that I know far too little to say much of anything with confidence about early Islam. In effect I have become an agnostic about how Islam came into being, what Muhammad thought he was doing, and what the earliest reciters of the Qur'an believed. Given the state of the field, this seems to be an eminently reasonable position. Strangely though, such agnosticism seems to be almost never embraced. Why

---

201. Speakers' Corner is in London; it claims to be the oldest place of free speech in the world.

not? Should it be so hard to admit that we just don't know, with any degree of confidence, what happened?

Such historical agnosticism might have several virtuous effects. First, it seems to me that it forestalls polemics. Honest doubts may make me agnostic; to transform those doubts into confident polemics renders me a sort of atheist. How can I polemicize about what I honestly don't know? Consequently, a virtue that seems likely to accompany historical agnosticism is humility. Humility would forbid us to use *any* claims about early Islamic origins polemically because we just don't know enough to be able to deploy polemics with integrity. It does not matter much whether these are old and out-of-fashion polemics or more recent and fashionable polemics. Second, in the realm of Christian-Muslim interaction, an agnostic position forces me to take refuge on more solid (and later) historical ground. I cannot pin my hopes for a reset in Christian-Muslim relations on some more positive reconstruction of early Christian-Muslim relations because such a reconstruction is likely to be pure imagination. The basic terms of debate were set by the third-century AH literary sources and later, are deeply embedded in these sources, and are unlikely to be reset by hopeful re-mythologization. Thus in the area of practical Muslim-Christian interaction, a phenomenological starting point probably makes the best sense. Third, in our teaching and writing about Islam, I think historical agnosticism requires that we show a great deal less confidence than we normally do in teaching about the origins of Islam. When we teach about the first two centuries of Islamic history, we are almost always teaching the vision of Islamic origins left to us by Muslim scholars of the third century of Islamic history and after. This does not make this vision of history unimportant, or unworthy of being taught – just the opposite – but we should not thoughtlessly purvey third-century versions of Islamic origins as What Really Happened.

In the end, my argument reduces to a simple appeal for humility. And although humility is not a virtue for which either scholars or polemicists are well-known, it is a characteristic Christian virtue. Whatever other arguments we may have about appropriate Christian approaches to Islam, I feel that I am on unassailable ground if I conclude by suggesting that whatever approach we adopt, it is not Christian if it is not first of all marked by deep humility, both scholarly and personal.

5.3 Hermeneutical Hinges: How Different Views of Religion and Culture Impact Interpretations of Islam

Warrick Farah

As Martin Accad has proposed, "Your *view* of Islam will affect your *attitude* to Muslims. Your *attitude* will, in turn, influence your *approach* to Christian-Muslim interaction, and that *approach* will affect the ultimate *outcome* of your presence as a witness among Muslims."[202] I would like to add a more foundational layer to this proposal, namely, that your *understanding* of religion and culture will affect your view of Islam. In other words, your view of Islam inevitably hinges upon your approach to religion and culture and, specifically, the relationship between the two.

In this contribution, I would like to show how these ideas play out in the missiological discourse of ministry to Muslims. In the interest of space, I will not focus on a theology of religion (although the discerning reader will see hints of it throughout). Instead I will focus on the more basic concepts of religion and culture. I will also limit my survey of the Christian-Muslim encounter to those approaches within evangelical missiological discourse. As we will see, the contemporary debate concerning approaches of ministry to Muslims is complex, and different presuppositions about culture and religion can lead to drastically different understandings of Islam.

Culture: Secular, Evil or Theological?

Richard Niebuhr's classic work *Christ and Culture* often stands as a starting point for different ways to understand culture and its relationship to biblical faith.[203] His five options (a spectrum of views) include Christ against culture, Christ of culture, Christ above culture, Christ in paradox with culture, and Christ the transformer of culture. As influential and important as Niebuhr has been, his analysis has recently been critiqued by many.[204] Niebuhr built his understanding of culture on the framework of secular anthropology. He

---

202. Martin Accad, "Christian Attitudes toward Islam and Muslims: A Kerygmatic Approach," in *Toward Respectful Understanding and Witness among Muslims: Essays in Honor of J. Dudley Woodberry*, eds. Evelyne A. Reisacher et al. (Pasadena: William Carey Library, 2012), 31, emphasis original.

203. Richard Niebuhr, *Christ and Culture* (New York: Harper and Brothers, 1951).

204. Timothy Tennent, *Invitation to World Missions: A Trinitarian Missiology for the Twenty-First Century* (Grand Rapids: Kregel, 2010), Kindle 1707ff.

defines "culture" as a process that "is the work of men's minds and hands."[205] According to Timothy Tennent, Niebuhr is unable to account theologically for the incarnation, where Jesus obviously did not become a general "human being," but a person within a specific cultural context. Tennent notes, "To create a barrier between Christ and culture is to relegate God to the supra-cultural category, which is maybe acceptable to some Islamic theologians but can scarcely be accepted as a thoroughly Christian view."[206] Writing in the mid-twentieth century, Niebuhr assumed Christendom's presupposition of the church's cultural and political superiority. His understanding of culture was also monocultural and is unsuitable for the globalizing forces and multicultural realities of today.[207]

Still, there are many who view culture exclusively through a secular lens. Some of these propose that much of Islam is simply culture and therefore neutral. For instance, Rick Brown states, "Muslims view Islam as a complete culture, with its own historical heritage, art forms, greetings, holidays, books, customs, ethics, politics, values and beliefs. They view Christianity the same way, not as a relationship to God through Christ but as a contrasting socio-religious grouping."[208] The implication is that Muslims who choose to follow Christ can retain a "Muslim" identity, since Islam is basically a culture.

Christians ministering to Muslims do not all share the same theological or secular perspectives on culture, however. Some believe that much of Muslim culture is *Islamic* – in a negative and spiritually-loaded sense.[209] For example, Jeff Morton believes that since all people are sinful and sinful people create sinful structures, culture is a prison from which we all need to escape. To build his case, Morton quotes from Sherwood Lingenfelter. However, I believe he has misunderstood Lingenfelter's thesis. Christians must become cultural pilgrims to free themselves from cultural bias, not from culture itself. In Lingenfelter's view, culture is not only a prison but also a palace that

---

205. Niebuhr, *Christ and Culture*, 33.

206. Tennent, *Invitation to World Missions*, Kindle 1764.

207. To be fair, I recognize that Niebuhr was as much a product of his time as we are of ours today.

208. Rick Brown, "Biblical Muslims," *International Journal of Frontier Missiology* 24, no. 2 (2007): 68.

209. Andrei Kravtsev, "Aspects of Theology of Religion in the Insider Movements Debate" (Unpublished Paper, 2015), 20.

paradoxically reflects much of God's goodness.[210] "Every follower of Jesus, every Christian, is on a pilgrimage away from his culture, his prison of bondage, and into full obedience to Jesus. . . . This view of culture permits new converts to see Islam for what it is: a pit, a prison, a noose and a snare of the devil."[211] This view contrasts sharply with that of Charles Kraft who believes it is not the structure or system of culture itself that is evil but the sinful choices of people that determine whether or not a specific culture will be used for ungodly purposes. Culture is not a person; it does not "do" anything.[212]

However, instead of a secular-neutral understanding and an understanding of culture as evil, others such as Tennent maintain that we should view culture *theologically*. If we are created in the image of God, and culture surrounds us like the air we cannot live without, then we are, by nature, *cultural beings*. As Karl Barth famously said, "theology has become anthropological because God has become man."[213] Others who hold a theology of culture framework maintain that the boundary between cultural anthropology and theology is artificial, constructed by modern thinking and not founded on biblical theology.[214] This theological understanding of culture affirms that an eschatological future, known as the "New Creation," has already broken into the present in Christ: "By relating the entire cultural process to the inbreaking of the New Creation, we are able to provide a vantage point from which to prophetically critique and enthusiastically celebrate as the gospel is embodied afresh in a potentially infinite number of new global contexts."[215]

Those with a more theological view of culture (i.e. that culture provides a necessary context of human existence) will see the good and bad in each culture, but through the incarnation as an example, they believe the gospel can take shape in any culture. Tennent, for example, argues that Muslims

---

210. Sherwood Lingenfelter, *Transforming Culture: A Challenge for Christian Mission*, 2nd ed. (Grand Rapids: Baker, 1998). See Warrick Farah, "Exegeting Culture with Lingenfelter," circumpolar, 24 March 2013, http://muslimministry.blogspot.com/2013/03/exegeting-culture-with-lingenfelter.html.

211. Jeff Morton, "IM: Inappropriate Missiology?," in *Chrislam: How Missionaries Are Promoting an Islamized Gospel*, ed. Joshua Lingel, Jeff Morton, and Bill Nikides (Garden Grove: i2 Ministries, 2011), 144.

212. Charles H. Kraft, *Anthropology for Christian Witness* (Maryknoll: Orbis, 1996), 34–35.

213. Quoted in Eric G. Flett, "Trinity: Conceptual Tools for an Interdisciplinary Theology of Culture," in *On Knowing Humanity: Insights from Theology for Anthropology*, ed. David Bronkema and Eloise Meneses (New York: Routledge, 2017), 209.

214. Gailyn Van Rheenen, "A Theology of Culture: Desecularizing Anthropology," *International Journal of Frontier Missiology* 14, no. 1 (1997): 33.

215. Tennent, *Invitation to World Missions*, Kindle 2094–2095.

who follow Christ could remain in their context *culturally*, but not *religiously*.[216] This however begs the questions: What is religion, and can it really be separated from culture?

Religion: Western Invention, Belief System or Subset of Culture?

Like culture, religion is a notorious and nearly impossible concept to define.[217] In the field of religious studies, there is no consensus of definition; this fact alone should infuse great caution as we try to frame this discussion. Some maintain that the very concept of religion is a Western invention with roots in modernity and in privatized, Protestant Christianity. Categorizing something as a "world religion" is a part of the heritage of colonialism that attempted to label people or events into groupings determined by the Enlightenment. In the end, this categorization confuses and distorts large, diverse parts of the world that do not fit into modern, discrete boundaries. In his article *Religious Syncretism as a Syncretistic Concept: The Inadequacy of the "World Religions" Paradigm in Cross-Cultural Encounter*, H. L. Richard argues that "the 'change of religion' terminology needs to be abandoned as a meaningful way to speak of someone becoming a disciple of Jesus."[218] For those with this view of religion, concepts of dual-belonging, hybridity and liminality offer more helpful tools for discipleship and for describing Islam (or actually *Islams*) in our globalized world today. Kyle Holton believes we should not focus on the abstract classification of religion or on rigid doctrinal statements, but on the formation of a people. Concentrating on a community of people "in Christ" helps us reframe the conversation "away from a non-localized, abstract confession to a life pattern that is analogous to the way of Christ."[219]

However, many evangelicals involved in Muslim ministry directly refer to religion as an encapsulating system of beliefs with discrete boundaries. In this sense, religion is basically reduced to a theology or a sphere of faith

---

216. Timothy Tennent, "Followers of Jesus (Isa) in Islamic Mosques: A Closer Examination of C-5 'High Spectrum' Contextualization," *International Journal of Frontier Missiology* 23, no. 3 (2006): 101–115.

217. Brent Nongbri, *Before Religion: A History of a Modern Concept* (New Haven: Yale University Press, 2013).

218. H. L. Richard, "Religious Syncretism as a Syncretistic Concept: The Inadequacy of the 'World Religions' Paradigm in Cross-Cultural Encounter," *International Journal of Frontier Missiology* 31, no. 4 (2014): 213.

219. Kyle Holton, "(De)Franchising Missions," in *Understanding Insider Movements*, eds. Harley Talman and John Travis (Pasadena: William Carey Library, 2015), 315.

allegiance that is distinct from culture. Islam is thus seen as an opposition force to Christianity. By sidestepping the question of whether Islam is a religion, a culture, or a combination of the two, Jeff Morton claims that, "If Islam does not have Jesus, the kingdom, the gospel, or the church, then it must have spiritual darkness as its primal substance. Therefore, it is a system that must be turned from as part of one's turning to the light."[220] For those with this view, there is usually very little talk of the different expressions of Christian faith around the world; there is only Christianity. For example, Bill Nikides proposes that Islam and Christianity are two competing "faith systems."[221] By directly equating false religion (Islam) and idolatry, Nikides claims that "all of the religions are false save one."[222]

This "belief system" understanding of religion should be contrasted with anthropological approaches that posit religion as a subset of a culture.[223] According to this perspective, it is reductionistic to claim that religion can be limited to the cognitive realm or an encapsulating (and encapsulated) domain of life. Instead, religion should be seen as a multidimensional, lived reality for its adherents. Throughout human history and across human religious symbol systems, religion enables people to cope better with and to control their environments.[224] Thus religion (and even secularism, which may be seen as a type of religion) serves as an important and unavoidable function in human society.

Those who conceptualize religion as a part of culture, and culture as a part of religion, believe it is a vital concept for the Christian. If all cultures are simultaneously a reflection of both the goodness of God and sinful human nature,[225] then all religions have at least some truth, and no religion is without flaw. This does not inevitably lead to relativism or pluralism. "Rather than comparing and contrasting Christianity with other religions, we measure all religions, including Christianity, against the revelation of Jesus Christ, who

---

220. Morton, "IM: Inappropriate Missiology?," 136.

221. Bill Nikides, "One-ist Missiology: Insider Movements and Theology of Religions," (2011): 16. http://www.pefministry.org/Nikides_files/One-ist%20Missiology%20and%20Insider%20movements%20copy.pdf.

222. Nikides, "One-Ist Missiology," 19.

223. Kevin Higgins, "Inside What? Church, Culture, Religion and Insider Movements in Biblical Perspective," *St. Francis Magazine* 5, no. 4 (2009): 83; Brian Howell and Jenell Williams Paris, *Introducing Cultural Anthropology: A Christian Perspective* (Grand Rapids: Baker Academic, 2011), 177.

224. Terry Muck, *Why Study Religion? Understanding Humanity's Pursuit of the Divine* (Grand Rapids: Baker Academic, 2016), Kindle 1339.

225. The Lausanne Movement, *The Cape Town Commitment: A Confession of Faith and a Call to Action* (Hendrickson, 2011), paragraph 7b.

is the embodiment of the New Creation."[226] This perspective also recognizes the contributions that different cultures bring to Christian theology, which is globalizing and multicultural.[227] If religion is seen as a multidimensional, socio-political phenomenon, and religion and culture are distinct yet inseparable, then disciple-makers can interact with and build upon certain elements within Islam as a bridge to biblical faith. However, there is no straightforward formula for how to do so. For some, since Islam is a total way of life, conversion should not entail a change of religions, and thus you can have "Messianic Muslims"[228] who remain in their cultural context. For others, like Tennent as mentioned previously, conversion means that Muslim background believers (MBBs) should follow Christ and remain in their context *culturally*, but not *religiously*. Clearly, the difference between the two is not always clear. The important concept is that religion and culture are distinct yet inseparable.

So, what does "religion" mean when applied to Islam? Hopefully this section has shown some very different trajectories that do not fit neatly on a spectrum of views. But this begs another issue: How should we study religion?

Epistemological Perspective: Top Down or Bottom Up?

Evangelicals use two general "ways of thinking" to conceptualize Islam. These epistemological processes are of considerable significance in research. Depending on the approach, different conclusions can be reached regarding the question, "What is Islam?" These two perspectives can be called "top down" and "bottom up."

The top-down perspective has a privileged place in evangelical approaches to understanding Islam. We typically believe that the Bible plays a central role in our lives and purpose, so we assume the Qur'an (and the Hadith) play a similar role in the lives of Muslims. It makes perfect sense for us to study the sacred texts of Muslims. The result of this inquiry is usually a description of the doctrines of Islam, or concepts such as "the Muslim worldview" or the "metanarrative" of Islam. According to Joshua Lingel, "Without reading the biography of Muhammad a person doesn't understand Islam. After reading

---

226. Tennent, *Invitation to World Missions*, 223.

227. Harold Netland and Craig Ott, *Globalizing Theology: Belief and Practice in an Era of World Christianity* (Grand Rapids: Baker Academic, 2006).

228. John Travis, "Messianic Muslim Followers of Isa: A Closer Look at C5 Believers and Congregations," *International Journal of Frontier Missiology* 17, no. 1 (2000): 53–59.

the biography of Muhammad a person understands Islam."[229] This type of statement is indicative of the top-down approach.

In contrast, others approach Islam from the bottom up. They tend to focus on Muslims themselves in their contexts. As is often taken for granted, many Muslims are indeed nominal, doctrinally aberrant, or just simply know little about the formal creeds of Islam. A preoccupation with "Islam" as a category at times obscures the realities of Muslims on the margins of Islam.[230] The bottom-up approach might also be called the anthropological approach to Islam.

The top-down approach tends to search for grand theories for understanding Muslims. This approach acknowledges diversity in the Muslim world, but Muslim culture and Islam are still described in (what claims to be) an all-encompassing system. Conversely, the bottom-up approach is skeptical of these theories. Instead, Islamic traditions are described in theories of the "middle-range."[231] Middle-range theories maintain that no single theory can describe all Muslims in the world. Islam is thus understood in whatever form it takes in a specific context. Far from being a non-theological perspective, the bottom-up approach adds to and enriches our theological understanding of Muslims:

> Can one develop an adequate theology of religions without carefully observing and understanding the actual beliefs and practices of particular religious communities? . . . If it is really a theological framework for understanding the religious realities in our world that we are seeking, then our theological reflection must focus upon the actual lived realities of various religious communities.[232]

As we seek to interpret Islam, both of these perspectives are important. Top-down and bottom-up approaches are often competing, but instead they should complement and critique each other. It is far too easy (and occurs far too frequently) to generalize all Muslims into some sort of category, i.e. Islam, that either simplifies, dehumanizes, or stereotypes them. And yet it is also easy to say there is no such thing as "Islam" and to minimize the effect that

---

229. Joshua Lingel, "Foundations of Islam," in an i2 Ministries resource, 2017. https://i2ministries.org/.

230. Gene Daniels and Warrick Farah, *Margins of Islam: Ministry in Diverse Muslim Contexts* (Littleton: William Carey, 2018).

231. Peter Hedström and Lars Udehn, "Analytical Sociology and the Theories of the Middle Range," in *The Oxford Handbook of Analytical Sociology*, eds. Peter Bearman and Peter Hedström (Oxford: Oxford University Press, 2009).

232. Harold Netland, "Evangelical Missiology and Theology of Religions: An Agenda for the Future," *International Journal of Frontier Missiology* 29, no. 1 (2012): 7.

various Islamic interpretations of the Qur'an and Hadith can have on Muslims. Both the texts and the contexts of Muslims have important perspectives for our understanding of Islam, and a robust "biblical theology of Islam" is best formed in a dialogue among Islamicists, anthropologists, theologians and missiologists.[233]

But we still need to discuss the relationship between culture and religion. One other concept greatly assists us in this regard: the form-meaning interplay.

Form and Meaning: Equated, Separate or Corresponding?

Dancing? What does it mean? How does it look? In some religions, dance is an integral expression of faith. In others, dancing is strictly forbidden. Obviously, different sects within the same religion sometimes disagree over whether dancing is acceptable behavior or not. So again, what do I mean by dancing? Depending on your religious background and culture, the word likely invokes drastically different images in your mind! This is the issue of "form and meaning."

There are three main ways to describe the relationship between form and meaning (or message). The first is that form is *equated* with meaning – that the relationship between the two is so strong, they cannot be separated. In our discussion of Islam, this position would say that Muslim religious forms are completely tied to Islam. For example, traditional Islamic piety such as *ṣalāt*-style prayers could never be reused or appropriated by a follower of Jesus. To do so is to mix religions and constitutes idolatrous behavior.

The same goes for the use of Islamic language. For example, Christians should never use 'Isa (Jesus's name in the Qur'an) because it is Islamic. Those in this camp also usually understand culture as inherently sinful and religion as an encapsulating belief system with discrete boundaries. For example, notice the relationship between form and meaning in this image of Islam:

> Is Islam a religion we can play with, taking bits and pieces and fiddling with it as if it were a tinker toy? I don't believe the Bible takes this view of other religions . . . I have already conceded that the forms of Islam were borrowed from Judaism and Christianity, but what I cannot concede is that the forms are now separable

---

233. Warrick Farah, "Outlining a Biblical Theology of Islam: Practical Implications for Disciple Makers and Church Planting," *Evangelical Missions Quarterly* 55, no. 1 (2019): 13–16.

from Islam or redeemable due to the irreconcilable problem that Islam has a demonic source.[234]

We will deal with the spiritual source of Islam in another section,[235] but for now, the implication of this encapsulating understanding of Islam is clear: form and meaning are equated.

In contrast, a very different position on the relationship between form and meaning is that the two are *separate* or arbitrarily related. Muslims who follow Jesus do not have to leave their "religion" and can use Islamic forms but with a new, Christ-centered "dynamic equivalence" of meanings. One of the chief proponents of this view is Charles Kraft.[236] In Kraft's proposal, meaning exists only in the hearts and minds of people. Messages can be transmitted in different forms because forms are neutral and have no inherent meaning. According to Kraft, the important thing in discipleship is to change the internal meanings and the faith allegiances that people construct, but not the outward forms or the structures themselves.[237] Thus Kraft discusses what a form-meaning separation looks like for MBBs:

> What would be the right forms of prayer for Muslims who commit themselves to Christ? Their background would lead them to want to face in the direction of Mecca (and Jerusalem). They would probably be inclined to pray five times a day with particular postures at specified times . . . I doubt that any of these things would bother God. . . . Just like with the Hebrews, God can start with virtually anything culturally or religiously, as long as the allegiance issue is settled.[238]

Those in this camp understand Islamic piety as a neutral set of forms that can be filled with new meanings. The important thing is for people to come to faith through the gospel alone, in which conversion is usually defined as a new faith allegiance to Christ.

Finally, a third, mediating position hovers between the form *equated* with meaning position and the form *separate* from meaning position. Paul Hiebert

---

234. Jeff Morton, *Insider Movements: Biblically Incredible or Incredibly Brilliant?* (Eugene: Wipf & Stock, 2012), 83.

235. See "Discerning Spiritual Realities in Islamic Contexts," section 9.5.

236. Kraft, *Anthropology for Christian Witness*, 132ff.

237. Scott Moreau, *Contextualization in World Missions: Mapping and Assessing Evangelical Models* (Grand Rapids: Kregel, 2012), 84.

238. Kraft, *Anthropology for Christian Witness*, 213–214.

is most well-known for his position that form and meaning are *corresponding*.[239] Meaning *corresponds* to form, and the strength of correspondence varies according to case. Hiebert rejects both the form-meaning separation and equation. For him, a form-meaning separation stems from a dualistic mode of thinking inherited from and biased by Western culture. But Hiebert also emphasizes the danger of equation. Examples for such equation can be seen when we automatically reject various local cultural symbols because the forms of the symbols are sometimes identified with idolatrous worship.[240]

Instead, Hiebert's approach is what he famously called "critical contextualization."[241] Applied to an Islamic context, Muslim religious forms should not just be uncritically denied or uncritically accepted. Neither should "Christian" (often Western) religious forms be uncritically imported. Either could result in syncretism or the gospel being rejected because it is perceived as foreign. Instead, Muslim forms of faith should be studied thoroughly and evaluated in the light of scripture. Then when appropriate, a new, contextualized biblical practice with local forms can be created in its place.

It helps to note an important difference between Kraft and Hiebert.[242] Kraft is more focused on linguistics in his approach, and the disassociation of form and meaning is most easily seen in communication theory. Words and their meanings clearly change over time and across languages and cultures. Hiebert, on the other hand, uses the tools of symbolic anthropology and sees less freedom in the ability to repurpose religious forms in contextualization. He is much more cautious about reusing Islamic rituals for biblical purposes. At the end of the day, how we understand the form-meaning issue is essential for how we understand Islam.

Islam: Cultureligion or Religiolatry?

So far, I hope I have shown how a few topics related to culture and religion play foundational roles on Islam's conceptualization in evangelical missiology. We have covered primary concepts such as culture, religion, epistemological perspective, and the form-meaning interplay. We cannot define Islam without simultaneously reflecting on our understanding of religion and culture. The

---

239. Moreau, *Contextualization in World Missions*, 84.
240. See Yoshiyuki B. Nishioka, "Worldview Methodology in Mission Theology: A Comparison between Kraft's and Hiebert's Approaches," *Missiology* 26, no. 4 (1996): 465.
241. Paul Hiebert, "Critical Contextualization," *Missiology* 12, no. 3 (1984): 287–296.
242. Kravtsev, "Aspects of Theology of Religion," 22.

relationship between the two acts as a hermeneutical hinge for our interpretation of Islam. The implications for missiology from divergent understandings of these concepts are complex.

At the risk of being simplistic, I will summarize our preliminary discussion into two approaches to working with Muslims that are often applied in missiology. Then I will offer a brief missiological critique of both in the conclusion. But first we need to introduce another concept into our analytical framework: idolatry.

I introduced this topic above *(see section 3.5)*,[243] so I will not repeat myself here. I will simply say that a recurring theme in the Bible is the adversarial role that idolatry plays in keeping people from glorifying God in Christ. Throughout salvation history and up to the present, God has actively opposed idolatry in order to redeem people so they can worship him alone. God does this in more than one way, and he calls his church to be involved in the adaptive process as well. So in the following analysis, I will hold three items in creative tension: culture, religion and idolatry.

The first approach is what we might call *the merger of religion and culture*, or "cultureligion." In this understanding, the two are so closely linked they can barely be distinguished. Idolatry exists as a concept separate from cultureligion. One significant example of this approach is the book *Insider Jesus* by William Dyrness.[244] Dyrness proposes that religions provide "indispensable hermeneutical spaces" that allow people the room to seek God and the latitude for believers to work out the meaning and implications of Christ's life and work.[245] Although some changes to the religion will be made when disciples of Jesus begin to follow him in the cultural structures of their practice, religion is still basically a manmade construct, humanity's honest yet broken attempt to know God.

For instance, the unique factor of the Old Testament Israelite community was not their religious practices but the God they worshiped. Circumcision, dietary restrictions and animal sacrifices were already common to many ancient Near Eastern peoples. Israel's religion was a means to know Yahweh, not an end in itself. God does not care about a perfect religion; only Christ can save people and restore them to himself. God does not wish to supplant religions, only to reform them from within, ultimately for his glory and for

---

243. *See section 3.5*, "Adaptive Missiological Engagement with Islamic Contexts."

244. William Dyrness, *Insider Jesus: Theological Reflections on New Christian Movements* (Leicester: IVP Academic, 2016).

245. Dyrness, *Insider Jesus*, 67.

human flourishing. So when people from non-Christian backgrounds initially begin to consider Jesus or to incorporate the Bible into their religions, even when the applications prove largely unorthodox, their efforts are evidence of the work of the Holy Spirit.

In this cultureligion approach, Islam stands as a natural part of human existence. Muslims use it in an honest attempt to reach God; what is lacking is Christ. God intends for Muslims to continue working out what it means to know him within the cultureligion of Islam. One benefit of this approach is that it avoids the worldly competition of religions. Christians can work alongside Muslims for the common good of society and still graciously present Christ (only the Holy Spirit brings people to faith).

Contrasting with cultureligion, which is distinct from idolatry, is another approach we might call religiolatry, where religion and idolatry are merged together and then segregated from culture. Speaking on behalf of a number of missiologists, Joshua Lingel claims that the overall redemptive flow of scripture represents a "covenantal, exclusive faith against the idolatrous religions of the nations."[246] In his view, approaches to non-Christian, unbiblical traditions that view religion in anthropological or cultural terms ignore false religions' fallen, satanic nature as ungodly imitations of the truth. Islam is a "poisonous faith system that eventually must corrupt and distort its practitioners." Lingel continues by asserting that in the Christian-Muslim encounter, errors are made when one values the positives of culture too highly: "It is as though the culture is the ultimate, irreducible reality."[247] Christianity and Islam are opposed to one another; there could never be any sense of mixing. According to Lingel, the proper Christian response "is to war against Islam with spiritual weapons. These weapons are in the realm of love and learning, knowledge, ideas, thoughts and arguments."[248]

As I have attempted to demonstrate, interpretations of Islam in missiological discourse are profoundly influenced by divergent understandings of religion and culture, and specifically, the relationship between the two. So, where do we go from here?

---

246. Joshua Lingel, "Recap of 'The Insider Movement Conference: A Critical Assessment II,'" 2010. See https://i2ministries.org/.

247. Joshua Lingel, Jeff Morton, and Bill Nikides, eds., *Chrislam: How Missionaries Are Promoting an Islamized Gospel*, rev. ed. (Garden Grove: i2 Ministries, 2012), 5.

248. Joshua Lingel, *Islam's Issues, Agendas, and the Great Commission* (Garden Grove: i2 Ministries, 2016), 149.

Concluding Reflections: Getting Comfortable with Ambiguity

We are unlikely ever to reach a consensus on a proper biblical theology of religion and culture. With the publication of *Christ and Culture* in 1951, Niebuhr called this issue an "enduring problem" for the church through the ages. While we can make some general clarifications, as I have done here, it seems to me that many of these issues can't be solved at the abstract, theoretical level. There is simply too much knowledge rooted in experience and context making the issues extremely difficult to evaluate in a historically "Western" way (i.e. in the realm of ideas).

Interestingly, during the infamous Jerusalem Council in Acts 15, the assembled reflected on the *experience* of God's work among them. A next step in this discussion would be to put approaches of ministry to Muslims in dialogue with the Muslim and MBB *experience* of Islam (religion? culture? both?), which, as we already know, varies.[249] I am very sympathetic to the charge that this discussion has been dominated by Western voices. And yet I find that non-Westerners and MBBs have similar discussions and similar disagreements around these concepts.

Still, we may offer some concluding critiques of the discussion. Many of the approaches to contextualization surveyed here assume that Muslims are practicing, not nominal, Muslims. In my experience, however, many Muslims, if they are practicing at all, use Islamic piety to keep God at a distance, either because they are afraid of punishment or because he is seen as unknowable. A Muslim friend once told me he was looking forward to eternity in paradise because in heaven, there "was no more worship." For him, heaven was a man-centered place of sensual indulgence; God was present only in theory.

Additionally, Muslims do not all share the same attachment to Islam. It should go without saying that, depending on the context, sometimes you do not have to do anything according to the context! Many Muslims do not desire to follow Christ in ways that are culturally or religiously familiar to them, although some indeed do. And yet the gospel has all too often been presented in Western forms, causing it to be rejected as foreign. While this may partially explain some of the tension in our discourse, it does not explain all the historical reasons for the resistance to the gospel in Muslim lands. In some Muslim contexts, there is often a very strong connection between form

---

249. L. D. Waterman, "Different Pools, Different Fish: The Mistake of 'One Size Fits All' Solutions to the Challenge of Effective Outreach among Muslims," 2017. https://sparks.fuller.edu/global-reflections/2017/01/18/different-pools-different-fish-the-mistake-of-one-size-fits-all-solutions-to-the-challenge-of-effective-outreach-among-muslims/.

and meaning. For many Muslims and MBBs, some of the forms are linked with meanings that are nearly impossible to modify.

On the other hand, the automatic equation of form and meaning practically villainizes particular Islamic cultures.[250] For mission in a postcolonial world, we must ensure that our theology of Islam does not speak pejoratively of Muslims and Islamic cultures. Unfortunately, evangelicals have a long history of failing to obey the Golden Rule of ethics, "do to others what you would have them do to you" (Matt 7:12). If we understand Christianity as a religious system, we can also demonstrate that "Christianity" has (at numerous times throughout history) done evil things seemingly rooted in the demonic. Does this also mean that "Christianity" has a demonic source? Furthermore, if God saves us from our culture (as some maintain), to what culture do we turn? What is "Christian" culture? Answers only add to the ambiguity.

So how can we understand Islam? Islam is a process of "meaning-making" undertaken by Muslims as they interact in their context with the revelation (according to their tradition) given to Muhammad. Islam includes diverse cultural traditions, access to social networks, a sense of belonging with others, and rituals and ceremonies.[251] Phrases such as "leaving Islam" or "remaining in Islam" are often too vague to be meaningful and can actually be confusing in discipleship. For some, "leaving Islam" could mean that a Muslim who comes to Christ must also leave his culture and community, while for others, "remaining in Islam" could mean it is automatically permissible to participate in Islamic rituals. Issues of socio-religious identity are not always clear either. What does a "Muslim" or a "Christian" identity mean within a specific setting? Answers vary with contexts. When we look at Muslim contexts, Islam is not all we see; it is one strand in the braided rope of Muslim societies.[252]

Finally, we haven't discussed other important issues such as the nature of the kingdom of God, the church and the gospel. These are also disputed concepts in evangelical missiology. Although we might not agree, and although we need to become more comfortable with ambiguity and messiness, we should still strive for as much Christocentric clarity as possible as we witness to Muslims in diverse contexts. Let us not forget the command to love one

---

250. Kravtsev, "Aspects of Theology of Religion," 20.

251. Warrick Farah, "The Complexity of Insiderness," *IJFM* 32, no. 2 (2015): 85–91.

252. Warrick Farah, "How Muslims Shape and Use Islam: Toward a Missiological Understanding," in *Margins of Islam: Ministry in Diverse Muslim Contexts*, eds. Gene Daniels and Warrick Farah (Littleton: William Carey, 2018), 13–21.

another and to love the religious other as we make disciples of Jesus among all nations.

5.4 Testimony 1: Hanane on Following Jesus in Morocco

interview by Martin Accad

We come to the first testimony of part II which is presented as an interview.

Martin: Hanane, welcome. Where are you from?

Hanane: I am Moroccan, from the center of the country viewed on a north-south axis, but nearer to the coast than the mountains in the east.

Martin: I met you when you came to study at ABTS. Please tell us about your journey to Christ and with him as a disciple.

Hanane: I came to faith in Jesus in 1999 and subsequently married a fellow believer. We came to ABTS in 2011 as a family of four. I graduated in 2014, and we returned to Morocco as a family of five. I am involved in children's ministry, and my husband works in Bible translation projects. We were active in Christian work before coming to ABTS; indeed this was essential for our being accepted as students.

Martin: Extended family is important in Morocco, as it is in many countries. How have family members reacted to your faith and ministry?

Hanane: There are a number of believers in our extended families, a picture that has changed over time. Praise God! Initially, telling family was difficult, although some had noticed the changes in our attitudes, behavior and lifestyle. Some responded by instructing us to choose between family and Christ. We assured them that we loved them but would not leave Christ. With hindsight, our children played a significant role in our speaking with family members: the children could not keep quiet.

Martin: How did your parents react to your marriage?

Hanane: I would have left my family if they had attempted to force me to marry a man who was not a Christian. My husband worked for a Christian radio station when we married. Consequently, we could not hide the conversion issue. His name being Muhammad was perceived as making him a safe choice despite his being considered an "apostate." His calmness and love were considerable assets in handling family relationships, as was his strong commitment to remain in the region.

Martin: What Islamic practices have remained with you?

Hanane: Muslims often ask me how I pray. Typically, many Christians like me either go very Western or stay with the Islamic forms that they practiced before conversion. I was raised as a Muslim but practically, with little if any relating to God. During my teenage years, I was searching for God and felt that my lifestyle was inadequate or wrong, and what religious rituals I knew did not satisfy me. I now regard prayer as being linked to God. I found Christian worship songs profoundly moving when I first encountered them. I have kept being very hospitable, which is very Moroccan.

Martin: What have you found significant in the material presented today (now the three core sections of this chapter)?

Hanane: I find the study of Islam's origins interesting. What I long for is to understand my neighbors and family, why they behave as they do, and where their religious beliefs and practices originate. My desire is to win people, not arguments. Misuse of religion can happen anywhere. I have seen argumentative types both among Muslims and within the church. I find it humbling to realize what we do not know about the origins of Islam. What we know about the other should not be used to assault them.

One aspect that affects us deeply in Morocco is the intertwining of religion and culture. There is nothing cultural in pilgrimage, it is profoundly spiritual and religious. Yet in these days, I notice some people going on the hajj who are motivated purely by acquiring the social title, so what was religious has become cultural for some. Traditional Moroccan dress and cuisine predate Islam; it was cultural long before some perceived it to be religious. My Lord left the glory of heaven to become incarnate for us. So in returning to relate to wider family, why would I not wear what my in-laws find appropriate? It is cultural, not religious what we wear, what we eat, or how we sit. I am pleased to do what helps to make Jesus accessible and attractive to them.

Martin: Wow! So are there examples of where you choose to be distinctive?

Hanane: One example is that as a married couple, my husband is supposed to bring a lamb for the Eid feast, but my Muhammad refuses to do so. He does so to be distinctly Christian. We keep demonstrating that we believe in God, and we are observably prayerful. We endeavor to be distinctive and to make Christ attractive to others.

Martin: How do you view Islam in Morocco in the light of what you have heard today?

Hanane: Personally, I see Islam as an alternative form of Judaism. Much of the time in Morocco, I simply describe what I see. Islam is diverse even within my country. It is under pressure from globalization and secularism. These pressures do not mean that Christianity will inevitably flourish, but it does give a context in which we can make Christ known.

Martin: Finally, how do you find being Moroccan and Christian given that there is no legally recognized national church in Morocco?

Hanane: In 1999 when I first believed, I thought that the culture was suffocating. I could not enter a building and worship as I desired. I was envious of those who were able to do so openly, to be freely Christian. Since then I have become aware that even in Lebanon there are things that restrict worship for some; I also know of believers who feel it necessary to relocate within this country. For myself, I now sense God's presence and protection in such things.

5.5 A Conversation among Friends: Exploring Missiological Implications

Moderator: Welcome. How do you think a Muslim might react to Dan's presentation?

Jewish-Background Disciple (JBD): It would vary widely by context. You would get different responses from different audiences. I think that it is easy to raise these questions in some circles, for example in places where there is a longstanding awareness of Hadith criticism and some academic engagement therewith.

Moderator: How should we speak clearly to Muslims about our faith? How would we recommend that Christ's followers from Muslim backgrounds tell their family?

Christian-Background Disciple (CBD): We do not have to be brave, bold and direct in a first conversion: announcing everything in one go rarely works well in practice. A wiser approach is to prepare people and find a narrative that makes sense to them and also to their family and friends. My usual approach with those from Muslim backgrounds is to encourage them to start with trusted friends, not family.

Muslim-Background Disciple (MBD): I am a disciple of Jesus from a Muslim background. This is a lifelong journey for many people like me. There are similarities with sanctification and lifelong discipleship. We need to demonstrate our faith in everyday life. At the education center where I work, we explore how we can be different. One example is to not see people just as customers. We have the arguments, the theological discussions, yet it is rare that these lead people to Christ. Our lives must show the difference that Christ makes. We must not hide life.

Moderator: How helpful is scientific enquiry to draw people into the knowledge of Christ?

JBD: Dan's approach in this chapter enables us to speak the truth with some humility. We need to give disciples of Jesus the foundations from which to speak with Muslims about what we do and do not know. We need to expose our own biases and views of Muhammad and the Qur'an. I think that doing so helps us reinforce our knowledge of Christian theology. Also, those who study history see the depth and strength of early Christians' faith in Jesus.

Moderator: How do you, CBD, justify your ministry to financial supporters in the West when you are not directly engaging with Muslims?

CBD: I see my work as providing active support to academic study in the region. Much of this is about enabling the conversations that people have with Muslims to go into deeper levels. I believe that theology, missiology and anthropology combine well, and that this combination assists the church with discipleship and witness.

JBD: I am sure that there is an internal battle within each Westerner raising financial support to enable them to live and work in the MENA region. How do they imagine what supporters at home think of what they are doing? I regard integrity as crucial. They need to be clear about what they are doing and aware that God calls people to many different activities.

MBD: I affirm the importance of theological study since it brings clearer thinking which leads to better speech. In my situation in my country, Christians and Muslims are engaged in a complex dialogue.

Moderator: Moving on, for disciples of Jesus that come from a Muslim background, what typical Muslim religious practices remain acceptable?

CBD: I think that there is no straightforward answer to this. To me, all forms of Islam are borrowed from Judaism and Christianity, a consequence of the history of Islam. However, I do ask to what extent are Muslims comfortable with this observation. Likewise, how comfortable are Christ followers, especially those from Islam?

JBD: If we give actual examples, then some boundaries might emerge. For example, many in the Muslim world will use an amulet or small piece of jewelry with scripture inside of it, believing that it will give them protection against evil, danger or disease. Is this acceptable after someone becomes a disciple of Jesus? Incidentally, similar issues emerge for Christ's followers from religious backgrounds other than Islam.

MBD: Practices rooted in the occult are clearly not acceptable, albeit there are fuzzy lines of what is occultic and what is not.[253] A common question is whether someone like me can continue to go to a mosque. Can I participate in non-Christian worship? In 2 Corinthians it is clear that we should disassociate ourselves from pagan rituals; however, the contexts are not quite analogous. I suggest that the criterion is where is Christ in whatever practices one adopts? For example, can someone continue to pray in a mosque with the aim of being a witness to Christ? Another aspect is what is social and cultural rather than religious. This is often far from clear.

Moderator: What about praying in a synagogue, a similar issue for those who are Jewish and come to worship Jesus as Messiah?

CBD: The issue is with corporate worship that is not Christocentric. For me, the key criterion is whether Jesus is there or not.

JBD: Agency must be given to the person with the challenge. We cannot make the decision for them, nor instruct them to follow one particular path. The corollary to this is the necessity of acceptance of the diverse approaches

---

253. Note from the editors: In sections 1.6 and 3.2 above, Rose Mary Amenga-Etego raises many of the sensitive issues related to the missionary task of bringing the gospel to regions where traditional religious practices form the underlying substratum of the host culture. In section 9.4 below, Lawrence Oseje also addresses the liminal space of faith and traditional religious practices. These voices, particularly for the modern Western reader, represent an important and moderate post-colonial critique that must at the very least be heard.

we see our sisters and brothers adopting. *(Section 8.5 deals with the heart of this question.)*

Moderator: Moving on, in interaction with non-scholar Muslims, does our having a theology of Islam have anything to contribute?

CBD: We all have a theology of Islam, although we might not be explicit about what it is. This book is endeavoring to make it more explicit.

JBD: Our theology affects how careful and considered we are in dealing with all Muslims; it aids us in avoiding some misunderstandings. We need to beware of the popular understanding of Islam influencing our dealings with all Muslims; in other words, of it obscuring the diversity among Muslims.

MBD: I think that we need to apply the insights derived in our studies to reach all Muslims. Why? Because academic study only for Islamic scholars would give us a small audience.

Moderator: So what about Islam in places of limited education?

MBD: I suggest that we need to be aware of being too goal-oriented. Let us think strategically and be proactive, not simply reactive to others. I urge that we keep studying and focused on God, seeking his wisdom and building respect and love for all people.

Moderator: Why might we fear Muslims turning to secular agnosticism?

JBD: This moves people from one inadequate worldview to another. So we should not fear it, but neither should we rejoice. People have freewill, and many are making such a move. We need to stand with them, whether we agree with their decision or not, since it might have involved much pain and loss. Later, we might be a route for them to regain in Christ what they lost when leaving their religion.

MBD: One aspect is spirituality. We should not seek to develop indifference to religion in others since to do so has no benefit for the gospel message.

Moderator: What changes would you ask Western church leaders to make to facilitate reaching Muslims for Christ?

CBD: The words "Muslim" and "Christian" are confusing, especially for disciples of Jesus from Muslim backgrounds. There are many variations within both religions and also political expressions of both. I urge that we keep Jesus at the center of our message and methods.

JBD: I suggest being aware of other idols that are widely embraced in the West, such as money and economic power. All churches are faced with some forms of idolatry. We need prophetic voices, and I lament that not many are speaking at present.

MBD: The challenge is to give Muslims the opportunity to meet Jesus. So much has been shaped by Western values, so we need to ask whether the message of the gospel has been obscured. The Western church needs to allow the rest of the global church to shape the presentation of the gospel for their contexts. Western missionaries should come with the gospel, not a cultural model that includes some Christianity.

JBD: Beware the differences between phenomenal and historical agnosticism. Most academics do not like empty space in knowledge and attempt to fill in the gaps. We need to hold such spaces lightly, recognizing that such spaces exist. In practice, I start with the people in front of me. I ask myself, "how do they see their situation?" and then, "how do I go about engaging them with the gospel?" Religions in how they develop do have a life of their own, so we cannot draw a simple straight line from their origin to present-day expressions.

Moderator: Which lens do you use to look at the practices seen?

CBD: The existential approach, namely what does Islam teach Muslims, and hence how do we present the gospel so that it is accessible to them? One observation is that some Christians who have become involved in mission to Muslims have become uncurious because they think that they know all the answers. This is not helpful. Religious texts are important, but genuine dialogue requires engaging with what those we are with actually think.

Moderator: Do we need to find a balance?

CBD: Yes, we need a balance between the forms and meaning of religion. I suggest being aware of the possibility of a modern **Gnosticism**. So we need to keep studying both.

Questions for Discussion

1. How might we use awareness of the uncertainties surrounding Islam's origins in our engagement with Muslims? What variety of approaches are we aware of?

2. What do we think of Dan Brown's suggestion that it is bad theology that leads to both the extremes of syncretistic and polemical approaches to Islam and Muslims?

3. Do we agree that humility is a crucial Christian virtue? If so, how can we display this godly characteristic to religious others, particularly Muslims?

4. Do we agree with Warrick Farah that, "Islam is a process of 'meaning-making' undertaken by Muslims as they interact in their context with the revelation (according to tradition) given to Muhammad?" Does this statement account for the vast diversity within Islam? How might we use the opportunities this idea creates to engage in theological conversations with Muslims?

5. How do our lives show the reality of Christ to the religious others we encounter?

6

Thinking Biblically about the Qur'an

Poetry by Anna Turner
Estuary Roots
    My roots are buried in estuary sand,
    I grew with my feet in the river's mouth,
    And hand in my Dad's hand
    I'd run along the walls,
    That stopped the river invading our land.
    Yes, my roots are buried in estuary sand;
    I know the rhythm of the turning tides,
    I've jumped the waves that tug at my country's side,
    But stood at waters only river wide.
    I know the feel of waters mixed
    And they've taught me tricks,
    For living in a world that isn't fixed,
    For living between and betwixt.
    In the place where waters meet,
    Sea salt and river sweet,
    I've learned that lives can be different, but great;
    River is river and sea is sea
    But they meet,
    And that place for me is home.
    And in the waves topped with foam,
    At the mouth of horizons unknown,
    My roots were forged and grown,

For my roots are buried in estuary sand,
So wherever my boat travels and lands,
My roots will be where I stand,
At the edge of waters mixed,
Living in the between and the betwixt,
At the mouth of horizons unknown,
My soul's roots firmly grown
In the sandy bay and salt filled foam
Of the estuary that was my home.

Anna Turner's poem expresses the tension resulting from tradition meeting innovation, where traditionists are challenged by the views of revisionists and the feelings experienced by those who, standing at the juncture of the river and the sea, have to live with a life "between and betwixt." In the next three chapters, after the opening biblical reflection, the IMES team has put together three case studies, one on the Qur'an, one on Muhammad and one on salvation. These studies are designed to set the tone for the ensuing sections by asking the questions that Muslim followers of Jesus struggle with when they turn their lives over to Christ. In the conclusion of this book, we will revisit some of these questions and consider in what ways they have been addressed and how much progress we have made in our endeavor to set the foundations of a biblical theology of Islam.

6.1 Opening Reflection: Is Intellectual Conviction Enough?

Hanane

John chapter 3 is an amazing passage of scripture describing Jesus's conversation with Nicodemus. Chapter 2 ends with a description of a confrontation in Jerusalem and notes that there is much amazement at what Jesus is doing and teaching, but there is little evidence of deep faith (John 2:23–24). In John's structure, Jesus's visit to Jerusalem follows his activity in Capernaum and the first miracle performed in Cana. So dialogue follows action.

Nicodemus comes at night: why? From the human perspective, he looked like an ideal person, an educated nobleman. The conversation focuses on new life and new beginnings with God. This dialogue continues John's theme of newness, of which the wine in Cana is also an example. Jesus takes Nicodemus step by step through the necessity for new birth.

A second theme is that of authority. The understanding of Nicodemus was being reshaped. He recognized the authenticity and authority in Jesus's actions. Yet Jesus took him beyond looking at the signs to see the significance and necessity of new birth. Nicodemus appears almost childlike in his wondering and enquiring and displays a willingness to oblige. He is being led beyond normal human intellect to the spiritual realm.

The dialogue moves toward a conclusion, to a verdict on the claims of Christ, to judgment. It is not about scaring people; it is about expressing the love of God. There is no embellishing or sugar-coating of the message. The need for, and possibility of, being born again is stated more than once.

We meet Nicodemus later in the gospel story when he is involved in caring for Jesus's body (John 19:38–39), an act that demonstrated his willingness at this time to be more open about his identification with Jesus.

Do we want to see more people doing what Nicodemus did, seeking to meet with Jesus, exploring the claims of Christ, seeking salvation? In these days, many such people, including many Muslims, are coming. Do we attract people to ask, to seek us out? Are we living for the sake of those outside the kingdom who are searching for truth?

In this story, Jesus engages in a verbal battle while being attentive to the other person. He is alert to moments of openness. Likewise, we need to live and dwell with people. I love academics and digging deeper into the faith. Yet we must be careful about complexity in life and testimony. Is there an intellectual ground we can use to reach Muslims? Undoubtedly. It is good to build bridges and to become closer to the other. This is, I believe, part of being faithful to God and seeking a harvest.

So what kind of message are we giving when we relate to the religious other? Is it sufficient to speak about ethical living and about kindness and goodness? Sometimes we need to take a stand on the message of Christ. We need to ask God to use everything about us to express the need for salvation to those with whom we engage.

6.2 Qur'an Case Study: Questions the Church Asks

This case study introduces some of the diverse views of the Qur'an held by Christians. It was constructed by the IMES team from the experiences of several people. The characters are fictitious, but the questions raised occur in many settings.

Muhammad was raised in a strict Muslim family, wherein he memorized the Qur'an and learned the basic foundations of Islam. Muhammad pursued his studies in Islam until he eventually became a preacher and a lecturer on Islam. After a period of researching and studying the Bible in order to prove that it is corrupted, Muhammad became a follower of Jesus Christ. He then decided to spend an extensive period of time studying the Bible.

During a Bible study group with other believers mainly from a Christian background, a conversation about Islam took place, specifically touching on the topic of the Qur'an. Samira, an evangelical Christian who regularly follows Christian television programs that speak negatively about Islam, shared what she had heard on one program that the Qur'an is demonic because it contains passages about killing and illicit sexual behavior that goes against humanity and the will of God. Samira went on to say that the God of Islam is indeed the devil because he orders his followers to kill.

There was silence for a few moments until Hakim, a devout Christian who occasionally attends the church, broke the silence by saying, "Not everything in the Qur'an is wrong. Why do you, Samira, say that?"

Samira replied in anger saying, "You, the Orthodox, are like Muslims in the way you think and worship!"

Then Samira turned to Muhammad and asked, "What do you think of the Qur'an and its content?"

Muhammad thought for a short period and then responded in defense of the Qur'an by questioning the Old Testament's inclusion of certain violent passages and events such as those in the book of Joshua. He also pointed to some other passages that are characterized by sexual imagery and language, such as in the Song of Songs. When Samira heard this, she got angry and responded aggressively to Muhammad, refusing to compare the Old Testament with the Qur'an. In her anger, Samira decided to leave the room. While the rest of the group tried to defend the Old Testament, Muhammad attempted to help them develop a fair reading of the Qur'an.

The next day, Muhammad received a phone call from one of the attendees, Milad, who asked Muhammad not to try to defend the Qur'an but to acknowledge its deceptive teaching. Milad further explained to Muhammad that his view of the Qur'an was leading Samira to question the legitimacy of his faith in Christ.

Questions for Discussion

1. Discuss the various perspectives about the Qur'an represented in the case study. Explain the motives behind each viewpoint. What

factors do you think influenced each participant with regard to their view of the Qur'an?

2. What in your opinion was Muhammad's goal in trying to compare the Old Testament to the Qur'an? Did his Islamic background influence his point of view concerning the Qur'an?

3. How do you explain Milad's request to Muhammad?

4. How do you explain Samira's questioning of Muhammad's faith in Christ because of his view of the Qur'an?

5. How might similar situations affect, positively or negatively, the practice of discipleship in the church?

6.3 Testimony 2: Amal Gendi on Ministry to Muslims in the West

interview by Emad Botros

Emad: We are two Egyptian men in conversation. Amal, do please introduce yourself.

Amal: I describe myself as Egyptian by birth, Canadian by choice and Christian by grace.

Emad: Well you might live in the West, but I understand that your work is focused on Arab people. Please summarize your portfolio of Christian ministry.

Amal: I work in education with a focus on discipleship and training for those from Muslim backgrounds. Above all, I long to equip local people as pastors within their communities. One emphasis has been on the Arabian Peninsula, which was the focus of my doctorate.[1] In Canada, I am active in teaching. I am also involved in raising awareness of Islam among Christians in Canada with the central message of "love your Muslim friend," urging people to explain the gospel to Muslims in the light of the fact that Islam is not all about killing people. Islam denies the reality of who Christ is; we must reach out with a message of hope to Muslims.

---

1. Amal Gendi, "Identifying and Addressing Barriers to the Discipleship of Believers from Muslim Background in the Arabian Peninsula" (doctoral diss., Tyndale University College and Seminary, 2015).

Emad: The case study above is based on a real event. What do you think of the characters?

Amal: Muhammad's behavior is natural, rooted in his tribal heritage: he responds to any attack on the Qur'an as an attack on himself. He cannot move beyond this reaction overnight. Is he challenging Christians here? This is his initial response. Samira appears superficial and heavily influenced by the media; she has not studied the Qur'an for herself. She attacks Muhammad and then leaves the room. In such scenarios, some people try to compromise while others try to be peacemakers. I want to discuss Hakim's approach without condemning him. In my opinion, it is better to ask questions than to make statements. Why? Because this is a route to dialogue, to engagement with the other in order to help them explore further. I handle the Bible passages about war by assisting people to explore the context as a route to understanding.[2] I encourage others to apply the same methodology to the Qur'an. I think that we should not be afraid of the Qur'an. It is the sacred text of Islam, and I believe that it is beneficial to us to study it.

Emad: How should we respond to the qur'anic passages that deny the divinity of Christ?

Amal: We might see them as demonic. Yet this does not detract from the other contents.

Emad: Do you use the Qur'an in your ministry?

Amal: My aim is to assist Muslims to explore truth. So one approach is to start with the Qur'an and then move to the Bible. One thing I find helpful is to use any reference to sacrifice as a bridge to Christ on the cross.

Emad: In the case study, Samira reacts strongly to Hakim's view of the Qur'an. She addresses him in a very negative, even derogatory tone.

Amal: We need to be careful in our use of the Qur'an. I make it clear that I handle it as the sacred text of another religion, but it is not the sacred text of my faith. Consequently, I do not regard it as divine revelation.

Emad: What do you think that the characters in the case study need the most?

---

2. *See section 2.5 above.*

Amal: Muhammad needs more spiritual growth and discipleship in order to be better equipped to use the Bible wisely. Samira needs to look at the Bible more deeply and be less influenced by stereotypes presented in the media. Milad, well, he spoke from his heart.

Emad: Can we discuss the role of the media in Western contexts in terms of demonization of Islam? Further, how might we critique similar presentations in the church?

Amal: I am not in favor of polemical approaches, although I do recognize that God can make use of such methods. The gospel is based on love, and a complete and full presentation must be centered on love. As Christians, we should be using media to present a positive message about Christ. Media are powerful, both Christian and otherwise, and many Christians are influenced by them. We must be aware of the negative, hateful view of Muslims that is presented by some. Jesus was compassionate with lay people but sharply rebuked many religious leaders. In a similar manner, we must distinguish between Islamic ideology and Muslims as people. We might critique the former, but we must always be loving toward Muslims as people.

Emad: Thank you for sharing with us.

6.4 The Honorable Qur'an: From Revelation to the Book

Issa Diab

The Qur'an is considered by Muslims as the word of God, revealed directly to Muhammad in Arabic, both literally and in substance. Accordingly, to all Muslims regardless of their sects and schools, the Qur'an is viewed as the primary source of doctrine, legislation and jurisprudence, as well as the ultimate reference in every issue pertaining to doctrine and conduct. Muslims likewise believe that the Qur'an in their possession today is the same as the one that was revealed to Muhammad, whether in its wording, text or content, with no alteration or modification whatsoever across the ages.

The Honorable Qur'an: An Overview

The Qur'an: the word of God sent down on his Prophet Muhammad and recorded in the *maṣāḥif* (plural of ***muṣḥaf***: "physical book"): "It is We who have sent down the Qur'an to you in gradual revelations" (*al-Insān* 76:23). The *Muḥiṭ al-Muḥiṭ* dictionary defines the Arabic word *Qur'an* as follows: "The Qur'an is the precious *tanzīl* (literally, sending down), made to precede, for its honor, what came before it in a simpler fashion." The words of God (May he be exalted!), which he sent down upon his Prophet, are referred to as the *kitāb*, the *qur'ān* and the *furqān*. *Qur'an* means "to bring together." It was so called because it grouped the sūras and combined them.

The Qur'an is composed of 114 sūras,[3] each encompassing an opening and an ending. The first sūra is entitled *al-Fātiḥa* (The Opening), and the last one is *an-Nās* (Humankind). Some of these sūras are long, such as *al-Baqara* (The Cow), comprising 286 verses, while others are short, such as *al-Fātiḥa* with seven verses. These sūras can be divided into two categories: the Meccan sūras, which were sent down upon Muhammad in Mecca before the migration to Medina in AD 622, and the Medinan sūras, which were given to Muhammad during his sojourn in Medina. There is no consensus as to the "ordering of the qur'anic sūras," whether it was divinely conceived or left to the discretion of the Prophet's Companions.[4] There are also diverse opinions concerning certain verses in Meccan sūras, which could be from the Medinan period, and vice versa.

A great number of verses and sūras were pronounced by Prophet Muhammad on specific occasions, referred to as **asbāb an-nuzūl** (the occasions of the revelation). Numerous Islamic books describe those "occasions." Sometimes sūras and verses would relate to personal situations, such as *Sūrat al-Masad* (The Palm Fiber, number 111), through which Prophet Muhammad addressed the situation of his uncle Abū Lahab and his wife.[5]

At other times, sūras were sent down to solve a problem or because Muhammad faced a deadlock and needed a way out. *Sūrat al-Anfāl* (The Spoils of War, number 8) is one such example, where a dispute and disagreement had

---

3. The sūra is a qur'anic passage comprising verses with an opening and an ending. The word *sūra* might mean "what has descended from an edifice," wherefore it meant to signify that the sūras of the Qur'an were split one from another. Moreover, according to the *Lisān al-'Arab* dictionary, the origin of the word "su'ra," with a softening of the glottal stop, might possibly mean "the remnant." Finally, a considerable number of Orientalists, Richard Bell and Charles Torrey, for instance, trace back the word sūra to Aramaic or Hebrew. The word itself appears in eight places in the Qur'an.

4. Abdallah Ibrahim Jalghoum, *The Wonder Miracle of the Ordering of the Suras and Verses of in the Honorable Qur'an* (Amman: n.p., 2005), cited from Arabic Wikipedia, at https://ar.wikipedia.org/wiki/سورة#cite_note-3.

5. "Doomed are the hands of Abū Lahab, and he is doomed too (1). His wealth and all that he gained would not help him (2). He will burn in a fire strongly glowing (3). And his wife as well, the carrier of firewood (4). Around her neck is a rope of palm fiber (5)."

arisen among the followers of Muhammad concerning the booty taken after the Battle of Badr.[6] Muslim scholars have developed a list of the sūras according to the chronology of their revelation. However, the Qur'an characteristically does not follow any topical or historical order. Its sūras, especially the longer ones, often comprise miscellaneous unrelated topics, even differing from the substance of the sūra itself or its title. We often find various parts of one of the prophets' stories told in several sūras with no chronological markers. The reader remains uninformed about which event of this prophet's story took place first and which came last. The reader may be helped in rearranging the events in the stories according to a logical order by going back to the Old Testament narratives and the extracanonical Jewish literature. Islamic literature labeled these references *Iṣrā'īliyyāt* (literally, Israelite stories).

Qur'anic interpreters often made use of these stories, causing some Muslim scholars and leaders to want to expunge the commentaries of them. The Qur'an was divided into seven parts in the days of the Prophet's Companions, who would complete their recitation in seven nights. The Qur'an was also organized into thirty sections, a division that aimed at facilitating memorization by determining specific portions for recitation and completion. This division is not mandatory but a matter of opinion, since there is no agreement as to where these sections and parts commence. This is why you will find various signs indicating quarters, eighths and parts, depending upon the milieus and the schools, as well as on specific versions and editions. Despite all of this, variations remain limited in number.

When reading the Qur'an, the reader ought to know the chronological order of the revelation of the verses, for if two verses are found handling the same judicial (and not doctrinal) topic but providing each a different ruling, the verse that was revealed last will abrogate the previous one. In other words, the later ruling annuls the earlier one and replaces it. This is what is known in qur'anic sciences as **an-nāsikh wa al-mansūkh** (literally, the abrogator and the abrogated), a process governed by complex rules that cannot possibly be studied in this summary.

Muslims believe that the Qur'an was sent down, both literally and in substance. In other words, both the Arabic wording and content of the verses are inspired. This is why Muslims consider that it is not the Qur'an itself which is "translated" from Arabic into other languages, but only its "meanings."

---

6. "They will ask you (Prophet) about the spoils of war. Say, 'This is a matter that will be dealt with by God and His Messenger.' So, remain mindful of God and settle your differences, and obey God and His Messenger if you are Believers" (1).

Translations are thus not considered true revealed Qur'ans from which commentaries may be derived.

The Honorable Qur'an: From Inspiration to Text

Prophet Muhammad did not produce the Qur'an in one shot, but rather over a span of twenty-three years (610–632), thirteen in Mecca (610–622) and ten in Medina (622–632), according to specific occasions called *asbāb an-nuzūl* (the occasions of the revelation). Muslims believe that the Qur'an *descended* in its entirety during the lifetime of Muhammad (570–632), some of the verses having been put down in writing, while a majority of them were kept by memorization "in the hearts of men."

The Qur'an went through three stages of composition before reaching us in the form we know today:

1. Inspiration and Memorization
2. Compilation and Putting into Writing
3. The *'Uthmānic* Qur'an

The Stage of Inspiration and Memorization

The stage of inspiration, *waḥī*, began when Muhammad b. 'Abdallah was in spiritual seclusion at Mount Ḥirā' in AD 610. According to *Sūrat al-'Alaq* (The Clot, number 96), the angel Gabriel made him hear the following words of God:

> Recite in the name of your Lord who created (1), created the human being from a clinging substance (2). Recite, and your Lord is the most Generous (3), Who taught by the pen (4). He taught the human being that which he knew not (5).

It is at that point that Muhammad understood he was a prophet and that God was sending him to his people. At first, the revelation would stop, then resume, until it finally became continuous throughout the life of Muhammad.[7] The longest period of time in which the *waḥī* ceased occurred after the death of Waraqa b. Nawfal. Muslims believe that Prophet Muhammad used to listen to

---

7. The revelation to the Prophet Muhammad (Peace be upon him!) became lukewarm [in the sense of got interrupted] twice: once at the beginning of the revelation, a pause followed by the *coming down* of *Sūrat al-Muddathir* (The Enrobed), and a second time after the *coming down* of several qur'anic sūras. With *Sūrat aḍ-Ḍuḥa* (The Morning Light), the inspiration resumed, not to be interrupted again.

the verses, then recite them to his Companions. After that, the verses and sūras of the Qur'an would be written on vellum and palm fronds, and memorized in the hearts of men. The process of recording was done by men known as the *waḥī* scribes.

Among the most prominent of these scribes was Zayd b. Thābit, who was entrusted with the collection of the qur'anic text during the rule of the first caliph, Abū Bakr aṣ-Ṣiddīq. It would seem that some of these scribes were of Christian, Jewish or pagan origins. After having recorded the Qur'an for Muhammad, they apparently recanted Islam and turned back to their kinsfolk, as reported in a Hadith narrated by Muslim Ibn al-Ḥajjāj.[8] It is important to note that the Islamic sources do not mention the size of those qur'anic materials recorded on vellum and palm fronds, nor of those that remained memorized in the hearts of men during the lifetime of Prophet Muhammad. In any case, memorization seems to have remained the prevailing means by which the Qur'an had spread among people. This became the main motivation for the collection of the Qur'an in written form, as we shall see later, following the death of most of the Qur'an's memorizers during the Battle of Yamama in AD 632, under the rule of Caliph Abu Bakr aṣ-Ṣiddīq, when Muslims feared the loss and disappearance of the Qur'an.

---

8. Abu Muʿammar reported that Abdul-Wārith reported that Abdul-Azīz reported what Anas (May God be pleased with him!) said:

> There was a Christian [from the Banī Najjār tribe, according to Muslim Ibn al-Hajjāj] who embraced Islam and read the Sūras al-Baqara and Āl-ʿImrān, and he used to write (the revelations) for the Prophet. Later on, he returned to Christianity again and he used to say: "Muhammad knows nothing but what I have written for him." Then Allah caused him to die [according to Muslims, God severed his head from his body] and the people buried him, but in the morning, they saw that the earth had thrown his body out. They [the man's family] said: "This is the act of Muhammad and his companions. They dug the grave of our companion and took his body out of it because he had run away from them." They again dug the grave deeply for him, but in the morning, they again saw that the earth had thrown his body out. They said, "This is an act of Muhammad and his companions. They dug the grave of our companion and threw his body outside it, for he had run away from them." They dug the grave for him as deep as they could, but in the morning, they again saw that the earth had thrown his body out. So, they believed that what had befallen him was not done by human beings and had to leave him thrown (on the ground).

Al-Bukhārī, 61, "Virtues and Merits of the Prophet (PBUH) and His Companions," Part 4, 545, narrated by Anas, quoted with minor additions from Sunnah.com, https://sunnah.com/bukhari/61/124.

The Stage of Compilation

A Hadith from *Ṣaḥīḥ al-Bukhārī* tells us that it was the first caliph, Abū Bakr aṣ-Ṣiddīq (632–634) who, strongly urged by ʿUmar Ibn al-Khaṭṭāb, worked on compiling the sūras and verses of the Qur'an. His endeavor saw the light in 632, after the Battle of Yamama between the Muslim army and the Renegades, in which a great number of Qur'an memorizers were killed.[9] *Ṣaḥīḥ al-Bukhārī* reports that ʿUmar Ibn al-Khaṭṭāb, one of the Companions, exhorted Abū Bakr to send for Zayd b. Thābit, one of the scribes of the Qur'an from Muhammad's lifetime. When this Zayd b. Thābit arrived, Abū Bakr disclosed to him the fierceness of the Battle of Yamama that had led to a great number of casualties among the Qur'an memorizers, and expressed his concern that parts of the Qur'an might get lost. Then Abū Bakr ordered Zayd to compile the Qur'an.

---

9. From Ṣaḥīḥ al-Bukhārī: Mūsa b. Ismāʿīl reported that Ibrāhīm b. Saʿīd reported that Ibn Shihāb reported that ʿUbayd b. as-Sibāq reported that Zayd b. Thābit (May God be pleased with him!) said:

> 'Abū Bakr aṣ-Ṣiddīq sent for me ... and found ʿUmar Ibn al-Khaṭṭāb sitting with him. Abū Bakr then said [May God be pleased with him!]: "ʿUmar has come to me and said: 'Casualties were heavy among the *Qurrāʾ* [reciters] of the Qur'an on the day of the Battle of Yamama, and I am afraid that more heavy casualties may take place among the *Qurrāʾ* on other battlefields, whereby a large part of the Qur'an may be lost. Therefore, I suggest you (Abū Bakr) order that the Qur'an be collected.' I said to ʿUmar: 'How can you do something which Allah's Apostle did not do?' ʿUmar said: 'By Allah, that is a good project.' ʿUmar kept on urging me to accept his proposal until Allah opened my chest [He convinced me] for it and I began to realize the good in the idea which ʿUmar had realized." Then 'Abū Bakr said (to me). "You are a wise young man and we do not have any suspicion about you, and you used to write the Divine Inspiration for Allah's Messenger [May God bless him and keep him!]. So, you should search for (the fragmentary scripts of) the Qur'an and collect it in one book." By Allah, If they had ordered me to shift one of the mountains, it would not have been heavier for me than this ordering me to collect the Qur'an. Then I said to Abū Bakr: "How will you do something which Allah's Messenger [May God bless him and keep him!] did not do?" Abū Bakr replied: "By Allah, it is a good project." Abū Bakr kept on urging me to accept his idea until Allah opened my chest for what He had opened the chests of Abū Bakr and ʿUmar. So, I started looking for the Qur'an and collecting it from (what was written on) palme stalks, thin white stones and also from the men who knew it by heart, until I found the last Verse of *Sūrat at-Tawba* (Repentance) with Abū Khuzayma al-Anṣarī, and I did not find it with anybody other than him. The Verse is: "Verily there has come unto you an Apostle (Muhammad) from amongst yourselves. It grieves him that you should receive an injury or difficulty ... (till the end of *Sūrat Barāʾa* [v. 128, alternative name for *Sūrat* at-Tawba]). Then the completed manuscripts (copy) of the Qur'an remained with Abū Bakr until he died, then with ʿUmar until the end of his life, and then with Ḥafṣa, the daughter of ʿUmar [May God be pleased with both of them].

Al-Bukhārī, 66, "Virtues of the Qur'an," Part 6, 415, quoted with editing from Sunnah.com, https://sunnah.com/bukhari/66/8.

After some hesitation on the part of the latter, due to the absence of a clear command from the Prophet of God to do so, Zayd yielded to Abu Bakr's insistence and started tracing the sūras and verses, collecting the text from palm fronds, stones and the hearts of men (those parts orally memorized). Thus as reported by the above mentioned Hadith, "the books remained in the possession of Abu Bakr until he died. Then, they were kept by ʿUmar for the rest of his life, and then they were preserved by Ḥafṣa, the daughter of ʿUmar [one of the wives of Muhammad], may God be pleased with both of them." Based on this Hadith, the Qu'ran seems to have been compiled during the caliphate of Abū Bakr aṣ-Ṣiddīq, then entrusted to Caliph ʿUmar Ibn al-Khaṭṭāb (634–644), to be finally committed to Ḥafṣa, daughter of ʿUmar and wife of Muhammad.

The Book, or Muṣḥaf, of Ḥafṣa, daughter of ʿUmar

Ḥafṣa became the "keeper of the Qur'an," which remained under her custody despite all the tribulations that the Islamic State went through, up to the time of Muʿāwiya. Certain sources ascertain that it only left her house twice, whereas others speak of one occasion only. The first time occurred when ʿUthmān, revolted by the many ways of its recitation, borrowed it to make his own copy. The second time, other sources say, occurred when it was burned at the hand the governor of Medina, then ʿAbd al-Malik b. Marwān. Some sources also report that this copy was returned to Ḥafṣa after it was used to make ʿUthmān's *Muṣḥaf*, at which point it remained in her house until her death during the month of Shaʿbān, in the year 41 of the **Hijra**, at the beginning of Muʿāwiya b. Abī-Sufyān's caliphate. Before dying, she had bequeathed it to her devout and pious brother, ʿAbdallah b. ʿUmar. We do not possess any certified information concerning the destiny of Ḥafṣa's *Muṣḥaf*.

The Muṣḥaf of Ali b. Abī Ṭālib

The Shiʿite Imāmiyya sect believes that Imam Ali b. Abī Ṭālib was dictated the Qur'an by the Apostle of Islam, Muhammad. However, its members disagree on its content. Some believe that the copy was seventy cubits long, containing every legal judgment people needed, and was called the "Collection." Others, however, claim that it contained the qur'anic text as collected and organized by Imam Ali. The *Muṣḥaf* of Ali is no longer extant, and tales affirm that he hid it from people. Other sayings certify that the imam approved of ʿUthmān's *Muṣḥaf* upon its publication.

In 2011, Turkish scholar Tayyar Altıkulaç published an exact reproduction of the *Muṣḥaf* attributed to Ali b. Abī Ṭālib in Ṣanʿā' under the title *The*

Honorable Muṣḥaf Attributed to Ali b. Abī Ṭālib: The Ṣanʿāʾ Version. This *Muṣḥaf* contains 86 percent of the qurʾanic text.[10]

The Muṣḥaf *of Abdallah b. Masʿūd*

Abdallah b. Masʿūd was an exception among the Qurʾan scribes; he worked hard on the writing and collection of the qurʾanic text in an eponymous book, *The Muṣḥaf of Ibn Masʿūd*. It is clear that at the time when Ḥafṣa's *Muṣḥaf* had not been in circulation yet, Ibn Masʿūd's was the most widespread, particularly among the people of Iraq. In reaction to ʿUthmān's initiative to unify the various versions into a single one – the *Muṣḥaf* of ʿUthmān, which was copied from that of Ḥafṣa, Abdallah b. Masʿūd violently opposed him, especially since Zayd b. Thābit had been the one who had both compiled the Qurʾan under Abu Bakr and copied the *Maṣāḥif* under ʿUthmān. In Ibn Masʿūd's words, Zayd had been in his father's loins at the time when he himself had received the Qurʾan from the very mouth of the Prophet and written it down in his *Muṣḥaf*.

A major crisis broke out between Ibn Masʿūd and Caliph ʿUthmān b. ʿAffān. The latter used his authority as governor, while the former took advantage of his influence and prestige among Muslims, having been the "Reciter of the Prophet." Ibn Masʿūd clung to his *Muṣḥaf* and, upon ʿUthmān's command that all diverging qurʾanic copies should be burned, urged those around him to hide their copies before the caliph could take hold of them. Ever since that episode, there has been great interest among historians to examine Ibn Masʿūd's *Muṣḥaf* in order to discover any variants between his *Muṣḥaf* and ʿUthmān's, contained primarily in various semantic and syntactic differences that appear in a number of qurʾanic verses in Ibn Masʿūd's *Muṣḥaf*. More critically, some scholars allege that Ibn Masʿūd's *Muṣḥaf* discarded two sūras found in ʿUthmān's recension (the sūras of *al-Falaq*, The Daybreak, and *an-Nās*, Humankind), on the claim that they did not belong in the Qurʾan. This issue is worth pondering and discussing.

Ibn Masʿūd was the Prophet's closest Companion and used to receive the Qurʾan from his mouth and write it down in a *Muṣḥaf* named after him, "The *Muṣḥaf* of Abdallah Ibn Masʿūd." This fact raises a serious question as to why the three Rightly Guided Caliphs – Abu Bakr, ʿUmar and ʿUthmān – did not refer back to him when they decided to collect, unify, and copy the qurʾanic text.

---

10. For photos of the document, see "The Qurʾan of Ali b. Abī Ṭālib (The Sanʿāʾ Muṣḥaf)," from first/second century of the Hijra, https://ar.wikipedia.org/wiki/ع.

The Muṣḥaf of Ubayy b. Kaʿb

Ubayy b. Kaʿb was one of the Prophet's supporters (**Anṣār**) who protected him upon his migration to Medina.[11] It is said that he was among those who penned the treaty with the Jerusalemites (Ibn Kathīr 2:322). He also became an expert in collecting the *waḥī* material, and it is said that he was one of four to whom Muhammad referred his followers when they needed advice on qurʾanic issues. In other words, his authority in qurʾanic matters was greater than that of Ibn Masʿūd. He was known as the Master Reciter, and we are told that the Prophet himself praised him as "the Master Reciter of my *Umma*," acknowledging that God had commanded him to listen to Ubayy's recitation of parts of the revelation. This means that Ubayy was the recipient of materials of a judicial nature and was asked by the Prophet to recite them to him from time to time. Arthur Jeffrey noted that we do not know exactly when Ubayy's *Muṣḥaf* was collected, but there is some inconclusive evidence that it was in circulation in Syria before the appearance of ʿUthmān's textus receptus. Jeffrey also notes that Ibn Abī Dāwud narrated how some Syrians had produced a *Muṣḥaf* which they brought to Medina for examination with Ubayy. Though the standard text was already in use, no one dared to refute Ubayy's variant readings. It appears that he played an active role in the production process of ʿUthmān's textus receptus in Medina. His name appears at different levels in these stories, but the narrative itself is so corrupt that it does not provide us with accurate information on his contribution.[12]

The Stage of Production of ʿUthmān's Qurʾan

Abu Bakr's work constituted the first stage in the fixing of the qurʾanic text, a recension that came to be known as ʿUthmān's *Muṣḥaf*. The following phase would prove to be determinant and occurred under the caliphate of ʿUthmān b. ʿAffān (644–662) who, according to a Hadith from *Ṣaḥīḥ al-Bukhārī*, played an essential role in providing Muslims with a unified qurʾanic text.

The above mentioned Hadith states that Muslims, during their conquest of Armenia and Azerbaijan, were overheard repeating qurʾanic verses in differing readings and Arabic dialects. The one having overheard them ran to Caliph ʿUthmān and told him: "O Commander of the Faithful, give knowledge to

---

[11]. Among the sources that contain his biography are an-Nawawī, 140–141; *The Tabaqāt* of Ibn al-Jazrī, no. 131; Ibn Saʿad, 3, 2, 59–62; *Usd al-Ghāba*, 1, 49–50; *The Iṣāba* of Ibn Ḥajar, 1, 30–32; *Tahdhīb at-Tahdhīb*, 1, 187–188.

[12]. Arthur Jeffery, *Materials for the History of the Text of the Qurʾan: The Old Codices* (Leiden: Brill, 1937).

this nation before they fight over the Book as the Jews and Christians did over theirs." In other words, hasten and save the Islamic nation from the danger of variant readings of the Qur'an, this snare into which Jews and Christians fell. Following this appeal, 'Uthmān asked Ḥafṣa, daughter of 'Umar and wife of the Prophet Muhammad, to send him Zayd b. Thābit, Abdallah b. al-Zubayr and other scribes with the qur'anic texts collected during Abu Bakr's caliphate and entrusted thereafter to her. When these came with Ḥafṣa's *Muṣḥafs*, 'Uthmān required they copied them into one volume, that is, the whole of the Qur'an in the dialect of Quraysh, because the Qur'an had been sent down in that very same dialect. Once they had completed their work, 'Uthmān gave the books back to Ḥafṣa, then sent a copy of the unified Qur'an to every corner of the lands under Muslim control, so that there would be one and the same Qur'an read by all people. He then commanded that the version of the Qur'an he sent be adopted and every other *Muṣḥaf* burned. What happened then to all the aforementioned *Muṣḥafs*?

As far as Ḥafṣa's is concerned, the stories are conflicting; some claim it was burned, others that it was returned to Ḥafṣa who, in turn, entrusted it to her brother before her death. As for Ali's *Muṣḥaf*, we do not possess any information, apart from the fact that Imam Ali consented to 'Uthmān's.

The critical problem lies with Ibn Masʿūd's Qur'an. When 'Uthmān b. 'Affān had the extant *Muṣḥafs* burned after confirming his as the sole legitimate one, Ibn Masʿūd fiercely opposed his decision and spoke of the greater legitimacy of his Islam over that of Zayd b. Thābit, who had been charged to redact the *Muṣḥafs*. As narrated by Ibn Kathīr in his work entitled *Al-Bidāya wa an-Nihāya* (*The Beginning and the End*), Ibn Masʿūd ordered his companions to hide their *Muṣḥafs*, citing God's words (May he be exalted!): "And whoever deceives [here understood as hides something] will be faced with his deceit [what he has hidden] on the Resurrection Day" (*Āl-ʿImrān* 3:161). However, 'Uthmān (May God be pleased with him!) is said to have invited him by letter to follow the Companions' decision as to the recension adopted and their rejection of any conflict for the sake of all. This appeal seemingly led Ibn Masʿūd to repentance and paying allegiance to the common cause, thereby putting an end to the dispute (May God be pleased with all of them!). In reality, however, Ibn Kathīr's narrative contradicts general knowledge about the fact that 'Uthmān had Ibn Masʿūd brought and beaten until his ribs were broken, then he deprived him of his stipend because he clung to his *Muṣḥaf*. It is also attested that Ibn Masʿūd's *Muṣḥaf* remained both in the possession of the people of Kūfa and in circulation. All scholars who have studied the history of the collection of the Honorable Qur'an have noted a remarkable number of variants in Ibn Masʿūd's *Muṣḥaf* when compared to that of ʿUthmān.

The Honorable Qur'an and Textual Criticism

We deduce from the above that it is difficult, if not impossible, to reconstruct the history of the qur'anic text before the production of ʿUthmān's Qur'an for the following reasons:

1. The absence of manuscripts dating back to that epoch.
2. The contradictions among stories told by Islamic sources.
3. The nebulous state of the Arabic language at this particular phase of its development.

Scholars who have worked on the reconstruction of the Qur'an's history through textual criticism, such as Nöldeke and Jeffery, have questioned the authenticity of the Islamic version on the genesis of the qur'anic *Muṣḥaf*. They subsequently worked on the variants in these stories, since they did not possess any manuscript at hand whose content contradicted the current qur'anic text. However, the discovery of the Birmingham and the Ṣanʿāʾ manuscripts offers us a new perspective in the study of the qur'anic text.

The Birmingham Qur'an Manuscript

The oldest manuscript of a qur'anic text that we currently have in our possession is the Birmingham Qur'an Manuscript. It consists of two pages of the Honorable Qur'an found at the University of Birmingham. A radiocarbon test determined it was 1,370 years old, which makes it one of the oldest copies of the *Muṣḥaf* in the world. While studying elements of a collection of Middle Eastern manuscripts in the context of her doctoral research, Alba Fedeli came across two previously unidentified pages of a *Muṣḥaf* dating back to the seventh century. She organized their radiocarbon examination in a radiocarbon data analysis unit at the University of Oxford; with an accuracy percentage of 95.4, the manuscript was estimated to date back to the years 568 to 645.[13]

---

13. Photos of the document may be found at "Manuscript of the Qur'an at the University of Birmingham," https://en.wikipedia.org/wiki/Birmingham_Quran_manuscript.

This means that the manuscript was written by a contemporary of Muhammad whose prophetic period spanned 610 to 632.[14]

Dr Wali, an eminent British Library expert in Persian and Turkish manuscripts, stated: "We know that these two folios, in a beautiful and surprisingly legible Hijazi hand, almost certainly date from the time of the first three Caliphs."[15] The Hijazi script is one of the Arabic scripts used to write down the Qur'an in the first century of the Hijra, thus proving the Birmingham document to be one of the oldest copies of the Qur'an in the world. Dr Wali also affirmed: "The discovery of this manuscript, with its beautiful and downright content, as well as its excitingly clear Hijazi script, constitutes news that will bring joy to the heart of Muslims."[16]

The manuscript consists of two pages of the Honorable *Muṣḥaf*. The first one includes verses 22 to 31 of *Sūrat al-Kahf* (The Cave). The second one comprises two separate sections of text. The first section consists of the last five verses of *Sūrat Maryam* (Mary), while the second section of the same page contains the beginning verses of *Sūrat Ṭā Hā*. This manuscript confirms that at least some portions of the Qur'an were written close to the lifetime of Prophet Muhammad, contrary to previous beliefs that the Qur'an was collected and expanded after the death of the Noble Prophet.

The Ṣanʿāʾ Manuscripts

Excavation works in the Great Mosque in Ṣanʿāʾ, Yemen, during the 1970s uncovered a considerable number of qur'anic manuscripts dating back to the first century of the Hijra.[17] The construction of the Great Mosque goes back to the sixth year of the Hijra, when Prophet Muhammad (May God bless and keep him!), charged one of his companions to build it. The Mosque witnessed several expansions in the course of its history which were carried out by Muslim governors and imams.

In the year 1385 of the Hijra (AD 1965), heavy rains in Ṣanʿāʾ caused damage to the northwestern corner of the mosque's ceiling. During the exploratory

---

14. Katharine Lackey, "Quran Dating Back to the Time of Mohammed Dated," USA Today, 22 July 2015, https://www.usatoday.com/story/news/world/2015/07/22/old-quran-manscript-found-united-kingdom/30509965/.

15. Dr Wali quoted in Lackey, "Quran Dating Back."

16. *Note from the editors: see the following with due note that the contributor wrote the text based on sources in Arabic and that the referenced source uses a different transliteration for some cited quotes; https://eu.usatoday.com/story/news/world/2015/07/22/old-quran-manscript-found-united-kingdom/30509965/.*

17. For photos of the documents, see "The Ṣanʿāʾ Manuscript," https://en.wikipedia.org/wiki/Sanaa_manuscript.

Thinking Biblically about the Qur'an 229

works, a big chest was found containing thousands of qur'anic and historical manuscripts. In 1979, upon the request of the magistrate Ismāʿīl al-Akwaʿ, then director of the Yemeni Department of Antiquities, Germany agreed to help in the restoration and maintenance of the manuscripts. The project cost 2.2 million German marks. It was launched in 1983 and carried through until 1996, a span of time during which the team was able to restore 15,000 qur'anic pages out of the 40,000 discovered manuscripts. Of the former, 12,000 were qur'anic vellum parchment which were opened, cleaned, treated, categorized and assembled. The Ṣanʿāʾ collection consists of around 4,500 qur'anic manuscripts and parchments written in Kufic and Hijazi scripts as well as in other non-pointed scripts, and some of these manuscripts are considered among the oldest extant qur'anic texts.

Among a number of historical manuscripts, a palimpsest (manuscript with two layers dating back to two different periods) was discovered in the Great Mosque of Old Ṣanʿāʾ in 1972 and was dated back to the first Islamic centuries. It is believed that some of this palimpsest may have been written by Ali b. Abī Ṭālib himself.[18]

The manuscript's visible upper layer corresponds to the standard qur'anic text (ʿUthmān's *Muṣḥaf*), whereas the lower subjacent text (underneath and indistinct) contains numerous variants from the textus receptus. A copy of the subjacent text was published in 2012. With 99 percent accuracy, the radiocarbon test dated the antique parchment to AD 671.[19] The order of the sūras is identical to that of our modern copies of the Honorable Qur'an.

These manuscripts are still under study. Some preliminary results allow us to think that there are variants between the *Muṣḥafs* that preceded ʿUthmān's recension, on one hand, and ʿUthmān's *Muṣḥaf* itself on the other. The following table shows some of these variants, as revealed by the lower text of the palimpsest.[20]

---

18. Geoffrey Roper, ed., *World Survey of Islamic Manuscripts*, Vol. 3 (London: Al-Furqan Islamic Heritage Foundation, 1992).

19. Behnam Sadeghi and Uwe Bergmann, "The Codex of a Companion of the Prophet and the Qur'an of the Prophet," *Arabica* 57 (2010): 353.

20. See https://en.wikipedia.org/wiki/Sanaa_manuscript. *Note from the editors: the material for this table and the one in Wikipedia is based on Behnam Sadeghi and Mohsen Goudarzi, "Ṣanʿāʾ 1 and the Origins of the Qurʾān," (Walter de Gruyter, 2012), 41–129, https://bible-quran.com/wp-content/uploads/2013/01/Sadeghi-Goudarzi-sana-Origins-of-the-Quran.pdf.*

Location	Visible Traces	Reconstruction	Standard Text
Qur'an al-Baqara 2:191 Stanford folio, recto, l. 4, p. 44	د لک ح / مں/لو کح	حتى ىٯىلو کم	حَتَّىٰ يُقَٰتِلُوكُمْ فِيهِ
Qur'an al-Baqara 2:191 Stanford folio, recto, l. 5, p. 44	د لک جر ا الکعر ىں	دلک جزاء الکافرىں	كَذَٰلِكَ جَزَآءُ ٱلْكَٰفِرِينَ
Qur'an al-Baqara 2:192 Stanford folio, recto, l. 5, p. 44	ا ىىر (ه) و	اىىهو	ٱنتَهَوْا۟
Qur'an al-Baqara 2:193 Stanford folio, recto, l. 6, p. 44	حىا	حىا	حَتَّىٰ
Qur'an al-Baqara 2:193 Stanford folio, recto, l. 7, p. 44	و ىکو ں ا لد ىں کلـه لرا[ل]	و ىکون الدىں کله لله	وَيَكُونَ ٱلدِّينُ لِلَّهِ
Qur'an al-Baqara 2:194 Stanford folio, recto, l. 10, p. 44	و مں اعىدى	و مں اعىدى	فَمَنِ ٱعْتَدَىٰ
Qur'an al-Baqara 2:194 Stanford folio, recto, l. 11, p. 44	ڡا عدٮ و	فاعىدو	فَٱعْتَدُوا۟
Qur'an al-Baqara 2:194 Stanford folio, recto, l. 11, p. 44	ما اعىد ى علىکم ٮه	ما اعىدى علىکم ٮه	مَا ٱعْتَدَىٰ عَلَيْكُمْ
Qur'an al-Baqara 2:196 Stanford folio, recto, l. 17, p. 44	ڡم//ٮسر من الهد ى	ڡما ٮٮسر من الهدى	فَمَا ٱسْتَيْسَرَ مِنَ ٱلْهَدْىِ
Qur'an al-Baqara 2:196 Stanford folio, recto, l. 17, p. 44	و لا ٮحلٯو ا	و لا ٮحلٯوا	وَلَا تَحْلِقُوا۟ رُءُوسَكُمْ

Thinking Biblically about the Qur'an 231

Location	Visible Traces	Reconstruction	Standard Text
Qur'an al-Baqara 2:196 Stanford folio, recto, l. 18, p. 44	و ا ن كا ن ا حد ملكم	فإن كان أحدٌ مِنكُم	فَمَن كَانَ مِنكُم
Qur'an al-Baqara 2:196 Stanford folio, recto, l. 19, p. 45	ڡد ٮه	فَديَةٌ	فَفِديَةٌ
Qur'an al-Baqara 2:196 Stanford folio, recto, l. 20, p. 45	من صىم او نسك	مِن صِيَامٍ أَو نُسُكٍ	مِّن صِيَامٍ أَوْ صَدَقَةٍ أَوْ نُسُكٍ
Qur'an al-Baqara 2:209 David 86/2003 folio, recto, l. 5, p. 46	(ما)ح[ا]كم الر(ه) [ك] ؟	مِن بَعدِ ما جاءَكُم الهُدى	مِّن بَعْدِ مَا جَاءَتْكُمُ الْبَيِّنَاتُ
Qur'an al-Baqara 2:210 David 86/2003 folio, recto, l. 6, p. 46	هل د/ىطر (و ن) ا لا ا ں ٮا ٮٮكم ا شه ؟	هَل تَنظُرونَ الهُدى أَن يأتيَكُمُ اللهُ	هَلْ يَنظُرُونَ إِلَّا أَن يَأْتِيَهُمُ اللَّهُ
Qur'an al-Baqara 2:211 David 86/2003 folio, recto, l. 9, p. 46	العوٮ	العِقابِ	الْعِقَابِ
Qur'an al-Baqara 2:213 David 86/2003 folio, recto, l. 12, p. 46	ڡا ا (س)ل الله	فَأَرسَلَ اللهُ	فَبَعَثَ اللَّهُ
Qur'an al-Baqara 2:213 David 86/2003 folio, recto, l. 13, p. 46	لٮحكمو ا ٮٮں الىا س	لِيَحكُمو بَينَ النّاسِ	لِيَحْكُمَ بَيْنَ النَّاسِ
Qur'an al-Baqara 2:213 David 86/2003 folio, recto, l. 15, p. 46	ا لٮ(ٮ)ٮٮٮ	البَيِّناتُ	الْبَيِّنَاتُ بَغْيًا بَيْنَهُمْ
Qur'an al-Baqara 2:214 David 86/2003 folio, recto, l. 17, p. 46	ا (حس)ٮٮم	حَسِبتُم	أَمْ حَسِبْتُمْ

232　The Religious Other

Location	Visible Traces	Reconstruction	Standard Text
Qurʾan *al-Baqara* 2:214 David 86/2003 folio, recto, l. 17, p. 46	ا الـ[ـد]ٮ(ں)(ﻫ)[ﻢ]لـكم	الَّذِينَ مِن قَبْلِكُم	الَّذِينَ خَلَوْا مِن قَبْلِكُم
Qurʾan *al-Baqara* 2:214 David 86/2003 folio, recto, l. 18, p. 47	ا لٮٮا	الْأَنْبَاءُ	الْأَنْبَاءُ
Qurʾan *al-Baqara* 2:215 David 86/2003 folio, recto, l. 20, p. 47	ٮـسا لو ٮک	يَسْأَلُونَكَ	يَسْأَلُونَكَ
Qurʾan *al-Baqara* 2:217 David 86/2003 folio, recto, l. 25, p. 47	[و] عں الـسٮهر الحر(م) وعں ٯٮل ڡٮه	عَنِ الشَّهْرِ الْحَرَامِ وَعَنْ قَتْلٍ فِيهِ	عَنِ الشَّهْرِ الْحَرَامِ قِتَالٍ فِيهِ
Qurʾan *al-Baqara* 2:217 David 86/2003 folio, recto, l. 26, p. 47	ں/[و](ﺻ)[د] عں/ ا ـ/ ـ ؛	[وَصَدٌّ19] عَن سَبِيلِ اللَّهِ	وَصَدٌّ عَن سَبِيلِ اللَّهِ وَكُفْرٌ بِهِ
Qurʾan *Hūd* 11:105 Folio 4, recto, l. 1, p. 51	؛{------} ا مں (لا) ا	إِلَّا مَنْ أَذِنَ لَهُ	إِلَّا بِإِذْنِهِ
Qurʾan *Hūd* 11:122 Folio 4, verso, l. 4, p. 52	؛{------}/ا[ٮ]ـ(ﺻ)/ ا/ ا	إِنَّا مَعَكُم مُّنتَظِرُونَ	إِنَّا مُنتَظِرُونَ
Qurʾan *al-Anfāl* 8:2 Folio 4, verso, l. 12, p. 52	ڡر ٯٮ	فَرِقَتْ	وَجِلَتْ
Qurʾan *al-Anfāl* 8:2 Folio 4, verso, l. 13, p. 52	ا ٮـاٮـ(ـه)	آيَاتُهُ	آيَاتُهُ
Qurʾan *at-Tawba* 9:122 Folio 22, recto, l. 3, p. 62	ما[ك]ا ں	مَا كَانَ	وَمَا كَانَ

Thinking Biblically about the Qur'an   233

Location	Visible Traces	Reconstruction	Standard Text
Qur'an *at-Tawba* 9:122 Folio 22, recto, l. 4, p. 62	من كل ما	مِنْ كُلِّ أُمَّةٍ	مِنْ كُلِّ فِرْقَةٍ
Qur'an *at-Tawba* 9:124 Folio 22, recto, l. 9, p. 62	و ا د ا ا ىر ل	وَإِذَا أَنْزَلَتْ	وَإِذَا مَا أُنْزِلَتْ
Qur'an *at-Tawba* 9:125 Folio 22, recto, l. 12, p. 62	فى قلو ٮهم ر حس	فِي قُلُوبِهِمْ رِجْسٌ	فِي قُلُوبِهِمْ مَرَضٌ
Qur'an *at-Tawba* 9:125 Folio 22, recto, l. 13, p. 62	ر حر ا الى ر حس[ه]م	رِجْزًا إِلَى رِجْسِهِمْ	رِجْسًا إِلَى رِجْسِهِمْ
Qur'an *at-Tawba* 9:125 Folio 22, recto, l. 13, p. 62	و ما ٮو ا و هم ڡٮسڡ[و]ں	وَمَاتُوا وَهُمْ فَاسِقُونَ	وَمَاتُوا وَهُمْ كَافِرُونَ
Qur'an *at-Tawba* 9:126 Folio 22, recto, l. 13, p. 62	ا ىر و // [و] ا	أَوَلَا يَرَوْا	أَوَلَا يَرَوْنَ
Qur'an *at-Tawba* 9:126 Folio 22, recto, l. 15, p. 62	و لا ٮٮ[د]ٮكر و ں	وَلَا يَتَذَكَّرُونَ	وَلَا هُمْ يَذَّكَّرُونَ
Qur'an *at-Tawba* 9:127 Folio 22, recto, l. 15, p. 62	و ا د ا ٮ(ا)ٮر [ٮ]	وَإِذَا أَنْزَلَتْ	وَإِذَا مَا أُنْزِلَتْ
Qur'an *at-Tawba* 9:127 Folio 22, recto, l. 16, p. 62	هل ٮر ں	هَلْ يَرَاكَ	هَلْ يَرَاكُمْ
Qur'an *at-Tawba* 9:127 Folio 22, recto, l. 17, p. 62	ا (ٮ)ا ٮصر ڡو	فَانْصَرَفُوا	ثُمَّ انْصَرَفُوا

Location	Visible Traces	Reconstruction	Standard Text
Qur'an *at-Tawba* 9:127 Folio 22, recto, l. 17, p. 62	فصر ف الله	فَصَرَفَ ٱللَّهُ	صَرَفَ ٱللَّهُ
Qur'an *at-Tawba* 9:127 Folio 22, recto, l. 17, p. 62	لا ٯو م (ه) [ح]/(ٮ)ٮڡهو ں	ذَلِكَ بِأَنَّهُمْ قَوْمٌ لَا يَفْقَهُونَ	بِأَنَّهُمْ قَوْمٌ لَا يَفْقَهُونَ
Qur'an *at-Tawba* 9:128 Folio 22, recto, l. 18, p. 62	و لـﺪ حاـكم	وَلَقَدْ جَاءَكُمْ	لَقَدْ جَاءَكُمْ
Qur'an *at-Tawba* 9:128 Folio 22, recto, l. 19, p. 63	ر سو ل مں(ﻛ)ـم	رَسُولٌ مِنْكُمْ	رَسُولٌ مِنْ أَنْفُسِكُمْ
Qur'an *at-Tawba* 9:128 Folio 22, recto, l. 19, p. 63	عر ٮر (ع)لـ(ٮ)ـ(ه) ما عٮٮكم	عَزِيزٌ عَلَيْهِ مَا عَنِتُّمْ	عَزِيزٌ عَلَيْهِ مَا عَنِتُّمْ
Qur'an *at-Tawba* 9:129 Folio 22, recto, l. 20, p. 63	ڡا (ں)ٮو لو ا	فَإِنْ تَوَلَّوْا عَنْكَ	فَإِنْ تَوَلَّوْا
Qur'an *at-Tawba* 9:129 Folio 22, recto, l. 21, p. 63	هو لا ا(لـ)ـى ا	الَّذِي لَا إِلَٰهَ إِلَّا هُوَ	لَا إِلَٰهَ إِلَّا هُوَ
Quran *Maryam* 19:2 Folio 22, recto, l. 24, p. 63	ر حمـﻪ	رَحْمَةِ	رَحْمَتِ
Qur'an *Maryam* 19:3 Folio 22, recto, l. 25, p. 63	ا ڊ ٮا د ى ر ٮک ر کر ٮ ا	إِذْ نَادَىٰ رَبَّهُ زَكَرِيَّا	إِذْ نَادَىٰ رَبَّهُ
Qur'an *Maryam* 19:4 Folio 22, recto, l. 25, p. 63	و ٯا ل ر ٮـﻰ	وَقَالَ رَبِّي	قَالَ رَبِّ

Thinking Biblically about the Qur'an   235

Location	Visible Traces	Reconstruction	Standard Text
Qur'an *Maryam* 19:4 Folio 22, recto, l. 26, p. 63	‏ٮ ڡل ر ٮی ا سٮعل الر ا س سٮٮا	وَقَلْ رَبِّي ٱشۡتَعَلَ ٱلرَّأۡسُ شَيۡبًا	قَالَ رَبِّ إِنِّي وَهَنَ ٱلۡعَظۡمُ مِنِّي وَٱشۡتَعَلَ ٱلرَّأۡسُ شَيۡبًا
Qur'an *Maryam* 19:4 Folio 22, recto, l. 26, p. 63	و لم اکں ر ٮ ٮد(ع)ا ک	وَلَمۡ أَكُن رَّبِّ بِدُعَآئِكَ	وَلَمۡ أَكُنۢ بِدُعَآئِكَ رَبِّ
Qur'an *Maryam* 19:5 Folio 22, recto, l. 27, p. 63	ا [ر] و ح(ڡ)ٮ المو ل مں و ر ا ی	وَخِفۡتُ ٱلۡمَوۡلَ مِن وَرَآءِي	وَإِنِّي خِفۡتُ ٱلۡمَوَٰلِيَ مِن وَرَآءِي
Qur'an *Maryam* 19:7 Folio 22, verso, l. 2–3, p. 63	و (مں) { --------- } هٮا لک علا م کٮا و ٮسر مں (ٯ) { --------- } مں ٯٮل سـ/ـمٮا	وَ﴿﴾ إِنَّا ۜ قَدۡ وَهَبۡنَا لَكَ غُلَٰمًا زَكِيًّا وَبَشَّرۡنَٰهُ ﴿يَحۡيَىٰ﴾ مِن قَبۡلُ ۖ لَمۡ نَجۡعَل لَّآ﴾ [سَمِيّٗا]	يَٰزَكَرِيَّآ إِنَّا نُبَشِّرُكَ بِغُلَٰمٍ ٱسۡمُهُۥ يَحۡيَىٰ لَمۡ نَجۡعَل لَّهُۥ مِن قَبۡلُ سَمِيّٗا
Qur'an *Maryam* 19:8 Folio 22, verso, l. 3–4, p. 63	ا ی ٮک(ک)و ں لی علـ(ـم) // و ٯـ[ا]لـ(ـد) عٮـ	أَنَّىٰ يَكُونُ لِي غُلَٰمٌ وَقَدۡ بَلَغۡتُ مِنَ ٱلۡكِبَرِ عِتِيّٗا	أَنَّىٰ يَكُونُ لِي غُلَٰمٞ وَكَانَتِ ٱمۡرَأَتِي عَاقِرٗا وَقَدۡ بَلَغۡتُ مِنَ ٱلۡكِبَرِ عِتِيّٗا
Qur'an *Maryam* 19:9 Folio 22, verso, l. 5, p. 63	و لم ٮک سا ی	وَلَمۡ تَكُ شَيۡـًٔا	وَلَمۡ تَكُ شَيۡـًٔا

Location	Visible Traces	Reconstruction	Standard Text
Qur'an *Maryam* 19:11 Folio 22, verso, l. 7, p. 64	ڢا-حد حر ح	ڢَاحَدٌ حرحَ	فَحَرَجَ
Qur'an *Maryam* 19:11 Folio 22, verso, l. 7, p. 64	ٯع(ل)م الرٮ(ٯ)ی (و) ا	اوحى النبیٖ	فَاوحى النَبیٖ
Qur'an *Maryam* 19:12 Folio 22, verso, l. 8, p. 64	و علىه الر(ح)کم	و عَلَمَا الحُکَم	وَاٰتَیْنَاهُ الْحُکْمَ صَبیّا
Qur'an *Maryam* 19:13 Folio 22, verso, l. 9, p. 64	حنا	حَنَٰنا	وَحَنَانًا
Qur'an *Maryam* 19:14 Folio 22, verso, l. 10, p. 64	و لم ىک	وَلَم یَكُ	وَلَمْ یَكُنْ
Qur'an *Maryam* 19:15 Folio 22, verso, l. 10, p. 64	و علىه السلم	و عَلَیه السلٰم	وَسَلٰمٌ عَلَیهِ
Qur'an *Maryam* 19:19 Folio 22, verso, l. 15, p. 64	انىٮ	اَنَیٖبَ	لِاَهَبَ
Qur'an *Maryam* 19:21 Folio 22, verso, l. 17, p. 64	و هو عل/اں هل-ٮں (؟)	وَ هُوَ عَلَیَ هَیِّن	هُوَ عَلَیَّ هَیِّن
Qur'an *Maryam* 19:21 Folio 22, verso, l. 18, p. 64	و مر [ ] مر ا معصا	وَ اَمرَ مَقضِیّا	وَكَانَ اَمْرًا مَقْضِیّا
Qur'an *Maryam* 19:22 Folio 22, verso, l. 18, p. 64	ڡحملٮ	ڡَحَمَلَتہُ	فَحَمَلَتْهُ

Thinking Biblically about the Qur'an 237

Location	Visible Traces	Reconstruction	Standard Text
Qur'an *Maryam* 19:23 Folio 22, verso, l. 19, p. 64	فلم[ ]حا ها المحص	فـلـمّـا اجـاءهـا المخـض	فَأَجَاءَهَا ٱلْمَخَاضُ
Qur'an *Maryam* 19:23 Folio 22, verso, l. 20, p. 65	م [و](ر)[ ] هد هل م	قـبـل هـذا الـيـوم	قَبْلَ هَٰذَا
Qur'an *Maryam* 19:24 Folio 22, verso, l. 20–21, p. 65	ا[ ]حر ى/حـحف من يا[ ]حـ[ ]حا [ ]د	فـتـنـاديـا مـن تـحـتـهـا/[مـلـكًا] الا تـحـزنـى	فَنَادَىٰهَا مِن تَحْتِهَا أَلَّا تَحْزَنِى
Qur'an *Maryam* 19:26 Folio 22, verso, l. 23, p. 65	ى ٮعـ [ى](ر)ڡ و	وقـرّى عـيـنًـا ⬭	وَقَرِّى عَيْنًا
Qur'an *Maryam* 19:26 Folio 22, verso, l. 24, p. 65	صحـ[ا] [م](و) [ا] صو	صـومًـا وصـمـتًـا	صَوْمًا
Qur'an *Maryam* 19:26 Folio 22, verso, l. 24, p. 65	كل لن	لـن أكـلّـم	فَلَنْ أُكَلِّمَ
Qur'an *Maryam* 19:27 Folio 22, verso, l. 25, p. 65	ا [ڡى] ڡو ٮ[ا](ٮ)ت ا	فـأتـت بـه قـومـى	فَأَتَتْ بِهِۦ قَوْمَهَا
Qur'an *Maryam* 19:27 Folio 22, verso, l. 25, p. 65	ٮٮت لـٯد	لـقـد جـئـتِ	لَقَدْ جِئْتِ
Qur'an *Maryam* 19:28 Folio 22, verso, l. 26, p. 65	[و]/ا [ا](ٮ) سـو [ا](ك)ٮ ابـ ا كـا مـا	مـا كـان ابـوكِ ابـا سـوء	مَا كَانَ أَبُوكِ ٱمْرَأَ سَوْءٍ
Qur'an *Yūsuf* 12:19 Folio 31, recto, l. 4–5, p. 71	ا/ا[سـ]؛ [ا]ا[سـ]ـحـ{ }(عـلـ)[ٮـ] سـ[ـحـ](١) و	و {جـاءت عـلـيـه بـعـض} الـسـيـارة	وَجَاءَتْ سَيَّارَةٌ

238 The Religious Other

Location	Visible Traces	Reconstruction	Standard Text
Qur'an *Yūsuf* 12:19 Folio 31, recto, l. 6, p. 71	و قل	وَقَلَ	قَالَ
Qur'an *Yūsuf* 12:19 Folio 31, recto, l. 7, p. 71	و {الـ(١)} علا ح سر(١) بـصطرلں	وَٱللَّهُ عَلِيمٌ بِمَا يَفْعَلُونَ	وَٱللَّهُ عَلِيمٌ بِمَا يَفْعَلُونَ
Qur'an *Yūsuf* 12:28 Folio 31, verso, l. 4, p. 72	قل [ا](ں)[ـہ] کں	قَلَ إِنَّهُ كَيْدِكُنَّ	قَالَ إِنَّهُ مِن كَيْدِكُنَّ
Qur'an *Yūsuf* 12:30 Folio 31, verso, l. 5, p. 72	ٮسو (ه) مں ا(هل) الـد ا**ٮـہ**	نِسْوَةٌ مِنْ أَهْلِ ٱلْمَدِينَةِ	نِسْوَةٌ فِي ٱلْمَدِينَةِ
Qur'an *Yūsuf* 12:30 Folio 31, verso, l. 5–6, p. 72	{--------}؛ / فرد س(١)/ (ڡ)//(ح)ٮـ(١)/ٯـ	[سقط] {اِمْرَأَتُ ٱلْعَزِيزِ} قَد شَغَفَهَا حُبًّا	ٱمْرَأَتُ ٱلْعَزِيزِ تُرَٰوِدُ فَتَىٰهَا عَن
Qur'an *Yūsuf* 12:31 Folio 31, verso, l. 7, p. 72	ڡلما سمع[هـ]ں / /مکـ(۱)ہں	فَلَمَّا سَمِعَتْ مَكْرَهُنَّ	فَلَمَّا سَمِعَتْ بِمَكْرِهِنَّ
Qur'an *Yūsuf* 12:31 Folio 31, verso, l. 8, p. 72	و{---------}/ ح(ح)ٮـ(ا)/د(ا)ٮـ(ں)	وَجَعَلْنَ لَهُنَّ مُتَّكَأً	وَأَعْتَدَتْ لَهُنَّ مُتَّكَأً
Qur'an *aṣ-Ṣāffāt* 37:15 Folio 28, recto, l. 1, p. 102	و ڡلو ا هد ا /ا ٮـس(---) مٮـٮں	وَقَالُوا۟ إِنْ هَٰذَا سِحْرٌ مُبِينٌ	وَقَالُوا۟ إِنْ هَٰذَا إِلَّا سِحْرٌ مُبِينٌ
Qur'an *aṣ-Ṣāffāt* 37:19 Folio 28, recto, l. 4, p. 102	/ڡا د ا ه[ـم] مح(١)ـص(ر)ر	فَإِذَا هُمْ مُحْضَرُونَ	فَإِذَا هُمْ يَنظُرُونَ
Qur'an *aṣ-Ṣāffāt* 37:22 Folio 28, recto, l. 6, p. 102	ا ـعـ(ر)و	اِبْعَثُوا	اُحْشُرُوا

Thinking Biblically about the Qur'an 239

Location	Visible Traces	Reconstruction	Standard Text
Qur'an *aṣ-Ṣāffāt* 37:22 Folio 28, recto, l. 6, p. 102	ط[ح]ا و // ا{}{}	الذين ظلمو	الَّذِينَ ظَلَمُوا وَأَزْوَاجَهُمْ
Qur'an *aṣ-Ṣāffāt* 37:23 Folio 28, recto, l. 8, p. 102	صر بط ا(ح)حىم	صر بط الجحىم	صِرَاطِ الْجَحِيمِ
Qur'an *aṣ-Ṣāffāt* 37:25 Folio 28, recto, l. 9, p. 103	// لا ىىصرو	صرون ro لا ىں ںں ںىصرون	لَا تَنَاصَرُونَ
Qur'an *aṣ-Ṣāffāt* 37:27 Folio 28, recto, l. 10, p. 103	ھ ا(ٯ)ىل	فا ٯںل	وَأَقْبَلَ
Qur'an *aṣ-Ṣāffāt* 37:48 Folio 28, verso, l. 3, p. 103	[د](د) ھم	عندهم	وَعِندَهُمْ
Qur'an *aṣ-Ṣāffāt* 37:50 Folio 28, verso, l. 4, p. 103	عل	عل	عَلَىٰ
Qur'an *aṣ-Ṣāffāt* 37:54 Folio 28, verso, l. 7, p. 103	ڡھل	ڡھل	هَلْ
Qur'an *aṣ-Ṣāffāt* 37:56 Folio 28, verso, l. 8, p. 103	لا(ح)و ںں	لںردںں	لَتُرْدِينِ
Qur'an *aṣ-Ṣāffāt* 37:58 Folio 28, verso, l. 9, p. 103	و ما ںحں	وما نحں	أَفَمَا نَحْنُ

Conclusion

Muslims believe that God preserved the Qur'an exactly as it was sent down to Muhammad, despite all the stages it went through, on the basis that the Qur'an itself claims that God has said: "It is We who sent down this Reminder and We will preserve it" (*al-Ḥijr* 15:9). This is doubtless a matter of faith. However, our analysis here based on textual criticism allows us to deduce the following:

1. The recording of the Qur'an indeed started during the lifetime of the Prophet and became more active in the phase of the **Rāshidīn**, Rightly Guided Caliphs.

2. The reconstruction of the Qur'an's textual history is no easy task.

3. Faith set apart, there are numerous lacunae (i.e. gaps) in the theory asserting that the qur'anic text remained unaltered, though the changes it underwent were slight from the time of Muhammad up to the production of ʿUthmān's Qur'an.

4. The discovery of the Ṣanʿāʾ manuscripts thrust the field of study of qur'anic history into a new phase open to numerous bombshells. It also certainly proves wrong the old critical theories claiming that the Qur'an was merely oral before being transcribed in its entirety.

6.5 The Reception of the Character of Jonah in the Qur'an: Toward a Better Understanding of the Qur'an and Practical Implications for the Church

Emad Botros

Ordinary Christians throughout history have made various unconscious but common assumptions about the Qur'an, often derived from a misunderstanding about the nature and function of what they call "biblical" narratives in the Qur'an.[21] One of those assumptions is that the Qur'an is a corrupted text since the Qur'an does not tell the "exact" same version as the biblical prophetic narratives. Those who hold this view assume that Muhammad, with ill-will, purposely attempted to create his own version of the biblical prophetic narratives. Such approaches attempt to defend the "authenticity" of the biblical

---

21. The term "biblical" is a misleading designation to describe prophetic narratives in the Qur'an as the term assumes that what we have in the Qur'an is straightforward "biblical" material. It is better to refer to what we have in the Qur'an as Jewish and Christian material combining both biblical and extra-biblical traditions.

narrative by claiming that the Bible is the "older" version, and therefore the "correct" one. In such views, originality is always ascribed to the "older" version of any text, and in this sense the "originality" of the Qur'an is denied. The practical implication of such an approach is its critique of the Qur'an which leads to a denial of its claimed status as the word of God. These assumptions, in turn, affect the church's engagement with the Qur'an, and consequently with Muslims, as it leads many Christians today to avoid any interaction with the Muslim sacred text. In addition, we rarely can find, at least in a Middle Eastern Islamic context, a serious engagement with the Qur'an by Christian theologians where commentators develop a relevant theology for their context. Such reality leads to the conclusion that our view of the Qur'an influences the way in which we engage with the Qur'an.

The purpose of this study is to develop a biblical approach to the Qur'an by investigating the function of prophetic narratives in the Qur'an with particular reference to Jonah. I will argue that the qur'anic hermeneutical approach to prophetic narratives is typological and homiletic in nature, particularly in the case of Jonah. The goal is to encourage Middle Eastern Christians and their Western counterparts to seriously engage with the Qur'an as they develop a viable biblical theology for the Muslim world with implications for discipleship. This contribution will be divided into three sections. First, I will begin with a brief survey of various approaches to prophetic narratives in the Qur'an. The survey will highlight the absence of any serious consideration of Islamic literature, particularly the Qur'an, as a vital element in the **reception history** of the Bible, and thus argue for the necessity of taking a reception history approach to the analysis of Jonah in the Qur'an. Second, I will analyze the narratives of Jonah in the Qur'an by employing a reception history methodology. Questions such as how the character of Jonah was received by the early qur'anic Muslim community and how the character of Jonah functions in the Qur'an will be addressed. Third, I will conclude with some remarks about the implications for the church's engagement with Muslims today.

A Survey of Approaches to Prophetic Narratives in the Qur'an

Scholars have employed various approaches to study the Qur'an and the Bible.[22] These can be categorized into five main approaches to prophetic

---

22. Scholars have devoted extensive studies to the Genesis narrative that share with the Qur'an common figures (Adam, Abraham, Joseph, etc.) and themes (creation, sin, flood, etc.). See for example Ida Glaser, *Thinking Biblically about Islam: Genesis, Transfiguration*

narratives in the Qur'an. A well-recognized approach is the theological comparative, represented by scholars such as Michael Lodahl, George Bristow and John Kaltner. Lodahl uses a thematic, comparative, theological approach "to interpret and reflect upon what the text either implies or directly claims about God and God's relation to the world."[23] Bristow challenges the classical notion of "Abrahamic religions" by showing how the character of a common figure, like Abraham, represents in the Qur'an a different theological view from that of the Bible. Interreligious dialogue, for him, aims to serve "the interests of persuasion and/or apologetics,"[24] since "the very 'DNA' of these faiths [Muslim and Christian] calls for mission/*da'wah*, [invitation]," and if this is the case, "how can deeper encounter avoid it?"[25] While Bristow challenges the notion of "Abrahamic religions," Kaltner uses an "intercanonical criticism" method, where he attempts to "study texts from different canons or religious traditions in relationship to each other."[26] The goal of his work is "to lay the foundation for a family reconciliation" among all three Abrahamic religions.[27]

Other scholars employ literary approaches to study common narratives in the Bible and the Qur'an in their respective literary contexts. Marilyn Waldman

---

and Transformation (Carlisle: Langham Global Library, 2016); Marilyn Waldman, "New Approaches to 'Biblical' Materials in the Qur'an," *Muslim World* 75 (1985): 1–13; M. A. S. Abdel Haleem, "The Story of Joseph in the Qur'an and the Old Testament," *Islam and Christian-Muslim Relations* 1 (2007): 171–191. Outside of Genesis, Moses and David receive considerable attention, while little attention is given to lesser characters such as Jonah. See for example Roberto Tottoli, *Biblical Prophets in the Qur'an and Muslim Literature* (New York: Routledge, 2002); John Kaltner and Younus Y. Mirza, *The Bible and the Qur'an: Biblical Figures in the Islamic Tradition* (London; New York: Bloomsbury T&T Clark, 2018); John Kaltner, *Ishmael Instructs Isaac: An Introduction to the Qur'an for the Bible Reader* (Minnesota: Liturgical, 1999); John Kaltner, *Inquiring of Joseph: Getting to Know a Biblical Character through the Qur'an* (Collegeville: Liturgical Press, 2003); Gabriel Said Reynolds, *The Qur'an and Its Biblical Subtext* (New York: Routledge, 2010); Khaleel Mohammed, *David in the Muslim Tradition: Bathsheba Affair* (London: Lexington Books, 2015).

23. Michael Lodahl, *Claiming Abraham: Reading the Bible and the Qur'an Side by Side* (Grand Rapids: Brazos, 2010), 3.

24. George Bristow, "Abraham in Narrative Worldview: Reflections on Doing Comparative Theology through Christian-Muslim Conversation," in *Reading the Bible in Islamic Context: Qur'anic Conversations*, ed. Daniel Crowther et al. (Oxford: Routledge, 2018), 35.

25. Bristow, "Abraham in Narrative," 40.

26. Kaltner, *Ishmael Instructs Isaac*, 23. Kaltner in *Inquiring of Joseph* also uses a comparative approach to study the Joseph story between the Qur'an and the Bible, but he applies two different methodologies there: narratology and rhetorical analysis. Though Kaltner values the literary historical approach and observes how it dominated the field of biblical studies for years, he prefers to use a narrative approach applied on both the Qur'an and the Bible by dividing the story into six narrative sequences: beginnings, narrators and characters, events, repetition, gaps and endings.

27. Kaltner, *Ishmael Instructs Isaac*, 19.

shows dissatisfaction with historical approaches to these traditions, as they investigate the transmission of materials between them assuming that "earlier materials are normative and later ones derivative."[28] According to Waldman, it is not helpful to think of the qur'anic Joseph story, for example, as a version of the biblical one since "it precludes us from approaching both as equally 'basic' tellings whose 'real' form logically can never exist apart from a given telling."[29] Applying a narratological approach, Waldman attempts to focus on the shape and function of characters in each narrative in their respective literary context as well as understanding the art of qur'anic narrative. This way, Waldman argues, we can still compare the two narratives with an emphasis that differs from that of the historical approach. Muhammad Abdel Haleem also calls for a study of both traditions that attempts "to identify the differing functions and preoccupations of the two accounts in their respective contexts, to show how these differences affect the choice of material and the treatment given to it."[30] In his treatment of the story of Joseph in the Qur'an and the Old Testament, Abdel Haleem encourages both Muslims and non-Muslims to "approach the two versions with this difference in mind in order to appreciate the message and the qualities of each."[31]

Recent studies attempt to employ methodologies that aid readings of the Bible in Islamic contexts. Ida Glaser, for example, offers a "multi-layered approach to reading the Bible";[32] that is, looking at the world behind the text, the world of the text, and the world in front of the text.[33] The first world is defined as the world in which the text has been written, looking "for parallels between the Bible's historical background and Muslim societies."[34] The second is to "*pay attention to the composition of the text itself* . . . [where] we need to consider what a passage means in the context of the book it is in and in relation to the rest of the Bible . . . [and looking] carefully at the nature and structure of the text."[35] The third is "to ask the significance of the message to ourselves and our world and to how we relate to it."[36] The Islamic world

---

28. Waldman, "New Approaches," 1.
29. Waldman, 13.
30. Abdel Haleem, "Story of Joseph," 171.
31. Abdel Haleem, 171.
32. Glaser, *Thinking Biblically*, 21.
33. Glaser, 21–24. *(Note from the editors: See also section 2.6 above.)*
34. Glaser, 22.
35. Glaser, 22.
36. Glaser, 23.

in front of the text, however, is different from any other context, as it has a sacred text, that is the Qur'an, attached to it. Moreover, Glaser observes how scholars have recognized the intertextual relationship between both traditions, but these conversations took place between *texts*, not people. Glaser therefore calls for a move beyond conversations between texts to conversations with persons and communities,[37] as the biblical text was read by many throughout history, including Muslims, and we should consider such readings.[38] For this conversation to take place, as this study suggests, there is a need for a wider engagement with Islamic literature as it reflects the values of the Muslim community and how it views itself in light of other texts (or traditions). In other words, there is a need to consider Islamic literature as a vital element of the reception history of the Bible in order to understand how the Muslim community received, interacted with, and was influenced by the biblical text.

Defining Reception History

The history of the reception-history approach goes back to Hans Georg Gadamer and Hans Robert Jauss.[39] Scholars since Gadamer and Jauss have demonstrated increased interest in reception history theories.[40] This interest has generated a discussion on issues related to reception history: its terminology, its relation to historical approaches and biblical studies, its significance, and its challenges.[41] I will briefly offer my own hermeneutical understanding of reception history by applying it to the following analysis of Jonah in the Qur'an. First, reception history aims to focus on meanings produced through

---

37. Glaser, 5.
38. Glaser, 23.
39. For a full survey on the history of this school, see Timothy Beal, "Reception History and Beyond: Toward the Cultural History of Scripture," *Biblical Interpretation* 19 (2011): 357–372; Emma England and William J. Lyons, "Exploration in the Reception of the Bible," in *Reception History and Biblical Studies: Theory and Practice*, eds. Emma England and William J. Lyons (London: Bloomsbury T&T Clark, 2015), 3–16; Jonathan Roberts, "Introduction," in *The Oxford Handbook of the Reception History of the* Bible, eds. Michael Lieb, Emma Mason, and Jonathan Roberts (Oxford: Oxford University Press, 2011), 1–8.
40. For a list of new projects in this area of research see Beal, "Reception History," 360.
41. See for example Caroline Vander Stichele, "The Head of John and Its Reception or How to Conceptualize Reception History," in *Reception History and Biblical Studies: Theology and Practice*, eds. Emma England and William J. Lyons (London: Bloomsbury T&T Clark, 2015); Christine E. Joynes, "The Reception of the Bible and Its Significance," in *Scripture and Its Interpretation: A Global, Ecumenical Introduction to the Bible*, ed. Michael J. Gorman (Grand Rapids: Baker Academic, 2017); Brennan Breed, *Nomadic Text: A Theology of Biblical Reception History* (Indiana: Indiana University Press, 2014); Beal, "Reception History."

interaction between text, reader and context.[42] This understanding of reception history welcomes the plurality of meanings and presupposes that the text functions differently in various contexts and that its meanings cannot be discovered in isolation from the interpreter's own context. Therefore our analysis of Jonah in the Qur'an discusses how the narrative of Jonah functions in its various literary contexts, and thus an examination of the immediate literary context is necessary. However, our examination of the literary context will be brief due to the space available in this study.

Reception history aims at examining how the text influences readers as it speaks into their contexts. Texts speak, and they generate a response within our own context. The prophetic narratives, in general, are not exceptional, and this is particularly the case with the biblical text as a theological discourse. Biblical texts as theological discourse are more than a source for reconstructing human history and religion. Rather, they are texts that testify to God's revelation of himself in history and his relationship with his own people and the world. Throughout the Bible, God speaks in various times and in various ways (Heb 1:1–3). Biblical texts are "God-breathed" and authoritative to correct, reprove and instruct (2 Tim 3:16).[43] Reception history aims to focus not only on the Christian and Jewish reception of the story of Jonah, but also on the Islamic reception. Our investigation of the Islamic reception history affirms a close relationship between the Bible and the Qur'an. In this relationship, the Qur'an is not seen as a text that contradicts the Bible, but rather as a vital element of its reception history. The purpose then is to analyze how the Muslim community interpreted the story in its own context.

Literary Analysis of Jonah (Yūnus) in the Qur'an

The character of Jonah appears six times in the Qur'an. Four of those occurrences will be the focus of this contribution, as they provide narrative sections about *Yūnus*. These are *al-Qalam* 68:48–50, *al-Anbiyā'* 21:87–88, *aṣ-Ṣāffāt* 37:139–148 and *Yūnus* 10:98. Other texts for Jonah are found in *an-Nisā'* 4:163 and *al-An'ām* 6:86. Though classical **mufassirūn** (interpreters) exegete the narratives of *Yūnus* based on the qur'anic text, it can be argued that they

---

42. William J. Lyons, "Hope for a Troubled Discipline? Contributions to New Testament Studies from Reception History," *Journal for the Study of the New Testament* 33, no. 2 (2010): 207–220.

43. Mark Boda, "Biblical Theology and Old Testament Interpretation," in *Hearing the Old Testament: Listening for God's Address*, eds. Craig Bartholomew and David Beldman (Grand Rapids: Eerdmans, 2012), 130.

fail to take into consideration the qur'anic literary context as they attempt to accomplish three main tasks. First is to create a basic sequence of all these narratives; second is to "fill the gap" as they attempt to search for more details to aid their exegetical work; and third is to illuminate obscure statements by employing the hermeneutical principle of interpreting the Qur'an by the Qur'an (*tafsīr al-Qur'ān bi al-Qur'ān*).

As we attempt to take the qur'anic literary context seriously, each narrative will be discussed separately in light of the literary context of the whole sūra. This literary narrative approach to the narratives of *Yūnus* is based on the fact that the Qur'an uses various methods to deliver its message, one of which is the allusion to the stories of former prophets. Muhammad Abdel Haleem observes how the histories of prophets who preceded Muhammad are "a salient feature of the qur'anic discourse."[44] With the exception of a few cases, these prophetic narratives appear, in general, in the form of a chain, and they share common themes as each chain attempts to serve a particular purpose and to address a particular situation related to the surrounding literary context. Such a literary feature, therefore, requires the interpreter to discuss all other prophetic narratives in this chain, even when he or she seeks to focus only on a particular figure like *Yūnus*.

As an illustration, the examination of how these narratives in a particular chain relate to the overall literary context of the sūra is necessary. Due to the limited space in this contribution, the narrative of Jonah in *aṣ-Ṣāffāt* 37:139–148 will function as the main example, while the other three accounts will be mentioned briefly. The reason behind this choice is twofold. First, *aṣ-Ṣāffāt* provides a full account of the narrative of Jonah; and second, it serves the purpose of this contribution well. Our analysis begins by briefly introducing the qur'anic literary context, which is polemical in nature. We will focus on the main themes running throughout the sūra and then examine how the narratives of the prophets relate to this polemical context. Though we will not be entering the scholarly debate on the unity and coherence of the sūra in the Qur'an, our analysis assumes some type of unity and coherence, particularly where the stories of the former prophets occur.

Aṣ-Ṣāffāt – The Ranks 37

In this sūra, we learn about those unbelievers who reject the message of the Prophet and deny its divine source (*aṣ-Ṣāffāt* 37:12–17). As the unbelievers

---

44. Abdel Haleem, "The Qur'anic Employment of the Story of Noah," *Journal of Qur'anic Studies* 8 (2006): 38.

mock the Prophet, he wonders at the fact that they refuse to learn from his message and reject any sign that proves its authenticity (vv. 12–14), claiming that "this is mere magic" (v. 15). Moreover, they described Muhammad as a possessed poet (v. 36). The result of this insult of the Prophet is the judgment of the unbelievers by God, while "God's devoted worshipers" will be rewarded in heaven since they believed the Prophet's message. A description of this reward is given (vv. 41–49).

As the sūra unfolds, the unbelievers' fate is discussed in a story-telling form among those who are in heaven (*aṣ-Ṣāffāt* 37:50–71). The concluding statement of this discussion reminds the Prophet of the fact that many nations in the past "went astray," as the surrounding rebellious community of the Prophet also does (v. 71), despite the fact that God sent many prophets to warn them (v. 72). This last verse reveals one aspect of the prophetic office, which is "to warn." The prophet, however, is encouraged to take note of the consequences on those who have been warned (v. 73), while God saved the "devout worshipers of God" (v. 74). This last expression, "the devout worshipers of God (*'ibādu Allāh al-mukhliṣīn*)," appears five times throughout the sūra (vv. 40, 74, 128, 160, 169) to compare the devout worshipers with the unbelievers.

It is important to note that this theme is echoed throughout the following section recounting the narratives of the prophets, but using a synonym expression, each time addressing another one of the prophets with the words, "for he was among Our believing worshipers (*innahu min 'ibādinā al-mu'minīn*)." In this context, the life stories of the former prophets are narrated, beginning with Noah (*aṣ-Ṣāffāt* 37:75–82) and moving on to Abraham (vv. 83–113), Moses and Aaron (vv. 114–122), Elijah (referred to as *Elyās* and *El-Yāsīn*) (vv. 123–132), Lot (vv. 133–138) and finally Jonah (*Yūnus*, vv. 139–148).

The stories of former prophets share some common themes. All prophets endured rejection, called upon God, and had their prayers answered, resulting in their own salvation as well as that of their people. They saw their opponents punished, while "the devout worshipers of God" were rewarded, honored and granted victory. It is in this context that the narrative of *Yūnus* is recorded in *Sūrat aṣ-Ṣāffāt* (37:139–148):

> Jonah was one of the messengers (139). He ran away to a loaded ship (140), but they cast lots, and he lost (141), (so they threw him into the sea [not in the Arabic]), and a great fish swallowed him, for he was blameworthy (for what he had done) (142). And had he not been one of those who glorify (God's limitless glory [not in the Arabic]) (143), he would have remained inside its

belly until the Day they are resurrected (144). But We cast him, ill, on an open shore (145), and We made a gourd vine to grow over him (146), and we sent him to a hundred thousand people or more (147). They believed, so we let them enjoy their life (148).

It is important to mention that the *Yūnus* narrative differs from others in that the full account of his story is narrated in a single breath, without any external features, though it is brief and condensed. In other prophetic narratives, only portions of their stories are mentioned. But although the *Yūnus* narrative differs from other prophetic narratives, it still shares common themes with them. As with other prophets, it is mentioned that *Yūnus* was a messenger of God (*aṣ-Ṣāffāt* 37:139), that he called upon him and his prayer was answered (v. 134), that he was sent to more than a hundred thousand (v. 147) and that the believers were rewarded (v. 148). Intriguingly, the formula of honor and reward are missing at the end of the Jonah narrative, which may raise questions regarding motivations. Yet God's mercy still reaches *Yūnus* as he calls upon or praises God. This mercy appears in the actions that God takes in favor of *Yūnus* (vv. 146–147).

The point of comparison between Muhammad and Jonah is twofold. First, Jonah like other prophets was rescued by God when he called upon him while in the belly of the great fish. Here we can hear the message that Muhammad, like Jonah, will be rescued from this severe criticism. As he calls upon God, he will receive God's care as *Yūnus* did. Second, the people to whom *Yūnus* was sent believed in his message, repented and were rewarded. This story functions not only as a message of hope for Muhammad, but also as a positive example for the people of Mecca to follow. The prophet *Yūnus* and these people thus were an example of those sincere and devout servants of God.

Al-Qalam – The Pen

The final pericope of *Sūrat al-Qalam* 68 (vv. 43–52) offers counsel to Muhammad as it reveals God's plan for dealing with those who deny the authenticity of the revelation, instructing him on the virtues with which he is expected to act.[45] It begins with God assuring his prophet that though he may be patiently addressing their rejection, he alone, and not Muhammad, will punish those who disbelieve (vv. 44–45). In this intense context, the example of "the fellow of the whale" is given to urge Muhammad to wait patiently for

---

45. Early in the sūra, we can see again how the surrounding community accuses the prophet of being insane or possessed. God, however, affirms the opposite in an intense direct speech: Muhammad is not a possessed person, and this is by the grace of God (68:2).

the judgment of the Lord on the unbelievers. Muhammad is encouraged not to be a *Yūnus*-like prophet, as *Yūnus* called upon God in anger while in the belly of the fish (*idh nāda wa huwa makẓūm*) (v. 48). Patience is therefore needed, as God promises his prophet that he will see his judgment over the unbelievers (v. 50). Jonah, in this sūra, is a prophet offering an example of behavior that Muhammad is not to follow.[46]

Yet the Qur'an reports how God's grace reached *Yūnus* in time of distress. Without the grace of God, *Yūnus* would have been "abandoned on a naked shore" as a sign of being guilty. By the grace of God, moreover, *Yūnus* is chosen by his Lord as a prophet and sent to his own people, and this act of grace granted *Yūnus* the status of "the righteous" (*al-Qalam* 68:50). Koloska observes:

> Particularly striking is the designation of Jonah as among the righteous (*min al-ṣāliḥīn*) and not explicitly as a prophet or messenger so that he may serve as a general example and not just as a parallel to the prophet in salvation history. That he is not named, but referred to by an epithet, might also stress his role as an afflicted person instead of as one on a prophetic mission. Thus, Jonah serves as a model for a wrongdoer whose prayer, uttered in despair, was answered.[47]

Moreover, Johns observes another parallel between *Yūnus* and Muhammad: Jonah received a grace from his Lord, and because of this grace, he was not abandoned on a naked shore. In the same way, Muhammad received a grace from his Lord, and because of this grace, he is not possessed as the unbelievers describe him.[48] Thus, if Muhammad patiently waits for the judgment of his Lord, and believes in the grace granted to him, he will be rewarded, like *Yūnus*, as one of the righteous. In other words, Muhammad by the grace of God is considered one of the prophets and given the status of the righteous.

Al-Anbiyā' – The Prophets 21

The context of this chapter in *al-Anbiyā'* is, to some extent, similar to those of *al-Qalam* and *aṣ-Ṣāffāt*. The chapter begins with a tension between objections

---

46. A. H. Johns, "Jonah in the Qur'an: An Essay on Thematic Counterpoint," *Journal of Qur'anic Studies* 5 (2003): 53.

47. Hannelies Koloska, "The Sign of Jonah: Transformations and Interpretation of the Jonah Story in the Qur'an," in *Qur'anic Studies Today*, eds. Angelika Neuwirth and Michael A. Sells (London; New York: Routledge, 2016), 87.

48. Johns, "Jonah in the Qur'an," 53.

to Muhammad and God's response to them. Particularly, Johns suggests, the chapter addresses "the period of respite between the threat of divine punishment and its execution, leading unbelievers to regard it as empty."[49] This point is explained later, when Muhammad's original audience question the authenticity of his message (*al-Anbiyā'* 21:36–46), particularly as they ask, "When will this promise be fulfilled, if you are telling the truth?" (v. 38). The chapter begins with the affirmation that the Day of Judgment draws near (v. 1). The dispute thus is related to eschatological issues.[50] Rather than paying attention to that Day, Muhammad's hearers question his prophethood, claiming that he is just human like them. They dismiss what he claims to be a revelation as nothing but magic, a collection of dreams, poetry from a poet.

In order for Muhammad to prove his prophethood to them, they ask for a sign similar to that of the former prophets (*al-Anbiyā'* 21:3–5). The divine response affirms the uselessness of providing a sign as people did not believe when God sent his punishment as a sign in the past (v. 6). Moreover, God affirms that he has sent prophets before who were human beings, and if they are not sure of this fact, they can ask the People of the Book (v. 7). While those prophets were rescued, the unbelievers were punished (v. 9). The punishment of the unbelievers resulted in self-examination, which led to their confession of faith: "They said, 'Woe to us! We were truly wrongdoers'" (v. 14).

The narrative of *Yūnus* appears in the middle of a chain of former prophets, and there are several common themes between them. There were four prophets who called to God (*idh nāda rabbahu*), and God answered them (*fa 'stajabnā lahu*): Noah (*al-Anbiyā'* 21:76), Job (vv. 83–84), *Yūnus* (vv. 87–88) and Zechariah (vv. 89–90). Four others were saved by God (*najjaynāhu*): Abraham (v. 71), Lot (v. 74), Noah (v. 76) and *Yūnus* (v. 88).[51] Moreover, Johns observes the emphasis on patience with Job (vv. 83–84), Ishmael, Idris and *Dhā al-kifli* (v. 85). Johns then states that, "There is thus a delicate emphasis on the fact that patience, when Jonah *departed enraged* (*mughādiban*, v. 87), was a quality in which Jonah had fallen short."[52] With Job, Ishmael, Idris and *Dhā al-kifli*, moreover, there is emphasis on God's mercy. God appears as the "Most Merciful" (vv. 83, 86). Though the narrative of *Yūnus* does not explicitly speak of God's mercy, we can see God's answering of prayer and *Yūnus's*

---

49. Johns, 61.
50. Koloska, "Sign of Jonah," 90.
51. Johns, "Jonah in the Qur'an," 60.
52. Johns, 60–61.

deliverance as a sign of his mercy (vv. 78–88).[53] We can thus conclude that there are major themes appearing in the narrative of *Yūnus*: the importance of calling to God, God's answering of prayer, God's salvation, God's patience and God's mercy.

The narrative of *Yūnus* in this sūra begins with his name: *Dhū an-nūn* (the man of the fish), which defines and refers to *Yūnus* in terms of the best known event of his life.[54] The narrative continues with *Yūnus's* thoughts while he was running away in anger, revealing that God had no power over him (*al-Anbiyā' 21*:87). *Yūnus's* line of thought may reflect the thoughts of the unbelievers early in the chapter, as they thought that Muhammad's threat of punishment had no value because of the period of respite between the threat and its fulfillment (v. 1). In other words, the unbelievers, like *Yūnus*, thought that God had no power over them to fulfill his threat as proclaimed by Muhammad. In this sense, *Yūnus* reflects or represents the attitude of the unbelievers toward God and toward his messenger Muhammad.

The call and the prayer of *Yūnus* here clarifies other qur'anic references to *Yūnus's* prayer (*aṣ-Ṣāffāt* 37:144; *al-Qalam* 68:48). It came from a dark place, that is from the belly of the great fish and the bottom of the sea. This prayer affirms, in contrast with *Yūnus's* earlier thoughts, the **inimitable** sovereignty of God: "There is no God except You; May You be exalted in your glory" (*al-Anbiyā' 21*:87a). In this prayer, *Yūnus* is not only confessing the glorious qualities of God, but also his own guilt: "I have been among the unjust" (v. 87b). This is a self-declared confession, while in two other narratives (*aṣ-Ṣāffāt* 37:144; *al-Qalam* 68:48), the confession is in the form of a narrative in the third person. God hears *Yūnus's* prayer and delivers him from grief (*al-Anbiyā' 21*:88a). Thus *Yūnus* becomes the model of a man of prayer for all Muslims, and particularly for Muhammad. It is important to notice how the narrative of *Yūnus* ends with a didactic formula: "This is how we save the believers" (v. 88b). *Yūnus's* prayer, therefore, plays a major role not only because of its occurrence in the other two narratives that speak of *Yūnus*, but also because it becomes a typical daily prayer, or a "formulaic prayer," for all Muslims during

---

53. Koloska suggests that the chapter "emphasizes God's mercy often, by the use of the divine epithet "*'ar-raḥmān*" (Koloska, "Sign of Jonah," 90).

54. On the meaning of the term *dhū an-nūn* and the possible external influence on the Qur'an regarding this name, see Reynolds, *The Qur'ān*, 129.

times of distress. This prayer grants a hearing from God and thus serves as "an antitype for a penitent and saved person."[55]

In summary, *Yūnus's* thought reflects the skeptical attitude of the unbelievers toward God's power to fulfill his threats declared by Muhammad. Just as *Yūnus* thought that God had no power over him, the unbelievers also assumed that God had no power to judge them. The declaration of the inimitable sovereignty of God and the self-declared confession by *Yūnus* from the darkness, however, reveals the opposite to this group of people; that is, *Yūnus* mistakenly underestimated the power of his God, and God's judgment was closer than he thought. It follows that this group should reconsider the whole notion of questioning Muhammad's warning of God's judgment (*al-Anbiyā'* 21:1). On the other hand, Muhammad, like all believers, is invited to become like *Yūnus* in the midst of emotional and physical distress by calling upon God and trusting that the one who delivered *Yūnus* will deliver him and all the believers. This deliverance is a sign of God's mercy toward his Prophet Muhammad, as it was to *Yūnus*. As God showed his mercy to *Yūnus*, Job, Ishmael, Idris and *Dhā al-kifli*, Muhammad will also experience the hand of the Most Merciful.

Yūnus – Jonah 10:98

It is remarkable to note that though this sūra bears *Yūnus's* name, it has only one verse that speaks of the people of *Yūnus*.[56] This makes our task unique, as we have to navigate through the whole chapter in order to understand the function of the narrative of *Yūnus* and his people. Though it is a single verse, the verse is key to the sūra's structure and purpose. It stands in contrast to the other two prophetic narratives of Noah and Moses, and it functions as the climax of the Sūra. To begin with, this sūra argumentatively deals with the unbelievers' rejection of Muhammad and his message. It is a response from God to a string of accusations levelled at the Prophet and the Qur'an by the unbelievers (*Yūnus* 10:2, 15, 20, 38). The rhetorical question at the beginning of the chapter (v. 2) sets the tone, explaining the reason for what will be revealed next. There are those who reject the whole notion of "the Day of the Resurrection," as reflected in the way they live. People in Muhammad's

---

55. Koloska also states that, "The passage reveals a strong relation to the Jewish and Christian image of Jonah as known from liturgical traditions and from pictorial representations, but at the same time, Jonah is transformed into a more qur'ānic figure due to increased inner-textual references and the solace of the believers (v. 88)" ("Sign of Jonah," 91).

56. On the relationship between the sūra and its name, see Johns, "Jonah in the Qur'an," 65–67.

audience are more interested in the here and now, and they live their life accordingly (vv. 6–7). As they sarcastically hasten the Day of Reckoning (v. 11), they ask, "When will this promise be fulfilled, if you are telling the truth?" (v. 48).

Another challenge raised by Muhammad's audience is that of requesting a sign from him, similar to those of previous prophets (*Yūnus* 10:20). Even though these same people had experienced God's signs and mercy, having been rescued from crisis, they returned quickly to their evil ways and forgot the promises they made to God. They insist on disbelieving, regardless of whether God had fulfilled his promises to previous prophets (vv. 21–33). The allegations continue as the unbelievers claim that the Prophet had fabricated (created) the Qur'an (v. 38). Three major allegations thus run through the whole chapter: the rejection of Muhammad and his message, since he was human like anyone else (vv. 2, 15, 20, 38); the rejection of the whole notion of the Day of the Resurrection (vv. 6–7, 11); and the request for a sign (v. 20).

The Qur'an then offers a series of prophetic stories as examples of how God previously punished those who rejected the message of former prophets Noah (*Yūnus* 10:71–74) and Moses (vv. 75–97). The exemplary belief and salvation of the people *Yūnus* spoke to (v. 98) thus stand in contrast with the disbelief of Noah's contemporaries and Pharaoh.[57] Indeed, the example of the people of *Yūnus* is unique, since it functions as a model for the people of faith, in contrast to those who refused to believe. What is unique about the faith of the people of *Yūnus* is that they believed before seeing the severe punishment of God. The faith of the people of *Yūnus* was thus unlike Pharaoh's, who believed after seeing God's punishment (v. 90). Theirs was a response to God's warning of punishment.[58] The Qur'an thus portrays the people of *Yūnus* as a source of encouragement to the Prophet, and as a model that his people should follow.[59] Koloska states:

---

57. Reynolds has pointed out that the verse reflects a similar interpretation of the "sign of Jonah" as we find in Matthew and Luke: "The Qur'ān refers to the Jonah story in precisely the same way: to contrast the repentance of Jonah's people with the stubbornness of its audience" (*The Qur'ān*, 129).

58. Wahbah Zuhayli, *Concise Interpretation of the Grand Qur'an with the Causes of Descent and Rules of Reciting* (Damascus: Dar Al Fikr, 1994), 221.

59. Johns however wonders: "Is there perhaps concealed within this sūra a yearning that this people of Muhammad might be as the people of Jonah, who after first rejecting their prophet, accepted him, and were spared the final punishment? There is still time for the Meccans to believe, and their faith to avail them" ("Jonah in the Qur'an," 66).

> The verse forms a climax within the sūra because the Ninevites form an exception from the warned people who always turn their backs. They constitute an exemplar of another possible behavior than the attitude of the adherents of the prophet and his community.... [Moreover] The people of Jonah serve as an example; they are a "sign" (v. 97) in the sense that they confirm the truth of the message, but they do not serve as accusant on Judgment Day. The opposite is the case: they are spared punishment in this world, but they will be judged in the world to come. Thus the "sign of Jonah" is a positive sign, stressing also God's forgiveness.[60]

Though the narrative of the people of *Yūnus* gives hope to the disappointed Muhammad, it helps him to realize how the history of the former prophets affirms the fact that, while many rejected their message, a few did accept it. Indeed, this simple fact corresponds with God's will, as we read: "Had your Lord willed, all the people on earth would have believed" (*Yūnus* 10:99). But since this is not the case, the prophet is encouraged not to act against the will of God, as the rhetorical question that God posed to Muhammad suggests: "Is it, then, up to you (Prophet) to compel people to believe?" (v. 99). It is expected that the prophet will act in accordance to God's will, particularly since he knows that, "No soul can ever believe except with God's permission" (v. 100).

Conclusion and Implications

Our analysis of the four qur'anic accounts of *Yūnus* in their respective literary contexts has revealed potential common features with the overall socio-religious environment of Muhammad, as it seems to be reflected in various sections of the qur'anic text. We can describe the contexts as polemical and hostile in nature. The repetitive questions and criticisms raised in each sūra indicate that there were major issues common to Jonah's community and that of Muhammad regarding his prophethood, his character and his message: the rejection and refutation of the Qur'an, the description of signs as obvious magic, the denial of the whole notion of the Day of Resurrection, the questioning of Muhammad's moral character and his description as a possessed poet, and the fate of the unbelievers.

As a first conclusion, let us sum up some of the common characteristics of prophetic narratives in the Qur'an. The narratives are brief and condensed.

---

60. Koloska, "Sign of Jonah," 92.

The character of Islam's prophet appears in various contexts and in the middle of a chain of former prophets. In each context, the narratives of former prophets correspond thematically with the literary polemical context, and there is an implicit literary contrast between various prophetic narratives. In each context, the character of a prophet corresponds thematically with other prophetic narratives. And all these examples of literary features of the accounts of *Yūnus* show how prophetic narratives in general, and *Yūnus* in particular, are purposefully situated in their literary context, functioning accordingly. Understanding the characteristics of prophetic narratives in the Qur'an, as outlined above, refutes the assumption that the Qur'an is a corrupted text because its accounts of prophetic narratives differ from those of the Bible. As we have seen, the Qur'an does not re-tell the exact accounts of the prophetic narratives, nor does it reflect a "corrupted" version of the Bible. Rather, the narratives are illustrations that suit well the immediate literary context. Moreover, to think of the prophetic narratives in the Qur'an as "versions" of the Bible is to mistakenly assume that the qur'anic author had direct access to the Bible. Rather, Muhammad, his community and the author of the Qur'an had access to the Jewish-Christian religious heritage through various means.

On a personal level, seeing the Qur'an as a vital element in the reception history of the Bible, and understanding the characteristics of its prophetic narratives, has changed my own perspective on the Qur'an. It has helped me to seriously take the Qur'an into consideration as I work on developing a biblical theology in a Middle Eastern Islamic context. Such engagement with the qur'anic text is necessary as we attempt to interpret the Bible in the context of Islam. It makes our presentation of the biblical Christian faith more relevant to our context. This is a call to Middle Eastern Christians and their Western counterparts to reconsider the Qur'an as a vital part of the reception history of the Bible as we seek to share our biblical faith with our Muslim neighbors.

My second conclusion is that the Qur'an interprets the narrative of Jonah typologically, and therefore a biblical interpretation of Jonah in the context of Islam should be homiletic and morally oriented. Our analysis has shown that the characteristics of *Yūnus* and his people serve as a typological background for the life and circumstances of Muhammad and his community. We can see in *Yūnus's* narratives how Muhammad and his early hearers relived the experiences of *Yūnus* and the Ninevites. *Yūnus* and these people become a prefiguration of Muhammad and his community. Muhammad and his early hearers function as the antitype of *Yūnus* and the Ninevites. Neuwirth observes that this hermeneutical feature of **typology** in qur'anic narratives is familiar to narratives in the Bible. She states, "It is little surprising to find a particular hermeneutic trait familiar from the Bible and especially the gospels prominent again in qur'anic narrative: typology. 'Types' are exemplary representations in scripture of more momentous events or more significant figures still expected to come."[61] However, Neuwirth explains how "the paradigm of typology at work" is different from that of the Bible, as Muhammad did not come to fulfill a biblical promise. She sees in the story of Moses, for example, that the paradigm of typology at work is that of *taṣdīq* (validation) "where the older tradition comes to confirm the new."[62] In the case of *Yūnus*, the paradigm of typology at work is that of imitation in the sense of a moral lesson (*'ibra*) where the antitype is invited to reflect and learn from the type. The type, as in the case of Jonah, can function as a source of encouragement, a moral figure and a guide. In this sense, *Yūnus* becomes the example of a prayerful and repentant figure whom God saves, a guidance for how Muhammad and his community should respond in the face of severe criticism by calling upon God and being patient, and a source of encouragement for the disappointed prophet. The people of *Yūnus*, on their part, also become an example to those who will believe in Muhammad's message. Those typological categories suit well the qur'anic use of the stories of the prophets, by the Qur'an's own account:

> So, (Prophet), We have relayed the accounts of the (earlier) messengers to you in order to make your heart firm. The truth comes to you through these accounts, as well as lessons and reminders for the believers. (*Hūd* 11:120)

> In the stories of these men, there is a lesson for those who understand. (As for this Qur'an), it could not possibly be a discourse invented (by the Prophet). No, it is a confirmation of what is available to him from prior revelations, clearly spelling out everything, and (offering) guidance and mercy to people who will believe. (*Yūsuf* 12:111)

This understanding of the hermeneutical features of the Qur'an's typological interpretation of the stories of the prophets and its moral orientation invites us to view Muhammad and his community in the Qur'an as a community that is inspired by the wonders and the experiences of ancient heroes. Those heroes are meant to exemplify moral behaviors and "to illustrate – again and

---

61. Angelika Neuwirth, "Qur'an and History – A Disputed Relationship: Some Reflections on Qur'anic History and History in the Qur'an," *Journal of Qur'anic Studies* 5 (2003): 15.

62. Neuwirth, "Qur'an and History," 9.

again – how the true Believer acts in certain situations."[63] This perspective on the Qur'an, moreover, inspires us to focus more on the theological and homiletic message of the prophetic narratives in the Old Testament as we develop discipleship curricula in the context of Islam. Our interpretation of those narratives, however, must be typological rather than allegorical. While the latter attempts to see Jesus in every story in the Old Testament and to use it as an entry point to sharing Jesus in the context of Islam, the former takes seriously those narratives in their historical context, further interpreting them in light of the coming of Christ. This understanding of the typological reading of Old Testament prophetic narratives will help the church discover the relevance and centrality of the Old Testament as Christian scripture that serves the proclamation of the gospel.

6.6 Where Do Scriptures Come From?

Daniel Brown

We can begin thinking about doctrines of revelation with a statement of faith that is affirmed by a significant number of Christians from a wide range of denominations and contexts. Adherents to the Lausanne Covenant affirm "the divine inspiration, truthfulness and authority of both Old and New Testament scriptures in their entirety as the only written word of God, without error in all that it affirms, and the only infallible rule of faith and practice."[64] We could offer many similar examples, but the exercise would add little. Evangelical Christians are generally agreed: The Bible is the revealed word of God. God has spoken to us through it. It is unique in its authority. We might have interesting discussions about exactly which words we should use – infallible? inerrant? – and about what these words mean, but we generally have little difficulty agreeing that the Bible is uniquely and exclusively authoritative and that this authority makes it categorically different from all other books.

Similarly, an early Muslim creed affirms that, "The Qur'an is the speech of Allah, written in the copies, preserved in the memories, recited by the tongues, revealed to the Prophet. Our pronouncing, writing and reciting the Kuran is created, whereas the Qur'an itself is uncreated."[65] Another affirms that "the

---

63. Reynolds, *The Qur'an*, 238.

64. Lausanne Covenant, www.lausanne.org/content/covenant/lausanne-covenant#cov.

65. Fiqh Akbar II quoted in A. J. Wensinck, *The Muslim Creed: Its Genesis and Historical Development* (Cambridge: Cambridge University Press, 1932), 189.

Qur'an is the speech of Allah, uncreated, his inspiration and revelation, not he, yet not other than he, but his real quality, written in the copies, recited by the tongues, preserved in the breasts, yet not residing there." And warns that, "Whoso sayeth that the speech of Allah is created, he is an infidel regarding Allah."[66] Popular modern statements often go further: The Qur'an is the only religious text that "remains as pure as the day it was revealed. Nothing has been added, removed or modified from it, since its revelation over 1400 years ago."[67] It is "the last testament in a series of divine revelations from God. It comprises the unaltered and direct words of God."[68]

Clearly, viewed through the lens of doctrine, these two books are competing for the same space. Although the particular credal preoccupations and formulations vary, the result is similar: two different canons of scripture both claim to be God's word, and hence uniquely authoritative. This is not to ignore the considerable differences between Christians and Muslims in what we mean by calling a book God's word. We will return to some of these below. But the claims are clearly overlapping, and we therefore often find ourselves in a zero-sum game – choose one word of God or the other, not both. This zero-sum competition, in which we seek to bolster the authority claims of one book at the expense of the other, is reflected especially in polemical exchanges, but also in our apologetics and often too in our most casual interreligious conversations.[69]

Of course, this is not quite fair. In reality some Christians and some Muslims do seek to soften these boundaries in order to squeeze both books into the category of scripture. This usually involves a claim to hierarchy or supersession among scriptures. In the case of Islam, the notion of multiple scriptures comes ready-made. The Torah, ***Zabūr*** and ***Injīl*** are by definition scripture because the Qur'an says they are. But most (though not all) Muslims hold that these are unavailable in their original revealed form, and all Muslims hold that the authority of the Qur'an supersedes them. The concept of **abrogation** in the Qur'an (in contrast with the later legal doctrine of ***naskh***) reflects a clear ordering of revelation whereby earlier scriptures are successively abrogated

---

66. Waṣīyat Abī Ḥanifa, art. 9, quoted in Wensinck, *Muslim Creed*, 127.

67. "What Is the Qur'an?," Islamic Pamphlets, http://islamicpamphlets.com/the-quran-the-final-revelation-to-mankind.

68. "The Origin of the Quran," Why Islam?, 9 October 2017, www.whyislam.org/islam/originofquran/.

69. For some early examples and a succinct statement of this tendency, see Clare Wilde, "The Qur'ān: Kalām Allāh or Words of Man? A Case of Tafsīr Transcending Muslim-Christian Communal Borders," *Parole de l'Orient* 32 (2007): 402, 413–414.

by later ones, culminating with God's final word in the Qur'an.[70] The assertion that Muhammad is the seal of the prophets is another way of reinforcing this hierarchy of revelation. But qur'anic validation of the Torah, *Zabūr* and *Injīl* gives Muslims reason to be at least mildly conflicted about how seriously to take the Bible; and Christians have some grounds for arguing that their Muslim friends should take it more seriously than they sometimes do.

Christian arguments for accepting the Qur'an as a form of scripture are more complex. One strategy has been to enlarge the category of Old Testament prophecy in order to include Muhammad. *Prima facie*, much of Muhammad's message fits snugly into the tradition of Old Testament prophet-warners. But while this fits well with qur'anic ideas of prophethood, it fits badly with Christian understanding of prophecy as *praeparatio evangelica* and seems to make a mess of biblical-historical chronology. Objections to seeing Muhammad as a sort of untimely Old Testament prophet are the subject of section 7.4 of this book, so it need not take up space here.[71]

A more radical strategy adopted by a smaller subset of both Christians and Muslims would dissolve the problem altogether. A radical pluralist theology of religions will allow both the Qur'an and the Bible to coexist as co-equal scriptures – and not just the Qur'an and the Bible, but also the Vedas, the Tao te Ching, the Tripitaka, the Analects and the Book of Mormon – but only at the expense of seriously curtailing their claims to ultimacy. If we are willing to become John Hick style pluralists, then all scriptures will share the same status because all of them have been rendered subsidiary to the superior philosophical mind of the pluralist, or the experience of the mystic.[72] But for ordinary believers, pluralism of this sort is a hard sell. Consequently, whether polemical, apologetic or dialogical, our scriptural conversations often end up in a *cul de sac*.

Approaches to Interpretation

To begin exploring ways out of this apparent impasse, we move from **systematics** to hermeneutics. When we put aside apologetic or systematic concerns

---

70. John Burton, *The Sources of Islamic Law: Islamic Theories of Abrogation* (Edinburgh: Edinburgh University Press, 1990).

71. See also George Bristow, *Sharing Abraham? Narrative Worldview, Biblical and Qur'anic Interpretation & Comparative Theology in Turkey* (Cambridge: Doorlight Academic, 2017).

72. John Hick and Paul F. Knitter, eds., *The Myth of Christian Uniqueness: Toward a Pluralistic Theology of Religions* (Eugene: Wipf & Stock, 2005).

to focus on interpretation, we find that the landscape changes in ways that may open up new possibilities, or at least suggest more constructive ways of communicating about our sacred texts.

A Qur'anic Case Study

In a seminal article outlining the chief characteristics of the genre of *tafsīr*, Norman Calder uses the case of Abraham,[73] and I will draw heavily on his analysis here.[74] Qur'an *al-An ʿām* 6:74 reads, "Remember when Abraham said to his father, Azar, 'How can you take idols as gods? I see that you and your people have clearly gone astray.'" Abdel Haleem's translation,[75] along with every other English translation, adopts the most obvious reading of this verse: Āzar is the name of Abraham's father. But Muslim interpreters knew that Abraham's father was called Terah in the Bible and in Jewish tradition, and they proposed numerous possible explanations for the apparent discrepancy, which Calder enumerates: Āzar is the correct name, and the Bible is in error; or like Jacob/Israel, Abraham's father had two names, and perhaps the two names corresponded to a *laqab* (nickname) and an *ism* (proper name); or *āzar* is not a name at all but means "fool"; or it has a Persian derivation and means "old man"; or it means one who errs, a wrongdoer; or it means "to help," indicating that Abraham's father helped his people worship idols; or it is related to power or force resulting in the meaning, "Is it through force that you take idols?"; or it is the name of an idol ("Do you take *Azr* as idols?"). Grammar also figures in, so that if, for example, *āzar* is taken to mean fool, the verse might be read either as "Abraham said to his father, a fool, 'Do you take idols?'" or "Abraham said to his father, 'Fool, do you take idols as gods.'"[76]

Examples like this could be easily multiplied. Calder shows that this kind of polyvalent reading of the text is characteristic of the classical genre of *tafsīr*,[77] and that this indicates a willingness to accommodate a multiplic-

---

73. For an overview of treatments of Abraham in the Bible and the Qur'an, see Bristow, *Sharing Abraham*.

74. Norman Calder, "Tafsīr from Ṭabarī to Ibn Kathīr: Problems in the Description of a Genre, Illustrated with Reference to the Story of Abraham," in *Approaches to the Qur'ān*, eds. G. R. Hawting and A. Abdul-Kader Shareef (London: Routledge, 1993).

75. Unless otherwise indicated, all citations in this contribution (as opposed to elsewhere in this book) are from M. A. S. Abdel Haleem, trans., *The Qur'an: A New Translation* (Oxford: Oxford University Press, 2008). This was done in order to preserve Calder's argument, who uses the translation.

76. Calder, "Tafsīr," 102.

77. Calder, 103.

ity of meanings without thereby undermining the authority of the text.[78] This accommodation of a multiplicity of meanings in no way undermines the interpreter's doctrinal presupposition that the Qur'an is God's word. On the contrary, the incentive for interpreters to work so hard at collecting every possible meaning is precisely that the text *is* authoritative and therefore is of immense, indeed ultimate importance. But at the same time, it is clear that even the most skilled human interpreters often have only the vaguest notion of what God actually means to communicate to us. We must put in our best efforts, but in the end, God knows best. To put it another way, the interpreter knows that he is not God, and he knows he does not speak for God. The best he can do is struggle to hear and understand. This perspective acknowledges a canyon-like gap between the text and its meaning, and it makes clear that authority resides in the text, not in any particular meaning that an interpreter may derive from it.

This example is instructive for another reason. Because it involves an apparent conflict with the Bible, it indicates something about the interpreter's attitude toward the biblical text, and it is noteworthy that many (though not all) of the solutions seek harmony with the biblical text rather than dismissing it.

A Biblical Case Study

Something analogous happens in the case of biblical interpretation, and we can use another Abraham example to illustrate.[79] In Galatians 4, Paul famously applies the narrative of Hagar and Sarah (figuratively? allegorically? typologically?) to his Galatian audience to reinforce his argument about law and freedom. Paul takes the two women to represent two covenants: Hagar, the covenant of law at Mount Sinai resulting in slavery; Sarah, the covenant of faith leading to freedom. Now this passage is potentially of enormous importance to how followers of Jesus think about Judaism, and by extension how they think about Islam. Yet neither the context nor the precise meaning of some details in the passage are easy to discern. One crucial point in the text, verse 25, has especially puzzled interpreters. Fung lists five possibilities for how we might understand Paul's meaning in this verse: (1) A geographical reading: Sinai is a mountain in Arabia; (2) A cultural reference: Hagar represents Mount Sinai *among the Arabians*; (3) A linguistic reference: the word "Hagar" means Mount Sinai *in Arabic*; (4) We have no idea why Paul

---

78. Calder, 104.

79. Galatians 4:21–5:1; Ronald Y. K. Fung, *The Epistle to the Galatians* (Grand Rapids: Eerdmans, 1988), 204–220.

links Hagar and Sinai because the meaning is lost to us; (5) Fung's favored reading, "Now Hagar *stands for* Mount Sinai in Arabia."

Now arguably the impact of this one particular uncertainty has only a trivial impact on our overall understanding of Paul's point about law and freedom. But it would be nice to know what Paul (and God!) wants us to understand in this particular verse. And the cumulative effect of uncertainties like this is significant. Fung's commentary on the larger passage, like most responsible biblical commentary, is riddled with the language of probability, inference and preference: "He is *possibly* thinking . . . It *would appear* . . ."[80] "The first part of this verse presents us with a well-known *crux interpretum* . . . this view faces the objection, . . . *in all probability*, therefore . . ."[81] "The *apparent untenability* of the above views . . . The latter is to us *much the preferable course* . . ."[82] "The context as a whole . . . *would seem to imply* the latter . . . If, *as seems reasonable*, we may interpret this promise in the light of earlier references . . ."[83] "It is, however, *more satisfactory* . . . *if we are right* in understanding . . . The verse *seems intended* . . ."[84] "The *natural inference* is that there was a special reason for its use here . . . A *convincing reconstruction* of the probable historical setting . . ."[85]

While Fung doesn't quite come out and state at the end of the passage that only God knows best, such a response would not seem out of place. Of course as a modern commentator operating in the Western academy, Fung is obliged to argue in favor of one particular meaning; he doesn't have the same freedom of some medieval commentators (both Christian and Muslim) to contemplate the possibility that God himself intended multiple meanings. But as a thorough and careful scholar, he also faces us honestly with all of the uncertainties, and most Christians are unlikely to be shocked by this. We are so used to reading language like this in biblical commentary that it hardly registers. We know we are reading the word of God; and at the same time, we are frequently unsure about which words in our manuscripts are the words God chose to use, let alone what meaning he wants us to hear in them. In the end, we are left with a great deal of uncertainty about what was going on among Paul's Galatian

---

80. Fung, *Galatians*, 204. Italics here and in the following examples are mine.
81. Fung, 207.
82. Fung, 208.
83. Fung, 212.
84. Fung, 214.
85. Fung, 219.

recipients that led Paul to draw this Abrahamic analogy, and therefore we are left with a good deal of uncertainty about what he means and how to apply it.

Shared Challenges

These cases reveal a problem shared by readers of both the Qur'an and the Bible. When we move from doctrine to the hard work of interpreting our scriptures, the gap between the text and our capacity to understand the text looms large. We receive and experience the text from across a vast canyon created by the uncertainties of original context, of historical transmission and of language. Our doctrines of scripture concern the reality on the far side of the canyon, affirming that the original text is the authoritative word of God. But this is not where we live, work, or do hermeneutics. We do hermeneutics on the near side, where we are confronted with all of these uncertainties and human frailties of understanding and interpretation.

The case of the Qur'an is, in theory, less complex than that of the Bible. It is a far shorter work, (probably) the work of a single author over a far shorter period, (mostly) in a single language, and a mere thirteen centuries distant from us. The Qur'an itself calls its message clear and reassures us that it is written in "clear Arabic" (*an-Naḥl* 16:103; *ash-Shuʿarāʾ* 26:195). And it is true that the overall monotheistic message of the book is clear enough. But classical interpreters of the Qur'an still found plenty of puzzles to keep them busy, and some characteristics of the Qur'an make it especially difficult to interpret. The allusive quality of qur'anic narratives assumes that the reader will already know the story; often many of the details of those narratives are in tension with sources external to the Qur'an; and the language of the Qur'an was often opaque even to the earliest interpreters. The Qur'an does not provide its own narrative frame or easily reveal its own context, so that establishing historical or literary context presents enormous difficulties. The Islamic tradition seems to provide extensive data on the context of particular passages especially via the *asbāb anl-nuzūl* literature (the occasions of the revelation). But even if we ignore serious questions about the authenticity of these traditions, the sheer volume and variety of the material often presents interpreters with multiple options from which to select in establishing the context of any particular passage. The classical tradition of *tafsīr* acknowledges all of this variety, and indeed, these challenges of interpreting the text are the very *raison d'être* for *tafsīr*.

Interpreters of the Bible face corresponding, though even greater, challenges.[86] The historical gap is many centuries wider. Biblical literature is more varied and complex, unfolding over millennia of history. The biblical canon brings together the contributions of roughly forty human authors, many anonymous, writing in multiple languages, deploying multiple genres, and from strikingly varied historical and cultural contexts. We rightly assume that responsible handling of God's word will require an enormous amount of effort to bridge the gaps of time, of culture and of language that separate us from the original texts. Much of what we learn in seminary aims at helping us to bridge this gap.

Divergent Strategies

The general challenge is a shared one: Muslims and Christians claim to hear God speak through ancient texts, but we are separated from those texts by many centuries, by language and by culture. How will we bridge this gap? It turns out that the tools and methods we use are strikingly different. Textual criticism is the most obvious example. In even the most basic lay Bible study, Christians find themselves discussing not just what a word means, but whether Isaiah, or Paul or God intended to use that particular word at all. We are unsurprised by marginal notes indicating textual variants. Ordinary Christians have, to a large extent, accommodated themselves to text-critical methods. Indeed, the huge number and variety of manuscripts and the complexity of transmission history of the biblical text made the development of such methods indispensable, and study of the Bible became one of the great engines for the refinement of techniques of textual and manuscript criticism.

Many Christians are willing to go well beyond such basic textual criticism. Few scholars shy away from discussions of the documentary hypothesis, the authorship of Isaiah or the synoptic problem. Indeed, such discussions are more or less obligatory in modern biblical commentary. Christian doctrines of inspiration pose no insuperable obstacles to this kind of scholarship. Yes, the Bible is the inspired word of God; it is also the words of David, Isaiah, Matthew, Paul, and dozens of other prophets, poets, historians, evangelists and theologians, many of them anonymous. Accepting that the Bible can

---

86. For evangelical perspectives on biblical hermeneutics, see Grant R. Osborne, *The Hermeneutical Spiral: A Comprehensive Introduction to Biblical Interpretation* (Downers Grove: IVP, 1991); Graeme Goldsworthy, *Christ-Centered Biblical Theology: Hermeneutical Foundations and Principles* (Downers Grove: IVP, 2013); Graeme Goldsworthy, *Gospel-Centered Hermeneutics: Foundations and Principles of Evangelical Biblical Interpretation* (Downers Grove: IVP, 2014).

at the same time be both divine word and human word is unlikely to pose an insuperable problem for people who confess that the Creator God of the universe entered history as a Jewish baby.

Muslim interpreters of the Qur'an will countenance none of this. They will not "consider a word or passage as incomplete or corrupt, a victim of scribal transmission," nor will they "entertain theories about cultural borrowing or extra-Islamic influence."[87] Consequently, "most of the questions that fuel the historical-critical method of the biblical scholar are, for their qur'anic counterpart, non-questions or even blasphemies."[88] The uncertainties acknowledged by Muslim interpreters are always uncertainties of meaning, never of the text itself. We can discern here the burdens of the Muslim doctrine of revelation whereby the Qur'an is pure speech of God, free of any taint of human influence, and in no way the word of Muhammad. The doctrine of the inimitability of the Qur'an further reinforces the purely divine origins of the text. In light of such doctrine, certain questions about the text are ruled out *a priori*. This tendency has hardened in the modern period,[89] and since 1924, all variations, even in the vowelling of the text, have been obscured by the remarkable success of a uniform Egyptian edition.

We also use very different tools to establish context. Muslims rely almost exclusively on traditions transmitted independently of the Qur'an to match texts of the Qur'an to the events of Muhammad's life and to his words and deeds. Muhammad becomes the "living Qur'an," and his life and example is its essential hermeneutical key. Christians have no such authoritative tradition, but are accustomed instead to amass and weigh evidence from a wide range of historical sources, which vary, of course, depending on the particular biblical text, genre and historical period. And in the end, the interpretation of many biblical texts depends heavily on evidence internal to the scriptural canon, that is the witness of other biblical texts. We argue for a particular meaning of a word Paul uses in one place on the basis of the way he uses it in other places, or the Old Testament texts he is drawing on.

These divergences leave plenty of opportunity both for serious misunderstanding and for genuine disagreement. In the category of misunderstanding, the undeniable human element in the biblical text, and Christian

---

87. Jane Damen McAuliffe, *Qur'ānic Christians: An Analysis of Classical and Modern Exegesis* (Cambridge: Cambridge University Press, 1991), 30.

88. McAuliffe, *Qur'ānic Christians*, 30.

89. Daniel Brown, "The Triumph of Scripturalism: The Doctrine of Naskh and Its Modern Critics," in *The Shaping of an American Islamic Discourse: A Memorial to Fazlur Rahman*, eds. Earle Waugh and Frederick Denny (Atlanta: AAR, 1998).

acknowledgement of it, has been used polemically by Muslims to argue the unreliability and corruption of the Bible.[90] Christians in turn conclude that Muslims are naïve and uncritical, incapable of confronting key questions raised by the qur'anic text.[91] In both cases, we tend to read one another's scriptures through the lens of our own interpretive tradition. Christians come to the Qur'an expecting a good story and built-in contextual clues, and find it incoherent and difficult to decipher; Muslims read the Bible thinking God should be speaking, only to discover (as they may have expected all along), that they are instead reading stories about Jesus penned by Luke or letters written by Paul. Misunderstandings are multiplied when we read one another's scripture in uncharitable ways because we have already prejudged it to be false. Thus, it may seem obvious to the English reader of a translation of the Qur'an, oblivious to all of the interpretive uncertainties, that the Qur'an is simply mistaken about the name of Abraham's father and about a great deal of other biblical data. And similarly, Muslims who know that the Qur'an is perfect and that the Bible has been corrupted will have just as much certainty that that biblical text got it wrong, or has been changed.[92] Similarly, Paul's use of Sarah and Hagar and their sons to represent freedom and slavery will appear to directly clash with Islamic sacred history and will be easy for many Muslims to dismiss without ever struggling to understand what Paul means. Clearly taking refuge in hermeneutics will not shield us from the impact of doctrine. So have we taken a long detour just to return to the doctrinal impasse with which we began? Not necessarily.

Paths Forward

It is important to acknowledge these differences and to recognize that the task of interpretation cannot be hermetically sealed off from doctrinal predispositions. But our situations are similar enough to at least wonder whether we can work up enough mutual empathy to find a way out of our apologetic *cul de sac*. Figuring out what the Qur'an means takes hard work and is fraught with uncertainty; figuring out what Paul means is equally difficult. In both cases

---

90. Christians have less frequently explicitly argued the corruption of the qur'anic text, although Wilde describes an early case of a Christian, Theodore Abū Qurra, making this argument. Wilde, "The Qur'ān," 404–413.

91. A. T. Welch, "al-is Argument," *Encyclopaedia of Islam*, eds. P. Bearman, Th. Bianquis, C. E. Bosworth, E. van Donzel, and W. P. Heinrichs, 2nd ed. (Leiden: Brill, 1960).

92. For an extended treatment of how such misunderstandings have played out historically, see Accad, *Sacred Misinterpretation*.

we are seeking to understand ancient texts and uncertain contexts from which we are separated by huge gaps of time, language and culture. We discover that interpretation is a human, fallible enterprise which leaves plenty of room for argument and which demands humility. Can we harness the humility of the interpreter as a basis for constructive conversation? To put the proposal more precisely, what will happen if Christians read the Qur'an with the same level of humility and respect that we show toward the interpretation of the biblical text, seeking first to understand it rather than to score apologetic or polemical points? And similarly, what if Muslims were to interpret the biblical text with the same degree of respect they show to the text of the Qur'an?

Building a case for such an approach is not difficult. Muslims and Christians share a common humanity, and the Bible and the Qur'an address themselves not to some subset of humans, but to all. Therefore it becomes both the right and the responsibility of Muslims *as humans* to listen and respond to the challenge of the Bible, and similarly for Christians *as humans* to listen and respond to the challenge of the Qur'an. But to listen and respond, we must make a good faith effort to understand the message; and we can hardly expect to do this responsibly without learning from those who have worked within a centuries-long tradition of interpretation. Moreover, coming to these texts as humans, we also bring to them a full set of existential dilemmas that are also common to humans. We suffer, we face injustice and cruelty, and we are unjust and cruel. We feel guilt and shame; we experience meaninglessness, unexpected joy and unbelievable pain, sometimes all on the same day; and we die.

This logic alone should be enough to encourage us to venture out of our apologetic fortresses onto common ground. But we can say more. Beyond common humanity, we also share a set of monotheist theological assumptions that make the world challenging to decode. Were we polytheists, we would have no particular reason to expect ultimate justice, beauty or meaning. The gods and spirits of polytheism are often just as crazy and unpredictable as we are. By contrast, our shared belief in one all-powerful creator God, without beginning, end or limitation, who is also just, all-merciful and good, leaves us the kinds of shared existential tensions that give rise to the extraordinary poetry of Job, Isaiah, Rumi, Iqbal and Gerard Manley Hopkins. The vagaries of history and the challenge of finding meaning in it add further to the tension. Sovereignty and freedom, transcendence and immanence, election and choice, justice and mercy, law and grace. These are tensions Christians and Muslims share, and our theological strategies for thinking about them often overlap.

In other words, when we approach scripture, we come with a set of shared problems that arise not just from shared humanity but also from a shared monotheism and a sacred history that, while not entirely shared, overlaps in significant ways. Add to this the substantial common challenges, described above, that we face in interpreting and understanding our scriptures, and we have plenty to talk with each other about. My modest suggestion is that we make the starting point of our interreligious conversations these shared problems, and that we focus these conversations squarely on the human side of the hermeneutical canyon that separates the interpreter from the word of God.

Some Christian (and Muslim) readers may immediately be troubled by this suggestion and will cycle back to the doctrinal problems with which we began. Won't bracketing off the question of revealed authority in this way amount to a betrayal of our faith in the unique authority of the Bible (or the Qur'an)? If Christians take seriously another book that claims to be revealed, aren't we granting it an authority that belongs exclusively to the Bible? The solution seems to me quite simple, and Western Christians implicitly embrace it each time we read or quote Plato or Shakespeare. That we take these texts seriously, treat them with a certain cultural reverence, and expect to learn important lessons from them would be an understatement. Yet when we do so, we seldom feel that we are somehow endangering the unique status of the Bible. We have another category for such texts which assigns them a kind of authority, though not ultimate authority. We call them classics.

A Case Study

What might it look like in practice to grant one another's scriptures this degree of respect while still remaining loyal to our own? An extraordinary recent publication, Shabbir Akhtar's *The New Testament in Muslim Eyes: Paul's Letter to the Galatians*, presents us with a test case for the possibilities and limitations of such a project.[93] Akhtar writes his commentary from an explicitly Muslim viewpoint, but from a perspective informed by constructive interaction and relationship with Christians. Thus he jettisons key polemical tropes that have marked most previous Muslim responses to Paul and his epistles. He dismisses Muslim vilifications of Paul as "simplistic views, at best caricatures of Christian origins and possibly character assassination of Paul."[94] He writes,

---

93. Shabbir Akhtar, *The New Testament in Muslim Eyes: Paul's Letter to the Galatians* (London: Routledge, 2018).

94. Akhtar, *New Testament in Muslim Eyes*, 13.

"Muslims slander Paul when they assert that he wanted Christians to behave as libertines."[95] By contrast Akhtar sets out to write "with charity and clarity, not evasion and malice."[96] He assumes the textual integrity of Galatians, and he suspends judgment on Muslim accusations of *taḥrīf*.[97] His stated aim is "to enter into St Paul's mind and present fairly his vision to the Muslim (Gentile) reader."[98]

These are remarkable goals, unique in the history of Muslim commentary on Christian scripture. How does Akhtar's commentary measure up to these ambitions? As a test, I made a survey of his treatment of the Abraham material in Galatians 4:21–31, measuring my own reactions as a Christian and a fairly average reader of biblical commentary. I immediately found myself with a boatload of complaints. (But in case you are reading, Shabbir, please stay with me until the end.) Akhtar begins by labelling this Galatians passage as an allegory that is "ostensibly about Abraham's two sons."[99] Calling this an allegory is not particularly surprising, since Paul himself calls his treatment allegorical. But Akhtar skips any discussion of what Paul means by allegory and whether it is the same as what he might mean. Is it allegory? Or typology? Or analogy? Or illustration? More irritatingly, I suspect that Akhtar uses "allegory" pejoratively, since he goes on to say that Paul's use of Hagar, Sarah, and their sons in this way is "indefensible"[100] because, "Only when the literal is problematic does one need to, and therefore should, resort to a figurative reading."[101] Here Akhtar imports a distinctively Muslim distinction between figurative and literal verses of the Qur'an in a way that fits badly with the range of genres or complexity of biblical literature and its uses. Nor is this distinction even properly representative of the range of the Muslim *tafsīr* tradition. My more serious complaint, though, is that this dismissal short circuits any significant discussion of why Paul might have adopted an approach that is, admittedly, unusual for him. What was going on among his Galatian readers, and what were his opponents saying, that would lead him to bolster his argument with this kind of appeal, and why would he (presumably)

---

95. Akhtar, 12.
96. Akhtar, 12.
97. Akhtar, 11.
98. Akhtar, 1.
99. Akhtar, 179.
100. Akhtar, 182.
101. Akhtar, 183.

have thought it (*contra* Akhtar) both defensible and effective? On this question Akhtar won't help us, because he doesn't ask. Why not?

Akhtar wishes that this section of Galatians "had not been penned by the apostle."[102] Fair enough. We all feel that way sometimes, and Akhtar helpfully admits that he feels this way about some passages in the Qur'an, but that, regret it or not, we must nevertheless accept scripture as received.[103] What are his reasons for this regret? They have mostly to do with hypothetical anti-Muslim uses of the passage. "It is an obscure allegory," he complains, "plastic to interpretation and therefore one easily recruited for promoting anti-Islamic sentiment."[104] He fears that "adventurous or mischievous contemporary Christian preachers" could easily use these verses "to extract a negative notice of Islam" and the passage "can be readily prostituted to denigrate Hagar, Ishmael and thus Muhammad and Islam, including contemporary Islam."[105] I am sympathetic. Having read more than my share of anti-Muslim polemical literature, I know that these concerns are not just hypothetical, and Akhtar is careful to absolve Paul himself of blame for such misuses of scripture. What I find myself wishing is that Akhtar had spent less time complaining about hypothetical misuses, and spent more time carefully and patiently showing us how such readings conflict with a legitimate reading of Paul's argument. I am not satisfied that enough effort has gone into listening to Paul and seeking to bridge the huge historical and contextual gap.

Some of these limitations are a predictable consequence of Akhtar's goal, which is to provide commentary from an explicitly Muslim perspective. But sometimes he seems over eager to interject his Muslim perspective. I would occasionally like to hear more about how he responds as a human being to something Paul says, but he interjects the solution, the correct Muslim answer, sometimes too quickly and too confidently. At the end of one especially thought-provoking passage, for example, Akhtar concludes that Paul's emphasis on the ethical dimensions of the law and his spiritualization of the moral life "would both be alien – though not anathema – to Paul's Muslim readers." This is tantalizing, and I wish he would say more.

In a few places, my confidence is more severely shaken. For example in an astonishing dismissal of a huge volume of historical research, Akhtar minimizes the impact of Roman rule in first-century Palestine on the grounds

---

102. Akhtar, 180.
103. Akhtar, 180.
104. Akhtar, 180.
105. Akhtar, 186.

that his grandmother had grown up in rural pre-partition India oblivious of British rule![106] Earlier, in his introduction to the passage, he sums up Paul's covenant of the Spirit as "anti-Sinaitic, anti-Torah, anti-Mosaic," and says that Paul's intention is "to repeal and replace the older covenant of law."[107] Neither of these over-confident contentions display any awareness of the last several decades of research on Paul and the complexities of his approach to the law. This introduces my final complaint, which is that Akhtar too often seems to be neglecting the kind of lively, continuing conversation with prior commentators and scholars that is often a distinctive feature of good commentary, whether biblical or qur'anic. Too often it seems like a three-way conversation – Paul, the Qur'an and Shabbir. This is a very modern, even fundamentalist, way of reading.

Having unloaded all of these complaints, what is my assessment? It may come as something of a shock to say that I really like this book. Akhtar approaches Paul in a way that opens conversation rather than closing it down. Where I have disagreements or complaints, they are frequently the same kinds of complaints I might have of any biblical commentary. I face no temptation to throw the book across the room, which is more than I can say for many popular Christian books I have picked up. In other words, the book functions the way it should. It opens conversation, invites disagreement, confronts me with ways of reading the biblical text that are unfamiliar to me, makes me want to argue, and makes me think that it may actually be worthwhile to argue.

What enables this? At his best Akhtar, true to his aims, takes Paul with sufficient seriousness, honesty and charity to grapple with his argument. He really does want to hear what Paul has to say. Akhtar accepts the authority of the text as a given – not as ultimate authority, but rather the kind of authority we grant to any established text as a basis for exploring its meaning. He shelves upfront attempts to undermine or dismiss the text as corrupt or inauthentic, focusing instead on trying to understand the meaning of the received text. Does he do this with perfect consistency? No. His summary dismissal of Paul's use of Sarah-Hagar imagery as illegitimate, for example, circumvents basic hermeneutical questions. (What is Paul striving to accomplish by invoking this imagery? And why?) But this dismissal does not lead to an impasse. These are things we can talk about.

I find it extremely helpful as a Christian to read how an erudite Muslim responds to these passages. And while this will hardly pass as a great

---

106. Akhtar, 184.
107. Akhtar, 180.

compliment, reading Akhtar is far more interesting, more encouraging and rather more edifying than listening to Ahmed Deedat.

I have focused on Akhtar's work because it is a rare, indeed groundbreaking, example from a Muslim perspective. What about Christian cases? Akhtar's approach to Galatians bears comparison to Kenneth Cragg's approach to the Qur'an,[108] though the resemblance may seem ironic since Akhtar has remained consistently hostile toward Cragg's work.[109] In reality Cragg, like Akhtar, is a very modern reader, often coming to the text of the Qur'an relatively unencumbered by the classical *tafsīr* tradition. In this Cragg mirrors his modernist interlocutors. Also like Akhtar, Cragg was often quick, perhaps too quick, to interrogate the text in specifically Christian ways. But most importantly, he came to the text of the Qur'an assuming both its integrity and its authority – granting it far greater authority, in fact, than Akhtar is willing to grant to the biblical text. Joseph Cumming models a different, though similarly respectful approach, which takes much greater account of the Muslim interpretive tradition.

Do these models have any real significance for everyday conversations between ordinary Christians and Muslims? After all, not many of our Muslim friends will have Shabbir's grasp of Greek or be given the time or resources to study the biblical text in any depth, and few Christians will come close to Kenneth Cragg's mastery of qur'anic Arabic or his depth of sympathetic immersion in the text of the Qur'an. I have two responses. First, exercising hermeneutical humility requires no specialized training or gifts. One of the most obvious symptoms of such humility will be genuine curiosity. We should, in theory, be able to work side by side, and indeed to learn from each other without specialized training. Second, I think we need to ask why such expertise is so rare. Perhaps our institutional boundaries are too high. What if Christians invited Muslim students into our seminaries to share in our struggle to understand the biblical text? What if our Muslim friends invited us to study *tafsīr* with them? In the end, we would certainly retain grave disagreements.

---

108. On Cragg, see Nicholas J. Wood, *Faiths and Faithfulness: Pluralism, Dialogue, and Mission in the Work of Kenneth Cragg and Lesslie Newbigin* (Eugene: Wipf & Stock, 2009); and Christopher Lamb, *The Call to Retrieval: Kenneth Cragg's Christian Vocation to Islam* (London: Grey Seal, 1997).

109. In this book Akhtar dismisses Cragg as an apologist, offering him as an example of "competitive pieties locked in a deadlock – a religious form of rigor mortis" (Akhtar, *New Testament in Muslim Eyes*, 2). To be fair, Akhtar's trouble with Cragg seems to be his theology, not specifically his treatment of the Qur'an. At least I hope this is the case, because Cragg's treatment of the Qur'an is arguably rather more respectful than Akhtar's approach to the biblical text.

But we will have become fellow travelers in the shared struggle to hear and respond to the word of God.

6.7 Testimony 3: Senem Ekener on Following Jesus in Turkey

We pause with a testimony presented as an interview. We will meet the interviewer, Grant Porter, in chapter 8. One focus here is the growth of the church in Turkey.

Grant: Senem, please introduce yourself.

Senem: I am from Izmir in Turkey. I was raised in a nominal but traditional Muslim home. I have a degree in philosophy. I rejected Islam during my studies, so being "Muslim" was no longer part of my identity. I had a slow journey to Christ, making a decision to follow him when I was twenty-five.

Grant: So how do you identify yourself?

Senem: This is tricky. If I say that I am a Christian, then it will be presumed that I am of Greek or Assyrian ethnicity. There is the false notion in Turkey that to be a Turk is to be a Muslim. Yet I am a Turk who is a follower of Jesus Christ.

Grant: Please describe your role and ministry in Turkey.

Senem: My work as the country director for the Ravi Zacharias International Ministries is to lecture as a member of the speaking team.[110] This work gives me a varied portfolio of activities including speaking and sharing to defend the faith and teaching in church-based theological education programs. Our strapline is "Help the believer think and the thinkers to believe." I seek to express the love of Christ in all encounters with Muslims. I meet a wide variety of people in both urban and rural settings. I live in Istanbul but travel throughout the country. I am delighted to see a growing church in Turkey. I see Jesus as an amazing example and regard Acts as a textbook for mission.

Grant: In Turkey, what questions are people in the age range of eighteen to twenty-five typically asking?

---

110. Ravi Zacharias International Ministries, www.rzim.org.

Senem: I wish that they asked more! Some are desperate about the future, lacking hope or purpose, not feeling safe and perceiving that their lives have little meaning or significance. Many see the dominant faith very negatively; they are disenchanted with Islam. Some are agnostics or atheists, although most remain theists. They see themselves as not provided for and the victims of injustice. The gospel addresses all these concerns.

Grant: The rise of atheism in the Arab world is a huge surprise, even shock to many. Is the same happening in Turkey?

Senem: There are some, but it is mainly an underground trend. Few openly identify themselves as such, although some use nicknames on social media. In face-to-face encounters, it is common to find rejection of Islam. This leaves people not knowing or understanding God, which creates an incoherence in their minds with religious convictions not making sense. It results in anger, fear and numerous questions, often unasked. Few regard God as being even close to compassionate. This might look like a mind problem, but it creates a significant heart problem. One consequence is the need for sensitivity with people who first enter a church; the need is for careful exploration of their thinking and their exploration of religious matters.

Grant: The case study at the start of this chapter shows different reactions by the characters.

Senem: Their ages are not stated, nor is the length of time that they have been Christ's followers. Muhammad has engaged in religious study all his life. Yet this appears to not be respected or welcomed. His desire to study the Bible is commendable, including addressing the difficult passages. I have appeared on a Christian TV channel. I found it hard to be a presenter; I was fearful of stumbling. But I would like to spend time one-to-one with Samira. This would enable me to check her beliefs and discuss how she might live them out. It would, I think, be wrong to threaten her in her understanding of Christianity. It is rare in the Turkish context to have a new believer from a deeply Islamic context: most have drifted well away from Islam before coming to Christ, much as I did. So we rarely do comparative study because most Turkish believers have long since left the Qur'an.

Grant: How did you respond to Pastor Issa's presentation *(in section 6.4)*?

Senem: I only know the Qur'an from a translation into Turkish. In my context, it is very rare that people ask deep questions about the text, and few people are aware of the issues raised. Also, polemical approaches are rarely used in the Turkish context.

Grant: In the Turkish context, what is your typical advice to new believers on sharing with parents and other family?

Senem: One approach is to ask someone else from the church to speak with them. Typically, one can openly identify with Christ in Turkey, although there are elements that some choose to keep quiet about. I encourage people to be pretty open, not least because of the amazing transformative power of Jesus. So at least in urban contexts, there is no need to remain Muslim in the cultural sense. In remote areas there are people coming to faith through dreams and visions, and some organizations are trying to identify them and connect them with others. I am delighted that the actual numbers are higher than what is often claimed. For many Muslims, identifying as Christian is understood to mean adopting a full Western, worldwide perspective and culture. We constantly endeavor to challenge this, since there is a very rich history of Christianity in Turkey, including that approximately half the New Testament was written to or from the country.

Grant: Is there space for someone to say that they are a Muslim but follow Jesus's teaching or an equivalent?

Senem: There are Muslims reading the New Testament, coming to church, and sincerely searching for truth. I sometimes challenge them with the question, "You have met Jesus; would you like to accept him?" In urban contexts, friendship remains the number one reason that most people come to faith, so walking through life with people is crucial. This produces slow, steady church growth.

Grant: What is your dream for the Turkish church in twenty years' time?

Senem: Wow, that is a very emotional question. First, that it grows in every city. Second, that there are many followers of Christ, not simply students of the Bible or religious converts. Third, that there would be traffic issues on Sunday because of the number of people coming to church! More seriously, growth often comes with suffering, so in a strange way, we welcome suffering. We are very thankful for many missionary friends. Please pray for an increasing number of people being convicted by the Spirit in their hearts and minds. Harvesting is God's work and according to his timing. Please pray that many Turks come to know Jesus truly.

Grant: We will be pleased to pray with you for these things.

6.8 A Conversation among Friends: Exploring Missiological Implications

Moderator: Welcome. Let's begin by asking what humility looks like.

Jewish-Background Disciple (JBD): First before God, then before texts, and by extension before those whom God has made. "Consider others better than yourself" is a command to us all. Humility is toward that which demands respect. Humility does not mean compromise. Before God, humility can mean taking a stand which might be painful or costly, such as confronting the powerful about a matter of injustice. Conversely, bowing down to the powerful is not bowing down before God; that might not be humility.

Muslim-Background Disciple (MBD): Approaching the Qur'an, I need to listen and learn. I used to react negatively to the very idea of continuing to learn from the Qur'an. I have learned to respect all people not least because everyone has something to say, whether or not I agree with it. Learning from sources does not imply that one agrees with them.

Moderator: Being provocative, are we not being polluted by it?

MBD: Let us look at Jonah as an example. There is nothing in the Qur'an about Jonah that we could disagree with, and further, there are many common elements. One theme of the biblical account of Jonah is grace, since we see God acting in grace toward Jonah. This is an example of how much we learn about God from the Old Testament. I rejoice when I see Muslims recognizing that God operates in grace.

Christian-Background Disciple (CBD): I agree about approaching dialogue with humility and humble hearts. We should not be coming from above in order to dictate what we know. A better approach is to ask questions, to reach out to the other. We are not looking for a debate or a fight; we are seeking an exploration of truth.

Moderator: Great. But what if they are attacking the Bible or Jesus?

CBD: My response is to keep calm and ask why they have such misconceptions. My desire is that we start exploring together who Jesus is. I commend praying before, during and after all conversations with Muslims.

Moderator: Amen to that! What more can we add about the spectrum from compromise to bridge building?

MBD: What level of engagement are we talking about? Many conversations are within specific dynamics, such as childhood friends or a Muslim seminary student coming into a church, which are two very different scenarios. Most of the time it is the prejudices and misconceptions of the other that are being challenged. We need to let these come out since they need to be articulated. Then we can start bridge building. One exercise is to pick a biblical character and write a defense of the biblical view of that character in the light of qur'anic material on that same person. With Muslims, I often encourage them to look at the biblical text on Mary, Jesus and God; my desire is that they gain a biblical view of the historical facts about these characters.

Moderator: This looks like a bridge of ideas. Is there another level, such as relational, when they are putting us into a box?

MBD: Jesus was so counter-cultural! He shocked many by wanting to relate to people when they did not agree about faith or ethical behavior.

JBD: What do we mean here by compromise? My answer would be that which betrays my relationship with Jesus and my loyalty to him. What constitutes this varies by context: it could be silence in one setting and speaking out in another.

MBD: I re-examine my emotions. Middle Eastern culture typically insists that men be strong, say what they think and never display fear. As a male follower of Jesus, do I need to behave like this? I ask, what does it mean to be strong as a Christian man? How is my behavior understood by those around me?

Moderator: We have to be acting differently. I think that hospitality could be crucial for bridge building. Is it fair to say that the Qur'an is part of who Muslims are? Could we say something similar about an atheist? Or is it simply that someone who comes to Christ is lost and found?

CBD: I emigrated from the Arab world to the West twenty-five years ago. It took me time to deal with baggage from my country and to learn how to live well in Western culture. Similarly for those who become disciples of Christ: in their discipleship, it will take them time to deal with their former theological understandings.

MBD: I agree that we all come with various allegiances before we come to faith in Christ, and everyone's discipleship journey takes time.

JBD: I suggest that one approach would be to consider carefully how we regard the Qur'an and the religious literature of other non-Christian faiths. In a similar way to how literary classics are handled, we need to give them authority, status and respect without treating them as authoritative. Could a disciple from a Muslim background defend the Qur'an in a similar manner to a classicist with an ancient text?

Moderator: Some Muslims become interested in Jesus through reading the Qur'an. So is there a revelation of Christ within it?

MBD: I no longer regard the Qur'an as revelation. Muhammad did not reflect on a text: he did reflect on Jewish and Christian traditions. As we have seen in this chapter, God uses the story of Jonah to speak to people in many ways, for example praying in a time of crisis. Some Muslims read this and understand that God hears prayer. God is dealing with everyone in many different ways. We need to understand that God speaks through history in many ways, including through narratives about prophets.

JBD: Are there limits in creation and history as to how God can speak? For example, could he speak through a Hindu temple with many idols?

MBD: In my opinion, texts are authoritative, and so it is very difficult to set limits.

JBD: Likewise, I would not set many limits since God can reach down to speak to people anywhere. In my observation, he uses many things to draw people to himself.

CBD: I agree. Paul in Athens used the statue to the unknown God *(see section 2.3)*. We need to beware of focusing on dreams, visions, etc., and maintain a clear focus on his word.

Moderator: Being controversial, I know an Indonesian example of an imam who became a disciple of Jesus but is still leading a mosque as well as preaching in a church. He speaks from the Qur'an about Jesus. How legitimate is this?

MBD: What is the imam teaching in the mosque?

Moderator: It could be philosophical and fluffy. It is about ethics, not Jesus.

MBD: How does he continue to do his job? Clearly, he is known and accepted as a Muslim in the mosque and as a follower of Christ in the church.

Moderator: From the front in both the mosque and the church, he speaks about Jesus and ethics. With a small home group of followers of Jesus, he speaks about Jesus as God.

JBD: Important to me would be his integrity and loyalty to Jesus.

Moderator: Two key areas of our reflections are Muhammad and the Qur'an. People such as this imam redefine their understanding of them, a subject that we will return to later *(see section 8.5)*. Moving this conversation on, how do you balance your focus on academic, theological and relationship-based approaches to engaging Muslims?

JBD: I do not see them as separate things. I endeavor to speak with everyone at an appropriate level. Incidentally, I do the same in a church with apologetists and polemicists!

MBD: I think that the separation of academia and practice is damaging. Our purpose here is to bring the two together so that we all might learn from one another. Study has helped me to be clearer in my conversations with my Muslim family and friends, who all span a breadth of academic levels. Our studies can challenge Muslims since they enable us to sit and talk about the questions that Muslims are asking.

A colleague of mine is doing a master's degree in religious philosophy in a secular university and is having great conversations with class cohorts. We need to think creatively about being with Muslims. I find numerous topics very useful in conversations with them, one being theodicy – notably the question, "why do bad things happen to good people?"

Moderator: So if you meet a Muslim who you are unlikely to meet again, what one thing would you share about your faith?

JBD: God is love.

MBD: God is gracious and merciful.
God loves you; Jesus paid a price for you.

CBD: God loves you; please let me help you download the Bible app.[111]

Moderator: Many thanks to you all.

Questions for Discussion

1. How can we develop greater humility? What benefits might this bring to our engagement with religious others?
2. How should we regard the sacred texts of other faiths while maintaining our belief in the supremacy of Christ and the authority of the Bible? How should we describe sacred texts in our conversations?
3. How might we describe the origins of the Qur'an in ways that reflect the traditional view of most Muslims while maintaining scientific honesty and integrity given the contents of this chapter?
4. How do we understand the Qur'an's use of biblical characters? What similarities and differences are we aware of? How might we use this understanding in our engagement with Muslims?
5. What processes are most applicable for understanding sacred texts on their own terms? Can we apply the same methods to the Bible and the Qur'an?

---

111. One Bible app source is https://my.bible.com/ar/. Languages other than Arabic are also available here.

7

Thinking Biblically about Muhammad

Poetry by Yasser (translated by Martin Accad)
Will You Murder Me?

> Will you murder me, my brother, although I care for you?
> > Will you remove my spirit from my being and the blood from my veins?
> Will you slaughter me in God's name? In God's name will you harm me?
> > You call out "Akbar" into the open, and your call becomes the blade at my throat
> Jesus guides me, and he commands me to love you
> > He reminds me that God is present in both pieces of my severed body
> My head rests in your hand while my eyes look to heaven
> > And my brow bleeds in pain as the fire of the sword slices me
> In my heart are questions that sear me with a burning pain
> > Will the Lord accept your **takbeer** and reject my religion?
> I have a Lord in heaven who saves me and rescues me
> > From the fires of a sea of brimstone he protects me
> I forgive you for you are my brother, of the same flesh and mud
> > Despite the slaughter I have no remorse;
> > for my act of forgiveness is the zenith of religion.

أتقتلني؟

أتقتلُني وأنت أخي وأمرُك كان يعنيني؟
تُزيل الروحَ من روحي ودمي من شراييني؟
أبِسم الله تذبحني أبِسم الله تؤذيني؟
تنادي في المدى أكبر وكبرك نصل سكيني
يسوع كان يأمرني لحبك كان يهديني
يذكّرني بأن الله مقسوم على اثنيني
وبات الرأس في يدك وتنظر للسما عيني
وتنزف جبهتي ألمًا ونارُ السيف تصليني
بقلبي نارُ أسئلةٍ تعذبني وتكويني
أيرضى الرب تكبيرَك وينسالي أنا ديني
أنا لي في السما ربٌّ يخلصني ينجيني
من النيران في بحر من الكبريت يحميني
أسامحُك فأنت أخي ومِنّ لحمي ومن طيني
ورغم الذبح لن أندم سماحي قمّةَ الدينِ

7.1 Opening Reflection: Who Is This Man?

Senem Ekener

What is the most important thing about Jesus? Is he a gifted teacher? A miracle worker providing food for the hungry and healing for the sick? All are correct, but far from everything. The Bible presents him as a man correcting wrongs, striving against some aspects of the times. Further, he is described as Savior and the giver of eternal life. But what Jesus does is not what he is.

C. S. Lewis in his book *Mere Christianity* notes that Jesus's claims about himself mean that he is either divine or a liar or a con man; he is either mad, bad or God. Luke 5:17–26 describes the healing of a paralytic man. It is a complex scene and benefits from many camera angles. The parallel passage in Mark is helpful (Mark 2:1–12). Many people are present to listen to Jesus's teaching. Some are from the religious class (Luke 5:17a) and are there to evaluate his teaching and decide whether to include him among their number or reject him as outside of Judaism; they are there to pass judgment. In our days, many Muslims are doing likewise, evaluating Jesus's teaching and deciding how to respond. These are important questions; some linger over them for a long time. Is Jesus going to prove reliable for them?

In this story, Jesus is both teaching and healing: Luke's emphasis is on healing (Luke 5:17b), whereas Mark emphasizes the teaching aspects. In Jesus's era, prophets confirmed their status by miraculous acts. Many Muslims revere Jesus as a prophet and urge us to do likewise. The challenge for us is to encourage them to take the next step: to consider Jesus's claims to be more than a prophet.

We are not told where this story occurs. It appears that Jesus is in the main room, and the religious leaders have been given the best seats. Their desire is to control or manage him. Into the picture enter four men carrying a fifth man on a pallet. They have no hesitation in causing a disturbance. One wonders what the venue's owner thought as part of the roof was dismantled and dust fell into the room and onto some of those present. The four men made a considerable effort, displaying tremendous persistence, belief and a "do whatever it takes" attitude to put their friend immediately in front of Jesus. They ignored the opinions of others. How aware were they that "the power of the Lord was with Jesus" (Luke 5:17b)?

Jesus does the unexpected. He does not pronounce healing. Instead, he pronounces forgiveness of sins (Luke 5:20). We must note that Jesus saw the faith of the four men (Luke 5:20) which I take as an encouragement that our faith in Jesus can make a difference in bringing people before Jesus. Many are paralyzed or trapped by sin and assorted fears, yet we can bring them before our Lord.

My husband decided to follow Jesus before I did. He encouraged others to pray that I would follow him to Jesus. After I accepted Jesus, I received postcards from people that I did not know saying how they had been praying for me. Many people carried my metaphorical pallet and put me before Jesus. Who are we putting before Jesus in prayer? Who are we inviting to our places of worship? Social study suggests that it requires someone to know two to four people in a church before they are comfortable accepting an invitation to attend.

I wonder what the man and his four friends were thinking at this point. They came seeking and expecting healing, not forgiveness. Yet Jesus operated on a higher, richer level. Many people come to Jesus wanting help with all sorts of challenges; yet their key need is dealing with their deepest spiritual needs. The man got salvation and healing. In our day, Jesus may heal physically or not, yet he will certainly forgive the sins of all who ask. He is God in flesh; we have been ransomed. This is Jesus.

Many in the audience were shocked, none more so than the Pharisees. They now had a very clear answer to their question: Jesus was clearly, in their eyes, a blasphemous teacher.

Ultimately, all sin is against God (cf. Ps 51:4) and must be forgiven by God, hence Jesus's authority to forgive. In this instance, Jesus claimed that the healing proved his authority to forgive sins and the attendant claim of divinity (Luke 5:22–24). Forgiveness of sins is an invisible action, contrasting with the highly visible physical healing.

The outcome was that many were amazed and glorified God (Luke 5:26). Yet some were fearful. There are always mixed reactions to Jesus, especially to his claims to divinity. Is Jesus God incarnate or just a morally upright, good man?

7.2 Muhammad Case Study: Questions the Church Asks

This case study, compiled by the IMES team, is fiction based on oversimplified yet all too typical conversations among disciples of Christ. May it stir our minds and hearts as it introduces the subject of this chapter.

Boulos, an elder at the Church of Grace in Beirut, Lebanon, leads a small group of Muslim background believers (MBBs) as part of his church's outreach ministry. Boulos gets excited to see Muslims becoming Christians and, in the process, publicly renouncing Islam. He encourages these people to stand firm for the truth without compromise by telling their families that Muhammad is the Antichrist and a false prophet. He believes that this bold practice will shock Muslims and cause them to turn their eyes toward Jesus.

Imad, an MBB and member of the same church, leads a small group of MBBs in the Beirut suburb of Mansourieh. He is a friend of Boulos. Imad encourages MBBs in his group to become a living testimony to their families and to speak about the love of God, avoiding discussions about Muhammad as much as possible. Having once heard from a Western scholar of Islam that Muhammad might not even be a historical figure, avoiding the prophethood of Muhammad altogether makes sense to him. It is Imad's hope that Muhammad's influence in the lives of those he disciples will gradually diminish as they learn to follow and obey Jesus. To Imad, Muhammad was an ordinary person who had both good and bad issues in his life, but it is not necessary to label him as a false prophet.

Rima, also an MBB but a much more recent disciple and cousin of Imad, was visiting him at his home one day when Boulos dropped by to check on his friend. As the three were discussing ministry issues among MBBs, Rima said that whereas Jesus is Lord and Savior, Muhammad was nevertheless a good reformer for his time, not unlike the prophets of the Old Testament. Boulos became furious and accused Rima of compromising her faith and being syncretistic. Rima was surprised by Boulos's reaction, and as a result she left the room. Imad was embarrassed because of the awkward situation and stood by, silent but angry.

You are asked to gather together Boulos, Imad and Rima in order to help each of them understand the point of view of the others.

Questions for Discussion

1. With whom, among the three characters, do you most identify?
2. What would you see as being the goal or goals of such a conversation? Would you try to convince them to adopt a particular view on the issue, or would you simply seek to help them understand their different attitudes and positions?
3. How do Christians in your community typically view and talk about Muhammad? Do you think this view is consistent with the facts of history?
4. Suppose Muhammad never claimed to be a prophet, but instead, two hundred years after his death, the Islamic community fabricated his life's account and claimed he was a prophet whose ministry superseded and replaced previous revelations. Would this have any implications for how you think about Muhammad or your approach to ministry practice?

7.3 The Quest for the Historical Muhammad

Martin Accad

The Muslim world has lived with a particular representation of Muhammad that has emerged from traditional narratives developed during the first two centuries after Muhammad's death (roughly mid-seventh to mid-ninth centuries), which we may refer to as the "Muhammad of faith." The traditional narrative reports that Islam's prophet was born in Mecca, a city in the Hijaz in western Arabia, to the polytheistic Arab tribe of Quraysh, and that he invited his Arab people to embrace the worship of the One God of Abraham, Moses and other biblical prophets, warning them of eventual doom and hell's fire if they did not do so. It affirms that, after a period of rejection and persecution in Mecca, Muhammad migrated with his early followers to the northward city of Yathrib – later known as Medina – where he was invited by local tribes to take up a leadership position. In Yathrib, a city whose trade and leadership were dominated by Jewish tribes, Muhammad reorganized society within a political and legal structure that embraced all tribes and confessions in the city under one *umma* (nation), defined by *al-Islām*, a verb indicating "submission" to the One God of the Judeo-Christian tradition.

The instance of the Hijra (migration) in this narrative represents a turning point for Muhammad's followers, a shift from being an oppressed minority to a successful, all-embracing tribe ready to take their message of pure monotheism to the rest of the known world. Whereas the traditional narrative up to this point spoke of convergence between the faith of Muhammad's early community and that of the Judeo-Christian communities of Arabia, it begins now to speak of divergence. Jewish tribes, which up until then had accepted – or at least tolerated – the new leader from Mecca as sufficiently aligned with their beliefs so as not to disturb the social peace, began to perceive him as a threat from about the third year of his transition to their city. From this point onward, the traditional narrative begins to offer accounts of conflict and war between Muhammad and the Jews, reflected even in cultic practice in the qur'anic (and hence divinely revealed) instructions to shift the direction of their prayer from Jerusalem (the Jewish *qibla*) to Mecca (the second *qibla*).

But twentieth-century critical scholars, particularly in the West, have questioned the historicity of traditional Muslim narratives (Hadith), and by doing so have brought the whole classical representation of Muhammad – chiefly based on Hadith – to the brink of collapse. Some of these critical approaches are covered in Daniel Brown's contribution on Islamic origins in section 5.2 above and need not be repeated here. At the same time, these scholars have affirmed the ancientness of the Qur'an, whose earliest manuscripts date from the end of the seventh century. According to this new, revisionist scheme, the Qur'an would be a far more reliable source from which one may infer an identity of Muhammad that is more faithful to the original historical figure.

Where does that leave us with the question of who the "historical Muhammad" really was? What can we learn about him from a reading of the Qur'an, which is a rather opaque source of information from which to derive a biography? The present contribution will seek to draw an alternative picture of the "Muhammad of history," which differs from the "Muhammad of faith" usually held by Muslims. How does this alternative picture inform the church's mission in the world of Islam, including the ministry of discipleship and the formation of new communities of faith around Christ?

I have advocated in much of my writing and teaching over the past fifteen years for what I call the *kerygmatic* approach to Christian-Muslim interaction which moves away from the extremes either of syncretism or of polemics.[1] The former, which tends to minimize differences between the faiths, is inadequate when we engage in conversation with Muslims who care about their faith. True interfaith engagement should not shy away from our differences but seek rather to understand the other faith respectfully and authentically. The polemical approach, on the other hand, is even less adequate in our multifaith world where the church is called to be an agent of peace and transformation rather than of conflict. An aggressive approach not only breeds conflict, but as we will see in this section, it tends to rely as much on historically unreliable source materials as the classical Muslim approach to the biography of Muhammad. By contrast, the kerygmatic approach is Christ-centered, prophetic, scientifically honest and driven by missional motivation and outcome. In the concluding sections of the present piece, I will discuss how a quest for the historical Muhammad fits within a kerygmatic approach to Christian-Muslim interaction and why it serves the missional purpose of the church better than a simple acceptance of the classical Muslim portrait.

The Dual Message of the Qur'an and What It Tells Us about Muhammad

What we have to work with, then, is the Qur'an. The Qur'an is a text which, according to current manuscript evidence, originates at least in some of its parts from the second half of the seventh century.[2] We may safely assume that the Qur'an had an author. While the Muslim tradition has affirmed that God was its author, if we belong to a community that stands outside the Islamic tradition, we are not required to retain this assumption. The only confession we are bound to is a recognition that the Qur'an is an early text within the traditional Muslim chronology of Islam's emergence. In light of the brief introduction above, we must also affirm that the Qur'an is the most reliable source of information for anything we can know about its author, just as any piece of literature has much within its pages to reveal about its author.

---

1. My initial piece on the kerygmatic approach and the SEKAP Spectrum was published in Martin Accad, "Christian Attitudes toward Islam and Muslims: A Kerygmatic Approach," in *Toward Respectful Understanding and Witness among Muslims: Essays in Honor of J. Dudley Woodberry*, eds. Evelyne A. Reisacher et al. (Pasadena: William Carey Library, 2012), 29–47. I apply both my approach and spectrum in practice in my book on theological dialogue, Martin Accad, *Sacred Misinterpretation: Reaching across the Christian-Muslim Divide* (Grand Rapids: Eerdmans, 2019).

2. See the contribution of Issa Diab *(in section 6.4)* for a comprehensive treatment of the Qur'an's origins and the current status of textual studies.

In our quest for the historical Muhammad, we assume that the founder of Islam – a religion birthed out of the Qur'an's message – was also the Qur'an's primary author. We must then come to terms with its message as we would with any piece of literature. This means that we will not take for granted any of the traditional Muslim interpretations of the text. For traditional *tafsīr* has embraced the traditional biography of Muhammad – the Sira – as a reliable source of historical data for the reconstruction of the historical context of God's revelation of the text to his prophet. This has been referred to as ***asbāb an-nuzūl*** – the occasions of the revelation. However once we have accepted the Western critique of the Hadith, whose individual traditions form the building blocks of the Sira literature, none of this reconstruction may be accepted uncritically, which leads us to a re-reading of the Qur'an as a text with its own integrity.

We will therefore not assume the traditional division of Muhammad's life into a Meccan and a Medinan period. This structure was adopted by Muslim exegetes in order to make sense of the diverse and sometimes conflicting message of the Qur'an. The affirmation that Muhammad was a persecuted preacher and warner in the polytheistic context of Mecca, who turned into a community organizer, lawgiver and even military leader in Medina, has served as a helpful framework for Muslim exegetes. But as we have said above, this chronology is the fruit of a narrative reconstruction of building blocks whose authenticity have been seriously questioned. Critical revisionist scholars have even argued that the supposed "occasions of the revelation" were themselves the outcome of this exegetical exercise, forged in response to the need to fill out the numerous gaps in meaning left by a text that quickly lost the original socio-cultural and geographical setting in which it was composed. Once this chronological periodization became dogma, qur'anic commentators continued to attribute various portions of the Qur'an to the one or the other "period" in Muhammad's life, depending on whether they felt that their contents better fit the oppressed preacher or the victorious leader. As a result of this critique, classical Muslim exegesis emerges as a closed, circular and self-referencing hermeneutic that does more to hide the intended meaning and message of the text than to reveal it.[3]

Though we will therefore largely ignore this classical hermeneutic, we may nevertheless not ignore the reality of the Qur'an's dual message that is contradictory in some places and puzzling in others. The purpose of the next

---

3. For a book that argues to this effect, see Gabriel Said Reynolds, *The Emergence of Islam: Classical Traditions in Contemporary Perspective* (Minneapolis: Fortress, 2012).

part of this contribution is to propose other ways of making sense of this dual literary evidence. Can we make sense of the diverse message of the Qur'an without resorting to the **Mecca-Medina** schema? I propose some alternative options which will provide the background for the following exploration of what we might learn about the "historical Muhammad" through the pages of the Qur'an.

Anyone acquainted with the content and style of the Qur'an will agree that it represents a genre in itself. With its mix of preaching, eschatological warnings and promises, moral pleas and demands, prophetic narratives, kernels of legal prescriptions, and even elements of a philosophy of war and combat, it certainly cannot serve as a helpful source to reconstruct a biography in the traditional sense. But this does not make it useless as a source of information about its author. Our expectations, however, must be aligned with the possibilities offered by the text. What will emerge are the outlines of Muhammad's thinking and belief system, his self-perception vis-à-vis other ideologies of his day, and his convictions on what constitutes appropriate behavior for the believers in his faith community. Furthermore, to the extent that we are convinced that his retelling of prophetic stories from the Judeo-Christian tradition serve a moral and behavioral purpose, we may even propose that he carried out certain actions modeled on those prophetic stories narrated in the Qur'an. The logic here is that an author who integrates stories from previous sources into his own text always does so selectively. His choices may be assumed – for the most part – to serve a specific purpose, possibly to act as paradigm for his own behavior or serving as a reflection over, and justification of, his own behavior.

To be clear, the use of the Qur'an as a primary source for our understanding of the historical Muhammad will not yield a comprehensive story. Indeed, the text was not meant to offer such a story, and we do not do justice to a text by trying to make it say what it was not intended to communicate. Michael Cook, who took the revisionist critique of Islamic Hadith literature seriously, attempted to reconstruct the story of Muhammad in his book, *Muhammad*, first published in 1983 with a reissue in 1996. In his second chapter, entitled "Life," Cook asserts that his "aim here is simply to present the traditional account in outline – not, at this point, to interpret it or assess its reliability."[4] The rest of his endeavor in this book consists in deriving from the qur'anic text Muhammad's convictions regarding the nature of the universe (ch. 3), his view of history (ch. 4), his role as lawgiver (ch. 5), and the beginnings of his

---

4. Michael Cook, *Muhammad* (Oxford: Oxford University Press, 1996), Kindle 114.

political theory (ch. 6). This endeavor should give us pause as to the humble nature of the task of deriving biographical information about Muhammad from the Qur'an. Given the limitations of the present piece, I will not reiterate these points of doctrine that emerge from the Qur'an, and my survey of the life of Muhammad based on the traditional Muslim sources will remain limited to what I have already said in the preceding paragraphs.

What this contribution will focus on, therefore, is Muhammad's attitude toward people of other faiths in Arabia during his time. How he viewed other religions, particularly Judaism and Christianity, should tell us much about his understanding of his own mission. Did Muhammad intend to be the founding prophet of a new religion? Or did he perceive himself as a reformer and continuer of the Judeo-Christian tradition? Was his agenda captured by his later followers to serve socio-political and religious purposes that he had not sought himself? It is these questions above all others that will drive our present investigations.

Furthermore, the attitude and behavior of a person of faith toward people of other faiths tells us much about their moral character. Was this not the primary assumption both of the Middle East Consultation 2018 on "Jesus Christ and the Religious Other" and of 2019 on "Thinking Biblically about Muslims, Muhammad and the Qur'an"? We consider it as of primary importance for the mission of the church today to develop a view of the religious other – and of Muslims and Islam's core components – which aligns both with the biblical imperative to love our neighbor and which facilitates the formulation of a theology of Islam within the boundaries of biblical salvation history.

The final section of this contribution will address the all-powerful question, "so what?" Material emerging from a piece entitled "The Quest for the Historical Muhammad" could indeed be used for the purpose of polemics against Islam. But just as "historical Jesus" quests have been used in biblical studies by some liberals and agnostics for theologically destructive purposes, while others have used them in pursuit of greater scientific knowledge and in support for the truth, I believe that "historical Muhammad" quests may also be used in pursuit of the truth and in collaboration with Muslim scholars who are committed to their Muslim faith. In fact, I will argue in the final section that our quest for the "historical Muhammad" will contribute more effectively and honestly to discipleship and interfaith peace than an embrace of the "Muhammad of tradition." In the final analysis, the "Muhammad of history" will continue to serve as the "Muhammad of faith," perhaps even more effectively than the "Muhammad of tradition."

Historical and Ideological Duality in the Qur'an

The reader of the Qur'an is confronted with tensions between a message of continuity and affirmation of the Judeo-Christian tradition on the one hand and a message of dissociation and polemics against any other message than Islam on the other. Some verses clearly argue that the message of the Qur'an is no different than preceding revelations. Muhammad considered that the message he was bringing in the Qur'an was basically a contextual reinterpretation of what God had revealed to Jews and Christians in the Torah and the *Injīl*:

> He has sent down the Book to you with the Truth to confirm what is available of other revelations, as it is He who sent down the Torah and the Gospel beforehand as guidance to people, and He revealed the standard by which we judge right from wrong. Those who do not believe God's signs will have severe punishment. God is Almighty and capable of revenge. (*Āl-'Imrān* 3:3–4)

The affirmation of the Qur'an's continuity with the Judeo-Christian tradition is based on the sense expressed in the Qur'an that it is an Arabic version of preceding revelations. There is ample evidence in the Qur'an itself that Muhammad viewed his message as essentially an Arabic version, expansion and interpretation of the scriptures of Jews and Christians, which at the time circulated in Arabia in languages that were foreign to Arabs (emphases are mine):

> This (Qur'an) is the revelation sent as you received it from the Lord of the worlds, and brought down by The Trustworthy Spirit to your hearts, that you may (Prophet) be of the warners *in a clear perfected (Arabic) tongue*. It is mentioned in the Scriptures of the ancients. Is it not a sign that the scholars of the Children of Israel knew it? (*Ash-Shu'arā'* 26:192–197)

> Yet before it, was the Book revealed to Moses, a guide and as a mercy. And this *a Book confirming it in Arabic tongue* to warn those who are unjust and to bring good news to those who do good. (*Al-Aḥqāf* 46:12)[5]

---

5. Another nine verses that emphasize the importance of the Arabic medium of the Qur'an are *Yūsuf* 12:2; *ar-Ra'd* 13:37; *an-Naḥl* 16:103; *Ṭā Ha* 20:113; *az-Zumar* 39:28; *Fuṣṣilat* 41:3, 44; *ash-Shūra* 42:7; and *az-Zukhruf* 43:3.

In one verse, Muhammad seems to address his followers as the "People of the Book," a term generally reserved for Jews and Christians, inviting them to believe in the Torah and the gospel in addition to his own message:

> Say, "People of the Book, You have no valid ground for your beliefs, unless you (truly) observe the Torah and the Gospel, and all that has been sent down to you from your Lord." Yet all that has been sent down to you (Prophet) by your Lord is bound to make many of them more stubborn in their arrogance and in their denial of the truth. Do not worry about unbelievers. (*Al-Mā'ida* 5:68)

At the end of the verse, Muhammad is already aware that some will reject his invitation, both from among Jews and Christians, as well as from among those who had become his followers. Generally, Muhammad's attitude toward Jews differed from his attitude toward Christians, even though he expressed hope that Jews and Christians would receive his message with open arms. This tension is strongly reflected in the following verse:

> You (Prophet) are sure to find that the most hostile to the believers are the Jews as well as those who are bent on ascribing partners to God. While, you will find that the nearest in affection towards the believers are those who say, "We are Christians," because there are priests and monks among them, and because these people are not given to arrogance. (*Al-Mā'ida* 5:82)

From verse 83 of the same Sūra, it would even seem that many Christians were positively affected by his message:

> For, when they understand what has come down to this messenger, you can see their eyes tear up because they recognize the Truth in it, and they say, "Lord, we do believe. Make us one with all who bear witness to the Truth." (*Al-Mā'ida* 5:83)

The same idea is reflected in another verse, where the Qur'an rebukes polytheists for not believing the message, in contrast with the People of the Book who recognized in it the commonality with what they had received before:

> Say, "Believe it or do not believe it." When it is recited to those who have been given knowledge before, they fall down on their faces in prostration, saying, "May our Lord be exalted in His glory! Truly, our Lord has fulfilled His promise" and they

fall down, weeping. It (the Qur'an) fills them with humility. (*al-Isrā'* 17:107–109)

Other verses express frustration and disappointment with Christians and Jews because they rejected Muhammad's message. One verse reflects the view that the problem is not with the Judeo-Christian scriptures, but rather with the Jews' and the Christians' lack of obedience to their teachings:

> And if they would truly observe the Torah and the Gospel and all that has been revealed to them by their Lord, they would have been given an abundance of grace from heaven and earth. Some of them are on the right course, but most of them do what is evil. (*Al-Mā'ida* 5:66)

The Qur'an can get quite polemical with such people. The following is a verse that likens Jews to donkeys who were given precious knowledge but were not worthy of it:

> The example of those who were entrusted to uphold the Torah, but then failed to uphold it, is that of a donkey carrying volumes of knowledge. Terrible is the example of the people who reject the signs of God. God does not guide the unjust People. (*Al-Jumuʿa* 62:5)

Christians, too, are accused of the same sin:

> Let the followers of the Gospel judge according to what God has revealed in it. *Those who do not judge in light of what God has revealed are deviators*. (*Al-Mā'ida* 5:47, emphasis is mine)

Some verses indicate that Muhammad was skeptical of Jews and Christians, as he realized that all did not actually agree with his message and considered that he was not a true messenger of God. The Qur'an's statement about them can be rather negative and aggressive, and it contains a warning to Muhammad's followers if they follow their skepticism:

> The Jews and Christians will not be pleased with you until you follow their ways. Say, "God's guidance is the guidance." If you follow their whims, after having received knowledge, you will not have anyone to protect you from God or to help you. (*Al-Baqara* 2:120)

The Qur'an thus warns the followers of the new message against forming alliances with Jews and Christians. But as Safi Kaskas, whose English translation of the Qur'an is used in most of the citations in the present book, points out in a note regarding this verse, such verses seem to warn against political alliances rather than day-to-day friendships:[6]

> Believers, do not take the Jews and Christians as allies. They are only allies with one another, and whoever allies himself with them becomes one of them. God does not guide such unjust people. (*Al-Mā'ida* 5:51)

This verse reflects that Muhammad at some point had attained political power and that he viewed his movement as a challenge to other political powers of his day. It probably constituted a warning against forming alliances with Christian Byzantium or with other powers that were challenging his rising dominance in Arabia.

Doctrinal and Political Duality in the Qur'an

The reader of the Qur'an is, moreover, confronted with tensions between a message of social and religious tolerance on the one hand and a message of political and military dominance on the other. There is a clear duality in the Qur'an's attitude toward Jews and Christians. Some verses emphasize the necessity to embrace and affirm adherents of the preceding revelations:

> Truly those believers in this message, as well as the Jews, the Christians, and the Sabeans, whoever believes in God and in the Last Day and does righteous deeds will have their reward from their Lord, and will not have fear, nor will they grieve. (*Al-Baqara* 2:62)

> The believers, as well as the Jews, the Sabeans and the Christians: all who believe in God and the Last Day and do righteous deeds, will have nothing to fear and they will not grieve. (*Al-Mā'ida* 5:69)

The message of tolerance preached in these verses is based on the preacher's conviction that Jewish, Christian and Sabean beliefs will lead their adherents to salvation. The bar to reach salvation in these verses is quite low: a belief in God and "the Last Day," and a life of righteous deeds. Based on this conviction, the author of the Qur'an enjoins his followers not to engage in pointless polemics with the People of the Book. The only legitimate reason to engage in polemics is if any of these people are "unjust." There is a clear

---

6. See note 26 in Safi Kaskas, trans., *The Qur'an: A Contemporary Understanding* (Fairfax: Bridges of Reconciliation, 2015), Kindle 2309.

belief expressed that the God that Muhammad is proclaiming is the same God that Jews and Christians believe in:

> If you argue with the People of the Book then argue only in the kindest way, except with those among them who are unjust, and say, "We believe in what was revealed to us and in what was revealed to you. Our God and your God is one; and we are submissive to Him." (*Al-'Ankabūt* 29:46)

In other verses, however, Muhammad seems less convinced of Jews' and Christians' correct beliefs, partly it seems because Jews and Christians condemned each other. But ultimately, he believed that God would judge between right and wrong belief on the Day of Judgment and that it was not his role to bring down on them earthly punishment:

> The Jews said, "Christians are without valid ground," and the Christians said, "The Jews are without valid grounds," while they chant the Book. The ignorant speak similarly. God will judge between them on the Day of Resurrection concerning their differences. (*Al-Baqara* 2:113)

Muhammad was clearly frustrated by Jewish and Christian claims that they held exclusive truth. He knew from stories about the children of Israel that had reached him that God did not always vindicate them in their self-confidence. He affirmed that God alone was the ultimate judge and holder of the truth, which would be revealed at the end days:

> The Jews and the Christians say, "We are God's children and His loved ones." Say to them, "Why does He punish you for your sins? No, you are only human beings of His creation. He forgives whomever He wills, and He punishes whomever He wills, for God has control over the heavens and the earth and everything in between. All journeys lead to Him." (*Al-Mā'ida* 5:18)

Further, it seems that even though Muhammad believed that Judaism and Christianity were in essence true, he was also aware of certain beliefs they held that were clearly contrary to his own convictions about God's unicity. But here again, he did not set himself as judge against them and left it for God to vindicate his truth in the end:

> As for those who believed, the Jews, the Sabeans, the Christians, the Magians and those ascribing divinity to other than God – God

will judge between them on the Day of Resurrection. God witnesses all things. (*Al-Ḥajj* 22:17)

The Qur'an's duality with regard to Jews and Christians is reflected in verses where Muhammad appears to have thought that he did not only have the responsibility to preach the message of monotheism, but also that of enforcing his message with political and military force. Traditional Muslim exegetes ascribed such verses to the Medinan period, when Muhammad is supposed to have been not only the preacher, reformer, social leader and legislator of a community but also a military leader. If we put this hermeneutical lens aside, however, what we are left with is qur'anic ambivalence toward preceding revelations. We will look at the way that the Muslim tradition has dealt with this duality later in this section. Here we will simply cite the so-called "sword verse" (*āyat as-sayf*):

> Fight those People of the Book who do not believe in God and the Last Day, those who do not forbid that which has been forbidden by God and his Messenger, and do not follow the religion of Truth, until they pay the exemption tax after having been subdued. (*At-Tawba* 9:29)

It is important to note, at the same time, that the legislation of war in the Qur'an's message is based strictly on the principle of self-defense, and the fighting had to be carried out only against those who actively and militantly opposed the message of Muhammad and subjected his followers to persecution. If they ceased their persecution, Muslims were to stop the fight as well:

> Fight in God's path against those who fight you, but do not be aggressors, for God does not love aggressors. . . . Fight them until there is no more persecution and until all worship is devoted only to God. If they stop, there should be no aggression – except toward the unjust. (*Al-Baqara* 2:190, 193)

Muhammad's issue with some Christians, as reflected in specific verses of the Qur'an, tended to be doctrinal. Where their beliefs led them to reject him, the Qur'an adopted a more polemical attitude toward them. But we should note as well that the beliefs ascribed to Jews and Christians in the Qur'an are often hard to reconcile with orthodox doctrine and may in fact have reflected the sectarian beliefs of some of these communities in Arabia. An example is the description the Qur'an gives of Jewish beliefs concerning Ezra. Here again, the assertion of the Qur'an is that it is ultimately God's responsibility to punish and destroy them:

Some Jews say, "Ezra is God's son," while some Christians say, "The Messiah is God's son." This is what they say with their own mouths. They repeat the assertions made before by unbelievers. "May God destroy them." How perverted are their minds. (*At-Tawba* 9:30)

Making Sense of Qur'anic Duality: A Hermeneutic of Supersession or of Redaction and Interpolation?

How have Muslim Qur'an commentators harmonized these texts that reflect duality regarding Jews and Christians? They have proposed a variety of exegetical solutions. When confronted with conflicting commands in the Qur'an, Muslim exegetes first established which of the verses were revealed in Mecca and which ones in Medina. The second step consisted in giving primacy to one set of verses over others. We have evidence of two approaches.

By far the most widespread exegetical device during the classical period was the principle of **abrogation** (*an-nāsikh wa al-mansūkh*). The verse revealed later had abrogated – meaning changed, replaced or corrected – the earlier one. Since those verses containing political, legal and military injunctions are largely considered to have been revealed during the Medinan period, the nature of this abrogative Islam became primarily one of political and military domination. Indeed, much of Islamic history can be understood through this hermeneutical lens.

A second solution to this dilemma was to affirm another exegetical principle – that of "the universal versus the particular" (*al-ʿāmm wa al-khāṣṣ*). Traditionally, this principle has represented a minority voice within Islam, primarily present among the more peaceful tradition of Sufi Islam and the more quietist currents of historical Shiʿism. One of its strongest proponents in the modern era was Mahmoud Mohammed Taha (1909–1985), a Sudanese reformer who believed that universal Islam was represented primarily in the Qur'an's Meccan message. Though he considered moderate, non-militant Meccan Islam to represent "authentic" Islam, he believed that Muhammad's community was not ready for its pure message in the seventh century. Thus, God had abrogated that message for a time, until believers would be able to subscribe to Islam's original prescriptions. This is how he explained the more legislative, political and even militant verses revealed during the Medinan period. Taha, therefore, allowed for the principle of abrogation, but he reduced its validity to a limited time in history, beyond which the principle of Meccan universalism superseded Medinan temporality. As a result, he considered that much of Islamic practice today was in error, and in his book entitled *The Second Message of Islam*, he advocates the return to Meccan Islam: "Many aspects of the present Islamic Sharīʿa are not the original principles or objectives of Islam. They merely reflect a descent in accordance with the circumstances of the time and the limitations of human ability."[7]

In this day and age, a form of Meccan Islam is often assumed implicitly by the majority of Muslims who swiftly distance themselves from violent streams among some of their coreligionists. The affirmation of Meccan Islam's primacy is increasingly the leaning of Muslim moderates, both in the Western world and outside of it. Qur'anic injunctions to fight were limited to the particular historical context of early Islam in Medina. Safi Kaskas, for instance, provides several notes in his translation of the sword verses. Regarding verses 29 and 30 of *Sūrat at-Tawba* (9), he explains that they referred to "those idol worshipers Arabs who violated their peace treaties by waging war against the Muslims," adding on the authority of qur'anic commentator Abu Bakr al-Jassās (d. 370 AH), that "these verses are particular to the Arab idolaters who were in a state of war with the Muslims, and do not apply to anyone else."[8] Regarding *Al-Baqara* 2:190–193, he explains:

> To understand the verses 2:190–193 and those it is referring to, it is important to understand its context. Ibn Abbas, the famous companion of the Prophet and qur'anic exegete, says that this passage was revealed in reference to the Quraysh. The Quraysh tribe had persecuted the Muslims and tortured them for thirteen years in Makkah. They had driven Muslims out of their homes, seized their properties and wealth, and fought battles against them after the Muslims sought refuge in Madinah. The Muslims were apprehensive about another attack occurring during their sacred pilgrimage when fighting was prohibited for Muslims. This is why these verses were revealed to reassure the Muslims that they would be able to defend themselves against a Qurayshi attack during pilgrimage. Such fighting never actually took place between them and Quraysh, for a peace agreement was upheld and the pilgrimage was permitted.[9]

---

7. Mahmoud Mohammed Taha, *The Second Message of Islam*, trans. Abdullahi Ahmed An-Naʻim (Syracuse: Syracuse University Press, 1987), 137.

8. Kaskas, *The Qur'an*, Kindle 3562, no. 35.

9. Kaskas, Kindle 1424, no. 9.

Clearly the qur'anic permission to fight is troublesome to some contemporary Muslims. But since the verses are found in the Qur'an, they have to find a way to dismiss their universal legitimacy by some hermeneutical means. This is done by relativizing such verses and relegating them to a historical past. The universality of the moderate Meccan message, on the other hand, is upheld as applicable to every day and age. Contrary to Taha's acceptance of the principle of abrogation that applied for a limited historical period, however, Kaskas rejects the principle of abrogation altogether. In his glossary of terms, he explains the meaning and limitations of the qur'anic principle of *naskh*. "It generally refers," he explains, "to the qur'anic verses said to be abrogated or nullified by later verses. However, in time, new theological and philosophical theories emerged denying that any verses in the Qur'an abrogate others. The abrogation mentioned in 2:107 refers to the Qur'an abrogating previous messages."[10] Kaskas thus rejects the idea that later-revealed verses could have abrogated earlier ones. The only abrogation he admits is that of the Qur'an's abrogation of previous revelations in the sense of supersession.

Another way of looking at the duality in the Qur'an's attitude toward preceding revelations is to admit the possibility that interpolations had entered certain passages at some stage after their original proclamation. These interpolations could have taken place during Muhammad's own lifetime and originated from him, in which case they would reflect a development in his own thinking. This suggestion may be sustained without necessarily agreeing with the traditional Mecca-Medina trajectory. They would be the result of doctrinal developments in his own thinking rather than resulting from such a dramatic historical turning point as the Hijra.

A more radical hypothesis would be to ascribe the Qur'an's duality toward preceding faiths to post-prophetic interpolations. If we allow for this possibility, the original profile of the historical Muhammad may differ in any degree from the one inherited from the later Muslim tradition. The current state of research into the integrity and coherence of the qur'anic text provides neither for the dismissal of, nor for overconfidence in, such a theory. One Qur'an scholar today, Nicolai Sinai, in his most recent book exploring the Qur'an from a historical-critical perspective, joins earlier scholars in identifying a few passages in the Qur'an that may signal later interpolation. Though he affirms that such interpolations need to be cautiously considered as "inevitably probabilistic," he nevertheless maintains that "the hypothesis of secondary interpolation nonetheless constitutes an important part of a qur'anic scholar's

---

10. Kaskas, Kindle 10737.

explanatory toolkit."[11] For the purpose of the present piece, I will not attempt further to demonstrate the strength of such a hypothesis. Suffice it to maintain that later interpolation into the text is a possibility, in our broader attempt to recover the original attitude of the Muhammad of history toward other religions, whereas a more detailed pursuit of the theory will need to be undertaken through more extensive research.

In Quest for the Historical Muhammad

Having examined the Qur'an's attitude to preceding revelations, and having considered this to represent Muhammad's own position, we now come to some conclusions about what this feature of the Qur'an can tell us about the identity of the historical Muhammad. What difference does it make if we read these passages from the perspective of classical Muslim exegesis, through a more progressive hermeneutical lens, or through the hypothesis of later interpolation?

The Muslim Muhammad

If we accept the classical Muslim exegesis of the Qur'an, we must come to terms with the fact that Muhammad's preaching underwent a major shift after the Hijra from Mecca to Medina. Muslim exegetes, as we have just seen, have been well aware of this, and they have proposed various hermeneutical solutions to this dilemma. The tension resides in that an acknowledgment of such a shift would have to conclude on a first reading either that God changed his mind about his purpose in sending his messenger, or that the messenger himself had initially misunderstood his calling and that God later set him back on the right track. Neither of these two solutions is readily acceptable to a Muslim believer convinced both of God's immutability and of his prophet's infallibility. The two exegetical principles of *asbāb an-nuzūl* (the occasions of the revelation) and of *an-nāsikh wa al-mansūkh* (the theory of abrogation) have generally come to the rescue of classical exegesis here.

As Qur'an commentators have generally placed the verses affirming continuity in the Meccan period and those stressing discontinuity in the Medinan period, they have been able to argue that a parting of the ways between Islam and preceding religions had taken place during the Medinan period, based on the theory of abrogation. From this view derived the doctrine that Islam

---

11. Nicolai Sinai, *The Qur'an: A Historical-Critical Introduction* (Edinburgh: Edinburgh University Press, 2017), Kindle 2700.

was the final revelation that came to supersede and replace Judaism and Christianity. The "change of heart" is explained primarily by means of a narrative from Muhammad's traditional biography that tells of rising tensions and conflict that are supposed to have occurred between Muhammad and the Jewish tribes of Medina during the second year of the Hijra: "About this time the Jewish rabbis showed hostility to the apostle in envy, hatred, and malice, because God had chosen his apostle from the Arabs."[12]

In addition, as we have seen above, there are varied views of Jews and Christians and their doctrines expressed in the Qur'an – ranging from affirmation, to great expectation, to disappointment, to harsh criticism. Viewed through the Mecca-Medina framework, affirmation and expectation were set in the context of Mecca, whereas disappointment and criticism were set in the context of later Medina.

The Muhammad of the Muslim tradition is therefore a man who initially affirmed continuity with Judaism and Christianity by proclaiming that his message was no other than a new and refined expression of previous revelations. He affirmed this by emphasizing the centrality of the lowest common denominator in terms of doctrine. But once Jews and Christians had rejected the authenticity of his prophethood, he rebuked them, not by dismissing their religions, but by accusing them of having wrongly and unfaithfully interpreted their scriptures. The Muslim Muhammad, then, emerges as the final prophet in a long line who brought to humanity the final and perfect scripture that fulfilled and completed all preceding ones.

The Judeo-Christian Sectarian Muhammad

If we stand outside the Muslim faith tradition, we have access to more than simply exegetical devices to make sense of the complex and seemingly conflicting message of the Qur'an regarding preceding religions. If as Christians we may not feel comfortable either with the idea that God sent a messenger with a new message after Christ, or that he changed his mind in the process of his guidance of that prophet, we will then retain the possibility that Muhammad set out with one mission and mandate, which may perhaps even have been inspired by God, but that he later shifted course for utilitarian political purposes.

This approach may either retain the classical division of qur'anic verses into Meccan and Medinan, or it may largely dismiss this framework.

---

12. Alfred Guillaume, *The Life of Muhammad: A Translation of Ibn Ishaq's Sirat Rasul Allah* (Oxford: Oxford University Press, 2002), 239.

Essentially, though, this view will consider that the historical Muhammad had far more affinity with the Jewish and Christian communities of Arabia than is admitted by the traditional Muslim view. Muhammad must have belonged to some syncretistic Judeo-Christian sect of Arabia, which explains why he was himself conflicted in his attitude toward both faiths.

There are a number of elements in the Qur'an that would seem to support this position. For one thing, the traditional profile of Muhammad as a pagan man with no original connections with the Judeo-Christian tradition does not explain why his message was so replete with biblical and extrabiblical allusions from these traditions. A pagan Qurayshi who wanted to establish himself as a new prophet, endowed with divine authority and a message received directly from God through no human intervention, would have had no reason to affirm any Judeo-Christian sacred narratives. This would only have drawn accusations of plagiarism, as it in fact did. For comparison's sake, if Jesus or Paul had not affirmed their Jewish identity but had instead claimed to have received a completely new revelation, we would not have expected to find them relying so heavily on the Jewish scriptures in their teaching. As things stand, however, our understanding of the Jesus movement as a fulfillment of Judaism fits naturally with the fact that Jesus was a respected rabbi and that Paul was a high-caliber Midrashist[13] who was able to make sense of the Hebrew scriptures in a new way in light of the Christ event.

The Judeo-Christian Muhammad would therefore have been an Arab man who grew up with much affinity with Judaism and Christianity. His family may even have belonged to a Judeo-Christian sect of Arabia, where mostly oral traditions – both biblical and extrabiblical – were deeply and abundantly familiar. Qur'anic anachronisms; biblical name confusions; prophetic stories often reflecting later Jewish narratives from the **Midrash** and Christian narratives from the apocrypha rather than from the Bible; and references to the gospel (*Injil*) consistently in the singular and reflecting no knowledge of the four gospels are all elements that reflect Muhammad's knowledge of the Bible primarily through oral tradition. The Judeo-Christian sectarian Muhammad would have initially viewed himself as a reformer of Judaism and Christianity, with a mission from God to call pagan Arabs to the worship of the One God of his tradition. After being rejected by more orthodox Jews and Christians whom

---

13. Strictly speaking, the Midrash is the Jewish process of interpretation of the Hebrew scriptures undertaken by the rabbinic school from the second century AD onward. But ultimately, and as used here, any exegesis of the Hebrew scriptures may be referred to as Midrash. A "Midrashist" is the author of such exegesis.

he met in some cities of Arabia and through his trade journeys into *Bilād ash-Shām*, he would have continued to affirm his own version of Judeo-Christian monotheism over and against other forms of the two religions. The profile of a Judeo-Christian Muhammad has no need for a radical parting of ways such as we find in the Muslim tradition, and understanding the Qur'an's message in this way can do away with the Mecca-Medina framework.

The Judeo-Christian Redacted Muhammad
A third solution to our quest for the Muhammad of history that would help us make sense of what appears to be the Qur'an's conflicted position regarding the core message of Islam and its relationship with other religions is to assume, as we have seen above, that later interpolations occurred in the text of the Qur'an. This would be akin to a redactionist critique of the text of the Qur'an. The Judeo-Christian redacted Muhammad would have historically been and remained far closer to biblical orthodoxy – albeit one based primarily on oral narratives – than is eventually reflected in the Qur'an. In this scheme, places where the qur'anic message departs too radically from biblical orthodoxy, and others where Jews and Christians become legitimate targets of war, would be viewed as the result of later interpolations into the text, introduced post-Muhammad by Muslim leaders to justify and serve an ideological and political agenda.

I referred in the introduction to what I call the kerygmatic approach to Christian-Muslim interaction. Elsewhere I describe the *kerygma* – "proclamation" in Greek – as one that avoids "polemical aggressiveness, apologetic defensiveness, existential adaptiveness, or syncretistic elusiveness."[14] In these concluding paragraphs, I want to suggest how the kerygmatic approach will deal with the question of Muhammad's historical identity, and in the end how a revised understanding of the historical Muhammad will better serve the mission of the church than the traditional one. The kerygmatic approach will turn down the traditional narrative of the Muslim Muhammad, whether used positively or negatively, for two reasons. A positive use of the Muslim Muhammad requires that we acknowledge that he was a prophet sent from God, on par with biblical prophets. A rejection of this scenario does not derive from a denigration of Muhammad but from an affirmation of the finality of Christ and his redemptive life that culminated at the cross, leaving no room for a supplementary prophet and message. It is therefore the Christ-centered nature of the kerygmatic approach that prevents us from accepting the positive

---

14. Accad, "Christian Attitudes," 38.

Muslim use of Muhammad's traditional portrait. A negative use of the Muslim Muhammad on the other hand – one that uses the Sira and other Hadith narratives as "historical evidence" to *prove* that Muhammad was motivated by bad intentions, or that he experienced demonic oppression when he was receiving the Qur'an, or any such fodder of classical Christian polemics against Islam – is, from a critical revisionist perspective, as misguided and unjustified as the Muslim claims to the historicity of the Muhammad of tradition. The kerygmatic approach seeks to be scientifically consistent and honest. It cannot consider as historically reliable material whose historical usefulness has been seriously questioned by a vast array of academic scholars who have been critical of this material.

From a kerygmatic perspective, therefore, we are drawn to the Judeo-Christian Muhammad, either sectarian or redacted. In both cases we would view him as having understood himself to be a reformer of the Judeo-Christian tradition as he encountered it in Arabia. But whereas in the first scenario he would have strayed away from his original mission due to doctrinal misinformation about Judaism and Christianity, in the second it would be his followers who would bear the blame for twisting his message, either intentionally or due to historical expediency and geographical distance from the original context of the qur'anic message.

If one objects that this choice is arbitrary, they would not be entirely wrong. But as emerges from the present book, hard historical evidence to reconstruct Islam's early emergence is so slim that adopting the Muslim Muhammad of the classical tradition seems to me no less arbitrary. If that is the case, then what should drive our choice is not the weight of historical evidence – for it is all but absent – but rather our motivation should lie in the pragmatism of ministry within a theological framework which is biblically legitimate and faithful.

The Muhammad of History and Implications for Ministry

So far, not only has our inclination to adopt certain scenarios about the identity of the historical Muhammad over others seemed arbitrary, but it may also seem that our discussion of the "Muhammad of tradition" versus the "Muhammad of history" was undertaken entirely for theoretical purposes – a sort of intellectual exercise with no implications for the life and ministry of the church. But nothing could be further from the truth.

In these closing sections, I will argue that the outlines of the Muhammad of history, the primary author of the Qur'an, are far more useful in our quest for a constructive and fruitful ministry among Muslims today, for it allows us legitimately to declare a moratorium on the polemical approach to Islam. From here, we are able to reconstruct an understanding of Muhammad that serves the church's ministries of peacebuilding, gospel proclamation and discipleship as we work for the common good of our societies.

Implications for Christian-Muslim Relations
At the heart of the gospel is Christ's invitation to his followers to be peacemakers. It is when we are ambassadors for peace and reconciliation that we are truly God's children (Matt 5:9). In today's world of extensive people migration, where savage conflicts and wars have ravaged millions of people and their communities, and where societies globally have become more diverse and multifaith than ever before in history, the church's message should focus on peace, reconciliation and healing. This is how the incarnation and the cross will come back into relevance for Muslims, after having been rejected for centuries. It is when we love one another, and when that love overflows into our relationships with our non-Christian neighbors, that Christ shines as a radical challenge to worldly understandings of power and leadership.

It is when the message of the gospel expresses itself in this way that the Christ-centered *kerygma* becomes uncompromising. Followers of Jesus engaged in kerygmatic Christian-Muslim dialogue can proclaim Christ while avoiding the trappings of entering the cosmic battle of interreligious competition. Kerygmatic engagement can talk about Muhammad and the Qur'an positively without giving up the centrality and finality of Christ, the divine incarnation and the cross. The Muhammad of history, reframed in the way suggested in this contribution, can thus fit the profile of the Muhammad of faith for Muslims who are willing to lay aside for a time their venerable exegetical traditions for the sake of dialogue and the common good.

Implications for the Church's Message
By largely dismissing the historical reliability of the classical Muslim portrait of Muhammad, we have also debunked the legitimacy of using that portrait for polemical purposes. I would argue that the polemical approach in our interaction with Muslims is not only destructive and conflictual, but it is also unscientific and possibly dishonest given the current state of critical research into Islamic studies. The message of the church is the gospel – the *evangelion* in Greek – which means the "good news." If the good news is our *kerygma*, then it should be focused on an affirmation of Christ rather than on a negative discourse about Islam, Muhammad or the Qur'an. The positive *kerygma*

does not need to destroy anything in order to affirm itself. The message of the gospel is God's invitation to humanity into relationship with himself through Christ, and this is certainly good news! It needs "no militant enforcers, no fanatic defenders, no smart adapters, and no crafty revisers."[15] The church's message to Muslims, when it is based on an honest search for the historical Muhammad, can affirm Christ without dismissing Muhammad.

Islam's prophet, in this perspective, can be affirmed as a man who viewed himself as an honest religious reformer. On the reasons why the Qur'an ended up inspiring a new religion, one that eventually drove its adherents away from the finality of Christ and the cross as the essential components of the gospel, we can for now suspend judgment. Certainly, Muhammad succeeded in bringing the totality of the Arab tribes of Arabia to the worship of the One God of Abraham and the biblical tradition. Like Moses, he was able to unite them under a legal and political system that would have been quite progressive compared to the tribal laws of seventh-century Arabia. Women, slaves and Arab people generally became better off as members of Arab societies as a result of his life and preaching. The Qur'an's message, particularly its moral and ethical contents – which represent the greater part of it – inspire, for those who will hear it, good conduct, magnanimous hospitality and loving neighborliness. This is why those of us who will take the time to build relationships with Muslims will find in them loyal friends and trustworthy neighbors.

As I say elsewhere in this book, I believe that the greatest challenge to the church's message to Muslims today is our failure until now to develop a consistent and mature theology of Islam, Muhammad, and the Qur'an. Every theology needs to develop a comprehensive understanding of the context in which it works, for theology has to be thoroughly contextual if it is to address its audience effectively and bring helpful and godly answers to the challenges of every generation. Without addressing this contextual concern adequately, the church's *kerygma* will create converts who are alien to their own contexts. Sadly, much of the church's work of evangelism in the Muslim world has alienated Muslim converts from their families and communities by failing to help them develop a discourse that maintains their witness in their societies. By adopting alternative ways of thinking and speaking about Muhammad, we are offering recipients of our message the gift of the possibility of continued belonging and rootedness in communities within which they are so tightly knit that ripping them out of them has been akin to the experience of deep loss that has often led to despair.

---

15. Accad, "Christian Attitudes," 38.

Implications for Discipleship

The other great challenge in the church's ministry to Muslims is the challenge of discipleship. Too much of the church's work of discipleship among Muslims who come to faith in Christ has encouraged them to dissociate themselves radically from their former faith. Methods of discipleship that include a radical dismissal of Islam drive a wedge between Muslim followers of Jesus and their Muslim families and communities. How are they to obey Christ's invitation to be salt and light if they are completely extracted from their communities? By integrating a more positive understanding of Muhammad into our discipleship methods, we help followers of Jesus from Muslim backgrounds to salvage their witness to their families and communities. As they learn to develop a discourse that is conciliatory rather than polemical, their transformation and growth in Christ becomes a source of inspiration, and they become objects of emulation for their friends. From traitors to their families they can become peacebuilders, reformers and ambassadors of reconciliation to the many conflicts and tragedies that are currently ripping apart their communities and societies.

Over the past few years, I have worked with converts from Islam that had become so completely cut off from their families as to be led to despair and hopelessness. Many who had been influential and respected leaders in their communities had, as a result of leaving Islam, had no choice but to hide behind pseudonyms in order to be able to speak about their faith on the internet and from a distance. They had developed an aggressive discourse that seldom led to any fruit and contributed to further conflict and division rather than to peace and reconciliation. They had experienced persecution and rejection as a result of the aggressive message they had heard and of the polemical methods they had learned. As they learn to develop a more positive discourse about Muhammad and the Qur'an, many are gradually able to reintegrate into their communities and to have rich and open conversations about Jesus with their families. They are not hidden Christians, nor are they stealthy pretenders. Rather they are able to develop a new identity of honest disciples of Jesus who has called them to love, build peace and be reconcilers. They have truly become "born again" into Christ rather than into Christianity. Their message to their Muslim community is truly good news in a world that so needs it.

7.4 The Seal of the Prophets: Reflections on John the Baptist and Muhammad

George Bristow

"So, what do you think of Muhammad?" During my thirty-one years in Turkey, I have often been confronted with this challenging question. Sometimes I answer, "Jesus said, 'I am the First and the Last,' so I believe that he will be with his followers until he returns at the end of this age,"[16] without giving reasons for rejecting Muhammad as the final prophet. Sometimes I talk about Joseph Smith, whom Mormons believe to be a great prophet. Yet because the Book of Mormon which he communicated radically subverts the biblical storyline, I cannot affirm Smith's claims even though he spoke highly of Jesus Christ. Because of obvious parallels with Islam (alleged divine revelation and a "final" prophet centuries after Christ), Muslim questioners understand my Christian position regarding Muhammad without requiring that my position be spelled out.[17] The point is clear: because these later writings (the Qur'an or the Book of Mormon) do not cohere with the biblical witness to God's final act through Jesus, I do not see their proclaimers as trustworthy prophets.

In a provocative article, Harley Talman offers a very different answer to this challenge, arguing that there is "theological, missiological, and historical sanction for expanding constricted categories of prophethood to allow Christians to entertain the possibility of Muhammad being other than a false prophet."[18] Talman's argument has stimulated thoughtful responses from Ayman Ibrahim and John Azumah,[19] but because of the importance of this subject for missiology, I wish to revisit the question from the perspective of comparative theology and from my own experience and research in Turkey.

To treat this issue adequately, we must think through a biblical theology of prophethood. But we must also examine the qur'anic picture of prophethood in a way that shows Muslim scholars that we are presenting the nature of prophethood in the Qur'an fairly, particularly in relation to Muhammad.

---

16. Rev 1:17–18; see also Matt 28:18–20.

17. There are also parallels between Muslim and Mormon writings in their relationship to Jewish extra-biblical literature. See Bradley J. Cook, "The Book of Abraham and the Islamic Qiṣaṣ al-Anbiyā' (Tales of the Prophets) extant literature," *Dialogue: A Journal of Mormon Thought* 33, no. 4 (2000): 127–146.

18. Harley Talman, "Is Muhammad also among the Prophets?," *International Journal of Frontier Missiology* 31, no. 4 (2014): 169–190; http://www.ijfm.org/PDFs_IJFM/31_4_PDFs/IJFM_31_4-Talman.pdf.

19. See *IJFM* issues 32 (2015) and 33 (2016).

Much of what the Qur'an says about prophethood is found in the so-called "prophet stories," some of which partially overlap biblical narratives. In my research on Abraham, I argue that we need to theologically compare these overlapping biblical and qur'anic narratives, noting both commonality and dissonance.[20] We must notice both what is present and what is absent from these stories. Otherwise, our first impressions of similarity may turn out to be *false positives*, incorrectly indicating commonalities that do not stand up to scrutiny. Later in the presentation, I will focus especially on accounts of John the Baptist, son of Zechariah, as an instance of such partially overlapping narratives.

As we look at qur'anic and biblical concepts of prophecy and prophets, I will defend three propositions. First, Muhammad's prophethood is inseparable from the qur'anic prophet story pattern and needs to be examined as the epitome of this element of Muslim worldview. Second, biblical prophethood or prophecy is inseparable from the overarching biblical narrative which reaches its fulfillment with the coming of Jesus. Third, these two perspectives on prophethood are fundamentally incompatible.

Muhammad and the Qur'anic Prophets: Muhammad as the "Seal"

Talman states his intent to "broaden our base of theological, historical and missiological understandings of prophethood in general and of the person of Muhammad in particular." Since he rejects Islamic tradition as a reliable guide to understanding Muhammad,[21] I will focus on the qur'anic prophethood material, particularly the "prophet stories" found throughout the text. Concerning the overall unity of the Qur'an, Malise Ruthven writes, "The seemingly chaotic organization of the material ensures that each of the parts in some way represents the whole . . . any one of the sūras will contain, in a more or less condensed form, the message of the whole."[22] This coherence is evident in the prophethood material.

Numerous prophet stories appealed to throughout the Qur'an flesh out the concept of prophethood. These narratives generally follow a pattern in

---

20. See George Bristow, *Sharing Abraham*.

21. Talman aligns himself with scholars who "maintain that Muhammad's message should be interpreted in harmony with the previous scriptures which it claimed to confirm, rather than rely on later traditions that contradict them" ("Is Muhammad," 170–171).

22. Malise Ruthven, *Islam in the World*, 3rd ed. (Oxford: Oxford University Press, 2006), 84.

which the community rejects the messenger, but God vindicates the prophet and punishes the unbelieving community. These fragmentary episodes provide moral examples, underscoring the danger of rejecting the messengers of God and warning the audience to beware how they receive the Prophet (Muhammad) and his message.

Qur'anic prophets are sent to different human communities to proclaim ethical monotheism: "We sent a messenger to every nation, saying: 'Worship God, and shun the powers of evil!'" (*an-Naḥl* 16:36). The Qur'an, which is disclosed to the final messenger, describes itself as "guidance to humankind" (*al-Baqara* 2:185). No society will be judged before being warned by a prophet, who may even testify against them in the judgment (*Yūnus* 10:47; *az-Zumar* 39:69). The final and universal prophet is Muhammad. Unless we deny that Muhammad is the primary addressee in qur'anic discourse, as some do,[23] we find him presented there as the very epitome of prophethood: "Muhammad is . . . the Messenger of God and last [literally, seal] of the prophets" (*al-Aḥzāb* 33:40).[24]

Muslim scholars have recognized that this qur'anic pattern diverges from the biblical salvation-history concept of God redeeming a particular people through a series of covenant-making acts. Al-Faruqi, for example, rejects the biblical pattern as unworthy of God:

> The so-called "saving acts of God" in Hebrew Scripture, Islam regards as the natural consequences of virtue and good deeds.
>
> The "Promise" of Hebrew Scripture, or the unearned blessing of any man or people, the Qur'an utterly rejects as inconsonant with God's nature and his justice; the Muslims being no more unfit for such favoritism than any other people.[25]

Whether or not al-Faruqi misrepresents the biblical concept of God's election of grace with the phrase "such favoritism," he correctly represents

---

23. Rippin says, "it does seem that in no sense can the Qur'an be assumed to be a primary document in constructing the life of Muhammad." Andrew Rippin, "Muhammad in the Qur'an: Reading Scripture in the 21st Century," in *The Biography of Muhammad: The Issue of the Sources*, ed. Harald Motzki (Leiden: Brill, 2000), 307.

24. This is one of four verses where Muhammad is mentioned by name. The others are *Āl-'Imrān* 3:144; *Muḥammad* 47:2; and *al-Fatḥ* 48:29. The word *khātam* means to *affix a seal* or to carry something to completion. When a document was sealed, it was complete. Thus the widely accepted meaning is that Muhammad is the culmination of prophethood or the last of the prophets.

25. Ismail R. al Faruqi, "A Comparison of the Islamic and Christian Approaches to Hebrew Scripture," *Journal of Bible and Religion* 31, no. 4 (1963): 286, 290.

the qur'anic position as deeply different from it. The lives of qur'anic prophets support its rhetoric and worldview, in which they function as models for believers. They exemplify this divinely guided life of "virtue and good deeds," above all by avoiding the unforgivable sin of *shirk* or idolatry (*an-Nisā* 4:48, 116; cf. *az-Zumar* 39:65; *Sabā* 34:22; *Luqmān* 31:13).

The close relationship between the qur'anic Abraham and Muhammad displays this prophet portrait clearly, especially the story of Abraham disputing with idolaters, which is found in eight Sūras in different forms.[26] The Qur'an narrates how Abraham deduces the reality of God from the evidence of creation and boldly rebukes his kinfolk (*al-An'ām* 6:78–84). In some accounts, Abraham is cast into a fire by his adversaries but is miraculously protected.[27] As Muhammad is being mocked by idolaters, God assures him that other messengers have been mocked before him (6:10) and that he has been guided into "a straight path through an ever-true faith – the way of Abraham" (6:161).

Like Abraham, John (*Yahya*) the son of Zechariah also functions in this role of model messenger in the Qur'an.[28] In *al-An'ām* 6:84–86, he is listed among the prophets whom God chose and "guided on a straight path." Like all qur'anic prophets, John's exemplary character is underscored: "He will be noble and chaste, a prophet and one of the righteous" (*Āl-'Imrān* 3:39; *Maryam* 19:12–14). His birth story, which forms part of Mary's story in the Qur'an, has elements in common with the narrative in Luke 1:5–20.[29] But we find nothing of his ministry or crucial New Testament role as Jesus's forerunner, which, as we will see below, is key for understanding the biblical perspective on prophets.

While stories of qur'anic prophets are found in a variety of detail and are certainly not identical to one another, their DNA is consistent. The qur'anic portrait of Muhammad as the ideal and final prophet is inseparable from this qur'anic prophet pattern.

---

26. Qur'an *al-An'ām* 6:74–87; *Maryam* 19:41–50; *al-Anbiyā'* 21:51–73; *ash-Shu'arā'* 26:69–102; *al-'Ankabūt* 29:16–27; *aṣ-Ṣāffāt* 37:83–100; *az-Zukhruf* 43:26–28; *al-Mumtaḥina* 60:4–7.

27. Though this material has no parallels in the canonical Abraham narrative, many are found in Jewish para-biblical writings. See Shari L. Lowin, *The Making of a Forefather: Abraham in Islamic and Jewish Exegetical Narratives*, Islamic History and Civilization (Leiden: Brill, 2006).

28. John is mentioned in four sūras: *Āl-'Imrān* 3:33–41; *al-An'ām* 6:84–90; *Maryam* 19:2–15; and *al-Anbiyā'* 21:83–91.

29. These include the angelic announcement to his father Zechariah as he prays in the sanctuary and his mother's barrenness. Zechariah's dumbness comes in answer to his request for a sign, rather than a punishment as in Luke's account.

Jesus and the Biblical Prophets: John as the "Seal"

Second, if Muhammad cannot be separated from the larger qur'anic narrative, neither can biblical prophets be separated from the overarching biblical narrative. The Hebrew prophets arise within Israel, the people uniquely chosen by God (Amos 3:2). With rare exceptions (e.g. Jonah), they prophesy in Israel, charging God's people to live by his covenant.[30] Jesus made this perspective clear to the Samaritan woman: "You Samaritans worship what you do not know; we worship what we do know, for salvation is from the Jews" (John 4:22). Biblically speaking, "the Jews have been entrusted with the very words of God" (Rom 3:2). As Kevin Vanhoozer says, "the task of interpreting Israel's history . . . fell first to the prophets. It was their interpretive words that made sense of God's saving deeds."[31] The New Testament apostles have a similar interpretive role and stand in explicit continuity with the Old Testament prophets. Thus, Christians are exhorted to "recall the words spoken in the past by the *holy prophets* and the command given by our Lord and Savior through your *apostles*" (2 Pet 3:2, emphasis added; cf. Heb 1:1–2 with 2:3–4; 1 Pet 1:10–12).

Biblical use of the category of prophetic activity is not systematic, but varied and complex.[32] It may therefore be useful to distinguish the activity of prophesying from the "vocation" of prophet as it came to be understood. Prophetic activity, for example, even included temple singers, though they were not considered prophets, "for the ministry of prophesying, accompanied by harps, lyres and cymbals . . . in thanking and praising the LORD" (1 Chr 25:1–3).

While the phenomenon of prophecy was prevalent throughout the ancient Near East, and similar terminology was used for these figures and the Hebrew prophets, there were also significant differences, above all the nature of the

---

30. Old Testament prophecy also includes judgments on Israel's neighbors: Babylon, Assyria, Philistia, Moab, Damascus, Ethiopia, Egypt, Edom, Arabia, Kedar, Hazor, Elam, Tyre, and Sidon (e.g. Isa 13–25; Jer 46–51; Ezek 25–32; Dan 4–5; Amos 1:3–15; Zech 9:1–7; and the books of Obadiah and Nahum).

31. Kevin J. Vanhoozer, *The Drama of Doctrine: A Canonical-Linguistic Approach to Christian Theology* (Louisville: Westminster John Knox, 2005), 50.

32. A search for the words prophet, prophecy, prophesy and cognates yields more than 550 verses across biblical genres. Of these, 35 percent refer to individuals who are called "prophet" (or "prophetess") of God; 25 percent are plural references to "the prophets" sent by God to Israel (e.g. Neh 9:26, 30); another 23 percent refer to "false prophets"; 12 percent refer to the "prophesying" activities of both true and false prophets; and 5 percent refer to "prophecy" as a phenomenon. For example, Daniel 9:24 speaks of an eschatological sealing of "vision and prophecy," and the New Testament refers to prophecy as a spiritual gift (1 Cor 12–14).

gods they served.[33] Another was that outside of Israel "there is no evidence that ancient Near Eastern prophecy ever fundamentally questioned the monarchy."[34] By contrast the "prophets of the Lord," who spoke his word whether favorable or not to the regime,[35] were frequently in conflict with false prophets who flattered the kings of Israel. These are typically either idolatrous "prophets of Baal and . . . prophets of the Asherah" (1 Kgs 18:19) or "who prophesy the delusions of their own minds," but claimed to represent the Lord (Jer 23:26). Often these false prophets served along with diviners, interpreters of dreams, mediums, or sorcerers (Jer 27:9). "The leading traits of their 'revelations' are mixing of falsity and truth (Jer 23:28) and stealing Yahweh's words from other sources," such as dreams and other prophets (Jer 23:30–32).[36]

At the core of genuine prophethood was "covenantal integrity" embodied in personal contact with the living God, obedience to covenant provisions, and loyalty to his Davidic kingdom promises.[37] God said of false prophets, "if they had stood in my council, they would have proclaimed my words to my people" (Jer 23:22). The life-changing calls of Isaiah and Ezekiel came from the throne of God symbolized by the ark of the covenant in the temple (Isa 6; Ezek 1; cf. Rev 4–5). The prophets relay both God's anguish over his disobedient children and his intent to restore a remnant after the inevitable judgment falls.

It is against this background that we should place Saul, with whom Talman begins his consideration of Muhammad's reputation among Christians. Saul's surprising "prophesying" prompted the reaction, "Is Saul also among the prophets?" (1 Sam 10:10–13). Yet Saul is not said to be a prophet, but only to have "joined in their prophesying" under the Spirit's influence. Years later Saul, controlled by jealousy, sent messengers to capture David, who had

---

33. See Karl Möller, "Prophecy and Prophets in the OT," in *Dictionary for Theological Interpretation of the Bible*, ed. Kevin J. Vanhoozer (Grand Rapids: Baker Academic, 2005), 689–692.

34. J. Stokl, "Ancient Near Eastern Prophecy," in *Dictionary of the Old Testament: Prophets*, eds. Mark J. Boda and J. G. McConville (Downers Grove: IVP Academic, 2012), 23.

35. 1 Sam 3:20; 1 Kgs 18:4, 13, 22; 22:7–8; 2 Kgs 3:11; 17:13; 2 Chr 18:6, 13; 20:20; 28:9; 29:25; 36:16; Ezra 5:2.

36. Ronald E. Manahan, "A Theology of Pseudoprophets: A Study in Jeremiah," *Grace Theological Journal* 1, no. 1 (1980): 88.

37. Simon J. De Vries, *Prophet against Prophet: The Role of the Micaiah Narrative (1 Kings 22) in the Development of Early Prophetic Tradition* (Grand Rapids: Eerdmans, 1978), 145.

been anointed king by the prophet Samuel.[38] Saul's messengers "also prophesied" when they approached the ecstatic company of prophets (19:20–24), yet the messengers were not called prophets. Although the Spirit had long since "departed from Saul" (16:14), he "prophesied" again (19:23–24). He finally consulted a banned medium when God no longer answered him. The experience of being moved to ecstasy and prophesying under the powerful influence of God's Spirit does not make one a prophet of God. Nor is the case of Saul a likely point of common ground with Muslims, since the comparison of Muhammad with sinful Saul contradicts the consistent qur'anic portrait of prophets as exemplary and protected by God from significant sin.

There are no clear biblical references to genuine prophets outside of the covenant people of God. Paul once quotes a pagan prophet as "one of Crete's own prophets" (Titus 1:12; cf. Acts 17:28), but not as a prophet of the Lord. Towner argues that "'Prophet' would then be a title of honor that attached itself to various historical (and legendary) figures known to have been great teachers and poets."[39] Balaam, who superficially appears to be an exception, on closer scrutiny turns out to represent a pattern of false prophecy. God's Spirit came upon Balaam, and he spoke divine oracles (Num 24:2). Yet Moses's soldiers later executed him for helping the Midianites lead Israel into idolatry (Num 31:8, 16). Moreover, in the most important New Testament reflection on Balaam, Peter speaks of "the prophet's madness," and uses Balaam as a memorable example of "false prophets" (2 Pet 2:1, 16).[40] Thus Balaam is clear evidence that simply communicating words from God does not make one a genuine prophet of God.

We see this same phenomenon in the New Testament. Even Caiaphas, the high priest who conspired to have Jesus executed, unwittingly but truly "prophesied that Jesus would die for the Jewish nation" (John 11:44–52). The outpouring of the Spirit makes prophecy a central reality of God's new covenant people (Acts 2:1–36). Yet even if New Testament prophecy can be both legitimate and fallible as some argue,[41] identifying and rejecting false

---

38. The role of Samuel, Nathan and other prophets in announcing the reign of David and the Davidic Messiah is crucial, as Peter reminds the Jews of Jerusalem in Acts 3:24; see also 1 Chr 29:29.

39. Philip H. Towner, *The Letters to Timothy and Titus*, NICNT (Grand Rapids: Eerdmans, 2006), 700.

40. See also Deut 23:4–5; Josh 13:22; 24:9–10; Neh 13:2; 2 Pet 2:15; Jude 1:11; Rev 2:14.

41. Most notably Wayne A. Grudem, *The Gift of Prophecy in the New Testament and Today*, rev. ed. (Wheaton: Crossway, 2000). Talman affirms this position in footnotes 64 and 114.

prophecy remains essential (1 Tim 4:1–3; 2 Pet 2:1; 3:1–2; 1 John 4:1–6).[42] The essential criterion is loyalty to the incarnate, crucified and risen Lord, whose apostolic gospel was once for all delivered to the saints by his apostles and prophets (Eph 2:20–22; 4:11; Jude 3).

A robust Christian understanding of prophecy must also reckon with the epochal change introduced by the arrival of Jesus Christ. Here we return to John the Baptist, who epitomizes biblical prophecy from the perspective of the Evangelists. We saw above that in the Qur'an, John is simply one of the prophets. But Jesus speaks of him as something more akin to the "seal" of the prophets (Matt 11:9–13):

> Then what did you go out to see? A prophet? Yes, I tell you, and more than a prophet. This is the one about whom it is written:
>
> *"I will send my messenger ahead of you,*
> *who will prepare your way before you."*
>
> Truly I tell you, among those born of women there has not arisen anyone greater than John the Baptist; yet whoever is least in the kingdom of heaven is greater than he. . . . For all the Prophets and the Law prophesied until John.

John was a genuine prophet of God, his calling announced by the angel Gabriel in the temple sanctuary and by Zechariah's prophecy (Luke 1:11–20, 76–79). John arose among the covenant community and proclaimed a baptism of repentance for the forgiveness of sins. But as the promised "messenger," whose coming heralds the arrival of God himself, he was "more than a prophet" and identified by Jesus as the greatest person born to that point. All four gospels begin their accounts of Jesus's ministry with John's arrival and cite Isaiah 40:1–11 and Malachi 3:1 to identify him as the promised forerunner. In both Old Testament passages, the one whose way is being prepared is the creator God, coming at last to restore his people.[43] Jesus thus gives his disciples a framework for understanding God's progressive self-revelation in relation to John and to himself:

Moses – prophets → final Old Testament prophet (forerunner) → THE SON[44] → New Testament prophets

---

42. Jesus repeatedly warned his followers of false prophets to come (Matt 7:15; 24:11, 24).

43. See Bristow, *Sharing Abraham?*, 30 endnote 42. On Jesus and the coming of God, see N. T. Wright, *Jesus and the Victory of God Vol. 2, Christian Origins and the Question of God* (London: SPCK, 1996), 615–621.

44. Jesus identifies himself in the context as the unique Son of God (Matt 11:27).

In the parable of the tenants, Jesus shows that God (the landlord), after sending many prophets (the servants), has finally sent his Son (Matt 21:33–46). He also announces to Jerusalem that as the Son, he will send them "prophets and sages and teachers" to announce his reign (Matt 23:34; see 24:14; 28:18–20). The author of Hebrews works within this same framework: God who spoke "through the prophets" in past ages is now speaking "in these last days . . . *by his Son*" (Heb 1:1–2).

John felt himself unworthy to be Jesus's lowly servant (Luke 3:16) and introduced him with glowing words brimming with Old Testament prophecy: "He who comes after me has surpassed me because he was before me" (John 1:15, 30); Jesus is the pre-existent Coming One (Ps 118:26; Mic 5:2; Mal 3:1). "He will baptize you with the Holy Spirit" (Luke 3:16); Jesus is the giver of the eschatological Spirit (Isa 59:20–21; Joel 2:30). "His winnowing fork is in his hand to clear his threshing floor and to gather the wheat into his barn, but he will burn up the chaff with unquenchable fire" (Luke 3:17); Jesus is the Lord of the harvest (Mal 4:1–3). "I saw the Spirit come down from heaven as a dove and remain on him" (John 1:32); Jesus is the Spirit-endowed Messiah and Servant-Priest (Isa 11:1–9; 42:1–9; 61:1–11). "Look, the Lamb of God, who takes away the sin of the world!" (John 1:29); Jesus is God's own sacrificial Lamb (Gen 22:8, 14; Isa 53:6–7). "The bride belongs to the bridegroom" (John 3:29); Jesus is the coming "Bridegroom" of God's people (Isa 62:4–5).

The New Testament apostles and prophets confirm and develop the witness of John the Baptist, preaching the crucified and risen Jesus as Lord to Jews and "God-fearers" with direct citations of the prophets,[45] and to Gentile hearers with the biblical metanarrative in the background (Acts 14:15–17; 17:24–31).[46] They insist that "all the prophets" proclaimed these messianic days (Luke 24:25; Acts 3:24; 1 Pet 1:10–12). New Testament prophets, along with the apostles, unfold the unsearchable riches of Christ to the people of God (Eph 3:4–10). The test of prophecy is henceforth full conformity to the Spirit-revealed testimony that Jesus is Lord (1 Cor 12:3).

---

45. Acts 2:21–36 cites Pss 16, 110 and 132; Acts 3:12–26 cites Deut 18:15–19 and Gen 22:18; Acts 4:8–12 cites Ps 118; Acts 4:24–28 cites Ps 2. Stephen (Acts 7:52) and Philip preach the good news about Jesus from the prophets (Acts 8:27–35). Peter (Acts 10:43), Paul (Acts 13:16–41, citing Pss 2 and 16; Isa 49 and 55; Hab 1) and James (Acts 15:13–18, citing Amos 9:11–12) believed that the gospel was precisely what *all the prophets* had announced beforehand. Several begin specifically from John the Baptist (Acts 1:22; see also 10:37; 13:24–25).

46. Note the movement from the ages before Jesus – "in the past generations" and "the times of ignorance" – to the emphatic "*but now . . .*" of the final, post-resurrection era in which all peoples are commanded to repent and take refuge in Christ (Acts 14:16; 17:30).

Thus, from the standpoint of biblical theology, Jesus's era is the finale of salvation history. There can be no return to pre-Jesus prophecy, at least none which does not submit to the corrective teaching of Christian evangelists (Acts 18:25–26) and to baptism in the name of the Lord Jesus (Acts 19:1–10). Paul makes this clear to the Athenians: "In the past God overlooked such ignorance, *but now* he commands all people everywhere to repent" (Acts 17:30, emphasis added). Despite suggestions by Talman that we might think of Muhammad as a BC-like prophet during an AD time frame,[47] we find no evidence in the New Testament for the possibility of another "preparatory economy" like God provided in Old Testament salvation history.[48]

In the Old Testament, prophecy highlights God's *dwelling place* in Jerusalem and the priestly worship based on the law of Moses and the commandments through David and the prophets (2 Chr 29:25–30; 36:15–16). Jesus's inauguration of the "new" covenant promised by prophets such as Jeremiah and Ezekiel brings not only the fulfillment of the Davidic kingdom through Jesus, son of David and Son of God, but also of the *priesthood* through Christ's once-for-all sacrifice and ministry at God's right hand (Heb 8–10), of God's law now written on hearts as the law of Christ (1 Cor 9:21; 2 Cor 3; Heb 8), and of Christ's worldwide "body" as the true dwelling place of God by the Spirit (1 Cor 3:16–17; Eph 2:19–22). The New Testament concludes with John's prophecy of Christ's "bride" as the holy temple-city (Rev 21:9–22:5). Considering this advancing purpose of God, there can be no return to a geographical center of worship on earth, whether Rome, Mecca or Salt Lake City.

Incompatible Perspectives on Muhammad's Prophethood

We can more clearly see the incompatibility of biblical and qur'anic concepts of prophethood by pairing the main elements of the qur'anic and biblical worldviews. Two provisional observations about the relationship between narrative and worldview may help prepare the ground: (1) Worldview is often articulated in narrative form; and (2) canonical master narratives undergird both Christian and Muslim worldviews.[49] Because narrative both shows and

---

47. Talman, "Is Muhammad," 179, citing Dudley Woodberry's lectures.

48. For discussion of proposals that the Qur'an be seen as preparatory for Muslims, see Doug Coleman, *A Theological Analysis of the Insider Movement Paradigm from Four Perspectives: Theology of Religions, Revelation, Soteriology, and Ecclesiology*, Evangelical Missiological Society Dissertation Series (Pasadena: WCIU Press, 2011), 128–129.

49. Bristow, *Sharing Abraham?*, 25.

shapes worldview, careful evaluation of related biblical and qur'anic narratives can lead to meaningful comparison of their respective worldviews.

I have argued elsewhere that the essential three elements of the Muslim worldview are *tawhid* (divine unity), prophethood and afterlife, and that these may be usefully juxtaposed with the elements of a biblical worldview framework summarized as "creation, fall, redemption, consummation," resulting in the following set of pairs or correspondences:

Creation-Fall – Tawhid;
Redemption – Prophethood;
Consummation – Afterlife

While the first and last of these pairings share some common ground, the middle pair, redemption and prophethood, radically diverge and ultimately tell different stories of God and humanity.[50] These divergent narratives also correspond to very different diagnoses of what is wrong with the world. In the biblical worldview, God brings redemption to *fallen* humanity (through Christ); in the qur'anic worldview, he provides reminders and guidance to *forgetful* humanity (through prophets). While the Bible underscores God's repeated entries into and powerful action within history, the qur'anic version of human history highlights God's repeated sending of prophets. The comparison of the biblical John as the coming Lord's unique forerunner with the qur'anic John sharpens this dissonance.

Muslim writers are clear that the biblical concept of *God coming tangibly into the world* is incompatible with the qur'anic *tawhid* principle. For Shah, the tension caused by the "amalgamation of anthropomorphic and transcendental tendencies" of the Hebrew Bible becomes unbearable in the New Testament: "Incarnational theology is not paradoxical. It is thoroughly and utterly contradictory."[51] Muslims see the Qur'an, revealed to Muhammad, as correcting the Jewish error of making God too immanent and the Christian error of deifying a prophet. Yet this biblical revelation of the God of Israel condescending to come among us is at the heart of its prophetic witness.

---

50. Bristow, 36–51.

51. Zulfiqar Ali Shah, *Anthropomorphic Depictions of God: The Concept of God in Judaic, Christian and Islamic Traditions: Representing the Unrepresentable* (Herndon: International Institute of Islamic Thought, 2010), 661.

Hebrew prophecy gives great significance to the *temple and priestly sacrificial system*,[52] looking for its fulfillment in the "last days" (e.g. Ezek 40–48).[53] The New Testament announces this fulfillment in Jesus and his new covenant kingdom of priests. But the qur'anic perspective not only allows neither "intercession" nor "ransom" in the "day when no soul can benefit another soul" (*al-Baqara* 2:48; cf. *al-An'ām* 6:164; *al-Isrā'* 17:15) but also, as traditionally understood, rejects Jesus's death by crucifixion (*an-Nisā'* 4:157)[54] and makes nothing of his present universal priestly role. Here the qur'anic John's simple prophet role diverges deeply from priestly born John's prophetic declaration of Jesus as the "Lamb of God."

The biblical John warns of the "wrath to come" and points to Jesus himself as the judge who will separate wheat from chaff (Matt 3:7–12). In the qur'anic message, belief in the afterlife is second only in importance to belief in God. The prophets continually remind forgetful humanity of God and "the Day."[55] Talman asserts that "the emphasis of [Muhammad's] eschatological proclamation was Christ's Second Advent."[56] Yet if we base our understanding of Muhammad's prophethood on the Qur'an, this is a dubious statement. While there is extensive para-qur'anic Muslim exegetical literature that expects Jesus's return in the eschaton, no qur'anic statement clearly affirms it. As Reynolds says: "None of the events which Jesus is said by the [Muslim] exegetes to accomplish in the eschaton – killing al-Dajjāl, leading believers in prayer, breaking Crosses, killing swine (and Christians), etc. – are mentioned in the Qur'an."[57] Despite similarities, there are deep differences between the qur'anic "afterlife" concept which emphasizes the soul's "return" to God and the biblical "consummation" concept which is built upon the resurrection and return of Jesus.[58]

Talman claims that "Jewish Christian Christology . . . would not have compromised the Abrahamic monotheism of the *ḥunafā,*' as did the aberrant

---

52. Hebrew prophecy also insists that insincere sacrifices are abhorrent to God (e.g. Mal 1).

53. On the "expanding end-time purpose of temples" in the Old Testament prophets, see Gregory K. Beale, *The Temple and the Church's Mission* (Leicester: IVP, 2004), 123–167.

54. This last verse is interpreted differently by some: "God (and not the Jews!) first made Jesus die, and then made him ascend to heaven." Gabriel Said Reynolds, "The Muslim Jesus: Dead or Alive?," *Bulletin of SOAS* 72, no. 2 (2009): 240. Nevertheless, in *Maryam* 19:33, Jesus's death is treated just as that of John in 19:15.

55. Bristow, *Sharing Abraham?*, 163–167.

56. Talman, "Is Muhammad," 185.

57. Reynolds, "Muslim Jesus," 250. See also Zeki Sarıtoprak, *Islam's Jesus* (Gainesville: University Press of Florida, 2014), 23.

58. Bristow, *Sharing Abraham?*, 47–51, 163–168.

Christologies of the Christians that Muhammad refuted in the Qur'an."[59] I have two concerns here. First, the biblical narratives diverge sharply from the Jewish exegetical narratives which parallel the Qur'an in many places. And the New Testament writings reject these "Jewish myths." Yet the Qur'an's use of the formula "remember . . ." when introducing its prophet narratives shows that it was precisely these traditional stories which were known to pre-Islamic Arabs.

Second, as Bauckham has demonstrated, the earliest Jewish Christian monotheism was a "Christological monotheism" which included Jesus "in the unique identity of this one God."[60] Thus the "Abrahamic monotheism" of the New Testament, in which Christ presents himself as the God of Abraham and the Lord of David (Matt 22:41–46; John 8:56–58), has little in common with that expressed in the Qur'an. It does however have a lot in common with the Christology of the churches present in the Hijaz at the time of the emergence of Islam. Despite intense controversy over how to formulate the mystery, "the Orthodox, the **Monophysites**, and the Nestorians were all agreed that He was both God and man."[61] Against this, the Qur'an insists that Jesus is only a messenger (*al-Māʾida* 5:72–75; *an-Nisāʾ* 4:171).

The presence of biblical concepts and para-biblical material in the Qur'an, especially given its use of the formula "remember . . ." when introducing prophet narratives, may be explained by their presence in the Jewish and Christian communities extant in the Hijaz. Yet we should remember that the New Testament explicitly warns against Jewish exegetical narratives and interpretive approaches which paint biblical figures in glowing colors (1 Tim 1:4; 4:7; Titus 1:14). Watson shows how Paul is in "conversation" with Second Temple narratives in which Abraham is a paragon of virtue.[62] It seems to me that the Qur'an expands on these Jewish para-biblical "hero" stories and presents a very different narrative from that of the Bible. While claiming to

---

59. Talman, "Is Muhammad," 173.

60. Richard Bauckham, *Jesus and the God of Israel: God Crucified and Other Studies on the New Testament's Christology of Divine Identity* (Grand Rapids: Eerdmans, 2008), 182.

61. Theodore Sabo, *From Monophysitism to Nestorianism: AD 431–681* (Cambridge: Cambridge Scholars, 2018), 1. As Cragg argues, "The clause, from Nicea, 'of one substance with the Father' was not in question." Kenneth Cragg, *The Arab Christian: A History in the Middle East* (Louisville: Westminster John Knox, 1991), 15–16. Block says, "It was Monophysitism that Muhammad likely encountered." C. Jonn Block, *The Qur'an in Christian-Muslim Dialogue: Historical and Modern Interpretations* (Abingdon, Oxon: Routledge, 2014), Kindle 911–912.

62. Francis Watson, *Paul and the Hermeneutics of Faith* (London: T&T Clark International, 2004), 167–269.

confirm the previous books,[63] it does not present a confirmation or a continuation, much less a concluding resolution, of this particular history.

A full biblical theology of Islam (or other religions) is beyond the scope of this contribution.[64] God is indeed at work among peoples outside of the covenant community in a variety of ways, not leaving himself without witness (Acts 14:17; Rom 1:20). God does speak through visions, angels and human representatives to individuals who need to hear the true prophetic word, such as Naaman whose servant girl told him of Elisha (2 Kgs 5:1–4), and Cornelius whom the angelic vision prepared to hear Peter's "message through which you and all your household will be saved" (Acts 11:14). But neither Naaman nor Cornelius were thereby made prophets. Deciding if there is a biblical category which can include Muhammad as a prophet of God is a different question, one which requires a thorough assessment of the qur'anic prophet story pattern and the role of prophets in the overarching biblical narrative.

Talman cites with approval Bavinck's view that "God dealt with Muhammad and touched him."[65] Bavinck does indeed argue that "Buddha would never have meditated on the way of salvation if God had not touched him. Muhammed would never have uttered his prophetic witness if God had not concerned himself with him. Every religion contains, somehow, the silent work of God." But he also insists that human beings always subvert this silent work of God through *repression* and *substitution*, that the church must humbly testify in harmony with all the prophets, and that in Jesus Christ alone do we hear God's voice and see his image.[66]

In my view, the Qur'an *substitutes* a different story for "the gospel of God – the gospel he promised beforehand *through his prophets* in the holy scriptures regarding his Son" (Rom 1:1–4, emphasis added). Consequently, the qur'anic prophet model personified by Muhammad is ultimately incompatible with the biblical model in which "it is the Spirit of prophecy who bears testimony to Jesus" (Rev 19:10).

---

63. For example, "He has sent down the Book to you with the Truth to confirm what is available of other revelations, as it is He who sent down the Torah and the Gospel beforehand" (*Āl-'Imrān* 3:3; cf. *al-Baqara* 2:91; *Āl-'Imrān* 3:81; *al-Mā'ida* 5:48; *Yūnus* 10:37).

64. A recent evangelical entry is Daniel Strange, *Their Rock Is Not Like Our Rock: A Theology of Religions* (Grand Rapids: Zondervan, 2014).

65. J. H. Bavinck, *The Church between Temple and Mosque: A Study of the Relationship between the Christian Faith and Other Religions* (Grand Rapids: Eerdmans, 1966), 125.

66. Bavinck, *Church between Temple and Mosque*, 200–205.

Missiological Implications

A gospel-centered hermeneutic is essential to seeing the Old Testament and New Testament writings as one book. As the seal of the biblical prophets, John the Baptist clarified this hermeneutic, announcing that the kingdom of God was at hand in the arrival of the Christ of God. After his resurrection, Christ taught his followers to read the scriptures in light of his suffering and subsequent glory (Luke 24:25–27, 32–34, 44–49; Acts 1:3). If we are going to use the Bible to evaluate Muhammad correctly and witness to Muslims convincingly, we must keep this interpretive grid clearly before us, which is, of course, essential to doing a biblical theology of any religion.

A reconstrual of Muhammad's prophethood which forces him into a quasi-Christian category as a prophet bearing fallible witness to Jesus does justice to neither the Bible nor the Qur'an. Respectfully confessing my belief in the uniqueness and finality of Jesus is therefore the best answer to the question of what I think of Muhammad. Telling the story of John the Baptist pointing to Jesus as the long expected Savior and Jesus's testimony to John as "more than a prophet" may give clearer understanding of why Muhammad does not fit into the biblical story.

Good witness often takes the hearers' worldview as a starting point, as Paul began his talk in Athens with a reference to the altar "to an unknown god" (Acts 17:23). But as Coleman notes, "Paul moved from commentary on the altar to a fairly significant rebuke of their worldview and practices while continuing to emphasize both their ignorance and culpability."[67] Witness to Muslims may well begin from their understanding of prophets and move to the gospel, as Pennington proposes.[68] However it is crucial in light of my findings here to keep in mind that biblical and qur'anic concepts of prophethood are deeply different. We should stress John's prophetic announcement of the glorious One who came after him and Jesus's own insistence that all the prophets spoke of him.

Whatever our biblical theology of religions, we do not respect Muslims by redefining Muhammad on our own terms. Rather we honor their seeking after God by standing with John, the prophet who was "more than a prophet," and directing them to the Lamb of God.

---

67. Coleman, *Theological Analysis*, 59. See 54–65 for a discussion of Acts 17:15–34, particularly engaging Kevin Higgins, "The Key to Insider Movements: The 'Devoted's of Acts," *IJFM* 21, no. 4 (2004): 155–165.

68. Perry Pennington, "From Prophethood to the Gospel: Talking to Folk Muslims about Jesus," *IJFM* 31, no. 4 (2014): 197–198. *Note from the editors: One resource that uses this approach is al-Massira (The Journey), www.almassira.org.*

7.5 The Messengers and the Message: A Biblical Perspective on Qur'anic Prophethood

Ida Glaser

Different Christians "thinking biblically about Islam" are thinking from different perspectives. Most are thinking as outsiders to Islam, trying to understand peoples who live in different countries, or at least in different communities than themselves, and who are definitely "other" than themselves. Many are thinking as outsiders to Islam but as neighbors of Muslims, trying to understand people who live alongside them but have another faith. There are also increasing numbers who grew up as insiders and who are thinking about the faith and the community to which they have belonged and, in many ways, may still belong. They are trying to understand their own heritage – not only their own families and communities, but also themselves. Interacting with the amazing range of thinking people at the consultation in 2019, I realize that I am thinking from yet another perspective: a Jewish Christian perspective which leads me to think about Islam as something which grew up alongside rabbinic Judaism as well as Orthodox, Nestorian and Monophysite Christianity.

Islam and rabbinic Judaism share much. They share a view of revelation in which prophets take a central role. They share a claim to be inheritors of the faith of Abraham. They share the view that it is incumbent upon God's people to follow very specific instructions, and they share in having sophisticated legal systems which have developed to interpret those instructions. In much Christian thinking, they share a more uncomfortable position: it is difficult to find a place for them within a Christian worldview. On the one hand, it is thought that the Jewish people should have recognized Jesus as their Messiah, so should be one body with Christian people; and the status of the ongoing Jewish people has been a matter of tension and debate throughout the Christian centuries. On the other hand, it is thought that special revelation ended with the New Testament writings, so there is simply no room for a prophet like Muhammad or for the Qur'an which he brought.

I have argued previously that the main place for Muslims (the people), as well as for people of all other faiths, in biblical thinking is as human beings, made in the image of God, fallen, and under the rainbow covenant of Genesis 9.[69] I have also argued that Islam (the system/systems) can be seen as having reversed the transfiguration and then built on from there, so that a starting point for theologizing about Islam might be that Islam is a form of Judaism, albeit

---

69. See section 2.6 above and Glaser, *Thinking Biblically about Islam*.

a form that differs from current rabbinic Judaism as well as from Judaism of the New Testament period in several important ways.

I want in this contribution to explore further the implications of the similarities and differences of Judaism and Islam for Christian thinking about Muhammad, and in a later contribution about the possible place of Islam in salvation history.[70] If we can relate Islam to Judaism, and if we can discern a special place for Judaism and Jewish people in a Christian worldview,[71] we may be able also to discern a special place for Islam and for Muslims in our thinking. At this stage in my own thinking, I am still trying to identify the right questions and have a long way to go before I can answer them. I have no doubt that there will be readers who will see the very questions as pointing toward theologically "unsound" conclusions; and, indeed, further exploration may yield answers which clash with current paradigms. But if we are to move toward biblical faithfulness, there is no alternative but to be rigorously honest and as thorough as possible in our questioning, and to be ready to change our ideas if scripture so directs. My prayer is that this contribution will not only shift our debates toward fruitful discussions and relationships, but also return us to the Bible with the expectation that God is well able to show us what we need to know in order to honor him.

What Was Muhammad Trying to Do?

As Daniel Brown's earlier contribution pointed out, there is much that we cannot know about Islamic origins.[72] However, it is clear from the Qur'an that Muhammad was trying to set up a monotheism, at least initially for Arab people. In this, he was greatly influenced by both Judaism and Christianity, which he seems to have seen as two variations on an underlying faith; and that underlying faith was what he saw himself as preaching. This is evidenced by the many characters from the shared history of Judaism and Christianity with whose message the Qur'an sees itself as continuous, and by the many qur'anic appeals to the previous scriptures.

To put it briefly, the Qur'an presents Christians as mainly good people who have confused and false beliefs. In contrast, it sees Jews as people who

---

70. See section 8.6 below.

71. I am indebted for stimulating my thinking about this topic to M. Kinzer, *Jerusalem Crucified, Jerusalem Risen: The Resurrected Messiah, the Jewish People and the Land of Promise* (Eugene: Wipf & Stock, 2018); and to S. Dauermann, *Converging Destinies: Jews, Christians and the People of God* (Eugene: Wipf & Stock, 2017).

72. See section 5.2 above.

have the right beliefs but who do not follow them properly.[73] The Qur'an uses Jewish and Christian history to urge Jews to right living and Christians to right belief, and to urge all those who have hitherto been of neither faith to both right belief and right actions. That combination of right belief and right actions is described as submission to God (*Islam*) and, with some variations in the required actions, is considered to have been the faith of all the prophets.

Muhammad was, then, proclaiming a reformed monotheistic faith that we could call "Judaic" in that it has a measure of continuity with the Judaic roots of Judaism and Christianity. However, this was a faith to be established outside the covenant people of Israel, and, although recognizing Jesus as Messiah, outside the new covenant people of Christianity.

Initially, this faith was established among another people – the Arabs – and it was seen as having foundations in the Abrahamic covenant through Ishmael. However, Islam rapidly became what we might call "universalized." That is, it became seen as the faith to which God was calling all people. We can see this as parallel with the New Testament's universalization of the faith of Israel, so much discussed in Acts, Romans, Corinthians and Galatians. The contrasts here are significant, as Islamic universalization was without the Holy Spirit and centered on the "final prophet" rather than on the Messiah. I would summarize the difference thus: Islam seeks to universalize the rule of God through law, while Christianity seeks to universalize the presence of God through the Holy Spirit.[74] A major result is that Islam has been linked with legal and political power since the **Hijra**.

The above formulation of the nature of Islam is, I think, consonant not only with the Qur'an's inclusion of biblical foundations, but also with what may otherwise seem to be strange omissions. The Qur'an mentions the **covenants** with Abraham, Moses, David and Jesus, but gives little of their content and seems to have a different view of their nature. In the case of the Abrahamic covenant, the repeated unconditional divine commitment to Abraham's descendants through Isaac is replaced by an insistence that unbelievers will forfeit the blessings (*al-Baqara* 2:124; cf. 2:133–134). Thus the Abrahamic covenant, as other qur'anic covenants, seems to be closer to the conditional Mosaic covenant: God gives the law, and people agree to keep it.

---

73. This formulation comes from my colleague Shabbir Akhtar (see next footnote).

74. This formulation has resulted from reflection on discussions with Shabbir Akhtar during the writing of his *The New Testament in Muslim Eyes: Paul's Letter to the Galatians* (London: Routledge, 2018).

While there is little in common between the biblical and qur'anic accounts of Abraham, the qur'anic Moses narratives are remarkably similar in content to the biblical Moses narratives. However, the Qur'an omits all the material pertaining to the tabernacle and priesthood and has only one passage which can be interpreted as referring to the sacrificial system (*al-Baqara* 2:67–71). This is highly significant in that it reduces the Sinai events to the giving of instructions and the problem of idolatry seen through the story of the golden calf (*al-A'rāf* 7:148–154; *Ṭā Hā* 20:85–97). We lose the dramatic meeting of God with the whole people of Israel, which constitutes the nation through the holiness system and results in the coming of the *shekinah* – the dwelling of God among his people which is, as I argue elsewhere,[75] the whole purpose of God in biblical salvation history.

The Qur'an will, like rabbinic Judaism, replace the tabernacle/temple and the sacrifices with the law and its study, though for different reasons and with different intent. Rabbinic Judaism will see the study of the sacrifices as effectively performing those sacrifices, while Islam will see the sacrifices as unnecessary. The Qur'an will minimize references to the coming of God (although it recognizes his omnipresence), and many Muslims will see God as a transcendent being of whom it makes no sense to say that he "comes."

In short, the Qur'an seems to see no need for the aspects of the biblical covenants which focus on the descendants of Isaac and Jacob. It is acknowledged that the lineage leads to the Messiah, but the purpose of the choice of Israel as the locus of prophethood is otherwise without explanation. It is, perhaps, this omission which enabled Muhammad to think it valid to go back to a putative link with Ishmael and reduce biblical salvation history to a series of prophets. The result of his doing so was that Islamic thinking would largely replace Jerusalem with Mecca, the Bible with the Qur'an, and the prophets of the Bible with himself. And it would do this in the context of development of political power.

Replacing Jerusalem with Mecca

Jerusalem was the place of the Davidic covenant, the place from which the messianic dynasty ruled. Jerusalem was the place of the temple, the center for the covenantal worship of the God revealed in the Mosaic covenant at Sinai.

---

75. Ida Glaser, *The Bible and Other Faiths: Christian Responsibility in a World of Religions* (Downers Grove: IVP, 2005); and *The Bible and Other Faiths: What Does the Lord Require of Us?* (Carlisle: Langham Global Library, 2012).

Jerusalem was also traditionally considered to be the site of the *akedah* – of the willingness of Abraham to sacrifice his son and the willingness of Isaac to be sacrificed – which seal the blessings of the Abrahamic covenant (Gen 22).

During the establishment of the new socio-political entity in Medina, the *qibla* was changed from Jerusalem[76] to the *Ka'ba* in Mecca, the ancient place of worship for the Arabs in the region. This change implies a deliberate move from worship continuous with Jewish and Christian history and establishment of a new, distinctively Arab focus for worship.

Yet the change in direction does not appear to change the object of worship – the One Creator God of Abraham, Moses and David. It seems likely that the *Ka'ba* was already linked not only with a variety of local gods, but also with the monotheistic worship of Allah – this word being cognate with Hebrew and Syriac biblical terms for God.[77] The monotheism and polytheism appear to have existed side by side.

There are records of others than Muhammad who claimed to be prophetic preachers of this one God, and it is possible that some Arabs already linked the *Ka'ba* to Abraham.[78] A Jewish tradition states that Abraham made two visits to see his son Ishmael in Arabia,[79] and Islamic tradition expands it to three, making the site of Ishmael and Hagar's home Mecca, and making the *Ka'ba* one of the places of worship which Abraham built.

Historians are still discussing when and how the Arabs came to identify themselves with the descendants of Ishmael.[80] Certainly there were Jews who thus identified the Arabs as far back as Josephus, and Christians shared this

---

76. This is the traditional account provided as an explanation to the qur'anic verse *al-Baqara* 2:144, as preserved in al-Wāḥidī's treatise, *Asbāb an-Nuzūl* (The Occasions of the Revelations). Al-Wāḥidī mentions in this regard that Muhammad received the instruction concerning the shift in the direction of the *qibla* sixteen months after his arrival in Medina. (An English translation of this work and the specific tradition on 2:144 can be found at: https://www.altafsir.com/asbabalnuzol.asp?soraname=2&ayah=144&search=yes&img=a&languageid=2.)

77. I. N. Shehadeh explores both the etymology of *allah* and the meaning it has come to have in Islamic and in Christian thinking; *God With Us and Without Us: Oneness in Trinity versus Absolute Oneness*, Vol. 1 (Carlisle: Langham Global Library, 2018).

78. For a classic study of possible Abrahamic and monotheistic roots of the *Ka'ba*, see Uri Rubin, "Ḥanīfiyya and Ka'aba: An Inquiry into the Arabian Pre-Islamic Background of Dīn Ibrāhīm," *Jerusalem Studies in Arabic and Islam* 13 (1990): 85–112.

79. *Pirke Rabbi Eliezer* 30. There is some discussion as to whether this tradition is pre- or post-Islamic. For a discussion of this topic and other aspects of Jewish thought at the time of Muhammad, see Reuven Firestone, "Jewish Culture in the Formative Period of Islam," in *Cultures of the Jews: A New History*, ed. David Biale (New York: Schocken, 2002), 267–304.

80. See M. Whittingham, *A History of Muslim Views of the Bible: The Bible and Muslim Identity Formation*, Vol. 1 (Berlin: De Gruyter, forthcoming).

tradition. A tantalizingly brief comment by the fifth-century church historian, Sozomen, claims that it was Jews who informed the Arabs of their Ishmaelite ancestry, although which Jews and when he does not say.[81] Sozomen also reports that some of the Arabs had adopted some Jewish practices, although again he does not elaborate. However, Josephus asserts that the Arabs practiced circumcision and did so explicitly as descendants of Ishmael and not Isaac, his evidence being that they circumcised at the age of thirteen, which was the age of circumcision of Ishmael.[82]

Whatever the historical route to the identification of the *Ka'ba* with Abraham and Ishmael, we can suggest that the change of *qibla* to Mecca indicates a deliberate turning from the religion of the descendants of Isaac and the establishment of a religion for the Arab descendants of Ishmael.

Centering on Muhammad

A significant number of qur'anic verses call believers not only to obey God, but also to obey his prophet. While those Sūras which are traditionally considered Meccan focus on the worship of the one God, those considered Medinan move more and more toward declaring the importance of following the lead of the prophet. As is well-known, future Sunni Muslims were to see that lead as so important that they would seek to follow it in every aspect of life; Shi'ites would revere his descendants; and the declaration of faith would include the prophethood of Muhammad in the same breath as the oneness of God.

The qur'anic passages about obedience to the prophet occur in relation to socio-political matters. In matters of worship, the qur'anic call is to accept the prophet's message and to obey God; but in matters of war and governance, the call is to loyalty and obedience to the prophet himself (e.g. *al-Anfāl* 8:1, 13, 20, 24, 27, 41, 46, 71). This signals not only the centrality of Muhammad, but also the role of Muhammad as a social reformer and political leader.

The Qur'an models its stories of the biblical prophets and characters on Muhammad; or perhaps it would be more true to say that it chooses the aspects of their lives which can be seen as similar to Muhammad because it is using

---

81. Sozomen, *The Ecclesiastical History of Sozomen: Comprising a History of the Church from AD 324 to AD 440*, trans. E. Walford (London: Henry G. Bohn, 1855), 6.38. https://archive.org/details/ecclesiasticalh00walfgoog/page/n7/mode/2up. See also Gabriel S. Reynolds, *Emergence of Islam: Classical Traditions in Contemporary Perspectives* (Minneapolis: Fortress, 2012), 161.

82. Flavius Josephus, *The Antiquities of the Jews*, trans. William Whiston (Project Gutenberg, Release Date 2009), 1.12.2, www.gutenberg.org/files/2848/2848-h/2848-h.htm.

the stories to affirm Muhammad and his prophethood. We might see this as a rewriting of biblical history which focuses on prophecy and Muhammad rather than on covenant, exodus and Messiah.

Jeroboam – A Biblical Parallel?

Christian discussions about the prophethood of Muhammad tend to focus on how far he shares the characteristics of biblical prophets as well as on how far his message is consonant with the Bible. The above analysis suggests that whatever the characteristics of Muhammad, he deliberately set up a religion outside the biblical covenant communities. He set up what might be called a universalizing Judaic faith which opted not to join the covenant communities either through entering a Jewish community or through the universalizing Messiah, Jesus. The reason why it is difficult to fit Muhammad into biblical salvation history is not only because his claimed prophethood is post-biblical, but because he himself stepped outside the flow of covenant history.

The religion developed by Muhammad and the early Muslims has, however, many characteristics which are shared with the covenant peoples. This, too, is deliberate. As we have said, the Qur'an acknowledges the God of the Bible and calls people to worship him. So our question about Islam and about Muhammad becomes, "How might we regard a faith which seeks to develop aspects of the faith of the Bible outside the biblical covenants?"

Different biblical prophets are regularly suggested as biblical analogies to Muhammad. Our analysis suggests a different sort of analogy. We are looking for someone who develops a new place of worship, outside of God's covenants with the Jews, and develops an alternative people for political purposes. The obvious biblical analogy is Jeroboam who set up worship outside Jerusalem and a kingship outside the Davidic covenant in order to keep the people under his rule. It has often been noted that there are strong parallels between the New Testament Samaritans and Muslims: perhaps there are also helpful parallels between the Old Testament Samaria and Islam.

Following the prophetic ***haggadah***[83] of the Northern Kingdom through the books of Kings, we find several concerns which parallel concerns in relation to Islam. First, there are questions of law, in particular of monotheism and of

---

83. Note that the books of Kings are categorized as prophetic books in the Hebrew Bible. As I explain in my last contribution *(section 8.6)*, "In rabbinic Jewish thinking, the covenant faith of the Torah can be described under two categories: *haggadah*, or stories, and *halakhah*, or law. *Haggadah* includes the whole narrative aspect of the Torah, which tells of God's relationship with the world and all the people in it, and especially with the Jewish people. *Halakhah*

social justice. These are two huge concerns in Islamic thinking, and here, at least in theory, Muslims are on the side of the prophets.

Second, there are questions of covenant. The Northern Kingdom stepped outside the Messianic covenant with David's descendants. Its people were, however, under the Mosaic covenant, even though they broke much of it simply by not having the temple with the Levitical priests. However, as such passages as 2 Kings 13:23; 14:27 and the book of Hosea demonstrate, the northern tribes are still very much part of the Abrahamic covenant, and God will fulfill his promises to them.

Third, there are questions of power. Jeroboam's kingdom began as a political power, and the pattern continued. There were regular power clashes between the north and the south, between the successive northern dynasties, and between both kingdoms and foreign powers. Throughout the books of Kings, and especially in the central accounts of Elijah and Elisha, we see the reign of God through the words and deeds of the prophets constantly encountering the human kings, and always prevailing. Accounts of the kings' battles and the prophetic confrontations with power and ministry to the weak are carefully interwoven to make the point.

Law, covenant and power – the concerns of the books of Kings suggest the major areas which need to be addressed in developing biblical thinking about Muhammad and Islam. I will use this framework in discussing the place of Islam and Muslims in God's salvation history in my later contribution *(see section 8.6)*.

7.6 A Conversation among Friends: Exploring Missiological Implications

Moderator: Welcome. I'll begin with a few direct questions. Is Muhammad a false prophet?

Christian-Background Disciple (CBD): Typically, concerns arise from within Muslim-majority contexts which make many of us reluctant to use the expression. Many might accept him as a prophet of Islam in a similar manner to the phrase "prophets of Baal" (1 Kgs 18:19). Muhammad's claim to be calling people back to the original monotheism proves untrue. He is a leader or spokesperson of his own, and there are many other such figures in history.

---

includes not only the written requirements of the Torah, but also their oral dimension and later legal discussions."

Moderator: The author of the Qur'an claims to be bringing words of God. Do we regard this claim as authentic or deceptive?

Muslim-Background Disciple (MBD): In her contribution, Ida has proposed an alternative approach. Whoever wrote the Qur'an is not from a pagan background, nor is their audience: this is what the text presumes. One could say it is the word of God in the sense of being an understanding of previous revelations accepted as the word of God. It respects the Judeo-Christian oral tradition. One observation that remains puzzling to me is that the word *Injil* is always singular in the Qur'an, never plural, which suggests that the author might be unaware of the Bible containing four gospels. This reaffirms the Qur'an's reliance on the oral tradition.

Jewish-Background Disciple (JBD): I suggest that we take apocryphal literature into account since there were other texts about in Muhammad's era. Further, the literary conventions of the time are unknown.

Moderator: How does the revisionist approach assist us on the street?

MBD: Radically in my attitude which, in turn, affects my speech. One implication is for polemical approaches since they become unscientific because they rely on the Hadith, which has been shown to be unreliable. Being unscientific doesn't help my Muslim-Christian dialogue globally. The reality is that we live within a global society which is changing, as we discussed in chapter 1; consequently, I adapt my approach. I have no interest in being aggressive. I desire to shine like Christ. I don't denigrate Muhammad, but I do not regard him as a prophet anymore because to do so would be incompatible with my Christology which leaves no place for a new prophet or a new religion. But I have much respect for Muhammad and regard the Qur'an as an interesting book.

JBD: Thinking about Muhammad's emotions can be helpful. I have heard a Christian scholar of Islam describe Muhammad as a failed prophet who tried to bring the Judeo-Christian faith alive for Arabs. He failed and became a ruler and developed a political system instead. We might grant him a measure of grief about his own people, in a similar manner to how Paul views his fellow Jews in Romans chapter 9.

Moderator: So, what would Muslims expect of you?

MBD: Today, since they expect me to be a Christian, they do not expect me to believe in Muhammad's prophethood.

CBD: If I were Muslim, then I would believe in Muhammad. As a Christian, I clearly do not believe the traditional Islamic view of Muhammad. I have read the Qur'an but find no place for it. I affirm Christ as the final, complete revelation of God. Muslims accept that I remain a Christian. I find it hard to say precisely what or who Muhammad is. We share the gospel because we have something that Muslims do not.

MBD: Not affirming Muhammad as a prophet in the Christian, biblical sense does not require us to label or pigeon-hole him. It is too easy to fall back on antichrist language, something that I find to be sloppy and lazy theology. We must ask, based on the Qur'an, how Muhammad seems to have viewed his role from the beginning. Did he think of himself as a reformer or as creating something new?

JBD: Equivalently, did a shift occur or not? If so, when and why? The switch to focusing on Mecca is significant in losing the covenants. I wonder how far the **Ka'ba** was already associated in some sense with Abraham and/or Ishmael? Historically we do not know. But we can look at what has grown out of the Qur'an. One effect is that Islam has replaced Jerusalem with all its symbolism with an Arab place of worship. But the Qur'an has so little material on Ishmael.

CBD: The linkage of Muhammad and Abraham in the Qur'an is strong. They are both linked to Mecca, but not otherwise geographically tied.

JBD: I wonder whether there was an Ishmael tradition among Arabs prior to Muhammad. A fifth-century source about Jewish mission labels Arabs as children of Ishmael, and hence they could adopt Jewish religious practices including circumcision at age thirteen like Ishmael. If there is an historic link, then it makes sense that Muhammad was calling people back to true monotheism. Some epistemological humility is needed; as noted before, we need to accept that there are some things that we don't know.

MBD: There is a challenge to Israel's claim to uniqueness. The attachment to Ishmael seems to universalize the role of Israel.

Moderator: What would you like to ask each other?

JBD: Can we think of Muhammad as reforming what existed, and is there evidence that some components of the Qur'an predate Muhammad, even if he is the catalyst that stimulated it being brought together?

MBD: That is a very interesting idea. One can show from the Qur'an that the author had more dealings with Judeo-Christian communities than many Muslims give him credit for.

CBD: It seems clear to me that much of the Qur'an is rooted in ongoing conversations about transcendence, Abraham and other matters.

MBD: Are we engaging in re-mythologizing? Are we open to such a charge, using creative thinking to fill in the gaps?

JBD: Personally, I cannot contribute to debate on the history of Muhammad, attempting to look at the Qur'an and what comes from it to find a religious category to describe it, and from that to identify what Muhammad was attempting to do. What I see is something that has lost its Jewish roots, seeking to tap below what underpins the covenants.

CBD: Concerning the covenants, there is a substitution, a universalizing with the whole of humanity, effectively signed before human beings were created. So, a replacement of covenants.

MBD: We should note that the Qur'an is very harsh on Israel for breaking its covenants.

JBD: Yet the Qur'an misses what the covenants were about.

Moderator: Some here are wondering whether the kerygmatic approach is useful for Christians outside of Muslim-Christian circles. Is it?

MBD: It was developed specifically for interfaith relations to broaden the understanding of Muslim-Christian dialogue and other aspects of engagement with Muslims. It is an incarnational method based on friendship. Other contexts are perhaps beyond its focus.

Moderator: Who has a closing comment?

JBD: Please pray for those grappling with these ideas.

Questions for Discussion

1. In what ways does a positive, constructive discourse about Muhammad and the Qur'an enable Christ's followers from Muslim backgrounds to be honest disciples bringing good news to their communities?
2. What were Muhammad's intentions and objectives?
3. How useful is the comparison of Muhammad with Jeroboam, first ruler of the Northern Kingdom of Israel?
4. What qualifies someone as a prophet? How do these qualifications vary in Judaism, Christianity and Islam? How do they differ in the Hebrew scriptures, the Bible and the Qur'an?
5. How do you distinguish between the Muhammad of classical Islamic faith and the Muhammad of history? How might this understanding inform our interactions with Muslims?
6. How do we respond to the dual message of the Qur'an? How do Muslims understand this aspect of their sacred text? In conversations with Muslims, how might we use their response to this aspect of the Qur'an?

8

Thinking Biblically about Muslims and Salvation

Poetry by Anna Turner
Outcast for the Outcasts

    Are we a boundary wall, or the "no one is outside this" edge?
    All-encompassing limit, or exclusive high towered defence?
    Have we forgotten that we are "the far off ones brought near?"
    We who were not a people are now a people here,
    And the one who bid us come as close as we like without fear,
    Is the one who commissioned us all to bring the far off near.
    His lips spoke welcome for the outcast,
    Compassion and truth for the lost,
    And He made a way for them all as he died outcast on the cross.
    Named criminal and blasphemer,
    From a place from "which no good can come!"
    He went to the edge for the outcasts, God's divine never sinning Son.
    And as we go to the edges
    With steps interspersed with fear,
    The funny thing is we meet people
    Who God is already bringing near.
    And though at first we may see them,
    As more unlike us than like,
    And although that may make us uneasy,
    Stomachs and minds uptight,
    I find at the edge, a little on edge with the other,
    Is where I'm most likely to find,

The Spirit and the Father,
And the Son who is hope for mankind.
The Holy Outcast for the outcasts,
The edge-dwelling Son of God,
In whose footsteps I follow
To seek the ones still far off.

8.1 Opening Reflection: From Shame to Honor

Hiba al-Haddad

Wherever Jesus was, there was often a crowd around him. In Luke chapter 7 he is at the home of a Pharisee named Simon (Luke 7:36, 40). Simon's motivation is not stated, nor do we know why Jesus accepted his invitation.

A woman enters the scene. We are not told her name. It is clear that her reputation is known throughout the vicinity (Luke 7:37). She saw this as an opportune time to seek Jesus's forgiveness. She overcame all the obstacles of making a scene in public. Jesus accepts her actions of wiping his feet with her tears and hair followed by pouring perfume on them (Luke 7:38). She is the image of humility. Could she not dare to look at him face to face? Are her initial tears an expression of repentance and remorse?

Simon's reaction is one of condemnation, of both the woman and Jesus, and denial of Jesus being a prophet (Luke 7:39). Such actions brought defilement from a ritually unclean woman.

Jesus addresses Simon's questions using a parable. The woman here needed his forgiveness and to feel and experience his love. This situation provides a number of sharp contrasts. Jesus is formally invited, but the woman simply enters. Jesus's words of love and acceptance contrast with the words of Simon. What the woman did is contrasted with what Simon did not do: there had been no washing of feet or anointing with oil (Luke 7:44, 46). Simon appears to have cared about hospitality and food but not about caring for his guests. I wonder whether Simon was fearful of what others would think of his relating to Jesus. He has invited Jesus into his house but not into his heart or life. The woman is open about her need for forgiveness whereas Simon is hiding behind a screen of (supposedly) upright appearances.

This woman has a lesson to teach us all. We need to approach Jesus acknowledging we are sinners and aware that he is waiting for us. The law says she should be stoned; but Jesus gives her honor before others. She is set free by Jesus and told, "Your faith has saved you; go in peace" (Luke 7:50).

What do we want to receive from Jesus? The woman is a role model for those seeking forgiveness, love and salvation.

The land at Jesus's feet is holy.

8.2 Salvation Case Study: Questions the Church Asks

George is a committed and well-known Christian leader with a ministry among students at the secular university where he is also studying. As a very popular student, George has many friends who have been positively influenced by his teaching.

Two of George's Muslim cousins, Hassan and Amina, were interested in George's Christian faith, and one of them, Hassan, eventually believed in Christ. Although Amina had witnessed Hassan's faith in Jesus, they never really discussed what had happened. Hassan was reluctant to declare his Christian faith to his broader family for fear of negative repercussions.

Additionally, Hassan was the older brother to three sisters, and his father, a man who was very curious about Jesus but who had not read much of the Bible, was struggling with cancer. Hassan shared the information about his father's medical condition with George, who encouraged Hassan to declare his faith to his father before he dies.

Imagine the following dialogue among George, Amina and Hassan:

George says, "Dear Hassan, now that you have become a Christian, you know that only Christians will be saved and have eternal life. Jesus said, 'Whoever believes in the Son has eternal life, but whoever rejects the Son will not see life, for God's wrath remains on them' (John 3:36). Therefore, he who does not believe in Jesus will perish. If you want to save your father, I suggest you should witness to him and urge him to become a Christian."

Hassan replies, "I know this, but my father has been on a **hajj**, and there are many obstacles to sharing the gospel with him. Besides, I happen to know that he has always been very curious about Jesus."

Amina becomes irritated by George and challenges him, "Are you saying that only Christians get into paradise? What about the good people that are really following God's commands and are true to their faith, whatever that might be? Are they all going to hell?"

George responds, "Yes, my friend! Christianity is the only way. Followers of Christ were called Christians in the Bible; therefore, salvation belongs only to people who follow Christ. Islam does not offer salvation or eternal life with God! Only Christianity does!"

As a result of this conversation, Hassan took the advice of George, and out of fear for the eternal destiny of his father, he asked him to consider converting to Christianity. The father, although seriously ill, reacted very negatively, threatening to cut Hassan off from the family if he did not come back to his senses. As a result, Hassan was never able to finish his studies and was rejected by most in his family.

Questions for Discussion

1. Is there anything in this case study that makes you uncomfortable?
2. What does Hassan's father need to believe in order to "be saved?" How do George's beliefs about the nature of salvation impact the way he expects Hassan to engage in witness?
3. Does biblical conversion necessarily entail a change in religious affiliation? Why or why not? How does your understanding of the nature of religion impact the manner in which you answer this question?
4. What other ways might there be to think about and engage in witness that could be seen as more positive, as "good news," to a Muslim than the manner in which George approached the issue?

8.3 Testimony 4: Shirin Bahrami on Following Jesus in Iran

Our next testimony is a conversation between two women. They are of different nationality and ethnicity. They share in common choosing to follow Jesus having been raised as a religious other.

Chaden Hani (Druze): Shirin, please introduce yourself.

Shirin: I was born in Tehran, Iran, and raised within a Muslim family. Throughout my childhood, I endeavored to please God by praying and fasting. Yet I felt that several deep longings within me were not being fulfilled. Why, I wondered, must I pray in Arabic and not my own language? Why must I cover my hair and legs? I did, though, always have a strong desire to search for and be closely connected with God. I moved to France to study for my degree, and it was there that people introduced me to Jesus. My first reaction to the *Injil* was rejection and a battle over religious beliefs. Steadily over time, by attending student events and by the faithful and attentive witness of several Christians, my heart opened to God, and this led to a changed life and belief system. Crucially, I have full assurance that I am going to be with Jesus forever.

Chaden: How did you inform your family about this life-changing choice?

Shirin: One year after my conversion, I returned to Iran. I had not seen my family for three years. I had spoken with them many times on the phone, including about God's love. Consequently, my family knew that my language about religion had changed, but they were unaware of the conversion that underpinned this. I did receive advice from friends on being very careful about telling my family and not to rush into doing so. However, the promptings of the Holy Spirit were different. I spoke with a fellow passenger about Jesus on the airplane and then with my family that evening. The positive outcome was that my sister came to faith that evening and promptly experienced physical healing. My father accepted me; my mother rejected me. But God was at work: within forty days, nine people had come to faith including my mother who promptly invited others to hear me speak about Jesus.

Chaden: The case study above is based on a real-life situation. How did you react to it?

Shirin: I respect the compassionate heart for salvation but do not agree with the approach of pushing someone to act without due consideration of their family situation. We need to practice presence before proclamation.

Chaden: Good point.

Shirin: The compassionate ministry of Jesus should be an inspiration to us. In my view, he came to reduce the pressure on human beings, not to add to it. I note how Jesus combined compassionate acts with helping people to realize who he was. Two examples are the woman at the well *(see section 4.3 above)*, where he was very direct in his approach, and the healing of the paralytic lowered through the roof *(see section 7.1 above)*, an occasion when he used an indirect approach. We must talk about salvation, just as Jesus did. He met people where they were and understood their religious perspective before sharing his own. We should do likewise, which implies that we endeavor to understand the spiritual aspects of the religious other's beliefs and situation in life.

Chaden: So what advice would you give to whom in the case study?

Shirin: George appears the more mature character, but he needs greater sensitivity about how he speaks with Muslims. I think he needs a broader view of scripture as a whole, especially concerning relating to religious others. He should go with a practical, loving heart and an openness to listen.

It is, I think, essential that we understand the person before us. We must beware of being perceived to be attacking people, which will, inevitably, prompt defensive barriers to be invoked. This is very normal human behavior when one's sense of inner self is perceived as being under threat; there are defense mechanisms within all of us. An illustration is my grandfather's reaction to the conversion of my mother and me: his first reaction was to speak with an imam, and he remained distant from us. Yet when he was seriously ill, my mother went to visit him and recommended that we be present and pray around him. Two days before he died, he asked that I pray with him during a phone call. I did so. Did he accept Jesus? Will I meet him in heaven? I am content to leave that in God's hands.

Chaden: That prompts me to ask what is your understanding of salvation in Islam?

Shirin: I am from a Shi'a background. In this strand of Islam there is clarity about God being the judge and the separation of all people into heaven or not. In Shi'a Islam, one cannot know about God's verdict on us prior to death; his decision is based on the balance of our good and bad deeds. Since nobody is perfect, then no one can have assurance that God will accept them. This is very different to the Christian doctrine of assurance rooted in Christ's actions on our behalf. Consequently, we seek to demonstrate by our lives that we are true followers, assured that our God knows our hearts and those of everyone else.

Chaden: Thank you for articulating this difference between Islam and Christianity. So what approach or approaches would you recommend in engaging with Muslims?

Shirin: I recommend regarding social sciences as instruments in our hands; in other words, we should apply what we know in ministry. Yet at all times we must trust the Holy Spirit who – among other activities – changes information into revelation in the minds and lives of Muslims. We should speak to God first, then to Muslims. I recommend keeping in mind that Muslims vary widely; they do not all experience Islam in the same way. This makes being attentive to where they are spiritually an essential element in our engagement with them.

8.4 Who Is the Other? Reconsidering "Salvation" through Classical Islamic Thought
Alexander E. Massad

> The cross is powerful and the crucifixion is sorrowful. But as I sit here I feel that while the cross speaks to me, it does not draw me in. Its mystery is moving, but I cannot incline towards what it says about a God in form, a God who undergoes this inexplicable agony for an inexplicable act of mercy. It is not the language of redemption which I cannot understand, it is the necessity of God's self-revelation for this act of redemption.[1]

This personal account from Mona Siddiqui, a professor of Islamic and Interreligious Studies at the University of Edinburgh, wrestles with the Christian tradition's redemption narrative. Siddiqui's reflection is insightful because she does not struggle with the notion of redemption in general. Rather, her struggle is with the particular Christian formulation of redemption as a *kenotic* love, love that takes the form of Christ's incarnation, death and resurrection. In particular, Siddiqui struggles to understand why it was necessary for God to do these acts to redeem creation. Later in the same book, Siddiqui says that for her, Islam is not concerned with human depravity *per se*. Islam, for Siddiqui, offers guidance so that people can return to God. Although Islamic doctrines may teach that God is transcendent, Siddiqui finds that within Muslim piety God is incredibly close. Thus, for her, redemption consists of God divinely guiding people back to himself because God is merciful and forgiving, willing and capable of redeeming us without a sacrifice.[2]

I bring up this example because Siddiqui is a Muslim scholar thoroughly acquainted with Christian beliefs and practices who shows vulnerability toward beliefs of another religious tradition. As she sits before the cross, she fully understands what the cross and the Christian tradition claim. Yet she

---
1. Mona Siddiqui, *Christians, Muslims, and Jesus* (New Haven: Yale University Press, 2014), 248.
2. Siddiqui, *Christians, Muslims, and Jesus*, 248.

finds more certainty and comfort in the Islamic tradition. Siddiqui presents a number of challenges to those of us who believe Christ is the way, the truth and the life of the world. First, how do we account for someone who fully understands the gospel and rejects it, not out of selfishness or spite, but out of serious reflection and piety? Second, do we take account of Siddiqui's understanding of God and salvation when communicating the gospel message, or do we simply proclaim Christian concepts? Or in other words, how can we consider the complexity of the religious other's identity so as not to impose Christian categories upon them? These are the questions that I want to engage with in this contribution.

I am going to answer these two questions in three parts. First, I will introduce the problem I see perpetuating within Christian beliefs about salvation when it comes to Muslims and non-Christians in general. I will argue that contemporary Christian conceptions of salvation deny Muslims their own identity by imposing a framework upon them. I suggest that a resolution to this problem is to open up our theological beliefs to becoming vulnerable to the Islamic tradition's beliefs and practices. Second, I will present a comparative theological exercise to exemplify the type of theological vulnerability I am advocating. Specifically, I will investigate Muhammad Rashīd Riḍā's (d. 1935) reinterpretation of classical Islamic soteriology. I will show how Riḍā reinterpreted aspects of Islamic soteriology concerning the status of sound-minded adults living after the Prophet Muhammad who do not believe in his message.[3] Through what I term "hermeneutical leaps of mercy," Riḍā reinterpreted the Qur'an to conclude that the overwhelming majority – if not all – of humanity would be saved. Finally, I will reinterpret Romans 1:18–23 in light of Riḍā's soteriology. I will take a "hermeneutical leap of grace" in reading this passage to show the possibility that Paul may not be condemning non-Christians simply for their rejection of the gospel.

Introducing Christian and Islamic Soteriology

Let us return to our first question: how do we understand someone who has heard the message, understood the message, but has chosen another path not out of malice or selfishness but out of piety and serious reflection? For Christians, this is a question of salvation and falls under a concept we call "soteriology," meaning beliefs about salvation, who is saved and who is not

---

3. Mohammad Hassan Khalil, *Islam and the Fate of Others: The Salvation Question* (Oxford: Oxford University Press, 2012), 18.

saved. Currently, Christians divide soteriology into three perspectives, which we call the theology of religions. First, there are the **exclusivists**. This position generally holds that there is no salvation outside of Jesus Christ, who is found only in the Christian tradition. Muslims, thus, have no hope for salvation. Next, there are the **inclusivists**. This position also believes that salvation only comes through Christ, but they believe the benefits of Christ's revelation and work can be found outside the Christian tradition. Muslims might be saved, but if they are, it is through an unconscious connection to Christ. Finally, there are the pluralists. This position affirms that people of all religions can find salvation through various ways. For the pluralist, salvation comes from correctly orienting one's life to the divine, not through the mediating work of Christ. In summary, contemporary Christian soteriology regarding the fate of the religious other has been divided into three categories – exclusivism, inclusivism and pluralism.

Although these three soteriological positions seem distinct, and they are, they all fall victim to the same problem – they all presuppose a particular Christian theology that they then impose upon the religious other, which suppresses the religious other's identity. Exclusivists reject Muslim claims to truth and salvation, favoring engagement through apologetics or polemics. Muslims are given little to no space to assert their identity on an equal footing with the Christian. Inclusivists accept non-Christian claims of truth and salvation as a form of Christ working mysteriously through another religious tradition. Muslim claims are accepted, but only as an outworking of the Holy Spirit. This Christianizes the religious other as a variant form of Christ in the world. Finally, the pluralist suppresses the uniqueness of religious traditions by arguing that all religious traditions ultimately say the same thing. This is a subtle form of religious intolerance because it denies a religion's uniqueness.[4] Thus exclusivism, inclusivism and pluralism fail to affirm the identity of the religious other as a legitimate alternative vision of the world by presupposing a Christian theological position before interacting with the religious other. This presupposition ends up imposing Christian beliefs on the religious other and results in the suppression of the religious other's unique identity.

One might argue that it is impossible for Christians to interact with Muslims and not see them through the lens of the Christian tradition. On this point I would completely agree. It is impossible for any person to escape her or his conceptual framework when interacting with the world. What I

---

4. James Fredericks, *Faith among Faiths: Christian Theology and Non-Christian Religions* (New York: Paulist Press, 1999), 164.

am arguing is that Christians and Muslims tend to uncritically assume their particular worldview is correct and then filter all their encounters through this singular worldview. This uncritical imposition of one's conceptual framework upon others raises serious ethical questions. I wonder, do Christians really love their Muslim friends or neighbors when they claim that what the other believes is incorrect simply because it conflicts with their own beliefs? How can such a person possibly interact with Muslims ethically, honestly and with love? I do not think that such a position shows love to the actual Muslim in front of us. Rather, this position loves a filtered vision of the Muslim identity.

What Christians need is a way to express their faith in relation to the beliefs and practices of other religions while affirming the religious other's identity.[5] For us in the framework of this book, we need an approach where Christians can express their faith in relationship with Muslims that is responsible to the gospel and does not impose our beliefs.[6] In short, how can we consider the complexity of the religious other's identity so as not to impose Christian categories upon them? To sum up what I have said so far, I am asking how Christians can account for Muslims who have heard the message and understood it but ultimately prefer their Muslim faith and do so in such a way that does not impose a Christian worldview upon them?

Let us take this question in light of Mona Siddiqui's statement above. How can a Christian account for Siddiqui's preference for the Islamic tradition, after serious engagement with the Christian faith, without imposing Christian categories such as depravity, demonic spirits or sin? I want to suggest that any attempt to resolve this problem requires two steps. First, there needs to be a personally vulnerable investigation of the transformative power of the religious other's faith and tradition. In our case, we need to investigate the Islamic tradition and how our Muslim friends and neighbors live out this tradition. Inclusively, we should do so with an openness to the transformative power and beauty that Muslims find in their tradition.

Second, we must reflect on our own beliefs and practices, burdened and energized with insights from our investigation. This introspection should prompt us to reconceptualize our beliefs and practices. Just as Christians are asking our Muslim friends and neighbors to rethink their beliefs and practices in light of the gospel, so too should Christians be open to rethinking their beliefs and practices in light of the Islamic tradition's claims. I believe this approach creates a more equitable relationship where Muslims can speak as

---

5. Fredericks, *Faith among Faiths*, 166.
6. Fredericks, 8.

equals and assert their identity. Such a practice does not remove our biased filters. Rather, this practice presents our biases before the religious other for revision. Such an approach, I believe, acts as a deterrent against suppressing the Muslim's voice in Christian-Muslim encounters.

To sum up my first point: There is a problem facing Christians when it comes to relating to people from another tradition. This problem is that the current framework of exclusivism, inclusivism and pluralism, which we all have adopted at some level, actually suppresses a Muslim's identity by imposing a Christian worldview upon her or him. A movement toward alleviating this problem requires two steps. First, one must be open to the transformative power of the Muslim's tradition and take the time to learn about Islam. Second, we should rethink our own Christian identity in light of the beliefs and practices that our Muslim friends are professing. This approach validates the Muslim's identity as equally important as our own. We begin to see the actual person before us according to her or his self-perceived identity and not through an identity filtered through a Christian lens.

Investigating Classical Islamic Soteriology: Al-Ghazālī and Rashīd Riḍā's Reinterpretation

I want now to apply this approach to our questions, how can Christians account for a Muslim who seriously investigates Christianity, but out of pious motivations remains a Muslim, and how can we do so without simply imposing Christian categories? To answer these questions, one must look at Islamic soteriology. It would be a mistake, however, to assume that "soteriology" is a category that exists within the Islamic tradition. To do so would be imposing a presupposed Christian doctrine upon the religious other, which would repress their identity. However, Mohammad Hassan Khalil argues that the Qur'an and the Islamic tradition as a whole have a concern for salvation in this world (***ad-dunyā***) and in the afterlife (*al-ākhira*).[7] The Qur'an has much to say about the Last Day (*al-yawm al-ākhir*), the Hour (*as-sā'a*), the Day of Resurrection (*yawm al-qiyāma*), and the Day of Reckoning (*yawm al-ḥisāb*).[8] It is on this Last Day that all souls will be judged according to their actions. However, humans are prone to error and generally need forgiveness and guidance. Thus, although the Qur'an and the Islamic tradition do not have a doctrine of original

---

7. Khalil insists that "salvation is arguably *the* major theme of the Qur'an." Khalil, *Islam and the Fate of Others*, 1.

8. Khalil, 3.

sin, there is a clear concern for our salvation from the human propensity to err.[9] It is from such a concern, and the Islamic thought that grows out of this qur'anic concern, that we can talk of an "Islamic soteriology."

Islamic soteriology operates within a tension between *īmān* (belief, sincerity or fidelity) and *kufr* (unbelief, ingratitude, or rejection).[10] Perhaps the most driving question within Islamic soteriology concerns the soteriological status of sound-minded adults living after the Prophet Muhammad who do not believe in the Prophet's message. This problem brings up two tensions that Muslim scholars have wrestled with since at least the eleventh century. The first tension is between God's wrath and God's mercy. On the one hand, Muslim scholars believed in the superiority of the Prophet Muhammad's message, which they tied to the notion that God deals out divine justice in relationship to one's acceptance or rejection of this message. On the other hand, they asserted the unbounded supremacy of God's divine mercy, which they associated with God's generous disposition to overlook punishment.[11] The second tension is between the Islamic concept of the *fiṭra*, the natural desire that all humans have to worship God, and the reality that many people do not do so even when they encounter the Prophet's message. Fundamental to this tension is the following question: if God's message resonates with our human *fiṭra*, and everyone has a *fiṭra*, then how do we explain those who hear the message and yet reject it?

In this section, I will focus on a seminal Muslim scholar within the modern era – Rashīd Riḍā. Riḍā was perhaps the most important Sunni Muslim scholar of the twentieth century. He was born in Tripoli, Lebanon, in 1865, and moved to Cairo to study with the reformist movement of Muhammad ʿAbduh (d. 1905) in 1897. ʿAbduh was the intellectual leader of the modern Salafi movement and a critical figure for the transition of Islamic thought from the classical to the contemporary era.[12] Although Riḍā initially propagated the reformist agenda of his teachers Jamāl al-Dīn al-Afghānī (d. 1897) and Muhammad ʿAbduh, under Riḍā's guidance their movement took a decidedly more conservative turn. As Riḍā came to appreciate Ibn Taymiyya's writings and the rising Wahhabi movement in the Arabian Peninsula, he began advocating for a return to a more pristine vision of Islam.[13] It is because of

---

9. Siddiqui, *Christians, Muslims, and Jesus*, 242.

10. Khalil, *Islam and the Fate of Others*, 3.

11. Khalil, 20.

12. Khalil, 110.

13. Khalil, 111.

Riḍā's work through his journal *al-Manār* (The Lighthouse) that his vision of Salafism and reformism quickly spread from the Middle East through North Africa and to the rest of the world.

When it comes to the question of salvation, Riḍā wrote a number of works dealing with non-Muslims and with Christians in particular. However, his commentary on the Qur'an, *Tafsīr al-Manār*, is perhaps his most relevant work about soteriology. This *tafsīr*, or commentary, bears the same name as his journal and in fact is the result of a compilation of numerous articles from Riḍā's journal over the span of several years. When it comes to the issue of salvation, Riḍā's commentary on *Sūrat al-Baqara* 2:62, *an-Nisā'* 4:115 and 4:123, *Āl-'Imrān* 3:19 and *al-Mā'ida* 5:69 are particularly poignant. For the sake of space and clarity, I want to focus on *al-Baqara* 2:62 and *an-Nisā'* 4:115, though I will refer to the other verses at times. I will discuss how Riḍā believed that true belief was *islām* but not the Islamic tradition, that only those who rejected the Prophet out of selfish desire were condemned, and that Riḍā made a hermeneutical leap of mercy by arguing that most people would go to heaven.

First, Riḍā proposed that true belief is *islām* but not the Islamic tradition. We find the beginning of this idea in Riḍā's commentary on *Sūrat al-Baqara* 2:62, which reads as follows:

> Truly those believers in this message, as well as the Jews, the Christians, and the Sabeans, whoever believes in God and in the Last Day and does righteous deeds will have their reward from their Lord, and will not have fear, nor will they grieve.

Riḍā, citing his teacher Muhammad 'Abduh, states that this verse must be read in conjunction with the preceding one (2:61), where the Israelites grumble to Moses that they had better varieties of food in Egypt. The Qur'an relates that, because of their grumbling,

> Humiliation and misery struck them, and they incurred the wrath of God because they persistently rejected his message and killed prophets contrary to all that is right. They were transgressors.

According to Riḍā, these verses teach that what matters soteriologically is not which religion or *dīn* one belongs to. What matters is one's "true faith" (*ṣidq al-īmān*) and one's service to God.[14] Riḍā further affirms this position later in his commentary on *Āl-'Imrān* 3:19, which states:

---

14. Khalil, 113; cf. 16.

> To God true faith is submission (Islam), and those who received the Book differed only after receiving knowledge out of contention. God will be swift in reckoning with those who deny His revelations.

Here, Riḍā comments that true religion (*al-dīn*) is in fact *islām*. But *islām* means submission to God. This *islām*, however, does not specifically refer to the religious tradition we call Islam. Rather, a true *muslim* is one whose faith and deeds are right no matter the context.[15]

Although Riḍā distinguishes between true *islām*, as true submission to God no matter the context, from Islam the religious tradition, he quickly remarks that God rebuked the People of the Book due to their deviations. This is because Riḍā believed that by the time of the Prophet Muhammad, the Jewish and Christian traditions no longer represented *islām*. The Prophet Muhammad's charge was to re-inaugurate a path for *islām*. Thus the qualification to be a *muslim* – one who follows the path of *islām*, which Riḍā thought equated following the path of the Prophet Muhammad and not necessarily the Islamic tradition.

Second, Riḍā believed that only those who reject the Prophet out of selfish desire are condemned. We find Riḍā discussing this concept in his concluding comments on *Āl-'Imrān* 3:19, where he argues:

> No one can be credited with belief (*īmān*) who knows [the Qur'an] and yet disagrees with it by preferring his own scriptures.... Everyone reached by the call (*da'wa*) of Muhammad and to whom its truth is evident, as is to [certain self-absorbed, stubborn People of the Book], but who rejects and resists, as they reject and resist, gains no positive credit for his belief in former prophets and their books.[16]

What is interesting here is that Riḍā limits condemnation of non-Muslims to those who have been "reached by the call of Muhammad and to whom its truth is evident." This is not a clear statement. What does it mean to be reached by the call of Muhammad? Does this mean simply hearing the message, or does it entail understanding what the message means? What is evident truth? If I hear the truth but I do not think it is the truth, does this qualify as evident truth, or is it not evident to me that the Prophet's message is true? There

---

15. Khalil, 114.
16. Khalil, 116; cf. 29.

are many questions that need clarification regarding the phrase "reached by the call."

We can begin to understand Riḍā's answer to these questions by going back to his commentary on *al-Baqara* 2:62, cited above, where he discusses the *ahl al-fatara*, the people of the gap, those who are truly unreached. Drawing on Abū Ḥāmid al-Ghazālī (d. 1111), Riḍā presents three categories of non-Muslims. First are those who have never heard of the Prophet Muhammad. Second are those who learn of the Prophet, but out of arrogance resist pursuing his message. Finally are those who are either "improperly" exposed to the Prophet's message or for whom the "preconditions" (*sharṭ*) for investigation are not satisfied, meaning that the message was not presented in a manner that stimulated a "sincere" investigation.[17]

Riḍā believed that only the second group will be condemned, because they properly heard the Prophet's truth, understood it, but declined to follow because of stubborn resistance. Riḍā concludes that the first and third categories of non-Muslims are both "unreached" and not necessarily condemned. The first group of non-Muslims is unreached because they have never encountered the Prophet's message. The third group of non-Muslims is also unreached because, although they have encountered a message, it was either a misrepresentation of the Prophet's message or they were not driven to investigate the message. Riḍā believed that having encountered an improper presentation of the Prophet's message is to have in fact not encountered the Prophet's message at all. Thus, this group of people is like the first group, unreached.

Now, what about those sincere, truth-seeking people who heard the Prophet's message, are motivated to investigate the Prophet's message, but do not follow the Prophet? In the June 1903 issue of Riḍā's journal, *al-Manār*, not to be confused with his *tafsīr* which is also called *al-Manār*, he responded to a letter asking if God's mercy extends to non-Muslims. Riḍā states that although God's mercy is universal, it is ordained only "for those who are conscious of God and pay the prescribed alms, who believe in revelations, who follow the Messenger."[18] God's mercy does not extend to those who properly hear the Prophet's message and reject it. Riḍā then clarifies that "God excuses both the unreached and the reached who investigate the message 'with sincerity' but who never succeed in discerning the truth."[19] Thus according to Riḍā, there are only two groups of non-Muslims who will receive God's punishment for

---

17. Khalil, 119; cf. 33.
18. Khalil, 118.
19. Khalil, 119.

rejecting the Prophet. First are those who encounter the message in its true form, and are provided with enough incentive to investigate it, but never do so. Second are those who investigate the Prophet's true message but reject it out of stubborn arrogance.[20]

What about those who reject the message for another reason besides stubborn arrogance? What about those who reject the message because they believe the message of another tradition is more convincing? What about us Christians who have a good grasp of the Prophet's message, have lived with and interacted with Muslims, and yet remain Christians? We can find a possible response in Riḍā's commentary on *an-Nisā'* 4:115, which reads:

> Whoever deviates, after guidance has been clearly given to him, contentiously opposes the Messenger and follows a path other than that of the believers, we will leave him on his chosen path and let him burn in hell, an evil destination.

Riḍā observes that this passage consists of a general divine threat to anyone who refuses to accept or investigate the Prophet's message after that message has been made clear to him or her.[21] But what does it mean for the message to have "been *made clear*?" Riḍā elaborates on ten different ways that individuals can interact with the Prophet's message. For the sake of time, I will look at only five of them. First are those who are absolutely certain of the Prophet's message. Second are those who may not be absolutely certain, but the Prophet's truth is accepted as divine guidance. Although Riḍā did not use this term, I will call this group the enlightened, because the truth has been made evident to them. If someone is from this enlightened group and subsequently rejects the Prophet's message, then Riḍā considered them worthy of damnation. However, Riḍā believed that there are only a few people who fall into this group of enlightened deniers. This is because Riḍā believed that the Prophet's message is harmonious with our natural *fiṭra*, our natural disposition for God. Because of our *fiṭra*, Riḍā believed that people preferred truth over falsehood, guidance over error, and good over evil. If the Prophet's message is divine truth, which Riḍā believed is the case, then people cannot resist the message's transformative power. In other words, if the message is made clear, then people cannot help but desire the Prophet's message. Thus, if the message is made clear to someone and they follow it, then rejecting the

---

20. *Al-Manār* 13, no. 8 (September 1910): 572–576. Riḍā finds support for this position in *an-Nisā'* 4:115; Khalil, *Islam and the Fate of Others*, 120; cf. 50.

21. Khalil, 120.

Prophet's message is equivalent to rejecting one's own *fiṭra*, which Riḍā found particularly contemptible. The only reason he could see for such a choice is either tribal stubbornness or the pursuit of desire over truth.[22] Thus those who are condemned are those who have faith in the Prophet's message but then reject it out of selfish desires.

The next eight types of individuals Riḍā discusses are those who experience various types of interactions with the Prophet's message but for whom the truth has not been made clear. I will focus on three of them. There are those who are exposed to an improper version of the message. Because they do not encounter the true message, they do not encounter that which would stimulate their *fiṭra* and lead to investigation. Riḍā believed that most non-Muslims during his time fell into this category. Next are those who sincerely investigate the message after encountering it but stop when the truth is not apparent to them. Finally are those sincere truth seekers who investigate the message and even when the complete truth of the message is not evident, they continue investigating. Riḍā claims that the verse in *an-Nisā'* 4:115 does not condemn any of these three individuals because the truth is never made evident to them. This does not mean that people from these groups will never be judged. Rather, they will be judged by what they know to be moral and true in relation to the Prophet's message and from their own rational deductions.[23] Again, the only people who are condemned are those who have heard the message, found it to be divine truth, and then rejected it out of stubborn, selfish desires.

Unlike previous generations of Muslim scholars who could make the argument that much of the world had not heard of the Prophet Muhammad, Riḍā could not. Here Riḍā makes the third point I want to highlight: he makes a hermeneutical leap of mercy to argue that most people will go to heaven. At the turn of the twentieth century, non-Muslims, especially more educated Western non-Muslims, had basic knowledge of the Islamic tradition that was pretty accurate. Now Riḍā believed that if the Prophet's message is made clear, then one's *fiṭra* cannot help but accept the message. Although some reject this clear message out of stubborn selfishness, Riḍā believed these are a minority. Thus, he had to account for the many people who have clear knowledge of the Islamic tradition and yet do not accept the message. From Riḍā's perspective, one's inability to receive the Prophet's message has less to do with one's sin or the corruption of one's heart, and more to do with the clouding of one's intellect. This is not a form of stupidity. Rather, the inability

---

22. Khalil, 121; cf. 58.
23. Khalil, 122.

to see because of a clouded intellect has to do with one's "social, cultural and political" worldview.[24] Riḍā acknowledges that people filter the world through social, cultural and political paradigms, and the Prophet's message will be unappealing in the light of some of these. Thus, Riḍā saw a need to "rehabilitate the tarnished image of Islam, to provide 'enough incentive' to at least some non-Muslims to take it seriously."[25]

Riḍā did not believe that the unreached are beyond condemnation. If that were the case, then hearing the Prophet's message would put their salvation in jeopardy, and it would be best to not have them hear the Prophet's message. This would make the Prophet's message, and other prophetic messages before him, harmful. This could not be the case because messengers are a mercy from God. Riḍā reconciles this problem by asserting that the unreached will be judged according to "what they know of the truth and falsehood, and good and evil."[26] Riḍā believed all people have an innate knowledge of good and evil and of truth from falsehood because all people have a *fiṭra*. Furthermore, Riḍā believed that there is a remnant of God's original message within the Torah and the Gospels. This means that Christians and Jews have some of God's merciful guidance through their texts and the *fiṭra* to guide them in discerning right from wrong. This is a hermeneutical leap of mercy. Riḍā went beyond the explicit statements in the qur'anic passages we looked at to affirm the existence of the righteous religious other. He recognized that God desires that people outside the Islamic tradition can find salvation through God's mercy, which takes account of human limitations. Thus, Riḍā conceived of an afterlife that includes Muslims as well as non-Muslims.

To sum up, Riḍā's soteriology consists of three elements that attempt to reconcile the tension between God's wrath and God's mercy, on the one hand, and the tension between the notion of a common *fiṭra* that desires God and the reality that not all people follow the Prophet Muhammad on the other. First, Riḍā believed that true belief is *islām*, but not the Islamic tradition. This means that God cares more about one's devotion to God than about the explicit tradition that one follows. Second, Riḍā affirmed that only those who reject the Prophet out of selfish desire are condemned. This means that those who have heard the message improperly, who are not given incentive to investigate the message, or investigate but find it wanting, are all excused. Finally, Riḍā made a hermeneutical leap of mercy by arguing that most people

---

24. Khalil, 124.
25. Khalil, 125, 77.
26. Khalil, 117; cf. 35.

will go to heaven because God takes into account human limitations due to social, political or religious contexts.

Reassessing Romans 1:18–23

Let us go back to our original question: How can a Christian account for a Muslim who has heard the message and understood it, but ultimately preferred their Muslim faith, and how can we do so in such a way that does not impose a Christian worldview upon them? At the beginning of this contribution, I argued that the current approach simply imposes a Christian worldview on Muslims, which in turn suppresses a Muslim's identity. I argued that in order to begin to alleviate this problem, we should investigate the Islamic tradition in such a way that we are open to its transformative power to revise our own beliefs and practices. We have just finished investigating Rashīd Riḍā's soteriology, but we have yet to see how this can lead to a revision of our own belief. To that end, I would like to end this contribution by interpreting, or perhaps reinterpreting, a commonly quoted passage of the Bible that supports the exclusivist position, but I would like to do so in light of Riḍā's soteriology. Let us go to Romans 1:18–23:

> The wrath of God is being revealed from heaven against all ungodliness and wickedness of people, who suppress the truth by their wickedness, since what may be known about God is plain to them, because God has made it plain to them. For since the creation of the world God's invisible qualities – his eternal power and divine nature – have been clearly seen, being understood from what he has made, so that people are without excuse.
>
> For although they knew God, they neither glorified him as God nor gave thanks to him, but their thinking became futile and their foolish hearts were darkened. Although they claimed to be wise, they became fools and exchanged the glory of the immortal God for images made to look like a mortal human being and birds and animals and reptiles.

This passage is often read as justifying the condemnation of non-Christians because they have suppressed the truth, whether it is the truth of creation or the truth of the gospel. However, we must remember that we too hold the same tensions that Riḍā did when engaging the Qur'an regarding the question of salvation. Although the Bible frequently mentions God's wrath being dealt out to those who reject God, the Bible is also filled with passages about

God's grace and patience (2 Pet 3:9). Also, there is the Christian doctrine that, being created in God's image, we are endowed with an inner desire for God. This stands in tension with the reality that many people do not seem to follow Christ, whom we believe fulfills the longing of the image of God within human beings. Thus when reading this passage, we must keep in mind this tension between God's wrath and God's grace on the one hand, and the image of God and the seeming rejection of that image on the other hand.

Turning back to Romans 1:18–23, here we have God's wrath revealed against ungodliness and wickedness. What do the ungodly and wicked do to earn such condemnation? They suppress the truth. What is the truth they suppress? God's power and divine nature that they know from creation. What else do they do? They do not honor or thank God. Instead, they claim to be wiser than God and begin worshiping images, giving them glory rather than God. This seems pretty straightforward, but this does not help us answer our question: what do we do with the sincere Muslim who knowingly rejects the gospel out of piety? Unlike the ungodly and the wicked in the passage, Muslims recognize God's presence in creation. Muslims recognize God's power and divine nature. Unlike the wicked and the ungodly, Muslims do not worship idols or images. Instead, Muslims are supposed to constantly thank God and give him praise and glory. If the ungodly and wicked are punished because instead of following the truth they know – that God is divine and powerful – they worship idols, and if Muslims do none of these things but rather claim to praise God and give him thanks, then it seems that Muslims do not fall under the Romans 1:18–23 category of the wicked and ungodly.

Does this then mean that Muslims are the same as Christians? No, it does not. How then can we reconcile the notion that Muslims and Christians differ with regard to the truth, and yet Muslims do not fall under the Romans 1:18–23 category of the ungodly and the wicked? It is here that I find that Riḍā's soteriology gives some insight to this question. As I have argued, Riḍā only condemns those people who fully know the truth but reject it out of stubborn selfishness. These people are not only denying the message, but they are also denying their *fiṭra*. The *fiṭra* desires God, and these people have heard the Prophet's message that resonates with our *fiṭra*. Yet they decide to reject their *fiṭra*'s yearnings and stubbornly pursue their selfish desires. Those who do not follow the Prophet's message because they are either introduced to a corrupted version of the message, are not given the proper preconditions to inquire, or inquire and find it wanting, are all excused because the message does not reach their *fiṭra*. If the message does reach their *fiṭra*, then according to Riḍā, one cannot help but know God's guidance. Because these people do not recognize the truth of the Prophet's message, their *fiṭra* has not been reached. Thus, they will not be judged for rejecting the Prophet's message.

How does this apply to our passage? Well, like Riḍā, we believe that all people have the image of God and that this image desires God. We also believe that the gospel resonates with the image of God and that when people truly hear the gospel, they cannot help but believe, because the image of God draws them to Christ. It seems that the people described in Romans 1:18–23 fully know God's truth and reject it. This means that the image of God within them responds affirmatively to God's truth. Yet they reject not only God's truth, but they also reject the image of God within them. This results in their worship of idols and their condemnation. If I may continue to apply Riḍā's hermeneutic to this passage, this entails that Muslims and those who sincerely investigate the gospel but do not find it convincing have not had the image of God within them inspired by God's truth. This means that they have not rejected God's truth because they do not know God's truth. Rather, they continue to follow the impulses of the image of God, which leads them into pursuing truth from falsehood and goodness from evil. If Romans 1 condemns people who reject God's truth because they know it and instead reject their own view of God, then, taking Riḍā's hermeneutic of mercy, it seems that Romans 1 does not condemn Muslims or those sincere, truth-seeking people who have investigated the gospel but found it wanting.

In this volume, Daniel Brown encourages us to be humble when interpreting the Qur'an. I want to expand on his call by asking that we not only be humble, but that we also be curious to learn more about the Islamic tradition and about our Muslim brothers and sisters. The hope is that we will develop a humble curiosity into the beauty of the Islamic tradition. A humble curiosity takes an interest in the Islamic tradition and the life of Muslims *because* there is a beauty to be found where we can deepen our life with God. The goal of this contribution is to show how opening up one's religious tradition to the insights of another religious tradition could open up new avenues for not only understanding other religions, but also for developing a deeper and more complex understanding of oneself. This practice I am advocating is a process, not a method or a theory. It is messy and at times disturbing. However, the more we pursue this type of practice and open ourselves up to be vulnerable to the insights of the religious other, the better we will understand not only how to communicate the beliefs we hold dear to our hearts, but we also come to better understand the religious other who stands as our friend and neighbor.

8.5 Salvation Made Plain: How Some New Fellowships from Muslim Background Create Community

Grant Porter

Jesus said to Zacchaeus, "Today salvation has come to this house" (Luke 19:9). What did the Lord Jesus mean? From the broader narrative of Luke/Acts, we could assume that Zacchaeus believed that Jesus is truly the promised Messiah and that Zacchaeus's declared actions as described by Luke were acts of repentance in keeping with that new-found belief. His generosity – "I give half of my possessions to the poor" – and his promised restitution – "If I have cheated anybody out of anything, I will pay back four times" (Luke 19:8) – demonstrate the transformation that had begun in Zacchaeus as a result of his faith in and his relationship with the Messiah.

In the same vein, people all around the world and – as this is a contribution focused on the Middle East – in the Muslim world in particular are making the same faith claims as Zacchaeus. What is the practical impact and outworking of those declarations of faith? These will surely vary to some degree from person to person and from context to context, albeit with a large degree of commonality. This variability is certainly true of the new ecclesial expressions of Jesus followers from Muslim backgrounds with whom I am acquainted. However, the practical outworking of these faith claims play a crucial role not only in the personal life of the adherents but also in both community formation and mission. Still, before drawing lessons from these expressions, I would like to describe my research over the last few years as a way of establishing context that has contributed to the observations that I will make.

Adopters, Negotiators and Reframers

Over a period of several years, I had the privilege of studying five fellowships whose members are from Muslim and Druze backgrounds in the Middle East region. Through a series of interviews, my research sought to answer questions around community formation and mission praxis. Unsurprisingly those two areas were intrinsically connected, while also being heavily influenced by how each community saw themselves in relation to each other, society and the wider Christian community. I was able to roughly group these fellowships into three categories based on how they view themselves, and as a result, how they relate both to their original community and to the Christian community with whom they now share a common faith.

First are those who believe that their faith convictions mean they need to join the existing Christian community. They see themselves as leaving Islam, and the cultural expressions that often go hand in hand with that religion, and joining a new community. Because of this, I call them *adopters*, as basically they say, "We would like to adopt Christianity, and we would like the Christian community to adopt us in turn." Those who choose this path often do so at a high price.

However, others feel that there are too many barriers to identifying with the wider Christian community. As one person expressed, "In the Middle East, unfortunately the Christians look down on the Muslims. And they consider them from a different tribe, from even a different kind of people. And these terms hurt the feelings of the newcomers from Muslim background who have come to Christ."

Another explained, "If I say I am a Christian, or if people see that I have friends that are Christians, people are going to think that I'm a Christian. One time, Mohammed and I went to visit somebody (a Christian), and that person's neighbor knew us, and he asked us, 'Have you become Christians?'" It is obvious from this statement that being perceived as a Christian, and by implication someone who is of the Christian community, was not a positive identifier for the speaker.

With these perceived tensions from both their own society and the Christian community, some followers of Christ look for alternative ways to identify themselves. This second group with whom I engaged I call *negotiators*. They are followers of Jesus from non-Christian backgrounds who have rejected the teachings of Islam but are unwilling to describe themselves as Christians and join the Christian community. In consequence, one of their primary goals is to remain embedded in their original community as non-practicing Muslims in order to share their faith convictions and maintain their core identity. Believing that one is able to splice culture and religion, these fellowships "negotiate" their way through life – hence my descriptor – deciding what is religious and what is cultural. Like the *adopters*, *negotiators* essentially do not see any unique truth within Islam and regard the Christian scriptures solely as authoritative.

The third grouping that I observed is one that I describe as *reframers*. These are Jesus followers who, like the *negotiators*, maintain their identity as Muslim but do not reject Islam or Islamic religious practices. They rather reinterpret or "reframe" Islam and the Qur'an through the lens of Christ and the scriptures. Where they see disagreement between the two, they discard the Islamic practice or belief. They remain embedded in their respective communities and are still regarded as Muslim (possibly as fringe Muslims) by family and friends. As those who are contextualizing their faith by remaining within the Muslim community, one wonders about the degree of influence that this starting point has on their decisions regarding what agrees with and what is in contradiction to the scriptures. Mosque attendance is possibly a good example. Some in the historical Christian community (including evangelicals) would regard such attendance as some type of compromise, whereas *reframers* have a more ambivalent view.[27] Similar to *negotiators*, they regard maintaining their core identity as Muslim as an aid to sharing about Christ. As one *reframer* indicated, "This makes it easier for . . . people to approach us. Because we aren't Christians . . . it makes it easier for us to share about Jesus wisely."

Even though each of these groups has a different self-description, with a resulting varied posture toward the wider society and the existing Christian community, they all seek to form and define their new faith communities. This is a powerful motivation that influences much of what they say and do. Two of the churches – one *adopter* and one *negotiator* – pursue community formation by employing an attractional model of church,[28] while others gather in homes. In both expressions, they have to some degree engaged a centered set approach, especially in evangelism. As they move into community formation, however, a more bounded set model is utilized by all as an aid to defining their community.[29] As someone from the *adopter* community said:

> About our ministry, we're a centered set . . . we just want people to be moving toward loving Jesus more. . . . About the gospel, we're a bounded set . . . we do feel like there is like a line that God knows about salvation; that's like you give your life to Christ and you cross that line . . . that's a bounded set.

---

27. In the words of an *adopter*, "They don't want to go to the mosque because what they learn in the mosque is contrary to what they've learned in the gospel. So, all of that stuff, I think it's understood that it's a package deal for them. Like Islam, you can't pick and choose one of the principles, like shall I continue fasting but not pray five times a day? Should I continue bowing down while I pray? It's a package deal, like this is an 'Islam brand.' So we see that these things stop, all of those Islamic forms; we don't do those."

28. An attractional model of church is a public gathering of Christians which anyone can attend, typically with programs for youth, children, women, etc., that would also attract the surrounding community. See Andrea Gray, Leith Gray, Bob Fish, and Michael Baker, "Networks of Redemption: A Preliminary Statistical Analysis of Fruitfulness in Transformational and Attractional Approaches," *IJFM* 27, no. 2 (2010): 89–95.

29. Hiebert, borrowing concepts from mathematics, introduced the concept of centered and bounded sets when describing types of churches. See Paul Hiebert, "Conversion, Culture and Cognitive Categories," *Gospel in Context* 11, no. 4 (October 1978): 24–29.

This "community with borders" paradigm comes about as each wrestles with their identity once they have made new faith commitments. As stated by one *negotiator* in describing the other people in his fellowship, "I'm responsible for them as part of my family. It's like Boaz spreading his blanket on Ruth. So we just flip the blanket . . . we just spread it a little bit further." For this fellowship, community is family. The question that needs to be answered, therefore, is, "Who is really my brother and who is my sister?" Essentially, a line has to be drawn. In the same vein, other communities ask, "Whom can I trust?" – a crucial question particularly for those communities facing antagonism for their beliefs.

That a community would seek to define itself by creating boundaries is not strange, it seems. Meeks, in the context of describing the early church movement, states, "In order to persist, a social organization must have boundaries, must maintain structural stability as well as flexibility, and must create a unique culture."[30]

Churches in other contexts sometimes appear to have designated the sacraments of baptism or the Eucharist (or both) as community markers. This is not the case among the fellowships of believers from Muslim backgrounds. In the five fellowships studied, both rituals are practiced but do not appear to indicate who is "in" the fellowship and who is "out" of the fellowship. Baptism is for those who request it and is seen as a further step in the life of a believer, rather than as a way to enter the fellowship. In regard to the Eucharist, the elements are served to all who are present. In two of the fellowships, visitors are encouraged to either refrain from sharing in the ceremony or to "think of Jesus" while they do. But in all five fellowships, no one is refused the bread or the cup if they are present. That would be considered inhospitable (a serious cultural faux pas) and the antithesis of the grace and generosity of God symbolized in the Lord's supper.

So if they are not able to follow the pattern adopted by other faith communities, how then can these faith communities define their community boundary? As I asked this question, the response was consistently the same: through observed behavioral change. This is from people who have been raised in a religion where one can convert by uttering a confession. As one *negotiator* stated, "It's a very important question: what changes have happened in your life when you became a believer? What happened? Are you still the same

---

30. Wayne A. Meeks, *The First Urban Christians: The Social World of the Apostle Paul* (New Haven: Yale University Press, 2003), 84.

person you were before you accepted Christ, or did you change? Because Muslim people are saying they're believers."

For *adopters*, part of this behavioral change seems to be making a clear public break with Islam and joining a church. This often results in a break with their traditional community, family and friends for a period of time for some and, sadly, permanently for others. Clearly, it is an indication of the willingness of these adherents to pay the cost and is often the first step in gaining the trust of the broader fellowship.

However, for others who are not seeking a clear public break with their communities, those boundary lines were often blurred. As one from a *reframer* community stated, "They just believe in Jesus . . . but they are not, well, followers 100 percent." When asked to distinguish between these two descriptions, it was communicated that "followers" were ones that read and obey the teachings of Jesus, as opposed to just declaring belief in Christ. This obedience begins with the core relationships of family and home. That same *reframer* added, "My family had a strong negative reaction to Jesus, but then when they saw the change in me, when they saw me sacrificing myself for them, wearing myself out worrying about their problems. . . . It made them see what it means to believe."

Other signs are a commitment to the gatherings (large or small), coupled with a consistent pattern of serving others in the fellowship. "We prayed together, and we declared our love one to another. Everybody, twenty-five or thirty of us, went to everybody else to pray with each other and ask them if there was any problem, and to be forgiven, and then to declare their love."

All members of the community are expected to be regularly (and sensitively) sharing about Christ within their circle of relationships. "You have to show people that you are a follower of Christ . . . in your relationship with your neighbors, in your relationship with your wife, with your kids. With your honesty, with your transparency."

And this does in turn often result in some form of persecution. As one *reframer* observed, "the leaders of the groups, and mostly all the members of the groups . . . have in mind the idea that they might be persecuted at any time (for the sake of) . . . the name of Jesus. Because we all read about Jesus and what happened with Jesus."

It is expected that the gospel will impact marriages, families, neighbors, friendships and work relationships. As far as possible, followers engage those relationships in grace and love, seeking to live in peace with everyone. In addition "followers," it seems in comparison with "believers," are more likely to participate in group ministry to the poor, be active in communal prayer and giving, and in time start and lead their own groups.

Interestingly, both *negotiators* and *reframers* face a similar problem in expressing a radically new "walk" that is aligned with their radically new "talk." As each of the interviewees described what this behavioral change looked like, in being more caring and attentive toward family and neighbors, generous and compassionate toward the poor, one could imagine that they were describing someone who was perceived to be "good" or "righteous" in any community, whether Christian or Muslim. Although these virtues are honorable and praiseworthy, they are not necessarily distinct enough to be countercultural and only give credence to the opinion held by some, that they are just very good people rather than Jesus followers. Externally, the characteristics of such a life differ little from what the surrounding society and religion idealize as a righteous life.

However, in at least one area there was a radical difference. Each community focused in its teaching and its witness on the issue of how one deals with his or her enemies. Whether the enemies are personal or of the wider society in which these communities exist, a righteous life is no longer just about how one treats one's family, neighbors and everyday relationships (love your neighbor), but also how one interacts with those who opposed and lived in enmity toward the individual Christ-follower, their family and their tribe or clan (love your enemy).

Time was spent in scripture study around this subject, and it became a behavioral distinctive of who is "in" and who is "out" – even to the point of church discipline. For example, one *negotiator* church leader stated:

> The reason I wanted to kick him out of the group is that I didn't want others to be influenced by him when it comes to taking revenge. . . . I told him clearly, if you want to obey the word of God, you have to obey it as it is. If you would tell me that you want to teach yourself how to love, I will help you. But if you keep insisting you love Jesus, but you hate . . . revenge is something not in the Bible. In Jesus there is no enemy; the only enemy is Satan.

In this regard, a position of compassion and forgiveness toward one's enemies, particularly those who are perceived to have attacked the community as a whole, can conceivably place one at odds with the rest of one's society. Often when someone shows love and acceptance to an enemy of the community or clan, the members of that clan naturally conclude that that individual is siding with the enemy. The implication is that this individual or group is betraying the community, which some of the new believers discovered despite emphasizing that "teachings of Christ mean we have to forgive and love our enemies, not condone their actions." In the end, often at great personal cost, obeying Christ's command to "love your enemies" became the unique distinctive that could not be hidden, and a shared conviction held by each fellowship regardless of where they most comfortably settled along the contextual spectrum.

Though this position created suspicion and opposition in some, it also simultaneously intrigued others. One member of the *reframer* community was asked to share at a large political rally. Because of the history and the suffering that this particular people group experienced and still continue to experience, the other speakers at the rally focused on the realization of political aspirations through violence. As a follower of Jesus, this believer pursued another tack. An observer reported, "he really felt that he should share a different perspective than what was being spoken about in that political meeting. So, he did; he shared some of the principles of love and forgiveness that he'd been learning from Jesus, and that sparked an interest from two religious teachers to meet with him, to study with him, and these have started their own study group within their communities based on the time that they've had with him."

This emphasis on true faith being proved and displayed in relationships, both to our neighbor and our enemy, particularly when seen in the context of community formation, is a challenge both to the churches and us. Obviously, this was not the only factor as they grew their churches. Coalescing around a shared belief in the person and work of Christ appears to be a key boundary marker. The different churches also articulated a sense of calling, a new understanding of who they are and their respective places in the world, which in turn adds to the distinctiveness of their new community, different from the rest of society. Nonetheless, obedience to Christ's teachings, particularly in our attitudes and actions toward our enemies as a boundary marker of a new community, demonstrates the extent to which relationships are valued, and a conviction that they are the main arena in which obedience is played out.

As authentic community is built on relationships of trust and commitment, it became clear from the interviews that each church is seeking a way to define the extent of their communities. They are creating boundaries. Entrusting oneself to whoever shows up to the weekly meeting is not sufficient it would seem, particularly in contexts where belief in the divinity of Christ places one in danger. The community needed definition.

Lessons for the Wider Church

This contribution has focused on just one aspect of the journey that these new emerging communities have embarked upon. Of course, there are many other facets to their story. As this story is shared, one has to ask what – if any – are the implications arising from what was expressed that could inform the wider Christian body, particularly as we engage the church that exists in other difficult contexts. I would like to suggest that there is much to be learned. The value of discovering what these Near Eastern churches from Muslim backgrounds actually do, and why they do it, cannot be underestimated and could serve as a useful example for other emerging churches in distressed contexts to reflect upon the "relatability" to their specific situations.

However, the conversation must be continued so that their valuable voices can be heard. I have ventured to make a few suggestions based on my interaction with these churches of how this dialogue can develop. These recommendations flow out of reflections on the conversations held with different members of the new churches. I had a unique opportunity to hear their thoughts and to examine both their model of mission and the way they formed community. Their insights I have found to be invaluable and enlightening.

First, I would suggest that we allow the community to create distinctions between themselves and the rest of their immediate society. In much of mission today, there is a continual push for new expressions of the church, particularly in hitherto unchurched areas (either geographical or social), to be culturally relevant and integrated into the wider society. This is particularly important so as to maintain access points for those interested inquirers currently outside the church to be able to connect with those inside the church, or for possible eventual discipling opportunities. I previously mentioned Hiebert, who, borrowing concepts from mathematics, introduced the concept of centered and bounded sets when describing types of churches. Bounded sets are churches with high expectations of conformity before joining, while centered sets are churches oriented toward a shared value, idea or teaching (e.g. the person and work of Christ). People are welcomed to the centered set church if they are moving closer to that central idea, value or teaching, no matter how far along the path they are. Church planters have increasingly adopted the centered set model as they seek to form communities of faith. Although this is an excellent evangelistic strategy particularly for individuals, in championing the model as a church planting strategy there remains a danger of losing community definition. I became convinced from my observations that clear boundaries that define communities are an aid to sustainability and longevity, particularly in difficult contexts.

As a caveat to the last paragraph, an emphasis on mission both in teaching and in lifestyle would also be helpful. It was impressed upon me as I interacted with the different fellowships that the concept of mission fosters a sense of community and identity, a sense of "specialness" that encourages adherents to join together with others who share that same sense of uniqueness. As has been demonstrated, community is key to sustainability and therefore should be a critical component of the discipleship process.

What impressed me from my interaction with these churches was their commitment to relationships. My second suggestion, therefore, would be to seek to always move from the programmatic to the relational as much as possible. Changing from the model of community that is similar to a voluntary association (like many well-established churches) focused on a weekly meeting to more of an intimate – even kinship-like – grouping-type structure seems to allow the community to develop more readily and to form closer bonds with a deeper commitment to relationships. Adherents are not so much attending an event as participating in a family-like gathering. When relationships in the community are strained because of the faith convictions held by adherents, a family-like community can be the support network that suffering people need. Particularly, but of course not exclusively in a collectivist society, adversity (and persecution) is most likely endured best as a community. Deep community relationships are also a powerful and attractive aid to the missional engagement of that community with the wider society, especially as it proclaims a message of reconciliation. An intentional and ongoing shift from the programmatic to the relational is a much-needed direction to help foster growth and sustainability.

Third, I believe that we do need to combat isolationism. Although cultural distinctiveness is a value to strive for, coupled with isolationism this distinctiveness may slide into tribalism. Some of the problems associated with mixing between the people groups – such as the question "Have you become a Christian?" – are highlighted in this contribution. However, a wealth of learning, challenge and mutual encouragement is missed when groups grow in isolation. A possible way to combat isolation is to explore ways for at least the non-Christian background churches to interact with each other. A greater openness to mix with other Christian communities, particularly at the leadership level, would expose each of the church fellowships to other communities' understanding of biblical values, truth and how the different fellowships tackled issues in their own particular context. This interaction is particularly relevant to the *reframers* as they seek to practice and declare their faith in the person and teachings of Christ within the framework of Islam.

However, it is also needed in the *negotiator* churches. In those congregations, as they seek to reject Islam while still embracing their culture, they attempt to discern what aspects of their lives are cultural and what are affirmations of their societies' host religion. This work has initially been undertaken by the individual church leaders who started the fellowships. However, this process should be more inclusive as time progresses. A coming together of contextual theologians, leaders of the new churches and mature adherents, if possible, would be a significant step in helping to retain these churches within orthodoxy and allow an authentic church expression to emerge within a new context. If left to themselves, particularly because some of these churches are quite isolated, the danger that culture is the final hermeneutic is quite real. Newbigin rightly identifies the great danger of allowing the context to dictate the terms on which the gospel message engages with society. He writes, "The result then is that the world is not challenged at its depth but rather absorbs and domesticates the gospel and uses it to sacralize its own purposes."[31]

Instead, Newbigin calls for a community that is truly local and truly ecumenical. He explains:

> Truly local in that it embodies God's particular word of grace and judgment for that people. Truly ecumenical in being open to the witness of churches in all other places, and thus saved from absorption into the culture of that place, and enabled to represent to that place the universality, the catholicity of God's purpose of grace and judgment for all humanity.[32]

Discreet efforts need to be made even now to quietly bridge the very real cultural and social divides (perhaps initially at leadership level) between these new churches and the broader Christian community.

As the number of these fellowships have grown, so the debate in the wider evangelical community has also grown regarding their status – "Are they really churches?" or "Is this just another foreign idea?" – and their validity – "Are these groups heretical?" However, what has become increasingly evident in the debate is a serious lack of actual engagement with these fellowships. Though at first glance the new churches seem very informal, disorganized, and at best "on the fringe" of evangelicalism in comparison with the institutionalized churches present in the Middle East today, they are not dissimilar in form to

---

31. Lesslie Newbigin, *The Gospel in a Pluralist Society* (Grand Rapids: Eerdmans, 1989), 152.

32. Newbigin, *Gospel in a Pluralist Society*, 152.

other early expressions of church. They have formed community, practiced rituals, established their own leadership, and continue to engage their society with the proclamation of the gospel message, even to the point of physical suffering. They are strongly Bible focused, possess a strong sense of calling, and seek to live God-honoring lives in their context. These are traits that would be common in any religious movement and stand in contrast to the more established institutionalized churches that often began as movements themselves.[33] Of concern, therefore, is not their structure but their body of theological beliefs and their potential to wander away from Christian orthodoxy.

It is fully understandable for established evangelical churches in the region to seek to absorb these new congregations in an effort to maintain the new churches' orthodoxy and to present a declaration of the new unity that the gospel can bring to Middle Eastern society. This joining would be particularly true for a house group in close proximity to an evangelical church in the city, though it would appear to be less practical for churches in more isolated areas far from established churches. However, this approach does not take into consideration the historical, strident denominationalism found particularly in evangelicalism and the wider Christian community in general, which has on occasion undermined the attempts to present a united congregation.

What was communicated to me was that this joining would also reduce the access points for seeking Muslims who are looking to inquire of the Christian faith. For the sake of mission, evangelical leaders have the opportunity to allow these new churches to continue and grow as the best viable means of effective witness and relevant discipleship in their respective communities. Historically, evangelical churches in the Near East have had until very recently little success in mission into other faith communities. Allowing these new churches to flourish outside of the registered Christian denominations creates more missional prospects. If evangelical leaders can accept that these new churches and networks of house churches are valid expressions of church, albeit in its early movement form, then they can also accept, for the sake of mission, the development of these new churches into their own unique institutions, independent of the evangelical denominations. In addition to allowing the new churches to develop outside of the official evangelical structure, evangelical leaders should still proactively seek to establish relational connections as

---

33. See Paul G. Hiebert, R. Daniel Shaw, and Tite Tiénou, *Understanding Folk Religion: A Christian Response to Popular Beliefs and Practices* (Grand Rapids: Baker Academic, 2000), 333–346.

brothers and sisters in Christ for the purpose of mutual encouragement, healthy discourse around gospel and culture themes, and mutual learning.

Concluding Reflections

This paper has been written in response to the emergence of an unusual phenomenon in the Middle East region. Faith communities based on the teachings of the Christian scriptures have begun to appear over the last twenty years in increasing numbers. What makes these faith communities unusual is the fact that the majority of adherents are from Muslim or Druze religious backgrounds and are choosing to congregate with others of like backgrounds to follow the teachings of Christ. As we engage with them, it is clear that they have a message which is evidenced by their uncompromising adherence to seek to walk in obedience to the command to love one's enemies. Those who were not willing to begin that journey, and a long journey it is, are regarded, in the words of one congregation, as believers but not yet followers. I think that the clarity of that definition can give the wider church pause for reflection.

It is hoped that this book will spark off many more conversations in the future between the new emerging fellowships and the wider Christian community, between the different new communities themselves, and finally within each unique community. I believe we will all benefit from a respectful but critical dialogue with multiple committed conversation partners, all engaging around the vital issues that these new fellowships will have to face. My hope is that this research has given these new fellowships themselves a clear voice both in this conversation and in the potential discussions in the future.

8.6 Is There a Place for Islam in God's Salvation History?

Ida Glaser

I introduce this contribution with the same opening paragraph as for my previous contribution, "The Messengers and the Message" *(section 7.5)*. Both share the same theologizing context within which my reflection is taking place. Different Christians "thinking biblically about Islam" are thinking from different perspectives. Most are thinking as outsiders to Islam, trying to understand peoples who live in different countries, or at least in different communities, than themselves, and who are definitely "other" than themselves. Many are thinking as outsiders to Islam but as neighbors of Muslims, trying to understand people who live alongside them but have another faith. There are also increasing numbers who grew up as insiders and who are thinking about the faith and the community to which they have belonged and, in many ways, may still belong. They are trying to understand their own heritage – not only their own families and communities, but also themselves. Interacting with the amazing range of thinking people at the consultation in 2019, I realize that I am thinking from yet another perspective: a Jewish Christian perspective which leads me to think about Islam as something which grew up alongside rabbinic Judaism as well as Orthodox, Nestorian and Monophysite Christianity.

I want in this contribution to explore the possible place of Islam in salvation history. As I affirmed earlier, if we can relate Islam to Judaism, and if we can discern a special place for Judaism and Jewish people in a Christian worldview,[34] we may also be able to discern a special place for Islam and for Muslims in our thinking.

Covenant, Haggadah and Halakhah: A Framework for Reflection

The covenants form the people of God. They tell us who those people are, how they relate to God, and what is their purpose in relation to other nations and to God's creative and eschatological purposes. They therefore have central socio-political significance as well as central theological significance – they relate to the power questions, to God's kingship and to how it relates to human kingship. They also relate to law.

In rabbinic Jewish thinking, the covenant faith of the Torah can be described under two categories: ***haggadah***, or stories, and ***halakhah***, or law. *Haggadah* includes the whole narrative aspect of the Torah which tells of God's relationship with the world and all the people in it, and especially with the Jewish people. *Halakhah* includes not only the written requirements of the Torah but also their oral dimension and later legal discussions. We might compare this categorization to the Islamic categories of *īmān* (faith) and *aʿmāl* (actions), and the Christian categories of "law" and "grace." These different categorizations can be a key to the discernment of how the "forms" of Christian, Muslim and Jewish practice relate to their meanings.

---

34. As noted in section 7.5, I am indebted for stimulating my thinking about this to M. Kinzer, *Jerusalem Crucified, Jerusalem Risen: The Resurrected Messiah, the Jewish People and the Land of Promise* (Eugene: Wipf & Stock, Cascade Books, 2018); and to S. Dauermann, *Converging Destinies: Jews, Christians and the People of God* (Eugene: Wipf & Stock, Cascade Books, 2017).

The Christian categories are about ways of salvation – are we saved through obeying the laws which God gave us, or by accepting the grace which God offers us? The answer is the latter, which leaves the God-given law in a somewhat ambiguous position. Too often it is deemed no longer necessary, except to show us that we cannot keep it. At worst, we have the irony that keeping God's law can be seen as a bad thing!

The Muslim categories are about human responses to the divine revelation – do we both believe it and obey it? In theory, the revelation enters time from eternity, so the stories which go with it are, in a sense, incidental. We only need them as illustrations of and confirmations of the revelation of the divine will.

The rabbinic Jewish categories are, then, instructive. The one has to do with the actions of God in history, and the other to do with God's revealed requirements. Together, the story and the law situate and direct God's people. Another way of putting this is that they define or form God's people.

The question of salvation, so often posed as central to Christian thinking about other faiths, is usually interpreted as meaning, "Who will go to heaven and escape hell?" It can further be interpreted as asking, "Who has forgiveness and a relationship with God here and now?" The Jewish categories suggest a slightly different question, "Who are God's people?" Their answer would be, "They are the people who are part of the story, and who walk in the ways of the law." It is important that *halakhah* and *haggadah* are linked. *Haggadah* gives the context and meaning for *halakhah*, and *halakhah* indicates the lifestyle which is appropriate to the people of the *haggadah*. As an influential twentieth-century Jewish philosopher writes,

> *Aggadah* (sic) deals with man's ineffable relations to God, to other men, and to the world. *Halakhah* deals with details, with each commandment separately; *aggadah* with the whole of life, with the totality of religious life. *Halakhah* deals with the law; *aggadah* with the meaning of the law. *Halakhah* deals with subjects that can be expressed literally; *aggadah* introduces us to a realm that lies beyond the range of expression. *Halakhah* teaches us how to perform common acts; *aggadah* tells us how to participate in the eternal drama.[35]

---

35. Fritz A. Rothschild, ed., *Between God and Man: An Interpretation of Judaism from the Writings of Abraham Heschel* (New York: Free Press Paperbacks, 1959), 175.

Together, *haggadah* and *halakhah* form the world in which the Jewish people live.[36] In the remainder of this section, we will consider how we might regard Islamic story and law alongside Jewish *haggadah* and *halakhah* and alongside the extended biblical narrative of Jesus the Messiah and the requirements which God has for his followers. In order to aid comparison, we will extend the use of the categories of *haggadah* and *halakhah* to describe Islamic and Christian story and law.

Thinking about God's People and Haggadah
Jews and Christians share the *haggadah* of the Hebrew Bible. This is the fundamental story shared by all Jewish people, and in which the flow of history from biblical times until now is understood. To this fundamental story, Christians add the story of Jesus as Messiah and of his people who understand themselves as part of this augmented story. The augmentation, of course, drastically revises interpretation of both the Hebrew Bible story and the story of the world since then. We see two faiths growing up from a common root, but taking different directions. The description in Romans 11 of this is that non-Jewish believers in the Messiah are being grafted into the stock of the Jewish people, while some of the Jewish people are being temporarily cut off from their own root. How far those who follow rabbinic Judaism might be considered as cut off branches until such time as they accept the Messiah, and how far a remnant of them might be considered as growing branches now, is difficult to determine from the text.

What about Islam? The Qur'an and Islamic tradition contain much that is recognizable as referring to the biblical *haggadah* – primarily from the Hebrew Bible, but also from the New Testament. However, the Qur'an adds the explicitly Islamic *haggadah* of the life of Muhammad and the founding of the Muslim *umma*, and it selects only such aspects of the biblical *haggadah* as fit into the Islamic *haggadah*. We might say that Islam effectively takes some branches from the tree and replants them in Arabian soil. The story which then develops is of the new growth spreading out from that new soil, and the key question in finding a place for Islam and for Muhammad in Christian thinking is, "How far can we see our *haggadah*s as being shared?"

---

36. For an incisive discussion of the interdependence of law and story, see Robert M. Cover, "The Supreme Court, 1982 Term – Foreword: Nomos and Narrative," *Faculty Scholarship Series* (Yale School of Law, 1983): Paper 2705, https://digitalcommons.law.yale.edu/fss_papers/2705/.

Thinking about God's People and *Halakhah*
Who are "God's people?" The New Testament would agree with rabbinic Judaism and Islam in calling them "righteous" (*dikaios, tsaddiq, ṣiddīq*). But what makes people "righteous?" How far are the assembly of "the righteous" in Psalm 1, for example, defined as participants in the *haggadah*, and how far are they defined as people who live by the *halakhah*? In rabbinic Judaism, as we have seen, both are essential: the people of the *haggadah* are required to live by *halakhah*.

In evangelical Christian thinking, the primary definition of God's people might be classified as participation in *haggadah* – acceptance of the story of the death and resurrection of Jesus the Messiah, and entering into the community of that story through faith. This is called "being made righteous (justification) by faith." There is, then, a range of understandings of how we should relate to the Torah and its *halakhah*. In thinking about Islam, it is essential that we reexamine these understandings.

Islamic identity is rooted in the simple *haggadah* of the unity of God and the prophethood of Muhammad. From that basis grows the righteous life which is regulated by *Sharī'a* – Islamic law. *Sharī'a* has much in common with rabbinic *halakhah*, both in its structures and methods and in its content. There are also important differences, for example, in regard to the basis of *halakhah* in the specific call of the Jewish people and in the idea of humanity made in the image of God.[37]

But even were Islamic law identical to biblical law and/or to rabbinic law, we would need to ask, "How valid is the practice of divine law apart from its context in the covenantal *haggadah*? How far does law depend on covenant? And how far does being able to keep the law depend on covenants old and new?" If *halakhah* and *haggadah* together make the Jewish thought world, then the story which focuses on Muhammad and the *Sharī'a* together make the Muslim thought world, and both have differences and similarities with any New Testament-based Christian thought world. This is an important way into thinking about the questions on the relationship between form and meaning raised elsewhere in this book. How does the form of what we do relate to the story which gives its meaning?

Here, I want to begin a discussion of these questions as they are addressed in the epistles to the Romans and to the Hebrews. Hebrews explains how the Messiah completes *haggadah* and fulfills *halakhah*. He does this through

---

37. See Jacob Neusner and Tamara Sonn, *Comparing Religions through Law: Judaism and Christianity* (London: Routledge, 1999).

a new priesthood which inaugurates a new law and a new covenant (Heb 7:11–22). In the context of thinking biblically about Islam, it is striking that the writer is explicitly dealing with the Mosaic covenant through the whole of the first ten chapters, with no reference at all to Abraham until chapter 11. By way of introduction, we learn that Jesus is greater than the angels, who were believed by many to have been the mediators of the Mosaic revelation, and that he is also greater than Moses himself. Because of this greatness, Jesus is also able to take his people where Moses and his successors could not take them (4:1–10). He does this through his new and perfect priesthood, which fulfills all the aspects of the Torah's *halakhah* which the Qur'an omits. As in Romans, it is by faith that people appropriate Jesus's fulfillment of the *halakhah*, so that sacrifices are no longer required of them (Heb 10:19–11:40). This does not mean that there are no longer laws about practice which believers in Jesus should follow – there is not only a way to be walked but a race to be run (12:1–2).

In short, the *haggadah* of Jesus so fulfills the *halakhah* of the tabernacle, the priesthood and the sacrifices that these are no longer necessary. This vision would have guided and reassured Jewish followers of Jesus through and after the destruction of the temple, the same event which would result in rabbinic Judaism's replacement of the priestly practices by the study of Torah. In contrast, the Qur'an removes all that is associated with priesthood, and Islamic theology removes the need for this essential part of Torah. In doing so, it raises questions not only about the nature of human beings and how they can be "righteous," but also about the nature and righteousness of God himself. These are the concerns of the epistle to the Romans.

Romans is well-known as expounding the universality of human sinfulness which requires the sacrifice of the Messiah in order to be made righteous. But its organizing concern is not so much our "righteousness" as the righteousness of God himself. Does Paul's gospel imply that God is unrighteous or unjust? The agenda is set in Romans 1:16–17, where Paul says that the opposite is the case. The gospel does not remove justice from God's character. Rather, the gospel reveals God's justice. Paul goes straight on to analyze God's uncompromising dealings with sin, wherever it is found. The implied injustice must be that God does not care whether human beings sin or not – that would certainly be a message that would bring shame on Paul and even on the Lord himself (cf. 1:16)! It is not uncommon for Muslims to ask Christians similar questions. Here, we will briefly explore the relationship between Torah, *halakhah* and *haggadah* in Paul's response.

First, Paul levels the ground by arguing that there is a place for law outside the covenants, or as he would phrase it, outside the Torah – which is what we suppose he means by the "law" in Romans 2:12–14. In the immediate context, the law outside the Torah is what has been called "natural law" – arising from human conscience and from observation of creation. If this law has validity at least as a basis for judgment, how much more does a law which can trace its roots to an interpretation of Torah have some validity in telling humankind what God requires? As Alexander Massad argues in his chapter *(see section 8.4)*, Muslims are much nearer to Jews than to the "Greeks and barbarians" described in Romans 1! On the other hand, being part of the Torah community does not of itself comprise righteousness – circumcision of the body is ineffective without circumcision of the heart (2:25–3:20). One may acknowledge both *haggadah* and *halakhah* and still not be righteous. So, although they are important for thinking biblically about Islam, our questions about how far Muslims share the biblical story and rabbinic law may not be relevant to the question of their righteousness.

The bulk of Romans goes on to explore the two central planks of God's righteous/just plan for the world: the law and the covenants given to the Jews. We can see this as roughly equivalent to our *haggadah/halakhah* distinction. The law, as Paul discusses it in Romans, is sometimes the whole Torah, but more often refers to the requirements of *halakhah*. The *haggadah* of the Hebrew Bible is the story of the covenants and of the covenant people, and Romans 4 roots Paul's teaching about justification and law in a discussion of how the *halakhah* fits into the *haggadah* of the covenants.

The specific questions are, "Is Paul saying that God no longer cares about people keeping his law? And is he saying that God is violating his covenant?" With regard to the former, Paul, like Jesus (Matt 5:17–20), insists that he is upholding the law (Rom 3:31) and argues this point at length, especially in Romans 6–7. He firmly asserts that the whole purpose of his ministry is the obedience of all peoples to God (1:5; 15:18; 16:26): the question is how that obedience can be won.

The latter concern is at least as important: if God can violate his own covenant, he is not honest or trustworthy. Romans 9–11 follows immediately from the assurance that nothing can separate us from the love of the Messiah (8:38–39). The implied question answered in Romans 9–11 is, "Can anything, then, separate the Jewish people from God's covenant commitment to them?" Paul's answer is that the covenant *haggadah* continues. It is God's *haggadah* – the story of his purposes. The Gentiles may join in the *haggadah* of the Jews through the Messiah, but that does not invalidate the master plan. The Jews may fail in *halakhah*, but God's *haggadah* cannot fail.

At the heart of Romans 9–11 comes the crucial explanation of what it is that Jews who reject their Messiah are missing, namely the circumcision of the heart which enables the keeping of the *halakhah*: The exegesis of Romans 10:1–10 of Deuteronomy 30.

Deuteronomy 30:11–14	Romans 10:5–10
Now what I am commanding you today is not too difficult for you or beyond your reach. It is not up in heaven, so that you have to ask, "Who will ascend into heaven to get it and proclaim it to us so we may obey it?" Nor is it beyond the sea, so that you have to ask, "Who will cross the sea to get it and proclaim it to us so we may obey it?" No, the word is very near you; it is in your mouth and in your heart so you may obey it.	Moses writes this about the righteousness that is by the law: "The person who does these things will live by them." But the righteousness that is by faith says: "Do not say in your heart, 'Who will ascend into heaven?'" (that is, to bring Christ down) "or 'Who will descend into the deep?'" (that is, to bring Christ up from the dead). But what does it say? "The word is near you; it is in your mouth and in your heart," that is, the message concerning faith that we proclaim: If you declare with your mouth, "Jesus is Lord," and believe in your heart that God raised him from the dead, you will be saved. For it is with your heart that you believe and are justified, and it is with your mouth that you profess your faith and are saved.

Today's rabbinic Jews read Deuteronomy 30:11–14 as a promise that they can indeed keep the Torah requirements. Paul reads it as a promise that all people will be able to obey God through the Messiah. As the rabbinic Jewish view is similar to the Muslim view that God has made his laws easy enough for us to keep, Paul's argument is worth examining.

Romans 10:5 is immediately preceded by a much-discussed verse which is sometimes taken as meaning that Christians need no *halakhah*: "Christ is the culmination of the law so that there may be righteousness for everyone who believes" (10:4). This verse, in turn, follows the statement that it is not their own righteousness that the Jewish people need, but God's righteousness. I read these verses not as negating *halakhah* but as confirming Paul's teaching that it is only through the Messiah and the Spirit that people are made "righteous," and that we can actually fulfill the requirements of the law, summarized in Romans 8:1–13. Romans 10:5–10 confirms this reading.

The context of the Deuteronomy 30 passage is important. Moses has indeed told the people that they will live if they keep the law, but he has also warned them that they may violate the law, incur God's anger and lose the land

(Deut 29:18–28). Chapter 30 begins, "When all these blessings and curses I have set before you come on you" (30:1). That is, it is looking forward to what will happen following their sin, when they want to return to God. There is a great promise of restoration (30:3–10). At the center of it is the declaration, "The LORD your God will circumcise your hearts and the hearts of your descendants, so that you may love him with all your heart and with all your soul, and live" (30:6), echoing the description of the words on the believing heart that qualifies the *shema* (Deut 6:6). It is thus that they will be able to keep all the commandments, and live (30:10).

We immediately recall Paul's comments on the necessity of heart circumcision in Romans 2:28–29. Clearly, Paul is reading Deuteronomy 30:11–14 as explaining how the promised heart circumcision, the coming of the law into the heart, will come about. There is no need to go up, because the Messiah has come down, and there is no need to go down, because the Messiah has risen. It is through faith in the Messiah that the word, the Torah, the *halakhah* is written on the heart and the person made righteous.

In our context, it is important to note the link here between *haggadah* and *halakhah*. The question here is not whether God wishes us to follow rabbinic *halakhah* or Islamic *Sharī'a* or some other code of law: it is how we can have the heart change that enables us to follow it. Indeed, the Deuteronomy passage finishes with a single word in Hebrew which Paul omits, but which is translated into English as "so that you may obey it" (Deut 30:14). The *haggadah* of the Messiah through which we enter the community of the righteous through faith may change *halakhah*, but it does not abolish it. On the contrary, it enables us to keep it.

It is this, says Paul, that can bring about the obedience not only of the Jews, but also of the Gentiles. It is this that so many of the Jews of his day had missed. Yet in faithfulness to his covenants, God will keep a remnant and eventually bring many to righteousness. We read Romans asking what ongoing place the Jews might have in God's salvation plan, and therefore in a Christian worldview. But what about Muslims who seek to uphold the law, but to do so outside of the covenants? What kind of sense can law make outside the covenant people and within a revised view of the covenants?

With Muslims, we have further questions to discuss. How far do we really need the *haggadah* of Jesus the Messiah in order to keep the *halakhah* of God's requirements, whether that be rabbinic law, Islamic law or Christian ethics? How far does the "righteousness" of God's people result from what they do, and how far and in what way does it derive from God's own righteousness?

And given the important role of the Holy Spirit in Romans, should we be focusing more on that role in enabling us to keep *halakhah*?

So, What Is the Agenda?

We finish this contribution by suggesting some of the areas in which the above analysis and framework might make a place for Muhammad, for Islam and for Muslims in our ongoing thinking.

A Place in Theologizing?

I shall leave it to the systematic theologians to ask what might be the implications of my reflections for the place of Muhammad, of Islam, and of Muslims within or in addition to their theological categories. Here, I want to point out that my analysis gives a place for Islamic thinking as an interlocutor in Christian theologizing. Historically, Middle Eastern Christians did much of their theology "in conversation with" Islam. Evangelical theology has traditionally been done "in conversation" with Roman Catholicism, and with the many issues of the European world and its Western progeny. The consultations on which this book is based represent recognition that today's theology needs again to be done in other contexts, and that the Islamic context is of global significance.

Thinking about story and law, about *haggadah* and *halakhah*, is theology proper: that is, it is in the end thinking about God. Our story and our law do not only tell us who we are. They tell us who God is.

God says, "I AM WHO I AM" (Exod 3:14). Classical Jewish interpretation links this double "I am" with the single "I will be with you" of Exodus 3:12. When asked his name, the Lord declares that he will be with his people in their current troubles and again in their future troubles, say such authorities as Exodus Rabbah, Rashi and Ramban in their comments on this verse.[38] That is, the God of the Bible is known not so much by words as by experience: theology is known through the *haggadah*, the story of God's dealings with his people.

If God is understood through his actions, then the theology of Islam is certainly different from the theology of either Christianity or of rabbinic Judaism.

---

38. Rabbah, *Midrash Rabbah, Vol. 3: Exodus* (London; New York: Soncino Press, 1983), III: 6; Rashi, *Pentateuch with Targum Onkelos, Haphtoroth and Prayers for Sabbath and Rashi's Commentary*, ed. and trans. M. Rosenbaum and A. M. Silbermann (London: Shapiro, Vallentine, 1946), 12; Ramban (Rabbi Moses ben Nahman), *Shemos: The Torah with Ramban's Commentary*, trans. Artscroll Mesorah (2007), www.sefaria.org/Ramban_on_Exodus.3.15?lang=bi.

On the other hand, there is enough commonality between biblical and qur'anic stories to make comparison fruitful, not only in establishing similarity and difference but also in throwing fresh light onto the biblical texts. There is a place for Muslims in the discussion of the stories and their theological implications.

The Torah also relates its *halakhah* to the character of God. A classic example is the *parashat* (weekly Torah section) called *qedoshim* (the holy ones) (Lev 19–20), in which we find the summary commandment to love our neighbor as ourselves (Lev 19:18, cf. 34). The title comes from the second verse: "Be *qedoshim* because I, the LORD your God, am *qadosh*" (Lev 19:2). The holiness required of the people is based on the holiness of their God. The point is made repeatedly throughout the *parashat* (Lev 19:3, 10, 12, 14, 16, 18, 25, 28, 30, 31, 32, 34, 36, 37; 20:7, 8, 24, 26). It is not only the broad "love" commandments which are based on "I am the Lord your God," but also commandments about the sabbath and other festivals; about economic, social and criminal justice; about food and farm management; and about sexual morality.

Our Christian theologizing often neglects the question of how God's requirements reveal the nature of God himself. Many Muslims are reluctant to acknowledge the possibility of knowing much about the nature of God, but perhaps there is an important place for discussion about the theological implications of the similarities and differences between the specific requirements of Christian ethics and Islamic *Sharī'a*, and perhaps consideration of rabbinic *halakhah* can facilitate this. Of particular importance could be discussion of the Qur'an's choice to omit the holiness *halakhah* of priesthood and sacrifice.

A Place in Salvation History?
Evangelical Christian discussions of salvation for people of other faiths usually focus on the question of the ultimate salvation of individuals after death. But biblical covenant faith is much more than this: it has to do with God's dealings with whole peoples. Of course, the eternal fate of individuals within those peoples is also important, but God's purposes have always been with families and peoples. That is evidenced in God's calling of Israel to carry his light for the nations, in contrast to the qur'anic pattern of the calling of prophetic individuals. God's covenants have always been with groups. So the question of the place of Muslims in salvation history has to do with the place of the whole Islamic movement and the many Muslim people groups that exist and have existed.

A common way of dealing with this question is to see Islam alongside Judaism and Christianity as an Abrahamic faith; but this is fraught with difficulties, because, as noted above, the biblical and the qur'anic Abraham are so different. The above analysis suggests that it might be more sensible to see Islam alongside rabbinic Judaism as a Mosaic faith, Muhammad alongside a kingly figure like Jeroboam as well as in comparison with prophets like Moses or Elijah, and Muslim peoples as branches waiting to be grafted into the vine. The question about Islam is, then, "Where can we place a faith which keeps much of *halakhah* and, indeed, which develops its own *halakhah* in its own context, but which rewrites the *haggadah*?"

But what about a place for Muslim communities, for the *umma* in all its diversity? We began by recognizing the difficulty which Christians have in finding a place for Islam in God's purposes for his world. There is a sense in which it should not exist. But exist it does, and as Ashoor Yousif's contribution indicates, Christians have been seeking a place for Islam in their worldview since its inception, variously seeing it as part of God's judgment, as part of his providence, and as part of his eschatological plans.

Perhaps Jeroboam's kingdom should never have existed. Certainly, it was an ongoing source of tension within the people of God, but God caught it up into his purposes for his people. On its story is built much of the Hebrew Bible, and eventually, many of the Samaritan people who occupied its land would be gathered into the people of the Messiah.

But Jeroboam's kingdom was within the covenant people. What about people who, like the Muslims, traced their origins to Abraham's family but not through the covenant line? The biblical insistence is, first, that God has enough blessing for all, and second, that even those who were outright enemies to the covenant people had their places within God's blessing and his messianic purposes.

Perhaps Ishmael should never have existed. But God blessed him and promised him progeny, and he was circumcised alongside Abraham (Gen 16:10–12; 17:20, 25–26; 21:13, 18). God has always been at work outside the covenant line as well as within it.

Esau may not have been the one chosen to father the covenant line (Gen 27; cf. Rom 9:12–13), and Isaac did not have enough blessing for Esau, but God had a place for Esau and enough for everyone. Esau as well as Jacob had plenty (Gen 33:9). The descendants of Esau as well as the descendants of Jacob are recorded in scripture (Gen 36). The land of the Edomites as well as the land of Israel were allocated by God (Deut 2:4–5). They would more often be Israel's enemy than their ally, but they were brothers, and therefore not to be hated or excluded (Deut 23:7–8).

Perhaps Israel's archenemies, the Moabites and the Ammonites, the result of Lot's incest, should never have existed, but the lands of the Ammonites and the Moabites were given to them by God (Deut 2:9, 19). They were not allowed even to come into the Jewish community (Deut 23:3–6). But both the Moabites and the Ammonites were needed in God's economy as part of the line of the Messiah – not through their men, but through their women – Ruth, the great-grandmother of David (Ruth 4:21–22; Matt 1:5–6), and Naamah, the mother of Rehoboam (1 Kgs 14:31; 2 Chr 12:13).

There are terrifying prophetic oracles of judgment on the Edomites, the Moabites and the Ammonites, but there are also oracles against Israel. The fact that peoples are at times enemies of God does not stop God from having a place for them in his world. We may find it difficult to find a place in God's purposes for Muhammad, for Islam, and for Muslim peoples, but that does not mean that they have no place. The limitation is ours, and not God's!

A Place in Current World History?
"Aye, there's the rub . . ." Islamic law developed as Islamic empire developed, while rabbinic law developed to sustain scattered and powerless minority communities. Christian readers will be familiar with Hebrews, "For here we do not have an enduring city" (Heb 13:14) – very literally true for Jewish Christians after the fall of Jerusalem in AD 70, about the time that Hebrews was written.

Hebrews solves the problem of the loss of temple, priesthood and sacrifice by seeing them all fulfilled in Jesus. Rabbinic Judaism solves the same problem by developing the study and practice of Torah. Both are in contrast to the Islamic establishment of the cities of Mecca and Medina, the conquests of Jerusalem and Damascus, and the building of Baghdad.

Since Babel, the dangerous fusion of religion and empire has been a recurrent aspect of humanity. So theologically,[39] we should not be surprised at this aspect of Islam. What is more surprising, and more challenging for the theological mind, is the fact that Christian history is no exception. Despite Jesus saying, "My kingdom is not of this world" (John 18:36), it has been marked (and marred) by empire and crusade, by colonialism and neocolonialism, by the cities of Rome and Constantinople, and by battles over Jerusalem both then and now. What difference, then, does the gospel make? How can we find a place for Islamic territory and Muslim rule without seeking mirroring Christian territory and rule? In what ways can we deal with the differences between *Sharī'a, halakhah* and Christian ethics in relation to socio-political

---

39. See Ida Glaser, *The Bible and Other Faiths: What Does the Lord Require of Us?* (Carlisle: Langham Global Library, 2012), especially 80–81.

matters? What is it that keeps us fighting for "lasting cities," and what is it that might stop our fighting?

In particular in our context of thinking about Islam alongside rabbinic Judaism, what is it that keeps us fighting over Jerusalem? It is not surprising that many Jews, after two millennia of homelessness, would like to have the city again. Neither is it surprising that Muslims generally would like to regain control of their third holy city, and it is even less surprising that Palestinians who have lost their land should wish to get it back. The concern is that so many people outside the Middle East, and especially evangelical Christians, join in the fight, and that they are often motivated by theologies which think about Jews and Judaism but do not take equal thought about Muslims and Islam.

Much of today's Christian discourse on the subject is polarized into those who emphasize the place of Jerusalem and the land in the biblical *haggadah*, and those who emphasize the importance of justice in the biblical *halakhah*. I wonder what would happen if we prioritized the question of how *haggadah* relates to *halakhah*, and if we thought about the development of Islam alongside the development of rabbinic Judaism rather than thinking about it, as so many do, as having developed in opposition to Christianity. Perhaps, then, even the most conservative of pre-millennialist thinkers might be able to see Muslim people alongside Jewish people as having a partial *haggadah* which needs filling out with the story of the crucified Messiah, rather than as enemies of Israel and of God.

A Salvific Place?
As I argue in my contribution in the first part of this book *(section 2.5)*, Muslims have their place in Christian theology as human beings, and all humanity needs salvation through the Messiah. For me, the soteriological question is not whether there is any salvation outside of the Messiah. Rather, it is who is given the free gift of gracious salvation through him. And if God alone, Father, Son and Holy Spirit, is the just judge who knows every heart, then how far can we as human beings know whom he will save? These are the questions which underlie all the discussions of "inclusivism" and "exclusivism," and which may be difficult to answer in the context of sincere believers from different faiths.

With regard to Jews, the questions are particularly poignant. If God's covenants with the Jews were not salvific for them, I think we have a big problem. From a New Testament perspective, it is very clear, especially from Hebrews, that the covenants were never salvific in themselves, but that they were pointing to the new priesthood and the new covenant and the new law in Jesus the Messiah (Heb 7–8). The newness in the Messiah may mean that the old ways are no longer necessary, but does it mean that they can no longer bring people into God's presence and loving, faithful forgiveness? The old ways were limited, but they were effective because they foreshadowed the new Way! At what stage, then, in the forty years between the rending of the temple curtain and the destruction of the temple, did the sacrifices there become ineffective? Today, there are no priests or sacrifices, but faithful Jews continue to study the priesthood and the sacrifices, seeing their study as their ongoing way of participating in the Torah covenant of forgiveness and fellowship with God and with each other.

One might argue that, at the time when Hebrews was written, any Jews who sincerely followed the old covenants should have recognized Jesus as the Messiah for whom they were waiting; and that it is those who did so who comprised the faithful "remnant" of Romans 11. Shifting to the twenty-first century, that argument cannot apply in the same way. A major reason for current Jewish rejection of Jesus has been, for centuries, persecution from Christians that has made Jesus seem to be the enemy of the Jewish people and not their Savior. Can it be that God would send Jewish people to hell because of the sins of Christian people? If not, then how might we judge which of today's Jews might be the "remnant?" Do we include only those who accept Jesus? Or might we include those who seek to keep the covenants by faith in the covenant-giving Lord – acknowledging, of course, that it is only that Lord who knows who they are?

With regard to Muslims, we have some different but related questions. The aspects of the covenant which Hebrews sees as fulfilled in the Messiah are steeped in *haggadah*. The details of temple, priesthood and sacrifice may be governed by *halakhah*, but they make no sense outside the story of God's dealings with his people and their purpose in his world. It is no surprise, then, that it is just these aspects of the Torah which are minimized or completely omitted from the Qur'an and from Islamic tradition and law.

Muslims have the *Sharī'a* which will show them something of what God wants from them, and as argued above, it also by implication shows them something of God himself. So we would expect to find Muslims who understand their need for salvation. Indeed, we can find plenty of Muslims who understand this but who would describe the need in different terms. They would see a need for God's mercy so that they can be forgiven, enabled to live better lives, and be admitted to paradise in the next life. What is missing from Islam is any basis for God's mercy. The question is, "Do people need to know the basis for God's mercy in order to receive that mercy?" Another way of putting this is that many Muslims see their need for what Christians know was achieved through the incarnation, death and resurrection of Jesus. If they believe that God and God alone can give them what they need, and ask him to do so, would we expect him to grant their request even if they do not understand that this can only be through Jesus? In some cases, we know that God has granted such requests by leading them to Jesus, but might there be other cases where that is not so?

This set of questions comes close to the more general questions that are asked about salvation and people of different faiths. What is special about Islam? First is the overlap with rabbinic Judaism and biblical Christianity concerning the law. Second is a measure of overlap concerning the *haggadah*. These mean that Muslims have access to more of God's special revelation than do people of other faiths, albeit usually seen through the different lens of the life of Muhammad.

But there is a third dimension which we have not so far explored: unlike most rabbinic Jews, Muslims have in their thinking a place for Jesus. They may not have the *haggadah* of the cross and resurrection which tells them about the significance of the Messiah, but they know that the Messiah is Jesus. And indeed, the Qur'an rebukes Jews for their rejection of their Messiah (*an-Nisā* 4:155–159). While the Qur'an includes material which is understood as negating the incarnation and the atonement, it also includes a remarkable amount of material which can inform the searching reader of Jesus's power of healing and life giving, and of the heart transformation which is available to those who believe in him (e.g. *Āl-'Imrān* 3:49; *an-Nisā* 4:171; *al-Ḥadīd* 57:27). It also contains references to Jesus's role in judgment and at the last day which has been developed in Hadith and tradition into eschatological expectations which have parallels with Christian expectations. There are also key differences, not least that it is the triumph of Islam which the second coming of Jesus is expected to inaugurate.

Experience confirms that the Islamic material about Jesus can point Muslims toward saving faith in him. There are even documented instances of groups of Muslims who have decided to take Jesus as their prophet on the basis of qur'anic information only, and without contact with the Bible or with Christian people.[40] How far and how many people there might be who

---

40. Probably the most documented example is the *Īsāwā* group of Nigeria. For a review of the literature on them, see C. D. Nguvugher, "Conflicting Christologies in a Context of Conflicts: Jesus, the Īsāwā, and Christian-Muslim Relations in Nigeria" (PhD diss., Universität Rostock, 2010), 317–320, https://doi.org/10.18453/rosdok_id00000667.

continue to identify as Muslims and yet have come to a saving knowledge of Jesus without direct access to the Bible is impossible to say. These observations in no way undermine the Great Commission to take the good news of Jesus to Muslim people – not least because there are countless Muslims who have been so taught about the qur'anic denials of Christian faith that they have turned away from Jesus rather than toward him. However, they do indicate a dimension for Christian thinking about Islam which differs from Christian thinking about rabbinic Judaism and about other faiths.

An Eschatological Place?
Eschatology is often the place where people try to discern answers to the questions about current world history. The eschatological dimension can obscure the questions of kingdom and of justice which we identified above. I would like to offer here what I think might be a more fruitful agenda for eschatological thought. If it is difficult to agree on common ground in our origins, might we get a more helpful perspective by looking forward?

A very important aspect of biblical salvation history and therefore of the question of salvation for people outside the covenants is eschatology: What will happen at the last day? Here Muslims, Jews and Christians have something very important in common: All are awaiting the coming of the Messiah as the just judge who will right all wrongs and deal with all evil. That is for all, the Messiah is indeed the savior of the world. We may not agree on the *haggadah* of the past, but we have a measure of agreement on the *haggadah* of the future!

Muslims and Christians agree that that Messiah is Jesus. Jews do not know who he will be, but from a Christian perspective, the Messiah for whom they are waiting is none other than the one they have missed for two millennia. Recognized or not, Jesus was and is and will be the Messiah of Israel. He does in fact rule over the Jews whether they know it or not, and he is the one who will bring all the righteousness and peace for which they are longing.[41]

As we look at biblical prophecy about the future, it is clear that God has some plans for his covenant people the Jews (Romans 9–11: God is faithful even when they are not!), and that eventually, many will accept Jesus. Many Christians see current movements toward Messianic Judaism as the beginning of the fulfillment of this plan of God. However, I have yet to hear people who have that view also seeing current movements of Muslims to Jesus as part of that eschatological fulfillment. Even if we discount Islam's aspirations to

---

41. For an important exploration of this idea, see Kinzer, *Jerusalem Crucified*.

Judaic roots, it is clear that the gospel going to all nations is part of the end-times scenario.

The ingathering of the Jews . . . the ingathering of the Muslims . . . could viewing these movements together as part of God's covenant faithfulness in the end times help Christians not only to accept that Jews and Muslims do exist, but also to find a place for them in God's good plans for his world?

8.7 Testimony 5: Gamal Zaki on Following Jesus in Egypt

interview by Emad Botros

Emad: Gamal, welcome. Please describe yourself and what you do.

Gamal: God has given me many gifts which are applicable to my work and ministry. I am an adviser to an Islamic institution. Egypt's president is very supportive of indigenous Christians. One example of this is the recent publication of the Gospel of John which was published and printed under the supervision of **al Azhar** which included two-page endorsements by six people and was distributed by various government organizations. Another recent initiative has been youth training which included taking groups to museums that have a Christian content. There are also activities in Minya governorate, an area that has seen numerous sectarian clashes.

Emad: How do you view God's involvement in placing you in such a position?

Gamal: I had an unusual journey to faith for someone in this role. I was raised in Shubra, a suburb of Cairo, and played near a church building. I was raised as a Muslim. I did though read the Bible, I think because of the influence of my mother. She came from upper Egypt and was a very prayerful person. I remember my mother warning me to accept how others worshiped, to recognize and appreciate diversity. I think I have a very rich heritage. I was aware of the influence of the Muslim Brotherhood within the school system. In my youth there were several assassinations. My response to violence in the name of religion was to reject all religions, especially when it became vicious and aggressive. The turning point came when I was a young adult. One day two women, Samira and Jinan, cautiously entered my office wanting to speak with me about some serious problems that they thought I could help them with in my professional capacity. The issues were addressed within a week. Something about them prompted me to ask them for a copy of their book, the

Bible. I had also had a vision of Christ. I began listening to a Christian radio station. The combination of vision, Bible and radio brought me to true faith.

Emad: So given your study of Christianity, how do you view Muhammad?

Gamal: As a social reformer. We should not over spiritualize or demonize him, nor should we dehumanize him. I think we should distinguish between him as a man, a person, and what he taught. It is worth exploring how he was raised and what his goals were. Finally, we should avoid exaggeration. Why should I hate him? The biblical mandate is to love the enemy!

Emad: Please explain how you maintain your identity and high-ranking position.

Gamal: I run away from church people! Many appear to forget that they have the ultimate truth, the credentials to make heaven accessible. So much of this comes from the social and cultural background, with perhaps just a tenth from your religion. When considering Christ's followers such as myself, then you do not want replicas of legally recognized Christians; that is simply not necessary to become a believer.[42]

Emad: How do you reconcile the content and form of previous religious practice with your faith in Christ?

Gamal: We must all explore what is manmade and what is from God. Orthodox rituals have a strong human element. We must examine what is Egyptian, what is Islamic and what is Christ-centered. Those of us from Muslim backgrounds have our own culture and language. Likewise, so does the younger generation. So do not try to restrict members of these communities: we need to be salt and light outside the church. Please do not force anyone into exclusively church or Christian settings.

Emad: Please talk more about Egyptian youth.

Gamal: Christian youth are witnesses and are authentically Egyptian. Many serve their fellow human beings. Further, many Egyptian youth are finding salvation. Starting from Abraham, all are looking to the finality of Christ. Historically, before Abraham the pharaohs built Egypt. So how did things

---

42. *Note from the editors: For the context in Egypt and elsewhere in the Middle East that makes the interaction of Christ's followers from Muslim backgrounds with those from Christian homes problematic, see for example Andrews,* Identity Crisis, *2016.*

work out for my ancestors? Were they condemned as outside of Christ, of being outside God's people? Of course not, since that would imply there being no mercy. Similarly, after the Christ event – that is the death, resurrection and ascension of Jesus – what do many know about Christ? The biblical text records Jesus saying, "My Father's house has many rooms" (John 14:2). How do we view this? In my view, if people live faithfully, then God will accept them.

Emad: So how did you find the presentations above on salvation?

Gamal: I much appreciated them. In my view, Christians cannot be compared to Jews. In Egypt, many are descended from the pharaohs, and so are far from the Abrahamic peoples, the Jews and the descendants of Ishmael. My ancestors were from Ham, not Shem.[43] I do not regard them as pagans. Be aware that many Muslims are not Arabs, even in the MENA region.

Emad: Many thanks, and may God bless you and all that you are involved with.

8.8 A Conversation among Friends: Exploring Missiological Implications

Moderator: Welcome. How does a disciple of Jesus from a Muslim background express his or her faith in Jesus and how do they worship?

Muslim-Background Disciple 1 (MBD-1): Worshiping with fellow followers of Christ can be difficult for me. I grew up with cleansing rituals for set times of prayer. I maintain some of these practices. At times, I feel obliged, even forced, to observe such practices. I find Nicodemus a helpful biblical example. How did he live? He came to Jesus at night and appears to have stayed in his position within his religious circles. How did he keep to Jesus's teaching? I note that he fulfilled a necessary practical role at Jesus's burial and grave site.

Moderator: What pressures do you face in normal life?

MBD-1: I do not have normal Christian support. So most of you have a privilege in worship that is denied to me. I did attend a church in my city for a period. However, I can do so no longer because of my employment and the presence of cameras outside their building.

---

43. A reference to the sons of Noah.

Moderator: You appear to be passing through a period where there is persecution, pressures and pain of certain kinds.

MBD-1: Yes. I used to be freer. One person said he had not seen me at a major event in my city that I always used to attend, but I was there at a work related stand. I have new opportunities and roles, with attendant pressures.

Moderator: How should we encourage those in the three categories that Grant described, the adopters, negotiators and reframers?

Christian-Background Disciple (CBD): Grant assessed five churches under these three categories and described what he observed. He did not set this up himself; it is a description of what he saw happening. So we are exploring the results of choices made by the believers. He heard their stories and affirmed each of them. It is not our role to tell anyone that they should act like those down the street. These groups, fellowships, are about a vibrant relationship with Christ. As such, they are the living body of Christ. They are not an experiment. They are all very Christocentric, vibrant and they each experience some form of suffering for Christ. I loved to hear about each expression. How might we encourage them? First, I think we should find where people are and encourage them in what they are doing. Second, we should remember that they are very fluid. One example Grant talked to me about is a group that began as twelve home groups that is now one meeting with three hundred participants. He observed some negotiators that later became adopters. Crucial no doubt is that they are studying the Bible and walking in transparency and integrity with servant leaders, not top-down leaders. Finally, for all of us disciples of Jesus, we need to be supportive of individuals as well as of communities.

Moderator: How should individuals adapt to be authentic followers of Christ?

MBD-2: As a disciple of Jesus from a Muslim background living outside the Muslim world, I face fewer challenges than those who, like MBD-1, are living inside. When I began following Christ, I was living in Europe and away from my family. Subsequently, they came to faith, which means that I do not face family rejection. In my country, there were pressures on me because I was known to have been to a church. I wondered what pressures might come on my mother after the church that she attended was closed down by the authorities. Who can join underground churches? This can be tough for many. The hard part for me is that I can no longer go to my country. I am thankful that I did have a window of opportunity to visit which coincided with my father's passing. We had to use Islamic burial rituals at his funeral for safety reasons. But we knew that he was with Jesus. We wanted to do a Christian funeral for him, but we had to think of other believers there. This was part of my family negotiating our way through the complexities of being disciples of Jesus.

CBD: I believe that one day God will redeem this. I have seen others buried in dishonor for the sake of Christ. This might appear superficial to some Westerners, but please be aware that it is a profound issue within Middle Eastern honor-shame culture.

Moderator: What are the unique aspects of Muslim tradition that we should consider based on Romans 8:28, of all things working together for good?

CBD: That is a broad question. I am interested in differentiating Muslim and Jewish traditions about fulfilling law from the Christian view of having law written on our hearts.

Jewish-Background Disciple (JBD): That too would be a long discussion. Islamic law is formulated in a different way to Jewish Torah. Islamic law is a classification of human actions, and one needs to know if each action is going to be rewarded or punished by God. In terms of practice, there are many parallels. One area is the food laws. Although the Islamic laws are more contextualized into Arabia, one example is about eating camels. In contrast, the reasons behind Jewish food laws is a long discussion. We could do more on the comparison. There are key differences in covenant and governing society in a more political manner.

Moderator: So what are the practical implications?

JBD: I am uncomfortable with the idea that ministry is something we do to a target audience. There is no difference, as noted above. Ministry is to all humans. We should avoid polarizations such as Muslim-Christian since there are many others, including secularists. This is one reason that I like triangular discussion including Jews: it eases the dualism and hence the tensions. Judaism is rooted in its scriptures. Either we are them or they are us: Judaism is a root into which one has been grafted, which engenders humility since our group cannot see themselves as the center of the world. We are called by God to responsibility and to service; yet many want to get rid of us.

Many stories in the Qur'an that appear strange to Christians relate to Jewish discussions; so suddenly Muslims are not strangers over there but close cousins. So, our attitude as Christians should not be that, "We have the Bible and must do this to them." Instead, we should see the Bible as a well of water from which we are offering a glass of water to a Muslim. Do we take it out with a Christian glass, examine the water and transfer it to a Muslim glass? Or do we just ask the Muslim to come and use their own glass?

Moderator: This prompts us to ask what does salvation mean? My recollection is that we have not yet given a definition.

CBD: There is no one answer.

JBD: So what are the questions?

CBD: There are many notions of salvation in both Christian and Muslim traditions. One definition might be atonement and the price paid by God for sin. Christian mystics would give something different, as would those who use eschatological visions in this context. Some questions would be, first, do we have salvation in this world? Second, is salvation the best life for people here? Seeking a definition is also problematic within Muslim traditions. I suggest that it is best not to start with a definition, but rather to seek to reach a definition by dialogue, and to be open to constant revision. Our conceptualization varies.

Moderator: So based on your reading of the Bible, what does salvation mean?

CBD: The Bible says many things about salvation. Primarily, it gives us a language to talk about it. Consequently, there are many definitions, all of which are based on the Bible. One's experience of the Spirit and the trinitarian nature of God are significant.

JBD: I agree that there is no simple definition. Be aware that the word means "safety," the idea of being in danger and being rescued. Salvation functions in many ways, including saving from sins, cleansing of the heart and changing of the heart so that one can live righteously. A common idea is escaping from the anger of God at the judgment. There are many clear ideas that are associated with salvation.

CBD: Salvation is the beautiful, multifaceted hope that we discover in Christ. Being saved from sin and having the Spirit with me and within me.

JBD: There are many dimensions to what we need to be saved from.

MBD-1: Jesus's sacrifice on the cross brought saving from original sin. This will go with us continuously. We should live diligently until Jesus comes again. I regard salvation as a process.

CBD: We are saved from but also saved to something. It is wonderful that we become one rich family. We are saved for this.

Moderator: The Bible speaks of Christ's followers being one body, living out mission as a community. So how can a disciple of Jesus from a non-Christian background live a Christian life away from the body of Christ?

MBD-1: As I said earlier, there are specific social circumstances that profoundly affect me. There are biblical examples that are relevant. Nicodemus is one. Another is Daniel, who played a role with a national leader. Some circumstances must be worked through. The early church had times of persecution including times of fleeing: where was community at such times? At times I too search for a community where I can be a participant. I see this as an expense, like a tax, that I have to pay. I believe that I manage it well. There are parts of my country where I can switch off my phone and join a Christian group. I am obliged to keep adapting how, where and with whom I can meet.

JBD: I honor you, brother, for the work that you are doing in the setting in which God has placed you. Another biblical example is God's mission to the pharaohs in which Joseph and Moses played a part.

MBD-1: Thank you. I have been involved in changing the law in my country concerning church buildings. The new law is not yet ideal, but it is progress. I asked a bishop about issues surrounding the acquisition of land for new church buildings. He urged me to keep promoting the big picture.

Moderator: Some of us cannot see the big picture like you can. Thinking back to the case study and about maintaining allegiance to Christ, are there any affiliations that we need to cut off?

JBD: Yes! Some things are clearly disapproved of by God; to be extreme, running a brothel. More specifically about Islam, anything concerned with black magic must be completely abandoned. Likewise, for other manipulative activities. Such matters do vary from person to person and from place to place. I should add, beware of emotional ties that, for survival, may need to be cut and moved on from.

Moderator: We are drawing toward closure. I am aware that we have explored a variety of opinions, and I am aware that not everyone will feel comfortable. Pastorally, what would you say to such people?

CBD: I have been surprised many times. Jesus is the Good Shepherd, and he does surprise us. If he is in the picture, then he will guide.

We need to act and speak out of love for the church and concern for God's people with our Muslim brothers and sisters.

JBD: Praise God for discomfort! We can remember God's grief over people (e.g. Gen 6:6). This might say something about our own inner struggles. Ask to be shown what is at the root of one's discomfort and to what one is reacting. Use what one discovers to honor and glorify God.

MBD-2: Trust the Holy Spirit, who will surprise you with wonder and miracles.

MBD-1: The Spirit is checking up on each of us. Be encouraged that change is happening in this part of the world. Our God is the source of joy.

Moderator: Thank you.

Questions for Discussion

1. Are we developing a humble curiosity about Islamic traditions? Are we open to the insights of religious others as one way of deepening our understanding of them, their story and their hopes as well as of ourselves and our faith?

2. What examples of, or equivalents to, *adopters*, *negotiators* and *reframers* do you see in your context?

3. What place do we see for Judaism and Islam, for Jews and Muslims in God's good plan for his creation?

4. Do we praise God for discomfort?! Are we willing to explore its roots within us? Do we see this as part of our own discipleship?

9

Thinking Biblically about Islam, Muslims and the Spirit World

Poetry by Teresa Sfeir

*My life once seemed to me
An interrupted melody,
A wandered upon the coast,
A heap of "maybe"s and "almost"s . . .*

*I'd stand on tiptoe
At my window
To steal a glance
At that last chance
Striding away into nevermore . . .*

*Somehow I had to end
This chase after the wind
And look upon my Lord
And all the joys I've missed
As I was busy wondering
How my life could've been . . .*

*It was His unseen hands
That diverted my way
And His unbending "no"s
That brought me here today.
And now there's nowhere I would be
Than in the life He chose for me.*

She passes through the valley wide
With filled up vessels on her side.
The poor and thirsty gather round
To hear her gentle voice resound.
A Flickering Flame in her had cried:
He is alive – the One who died!

The pure in heart, with soulful eyes
Whose faith has dumbed the doubtful wise,
From jars of water she would pour
Till fear of loss could stay no more.

Then came along after a while
Who chose to wear her gracious smile,
Her sandals worn, her tunic frayed –
An image of Him she conveyed.
This has become their heart's desire:
Inspired once so they inspire.

As she lay still, He stepped inside –
His eyes contain eternity.
He put the doubting mass aside –
Drew near with sure serenity.
Fear has no room where faith resides.
Fear not. Only believe.

As she lay still, He stepped inside –
A child He'd always loved and known.
Her heart would surely recognize
The One whose hands had shaped her soul.
Fear has no room where faith resides.
Fear not. Only believe.

He bent and reached down for her hand.
Their troubled hearts there almost sprang.
"O little one, rise up!" He smiled.
His gentle touch restored the child.
Fear has no room where faith resides.
Fear not. Only believe.

9.1 Opening Reflection: When Human Resources Are Inadequate

Shirin Bahrami

Let us see ourselves in John's account of the feeding of the five thousand, chapter 6 of his gospel. "When Jesus looked up and saw a great crowd coming toward him, he said to Philip, 'Where shall we buy bread for these people to eat?'" (John 6:5) In other words, Jesus was asking Philip to provide for their physical needs.

In my opinion Jesus asked this question for a reason: the disciples suddenly felt and sensed the weight of their own insufficiency. He wanted them to feel the weight of their own powerlessness and their own helplessness to meet people's needs. Jesus asked Philip this question and not Andrew. It is really interesting to know that the meaning of Philip's Greek name is "one who loves horses." In the Bible, the horse represents the strength of the flesh. In the Psalms we read that God's pleasure is not in the strength of the horse (Pss 33:17; 147:10) and that "no king is saved by the size of his army; no warrior escapes by his great strength" (Ps 33:16).

So for me as a counselor, where do I turn my eyes when the strength of the flesh is absolutely powerless to meet the need that is in front of me? Philip had no idea where to look. Andrew came and said to Jesus that there are two fishes and five loaves of bread but, compared to the need, that is insignificant (John 6:8).

In John 6:10, Jesus asked the disciples to make the men sit down. Men represented the strength of the flesh; men are proud of their strength. So when Jesus said make the men sit down, he was asking the strength of the flesh to sit down. The strength of the flesh is not needed here; the strength of flesh has nothing to offer here. As a counselor, I learned this lesson that I do not have the strength and power to meet people's needs.

This passage in John is a picture of more than five thousand people sitting and needing to eat, and there are just two fish and five loaves of bread to feed them. How insufficient, powerless and helpless it looked to meet this need. This is a picture of our lives. This is a picture of our ministry and a picture of our calling, whatever that may be. This is our ministry to the world. In ourselves, we are absolutely insufficient and powerless to meet the needs of people's lives. As a counselor, I work with people who come from different backgrounds, different cultures and religious experiences. I have met many people, believers and non-believers, who are suffering. I have seen those with weary souls, those who are lost because of the heavy burdens of their past, and those with skewed value systems and destructive ways of thinking and not knowing how to receive God's word for their daily walk.

We are living in a very needy world. Many people are so broken in spirit, so hurt and damaged, the need in their lives goes so deep. It is so deep that human knowledge, human strength, human resources and human help cannot go that deep. Only God can go that deep.

In my counselling work, many times I have faced a similar situation to Philip when Jesus said, "You provide for their needs." There have been seasons when I have recognized in myself that I have nothing that can go to these deep places in people's lives. I cry to God in my absolute despair, "Oh God with all my strength and all my talent and all my abilities, these things are absolutely powerless to go to those deep places in people's lives." I had this sense like Jesus was telling me, "You look at yourself and what you have because I want you to understand that without me you have absolutely nothing to give. There is nothing in your talent and your abilities and in your skills." There was, and still is, a time in my heart when I have to face my insufficiency, and I say to God, "Lord I may have talents, skills and ability, but in myself I have nothing that can meet the needs of these people's lives." But there is good news – God has a remedy for this broken world which is beyond human help.

In my opinion, sharing the gospel is not about leaning on our own understanding, putting our trust in the arms of the flesh and knowledge which is limited by our own reasoning powers and our own exposure to truth. In 1 Corinthians 1:30 we read what the Father has given us: Christ Jesus, who has "become for us wisdom from God." With him we find the answers we need and the reassurance that he is always in control. Sharing the gospel with Muslims is not being judgmental. Sharing the gospel is not attempting to sort out the problems of the others or expecting or encouraging them to behave in a way in which we may have behaved when confronted with a similar problem in our own life. Nor is it looking at people's problems from our own perspective, based on our own value system. There is no healing without the mighty love of our Lord and Savior Jesus Christ. His love and compassion transform our lives. At a time when we think we have lost what made us *us*, he restores what the locusts have eaten (Joel 2:25). He restores our hopes, our dreams, and he shows us that his strength is perfect in our weakness. He gives us stronger wings of faith (Isa 40:31).

I do believe that God is at work, drawing people to himself and transforming a generation of future leaders. God is using us in some of their lives to encourage them in their faith. For others, God is using us as a light to help them find their way. It is a privilege for us to work with people who come from different backgrounds, with different cultural and religious experiences. I am immensely grateful to God for the privilege of this task, which I believe will stretch us and allow us to use our gifts for his kingdom purposes.

9.2 Testimony 6: Michel and Janane Mattar on Following Jesus among Refugee Communities in Lebanon

interview by Elie Haddad

Elie: A warm welcome to Michel and Janane. Do please introduce yourselves.

Janane: We have been disciples of Jesus for thirty years. We lead a church and run an organization that assists Syrians, both children and adults. It also serves Iraqis and Lebanese people. We are very aware that many fear the other, especially in Lebanon due to the civil war; consequently, many Christians are scared of Muslims. Back in 2006, we were asking the Holy Spirit what we should be doing about displaced people and refugees in Lebanon. That summer many were internally displaced from the south during the conflict between Hezbollah and Israel. This crisis broke down the walls for us and others: we saw what God was doing. Since then, we have found it rewarding to serve the other, and our own fears have been broken completely.

Michel: I had a dramatic conversion and subsequent transformation. For example, I am a musician and now dedicate the material that I record to the Lord. I refer to Syrians as brothers and sisters; previously, I used the term enemies. Another example is that I no longer think or describe my brothers and sisters in Christ based on their background, Muslim, Christian, whatever; we are all simply people who know and love Jesus.

Elie: Our focus here is on the Holy Spirit. Please tell us more about the Spirit's role in your lives and ministry and in overcoming fear of the other.

Janane: The Spirit is essential in my life. I cannot build peace within myself, nor could I sustain fake peace if I tried. It must come from God whose love underpins everything. In my opinion, any activity toward the other must be Spirit-initiated, so we must interact with the Spirit accordingly.

Michel: In Corinthians we read that wisdom is the power of the gospel. This wisdom is from and through the Spirit. In practical terms, I have attempted to speak with people in camps about Jesus. In such encounters, I need the Spirit's guidance to express things in ways and terminology that they can hear and understand. Ultimately, they need to hear from God himself.

Elie: So how do you see concepts such as spiritual warfare and the spiritual realm in your dealings with Muslims?

Janane: Many people regard Satan as only an idea; however, he seems very real to me. In my opinion, demons are at work blinding people to truth. The Bible speaks of other gods and of spiritual warfare (e.g. Eph 6:10–18). We need the power of Christ and the Spirit, obtaining our authority from them, so that through us the presence of the Lord comes to people.

Michel: Jesus said that the enemy seeks to kill, so all people are at risk from Satan. Yet we are ambassadors of Jesus. So I avoid arguments and ask God for wisdom and appropriate words for each person. Many Muslims do not feel accepted. On several occasions, people have responded with tears when I spoke about being sons and daughters of God. Another encounter involved a man who had enmity toward his brothers, so he needed to hear about forgiveness and reconciliation. We must seek wisdom from the Spirit to know what life experiences have affected each person, what has influenced them, and hence how Christ can, through us, transform the critical challenges in their life.

Elie: I would like to pose what might be considered a controversial question: do you think that there is a demonic dimension in the Muslim world?

Michel: Thank you for asking. If I may, I will respond in an equally challenging manner. Christianity can likewise be demonic. Anything that is not worshiping Jesus is demonic! John the Baptist stated that he must decrease so that Jesus could increase (John 3:30). The same applies for all of us.

Janane: In my opinion, everyone who has not accepted Jesus as Lord has a demonic element within them, and every religion that denies Christ as Lord is demonic. We must distinguish between people and religions. I regard other religions as demonic, but people must be loved irrespective of their religion. So the Muslim to me is not a demon and is not to be judged by me. I must show each one love and proclaim Christ. Nobody but Christ can change hearts, hence new birth in Jesus. It is good for us to encourage love and changed behavior and attitudes, but the real, life-giving change must be made within.

Elie: With reference to your line of ministry, one controversial issue is whether there is space for evangelism within humanitarian initiatives. What is your view?

Michel: We are called to be with people and to share the hope of Christ. To do this, we must cultivate something within the other that allows us to express the gospel in a way that they can hear it. So it is always good to express Christ, but not always easy to do so in words: we must demonstrate the gospel by our attitudes and actions.

Janane: Some believe that Saint Francis said that we should proclaim the gospel at all times and use words when necessary. My life should demonstrate Jesus; words are the last thing I use. One practical expression for me is to avoid complaining. I endeavor to live the hope and peace of Jesus expecting that people will ask me about the source of what they see in me. Talking from now to eternity will not convince some about who Jesus is.

Elie: Let's return to the work of the Spirit. Please describe an extraordinary experience of the Spirit.

Janane: God started giving us something for Muslims in 2006. Prior to then, I used to isolate myself; I prayed but did not interact with Muslims. In 2006, I relied on the Spirit to teach me how to interact with Muslims. Typically, I start with Genesis which introduces the concept of sin, notably with Adam and Eve's ejection from Eden, and begins the journey to restoration in Jesus.

Michel: I will describe a dramatic act of the Spirit in my interaction with a person. Keep in mind my advice not to go to Muslims to have arguments but to keep asking God that we will be Spirit-led and humble. With one person, I had an intense inner struggle about speaking with him, and I thought something was preventing me from witnessing to him. Breakthrough came when he asked me if I knew and loved Jesus! This led to a conversation during which I told him my testimony which, in summary, is from drug addiction to Christ. A few days later he phoned me and asked me to pray. Why? He was facing detention by his employer, the army, because he had taken unauthorized time off to visit his mother who was sick. I prayed and felt prompted to suggest that he read John's Gospel while detained. This prompted my friend to pray to Jesus for his freedom. Shortly afterward, an official invited him to play soccer; he had to refuse because of being detained. However, the official got him released so that he could play. I believe that the Spirit was at work in my relationship with this person. In essence my approach when with Muslims is to focus on their need for Jesus and keep discussion of spiritual realities simple. I love Jesus, and I pray that they will decide to do likewise.

Elie: Here in Lebanon we have more latitude to speak with Muslims than is the case elsewhere in the MENA region. How would you advise those in other Arab contexts to seek to witness to Muslims?

Michel: I am aware that my friends in other Arab countries do not have as much freedom in religious matters as I do. So I recommend praying and fasting for Muslims, and God will give you space and opportunity for witness.

Elie: Thank you for sharing with us. May we each know the Spirit's promptings as you clearly do in all our engagements with religious others.

9.3 The Powerful Helper: A Narrative Study of the Holy Spirit in Mark

Nabil Habiby

Where is the Holy Spirit in the Gospels? Does the role of the third person of the Trinity only start after the day of Pentecost in Acts? This study will aim at answering the basic part of this question: a study of the Holy Spirit as a narratival character in the Gospel of Mark using **narrative criticism**. It will trace the presence and depiction of the Holy Spirit in the first narrative in the gospel and in the rest of the gospel. It will then attempt to draw a portrait of the Holy Spirit in Mark. The final picture should be able to speak of the characteristics of the narratival character of the Holy Spirit and the role he plays in the ministry of Jesus in Mark. The contribution will conclude with an attempt to draw out the practical implications of this picture for the church today. In light of the general thrust of this book, I will aim to link the conclusions regarding the characters in Mark with the way the church seeks to interact with Muslims today.

Methodology: How to Study the Holy Spirit in Mark

In the following study, I am approaching Mark as one unified narrative. Accordingly, I want to study it using narrative criticism. I chose a narratologist called Mieke Bal because she puts forward an organized theory that seeks to find meaning.

Bal puts forward a structuralist method for outlining the primary and secondary characteristics of a character. The first step is to put forth a number of semantic axes which are essentially binary opposite pairs of major characteristics (e.g. small/big). The choosing of the axes should be in such a way as to coincide with as many characters in the story as possible. Then every character will either be marked as positive (+) on the positive part of the pair for possessing the good side or negative (–) for possessing the opposite side of the pair and the weaker part, or be left unmarked on that axis if the character simply does not show any of the opposite characteristics of the pair.[1]

The reader obtains information about the character through "explicit qualification": the character's own words about themselves, in the words or actions of other characters toward them or in words by the narrator about them. "Implicit qualification" occurs when we know the characteristics of a character through their role or actions in the story, and through the actions of others toward them. This system, combined with the marked semantic axes, provides a good picture of a character.[2]

How do we choose actors? Bal argues that only actors who are related to functional events should be selected. Other actors are also important, but functional characters are more significant.[3] Bal defines "functional" events as events that create a choice, fulfill a choice, or reveal the consequences of a choice, thus leading to other events.[4]

Hence, I shall first prove that the Holy Spirit is a functional actor in Mark and worthy of study. Then I shall outline his main characteristics, along with those of the other main characters in Mark. Finally, I shall construct and analyze the semantic grid of the characters in Mark.

The Holy Spirit as a Functional Actor in Mark

A number of scholars have noted the importance of the Holy Spirit in the prologue of Mark's Gospel. "The presence of the Spirit in the transforming work of Jesus is assumed" in later passages.[5] Our task will be to study the six direct mentions of the Spirit in an attempt to see whether or not he is a

---

1. Mieke Bal, *Narratology: Introduction to the Theory of Narrative* (Toronto: University of Toronto Press, 1997; repr. 2004), 126–127.

2. Bal, *Narratology*, 129–131.

3. Bal, *Narratology*, 195–196.

4. Bal, 184–185.

5. Kent Brower, *Mark: A Commentary in the Wesleyan Tradition*, New Beacon Bible Commentary (Kansas City: Beacon Hill Press, 2012), 37.

functional actor/character bringing about functional events. The following is not an exegesis of the passages but a short foray into them as relates to the Holy Spirit.

The first mention of the Holy Spirit is in Mark 1:8. In verses 7–8, Mark shows the difference between John the Baptist and his successor in terms of might ("one more powerful"), value (only slaves undid sandals), and manner of baptism.[6] We have a clear contrast being made between water and the Holy Spirit.[7] Baptism in the Spirit has eschatological connotations and is a fulfillment of Old Testament hopes (Isa 44:3; Ezek 39:29; Joel 2:28).[8] The promise of the baptism of the Holy Spirit is reminiscent of God's presence with his people in the wilderness after the exodus.[9] The Holy Spirit, in this first mention, is related to a functional event: the fulfillment of an eschatological hope. This event will – and we use Bal's language – create a choice for people whether or not to participate in this baptism, and it will enact a change, a movement from water to Spirit. The new baptism will be done by/in the Holy Spirit. Hence, we can conclude that in this verse, the Spirit is a functional actor who looks as if he will be vital for the coming ministry of Jesus.

The second mention of the Holy Spirit is in Mark 1:9–11. We could categorize this occurrence as a slow motion scene, whereby we are invited to focus on the minute details of the baptism including the movement of Jesus, the opening of the heavens, the descent of the Spirit, and the voice from heaven rather than on the act of baptism itself.[10] The Holy Spirit mentioned in verse 8 now appears on the scene.[11] As Jesus exits the water, the Spirit comes down on him in a parallel motion. The descent of the Spirit on Jesus is the anointing of him. Jesus carries the Holy Spirit and thus is God's presence on earth. He is also the way through which people can be baptized in the Holy Spirit.[12] The gap between heaven and earth is crossed in Mark 1:10. The Spirit descends from the frame of heaven, the symbolic abode of God, into the frame of Jesus, who is now the abode of God in the frame of the earth. If the Spirit

---

6. Morna D. Hooker, *The Gospel According to Saint Mark*, Black's New Testament Commentary (London: A & C Black, 1991), 37–38.

7. Brower, *Mark*, 56.

8. Hooker, *Gospel according to Saint Mark*, 38.

9. N. T. Wright, *Mark for Everyone* (London: SPCK, 2001), 2–3.

10. Brower, *Mark*, 57.

11. Robert A. Guelich, *Mark 1–8:26*, Word Biblical Commentary, Vol. 34A (Grand Rapids: Zondervan, 1989), 31.

12. Gabrielle Markusse-Overduin, "Salvation in Mark: The Death of Jesus and the Path of Discipleship" (PhD diss., University of Manchester, 2013), 41–42.

was functional as an instrument of baptism in the first mention, here he is the carrier and authenticator of the divine proclamation and the in-dweller of the Messiah. His role is securely tied to this functional event, one in which a choice is fulfilled – the Father's choice to proclaim his Son as Messiah, and Jesus's choice to accept this anointing. This event gives Jesus his identity and launches him on his mission.

The third mention of the Holy Spirit in the prologue of Mark comes in 1:12–13. Two things are immediately clear from this section: The Spirit is the driving force behind the temptation scene,[13] and the "wilderness" is prominent in this passage, not the temptation.[14] Interestingly, Jesus is a "static" character, while the active verbs are attached to the Spirit and the angels.[15] The Greek verb used by Mark to describe the Spirit's leading of Jesus, ἐκβάλλει, is stronger than the more common word for led, αγειν.[16] Mark uses ἐκβάλλει to speak of exorcising demons.[17] We have the same Spirit who anoints Jesus leading him to the final stage before his ministry begins.[18] Four characters are present in the wilderness scene: the Spirit, Satan, wild animals and angels. Some see two warring teams with Jesus, the Spirit and the angels against Satan and the wild animals. Others see a peaceful coexistence with the animals, thus showing an Eden-like picture pointing toward God's eschatological salvation.

Once more, the Spirit is a functional actor in the prologue. He is the one who leads Jesus into the wilderness, thus enacting a change in the events and bringing about a functional event. The consequences of the previous choice of Jesus to be anointed by the Spirit are revealed; he is now in conflict with Satan. The prologue gives us a glimpse of the heavenly movement, the descent of the Spirit and the voice from heaven, and the character of Satan.[19]

The Spirit is functional as an instrumental means of baptism, he is functional as a conveyer of the divine proclamation. He is also functional as a leader of the Messiah – an instigator and helper in conflict with the powers of evil. The Spirit is mentioned three more times outside the prologue. It remains to be seen if he serves as a functional actor in those instances too.

---

13. C. K. Barrett, *The Holy Spirit and the Gospel Tradition* (London: SPCK, 1996), 49.

14. R. T. France, *The Gospel of Mark*, The New International Greek Testament Commentary (Grand Rapids: Eerdmans, 2002), 83.

15. France, *Gospel of Mark*, 83.

16. Guelich, *Mark*, 38.

17. Hooker, *Gospel according to Saint Mark*, 49.

18. Robert H. Stein, *Mark*, Baker Exegetical Commentary on the New Testament (Grand Rapids: Baker Academic, 2008), 62.

19. Hooker, *Gospel according to Saint Mark*, 31–32.

Outside of the prologue of Mark, the Holy Spirit is mentioned three times. First, we see him in Mark 3:29. In this rather infamous reference to the unforgivable sin and the Holy Spirit, we note with Brower the importance of taking the context of this scary verse into account: The warning of Jesus regarding those who "blaspheme against the Holy Spirit" is referring to those who reject the good news of Jesus, claiming that Jesus is the servant of Satan rather than the servant of God doing the work of God through the Spirit.[20] Simply put, the scribes, and earlier the family of Jesus, decline to attribute Jesus's authority to God, while his true family recognizes the work of God's Spirit in the work of Jesus.[21] This tells us that Mark sees Jesus as the "bearer" of the Holy Spirit in his work on earth.[22]

This passage (i.e. Mark 3:20–35) is a functional event that reveals the consequences of a choice: the choice to side with Jesus and see his work as the work of God through the Spirit will bring about forgiveness, while the choice to attribute the Spirit's work to Satan will see that person or group side with Satan in eternal condemnation. The Spirit is revealed to be a functional actor in the work of God through Jesus.

The Spirit is also mentioned in Mark 12:36. Jesus has made a public entrance into Jerusalem, causing a scene and inducing unto himself the fury of the religious leaders (11:18). This section from 11:27 to 13:2 shows us his confrontation by the different groups of religious men of the city.[23] The mention of the Holy Spirit gives a prophetic depiction of the words of David[24] and divine authority.[25] Although we may be hard pressed to see this event as a functional one in the story of Mark – we could say that Jesus is revealing the consequences of his choice to see himself as a mere son-of-David type of Messiah – it remains that the Holy Spirit proves to be active outside the narrative, for he is referred to as the one who gave words to David in the writing of the psalm in question. Hence, though this mention does not prove the Holy Spirit's functionality in Mark per se, he is functional in a separate narrative spoken about here where David was writing the psalm.

The final mention of the Holy Spirit comes in Mark 13:11. Verses 9–13 begin with the second "be on your guard," and it speaks of persecution.

---

20. Brower, *Mark*, 114.
21. Hooker, *Gospel according to Saint Mark*, 114–117.
22. Guelich, *Mark*, 180.
23. France, *Gospel of Mark*, 451.
24. Brower, *Mark*, 320–321.
25. Hooker, *Gospel according to Saint Mark*, 293.

Verse 11 would provide encouragement to a weak church, for the generally uneducated believers would be worried about their words in courts and before leaders.[26] The Holy Spirit will provide special help to the followers of Jesus in future times of persecution.[27] The disciples will face the consequences of their choice to proclaim the gospel before the rulers making this a functional, albeit future, event.

Up to this point, we have met the Spirit as a functional actor in the person of Jesus (and perhaps David), but here we meet functional actors in the community of Jesus's followers. Time and again, though the mentions are scarce, the Spirit is seen to take part in functional events in Mark. Now that this point has been sufficiently proven, we may begin constructing our semantic grid of the Holy Spirit and the other characters in the story of Mark.

Basic Semantic Character Traits of the Holy Spirit in Mark

As evidenced in the previous section, the Holy Spirit is rarely mentioned or characterized in Mark. However, we shall attempt to work with what we have, and using Bal's explicit and implicit characterization and our previous discussion, we shall glean the basic semantic traits of the Holy Spirit in Mark. Since the Holy Spirit is only mentioned six times, and since our previous section on his functionality had us cover them extensively, I will sometimes use the above conclusions to name the semantic characteristics of the Spirit in the following discussion.

I will first look at things said by or about the Holy Spirit. The Holy Spirit does not say anything in Mark, nor do any of the characters say anything about him. Concerning the narrator's depiction, the Holy Spirit is given a neuter grammatical gender in Greek (τὸ πνεῦμα). This does not indicate that the Spirit is an object. As Wallace explains, "Grammatical gender is just that: grammatical. The conventions of language do not necessarily correspond to reality."[28] In Mark 1:10, the Spirit descends "like a dove." The expression in this verse could be read adjectivally, "like a dove," or adverbially, "coming down as a dove does."[29] It is most probably adjectival and is describing the

---

26. Stein, *Mark*, 599–601.
27. Wright, *Mark*, 179.
28. Daniel B. Wallace, "Greek Grammar and the Personality of the Holy Spirit," *Bulletin for Biblical Research* 13, no. 1 (2003): 122.
29. Guelich, *Mark*, 32–33.

form of the Spirit, and no symbol is likely intended.[30] This adjectival use does not produce much in terms of semantic qualities, except perhaps to say that the Spirit, at least in one part of Mark, is tangible.

In our previous discussion in the functionality section, we saw that the Spirit is an active character, being named as the agent of baptism, descending on Jesus, taking him to the wilderness, playing a part in a pre-narrative writing of a psalm, and aiding the followers of Jesus in post-narrative conflicts with civil and religious leaders. Some see the active role of the Spirit in the prologue as continuing throughout the ministry of Jesus, where by the power of the Holy Spirit, he defeats uncleanliness (leprosy, impure spirits, etc.) with his holiness and redefines impurity and purity.[31] Furthermore, true to John's foretelling of Jesus having the power of the Holy Spirit, Jesus has no problem exorcising evil spirits, and they in return show utmost fear of and obedience to him.[32]

We can safely say that the character of the Holy Spirit in Mark is powerful. He has authority to lead Jesus into the wilderness, to give David words to say, and to aid the disciples in times of conflict. We can also tentatively add that the Holy Spirit is obedient. The image of him descending from the heavens onto Jesus gives the impression of sending. Perhaps we have the invisible God sending his Spirit onto the Son of God. The Spirit, in breaking through from the sphere of heaven into the sphere of earth, is obedient to the command of God.

Basic Semantic Traits of the Other Characters in Mark

The criteria used for choosing characters was simply that they are actors in the story of Mark and that they appear consistently in the story. I will study Jesus, the disciples, the religious leaders, the crowd and the impure spirits. There are more nuances and divisions in these broad categories, especially the crowd and the religious leaders, but for the sake of this contribution, I will stick with these broad groups. That being said, even the minor characters which we skip will fall in one of the two groups. The limitations of this contribution mean that I will only present brief conclusions regarding each of the above mentioned characters as we aim to move on to the semantic grid.

---

30. France, *Gospel of Mark*, 78–79.

31. David Rhoads and Donald Michie, *Mark as Story: An Introduction to the Narrative of a Gospel* (Philadelphia: Fortress Press, 1982; repr. 1984), 105–106.

32. Rhoads and Michie, *Mark as Story*, 77–78.

I start with Jesus. In Mark, Jesus shows authority.[33] He is able to heal the sick, exorcise impure spirits, ask people to follow him, prophesy about the future, explain the law, and control nature and even death.[34] Second, he is obedient unto death, drinking the cup that the Father gives him.[35] Third and finally, Jesus, unlike his cowardly disciples in the passion narrative, is faithful.[36] Jesus in Mark is powerful, obedient and faithful.

The disciples are a group made up of twelve men chosen by Jesus to walk with him. First, they are ignorant, failing to understand who Jesus is and why he should die.[37] The disciples manage to help Jesus in his mission of renewal by teaching and healing (e.g. Mark 6:7–13), but they do so by the authority of Jesus (e.g. see their failure in 9:14–29).[38] The disciples are, however, obedient, immediately responding to Jesus's call and aiding him along the way (e.g. 3:9).[39] They are faithful followers of Jesus, but toward the end, one of them betrays him, another denies him and all leave him (14:43–72).[40] The disciples oscillate between being noteworthy examples of willingness to follow Jesus, being invited to listen in on the secrets of the kingdom and taking part in the mission of Jesus, and being undesirable models of fear and lack of faith, of spiritual inability and of disloyalty to Jesus.[41] They are ignorant, powerful yet weak, obedient and faithful, but also fearful.

The religious leaders with their different sects are a group that is in constant opposition to Jesus.[42] The religious leaders are unified in their enmity

---

33. Hooker, *Gospel according to Saint Mark*, 20.

34. Richard A. Horsley, *Hearing the Whole Story: The Politics of Plot in Mark's Gospel* (Louisville: Westminster John Knox, 2001), 102–108.

35. Francis J. Moloney, *Mark: Storyteller, Interpreter, Evangelist* (Peabody: Hendrickson, 2004), 107–108.

36. Timothy J. Geddert, *Watchwords: Mark 13 in Markan Eschatology*, The Library of New Testament Studies (London: Bloomsbury Academic, 2015; Sheffield: Sheffield Academic Press, 1989), 102–103.

37. Brower, *Mark*, 35.

38. Moloney, *Mark*, 73.

39. Elizabeth Malbon, *In the Company of Jesus: Characters in Mark* (Louisville: Westminster John Knox, 2000), 88–90.

40. Some scholars argue that women are better followers than the disciples in Mark, but Malbon rejects how other scholars have simplistically painted the disciples as bad followers and women as good followers. She discusses the women figures in Mark, showing how some show true faith, but in the end – just like the disciples – they do not stick to Jesus at the trial and the cross (Malbon, *In the Company*, 46–50). Also note that at the empty grave, the women – like the disciples – act in fear and run away (Moloney, *Mark*, 112).

41. France, *Gospel of Mark*, 27–29.

42. James S. Hanson, *The Endangered Promises: Conflict in Mark* (Atlanta: SBL, 2000), 156–157.

toward Jesus, one which progresses from questioning him, to plotting against him, to bringing him to court, and finally to condemning him to the cross.[43] The religious leaders are powerful in the story of Mark, able to crucify Jesus, although their authority is different from that of Jesus (e.g. Mark 1:22). The religious leaders, like the disciples, show a lack of understanding. They are ignorant of the kingdom of God now come and of the scriptures which prophesy about Jesus, Elijah and the house of David.[44] Unlike the disciples, the religious leaders show unbelief and reject Jesus's words.[45] The religious leaders, then, are "a character" who has authority but is ignorant of Jesus's teachings and skeptical of him.

The ministry of Jesus sees him standing on the side of God facing Satan and also fighting the power of impure spirits.[46] The exorcisms are central in depicting this struggle, for they draw out the supernatural conflict happening behind the human story.[47] Exorcisms make up a major part of Jesus's ministry in Mark.[48] We can glean four semantic characteristics of the impure spirits in the gospel. First, they are powerful and able to make people they possess break chains (5:4) and become mute (9:17). But in front of Jesus the impure spirits are weak![49] Surprisingly, this leads us to the second characteristic of the impure spirits in Mark: they are obedient – it may be forced obedience, but it is obedience nevertheless. Jesus only has to speak a word, and the spirits obey and leave the possessed people. Upon meeting Jesus, the impure spirits show two further characteristics: fear and knowledge. A case in point is the first exorcism in Mark 1:23–26, where the narrator tells us that the unclean spirit shouts out to Jesus: "What do you want with us, Jesus of Nazareth? Have you come to destroy us? I know who you are – the Holy One of God!" The preceding statement, repeated with variations in other exorcisms, shows the fear of the unclean spirits at the approach of one stronger than they are who can demolish them, and it shows their knowledge of who Jesus is. Thus, the

---

43. Malbon, *In the Company*, 149.

44. Rhoads and Michie, *Mark as Story*, 118–119.

45. Thomas R. Hatina, *In Search of a Context: The Function of Scripture in Mark's Narrative*, Library of New Testament Studies, Book 232 (London: Sheffield Academic, 2002), 120–121.

46. Barrett, *Holy Spirit*, 46.

47. France, *Gospel of Mark*, 167.

48. Horsley, *Whole Story*, 121–122.

49. Rhoads and Michie, *Mark as Story*, 77–78.

impure spirits in Mark are both powerful and weak, their weakness stemming from their fear of, knowledge of, and obedience to Jesus.[50]

A final character is the crowd. The crowd is similar to the disciples in that both are followers of Jesus, but the disciples present a more intimate group around Jesus. The crowd as a character group is varied.[51] It is individuals from the crowd, not the disciples, who show understanding of the kingdom of God (e.g. the Syrophoenician woman in Mark 7:24–30).[52] However, some instances show the crowd unable to understand the parables of Jesus (4:11–12).[53] Though they cheer for the Messiah Jesus upon his entry to Jerusalem, like the disciples, they want an earthly king like David, and they do not understand the kingdom of God (11:1–25).[54] Similarly to the disciples, the crowd in Mark is ignorant of the true identity of Christ, though they identify him as one who has authority and is worthy of trust. The crowd is a passive receiver, always asking for more (1:37; 2:4; 10:48). Moreover, the crowd is not always believing but sometimes shows doubt (9:26).[55] This variation in the crowd's reactions to Jesus leads us to conclude that they oscillate between being believing and being skeptical. Regardless of the amount of belief they have, the crowd walks with Jesus (2:13–14; 8:34–38; 10:21) and shows faith in him (7:17–30; 9:24–28; 10:46–52).[56] However, the faithfulness of the crowd in showing trust in Jesus and following him breaks apart in a number of places. For instance, the mourners make fun of Jesus at Jairus's house (5:40).[57] The ultimate test is when Pilate asks the crowd what they want to do with Jesus, and they follow the inciting of the religious leaders, shouting: "crucify him!" (15:9–13).[58]

---

50. The miracles in Mark also point to the spiritual struggle and the work of God and the Holy Spirit through Jesus (Barrett, *Holy Spirit*, 69–93). But this discussion has sought to briefly study only the direct mentions of evil spirits and the kingdom of Satan in Mark, and not the implicit ones. The preceding link calls for a comparison between the exorcisms and the miracles in Mark, but that is beyond the scope of this study.

51. Rhoads and Michie, *Mark as Story*, 134–135.

52. Kelly R. Iverson, *Gentiles in the Gospel of Mark: 'Even the Dogs under the Table Eat the Children's Crumbs,'* The Library of New Testament Studies, Book 339 (London: T&T Clark, 2007), 179–180.

53. Hooker, *Gospel according to Saint Mark*, 21.

54. Moloney, *Mark*, 87–88.

55. Malbon, *In the Company*, 92.

56. Hooker, *Gospel according to Saint Mark*, 19.

57. Moloney, *Mark*, 71–73.

58. Whether or not the crowd in the scene with Pilate is different from the crowd following Jesus in his ministry is a question for historical inquiry. The narrator in Mark does not make any direct effort to distinguish between the two.

Thus the crowd is ignorant of the true person of Jesus, is both believing and skeptical, and is both faithful and fearful.

The Semantic Grid of the Main Characters in Mark

I now come to the final block of our building. I have thus far defended the usage of a narrative approach to the study of the character of the Holy Spirit in Mark and explicated a specific narrative structural approach to narrative studies according to Bal. I have also proven that the Holy Spirit is a functional character in Mark and worthy of our study. We have then moved on to find the basic semantic characteristics of the Holy Spirit and the main characters in Mark. I will now list the semantic axes, place them in one semantic grid, and attempt to analyze the implications of this system on the Holy Spirit.

Per our discussion of the basic semantic characteristics of the main characters in Mark, I can put forward the following five semantic axes which cover all of the characteristics discussed:[59] powerful/weak, obedient/rebellious, faithful/fearful, knowledgeable/ignorant, and trusting/skeptical. I shall now construct the semantic grid.

The Semantic Grid of the Main Characters in Mark

Characters	Powerful/ Weak	Obedient/ Rebellious	Faithful/ Fearful	Knowledgeable/ Ignorant	Trusting/ Skeptical
Holy Spirit	+	+	0	+	0
Jesus	+	+	+	+	+
Disciples	−	+	+/−	−	+
Religious Leaders	+	0	−	−	−
Impure Spirits	+/−	+	−	+	0
Crowd	−	+/−	+/−	−	+/−

The above grid shows the position of the characters with respect to the dominant semantic axes and with each other. The (+) sign means that the character reflects the positive part of the axis, while the (−) sign means that they reflect the negative part. Some characters display both parts of the axis, hence they take the (+/−) sign. Those characters displaying neither part of

---

59. The list does not show a priority of one axis over another.

the axis are marked (0) in that column. As discussed in the introduction, this table is rigid and does not account for the many nuances and degrees in every semantic quality. However, it will serve as a structure for drawing a basic portrait of the character of the Holy Spirit in Mark in relation to the other characters in the story. That will be the work of the concluding section of analysis and implications.

Implications of the Grid on Understanding the Character of the Holy Spirit

As is evident in the above grid, the Holy Spirit is similar to some characters, opposite to others, and simply different from others. We begin with the Holy Spirit and Jesus. They are almost a perfect fit. Where the Holy Spirit is marked positive, so is Jesus. Thus, both are powerful, obedient and knowledgeable. We did not discuss this third trait in our surveys of both characters, but Jesus did know who he is as evidenced by his recurrent order to the impure spirits and those whom he healed not to reveal his identity. Likewise, the Holy Spirit knows the true identity of Jesus. This first comparison reveals what others have already stated, that the Holy Spirit is active in the ministry of Jesus, for he is a character who is similar to Jesus, and hence working on his side.

We come to our next pair, the Holy Spirit and the disciples along with the crowd. The crowd scores the same as the disciples, so they will be discussed together. While the Holy Spirit is powerful, they are weak; and while the Spirit is knowledgeable, they are ignorant. Interestingly, they only meet on the trait of obedience. It seems that, whereas both characters are obedient – the Holy Spirit to God, and the disciples to Jesus – the crowd does not have the opportunity to demonstrate either obedience or the lack of it in the narrative. The Holy Spirit is a better follower or aide, for he has the power to help in the ministry of Jesus and understands who Jesus is, while the disciples and the crowd fail to understand and are weak characters, constantly dependent on Jesus. Consequently, we can timidly add that the disciples and the crowd need divine help, which here is the Holy Spirit, in order to properly understand who Jesus is and to receive his authority.

Both the Holy Spirit and the religious leaders are powerful characters in Mark. However as the grid shows, the Holy Spirit is on the side of Jesus, recognizing his identity, while the religious leaders are opposing Jesus, ignorant of his true mission and self. Hence, I can safely conclude that the Holy Spirit with his power is spreading the kingdom of God with Jesus, while the authorities, with their own powers, are opposing this same kingdom.

We now come to our most interesting set: the Holy Spirit and the impure spirits. They are very similar, for both are marked as powerful, obedient and knowledgeable. The only two differences are that the power of the impure spirits stops when it encounters the authority of Jesus – hence their obedience – and the impure spirits are fearful of Jesus. I do not have evidence from Mark to speak of the Holy Spirit trusting Jesus, but the one scene where the Holy Spirit descends on/into Jesus does not speak of fear. Hence, we have two similar characters whose only difference revolves around their relationship with Jesus. The impure spirits, unlike the religious authorities, recognize who Jesus is, and unlike the religious authorities, they are unable to fight him, for his authority overwhelms them. They are, like the Holy Spirit, obedient to God. But the Holy Spirit is an agent who walks with Jesus, helping him, while the impure spirits stand in opposition to him (or at least they try to). We can see a clear conflict between two types of spirits in Mark: The Spirit of God and the spirits of the devil.

What I can say with assurance is that the narratival character of the Holy Spirit in Mark is firmly aligned with Jesus and acts as a helper to him on his mission. I can also add that he is firmly in opposition to the religious leaders and the impure spirits, working against them with Jesus, and showing victory over them, especially in the case of the impure spirits. Though the Holy Spirit is mentioned but six times, our discussion has shown that he is a vital and essential character in Mark.

What about the Church Today?

This study has sought to draw a picture of the narratival character of the Holy Spirit in Mark. To that end, I have outlined using Bal's systematic method and proven the functionality of the Holy Spirit in Mark, outlined the basic semantic characteristics of the Holy Spirit and the main characters in the narrative of Mark, and finally constructed a grid of those characteristics that has enabled us to tease out the position of the Holy Spirit in Mark. The picture may be rather brief, but this is what Mark gives us. Nevertheless it is a picture, and one which perhaps will be used to ask more questions about the role, identity and presence of the Holy Spirit in Mark, in the other gospels, and in the New Testament in future studies.

In my Lebanese and Middle Eastern context, especially the evangelical one, we have different pictures of the Holy Spirit. In some churches, he is not part of the church worship or liturgy at all, while in others he is the main actor in the kingdom. We need to look once more at the picture of the Holy

Spirit in Mark and ask the question we asked of Mark: where is the Holy Spirit, or where should he be, in the church today? He is a powerful presence, but he works in the background, ever pushing Jesus forward on his mission of spreading the kingdom of God. The Holy Spirit is the "creative activity of God which calls into being the conditions of the Messianic era."[60] He is the one through whom the followers of Jesus are to be baptized. And we see the Holy Spirit in Mark being promised to aid the disciples as they stand in front of the authorities (Mark 13:11), much as Jesus stood. Perhaps the church today needs to remember that the mere presence of the Holy Spirit in Jesus and in our world speaks of a God of active holiness. Mark is telling us that Jesus wants to baptize each one of the disciples by the Spirit, so that they too may go out and preach the kingdom of "boundary-shattering" holiness.[61] The Holy Spirit works in power to challenge the forces of darkness in Mark. We as modern disciples are called to receive the help of the Spirit. We could also venture to say that we are called to be, like him and with his aid, helpers of God, challenging all that is dark in our world.

On another note, and as this book discusses the church's attitude toward the Muslim other, I make two final comments. First, we are in need of the Holy Spirit constantly. All and any authority we have as the church stems from him. We are not better than the Muslim. We are in need of constant empowerment. The above semantic grid reminds us that the disciples are ignorant and weak without the constant presence of Jesus. The disciples are not more powerful than the crowd. If anything, the disciples are weaker than the religious leaders and the impure spirits. Their only strength lies in their nearness to Christ and their dependence on the Holy Spirit.

Second, the Holy Spirit was in opposition to two characters: the religious leaders and the impure spirits. However, he was not in opposition to the crowds or the disciples. Could it be that the church today is the disciples, fearful yet obedient, yearning to understand? Could it be that the Muslims today are the crowd, seeking the power of Jesus but not truly comprehending his identity? Perhaps, above all, we need to point people toward Christ. In the end, he is the beloved Son, the locus of God's activity, the center of the work of the Spirit. Perhaps we should focus more on our attitude toward Jesus rather than toward the Muslim, so that our attitude toward the latter would become Christlike.

---

60. Barrett, *Holy Spirit*, 45.
61. Hanson, *Endangered Promises*, 177–189.

9.4 Christian and Muslim Perspectives on African Traditional Practices: A Case of Luo Funerals in Kendu Bay, Kenya

Lawrence Oseje

Africa for many years has been the home of Christianity and Islam. Islam was first adopted in many parts of Africa, including Kenya, in the seventh century, followed by Christianity in the early sixteenth century. Both religions came to Kendu Bay in Kenya between 1902 and 1906. While it is undeniable that these two religions have impacted the socio-cultural and religious perspectives of the African people, the rate at which Christians and Muslims easily revert to their African Traditional Religious (ATR) beliefs and practices at events such as death is quite alarming. With reference to East Africa, where Kenya lies, Shipton observes, "Neither Christianity nor Islam has managed to expunge aspects of indigenous religion in East Africa."[62] Among many occasions for ceremonies in Africa, death has the highest number of rituals. Death is not easily accepted as a natural occurrence in African thinking but is associated with supernatural powers such as magic, witchcraft and sorcery, as well as a result of breaking traditions such as wife inheritance.[63]

People carry out many elaborate rituals following the death of a loved one due to their belief in life after death, as Mbiti asserts: "For the Africans, death is a separation and not annihilation: the dead person is suddenly cut off from the human society and yet, the corporate group clings to him. This is shown through the elaborate funeral rites as well as other methods of keeping in contact with the departed."[64] But despite the many and elaborate rituals of death and widespread African belief in life after death, there are still many questions that linger in one's mind: What is it in ATR that makes them revert? How should one discern between what is religious and what is cultural and social in spiritual matters? How do the African church and the Muslim community view such reversion of their members? This contribution addresses

---

62. Parker MacDonald Shipton, *Mortgaging the Ancestors: Ideologies of Attachment in Africa* (New Haven: Yale University Press, 2009), 69.

63. Ruth Prince, "Christian Salvation and Luo Tradition: Arguments of Faith in a Time of Death in Western Kenya," in *AIDS and Religious Practice in Africa*, eds. Felicitas Beeker and P. Wenzel Geissler (Leiden: Brill, 2009), 68. See also Aloysius Muzzanganda Lugira, *African Traditional Religion*, 3rd ed. (New York: Chelsea House, 2009), 73; and John S. Mbiti, *Introduction to African Religion*, 2nd rev. ed. (Portsmouth: Heinemann Educational, 1991), 117–118.

64. John S. Mbiti, *The Crisis of Mission in Africa* (Mukono: Uganda Church Press, 1971), 46.

those questions. Some of the responses conveyed here were extracted from my book *African Traditions Meeting Islam*[65] which was developed from both field and library research for my dissertation.

Definition of Terms

Some of the recurring terms used in this contribution require definition. Below are the key terms.

ATR: African Traditional Religions represent the religious systems that developed among the people of Africa in the course of thousands of years, during which they were elaborated and which are still present in contemporary Africa.[66]

Culture: The term "culture" will be used to refer to the more or less integrated systems of ideas, feelings and values and their associated patterns of behavior and products which are shared by a group of people who organize and regulate what they think, feel and do.[67] The term derives from the Latin *cultura*, meaning cultivation of the soil. Culture is linked to the root of a people and is cultivated by the people and passed on to the following generations.[68] Culture is an integral whole or configuration, a magnifying glass through which people perceive the many facets of the world.[69]

Tradition or Traditional: These will be used as synonymous with terms such as "tribal," "indigenous" and "local."[70] The concept may be used similarly to the term "animism," which is derived from the word *anima*, meaning "soul" in Latin. It conceives of human beings as passing through life surrounded by

---

65. Lawrence Oseje, *African Traditions Meeting Islam: A Case of Luo-Muslim Funerals in Kendu Bay, Kenya* (Carlisle: Langham Monographs, 2018).

66. Ferdinand Nwaigbo, "Faith in the One God in Christian and African Traditional Religions: A Theological Appraisal," *OGIRISI: A New Journal of African Studies* 7 (2010): 56–68, https://www.ajol.info/index.php/og/article/view/57922.

67. Paul G. Hiebert, *Anthropological Insights for Missionaries* (Grand Rapids: Baker, 1985), 30. See also Allen Walker et al., *The New International Webster's Comprehensive Dictionary of the English Language* (Naples, FL: Trident Press International, 2003), 1386.

68. Mathew Ekechukwu Nwafor, "Integrating African Values with Christianity: A Requirement for Dialogue between Christian Religion and African Culture," *Mgbakoigba: Journal of African Studies* 6, no. 1 (2016): 2. See also Lesslie Newbigin, *Foolishness to the Greeks: The Gospel and Western Culture* (Grand Rapids: Eerdmans, 1986), 3.

69. Amaegwu Onyeka-Joe, *Globalization vs African Cultural Values* (Self-pub., 2013), 30.

70. Dean S. Gilliland, *African Religion Meets Islam: Religious Change in Northern Nigeria* (Lanham: University Press of America, 1986), 1.

the ghostly company of powers and elements which are mostly impersonal in character.[71]

Traditions: Particularly with reference to the Luo people in Kendu Bay, Kenya, the word also includes material objects and practices that are embedded in kinship relations and the sociality of everyday life that guide important events and experiences as common in the death of a person.[72]

Realities of ATR in the African Church and Muslim Community

The African indigenous religion, Christianity and Islam have been referred to as "Africa's Triple Heritage" or "Africa's Trinity of Cultures."[73] This means that they are interconnected. Can one be both a Christian and a follower of an African indigenous religion? Can one be both a Muslim and a follower of an African indigenous religion?[74] These are some of the questions explored in this contribution.

Forms of Realities in ATR

The relationship between ATR and other religions is characterized by both continuity and discontinuity, but also by synthesization. The coming of Christianity and the coming of Islam did not in any way replace or erase African traditional practices.[75] For example, in Senegal it is said that 90 percent of the people are Muslim, 10 percent are Christian, but 100 percent are animist.[76] Libation, blood sacrifice and memorial services are common examples.

---

71. M. C. Behera, *Tribal Religion: Change and Continuity* (New Delhi: Commonwealth Publishers, 2000), 93.

72. Prince, "Christian Salvation," 66.

73. Ali A. Mazrui, "African Islam and Competitive Religion: Between Revivalism and Expansion," *Third World Quarterly* 10, no. 2 (1988): 503.

74. Mazrui, "African Islam," 504.

75. Kwame Bediako, *Theology and Identity: The Impact of Culture upon Christian Thought in the Second Century and in Modern Africa* (Eugene: Regnum, 1992), 386. See also Mercy Amba Oduyoye, *Hearing and Knowing: Theological Reflections on Christianity in Africa* (Eugene: Wipf & Stock, 1986), 62; and John S. Mbiti, *The Prayers of African Religion* (Maryknoll: Orbis, 1975).

76. Doudou Diène and Jean Burrell, "A Dynamic Continuity between Traditions," *Diogenes* 47, no. 187 (1999): 16.

Nevertheless, the African traditional way of life has also been transformed by the values found in Christianity or Islam.[77]

In the final analysis, Christian and Muslim interaction with ATR has resulted in total or ultimate synthesis, leading to a single whole. There is therefore no dichotomy or dualism, as some scholars have pointed out.[78] Other scholars use hybridity or naturalization to explain the same. The majority of Christians and Muslims fall under this last category. They seem not to be aware of a boundary between what is religious, what is cultural and what is neither. This subconscious reality can be understood by looking at the characteristics and nature of ATR.

Characteristics and Nature of ATR

ATR dictates the terms of reference for both Christianity and Islam. "There is an African 'core culture' that basically decides the forms of expression of these religions [Christianity and Islam], as well as the dynamics of their progress or decline, on the continent of Africa."[79] ATR has been described as the substructure and as the software for both Islam and Christianity.[80]

Mbiti observes that there is for the African people, "no formal distinction between the sacred and the secular, between the religious and non-religious, between the spiritual and the material areas of life."[81] There is no separate traditional and Christian life to them; all life is one and complete, so they do not have to hide that they perform traditional rituals. "They do not see ancestral

---

77. Jacob K. Olupona, "Major Issues in the Study of African Traditional Religion," in *African Traditional Religions in Contemporary Society* (St. Paul: Paragon, 1991). See also Byang H. Kato, *Theological Pitfalls in Africa* (Kisumu, Kenya: Evangel, 1975); and Byang H. Kato, *African Cultural Revolution and the Christian Faith* (Jos, Nigeria: Challenge Publications, 1976).

78. Harvie M. Conn, *Islam in East Africa: An Overview* (Islamabad: Islamic Research Institute, 1978). See also Caleb Chil-Soo Kim, "Considering Ordinariness in Studying Muslim Culture and Discipleship," in *Discipleship in the 21st Century Mission*, eds. Timothy Park and Steven Tom (Kyunggi, Korea: East West Center for MRD, 2014); Caleb Chil-Soo Kim, *Islam among the Swahili in East Africa*, 2nd ed. (Nairobi: Acton, 2016); and Bill Musk, *The Unseen Face of Islam: Sharing the Gospel with Ordinary Muslims at Street Level* (Oxford: Monarch, 2004).

79. Diène and Burrell, "Dynamic Continuity between Traditions," 16.

80. Abraham A. Akrong and John Azumah, "Hermeneutical and Theological Resources in African Traditional Religions for Christian-Muslim Relations in Africa," in *The African Christian and Islam*, eds. John Azumah and Lamin Sanneh (Carlisle: Langham Monographs, 2013), 75.

81. John S. Mbiti, *African Religions & Philosophy* (New York: Praeger, 1969), 2.

practices as worship of ancestors, as suggested by missionaries, but as a way of appeasing or venerating them."[82]

Africans hold the spiritual world in high regard and are highly sensitive to it. The presence of a Supreme Being – or still more of a *Father* – is strongly recognized. This deep awareness and recognition results in a way of life that is imbued with a deep religious sense.[83] This is in line with Mbiti's assertion that, "Africans are notoriously religious."[84] African people had the concept of and belief in God, as well as various ways of worshiping in their religious life, long before foreign Christian or Muslim missionaries and travelers arrived in Africa.[85] The African person sees religion as a vehicle or medium through which God can be worshiped, related to and appreciated. In that respect, there is no single uniform image to represent God that Africans agree on. There is simply a general acceptance – consciously or unconsciously – that God is a spiritual being that cannot be quantified or measured.[86]

This fundamental belief in a Supreme Being draws a response of respect, fear and reverence for elders, authorities, the dead, kinship and extended family. The notion of family is not simply about the father, the mother and the children but also about other relatives, which explains why in many African communities, cousins, nephews and nieces are called brothers and sisters, while elderly uncles and aunts are called fathers and mothers.[87] The concept of *luwo* (derived from Luo) means to follow – e.g. burial customs and traditions passed on by the forefathers as well as socio-political issues.[88] Series of ritual feasts for the dead are performed because of people's strong fear and respect for the dead.[89] For example, a bull may be slaughtered for mourners, but the

---

82. L. Ntombana, "The Trajectories of Christianity and African Ritual Practices: The Public Silence and the Dilemma of Mainline or Mission Churches," *Acta Theologica* 35, no. 2 (2015): 114.

83. Nwaigbo, *Faith in the One God*, 63. See also Vatican II, 1965.

84. Mbiti, *African Religions and Philosophy*, 1.

85. John S. Mbiti, "The Encounter of Christian Faith and African Religion," *Christian Century* 97, no. 27 (1980): 817. See also Mbiti, "Challenges of Language, Culture, and Interpretation in Translating the Greek New Testament," *Swedish Missiological Themes* 97, no. 2 (2009): 146.

86. O. O. Asukwo, S. S. Adaka, and E. D. Dimgba, "The Need to Re-Conceptualize African 'Traditional' Religion," *African Research Review* 7, no. 3 (2013): 241.

87. Nwafor, "Integrating African Values with Christianity," 4.

88. Jude J. Ongong'a, *Life and Death: A Christian-Luo Dialogue* (Eldoret, Kenya: Gaba Publications, 1983), 7. See also Bethwell A. Ogot, *History of the Southern Luo* (Nairobi: East African Publishing, 1967), 108–112.

89. Wakana Shiino, "Death and Rituals among the Luo in South Nyanza," *African Study Monographs* 18, no. 3/4 (1997): 213.

same cannot be sold to cover medical bills or fees for the sick or needy.[90] A funeral is a very important social event that is believed to be vital in keeping in touch with the spirits of ancestors of the ethnic group.[91] Attending is a sign of belonging.

There is universal agreement that ancestors are commemorated in the rituals of traditional African societies and that they still have a significant role in religious practices, such as naming and marriage.[92] Killing – especially of a relative – is forbidden, as spirits are believed to torment people. At death, the soul changes into a spirit through what we might call a process of social elevation. At this point the spirit enters the state of immortality. The living are expected to take note of this development and render due respect to the departed through ritual.[93] Marriage and naming ensure continuity. Spirits are feared, for they are believed capable of causing harm, or even death, if not well treated or respected.

The Luo, more than any other ethnic group, are generally known in Kenya as a people who value ancestral land and are seriously concerned with their burial place.[94] S. M. Otieno is a Christian and a prominent lawyer who died in 1986 and was buried one year later due to a court case concerning where to be buried. His clan won the case against his wife, and he was buried in his ancestral land, representing his "home" and "house."[95]

ATR is dynamic, adaptive and accommodative. In one particular region, the community had recently changed from being just "Christians" to becoming "born-again Christians."[96] Still no extinction occurred of ATR traditions and practices. Beneath the new changes lies the subconscious mind of *zamani* (the past). Tribal life is only dormant, not dead.[97] African societies are community-oriented rather than individual-oriented. Mbiti's statement, "I am because we

---

90. Richard Kisiara, "Some Sociopolitical Aspects of Luo Funerals," *Anthropos* 93, no. 1/3 (1998): 130.

91. John W. van Doren, "Death African Style: The Case of S. M. Otieno," *American Journal of Comparative Law* 36, no. 2 (1988): 337.

92. Allan H. Anderson, *Spirit-Filled World: Religious Dis/Continuity in African Pentecostalism* (Gurgaon: Palgrave Macmillan, 2018), 82.

93. Lugira, *African Traditional Religion*, 52.

94. Shiino, "Death and Rituals among the Luo," 213.

95. Nancy Schwartz, "Active Dead or Alive: Some Kenyan Views about the Agency of Luo and Luyia Women Pre- and Post-Mortem," *Journal of Religion in Africa* 30, no. 4 (2000): 134. See also Patricia Stamp, "Burying Otieno: The Politics of Gender and Ethnicity in Kenya," *Signs: Journal of Women in Culture and Society* 16, no. 4 (1991): 823–824.

96. Anderson, *Spirit-Filled World*, 100.

97. Mbiti, *Introduction to African Religion*, 22.

are,"[98] centers on relationships, or *umma* in Islam. It implies interdependency and socialization, bringing to mind Genesis 2:18 that it is "not good for the man to be alone." This provides a sense of security.[99]

Another name for this community relationship is *ubuntu*, meaning voluntary participation, group solidarity, conformity, compassion, respect, human dignity, humanistic orientation, and collective unity and sharing of property.[100] While students of the Enlightenment would say, "I think, therefore I am," Africans say, "I belong, therefore I am."[101] An African is a being in community, sharing common values, norms, religion and identity.[102]

Polygamy has both social and religious value. One's true riches are related to the number of children and wives one has. When a husband and wife have marital problems, the whole community gets involved in an effort to reconcile the partners. Similarly, African people say, "We have been killed," when one member of their community has been killed. Not only the offender, but the whole community takes responsibility for the misbehavior. This community does not only include human beings, but also nature, the world of the spirits, ancestors and even God.[103] This brings to mind the story of Ruth – "Your people will be my people and your God my God" (Ruth 1:16). We may refer to this mindset as the "Ruth Syndrome." Among Muslims with folk religious practices, *jinn* or spirits are part and parcel of the family or community. The *ubuntu* spirit goes beyond religion. People come to a funeral to mourn "one of us."

---

98. Mbiti, 2–10.

99. Charles H. Kraft, *Worldview for Christian Witness* (Pasadena: William Carey Library, 2008), 234.

100. J. Broodryk, "Ubuntu in South Africa" (LLD Thesis, UNISA, 1997). See also Kraft, *Worldview for Christian Witness*, 234; and Lugira, *African Traditional Religion*, 17–18.

101. A. Meiring, "As Below, so Above: A Perspective on African Theology," *Hervormde Teologiese Studies* 63, no. 2 (2008): 735.

102. T. Adeyemo, "Clash of Two Worldviews: African and Western," *Orientation* 2, no. 87/90 (1998): 374. See also R. Gerloff, "Truth, a New Society and Reconciliation: The Truth and Reconciliation Commission in South Africa from a German Perspective," *Missionalia* 26, no. 1 (1998): 49; N. Ndungane, *A World with a Human Face: A Voice from Africa* (London: SPCK, 2003), 102; G. M. Setiloane, *African Theology* (Cape Town: Lux Verbi, 2000), 21; and D. M. Tutu, *No Future without Forgiveness* (London: Rider, 1999), 35.

103. C. Du Toit, "African Hermeneutics," in *Initiation into Theology: The Rich Variety of Theology and Hermeneutics*, eds. S. Maimela and A. König (Pretoria: Van Schaik, 1998), 398.

Christian View of ATR

There is a debate as to whether conversion to the Christian religion requires radical discontinuity between one's culture and what we might call "Christian culture," or whether it is legitimate to maintain continuity with those elements that are positive in the cultures encountered by Christianity. The discontinuity camp maintains that when becoming a Christian, one must become a new person with a totally different identity from one's original cultural identity. Others view conversion as involving substantial continuity between one's culture and the new "Christian culture."[104] This camp distinguishes between "the African-tradition-oriented Christianity and the Western-influenced Christianity."[105] The above evidence implies that the African church is divided concerning ATR.

Positive Christian View of ATR

Some clergy and other Christians view ATR and Christianity as compatible. For example, Presiding Bishop Henry Okullu of the Anglican Church was vocal in his support of S. M. Otieno's burial in his ancestral land. He was praised by members of parliament for highlighting the compatibility of Christianity and African traditions.[106] This position considers ATR – which often informs African theology, as quite compatible with the message and worldview of the Bible, even capable of enhancing our view of God.[107]

Culture, as sometimes expressed through languages, food and artefacts, brings a sense of belonging. It prevents a loss of identity. It is history without which there is no present and future. Christian converts who were under missionary authority became a group or a community that lived among the African people without reference to their traditional kinship-based social structures.[108] The Christian religion that Western missionaries brought to Africa was packaged in the "garb" of Western culture and values. This situation has led to

---

104. Nwafor, "Integrating African Values," 6.

105. James N. Amanze, "Christianity and Ancestor Veneration in Botswana," *Studies in World Christianity* 8, no. 1 (2003): 43. See also T. A. Matobo, M. Makatsa, and E. E. Obioha, "Continuity in the Traditional Initiation Practice of Boys and Girls in Contemporary Southern Africa Society," *Studies of Tribes and Tribals* 7, no. 2 (2009): 105.

106. Stamp, "Burying Otieno," 835.

107. Kwame Bediako, *Christianity in Africa: The Renewal of Non-Western Religion* (Edinburgh: Edinburgh University Press, 1995), 97. See also Mbiti, *African Religions and Philosophy*, 29; and John S. Mbiti, "African Theology," in *Initiation into Theology: The Rich Variety of Theology and Hermeneutics*, eds. S. Maimela and A. König (Pretoria: Van Schaik, 1998), 140–142.

108. B. A. Pauw, *Christianity and Xhosa Tradition: Belief and Ritual among Xhosa-Speaking Christians* (New York: Oxford University Press, 1975), 21.

an inauthentic Christian life and to syncretism among African Christians.[109] Everyone has a culture and traditions. Both missionaries and the local people have their own cultures, which do not always disappear.[110] Authors with a positive view of ATR emphasize its relational dimensions. They argue that ATR fosters love and mutual respect, maintains received values, abides by strict moral and ethical standards, encourages community participation ("I am because you are"), and maintains work solidarity.[111]

Some argue that certain traditions, such as traditional medicine, have originated from the supreme deity and operate through a tutelary divinity or spirits.[112] Others emphasize the divine and God-centered nature of ATR. They respond that magic and medicine were part of African scientific culture, rather than of religion per se.[113] Before the arrival of Christianity and Islam, Africans had the knowledge of God as Creator. Africans knew God as the all-knowing, all-powerful and all-loving who is greater than the works of human hands.[114] Africans see religion as the ground of human beings' relationship to God, creature to Creator, subject to Lord.[115] Western missionaries in the past focused their hearers' attention on a future hope (in heaven), while ignoring contemporary existential suffering.[116] ATR, on the other hand, deals with current realities, not just the future. Present realities such as sickness, calamities and death preoccupy the minds of most ordinary Muslims. They seek answers to these existential realities.

Defenders of a positive approach to ATR argue that it offers more freedom and is not as dogmatic and orthodox as Christianity. Some have documented how "[t]hose who were found to be contravening the missionary teaching were only allowed back to the church after undergoing the church ritual of repentance and cleansing, which included public confession and assurance that

---

109. Nwafor, "Integrating African Values," 1.

110. Hiebert, *Anthropological Insights for Missionaries*, 228.

111. Asukwo, Adaka, and Dimgba, "Need to Re-Conceptualize African 'Traditional' Religion," 240.

112. Emanuel B. Idowu, *African Traditional Religion: A Definition* (London: SCM, 1973), 199.

113. Pius O. Abioje, *African Ancestral Heritage in Christian Interpretations* (Beau Bassin: Lambert Academic, 2018), 95–100.

114. Asukwo, Adaka and Dimgba, "Need to Re-Conceptualize," 238.

115. Frederick Copleston, *A History of Philosophy: Medieval Philosophy* (New York: Continuum, 2010).

116. G. E. Dames, "Knowing, Believing, Living in Africa: A Practical Theology Perspective of the Past, Present and Future," *HTS Theological Studies* 69, no. 1 (2013): 3.

they would not do it again."[117] The freedom afforded by ATR includes what sometimes is referred to as "the leading of the Spirit." It is not uncommon in African churches to hear people talking about dreams that they feel were given to them by their dead relatives. Speech about generational curses and spirit exorcism are real.

Negative Christian View of ATR
While some Christians in many churches in Africa still revert to African traditional beliefs and practices in such events as birth, marriage and funerals, there are those who have minimized or abandoned these traditional customs and rituals. Most of these Christians are in the mainline churches. They have mainly inherited and adopted the missionary rejection of rituals as an official stance.[118] Through this lens, a lot of negativism is drawn against ATR.

Those who take this position argue that the Bible teaches that behind the genuinely extraordinary supernatural powers of ATR is the work of demonic spirits.[119] Therefore, any reversion to traditional practices is viewed as unbiblical. It is also viewed by many as promoting division along ethnic and tribal lines.

Some missionaries adopted a negative and derogatory view of African culture, equating African religion and culture with Satan, while associating Western culture with God. The African worldview and religion were seen as primitive,[120] inferior and demonic. They saw most of what Africans treasured and valued in their culture as devilish and as demons needing to be cast out.[121] Portuguese missionaries who came to Africa in the fifteenth century were warmly received, and they felt that Africans would give up their culture and beliefs. They viewed them as unstable and temporal. When this did not happen, the Portuguese became hostile and resorted to slave trade.[122]

---

117. Matobo, Makatsa, and Obioha, "Continuity in the Traditional Initiation Practice of Boys and Girls," 15.

118. Pieter François Theron, *African Traditional Cultures and the Church* (Pretoria: ISWEN, 1990). See also B. Afeke and P. Verster, "Christianisation of Ancestral Veneration within African Traditional Religions: An Evaluation," *In Die Skriflig* 38, no. 1 (2004): 50.

119. Richard J. Gehman, *African Traditional Religion in Biblical Perspective* (Wheaton: Oasis International, 2011), 118.

120. Peter Mutuku Mumo, "Western Christian Interpretation of African Traditional Medicine: A Case Study of Akamba Herbal Medicine," *Ilorin Journal of Religious Studies* 8, no. 1 (2018): 45. See also Edward Tylor, *Primitive Culture* (Cambridge: Cambridge University Press, 2010 [1871]).

121. Nwafor, "Integrating African Values," 1; Mumo, "Western Christian Interpretation," 41.

122. Lugira, *African Traditional Religion*, 24.

Due to Western missionary influence and generalizations, Western-influenced African Christianity came to regard all forms of African practices and rituals as "ancestral worship." Consequently, members were forbidden to participate in any of the rituals.[123]

Missionaries viewed African people as "pagans" and "uncivilized" and therefore as legitimate "objects" of missions. Missionaries were the "good Samaritans," bringing the civilizing influence of Christianity to Africa.[124] The word "pagan" is derived from the Latin word *paganus*, which means "village dweller."[125] Africans were thus incorrigible (not able to change) savages or beasts with no sense of religion and no sense of sin.[126]

Missionaries perceived most African rituals and practices as evil and referred to African people as "worshipers of demons" or "worshipers of ancestors."[127] They needed to be given new "Christian" identities. "The so-called Christian names in the form of biblical names like John, Joseph and Timothy were a symbol of new identity."[128] Due to their very strong connection with ancestors, and the performance of a number of rituals related to them, ATR was viewed as polytheistic and secretive. This impression was compounded by the fact that it was not possible for missionaries to know what was going on during the rituals, as they had no access to the ritual meetings.[129]

The intent of the missionaries was to bring Christianity to a continent they believed to have no true religion. They meant to stamp out African religious practices which they saw as superstition and ignorance and as a false religion.[130] Many have held that the ATR God is different from the Christian God. The fact that African people may have worshiped the Supreme Being did not mean that the God whom African people worshiped could simply be identified with

---

123. Wallace G. Mills, "Missionaries, Xhosa Clergy and the Suppression of Traditional Custom," (n.p., 1992), 1.

124. M. S. Clark, "Two Contrasting Models of Missions in South Africa: The Apostolic Faith Mission and the Assemblies of God," *Asian Journal of Pentecostal Studies* 8, no. 1 (2005): 143.

125. J. I. Omoregbe, *Philosophy of Religion* (Lagos: Joja, 1993).

126. S. Maimela, "Salvation in African Traditional Religions," *Missionalia* 13, no. 2 (1985): 65; S. Hayes, "African Initiated Church Theology," in *Initiation into Theology*, eds. S. Maimela and A. König (Pretoria: Van Schaik, 1998), 175.

127. Allan Anderson and G. J. Pillay, "The Segregated Spirit: The Pentecostals," in *Christianity in South Africa: A Political, Social and Cultural History*, eds. Richard Elphick and T. R. H. Davenport (Berkeley: University of California Press, 1997), 76.

128. Anderson and Pillay, "Segregated Spirit," 77.

129. Ntombana, "Trajectories of Christianity and African Ritual Practices," 109.

130. Lugira, *African Traditional Religion*, 24.

the God and Father of Jesus Christ.[131] Rituals contained too much exaggerated emotions, too much shaking, dance and manifestations of spiritism through communion with ancestral spirits.[132]

Muslim View of ATR

Although both Christianity and Islam have had influence on African Traditional Religion, it has taken a shorter time for Islam than for Christianity to penetrate African traditional society. Converts to Islam more readily identify with ATR than converts to Christianity, who sometimes feel like they are living in two worlds. Comparing both Christianity and Islam in relation to their impact on ATR, unlike Christians, many African Muslims live comfortably while still following their old customs and rituals. A good example is the Yoruba of Nigeria who, despite Christian or Muslim influence, still thrive in their practice of traditional customs and rituals. The reason why ATR thrives or co-exists alongside Islam can best be discovered by looking at the nature of Islam and its views of ATR.

Positive Muslim View of ATR

Islam and African Traditional Religion share several common features. One of these is multiple marriages. Actually, this cultural similarity of marrying several wives was one of the reasons why many African men were attracted to Islam.[133] In its interaction with Africans, Islam has always respected the ideals and values that ATR holds, such as the nature of relationships between genders, families, relatives and communal associations, and intolerance of abortion and prostitution.[134] Muslims view ATR as very hospitable and social, as accommodating to strangers and everyone in such events as funerals. Kings and chiefs received Muslims warmly, as exemplified in Kabaka Mutesa of Uganda.

---

131. K. Ferdinando, "Christian Identity in the African Context: Reflections on Kwame Bediako's Theology of Identity," *Journal of the Evangelical Theological Society* 50, no. 1 (2007): 127.

132. Agatha Onwuekwe Ijeoma, "The Socio-Cultural Implications of African Music and Dance" (PhD diss., Nnamdi Azikwe University Awka, n.d.), 175.

133. Lugira, *African Traditional Religion*, 22.

134. *Pew Forum on Religion and Public Life* (Washington: Pew Research Center, 2009), 53.

Negative Muslim View of ATR

Islam is ideally amenable with most of the African traditional customs. There is therefore not much opposition against its members who still revert to or practice some of the traditional rituals. However, there is always a very serious denial, and sometimes a disassociation from, fellow Muslims who are perceived or believed to be engaged in sorcery, witchcraft, evil eye, evil tongue and the domestication of *jinn* (spirits). These practices are mostly associated with popular or folk Muslims as opposed to orthodox or official Islam. There is also a current of strong rejection of ATR in Islam. The argument is that Islam has introduced the knowledge of a true God to a people who once had no religion. In the case of some burial rituals still practiced, their roots in ATR are often denied.

Reflections by the Church on Socio-Cultural and Religious Issues

The analyses in the previous sections have clearly shown that there are still some elements of African traditions in the beliefs and practices of many Christians and Muslims in different parts of Africa. Reverting to old traditional rituals and customs by Christians is certainly an issue that needs to be addressed so as to allow the church to grow holistically. By so doing, the church would simply be carrying out its mandate, as Robinson puts it, "The church continuously enters phases to engage creatively in its mission to change the world. Therefore, its relationship with the existing culture needs to be renewed."[135] Looking at ways to renew the church's relationship with the existing cultures is central. This section therefore proposes some approaches and ways that the church needs to engage so as to discern, distinguish, or draw a line between what is religious, social and cultural in the beliefs and practices of its people. The church should seek ways to address issues and challenges that Christians are grappling with, as Dames proposes, "Suffice to say that the church needs to find expressions of the Christian faith within both traditional and new cultural contexts. Theology is shaped by contextual factors such as people's socio-political, economic and cultural experiences."[136]

Newbigin underlines the value that Christian religion has in dealing with different cultures of the world: "Christian religion [is] fundamental to any

---

135. Martin Robinson, *Planting Mission-Shaped Churches Today* (Oxford: Monarch, 2006), 46.

136. Dames, "Knowing, Believing, Living in Africa," 2.

culture, a set of beliefs, experiences and practices that seek to grasp and express the ultimate nature of things, that which gives shape and meaning to life, that which claims final loyalty."[137]

While there is an admission of the missing gaps in ATR that some Christians still revert to, confronting and engaging them should be aimed at providing full loyalty and total allegiance to the lordship and authority of Jesus Christ in the cultural context of the people. Such relevance is what Mbiti proposes. The African should be free to express the Christian gospel, which remains basically universal and the same for all times, within the African language and cultural context that is the "medium of receiving, diffusing, tuning in and relaying the gospel."[138] Core to the spread of the gospel is the idea of cultivating a healthy relationship: In order to evangelize Africa, we must establish a relationship with the living revelation where God begins to speak through an apostle of a base community, using an African style to speak to Africans.[139]

Dealing with ATR in the African Church

Paul G. Hiebert in his book *Anthropological Insights for Missionaries* lays some fundamental guidelines on how the church and missionary can deal with the traditions that many Christians sometimes easily revert to, or areas where they find themselves unable to provide a clear distinction in light of their new-found Christian faith. The questions and the responses Hiebert poses are critical and insightful and are the bases upon which a theoretical framework on how to deal with ATR in the church has been developed. In dealing with traditions, Hiebert asks, "How should Christians respond to all this [rituals – religious fairs with markets and sideshows, drama or music performances and religious processions; public feasts and celebrations; sports events; and pilgrimages to distant shrines]?" How should new converts relate to their cultural past – to the food, dress, medicines, songs, dances, myths, rituals, and all the other things that were so much a part of their lives before they heard the gospel? What responsibility do missionaries have to young churches regarding all this? How far can the gospel be adapted to fit into a culture without losing its essential message? And who should make the decisions about the

---

137. Newbigin, *Foolishness to the Greeks*, 3.

138. John S. Mbiti, "Christianity and African Culture," *Journal of Theology for Southern Africa* 20 (1977): 27.

139. Jean-Marc Ela, *My Faith as an African* (London: Geoffrey Chapman, 1988), 45.

old culture?[140] Hiebert identifies the three approaches below that have been adopted in dealing with traditions.[141]

Denial of the Old and Rejection of Contextualization

Drums, songs, dramas, dances, body decorations, certain types of dress and food, marriage customs and funeral rites are rejected as "pagan" customs, hence unacceptable for Christians. The rejection is based on a form of **ethnocentrism** (religionism or monoculturism) which leads to the view that all other religions, denominations, cultures, etc., are bad.

However, it is not possible to draw a line in traditional cultures between religious and non-religious practices. First, problems with this approach include the fact that the rejection leaves a cultural vacuum that needs to be filled, and too often this is done by importing the customs of the missionary. This causes Christianity to be seen as a foreign religion and Christian converts as aliens in their own land. Second, old cultural ways of life merely go underground, so that you can have a formal wedding in the church, but then you go to the village for the traditional celebrations. The same applies in the negotiation between herbal and scientific medicine and in burial rituals. Finally, this approach turns missionaries and church leaders into a sort of police, which effectively prevents converts from growing by denying them the right to make their own decisions. A church only grows spiritually if its members learn to apply the teachings of the gospel to their own lives.

Acceptance of the Old and Uncritical or Naïve Contextualization

A second approach consists in accepting existing customs uncritically into the church, with very minimal or almost no changes at all. This can be thought of as "Gamaliel's approach," as we read in Acts 5:38–39: "if their purpose or activity is of human origin, it will fail. But if it is from God, you will not be able to stop these men." Old ways are seen as basically good, and few – if any – changes are seen as necessary when people become Christian. There is deep respect for humans and cultures and a recognition of the high value that people place on their cultural heritage. There is also a recognition that the "foreignness" of the gospel has been one of the major barriers to its acceptance in many parts of the world.

Some of the weaknesses with this approach are, first, that it overlooks the fact that there exist corporate and cultural sins as well as personal

---

140. Hiebert, *Anthropological Insights*, 183.
141. Hiebert, 184–190.

transgressions. Contextualization must lead to the communication of the gospel in ways that people understand, but it should also challenge them individually and corporately to turn from their evil ways. Second, it opens the door to syncretism of all kinds. If Christians continue with beliefs and practices that stand in opposition to the gospel, these in time will mix with their new-found faith and produce various forms of neopaganism. Change is never immediate, but Christians must grow in their Christian lives, and this demands that they continually test their actions and beliefs against the norms of the scriptures.

Dealing with the Old and Critical Contextualization
In this third approach, old beliefs and customs are neither rejected nor accepted without examination. We study them with regard to the meanings and places they have within their cultural settings and then evaluate them in light of biblical norms – for example weddings, birth rites and funeral rituals. Local church leaders and missionaries must lead the congregation in uncritically gathering and analyzing the traditional customs associated with the question at hand, such as funeral rituals. People should analyze their traditional rites – first describing each song, dance, recitation and rite that makes up the ceremony, and then discuss their meaning and function within the overall ritual. The purpose here is to understand the old ways rather than to evaluate them. The congregation should then evaluate critically their own past customs in light of their new biblical understandings, and they must make a decision regarding their use. In the end, if people themselves enforce decisions arrived at corporately, it is unlikely that the customs they reject will go underground.

Church leaders need to lead Bible studies related to the question under consideration. For example, a leader can use the occasion of a wedding or funeral to teach the Christian beliefs about marriage or death. There is a need for exegesis of biblical truth. It is important, however, that the congregation be actively involved in the study and interpretation of scripture so that they will grow in their own abilities to discern truth.

The pastor or missionary should help the congregation arrange the practices they have chosen into a new ritual that expresses the Christian meaning of the event. Such a ritual will be Christian, for it explicitly seeks to express biblical teachings. It will also be indigenous, for the congregation has created it, using forms the people understand within their own culture.

Conclusion

The foregone discussion has clearly demonstrated that the three religions of African traditions, Christianity and Islam are quite active and that they interact with each other extensively. The church should apply its missional and kerygmatic approach in dealing with ATR and Islam. Ignoring or failing to address adequately the real issues that affect ordinary people in Africa, such as the problems of death, sickness and other natural catastrophes, will only increase fear and uncertainty among people.

9.5 Discerning Spiritual Realities in Islamic Contexts: Missional Reflections of a Boring Charismatic

Warrick Farah

"Islam is not a religious system. It is an actual spiritual being that holds people in bondage. Pray with me to break the spirit of Islam!" exclaimed the conference speaker to begin a time of corporate prayer. The clear implication of his statement is that Muslims everywhere are imprisoned by the same malevolent force and all suffer the identical demonic oppression. Yet are there other ways to think of the spiritual conflict in ministry to Muslims? Merely asking such a mitigating question often leads to accusations of "minimizing truth" and failing to engage the "dark side of Islam." So, how do we discern the spiritual realities in Islamic contexts?

Since 9/11, Islam has frequently been denounced by some evangelicals as demonic and inherently violent.[142] Within the evangelical community, the opening quotation is neither an isolated incident nor even a particular rarity. Especially in the American context, demonization of Islam spans three centuries and finds deep roots in American history.[143] This kind of spiritualizing of a religion's adherents is often absent when considering Buddhists, Hindus or Mormons.[144] There are historical and political reasons that explain these tendencies, but my purpose here is not to explore these.

---

142. Daniel W. Brown, "Clash of Cultures or Clash of Theologies? A Critique of Some Contemporary Evangelical Responses to Islam," *Cultural Encounters* 1, no. 1 (2004): 69–84.

143. Thomas Kidd, *American Christians and Islam: Evangelical Culture and Muslims from the Colonial Period to the Age of Terrorism* (Princeton: Princeton University Press, 2009).

144. Harold Netland, "On Worshiping the Same God: What Exactly Is the Question?," *Missiology* 45, no. 4 (2017): 442.

Evangelicals who serve within a Muslim context frequently report confrontations with the occult and demonic oppression. Subsequently, there are many extraordinary stories of healing and miraculous divine intervention. Theological hermeneutics and denominational traditions play a large role in shaping practical responses to spiritual conflict, but again, a discussion of these issues goes beyond the scope of this contribution. It is all too easy to get caught in the philosophical/theological crossfire: colleagues of mine who minister in the "signs and wonders" camp claim I am not charismatic enough, while coworkers on the other side of the spectrum accuse me of being too supernaturally oriented. In finding my own place in these issues, I classify my personal theological stance on spiritual gifts and supernatural conflict in mission as that of a "boring charismatic." I do believe in all the supernatural gifts (although I'm still waiting for mine!), but I'm adverse to the sensationalism that often follows contemporary charismatic movements.

So rather than discuss the practical implications of supernatural ministry among Muslims, my emphasis here is more fundamental and pertains to our biblical theology of Islam. I will focus on *the nature* of the spiritual conflict in Islamic contexts. Does the spiritual conflict stem from Islam itself – as an evil spiritual covenant or as an actual demonic entity masquerading as a religion? In what ways are the evil, supernatural powers in Islamic contexts essentially different when compared with other religious traditions? Are military metaphors appropriate for conceptualizing our ministry to Muslims? What exactly are the spiritual realities we face in the Christian-Muslim encounter?

In this contribution, I hope to demonstrate how a biblically grounded approach to spiritual conflict (and to the "religious other") can make us more discerning and, in turn, fruitful in our missiological encounters with Muslims.

Spiritual Profiling?

Several years ago, I performed an informal ethnography on one of my Arabic teachers, a Muslim woman living in Beirut, Lebanon. She was very proud of her Sunni Muslim identity, but took pains whenever possible to distance herself from Sunni Arab Muslims of the Arabian Gulf. She claimed she had never read the Qur'an, which was quite strange considering her bachelor's degree in Arabic. In fact, when I quoted a few verses from the Qur'an in Arabic, her blank stare was due more to the unfamiliarity of the words than to my pronunciation. She was married, but she did not consider premarital sex or cohabitation before marriage as sinful. Neither did she think homosexual behavior was un-Islamic. To her, Muhammad was a role model of peace, equality and justice. Fasting during the month of Ramadan was very important to her as a pious act for every Muslim, and she adamantly believed that drinking alcohol was always wrong no matter the person or the occasion. She claimed she had never performed *ṣalāt*-style prayers in her life; instead, she loved to worship God through music.

With such an ambiguous connection to Islam, what does it mean that she is a Muslim? Does she participate in a Muslim worldview? Does understanding "Islam" help us know what is happening spiritually in her life? These inquiries beg another question: Can we view Muslims through the "Islam lens" and assess the spiritual realities they face without some inherent polarization of our own views? On one side, through the "rose-colored lens," Islam is a natural religion of peace, and Muslims are honest seekers of the truth who simply need Jesus. On the other side of the spectrum, through the "gray" lens, Islam stems from a demonic source, and all Muslims are, consequently, victims of a satanic scheme aimed squarely at Christianity. Interestingly, both approaches suffer the same fallacy; they paint all Muslims in unilaterally broad strokes by using "Islam" to categorize people spiritually.

One of the consequences of looking at Muslims through a totalizing lens of Islam, either rose-colored or gray, is the resulting practice of "spiritual profiling," or "spiritual stereotyping." On the one hand, if we gloss over spiritual realities in ministry to Muslims, then our ministry will be naïve and ineffective. One the other hand, if we assume that Muslims all struggle under the same "curse of Islam,"[145] then we can fail to recognize God's sovereignty (Acts 17:26) and the positive ways God is working in those contexts. In both cases, spiritual stereotyping prejudices Christian witness and incapacitates Christians for ministry because they already presume an understanding of every Muslim's spiritual condition. Especially at the earliest stages of the missional encounter, we are tempted to presuppose the stereotype characteristics most quickly.[146] Spiritual profiling effectively removes the need to listen and learn, which is a prerequisite for relevant disciple-making.

Within our own cultures, we might intuitively be more discerning of the unique characteristics of each person and his or her story, but when we engage

---

145. A variation on this idea are those who teach that ministers must "bind the strong man" of Islam, e.g. Mark 3:27. See Reza Safa, *Inside Islam: Exposing and Reaching the World of Islam* (Orlando: Creation House, 1996), 92.

146. John F. Dovidio, Miles Hewstone, Peter Glick, and Victoria M. Esses, "Prejudice, Stereotyping and Discrimination: Theoretical and Empirical Overview," in *The SAGE Handbook of Prejudice, Stereotyping and Discrimination*, eds. John F. Dovidio, Miles Hewstone, Peter Glick, and Victoria M. Esses (London: SAGE, 2018), 7.

other cultures – and particularly Islamic ones – the temptation to stereotype lures us, and we easily fall prey. My approach to witness with my Arabic teacher would have been skewed if I had assumed she believed and practiced what I think Islam teaches. Even provided that a faithful biblical theology explains the fallen nature of humanity and our need for redemption solely found in Christ, we need to be careful that our assumptions of the religious "other" do not deconstruct their dignity as fellow image bearers or lead us to presume we already know the spiritual, mental, emotional, cultural and physical challenges with which they wrestle. To holistically discern spiritual realities properly, we must become aware of this temptation.

Ordinary Muslim Piety

Most people are aware of the five pillars of Islam: the *shahāda*, daily *ṣalāt* prayers, fasting during Ramadan, almsgiving to the poor and the pilgrimage to Mecca. Performance of the five pillars, along with belief in the oneness of God and Muhammad as the final and greatest prophet, usually describes what people refer to as "traditional" or "orthodox" Islam. Yet around the world, many Muslims participate in practices more closely aligned with animism or the occult. These ordinary Muslims follow what is sometimes called "folk Islam," in contrast supposedly to the more "orthodox" form. This distinction is questionable, however, and imposes an impediment to solid, ethnographic research on Muslims because it assumes a normative Islam and relegates such "folk" practices to the margins of Islam.

Muslims engage in many different religious practices, many of which apparently involve the demonic. These customs were not simply absorbed into an otherwise form of pure, original Islam that was free from occult practices. Visiting the shrines of saints, the evil eye, curses, divination, qur'anic healing, etc., are all examples of Muslim practices even in places like Saudi Arabia. For instance, the Kaʿba, the center of the most important mosque in Mecca, features the "Black Stone," an object of veneration for many Muslims which can be considered an animistic power symbol of divine blessing. Additionally, the final two sūras of the Qur'an are claimed to have originated when a curse was put on Muhammad, and these two sūras are still used today to counteract curses.[147] These are just a couple examples of occult practices found in Islamic contexts.

Furthermore, *jinn*[148] are mentioned frequently in the Qur'an and Hadith. The way *jinn* are described in these texts portrays a belief in animism which is a common worldview element of Islamic contexts. Many Muslims operate with a mindset that has been called "*jinn* causality." They attribute the events in their lives, good or bad, to the activity of *jinn*. Anything from demon oppression to good fortune, sickness, or even marriage can point to *jinn* as the cause. "The fear of *jinn*, or the desire to subdue and use their services, are strong motivating forces in the practices of many ordinary Muslims."[149]

Sufism represents another important aspect of Islam for the purposes of our discussion. Scholars will, at times, present Sufism as a deviant form of Islam, and terms such as "Islamic mysticism" imply a negative value judgment against some sort of supposed, non-mystical Islam. Sufism has been variously defined and applied throughout history; thus, it is difficult to discern which Muslims have been Sufis. "On the practical level, Sufism explains how Muslims can strengthen their understanding and observance of Islam in order to find God's presence in themselves and the world."[150] For example, the *dhikr* ritual is common to many Sufis and involves chanting the names of God (often to the rhythm of drums) for long periods of time to achieve a trance-like state and thus unity with the divine. The point of Sufism lies in a personal experience of oneness with the Divine Reality.

Occult practices, *jinn* causality and Sufism are all common features of the spiritual realities in Islamic contexts. In mission, the conflict is indeed intense at times, and we do well to reject the rose-colored lens when looking at Islam. Historically speaking, Muslims have perhaps been more resistant to Christian witness than to that of any other religion. So then, from where does this spiritual resistance rise?

---

147. Warren Larson, "Ordinary Muslims in Pakistan and the Gospel," in *Margins of Islam: Ministry in Diverse Muslim Contexts*, ed. Gene Daniels and Warrick Farah (Littleton: William Carey, 2018), 84–85.

148. In addition to angels and demons, *jinn* are another category of supernatural beings in Islam.

149. Bill Musk, *The Unseen Face of Islam: Sharing the Gospel with Ordinary Muslims at Street Level*, 2nd ed. (London: Monarch, 2003), 33.

150. John O. Voll and Kazuo Ohtsuka, "Sufism," in *The Oxford Encyclopedia of the Islamic World*, Oxford Islamic Studies Online, ed. John L. Esposito (Oxford: Oxford University Press, 2009), http://www.oxfordislamicstudies.com/print/opr/t236/e0759.

Sources of Spiritual Conflict in Islamic Contexts

Does the Bible teach that non-Christian religions have a demonic source? Nations or peoples not part of the covenant people of God in the Bible are variously labeled: "unbelievers," "evildoers," "the wicked," "idolaters" and even "goats" (as opposed to "sheep"). Biblical scholar Chris Wright summarizes the Bible's teaching about the spiritual foundations of the religious other:

> In view of what we have noted about God's universal involvement with man, as his image, it seems to me an unbiblical exaggeration to assign all non-Christian religious faith and life to the work of the devil. Nevertheless, it is equally unbiblical to overlook the realm of the satanic and the demonic in human religions – often most subtly at its strongest in what appears as "the best" in them.[151]

Herein we see the biblical tension about the spiritual realities in any religious context. Wright's theological summary contradicts both of the two polar opposites from our previous discussion, that Islam is spiritually either a neutral religion of peace (a rose-colored lens) or an evil, satanic bondage (a gray lens). Whatever we believe about the origins of Islam, the socio-religious cultural milieu that Muslims occupy is not just a monolithic spiritual force. Wright continues, "At the very least it is clear that we cannot adopt simplistic categorizations, such as the view that all non-Christian religion is entirely demonic or that it is all purely cultural. The Bible's own subtle analysis of 'other gods' makes such binary opposites completely unsatisfactory."[152] It seems wise, therefore, to avoid spiritualizing generalizations when talking about Islam.

But a deeper problem of assuming a demonic source for Islam lies in the assumption's tendency to minimize personal responsibility for sin.[153] The Bible doesn't portray people as passive sufferers, but instead as active participants in the idolatrous influences surrounding them. A proper understanding of sin shows this clearly; we are victims but also perpetrators. Muslims shape and use Islam for various reasons and to meet various needs in various contexts. If there were no Muslims, there would be no Islam.

---

151. Christopher J. H. Wright, "The Christian and Other Religions: The Biblical Evidence," *Themelios* 9, no. 2 (1984): 5.

152. Christopher J. H. Wright, *The Mission of God: Unlocking the Bible's Grand Narrative* (Downers Grove: IVP Academic, 2006): Kindle 2010.

153. Such assumptions also read too much into the traditional Muslim account of the emergence of Islam. See Warrick Farah, "Outlining a Biblical Theology of Islam: Practical Implications for Disciple Makers and Church Planting," *Evangelical Missions Quarterly* 55, no. 1 (2019): 13–16.

Granted, there are false teachings and demonic strongholds in Islamic contexts, but we should not assume Muslims all suffer the same type of spiritual oppression. Reflecting on Romans 1:18 onward, missionary-theologian J. H. Bavinck encourages us to avoid spiritual stereotyping: "The history of religion, as well as missionary experience, teaches us that it makes no sense to paint all pagans with the same brush. We will have to observe with great care what has happened in every individual life."[154]

People are very different, and sin is very diverse. So are the idols we fashion for ourselves. Applied to the discussion at hand, we could say that an accurate understanding of Islamic diversity around the world reveals that all Muslims are not the same culturally, they are not the same religiously, and they are not the same spiritually. What is needed is a nuanced and sufficient response to the *varieties* of spiritual oppression among the *varieties* of Muslims.

How then can we be biblically balanced when trying to discern spiritual realities in different contexts? The Bible teaches that there are three forms of evil influences exerting power over the lives of people to lead them into sin and away from God. These three enemies are described in Ephesians 2:1–3 as the world, the flesh and the devil. According to Clinton Arnold, "In some passages of the Bible, one of these sources of evil influences might be discussed more than the other two, but in general, the Bible maintains a balance among these three evil influences."[155] Imbalance occurs whenever we either ignore or exaggerate the devil's influence. So, where does Islam fit into the biblical teaching on the nature of spiritual realities? Is it a false hope fashioned by the world, a personal sin made in the human heart, which is a "factory of idols," or is it a realm of demonic activity? Is it some combination of the three? Even better, *are these even the right questions to ask*?

In light of our preceding conversation, it seems best to focus *not* on Islam itself, but on the ways Muslims shape and use Islam. All contexts have an element of the "religious" that affects people spiritually. Though possibly simplistic, we will employ a biblical term as a means by which to explain the trio of evil influences tormenting people – the term "idolatry" – and we will include those individuals of ordinary Islamic piety. What idols do Muslims have? In light of the preceding section on unique features of ordinary Muslim piety, here is a list of potential idols and spiritual realities in Islamic contexts:

---

154. J. H. Bavinck, *The J. H. Bavinck Reader* (Grand Rapids: Eerdmans, 2013), 286.

155. Clinton E. Arnold, *3 Crucial Questions about Spiritual Warfare* (Grand Rapids: Baker, 1997), 32.

1. Prophetolatry[156]
2. Loyalty to a religious sect for salvation
3. Nationalism
4. Pride, personal/family/tribal reputation
5. Intercession of saints, mediators
6. Materialism, greed
7. Merit-seeking through good works to appease God
8. Folk religious practices, forms of magic
9. Strict, legalistic adherence to ritual and tradition
10. False teaching/doctrine and deceiving spirits
11. Grudges, bitterness, deception, jealously, rivalry, slander, etc.

This list ties together our previous discussion about ordinary Muslim piety and a balanced perspective on the evil influences assailing humanity. Looking at this list, it should not surprise us that Christians sometimes participate in similar idolatries. Spiritual battles continue to rage, conflicts designed to separate us from the beauty and sufficiency of Jesus Christ, our Lord and Savior. The point is this: it is better to engage Muslims not through the lens of Islam, but as the religious other who is as depraved as we once were without the gospel. To engage Islam is vague, but to focus on the idolatry issues I have outlined here helps us to be more specific when ministering to Muslims. Far from downplaying the demonic strongholds in Islamic contexts, this focus enables us to deliver a nuanced and specific missional response designed to set many Muslims free from whatever may turn out to be the unique footholds of demonic presence and activity in their lives.

Idolatrous Loyalty and Spiritual Oppression

At the heart of spiritual oppression towers the issue of loyalty or allegiance. Demonic oppression often occurs, both for followers of Jesus and for those who are not, at the place where people have a spiritual allegiance to something other than Christ. The "dual causation" principle of spiritual oppression

---

156. Salvation for many Muslims is a "prophetological concept," meaning "the logic of salvation has everything to do with one's relation to the Prophet Muhammad" (Perry Pennington, "From Prophethood to the Gospel: Talking to Folk Muslims about Jesus," *IJFM* 31, no. 4 [2014]: 198).

teaches that problems are caused both by human beings and by demons. By way of analogy, the rats (demons) come to places overflowing with garbage (sin and idolatry). The trash can be any one of the areas mentioned in the above section, occupying the cognitive, affective and behavioral dimensions of human life and experience. "When a person is carrying such garbage, it gives demons entrance, allows them to stay and gives them power."[157]

Ultimately, our allegiance issues pertain to worship. In 2 Corinthians 6:14–17, Paul exhorts the new believers in Corinth to disassociate from their previous places of worship, so they can find peace in Jesus and live in righteousness:

> Do not be yoked together with unbelievers. For what do righteousness and wickedness have in common? Or what fellowship can light have with darkness? What harmony is there between Christ and Belial? Or what does a believer have in common with an unbeliever? What agreement is there between the temple of God and idols? For we are the temple of the living God. . . . Therefore, "Come out from them and be separate, says the Lord."

The assumptions underlying this command are the spiritual realities involved in non-christocentric worship. In Corinth, the people of God were admonished to avoid the worship rituals of communities outside of the new covenant. For Paul, this was an issue of faith allegiance. He recognized the spiritual realities explicitly involved in the worship rituals of those who are not redeemed. Apparently, some in Corinth retained a worshipful connection with their context. But Paul warns decisively against this, "Come out from them and be separate!"[158]

The key difference between the pagans in Corinth and Muslims is, obviously, Islam's foundation in monotheism. Some might argue that the mosque is a place of monotheistic worship and is therefore not pagan, so these verses do not apply to Muslims. However, as we have seen, there are indeed many animistic or occultic worship practices in Muslim contexts. Yet the deeper issue is not monotheism versus polytheism, but allegiance/non-allegiance to the biblical Jesus. To argue that Muslims worship a different deity would

---

157. Charles H. Kraft, *Issues in Contextualization* (Pasadena: William Carey, 2016), Kindle 3893.

158. At the least, this would serve as a strong discouragement for believers from Muslim backgrounds to continue worshiping at the mosque. Much Islamic preaching, including various Islamic ideologies around the world, is filled with content that is noxious to the gospel. To be fair, this is true in every context.

not resolve the problem. Paul points to Jesus because no one redemptively approaches God without Christ. To worship with others in contexts *sans* Jesus is an opening for adverse spiritual realities. Christ is the ultimate measurement for discerning spiritual realities in Islamic contexts. Being under the influence of evil spiritual forces is a reality for all people, but it is especially prevalent when the lordship of Jesus is displaced or absent in a person because of idolatrous loyalty to another entity.

Beyond Military Metaphors for Mission

As I was writing this contribution, missiologist Evelyne Reisacher passed away after a long battle with cancer. Evelyne is perhaps best known for her book, *Joyful Witness in the Muslim World: Sharing the Gospel in Everyday Encounters*.[159] She was a colleague who helped me with my dissertation and also contributed a wonderful chapter entitled, "Who Represents Islam?" to a book I coedited.[160] In her work, Evelyne ties together the theology of joy with the motivation for mission.[161] She presents "joy" as an appropriate metaphor for the activity of the church in the world. "Joy in ministry does not result from names checked off on a conversion list, or winning the battle over souls between Muslims and Christians, but from sharing the joy that flows from God."[162]

At the news of her death, I wondered, *What would Evelyne think about my approach to spiritual realities in Islamic contexts?* Muslim ministry has often been discussed in the Christian-Muslim encounter in themes of warfare, conquest and suffering. But these are not the best metaphors for mission – especially in Islamic contexts. When Muslims hear the word "mission," they have the same emotional reaction as we do when we hear the word *jihad*.[163] I agree that a spiritual battle is always raging around us; it is clear our battle

---

159. Evelyne Reisacher, *Joyful Witness in the Muslim World: Sharing the Gospel in Everyday Encounters* (Grand Rapids: Baker Academic, 2016).

160. Evelyne Reisacher, "Who Represents Islam?" in *Margins of Islam: Ministry in Diverse Muslim Contexts*, eds. Gene Daniels and Warrick Farah (Littleton: William Carey Publishing, 2018).

161. The book by Michael W. Stroope, *Transcending Mission: The Eclipse of a Modern Tradition* (Downers Grove: IVP, 2017), argues that, in part because of its connection with colonialism, the modern metaphor of "mission" should be replaced with "pilgrim witness." While the issue is much deeper than semantics, we acknowledge that metaphors for "mission" in any language will always be imperfect.

162. Reisacher, *Joyful Witness*, 16.

163. This phrase did not originate with me, but I cannot recall or locate the exact attribution.

is not against "flesh and blood." But many still conceptualize ministry as a "battle" or a "war" waged by the church for the hearts and minds of Muslims.

In contrast to how evangelicals have employed metaphors for mission, it must be noted that the New Testament never uses military metaphors to describe the task of evangelism.[164] In a world of globalization, pluralism and terrorism, we would do well to avoid this metaphor when speaking of our mission to Muslims. "It is clear that in such a world, military metaphors for mission bring more baggage than the concept can bear. They do communicate, but they communicate the wrong things."[165]

The book *Christianity Encountering World Religions* proposes a better metaphor for mission – a gift, which the authors label *giftive* mission. "A metaphor cluster centered around gift giving has many advantages in a world filled with suspicion and mistrust of people bearing religious messages."[166] Taken together, "joy," "gift" and perhaps adding "love" present better metaphors that speak much more poignantly than those of warfare, *especially* in ministry to Muslims today. Twenty years ago, I used to teach that we must wage war against Islam because it is a destructive force intent on taking over the world. As a result, my relationships with Muslims were usually tense. Upon further reflection, I spent time only with Muslims who enjoyed debate and apologetics. I was viewing Muslims through the gray lens, and I had no framework for discernment, not to mention any hint of having fun with Muslims or enjoying them as people!

I do not argue against any type of spiritual warfare activity in our ministry to Muslims or suggest we should approach Islam with the rose-colored lens; we are, indeed, in the midst of a spiritual battle. The issue at hand refers to how we conceptualize the conflict. If our focus is faulty, our efforts may have unintended and disastrous consequences. For example, if we apply the gray lens, then we may regard the context of a Muslim background believer to such a negative extent that the only solution is to extract the new believer from their "Islamic" setting. Such practice often serves to stunt the growth of the church in that context as well as damage the emotional health of the new believer who becomes alienated from his or her social network.

When it is all said and done, we must minister with the humble confidence that Jesus is the Victor. We can trust in his sovereign rule initiated by his life,

---

164. Rick Love, *Glocal: Following Jesus in the 21st Century* (Eugene: Cascade, 2017), 34.
165. Terry Muck and Frances S. Adeney, *Christianity Encountering World Religions: The Practice of Mission in the Twenty-First Century* (Grand Rapids: Baker Academic, 2009), 312.
166. Muck and Adeney, *Christianity Encountering*, 328.

death and resurrection. We can learn to relate to Muslims not as the enemy or in a spirit of competition, but in joy, generosity and love. The greatest spiritual reality in every context is the Holy Spirit, the Comforter who simultaneously convicts people of sin and draws them to faith. The Bible teaches that every context has some providential testimony to God (Acts 14:16–17). These truths should fill us with hope and sober excitement in our mission.

Summary

I identified myself as a "boring charismatic" in this contribution for two main reasons. First, my charismatic emphasis denies the rose-colored lens and affirms the reality of oppressive supernatural conflict among Muslims wherein special gifts and persons are sometimes required to deal with these realities. Second, I am "boring" because I avoid the gray lens and the sensationalistic claims that Islam is either some extreme case or a monolithic, evil conspiracy against Christianity.

Understanding the various spiritual realities in Islamic contexts is an exercise in biblical discernment. We seek to relate to Muslims not under the triumphal metaphor of war and empire, but as people who are very similar to who we once were, including with many of the same idolatry and spiritual issues.[167] We must also become sensitive to the temptation of spiritually stereotyping all Muslims or of imagining the activity of Satan at greater or lesser degrees in Islamic contexts compared to all others.

Worship of God outside of Christ and an ultimate faith allegiance to anything other than Jesus opens everyone to spiritual oppression which is especially devastating for those who have not been given the Holy Spirit. In light of this, we proclaim the highest and only hope for Muslims: Jesus! Through faith in him alone we find the freedom we so desperately need. May God grant us the grace, wisdom and perseverance to minister with unwavering trust as we joyfully proclaim the liberating gift of the powerful gospel: "If the Son sets you free, you will be free indeed" (John 8:36).

---

167. While every context deeply impacted by the gospel should be transforming through the presence of the Holy Spirit, we recognize that this is an ongoing process requiring continuous reformation.

Questions for Discussion

1. Do we see Muslims as similar to the crowds that flocked to Jesus seeking his power yet not truly comprehending his identity? If so, do we simply pray for the Spirit to open their eyes, minds and hearts to the fullness of Christ? How might we cooperate with the Spirit in this?

2. What do we observe in our contexts of the interaction among different religions? How are they influencing each other? How is the uniqueness and centrality of Christ being expressed amidst such interactions? What other aspects of the kerygmatic approach are relevant?

3. What lens are we using when we look at Islam and Muslims? How aware are we of them? What additional lenses should we be seeking that keep us between demonization and idealization?

Conclusion

Poetry by Yasser (translated by Martin Accad)
We Shall Leave Our Gardens and Become a Field

Were it not for the pruning of a branch from its trunk
    Fields would not proliferate in our world
Our garden would bear no fruit
    And the universe would have turned yellow and shriveled
Jesus chose men for his gospel
    Great ones whose patience is remarkable
Disciples among whom we are now counted
    Though we face swords we do not bend
He told the parable of the mustard seed
    In whose shade the swallow finds protection
It stretches to heaven and becomes a home
    That embraces in its heart the wounded soul
Today we have become the Savior's men
    Our Lord's brothers to whom we declare
We will leave our branch and become a field
    And beautiful flowers will fill our gardens

سَنَتْرُك روضَنا ونَصيرُ حَقلاً
ولولا فَصْلُ غصنٍ عن حِماهُ   لما زادت بِدُنْيانا الحقولُ
لما صارت لِروضتنا ثِمارٌ   وصار الكونُ مصفرٌ هزيلُ
يسوعُ اختارَ للبشرى رجالاً   كبارٌ كان صبرهُم جميلُ
تلاميذٌ ونحنُ اليومَ منهم   تحاربنا السيوفُ فلا نميلُ
بحبةِ خردلٍ أعطى مثالاً   تُظلُ بفيئها ضُعفَ السنونو
فَتكبرُ للمدى وتصير بيتًا   فيحضنُ قلبها قلبًا عليلُ
ونحنُ اليومَ للفادي رجالٌ   مِنَ الأخوانِ للربِ نقولُ
سنترك غصننا ونصيرُ حقلاً   وتملئ روضَنا أحلى الزهورُ

Closing Reflections and Practical Applications: A Conversation among Some Contributors

The following conversation occurred as part of the process of concluding the 2019 consultation by formulating a theology of Islam. It was facilitated by Martin Accad and involved some of the contributors, namely George Bristow, Daniel (Dan) Brown, Warrick Farah, Ida Glaser, Alexander (Alex) Massad and Ashoor Yousif. It began with reflections on the major themes and moved on to discuss some critical questions.

Martin: Let's look at our topics in the order that we considered them. So, what are your reflections on the origins of Islam?

George: The Abraham link is significant. If the Qur'an is the crucial source for Islam's origin, then Abraham is linked to both Muhammad and the **Kaʿba** in Mecca. Abraham is also linked to the founding of the temple on Mount Moriah in Jerusalem. So there is direct linkage to centers of worship. Abraham is linked to Ishmael. So he is linked to nations both within and outside the covenants described in what Christians call the Old Testament.

Ida: Keep in mind the people, power and land triangle *(see section 8.6)*, which is my key biblical lens for viewing power structures. The early Christian response to Islam was to see the power dimension. The linkage of religion and political power is a common thread throughout human history.

Martin: What are your reflections on the Qur'an and Muhammad in light of what is emerging from global studies?

Dan: Islamic studies has typically been approached through either of two angles, which we often move between: classical academic study and the revisionist approach, including within Western academia. I believe we must constantly consider both. Within Western Islamic studies, two pictures emerge. First, the traditional Muslim understanding of the Qur'an's origins is confirmed with caveats; but second, serious doubt has emerged on the traditional history of Muhammad.

Ashoor: I would add the qualification that early sources have biases. So they are useful, but we need to be careful in assessing the motivations and objectives of those authors.

Martin: Moving on, what are your reflections on areas of ministry that you see emerging as we develop a more intentional theological study of Islam?

Warrick: The revisionist accounts of Islamic origins and the life of Muhammad are not just a binary, black or white choice. An important consideration for missiology is the trauma of disciples of Jesus from Muslim backgrounds which may well be exacerbated by simplistic, binary choices. We need to create more scope for our brothers and sisters from Muslim backgrounds to engage constructively with their family and the communities that they grew up within. We need kinder and gentler approaches, and we must help them find narratives to explain what has happened, is happening, and will happen to them.

Alex: I believe that both congregations, meaning a group of people with assorted relationships and churches as institutions, need to pursue humble, kerygmatic and curious programs. We need to engage fully and honestly, hoping for dynamic change in Muslims and in ourselves. We must act in love, allowing everyone to fully represent themselves, which might mean that we are not setting the agenda.

Martin: Let us move from reflections to some critical questions. Does a more friendly theological approach risk distracting us from the mission of God?

Ida: May I suggest a meditative approach to the question of motivation for mission based on the start of the Lord's Prayer. "Our Father" – we want people to know God as Father. "Hallowed be your name" – we desire to see Jesus honored. "Your kingdom come" – we long to observe the kingdom growing. "Your will be done" – so we go into all the world.

Dan: Theology is always being stretched as we encounter new developments. But theological adaptation has to be tested against faithfulness to scripture, so we need to be constantly critiquing our theology.

Ashoor: I affirm a positive and friendly attitude. The history of mission shows examples of positive and questionable results from various actions; one example from a previous era is colonialism within mission practices. So we need to constantly evaluate our attitudes and methods. A positive and friendly, we might say relational, approach is necessary but must be done carefully.

Alex: I believe that we must keep reviewing how we do church. In a previous era, colonization did not think through what church might and should look like away from its Western roots. So in this era, for us to omit consideration of ecclesiology would, I think, be dangerous. We must be open to new forms of church emerging that are faithful to Christ and fit local contexts well.

Warrick: I think that what we need is robust theology which clearly shapes our attitudes. Mission, I believe, is the bedrock of theology; one might argue that missiology has become theology. Yet we need major changes in mission practice, not least in recognition that 30 million people are born into Muslim communities each year.

Martin: So what are the implications for soteriology of our thinking more positively about Islam? Do Muslims need to hear the gospel?

Alex: I have been asked several times by Muslims why I am not a Muslim given that I am so appreciative of the Islamic tradition. We each need an answer to this when engaging with Muslims. On one occasion, I was discussing the name of God with a Sufi and I spoke about the notion of reconciliation and the Christian belief that God so loved us that he came down, restored our *fiṭra* (purity before God), and opened and cleansed our hearts of sin. This conversation struck me in that we were discussing a difference in our understanding of God's operation in salvation. I was affirming a more active role for the Holy Spirit in salvation, whereas my Muslim friend saw God's spirit as a principle that draws humanity toward God but not so much that God's Spirit actively enters into human history.

George: We cannot separate our understanding of God from that of salvation. What is the basic, key human need? The Qur'an presents mankind as forgetful but oriented toward God and consequently in need of prophets as reminders. The Bible takes a harsher view: mankind needs to be saved from sin by being renewed completely. Genesis chapters 1 to 11 have a theme of violence in the heart of mankind. God comes to save people with Abraham as the beginning of the salvation story, culminating in a Son of Man coming to save sinners. The two pictures are very different.

Martin: So can we distinguish salvation from developing a more positive view of Islam?

George: Do not demonize any human being. The context of the Bible is each nation with their god. Yet scripture asserts that there is one Lord, one God. Jesus told the Samaritan woman that she and her people worshiped what they did not know *(see section 4.3)*. We should go no further.

Ida: The Qur'an refers to the God of Abraham. We should be striving for a truthful view of Islam, whether positive or negative, whatever either of those terms mean when applied to a religion other than our own. That the Qur'an does not offer salvation in Christ is a simple, truthful statement. If they try to keep the law, which is based on Torah, then that is good, but, if we take Paul seriously, it will prove inadequate and point to the need for salvation. In the USA I have heard of some coming to Jesus in sickness (cheaper than the health-care system!), experiencing healing in Jesus's name and subsequently discovering that the gospel required something of them. If Muslims discover something good in the Qur'an, then hallelujah; it is a step on a journey.

Dan: Seeking to adopt either a positive or negative perspective is too simplistic. There are numerous forms of Islam, some of which are and should be condemned by all including Muslims.

Martin: On the spectrum from idealization to demonization, we are moving away from demonization. I suggest that we need to move well away from demonization without getting too close to idealization. The challenge then is do we need to go and preach the gospel to Muslims?

Ashoor: God called us to himself, and we are called to make Christ available to all. We must allow everyone to evaluate and decide what to do with the message. This is not about whether they are good or bad; it is about what we are commissioned to do. We have tasted the joy of knowing Christ as Lord and Savior, and we long for others to experience this.

Martin: I conclude that the gospel stands for itself, and it needs to be made known. In terms of spiritual dynamics and possible exposure to the demonic, should we think that Muslims are more prone to the demonic than other people?

George: Present darkness is not about Islam; it is about the god of this world in all sorts of manifestations. So I regard it as dangerous to label anything as more demonic than others. The blessing of Abraham is for all.

Ida: In my opinion, the greatest work of Satan at present is to deceive millions of Christians into fear and hatred of Muslims. Acting out of such attitudes is dreadful, and it is harmful to our engagement with the people whom God loves.

Warrick: Do we have nationalism tied up with our mission? This is a big topic. I think we need a contextual analysis of what idols are present. For example, can we see the demonic in certain expressions of American evangelicalism?

Can we see places with very little Christian presence? I think there are many senses of strongholds. I think it helps to leave spaces for mystery.

Alex: Keep in mind that there is something special about the work of the Spirit in the Christian. What is the Spirit doing in our lives and the temptations we face? The writer of the book of Hebrews warns us of the consequences if we ignore the Spirit's promptings and fall into temptation. What would happen if we ignored the Spirit because we were preoccupied with our preconceived notions of God apart from Scripture?

Ashoor: The exposure to the demonic is equal for all human beings. Christ was exposed to temptation. As Christians, we do have an advantage, namely the Holy Spirit. This gives us an additional tool aiding our ability to defend ourselves, to deal with attacks by Satan, demons, principalities, etc.

Dan: Paul wrote, "We are not unaware of the devil's schemes" (2 Cor 2:11), when addressing disunity in the church. My perception is that much of the time we are unaware of the demonic, because it takes such ordinary forms, and hence we are more vulnerable. As a simple example, when walking into a mall, we might say that we are encountering the demon of materialism. How do we respond to it?

Ida: In scripture it was Jesus who faced the most attacks because he, and he alone, resisted Satan to the end. Does this mirror the experience of many Christians?

Martin: Finally, what is the role of the Spirit in our ministry to Muslims?

Dan: The Spirit is present in every possible way, whether or not I am aware of him. Only the Spirit can open a mind to religious truth. In every way, he is the power that is present.

George: I do not naturally love anyone except my immediate family. I ask for love so that I may be patient with and gracious toward Muslim friends and government officials. I need the fruit of the Spirit.

Ida: I need the Spirit to turn the word of God into life-giving water.

Ashoor: I need the Spirit to fulfill my commitment to obedience, which is the engine to the power and path of God in this life and ministry.

Alex: The Spirit is the foundation of our relationships with Muslim neighbors and friends. The Spirit needs to not only work within us but also explicitly among us. Additionally, we must recognize the work of the Spirit within the Muslim community. Such a recognition ought to move us closer together in the Spirit of God toward God.

Warrick: I would like more of the Spirit's work within me, and I hope that I will always want more.

Martin: Thank you.

Summary and Conclusions: Toward a Biblical Theology of Islam, the Qur'an, Muhammad and Muslims – An Attempt at Answering the Church's Questions

Martin Accad

The first part of this book explored the concept of the "religious other" in general terms, providing a framework to make space for them in our worldview through theological, biblical and social science lenses. The second part zeroed in on the most significant "religious other" in today's global reality, namely our Muslim neighbor. This book does not intend to undermine the significance of other religions or those who profess no religion at all. Indeed, as our common humanity emerges though these pages as the most important foundation of our interfaith interaction, it should be clear that much of what derives from part I as applicable to Muslims in part II also provides an adequate framework to think about adherents of other faiths and of no faith.

In the introduction, I sought to propose a framework to think about the religious other in terms that we have found useful in our engagement with Muslims through the multiple initiatives of our Institute of Middle East Studies in Lebanon, from academic study and research, to interfaith dialogue to peacebuilding. This framework is what I refer to as the kerygmatic attitude and approach. This approach is elaborated through three pairs of characteristics described as (1) supra-religiousness and Christ-centeredness, (2) respect and love, and (3) prophetic stance and scientific honesty. These three pairs of characteristics are meant to establish the spirit, tone and foundation of this book. They also announce that the concept of the religious other will be examined through biblical-theological, ethical and academic lenses.

Part I then launches into this exploration by developing a biblical-theological method (ch. 1), establishing a biblical framework (ch. 2), and providing sociological lenses (ch. 3) to arrive at a multidisciplinary understanding of the religious other.

In chapter 1, we look at the challenge of religious diversity with several sections providing a helpful lens to look at the phenomenon of hybridity. The opening section explores the struggle of the prophet Jonah with God's unexpected initiative of grace toward Israel's enemies (1.1). We then try to wrap our minds around the reality of the massive migration and displacement of peoples and the implications of this phenomenon for global demographics. We ask what role the church has to embrace in this complex world, called as it is by its Lord to the missions of witness and peacebuilding (1.2). Then comes the testimony of a Druze woman whose decision to become a follower of Jesus has led to a life of negotiation between the various layers of her identity as she seeks to embrace the imperatives of the gospel while remaining culturally an active member of her community of origin (1.3). In an attempt to provide a framework for such hybridity, I then explore our attitudes and approaches to Islam on a theoretical spectrum between idealization and demonization, conscious that the church is called to spell out a careful understanding of the religious other which is both biblically faithful and mindful of the inherent diversity in all religions (1.4). This is followed by a second testimony, this time of a Muslim man in Egypt who has gone through a major paradigm shift in his understanding, from polemics against his former religion to a calling to reintegrate and be salt and light in his community of origin (1.5). The next section is an African challenge to our often rigid categories and religious boundaries. As a development worker from Ghana, Rose Mary Amenga-Etego comes from a social setting that is more naturally at ease with cultural and religious hybridity (1.6). Finally, the chapter closes with a reflection on Jesus's parable of the Good Samaritan (1.7). The hero of the story is presented as the model reflecting Jesus's ideal of how to behave in relation to the religious other, summarized as positive engagement with tender mercy and care.

Chapter 2 continues to explore biblical models that will instruct us on appropriate behavior toward the religious other. It reveals some interesting biblical responses to the exploitation of the vulnerable, beginning with the story of Naaman the Syrian (2.1) and followed by the story of Hagar (2.2). Both stories invite us to be on the side of God who looks after the vulnerable with compassionate care. We then look at the model of Paul in Athens who, as a passionate preacher and evangelist, considers every opportunity to establish common ground with the other as a legitimate way of building a bridge to the gospel with respect and truth (2.3). Section 2.4 continues the exploration of Paul. Here we are able to see him at work, removing obstacles to the gospel by affirming the equality of all human beings in their state of sinfulness, and hence their universal need for God's saving grace through Christ. We then move back to the Old Testament, with a reading of Genesis 1 to 11 focused especially on 4 to 11 (2.5). The point is similar to the previous section. It is a description of our world, a sinful and fallen world. It reveals that all people are religious, yet while religions are diverse, no person should be viewed as "other." Religious people are united in their search for God, their sinfulness, their search for meaning and their ultimate destiny to die, and what we learn from the Noah story is that all are under the rainbow covenant of God. The centrality of the Noah narrative in this section reflects God's concern for the whole of creation, and a reading from the New Testament perspective brings the judgment of the flood and the mystery of sacrifice (from that of Cain and Abel to Noah) together at the cross of Christ. We are reminded that God loves people of all religions and of none. Few issues in our world today reflect the tension between religion and power – so present in the Genesis narrative – as flagrantly as the Israeli-Palestinian conflict. Section 2.6 dives into this question, not only from a political theology and justice perspective, but also exploring this faith/power dynamic in the way that the ideology of Zionism, married to Christianity, negatively affects the work of the gospel in the MENA region. Finally, in the "conversation among friends" (2.7) our three imaginary friends – disciples of Jesus from Jewish, Christian and Muslim backgrounds *(see preface)* – revisit the key themes of the chapter: Abraham, Law and Grace, Zionism, sin, punishment and grace. The major takeaways of chapter 2 are that there are no religious "others," only religious people; that we are all the same because we are sinful; and that God is interested in us and has offered in the cross of Jesus an alternative to our obsession with religion, power and violence.

Chapter 3 shifts from biblical-theological perspectives on religion to insights into religious questions from the social sciences. From this new angle, we move into an exploration of anthropological roots of religions and their role in society, including modern tensions in the West between the religious and the secular (3.1). We then observe African societies where the community does not feel threatened by multiple religious belonging, because religions are all seen as means toward holistic peace, both through spiritual and physical health (3.2). From the context of India comes insight into the way that we ought to read and interpret sacred texts, both our own and those of religious others (3.3). The classic approach is to compare narratives and seek understanding by establishing lines of influence and questions of primacy. But this section encourages us to look beyond the written text and to search for influences on the minds of readers originating from broader literary and artistic vehicles, including virtual ones. It is a helpful reminder that our religiously plural world is not simply obsessed with comparative theology but is filled with other sources of influence that shape our diverse social realities and imaginations in rather eclectic ways. A concern for relevance in theology and mission has to take these realities seriously. The next two sections begin to move the conversation toward some focus on Islam, first through a comparison of different understandings of God's presence in Judaism, Christianity and Islam (3.4), and then through the search for a framework to understand religious diversity within religious societies generally and Muslim ones specifically as an important element in our search for relevance in mission (3.5). The chapter closes with a plea for those living in multi-faith societies not to focus all of their attention on orthodoxy and on delivering the right cognitive message, but just as importantly to be mindful of orthopathy and the message we deliver through our relational behavior and even through our bodily and facial features (3.6).

The last few sections of part I prepare us well for entering part II of the book, with its focus on Islam. Chapter 4 is designed to set the tone for the second part of the book and to establish a theological framework for the enterprise of developing a biblical theology of Islam. In section 4.1, I articulate my belief that there is a direct correlation between the polarized positions of rival evangelical camps on recent controversial issues in mission, and the conscious or subconscious views that members in these two camps have developed about Islam and Muslims over time. From this position I argue that if we are to reintroduce balance and reason into some of these controversies, we urgently need to develop a thoughtful and biblically faithful way of understanding Islam – in other words, the development of a Christian theology of Islam has become crucial. A "conversation among friends" follows (4.2), where our three imaginary friends recap among themselves the key takeaways of part I on the "religious other" as a foundation for the impending reflections and studies on Islam. This introductory chapter closes, like the end of part I, with a devotional reflection by Karen Shaw on Jesus's encounter with the Samaritan woman at the well in John 4, a paradigmatic story for every Christian about encountering the religious other (4.3). The tone is set by reemphasizing the central affirmation of the entire volume, that our presence among religious others fundamentally needs to move away from any thought that the church's mission is about promoting Christianity as a religion; the gospel is about

Christ, not Christianity. He is the source of living water, and he is God's vessel that draws our worship from geographical locus to truthful spiritual worship.

With these foundations laid out for part II, chapter 5 sets us on our journey through the five themes that ensue: Islam's emergence (ch. 5), the Qur'an (ch. 6), Muhammad (ch. 7), salvation (ch. 8) and the spiritual realm (ch. 9).

In section 5.1 of this chapter on Islam's emergence, Ashoor Yousif takes us on a journey into Middle Eastern Christian perceptions of Islam across the centuries. How they interpreted Islam's emergence and the formation of a Muslim people, the identity and function of Muhammad, and the nature and origins of the Qur'an and Islam as a new world religion were both diverse and progressive. Above all, it became clear that Christians developed their understanding of Islam in parallel with their continuous pursuit of self-understanding. The result was a blend of hermeneutics, apologetics and polemics that ultimately served as a lens to interpret their own life and raison d'être in the context of the Muslim world.

In section 5.2, Dan Brown brings us back to the present, asking important questions of the various directions that are being taken in recent scholarship on Islam, particularly in the West. In so doing, his contribution offers a helpful interpretation of the sources that Yousif presents to us. But in a way that is consistent with his conclusion, Dan helps us see what we *cannot* know for sure about Islam, rather than what we can affirm with confidence. His demonstration of the opacity of the origins of Islam, the Qur'an and Muhammad thus creates a helpful basis for the rejection of any arrogant approaches to the study of Islam, whether manifested in scholarly overconfidence or in haughty polemics. In the end, rather than choosing between the two, he offers the Christian in the context of Islam an alternative option, which he describes as "humble historical agnosticism." This is indeed an attractive position for evangelicals seeking civil and open relationships with their Muslim neighbors. It provides them with a framework that makes a balance between witness and dialogue possible. For the Christian scholar seeking the pursuit of truth, though agnosticism may not always be the best option to press forward with intellectual inquiry, humility is certainly a virtue that such scholars will do well to embrace if their scholarship is to be meaningful and relevant in conversation with Muslim scholars. We might say that humble historical agnosticism as a starting point is more likely to draw Muslim scholars into dialogue for the benefit of our multi-faith world. But as will transpire from other chapters in this book – including my own section 7.3 – some scholars will want to push for more confident hermeneutical scenarios when exploring alternative ways to understand the Muslim phenomenon. Humility, however, will remain of the essence.

In section 5.3, Warrick Farah brings the discussion of Islam's origins and the implication on its nature to full circle. With care and precision, he discusses various ways that the notion of religion has been understood vis-à-vis culture. Faith manifestations can only be understood within a specific time and culture, and culture is a slippery concept. His concluding invitation that we get comfortable with ambiguity offers a very helpful way for us to integrate the previous two contributions, which indeed offer sufficient skepticism about what we can know with confidence, to convince us that comfort with ambiguity may be the best way forward. With this position as our stepping-stone, Warrick invites us to engage in mission among Muslim communities with more confidence in the good news of God's salvation in Christ than in our ability to dislodge Muslim confidence in Islam.

The concluding interview (5.4) and conversation (5.5) of chapter 5 revisit some of the main themes of the chapter. One of the main discussion points addresses the question of whether the intellectual studies of our three core sections are adequate to engage the "common" Muslim person. A key takeaway is that Islam is diverse and that the Muslims we encounter day to day – like adherents of any religion – have a great variety of socio-economic and educational backgrounds. Thus, the learning provided in the chapter has to be adapted to each person at an adequate level. As churches living among diverse Muslim communities, we are called to communicate with human persons first, and to meet them each where they are. That is the core message of the incarnation.

Chapter 6 begins with a reflection on Jesus's loving attitude toward well-meaning religious leaders from his own religious tradition, in this case Nicodemus (John 3). Hanane dwells long on this attitude and entreats Christians today to learn from it (6.1). This reflection is followed by a case study (6.2) that presents three different positions on the Qur'an: (1) the aggressive (polemical) attitude of a sincere evangelical influenced by negative views of Islam in the media; (2) the defensive position of a Muslim convert to Christ struggling to express a meaningful comparative understanding of Muslim and Christian scriptures; and (3) the rather judgmental position of a religiously minded Christian who is concerned that a clear distinction between the Bible and the Qur'an should be maintained and emphasized. The case study is then discussed further in an interview (6.3) with a seasoned Christian minister who, though open to the use of the Qur'an in sharing the gospel with Muslims, is keen to emphasize the distinction that we should adopt between our attitude toward Islam and our attitude toward Muslims. These opening sections raise important questions regarding our theology of the Qur'an. They suggest that one might need to pay attention to specific factors that motivate a Christian to take a certain position on the Qur'an. Factors such as one's former relationship with Islam and whether one adopts a certain attitude for the sake of the gospel or primarily to defend the Christian religion against another are important. Each should stir in us a different reaction. Most important, perhaps, is the attention the case study draws to the primacy of discipleship. It incites us to push for more balanced and mature teaching in the church, to a fair and honest assessment of sources – both Bible and Qur'an – and to a constant return to Christ, the heart of the gospel, rather than to religious zealotry.

In section 6.4, Issa Diab takes us through a fairly detailed journey into the history of the emergence of the text of the Qur'an. After a helpful summary of its principal features, he helps us understand the transition from the stage of "inspiration" to those of memorization and compilation. The turbulent history of this transition, narrated by early Muslim scholars themselves, should be helpful in dislodging the enduring confidence that Muslims have in the immutability of the Qur'an. After this early history, Diab discusses some insights provided by recent Qur'an manuscript discoveries, which have brought to light a considerable number of "alternative readings." Even if, for now, these variants are not considered consequential for the essential meaning of the Qur'an, they do question the unfounded belief – rooted in faith rather than science – that the Qur'an stands to a great extent outside historical time. The table of variants provided in his chapter is a useful point of reference for Arab readers. Diab's overall thrust is far from polemical, even if his conclusions are troubling for a person of Muslim faith. His purpose is to show that a blind traditional faith is often dissonant with science and history. His contribution opens the way for the next two sections on the origins and function of sacred scriptures and on the relationship of the Qur'an to the biblical text.

In section 6.5, Emad Botros takes us on a fascinating exploration of the Jonah narrative in the Qur'an, distributed as it is over four different sūras. Steering away from the classic polemical approach that dismissively impugns the accusation of plagiarism on the Qur'an, he proposes a different way of reading prophetic narratives common to both scriptures through the typological approach. His ability to read the qur'anic version of a prophet's story in its original historical context, as a homily addressed to Muhammad's followers and a polemical warning against his detractors, allows us to do better justice to the narrative's originality. At the same time, Botros's approach establishes convincingly these narratives within the Judeo-Christian religious tradition, both canonical and extracanonical.

In section 6.6, Dan Brown speaks to us once more about the importance of humility in our approaching of each other's scriptures, and specifically in our Christian approach to the Qur'an. He argues for the separation of doctrine from hermeneutics, not permanently but during those times when we explore the Qur'an. He suggests that we should suspend theological judgment of Islam's scripture for the benefit of a more authentic reading. He proposes in effect that, as Christians, we should read the Qur'an as a classic, just as we would read Plato or Aristotle. By giving due reverence to this venerable text, we are encouraged to engage in joint hermeneutical efforts of both the Bible and the Qur'an, in partnership with Muslims, as we seek to listen to God's message addressed to both the pains and joys of our shared humanity.

Chapter 6 on the Qur'an concludes with a testimony in the form of an interview (6.7) and a conversation among friends (6.8). The focus of both is the relevance of an academic approach to the Qur'an in day-to-day conversations with Muslims. Senem's perspective from secularist Turkey helpfully frames the conversation. Is a scholarly understanding and approach to the Qur'an by a Christian helpful, when many in the Muslim world begin their journey to Jesus after experiencing disappointment with Islam, and when their rejection of the Qur'an's authority may have preceded their embrace of Christ and the Bible? Our three imaginary disciples from different religious backgrounds are clear that they do not consider the Qur'an to be revealed scripture, but this does not lead them to a denigration of the text and of its venerable place within the Muslim tradition. One suggests that we might focus on the positive moral and theological lessons the Qur'an provides and on the common beliefs it holds about the character of God, such as grace and mercy. Even where such attributes might be expounded somewhat differently, they can form important conversation threads in our relationships with Muslims. Another reaffirms his belief that the Qur'an can justifiably be held by Christians at least at the same level of respect as the great classics. This attitude is foundational to his recommendation that respect, humility and integrity should form the bases of our relationship with our Muslim friends and neighbors. On those three principles all our conversation partners agree. They also agree that genuine friendship is the starting point of authentic witness and the very manifestation of God's love for Muslims, as expressed in Christ.

Chapter 7 begins with a beautiful poem from a Syrian man called Yasser. It emerges right out of the pain and trauma he experienced from the devastating war that has ravaged his country since 2011. Yasser came to faith during his experience of displacement in Lebanon, and it is clear from his poem that what drew him most powerfully to Christ is the radical call to love our enemies, even as they sever our head. Yasser's poem conveys no anger or grudge, no judgment or desire for revenge, but only love and hope that his presumed executioner would come to know his Savior.

In the same opening section (7.1), Senem Ekener is with us again, now sharing a reflection from the Gospels. For her too, the focus is not to attempt a discrediting of Muhammad, but rather to highlight the awe-inspiring character of Jesus. Just like the various characters in the story of Jesus's healing of the paralytic, Ekener reminds us that all Muslims are attracted to Jesus because of his love and his power to heal. They look to him in hope for his touch in their own lives. Some walk out from this encounter shocked and scandalized by the claims of his divinity. For others it comes as a revelation that can no more be denied as they stand before his power and his claims. This was her own experience, and she believes that it happened because her husband and many of his friends had brought her before Jesus on her "metaphorical pallet" through prayer and faith.

The case study (7.2) puts before us three opinions about Muhammad. Was he a false prophet and the anti-Christ; was he an effective religious reformer for his time; or can we even know anything about him as a historical figure with confidence? The next three sections provide us with three studies on these questions as we seek to form our own opinions.

The three more substantial sections of chapter 7 begin with my section 7.3. Before beginning to speak about the most revered personality of a religious tradition, I explore who we are really talking about. We cannot begin to develop a theology of Muhammad if we do not begin by asking, "which Muhammad?" lest we end up analyzing a straw man. Building on the position of "humble historical agnosticism" of Dan Brown in section 5.2, I want to push the boundary beyond total agnosticism and propose that we can establish a starting point for our theology that is at least as valid as the confident affirmations about Muhammad in the traditional Muslim narrative, which I call the "Muhammad of faith."

I would describe my approach as bold but pragmatic. Equipped with the assumption that the Qur'an is the most reliable source for our knowledge of the "historical Muhammad," I examine what might be inferred from the text about its (presumed) author, as one would about the author of any text through his or her writing. That is the bold part. The pragmatic part has to do with missiology and the ministry of the church. I want, more than anything else, to debunk the polemical approach in which Muhammad is dismissed as an anti-prophet with the worst descriptions. I want to show that this portrait, that has for so long held central place among evangelicals, derives from the same scientifically unreliable sources from which traditional Muslims built their idealized portrait of their prophet. This leaves me, it is true, with a few speculative options needing further exploration. But it nevertheless allows me to propose a positive ground for the development of a theology of the historical person of Muhammad, a foundation on which to build both dialogue with Muslim scholars and more creative approaches to the church's ministries of witness and discipleship.

In section 7.4, George Bristow introduces one particular approach for looking at prophetic narratives in the Bible and the Qur'an comparatively. Arguing that prophetic narratives have to be read and understood within the literary patterns sanctioned by a particular scripture, he surmises that the qur'anic pattern is fundamentally incompatible with the biblical one. Whereas the biblical prophetic narratives reach their fulfillment in Jesus, he argues, the qur'anic narratives are designed to set the pattern for an understanding of Muhammad's prophethood. The idea is attractive, but as Bristow himself admits with reference to the Abraham narrative, the qur'anic prophetic stories that color outside the lines of the biblical stories are mostly inspired from extra-canonical Jewish stories, therefore continuing to belong to the Judeo-Christian tradition. I would also argue that reading biblical prophetic narratives primarily as leaning toward fulfillment in Jesus does not do sufficient justice to the original context of the scriptural stories. The biblical prophet stories belong first to the Jewish tradition and must be read in their own right within the Jewish interpretive tradition before being interpreted theologically and Christianly through their fulfillment in Christ.

Even though I agree with Bristow that the covenantal pattern of biblical prophethood is unique once it is read through its final fulfillment in the new covenant in Christ, I am not convinced that the qur'anic pattern differs greatly from the contractual dimensions of covenant in the Hebrew scriptures. I would point to the prominent position of the concept of covenant in the qur'anic narrative as well, as reflected in the often repeated qur'anic terms, *'ahd* (over forty-six times) and *mīthāq* (more than ten times). A comprehensive comparative study of the concept of covenant in the Bible and the Qur'an is beyond the scope of this book. There are certainly some significant differences. But in the Qur'an, God is described as being faithful to his covenants, and prophets and their peoples are invited to be faithful as well. Breaking the divine covenant is seen as a very serious sin, while faithfulness to it is expected. The covenantal commitment that God expects from his prophets and people is connected with monotheism, obedience and social justice. Faithfulness to covenant is the way to paradise, while covenant breakers cannot expect eternal reward.

The chief contribution of Bristow's section is to establish some boundaries around the concept of biblical prophethood, and many elements of his critique of Talman's article, which he uses as the basis for developing a biblical framework of prophethood, are on point. But I would argue that Bristow could have shown more flexibility in his interpretation of Muhammad's role within this framework. He helpfully clarifies the biblical definition of the prophetic office but perhaps does not do sufficient justice to the inherent variety present in the act of "prophesying." He does provide both negative (Saul and Balaam) and positive (OT priests and NT apostles) examples of individuals who prophesied under the influence of the Holy Spirit without making it to the status of prophetic office. Seen within this broader category, and given the little we know about the historical Muhammad *(see sections 5.2 and 7.3 by Brown and Accad)*, it may befit the "humble historical agnosticism" advanced by Dan Brown to leave the question open on whether that seventh-century ecstatic Arabian character ever prophesied to his people under the influence of the Holy Spirit.

Our Christ-centered theology is what prevents us from recognizing Muhammad as a prophet in the full biblical sense, since we embrace Christ as the fulfillment of all prophetic expectations, through whom our salvation is perfected. But to conclude that Muhammad is a "false prophet," given our current knowledge of early Islamic history, eliminates all nuance that Bristow himself provides in his distinction between the prophetic office or vocation and the occasional act of prophesying under the Holy Spirit's influence. To be fair, Bristow never explicitly comes to that conclusion, but the status of "false prophet" is the only implication that can possibly be inferred from his analysis.

At the end of the day, a biblical Christology has no need for a recognition of either prophetic office or prophetic act for Muhammad, and therefore from a purely Christian perspective, this whole conversation can safely be dismissed. But positive engagement between Jews, Christians and Muslims seeking to construct a common social good can certainly benefit from some careful nuance in the discussion of Muhammad's status. In this sense, missional interfaith engagement is ultimately teleological rather than ontological, driven by the purpose of relational rapprochement rather than by some gap inherent to the biblical-theological system.

In section 7.5, Ida Glaser provides us with another way of looking at Muhammad through a biblical lens. She ascribes more significance than Bristow does to the commonalities between Islam and Judaism – particularly rabbinic Judaism – and to their shared focus on monotheism and prophethood. This commonality provides a framework to understand Islam's ***shahāda***, with its strong confession both of the One God and of Muhammad's prophethood. Moving beyond the traditional discussions about Muhammad that compare him – either positively or negatively – with biblical prophets, Glaser suggests that Muhammad's significance in the overall biblical story of covenant reminds us in particular of the role of Jeroboam and Samaritan religion. From Israelite religion – both Judaic and Samaritan – Islam adopted its strong focus on monotheism. But following Christianity, it moved beyond the boundaries of God's covenant with Israel and universalized God's message beyond a particular people. The project of Muhammad, Glaser suggests, consists in a sort of displacement of the biblical narrative focus from Jerusalem to Mecca, from the Bible to the Qur'an, and from biblical prophets to himself.

Between the three core sections of chapter 7, we are exposed to three ways of thinking about Muhammad: the first from the perspective of Judeo-Christian continuity (Accad); the second from that of prophetic pattern discontinuity (Bristow); and the third through the lens of religious reframing (Glaser). Though the main focus of the chapter is an exploration of Islam's prophet, Muhammad, his relationship with the Judeo-Christian tradition, his character as retained by the Islamic tradition, and what we can and cannot know about him as a historical person, we are always drawn back to Jesus and his radical teaching of love and forgiveness. The closing conversation (7.6) reflects a somewhat dynamic debate between diverse ways of looking at Islam's central figure, raising perhaps more questions than providing definitive answers. But the overall focus on implications for ministry and passion and love for Muslims provides the common thread among all three conversation partners, with the various approaches and emphases reflecting the diverse personalities and contexts of each.

Chapter 8 focuses on salvation, a very thorny issue in the interfaith conversation. The opening reflection (8.1), offered by ABTS student from Syria, Hiba al-Haddad, sets the right tone. The gospel seems to tell us that our ability to receive salvation from God has to do more with the disposition of our heart than with our full grasp of a theology of salvation. The devotional reflection is followed by a case study (8.2). Once again, we stand before three characters who reflect two positions on salvation and one unenviable position where a Muslim man called Hassan has fallen victim to a theological debate at a very vulnerable time in his life when his father was dying. From this opening context, tension is expressed between the desire to see loved ones come to faith in Christ, social pressures about the implications of interreligious conversion, and dogmatic views about the nature of the gospel. Many complex questions are opened, awaiting to be addressed in the following sections.

The first response comes from Shirin Bahrami (8.3), an Iranian follower of Jesus from a Shiʻite background. For her, the most significant element of following Jesus is the assurance it gives her about her salvation. Though her family situation prompted her to witness quickly to them about Christ's saving grace, she expresses dissatisfaction with George's approach in the case study, which she considers insensitive. Gospel witness, she affirms, consists in the combination of both life and oral testimony. Timing and circumstances are of the essence.

In section 8.4, Alexander Massad proposes a new framework for thinking about salvation, about who stands inside and who stands outside of God's grace. His analysis is based on an exegesis of Romans 1:18–23, a classic passage often used by Christians to affirm the exclusivity of the Christian claim to salvation in Christ. But instead of reading the passage through the classical Christian soteriological categories of exclusivism, inclusivism and pluralism, Alex proposes to us the soteriological categories of the respected Sunni theologian of the past century, Muḥammad Rashīd Riḍā (d. 1935), whose thinking is based on a venerable Muslim line of thinking on the issue. Alex's invitation is for us to understand the methodology of Muslim theological thinking more authentically before imposing a theological framework which is alien to Islam and hence risks not doing justice to the Muslim worldview and missing the opportunity to communicate the gospel in terms that are familiar.

In a sort of exegetical tour de force, Massad is able to conclude, based on Romans 1, that sincere and godly Muslims who hear the gospel but still reject it are not necessarily condemned, for they will have done so either because they have been presented with a corrupt version of the gospel, or because their social, psychological or intellectual circumstances do not provide them with the ability to accept it, or because they are not convinced of it despite their honest inquiry. By adopting Riḍā's hermeneutic, Alex suggests that it is only those people who actually understand the gospel, are impacted and convinced by it, and then reject it out of stubborn selfishness, who stand condemned. What is unique about Massad's proposition is that it focuses the final verdict about salvation, not on the objective theological position of a Muslim toward the gospel, but on the subjective disposition of their heart in their search for the truth. What I find attractive about this approach is that Christians are placed in a non-judgmental position over Muslims in their witness to the gospel, ultimately having to rely on God's final judgment of a Muslim's intentions. This seems to me to be aligned with the biblical imperative that it is our responsibility to proclaim the gospel and God's responsibility to make it bear fruit and, ultimately, to judge.

In a second core section of the chapter (section 8.5), Grant Porter presents us with the findings of his research journey among various emerging communities of believers in Christ from Muslim backgrounds. He discovered fellowships made up essentially of one of three types of members, for which he proposes three categories. First are *adopters* who take on traditional forms of Christian fellowship usually after breaking away from their previous community, both in religious and cultural practice, through a public confession. Second are *negotiators* who, though having explicitly rejected Islam, maintain blurred boundaries with many cultural practices of their surrounding community and do not want to be identified as Christians, viewing behavioral change as the principal indicator of belonging. Third are *reframers* who are unwilling to reject either Islamic religious or cultural practices and instead reframe Islamic and qur'anic teaching in light of Christ and the Bible. What is fascinating about this exploration is that it blurs our usual distinctive soteriological categories. It puts us ill-at-ease because it takes away from us the ability to control who is "in" and who is "out" of the Christian fold. But there remain certain clear features that distinguish the *negotiators* and the *reframers* from their surroundings, notably their strong focus on practicing the teaching of Jesus, particularly giving up feelings of hatred and revenge and practicing radical love for enemies and persecutors. *Reframers* are particularly intriguing as they distinguish "believers" from "followers," the latter being the ultimate goal reflecting full belonging to the fellowship. It is interesting to observe that boundaries remain a key feature of a faith community, without which it would not be possible to speak of a church. But instead of doctrine or ritual, these more fluid communities are distinguished by practices that are aligned with the teaching of Jesus, particularly his radical teaching about love.

Ida Glaser's section 8.6 offers us a unique Jewish perspective on the question of the salvation of Muslims in the interfaith conversation between Judaism, Christianity and Islam. Her adoption of the Jewish categories of *haggadah* and *halakhah* to reframe our understanding of covenant and law, gospel and grace, Sira and Sharī'a, provide tremendous insight into our understanding of the character of God through his interaction with humanity and our journey with him. Ida reminds us that salvation history is ultimately God's initiative and God's story with his people. She reminds us that God has sufficient grace and blessing for all the peoples of the earth. As one deeply familiar with the Jewish tradition, she is careful not to undermine the seriousness of specific covenants and divine initiatives, whether the Mosaic covenant or the story of

God coming to us in Christ. But God's story with his people in the biblical witness clearly shows that he is not done with us, nor with the Jews nor with the Muslims. Glaser beautifully brings this point to a head by moving from the story of origins to the story of the eschaton – of the end days. All three traditions are steeped in the hope of the final coming of the Messiah, whether for the first time (Judaism), the second time (Christianity), or to reestablish true religion (Islam). Whereas a Christian might readily view the second coming of Christ as the fulfillment of an overdue recognition of Messianic hopes for the ingathering of the Jews in line with Romans 11, Ida suggests that we might also want to look to that moment as a part of God's plan for the ingathering of Muslims unto our glorified Messiah Jesus. As she aptly affirms, "We may find it difficult to find a place in God's purposes for Muhammad, for Islam, and for Muslim peoples, but that does not mean that they have no place. The limitation is ours, and not God's!"

In the closing sections of chapter 8, we have the privilege of meeting Gamal, an Egyptian follower of Jesus who is able to maintain his respected position in "high places" in Egypt and give his attention to the bigger questions of social cohesion and equal citizenship for all. With reference to Grant Porter's categories, we might view Gamal as a *reframer*. In the testimony interview with him (8.7), it is clear that he views his life as deriving from a high divine calling. Later during the conversation among friends (8.8), people like him are compared with Nicodemus and Daniel, both of whom lived in relative isolation from like-minded people of God because they were called by God for a specific mission at a critical time. Further, it is suggested that they might view themselves as a Joseph or a Moses whom God has decided to use in his mission to the pharaohs. Overall, chapter 8 is a very humbling chapter, raising very difficult questions and proposing tentative answers into an area that belongs to the realm of the divine. We tread on holy ground, so to speak, for who can affirm with confidence who will be saved? Recognizing our limits is a helpful reminder that our concern should be with the wonderful proclamation of God's coming to his people in Christ, rather than busying ourselves with opinions about who is included and who is excluded from God's gift of salvation.

Chapter 9, the final chapter, deals with the question of the spirit world and the demonic. While chapters 4, 5, 6 and 7 are more academic in nature and chapter 8 is more theological, chapter 9 takes us mostly beyond what can be studied intellectually and into the realm of experience and social studies, except for the narratival study of the Holy Spirit in 9.3. Section 9.1 opens with a devotional reflection from our Iranian guest, Shirin Bahrami. As a Christian counselor, she reflects on her own struggles in the face of human suffering and pain. The story of Jesus feeding the crowds with two fish and five loaves is a powerful symbolic expression of our human inadequacy in the face of other people's needs. Shirin shares about the way that this story made her face her own pain and how it taught her to rely on God and the Holy Spirit's guidance.

With section 9.2, we are offered a window into the ministry of a Lebanese couple, Michel and Janane Mattar. They have been involved in refugee outreach since 2006, when God led them to cross the boundaries of religion and overcome past fears and hurt brought about by Lebanon's history of civil war. Through answering Elie Haddad's leading questions, they talk about their own change of heart toward Muslims and of the opportunities they have in sharing their faith, more through their work of compassion than through words. Though they pastor a vibrant charismatic church, they do not feel that Islam is in itself more prone to the demonic than any other religion. Conversely, they express their belief that any person who is not a child of God in Jesus is to some extent under demonic influence. As in the case of Shirin, we hear the Mattars share about our constant need to be sensitive to the Holy Spirit's guidance, both in our work of witness and in the discernment of spiritual powers that may be at work against the advance of God's kingdom.

In the first core chapter contribution (9.3), Nabil Habiby takes us through a narratival journey into the Gospel of Mark with the purpose of comparing the main characters of the story. After demonstrating that the Holy Spirit is an active character in the gospel, the main contribution of the section is the contrast that Nabil draws between the characteristics of the Holy Spirit and those of impure spirits. Though both are revealed in the story as powerful, obedient and knowledgeable, the comparison stops when one looks more closely at their relationship with Jesus. Whereas the Holy Spirit comes across as an aid and supporter of Jesus, the impure spirits lose their power and are subjected to fearful obedience when they come into Jesus's presence and authority.

Habiby points out that the Gospel of Mark calls us, as Jesus's disciples even today, to rely on the Holy Spirit through whom we have been baptized as our aid in our call to challenge all of the darkness in the world. We are reminded that we are ignorant and weak without Jesus's presence with us, which is an important realization that can guide our relationship with the religious other, particularly with our Muslim neighbors. Finally, Habiby concludes that in the Gospel of Mark, the Holy Spirit, though in opposition to religious leaders and impure spirits, is never in opposition to the disciples and the crowd (another character in the story). Taking the crowds to symbolize Muslims today – followers ever-seeking to get closer to Jesus but fearful in their search for understanding – Nabil concludes that our primary task is to point people to Christ, striving to get right in our heart attitude to Jesus so that our attitude to Muslims will be more Christlike. As many in the evangelical church today view Muslims through the lens of the demonic, this section is an important reminder that in the gospels, even those crowds that oscillated constantly between faith and fear, trust and skepticism, and eventually called for Jesus's execution, were never the target either of Jesus's attack nor of the Holy Spirit's overpowering authority. Instead, they were always allowed to follow and explore through fear and doubt, even from afar, until such time as they would be ready to commit. The disciples' role was never to rebuke or fight them, but always to journey with them in their own weakness as they moved closer to Jesus. Such is the core instruction for us as the church in our relationship with Muslims.

Section 9.4 exposes us to certain questions that are not often part of interfaith conversations in the Middle East and North Africa region, but probably should be. Through personal experience, ethnographic research and keen insight, Lawrence Oseje of Kenya examines the historical forays of both Christianity and Islam in his ancestral land of Kendu Bay. While Nabil's examination of the contrast between the Holy Spirit and impure spirits in Mark (9.3) helps us embrace the reality of the spirit world in the biblical Judaic worldview, Lawrence puts forward a world where spiritual realities were always taken for granted long before the arrival of Islam or Christianity in these lands. That Islam came to Africa from the communal and spiritually vigorous regions of the East seems to have given it a strategic advantage on Christianity that came to the continent from the more individualistic and demythologized cultures of the West. Oseje is critical of both the rejectionist and the overly embracing missionary position toward African Traditional Religion. The first is dismissed as wholesale disrespectful and hostile to African culture, while the latter is looked on suspiciously as too uncritical, hastily embracing, and bereft of the vital theologizing role and responsibility of the church.

If we are to apply the organizational framework of Grant Porter in section 8.5 to the African realities described by Oseje, we can see that in Africa too there are tensions between *adopters*, *negotiators* and *reframers*. Both vis-à-vis Christianity and Islam, adherents of African Traditional Religion may be distributed between *adopters* who have rejected ATR in an effort to be "approved" by Christian and Muslim missionaries, *reframers* who may have been too quick to retain all former traditions, and *negotiators* who have sought to practice theologizing on individual rituals and traditions in order to come up with a case-by-case synthesis that should be faithful to the biblical witness. Lawrence Oseje seems to advocate for the latter position. He believes that this is the best way for the gospel to integrate appropriately into African culture and societies.

We learn that Islam has been more successful historically in its missionary efforts among Africans because of its greater openness to popular/folk religious practices, its great appreciation for communal social networks imbued with strong traditions of hospitality, and because of its liberal position toward polygamy. The implication of Oseje's section is that a readjustment of the Christian approach to the advance of the gospel in Africa would have to forge its own theological path by renegotiating many of these traditional issues. Given that the African church today has largely moved beyond the founding missionary era, the outlook of an African-led effort in this direction is promising. And I expect there will be much to look forward to in terms of collaboration between our two regions in trailblazing new ways into ministry with our Muslim neighbors.

The closing section of chapter 9 (9.5) provides us with an apt perspective on how to view the spiritual dimension of Islam, essentially by doing so as we would view the spiritual dimension of any other religion, including Christianity. Adopting a social sciences approach, Warrick Farah advances the view that a biblically faithful understanding of the spiritual phenomenon in religion will have to forge a framework diverse enough to do justice to the great variety of Muslim peoples and practices that exist around the world. As he puts it, "if there were no Muslims, there would be no Islam." The same, of course, applies to Christians and Christianity and to any other religious system.

As we reflect on the last two core contributions (9.4 and 9.5) in light of the gospel framework provided by Habiby in section 9.3, we are struck by the fact that no religion is sheltered from the reality of the demonic. It can be easy to forget as we inspect Islam or African Traditional Religion for essential demonic components that most of Jesus's acts of exorcism were performed on fellow Jews, the descendants of Abraham, the children of the promise, the very line of Messiah Jesus. This sobering fact holds up a mirror to us and our religious tradition. Nabil's contribution reminds us that a recognition of the reality of the demonic is an essential component of Jesus's worldview. Lawrence's contribution warns us not to be too cavalier about assuming the superiority of one culture or religious tradition over another as we consider the predisposition that each has for a "darker side." And Warrick's last contribution offers us a set of lenses through which to understand the phenomenon of religion in all of its rich diversity, preventing us from sliding into the essentializing tendency in understanding the complexity of our world, both material and spiritual. Chapter 9 is a good reminder that the safest protection from demonic influence and oppression is adherence to Christ who has authority over demons rather than by taking refuge in any particular religious system.

Conclusion

I would argue in closing that a biblical theology of Islam will ultimately strive to develop an "as positive as possible" view of the Qur'an, Muhammad and Muslims. As I stated previously, interfaith engagement that seeks to be missional is ultimately more teleological than ontological. We broaden the boundaries of our understanding of Muhammad's status and of the value of the Qur'an not because our biblical theology needs it, but out of the grace and empathy that are core to a biblical theology of the incarnation. If in Christ God committed the scandalous act of crossing philosophical categories of human reason for us by becoming human, then it is theologically robust for us to cross some of the traditional boundaries of our religious frameworks to the maximum admissible within a biblically faithful worldview. We do this out of love, for the sake of our Muslim neighbor, for the sake of many who are becoming followers of Christ from Muslim backgrounds and need to come to terms peacefully with their past, and for the sake of our increasingly multi-faith communities throughout the world that need us more than ever as church to answer our vocation as peace catalysts in the world.

Final Questions for Discussion

1. Can we see the diversity of religious others in the Bible?
2. Are we consciously building and evaluating our theology of religious others? How are we checking that our attitudes, which will be visible to others, are informed by our theology?
3. How are we handling any occurrences of the Jonah Syndrome – of not wanting the other to be blessed by God – that we see in ourselves or Christian friends?
4. What is our view of Islam, Muhammad and the Qur'an?
5. What do we learn from the comparison and contrast between Jeroboam, Samaritans and rabbinic Judaism on the one hand and Muhammad, Muslims and Islam on the other?

6. How might we express the supremacy of Christ with humility and openness to how the other responds?

7. How attentive to the Spirit are we in discerning the spiritual realities of each person and community that we encounter?

8. What are the implications of these studies for the discipleship of followers of Jesus from Muslim backgrounds?

9. How open are we to new forms of Jesus-centered worship, including those whose participants prefer not to use the term "Christian"?

Appendix 1

Transliteration of Qur'anic Sūra Names

The "a" in "al" of sūras beginning with the definite article should be capitalized only after a full-stop, with the exception of *Āl-ʿImrān*, which should always be capitalized because it means "family" and is not the definite article.

The sūra number follows the name.

al-Fātiḥa (1)	*al-Mujādala* (58)
al-Baqara (2)	*al-Ḥashr* (59)
Āl-ʿImrān (3)	*al-Mumtaḥina* (60)
an-Nisāʾ (4)	*aṣ-Ṣaf* (61)
al-Māʾida (5)	*al-Jumuʿa* (62)
al-Anʿām (6)	*al-Munāfiqūn* (63)
al-Aʿrāf (7)	*at-Taghābun* (64)
al-Anfāl (8)	*aṭ-Ṭalāq* (65)
at-Tawba (9)	*at-Taḥrīm* (66)
Yūnus (10)	*al-Mulk* (67)
Hūd (11)	*al-Qalam* (68)
Yūsuf (12)	*al-Ḥāqqa* (69)
ar-Raʿd (13)	*al-Maʿārij* (70)
Ibrāhīm (14)	*Nūḥ* (71)
al-Ḥijr (15)	*al-jinn* (72)
an-Naḥl (16)	*al-Muzzammil* (73)
al-Isrāʾ (17)	*al-Muddathir* (74)
al-Kahf (18)	*al-Qiyāma* (75)
Maryam (19)	*al-Insān* (76)
Ṭā Hā (20)	*al-Mursalāt* (77)
al-Anbiyāʾ (21)	*an-Nabaʾ* (78)

al-Ḥajj (22)	an-Nāziʿāt (79)
al-Muʾminūn (23)	ʿAbasa (80)
an-Nūr (24)	at-Takwīr (81)
al-Furqān (25)	al-Infiṭār (82)
ash-Shuʿarāʾ (26)	al-Muṭaffifīn (83)
an-Naml (27)	al-Inshiqāq (84)
al-Qiṣaṣ (28)	al-Burūj (85)
al-ʿAnkabūt (29)	aṭ-Ṭāriq (86)
ar-Rūm (30)	al-Aʿla (87)
Luqmān (31)	al-Ghāshiya (88)
as-Sajda (32)	al-Fajr (89)
al-Aḥzāb (33)	al-Balad (90)
Sabaʾ (34)	ash-Shams (91)
Fāṭir (35)	al-Layl (92)
Yā Sīn (36)	aḍ-Ḍuḥa (93)
aṣ-Ṣāffāt (37)	ash-Sharḥ (94)
Ṣād (38)	at-Tīn (95)
az-Zumar (39)	al-ʿAlaq (96)
Ghāfir (40)	al-Qadr (97)
Fuṣṣilat (41)	al-Bayyina (98)
ash-Shūra (42)	az-Zalzala (99)
az-Zukhruf (43)	al-ʿĀdiyāt (100)
ad-Dukhān (44)	al-Qāriʿa (101)
al-Jāthiya (45)	at-Takāthur (102)
al-Aḥqāf (46)	al-ʿAṣr (103)
Muḥammad (47)	al-Humaza (104)
al-Fatḥ (48)	al-Fīl (105)
al-Ḥujurāt (49)	Quraysh (106)
Qāf (50)	al-Māʿūn (107)
adh-Dhāriyāt (51)	al-Kawthar (108)
aṭ-Ṭūr (52)	al-Kāfirūn (109)
an-Najm (53)	an-Naṣr (110)
al-Qamar (54)	al-Masad (111)
ar-Raḥmān (55)	al-Ikhlāṣ (112)
al-Wāqiʿa (56)	al-Falaq (113)
al-Ḥadīd (57)	an-Nās (114)

Appendix 2

Arabic Transliteration Alphabet

The following table gives the transliterations used throughout this book.

A a – a Ā ā – ʾ	أ َ – ا آ – ء	Ḍ ḍ	ض
B b	ب	Ṭ ṭ	ط
T t	ت	Ẓ ẓ	ظ
Th th	ث	ʿ	ع
J j	ج	Gh gh	غ
Ḥ ḥ	ح	F f	ف
Kh kh	خ	Q q	ق
D d	د	K k	ك
Dh dh	ذ	L l	ل
R r	ر	M m	م
Z z	ز	N n	ن
S s	س	H h	ه
Sh sh	ش	W w – u Ū ū	و – ُ و
Ṣ ṣ	ص	Y y – i Ī ī	يـ ي – ِ يـ ي

Glossary

9/11 – attacks in New York City and Washington DC on 11 September 2001 involving crashing hijacked airliners into buildings

Abbasid – this empire succeeded the Umayyad Caliphate/Empire in 750 (see below), mostly ruled from Baghdad after they founded the city; forced to cede control of various areas to others at different times, while never managing to take control of Spain from the Umayyad's who ruled there from 756; control of territory ended in 1258 when the Mongols destroyed Baghdad; the Abbasid line of rulers was re-established in 1261 and based in Cairo; the dynasty claimed caliph status until the Ottoman conquest of Egypt in 1517

abrogation – principle applied to some qur'anic interpretation in which later revelations take precedence over earlier ones; presumes knowledge of the order of revelation

akedah – site where Abraham displayed his willingness to sacrifice his son and Isaac his willingness to be sacrificed; the event that sealed the blessings of the Abrahamic covenant *(see section 7.5)*

al-ākhira – the afterlife

al-'āmm wa al-khāṣṣ – exegetical principle of "the universal versus the particular"; in Islam the term is more common in peaceful (e.g. Sufism) and quietist (e.g. Shi'ism) traditions

al Azhar – leading academic institution within Sunni Islam (see below), located in Cairo, Egypt; head of al Azhar also holds the post of Grand Mufti or senior Muslim cleric of Egypt

a'māl – actions; an Islamic legal category alongside *īmān* (faith)

anomie – situation in which society provides little moral guidance to individuals; can arise from competing belief systems or from individuals rejecting overly rigid social norms and constraints; can be used to describe an individual whose actions are widely different from societal norms

Anṣār – supporters of Muhammad who joined his cause in Medina after he migrated to the city from Mecca

asbāb an-nuzūl – the "occasions of the revelation"; in traditional Islam, the historical circumstances when Muhammad received particular revelations in the Qur'an

āyat as-sayf – "sword verse" (*at-Tawba* 9:29) qur'anic verse about fighting Jews and Christians; considered a significant turning point in qur'anic hermeneutics; context of war usually understood as strictly occurring in self-defence *(see section 7.3)*

basmala – qur'anic and Islamic saying, "In the name of God, the Merciful, the Compassionate"

474 The Religious Other

Bukhārī – collection of Hadith (see below) regarded as authoritative by most Sunnis; compiled by Imam Muhammad al-Bukhārī (810–870) who was ethnically Persian and born in what is now Uzbekistan

Byzantine Empire – continuation of the Roman Empire in its eastern provinces: also referred to as the Eastern Roman Empire and Byzantium; survived the demise of the Western Roman Empire in the fifth century; endured until 1453 when it was conquered by the Ottomans; its borders varied during its long history; capital was Constantinople, modern Istanbul

caliph – leader of the Muslims; the first four were widely accepted by Muslims (see Rāshidīn caliphs below); subsequent ones were disputed

chiastic – literary structure with a central element and a series of matching or contrasting items before and after

Common Word, A – open letter in 2007 by 138 Islamic scholars inviting senior church leaders to meet for dialogue; some Christians argued that it was a trap or a cover for more sinister activities, others chose to engage[1]

companions of Muhammad – followers of Muhammad, often involved, according to Muslim tradition, in memorizing sections of the Qur'an

comparative literature – academic technique looking for lines of influence among different texts based on historic figures or similar concepts and ideas

covenants – agreements in the Bible between God and his people; define God's people, how they relate to God, how they relate to other peoples, and their place in God's creative and eschatological purposes; have central socio-political and theological significance

Daesh – name used by many political and religious leaders in the Middle East for ISIS (see below); derived from an approximate acronym of the group's name in Arabic; one reason for its use is that it avoids linking this group to Islam

da'wa – invitation to Islam, to become a Muslim; transliterated as *dawah* by some

dhimmitude – pejorative term coined by recent Western scholars engaged in the polemical study of Islam to emphasize the situation of non-Muslims being treated as second class citizens under the Islamic legal status of *ahl adh-dhimma*, literally, under Muslims' protection

dialogue – here in the sense of interreligious exchange, typically Muslim-Christian; occurs in formal settings and informal encounters; the contention in this book is that there is no authentic dialogue without witness; some argue that there is no true witness without dialogue

dīn – religion that one belongs to; distinguished in this book from one's "true faith"; religion in the sense of a social label and group identifier, not necessarily as a belief system

---

1. See www.acommonword.com/ which lists the senders and recipients together with other information.

Druze – ethnic religious group present in Israel, Lebanon and Syria; regarded by some as part of Islam

ad-dunyā – literally, this world, as opposed to the world to come, *al-ākhira*

ecclesiology – theory or study of what it means to be a church

Enlightenment – period of major cultural change in Europe in the seventeenth and eighteen centuries when reason became more prominent, (apparently) replacing the centrality of religion in society

eschatology – study or theology of the end times, day of judgment, etc., in Judaism, Christianity and Islam

ethnocentrism – discrimination based on ethnicity or ethnic-religious identity

ethnography – description of social life and culture in a particular social system based on multiple detailed observations of what people actually do; typically uses both qualitative and quantitative research methods used by sociologists

exclusivism – within Christian soteriology, the view that salvation is only through Christ and not available outside of Christianity; people must become Christian in order to be saved

fiṭra – in Islam, the concept that human beings are born with an innate nature of purity and innocence before God; some Muslims prefer the term "revert" rather than "convert" for those becoming Muslims since they are seen as returning to the status they had at birth; transliterated *fiṭrah* in some sources

Furqān – term found in the Qur'an as a synonym of Qur'an in the sense of scripture; gathering together of what is regarded as scripture; used in the Islamic sense of scripture being sent down from God

Gnosticism – prioritizing personal spiritual knowledge over orthodox religious teaching, practices and authority structures; from the Greek for knowledge; emerged in first century among adherents of Christianity and Judaism

Hadith – saying of the Prophet Muhammad; can mean one such or a collection (plural, *aḥādīth*); regarded as a complementary guide to the Qur'an by many Muslims; the historicity of many sayings is questioned by some *(see section 5.2)*

haggadah – stories element of the covenant faith of the Torah; the other element is *halakhah* (see below); includes the whole narrative aspect of the Torah which tells of God's relationship with the world and humankind, especially with the Jewish people

hajj – pilgrimage to Mecca; lasts four days with prescribed activities each day; all Muslims who are able to do so should undertake this at least once during their lifetime; one of the five pillars of Islam; also used to refer to someone who has participated

halakhah – law element of Torah; includes written requirements together with oral dimensions and later legal discussions

ḥanīf – often translated "monotheist"; refers either to a Muslim or a pre-Islamic monotheist such as Abraham; plural *ḥunafā'*, subst. *ḥanīfiyya* (Syriac *hanpa*, plural *hanpe*, subst. *hanputa, ahnap*)

Hijaz – area in western Arabia where Islam emerged; roughly equivalent to modern Saudi Arabia's Red Sea coast and plateau east of the Madyan Mountains; includes the cities of Mecca and Medina as well as Jeddah

Hijazi script – form of Arabic in the Hijaz at the time of the emergence of Islam

Hijra – when Muhammad moved from Mecca to Medina (according to the traditional timeline of the life of Muhammad); start of Islamic dating system, AD 622

īmān – belief, sincerity or fidelity

inclusivism – within Christian soteriology, the view that people can find salvation through Christ despite being outside of Christianity; consequently, religious others can be saved by an unconscious connection to Christ

inimitable – view that God cannot be imitated, particularly in his literal revelation of the text of the Qur'an for Muslims

Injīl – term used within Islam for the New Testament; literally, gospel

Insider Movement – practice of some disciples of Christ raised in Muslim communities of remaining within such communities and maintaining some Islamic practices; often motivated by the desire to be authentic witnesses to Christ

ISIS – armed group that arose in Iraq around 2006 before re-emerging in Syria in late 2011 or 2012; other armed groups have overtly affiliated with the original branch, a step that is primarily about endorsement of ideology and methods, not a shared political and military command; group's original official title was The Islamic State of Iraq and ash-Sham; referred to as The Islamic State in Iraq and Syria (ISIS) and The Islamic State in Iraq and the Levant (ISIL) in some sources because the Arabic phrase Bilad Ash-Sham can refer to Syria and also the entire Levant (see below); the group retitled itself The Islamic State in July 2014; the term Daesh (see above) is used pejoratively by some in the Middle East

Islamicists – those who study Islam, its history, theology and practices

Islamist – Muslims seeking to establish a political state or other entity governed according to Islamic principles; there is debate among such people as to what such a system of governance comprises; some are willing to use violent means typically referred to as jihadists

isnād – part of each Hadith; an ordered list of transmitters of the entry, ideally ending with a Companion of Muhammad; the *matn* is the substance of the saying

Iṣrā'īliyyāt – literally "Israelite stories"; the term in Islamic literature for Old Testament narratives and extracanonical Jewish literature used to arrange qur'anic material on prophets in chronological order

jihad – concept within Islam; literally, struggle; the greater *jihad* is the daily struggle to live a godly life; the lesser *jihad* is controversial, with some jihadists seeing it as the use of violent means to propagate the faith

jinn – spirits that are active in daily life; mentioned in the Qur'an and Hadith; common within traditional Islamic piety

jizya – tax levied exclusively on non-Muslims, ostensibly because non-Muslims do not serve in security and military services

Ka'ba – building located in the center of the Great Mosque in Mecca; forms part of the hajj when pilgrims circle it seven times; also known as The Cube

kerygmatic approach – explaining the gospel to non-Christians in a Christ-centered, prophetic, scientifically honest manner driven by missional motivations and outcomes; named from the Greek word *kerygma* meaning the proclamation

kufr – unbelief, ingratitude or rejection

Lebanese civil war – typically dated 1975–1991; involved numerous (estimated at 40) militias and armed groups; very sectarian on and, at times, within ethnic and religious lines

Levant – the lands around Damascus; typically understood to mean modern Iraq, Jordan, Lebanon and Syria; some usages include Israel, the West Bank and the Gaza Strip

liminality – in anthropology, the quality of ambiguity or disorientation that occurs during a rite of passage when participants no longer hold their pre-ritual status but have not yet begun the transition to the status they will hold when the rite is complete; used more broadly to refer to the uncertainties and fluidity that arise during periods of significant social or political change

matn – substance of a Hadith; see *isnād* above

Mecca-Medina schema – system in which each sūra is regarded as having been revealed in one of these two cities, hence Meccan or Medinan; underpins the use of abrogation to resolve conflicting passages; this schema collapses, along with the traditional chronology of Muhammad, with the undermining of the historicity of the Hadith

Mesopotamia – historical area of west Asia made fertile by the rivers Euphrates and Tigris; roughly equivalent to much of modern Iraq, Kuwait, northeastern Syria, southeast Turkey and areas along the Iran-Iraq border

Miaphysitism – christological view that Christ, the Word of God, is fully divine and fully human in one person; contrasts with the Chalcedonian christological dogma that Christ is one person in two natures, divine and human; historically significant; in modern era, a difference more in words than beliefs, practices or willingness to embrace the other

Midrash – strictly speaking, the Jewish process of interpretation of the Hebrew scriptures undertaken by the Rabbinic School from the second century AD onward; used here and elsewhere as any exegesis of the Hebrew scriptures; the author of any such exegesis is referred to as a "Midrashist"

minoritization – overt, conscious suppression of one group in society by another; more than marginalization; can be linked to being a minority, but there are situations in which a numerically larger group is minoritized by a smaller group that happens to control the political, economic, or religious power[2]

missiology – study or theory of mission; often summarized as *missio Dei*, the mission of God, reflecting that God is innately missional

Monophysite – major strand within Christianity, also known as the Oriental Orthodox Churches; distinct from the Eastern Orthodox Churches, from whom they separated following the Council of Chalcedon in 451 because of their rejection of the Christology statement adopted by the Council

mufassirūn – interpreters of sacred texts, usually of the Qur'an

murtadd – apostate from Islam; derived from the Arabic act of *ridda*, apostasy

Muṣḥaf – physical book; usually used to mean the Qur'an in the sense of its being the record of the words sent down by God; plural Muṣḥafs or Maṣāḥif

Muslim Brotherhood – within Sunni Islam, a movement calling for states to be run on Islamic lines; one element is the focus on *Sharī'a* as the basis for legislation; founded as a social reform movement by Hassan al-Banna in Egypt in 1928; views itself as peaceful and democratic; declared illegal in Egypt and several countries since 2013 due to being perceived as a threat to autocratic rule; shortened to Brotherhood in some contexts

Nakba – Arabic term used by Palestinians to describe the displacement of Palestinians between 1947 and 1949 inclusive, a period that included the declaration of the state of Israel; literally, catastrophe; transliterated *Nakbah* in some sources

Naksa – Arabic term used by Palestinians to describe the conquest of the West Bank and East Jerusalem by the state of Israel in 1967; literally, setback

narrative criticism – study of the stories used by a speaker or writer to analyze how they understand daily human experience; includes form, genre, structure, themes, characters and the communicator's perspective

naskh – legal doctrine within Islam; linked to abrogation

an-nāsikh wa al-mansūkh – literally "the abrogator and the abrogated"; exegetical method within traditional Islamic interpretation of the Qur'an whereby the later given revelation supersedes – changes, replaces or corrects – the preceding one(s); governed by complex rules; requires knowledge of the order of revelation

Nestorian Christianity – branch of Christianity named after Nestorius; it is unclear whether or not he actually subscribed to the views that are named after him

Orthodox Christianity – two traditions, Eastern Orthodox and Oriental Orthodox, within Christianity; two other major traditions are Catholic and Protestant

Persia – roughly modern Iran; a substantial empire at times during its long history, much of which predates the emergence of Islam

---

2. See Martin Accad, "From Minority Status to the Fateful Embrace of Minoritization," in *The Church in Disorienting Times*, ed. Jonathan Andrews (Carlisle: Langham Global Library, 2018), 87–98.

phenomenology – loosely defined as "the believer is always right" or by the tautology "the believer is always right about what the believer believes"; used in this book in the sense that Islam is whatever an individual Muslim says that it is

polemics – overt attack of the theology and philosophy of another's religious beliefs

prophetology – veneration of Muhammad; observed in some Muslims

qibla – direction of prayer; so the Jewish *qibla* is Jerusalem and the Islamic is Mecca, also referred to as the second *qibla*

rabbinic Judaism – form of Judaism developed following the destruction of the temple in Jerusalem in AD 70 with consequent ending of the system of animal sacrifices; based on studying and keeping of Torah; study of the sacrifices is perceived as effectively performing them

Rāshidīn caliphs – literally, rightly guided caliphs, *al-Khulafā' ar-Rāshidūn*, the first four caliphs succeeding Muhammad as the widely recognized leader of the Muslim communities; subsequent caliphs were recognized by some but not all Muslim communities

reception history – study of how texts were received when published and first distributed; examines how texts influenced readers (or hearers) in their contexts

as-sā'a – literally, "the hour"; term that occurs in some qur'anic passages relating to what Christians might term soteriology or eschatology

salam – peace in Arabic

ṣalāt – formal, ritualistic, set prayers; commonly performed five times per day

Ṣan'ā' Manuscripts – collection of approximately 4,500 qur'anic manuscripts and parchments discovered in the Great Mosque of Old Ṣan'ā' in 1972

Sassanian Empire – last Persian empire prior to the rise of Islam; ruled from 226 to 651; also known as the Empire of Iranians, Middle Persia and the neo-Persian Empire; succeeded the Parthian Empire

SEKAP spectrum – different ways of engaging with the religious other: syncretistic, existential, kerygmatic, apologetic and polemic

shahāda – Islamic creedal statement that declares "there is no God but Allah" and "Muhammad is the prophet of God"; Shi'a Islam adds a clause stating that Ali is the viceregent of God

shekinah – term in Judaism for visible evidence of the presence of God with his people

Shi'a – strand within Islam; distinct from the Sunni strand

ṣidq al-īmān – true faith, true belief

Sira – traditional biography of Muhammad, the founder of Islam

soteriology – study or theory of salvation; how people get to heaven or become acceptable in God's sight and presence

Sufi – adherents of a strand within Islam that emphasizes purity of worship and inward mystical experiences of Islam; occurs within both Sunni and Shi'a Islam; often involves an ascetic lifestyle

sumasum – among the Ashanti people of Ghana, coolness of heart in the sense of contentment; distinct from coldness of heart or indifference; distinct from hot-tempered aggression; also spelled *sumsum* or *sunsum*

Sunni – strand within Islam that literally means followers of the *sunna*, the paradigm or model of Muhammad; numerically the largest; has many sub-strands

sūra – qur'anic passage or chapter comprising verses with an opening and an ending; the Qur'an contains 114 sūras that vary widely in length; the word might mean "what has descended from an edifice" or "the remnant"; some Orientalists trace the word to Aramaic or Hebrew

"sword verse" – see *āyat as-sayf* above

syncretism – combining elements of different religions; often leads to the formation of a unique religious community that may or may not be accepted as a valid expression of a major religion

Syriac – ancient and indigenous language of the Middle East related to Aramaic

systematics – creation of a succinct, ordered and structured summary of the theological meaning of a sacred text

tafsīr – interpretation of the Qur'an; embraces a variety of exegetical and hermeneutic techniques

taḥrīf – corruption of scripture, whether in word or meaning; transliterated as *taHriif* in some sources

takbeer – magnification, affirmation or praise of God's greatness; used by many Muslims in *ṣalāt* (formal) prayer, the call to prayer, and (by some) as a battle cry (which is the usage in Yasser's poem in chapter 7), typically Allah Akbar; transliterated *takbīr* in some sources

Tanakh – Jewish term for the Hebrew scriptures, known as the Old Testament by Christians; written mostly in biblical Hebrew with a few passages in biblical Aramaic

Tawhid – divine unity; God is one; key tenet of Islamic theology

at-Tawrāt – qur'anic term for the Torah, the first five books of the Tanakh and Old Testament; in Islam, often a reference to the entire Hebrew scriptures or Old Testament

typology – systematic classification of a set of objects based on common characteristics; commonly applied in science and social sciences; one use in Christian theology is to see Old Testament characters and incidents as foreshadowing the New Testament

Umayyad – ruling clan of the Islamic Caliphate from 661 to 750; Uthman, the third Rāshidī caliph (see above) was of this clan; continued to rule much of Spain from 756 to 1031, although references to the Umayyad Caliphate or Empire typically ignore this fact

umma – concept within Islam that all Muslims are part of one global Muslim community; applied by some on regional or ethnic or language basis; some uses include non-Muslim monotheists; transliterated *ummah* in some sources

Verstehen **movement** – within sociology, looking at what religion means to people

waḥī – stage of inspiration for the compilation of the Qur'an

al-yawm al-ākhir – literally, the last day; qur'anic term for the day on which all human beings will be judged based on their actions

yawm al-ḥisāb – literally, the day of reckoning; occurs in some qur'anic passages relating to what Christians might term eschatology

yawm al-qiyāma – literally, the day of resurrection; occurs in some qur'anic passages relating to what Christians might term eschatology

Zabūr – qur'anic term for the Psalms, attributed to (Prophet) David

Zionism – pursuit of and support for a nation-state for Jewish people; has political forms; Christian Zionism is theologically based support of Zionism

Bibliography

Abioje, Pius O. *African Ancestral Heritage in Christian Interpretations*. Beau Bassin: Lambert Academic Publishing, 2018.

Accad, Martin. "Christian Attitudes toward Islam and Muslims: A Kerygmatic Approach." In *Toward Respectful Understanding and Witness among Muslims: Essays in Honor of J. Dudley Woodberry*, edited by Evelyne Reisacher et al., 29–47. Pasadena: William Carey Library, 2012.

———. "From Minority Status to the Fateful Embrace of Minoritization." In *The Church in Disorienting Times*, edited by Jonathan Andrews, 87–98. Carlisle: Langham Global Library, 2018.

———. "Mission at the Intersection of Religion and Empire." In *International Journal of Frontier Mission* 28, no. 4 (2011): 179–189.

———. "Mission in a World Gone Wild and Violent." *Global Reflections Blog* 2016, https://sparks.fuller.edu/global-reflections/2016/06/17/mission-in-a-world-gone-wild-and-violent-challenging-the-monochromatic-view-of-islam-from-a-silent-majority-position/.

———. *Sacred Misinterpretation: Reaching across the Christian-Muslim Divide*. Grand Rapids: Eerdmans, 2019.

Adams, Charles J. "Reflections on the Work of John Wansbrough." *Method & Theory in the Study of Religion* 9, no. 1 (1997): 75–90.

Adeyemo, T. "Clash of Two Worldviews: African and Western." *Orientation* 2, no. 87/90 (1998): 369–386.

Afeke, B., and P. Verster. "Christianisation of Ancestral Veneration within African Traditional Religions: An Evaluation." *In Die Skriflig* 38, no. 1 (2004): 47–61.

Al Faruqi, Ismail R. "A Comparison of the Islamic and Christian Approaches to Hebrew Scripture." *Journal of Bible and Religion* 31, no. 4 (1963): 283–293.

Akhtar, Shabbir. *Islam as Political Religion: The Future of an Imperial Faith*. Abingdon: Routledge, 2011.

———. *The New Testament in Muslim Eyes: Paul's Letter to the Galatians*. London: Routledge, 2018.

Akrong, Abraham A., and John Azumah. "Hermeneutical and Theological Resources in African Traditional Religions for Christian-Muslim Relations in Africa." In *The African Christian and Islam*, edited by John Azumah and Lamin Sanneh. Carlisle: Langham Monographs, 2013.

Albright, Madeleine. *The Might and the Almighty*. London: Macmillan, 2006.

Alford, Deann. "Unapologetic Apologist: Jay Smith Confronts Muslim Fundamentalists with Fervor." *Christianity Today* (13 June 2008). https://www.christianitytoday.com/ct/2008/june/21.34.html.

Alter, Robert. *Genesis: Translation and Commentary*. New York: W. W. Norton, 1997.

Amanze, James N. "Christianity and Ancestor Veneration in Botswana." *Studies in World Christianity* 8, no. 1 (2003): 43–59.

Anderson, Allan H. *Spirit-Filled World: Religious Dis/Continuity in African Pentecostalism*. Gurgaon: Palgrave Macmillan, 2018.

Anderson, Allan, and G. J. Pillay. "The Segregated Spirit: The Pentecostals." In *Christianity in South Africa: A Political, Social and Cultural History*, edited by Richard Elphick and T. R. H. Davenport, 227–241. Berkeley: University of California Press, 1997.

Andrews, Jonathan. *Identity Crisis: Religious Registration in the Middle East*. Malton: Gilead, 2016.

———. *Last Resort: Migration and the Middle East*. Malton: Gilead, 2017.

———, ed. *The Church in Disorienting Times: Leading Prophetically through Adversity*. Carlisle: Langham Global Library, 2018.

———, ed. *The Missiology behind the Story: Voices from the Arab World*. Carlisle: Langham Global Library, 2019.

Arnold, Clinton E. *3 Crucial Questions about Spiritual Warfare*. Grand Rapids: Baker, 1997.

Asukwo, O. O., S. S. Adaka, and E. D. Dimgba. "The Need to Re-Conceptualize African 'Traditional' Religion." *African Research Review* 7, no. 3 (2013): 232–246.

Ateek, Naim. *Justice, and Only Justice: A Palestinian Theology of Liberation*. Maryknoll: Orbis, 1989.

Aydin, Cemil. *The Idea of the Muslim World: A Global Intellectual History*. Cambridge: Harvard University Press, 2017.

Bailey, Kenneth E. *Jesus through Middle Eastern Eyes*. London: SPCK, 2008.

Bal, Mieke. *Narratology: Introduction to the Theory of Narrative*. Toronto: University of Toronto Press, 1997; reprinted 2004.

Barrett, C. K. *The Holy Spirit and the Gospel Tradition*. London: SPCK, 1996.

Bauckham, Richard. *Jesus and the God of Israel: God Crucified and Other Studies on the New Testament's Christology of Divine Identity*. Grand Rapids: Eerdmans, 2008.

Bauer, W., F. W. Danker, W. F. Arndt, and F. W. Gingrich. *A Greek-English Lexicon of the New Testament and Other Early Christian Literature*. Chicago: University of Chicago Press, 2000.

Bavinck, J. H. *The Church between Temple and Mosque: A Study of the Relationship between the Christian Faith and Other Religions*. Grand Rapids: Eerdmans, 1966.

———. *The J. H. Bavinck Reader*. Grand Rapids: Eerdmans, 2013.

Beal, Timothy. "Reception History and Beyond: Toward the Cultural History of Scripture." *Biblical Interpretation* 19 (2011): 357–372.

Beale, Gregory K. *The Temple and the Church's Mission*. Leicester: Inter-Varsity Press, 2004.

Bediako, Kwame. *Christianity in Africa: The Renewal of Non-Western Religion*. Edinburgh: Edinburgh University Press, 1995.

———. *Theology and Identity: The Impact of Culture Upon Christian Thought in the Second Century and in Modern Africa*. Eugene: Regnum, 1992.

Behera, M. C. *Tribal Religion: Change and Continuity*. New Delhi: Commonwealth, 2000.

Bellah, R. "Civil Religion in America." *Daedalus* 96, no. 1 (1967): 1–21.

Berger, Peter. *A Far Glory: The Quest for Faith in an Age of Credulity*. New York: Free Press, 1992.

———. "Epistemological Modesty: An Interview with Peter Berger." *The Christian Century* (29 October 1997): 972–978.

Bertaina, David. *Christian and Muslim Dialogues: The Religious Uses of a Literary Form in the Early Islamic Middle East*. Piscataway: Gorgias, 2011.

Best, Harold. *Unceasing Worship: Biblical Perspectives on Worship and the Arts*. Downers Grove: IVP, 2003.

Birt, Yahya, Dilwar Hussain, and Ataullah Siddiqui, eds. *British Secularism and Religion: Islam, Society and the State*. Markfield: Kube, 2011.

Block, C. Jonn. *The Qur'an in Christian-Muslim Dialogue: Historical and Modern Interpretations*. Abingdon: Routledge, 2014.

Boda, Mark. "Biblical Theology and Old Testament Interpretation." In *Hearing the Old Testament: Listening for God's Address*, edited by Craig Bartholomew and David Beldman, 122–153. Grand Rapids: Eerdmans, 2012.

Breed, Brennan. *Nomadic Text: A Theology of Biblical Reception History*. Bloomington: Indiana University Press, 2014.

Bristow, George. "Abraham in Narrative Worldview: Reflections on Doing Comparative Theology through Christian-Muslim Conversation." In *Reading the Bible in Islamic Context: Qur'anic Conversations*, edited by Daniel Crowther et al., 31–44. Oxford: Routledge, 2018.

———. *Sharing Abraham? Narrative Worldview, Biblical and Qur'anic Interpretation and Comparative Theology in Turkey*. Cambridge: Doorlight Academic, 2017.

Brock, Sebastian P. "Syriac Views of Emergent Islam." In *Studies on the First Century of Islamic Society*, edited by G. H. A. Juynboll, ch. 3. Carbondale and Edwardsville: Southern Illinois University Press, 1982.

Broodryk, J. "Ubuntu in South Africa." LLD Thesis, UNISA, 1997.

Brower, Kent. *Mark: A Commentary in the Wesleyan Tradition*, New Beacon Bible Commentary. Kansas City: Beacon Hill, 2012.

Brown, Daniel. "Clash of Cultures or Clash of Theologies? A Critique of Some Contemporary Evangelical Responses to Islam." *Cultural Encounters* 1, no. 1 (2004): 69–84.

———. "The Triumph of Scripturalism: The Doctrine of Naskh and Its Modern Critics." In *The Shaping of an American Islamic Discourse: A Memorial to*

Fazlur Rahman, edited by Earle Waugh and Frederick Denny, 49–66. Atlanta: AAR, 1998.

———, ed. *The Wiley Blackwell Concise Companion to the Hadith*. Chichester: Wiley, 2020.

Brown, Jonathan. *Hadith: Muhammad's Legacy in the Medieval and Modern World*. Oxford: Oneworld, 2009.

Brown, Rick. "Biblical Muslims." *IJFM* 24, no. 2 (2007): 65–74.

Burge, Gary. *Jesus and the Land: The New Testament Challenge to "Holy Land" Theology*. Grand Rapids: Baker Academic; London: SPCK, 2010.

Burton, John. *The Sources of Islamic Law: Islamic Theories of Abrogation*. Edinburgh: Edinburgh University Press, 1990.

Cairns, Alan. *Dictionary of Theological Terms*. Greenville: Ambassador Emerald International, 2002.

Calder, Norman. "Tafsīr from Ṭabarī to Ibn Kathīr: Problems in the Description of a Genre, Illustrated with Reference to the Story of Abraham." In *Approaches to the Qur'ān*, edited by G. R. Hawting and Abdul-Kader A. Shareef, 101–140. London: Routledge, 1993.

Casanova, José. *Public Religions in the Modern World*. Chicago: University of Chicago Press, 1994.

Chapman, Colin. "Going Soft on Islam?" *Vox Evangelica* 19 (1989): 7–32.

———. *Prophecy Fulfilled Today? Does Ezekiel Have Anything to Say about the Modern State of Israel?* Cambridge: Grove, 2018.

———. *Whose Holy City?* Oxford: Lion Hudson, 2004.

———. *Whose Promised Land? The Continuing Conflict over Israel and Palestine*. 4th edition. Oxford: Lion Hudson, 2015.

Clark, M. S. "Two Contrasting Models of Missions in South Africa: The Apostolic Faith Mission and the Assemblies of God." *Asian Journal of Pentecostal Studies* 8, no. 1 (2005): 143–161.

Cohen, Aryeh. "Hagar and Ishmael: A Commentary." *Interpretation* 68, no. 3 (2014): 247–256.

Coleman, Doug. *A Theological Analysis of the Insider Movement Paradigm from Four Perspectives: Theology of Religions, Revelation, Soteriology, and Ecclesiology*. Evangelical Missiological Society Dissertation Series. Pasadena: WCIU Press, 2011.

Cook, Bradley J. "The Book of Abraham and the Islamic Qiṣaṣ al-Anbiyā' (Tales of the Prophets) Extant Literature." *Dialogue: A Journal of Mormon Thought* 33, no. 4 (2000): 127–146.

Conn, Harvie M. *Islam in East Africa: An Overview*. Islamabad: Islamic Research Institute, 1978.

Cook, Michael. *Muhammad*. Oxford: Oxford University Press, 1983; repr. 1996.

Cooper, Alan. "Hagar In and Out of Context." *Union Seminary Quarterly Review* 55, no. 1–2 (2001): 35–46.

Copleston, Frederick. *A History of Philosophy: Medieval Philosophy.* New York: Continuum, 2010.
Cover, Robert M. "The Supreme Court, 1982 Term – Foreword: Nomos and Narrative." Faculty Scholarship Series. Paper 2705. New Haven: Yale School of Law, 1983.
Cragg, Kenneth. *The Arab Christian: A History in the Middle East.* Louisville: Westminster John Knox, 1991.
Dames, G. E. "Knowing, Believing, Living in Africa: A Practical Theology Perspective of the Past, Present and Future." *HTS Theological Studies* 69, no. 1 (2013): 1–9.
Daniels, Gene, and Warrick Farah. *Margins of Islam: Ministry in Diverse Muslim Contexts.* Littleton: William Carey Library, 2018.
Daube, D. "The Exodus Pattern in the Bible." In *All Souls Studies* 2, 23–38. London: Faber & Faber, 1963.
Dauermann, S. *Converging Destinies: Jews, Christians and the People of God.* Eugene: Wipf & Stock, 2017.
De Vries, Simon J. *Prophet against Prophet: The Role of the Micaiah Narrative (I Kings 22) in the Development of Early Prophetic Tradition.* Grand Rapids: Eerdmans, 1978.
Dharamraj, Havilah. "The Curious Case of Hagar: Biblical Studies and the Interdisciplinary Approach of Comparative Literature." *Journal of Asian Evangelical Theology* 23, no. 2 (2019): 49–71.
Dibelius, Martin. *The Book of Acts: Form, Style and Theology.* Series edited by K. C. Hanson. Translated by Mary Ling and Paul Schubert. Minneapolis: Fortress, 2004.
Diène, Doudou, and Jean Burrell. "A Dynamic Continuity between Traditions." *Diogenes* 47, no. 187 (1999): 11–19.
Domínguez, César, Haun Saussy, and Darío Villanueva. *Introducing Comparative Literature: New Trends and Applications.* Abingdon: Routledge, 2015.
Donner, Fred. "Early Muslims and Peoples of the Book." In *Routledge Handbook on Early Islam*, edited by Herbert Berg. New York; Abingdon: Routledge, 2018. https://www.routledgehandbooks.com/doi/10.4324/9781315743462.ch10.
Dovidio, John F., Miles Hewstone, Peter Glick, and Victoria M. Esses, "Prejudice, Stereotyping and Discrimination: Theoretical and Empirical Overview." In *The SAGE Handbook of Prejudice, Stereotyping and Discrimination*, edited by John F. Dovidio, Miles Hewstone, Peter Glick, and Victoria M. Esses, ch. 1. London: SAGE, 2018.
Dozeman, Thomas B. "The Wilderness and Salvation History in the Hagar Story." *Journal of Biblical Literature* 117, no. 1 (1998): 23–43.
Du Toit, Cornel. "African Hermeneutics." In *Initiation into Theology: The Rich Variety of Theology and Hermeneutics*, edited by S. Maimela and A. König, 373–398. Pretoria: Van Schaik, 1998.
Durie, Mark. *Liberty to the Captives: Freedom from Islam and Dhimmitude through the Cross*, 2nd ed. Melbourne: Deror Books, 2013.

Durkheim, Emile. *The Elementary Forms of Religious Life*. Oxford: Oxford University Press, 2001. First published in French, 1912.

Dyrness, William. *Insider Jesus: Theological Reflections on New Christian Movements*. Leicester: IVP Academic, 2016.

Ela, Jean-Marc. *My Faith as an African*. London: Geoffrey Chapman, 1988.

England, Emma, and William J. Lyons. "Exploration in the Reception of the Bible." In *Reception History and Biblical Studies: Theory and Practice*, edited by Emma England and William J. Lyons, 3–16. London: Bloomsbury T&T Clark, 2015.

Ess, Joseph van. *The Flowering of Muslim Theology*. Cambridge: Harvard University Press, 2006.

Exum, J. Cheryl. "The Accusing Look: The Abjection of Hagar in Art." *Religion and the Arts* 11 (2007): 143–71.

Farah, Warrick. "Adaptive Missiological Engagement with Islamic Contexts." *IJFM* 35, no. 4 (2018): 171–78.

———. "The Complexity of Insiderness." *IJFM* 32, no. 2 (2015): 85–91.

———. "How Muslims Shape and Use Islam: Toward a Missiological Understanding." In *Margins of Islam: Ministry in Diverse Muslim Contexts*, edited by Gene Daniels and Warrick Farah, 13–21. Littleton: William Carey Library, 2018.

———. "Outlining a Biblical Theology of Islam: Practical Implications for Disciple Makers and Church Planting." *Evangelical Missions Quarterly* 55, no. 1 (2019): 13–16.

Farah, Warrick, and Kyle Meeker. "The 'W' Spectrum: 'Worker' Paradigms in Muslim Contexts." *Evangelical Missions Quarterly* 51, no. 4 (2015): 366–377.

Ferdinando, K. "Christian Identity in the African Context: Reflections on Kwame Bediako's Theology of Identity." *Journal of the Evangelical Theological Society* 50, no. 1 (2007): 121–143.

Fewell, Danna Nolan. "Changing the Subject: Retelling the Story of Hagar the Egyptian." In *Genesis: A Feminist Companion to the Bible*, Second Series, edited by Athalya Brenner, 182–194. Sheffield: Sheffield Academic, 1998.

Firestone, Reuven. "Jewish Culture in the Formative Period of Islam." In *Cultures of the Jews: A New History*, edited by David Biale, 267–304. New York: Schocken, 2002.

Flett, Eric G. "Trinity: Conceptual Tools for an Interdisciplinary Theology of Culture." In *On Knowing Humanity: Insights from Theology for Anthropology*, edited by David Bronkema and Eloise Meneses, ch. 10. New York: Routledge, 2017.

France, R. T. *The Gospel of Mark*. The New International Greek Testament Commentary. Grand Rapids: Eerdmans, 2002.

Fredericks, James. *Faith Among Faiths: Christian Theology and Non-Christian Religions*. New York: Paulist, 1999.

Frymer-Kensky, Tikvah. Interviewed in Brett Schaeffer, "Five Scripture Scholars Pick Their Golden Oldies." *US Catholic* 61, no. 11 (November 1996): 21–26.

Fung, Ronald Y. K. *The Epistle to the Galatians*. Grand Rapids: Eerdmans, 1988.

Garrison, David. *A Wind in the House of Islam*. Monument: WIGTake Resources, 2014.
Geddert, Timothy J. *Watchwords: Mark 13 in Markan Eschatology*. The Library of New Testament Studies. Sheffield: Sheffield Academic Press, 1989; repr. London: Bloomsbury Academic, 2015.
Geertz, Clifford. *Islam Observed: Religious Development in Morocco and Indonesia*. Chicago: University of Chicago Press, 1971.
Gehman, Richard J. *African Traditional Religion in Biblical Perspective*. Wheaton: Oasis International, 2011.
Gerloff, R. "Truth, a New Society and Reconciliation: The Truth and Reconciliation Commission in South Africa from a German Perspective." *Missionalia* 26, no. 1 (1998): 17–53.
Gill, Brad. "Global Cooperation and the Dynamic of Frontier Missiology." *IJFM* 31, no. 2 (2014): 89–98.
Gill, David W. J., and Bruce W. Winter. "Acts and Roman Religion." In *The Book of Acts in Its Graeco-Roman Setting*. The Book of Acts in Its First Century Setting, Vol. 2, edited by David W. J. Gill and Conrad Gempf, 79–103. Carlisle: Paternoster; Grand Rapids: Eerdmans, 1994.
Gilliland, Dean S. *African Religion Meets Islam: Religious Change in Northern Nigeria*. Lanham: University Press of America, 1986.
Glaser, Ida. *The Bible and Other Faiths: Christian Responsibility in a World of Religions*. Downers Grove: IVP, 2005.
———. *The Bible and Other Faiths: What Does the Lord Require of Us?* Carlisle: Langham Global Library; Leicester: Inter-Varsity Press, 2012.
———. *Thinking Biblically about Islam: Genesis, Transfiguration and Transformation*. Carlisle: Langham Global Library, 2016.
———. "Towards a Biblical Framework for Christian Discipleship in a Plural World." In *Pursuing the Friendship of Strangers*, edited by H. Boulter, 22–32. Oxford: Oxford Diocesan Committee for Inter-Faith Concerns, 2009.
Goldsworthy, Graeme. *Christ-Centered Biblical Theology: Hermeneutical Foundations and Principles*. Downers Grove: IVP, 2013.
———. *Gospel-Centered Hermeneutics: Foundations and Principles of Evangelical Biblical Interpretation*. Downers Grove: IVP, 2014.
Goldziher, Ignaz. *Muslim Studies*. Translated by C. M. Barber and S. M. Stern. 2nd edition. London: Allen & Unwin, 1971.
Görke, Andreas, Harald Motzki, and Gregor Schoeler. "First Century Sources for the Life of Muhammad? A Debate." *Der Islam* 89 (2012): 2–59.
Gray, Andrea, Leith Gray, Bob Fish, and Michael Baker. "Networks of Redemption: A Preliminary Statistical Analysis of Fruitfulness in Transformational and Attractional Approaches." *IJFM* 27, no. 2 (2010): 89–95.
Green, Tim. "Identity Issues for Ex-Muslim Christians, with Particular Reference to Marriage." *St Francis Magazine* 8, no. 4 (2012): 435–481.

Greenlee, David, ed. *Longing for Community: Church, Ummah, or Somewhere in Between?* Pasadena: William Carey Library, 2013.

Griffith, Sidney H. "Christians and the Arabic Qur'an: Prooftexting, Polemics, and Intertwined Scriptures." *Intellectual History of the Islamicate World* 2, no. 1–2 (2014): 255–259.

———. "Disputes with Muslims in Syriac Christian Texts: From Patriarch John (d. 648) to Bar Hebraeus (d. 1286)." In *Religionsgespräche im Mittelalter*, edited by B. Lewis and F. Niewöhner, 257–258. Wiesbaden: Otto Harrassowitz, 1992.

———. "Disputing with Islam in Syriac: The Case of the Monk of Bêt Halê and a Muslim Emir." *Hugoye: Journal of Syriac Studies* 3, no. 1 (2000; repr. 2010): 29–54.

———. "Jews and Muslims in Christian Syriac and Arabic Texts of the Ninth Century." *Jewish History* 3, no. 1 (1988): 65–94.

———. "Muhammad and the Monk Bahîrâ: Reflections on a Syriac and Arabic Text from Early Abbasid Times." *Oriens Christianus* 79 (1995): 7–8.

———. "The Prophet Muhammad, His Scripture and His Message according to Christian Apologies in Arabic and Syriac from the First Abbasid Century." In *La vie du prophète Mahomet. Colloque de Strasbourg, Octobre 1980*, edited by Toufic Fahd, 99–146. Paris: Presses Universitaires de France, 1983.

———. "The Qur'an in Arab Christian Texts: The Development of an Apologetical Argument: Abu Qurrah in the Maglis of al-Ma'mun." *Parole de l'Orient* 24 (1999): 203–233.

———. "The Qur'an in Christian Arabic Literature: A Cursory Overview." In *Arab Christians and the Qur'an from the Origins of Islam to the Medieval Period*, edited by Mark Beaumont, 1–19. Leiden: Brill, 2018.

———. *Syriac Writers on Muslims and the Religious Challenge of Islam.* Kottayam: St. Ephrem Ecumenical Research Institute, 1995.

Grudem, Wayne A. *The Gift of Prophecy in the New Testament and Today.* Revised edition. Wheaton: Crossway, 2000.

Gruen, Erich. *Rethinking the Other in Antiquity.* Princeton: Princeton University Press, 2011.

Guelich, Robert A. *Mark 1–8:26.* Word Biblical Commentary, Vol. 34A. Grand Rapids: Zondervan, 1989.

Guenther, Alan M. "The Christian Experience and Interpretation of the Early Muslim Conquest and Rule." *Islam and Christian-Muslim Relations* 10, no. 3 (1999): 363–378.

Guillaume, Alfred. *The Life of Muhammad: A Translation of Ibn Ishaq's Sirat Rasul Allah.* Oxford: Oxford University Press, 2002.

Haleem, M. A. S. Abdel. trans. *The Qur'an: A New Translation.* Oxford: Oxford University Press, 2008.

———. "The Qur'anic Employment of the Story of Noah." *Journal of Qur'anic Studies* 8, no. 1 (2006): 38–57.

———. "The Story of Joseph in the Qur'an and the Old Testament." *Islam and Christian-Muslim Relations* 1 (2007): 171–191.

Hamilton, Victor. *The Book of Genesis: Chapters 1–17.* New International Commentary on the Old Testament. Grand Rapids: Eerdmans, 1990.

Hanson, James S. *The Endangered Promises: Conflict in Mark.* Atlanta: SBL, 2000.

Harrak, Amir. "Ah! The Assyrian is the Rod of My Hand!: Syriac View of History after the Advent of Islam." In *Redefining Christian Identity: Cultural Interaction in the Middle East Since the Rise of Islam*, edited by Jan J. van Ginkel, Hendrika L. Murre-van den Berg, and Theo van Lint, 45–65. Leuven: Peeters, 2005.

Hashemi, Nader. *Islam, Secularism, and Liberal Democracy: Toward a Democratic Theory for Muslim Societies.* Oxford: Oxford University Press, 2009.

Hatina, Thomas R. *In Search of a Context: The Function of Scripture in Mark's Narrative.* Library of New Testament Studies 232. London: Sheffield Academic, 2002.

Hausfeld, Mark A. "Folk Islam and Power Encounter." *AGTS Evangel University.* Summer 2018. http://agts.edu/wp-content/uploads/2018/05/Folk-Islam-AGTS-Syllabus-05.24.18.pdf.

Hawting, Gerald R. "John Wansbrough, Islam, and Monotheism." *Method & Theory in the Study of Religion* 9, no. 1 (1997): 23–38.

Hayes, S. "African Initiated Church Theology." In *Initiation into Theology*, edited by S. Maimela and A. König, 159–178. Pretoria: Van Schaik, 1998.

Hedström, Peter, and Lars Udehn. "Analytical Sociology and the Theories of the Middle Range." In *The Oxford Handbook of Analytical Sociology*, edited by Peter Bearman and Peter Hedström, ch. 2. Oxford: Oxford University Press, 2009.

Hick, John, and Paul F. Knitter, eds. *The Myth of Christian Uniqueness: Toward a Pluralistic Theology of Religions.* Eugene: Wipf & Stock, 2005.

Hiebert, Paul. *Anthropological Insights for Missionaries.* Grand Rapids: Baker, 1986.

———. "Conversion, Culture and Cognitive Categories." *Gospel in Context* 11, no. 4 (October 1978): 24–29.

———. "Critical Contextualization." *Missiology* 12, no. 3 (1984): 287–296.

———. "Power Encounter and the Challenge of Folk Islam." Paper submitted to the meeting of the Lausanne Committee for World Evangelization, Zeist, Netherlands, 27 June–4 July 1978.

Hiebert, Paul, R. Daniel Shaw, and Tite Tiénou. *Understanding Folk Religion: A Christian Response to Popular Beliefs and Practices.* Grand Rapids: Baker Academic, 2000.

Higgins, Kevin. "Inside What? Church, Culture, Religion and Insider Movements in Biblical Perspective." *St. Francis Magazine* 5, no. 4 (2009): 74–91.

———. "The Key to Insider Movements: The 'Devoted's' of Acts." *IJFM* 21, no. 4 (2004).

Holton, Kyle. "(De)Franchising Missions." In *Understanding Insider Movements*, edited by Harley Talman and John Travis, ch. 38. Pasadena: William Carey Library, 2015.

Hooker, Morna D. *The Gospel According to Saint Mark*. Black's New Testament Commentary. London: A & C Black, 1991.

Horsley, Richard A. *Hearing the Whole Story: The Politics of Plot in Mark's Gospel*. Louisville: Westminster John Knox, 2001.

Howell, Brian, and Jenell Williams Paris. *Introducing Cultural Anthropology: A Christian Perspective*. Grand Rapids: Baker Academic, 2011.

Hoyland, Robert G. "The Earliest Christian Writings on Muhammad: An Appraisal." In *The Biography of Muhammad: The Issue of the Sources*, edited by Harald Motzki, 276–297. Leiden: Brill, 2000.

———. "New Documentary Texts and the Early Islamic State." *Bulletin of the School of Oriental and African Studies* 69, no. 3 (2006): 395–416.

———. *Seeing Islam as Others Saw It: A Survey and Evaluation of Christian, Jewish and Zoroastrian Writings on Early Islam*. Princeton: Darwin, 1997.

Hughes, Paul Edward. "Seeing Hagar Seeing God: *Leitwort* and Petite Narrative in Genesis 16:1–16." *Didaskalia Spring* (1997): 43–59.

Ibrahim, Ayman S., and Ant Greenham, eds. *Muslim Conversions to Christ: A Critique of Insider Movements in Islamic Contexts*. New York: Peter Lang, 2018.

Idowu, Emanuel B. *African Traditional Religion: A Definition*. London: SCM, 1973.

Ijeoma, Agatha Onwuekwe. *The Socio-Cultural Implications of African Music and Dance*. Nnamdi Azikwe University Awka, n.d.

Iverson, Kelly R. *Gentiles in the Gospel of Mark: "Even the Dogs under the Table Eat the Children's Crumbs."* The Library of New Testament Studies, Book 339. London: T&T Clark, 2007.

Jalghoum, Abdallah Ibrahim. *The Wonder Miracle of the Ordering of the Sūras and Verses of in the Honorable Qur'an*. Amman: n.p., 2005.

Jeffery, Arthur. *Materials for the History of the Text of the Qur'an; The Old Codices*. Leiden: Brill, 1937.

Johns, A. H. "Jonah in the Qur'an: An Essay on Thematic Counterpoint." *Journal of Qur'anic Studies* 5, no. 2 (2003): 48–71.

Josephus, Flavius. *The Antiquities of the Jews*. Translated by William Whiston. Project Gutenberg. 2009. www.gutenberg.org/files/2848/2848-h/2848-h.htm.

Joynes, Christine E. "The Reception of the Bible and Its Significance." In *Scripture and Its Interpretation: A Global, Ecumenical Introduction to the Bible*, edited by Michael J. Gorman, ch. 8. Grand Rapids: Baker Academic, 2017.

Kaemingk, Matthew. *Christian Hospitality and Muslim Immigration in an Age of Fear*. Grand Rapids: Eerdmans, 2018.

Kaltner, John. *Inquiring of Joseph: Getting to Know a Biblical Character through the Qur'an*. Collegeville: Liturgical, 2003.

———. *Ishmael Instructs Isaac: An Introduction to the Qur'an for the Bible Reader*. Minnesota: Liturgical, 1999.

Kaltner, John, and Younus Y. Mirza. *The Bible and the Qur'an: Biblical Figures in the Islamic Tradition*. London; New York: Bloomsbury T&T Clark, 2018.

Kaskas, Safi, trans. *The Qur'an: A Contemporary Understanding*. Fairfax: Bridges of Reconciliation, 2015.

Kassis, Rifat, et al. "Kairos Document. A moment of truth: A word of faith, hope and love from the heart of Palestinian suffering." Kairos Palestine, n.d. www.kairospalestine.ps/index.php/about-kairos/kairos-palestine-document.

Katanacho, Yohanna. *The Land of Christ: A Palestinian Cry*. Eugene: Pickwick, 2013.

Kato, Byang H. *African Cultural Revolution and the Christian Faith*. Jos, Nigeria: Challenge, 1976.

———. *Theological Pitfalls in Africa*. Kisumu, Kenya: Evangel, 1975.

Keay, John. *India: A History*. London: Harper, 2010.

Keener, Craig S. *Acts: An Exegetical Commentary: Vol. 3*. Grand Rapids: Baker Academic, 2014.

Khalil, Mohammad Hassan. *Islam and the Fate of Others: The Salvation Question*. Oxford: Oxford University Press, 2012.

Kidd, Thomas. *American Christians and Islam: Evangelical Culture and Muslims from the Colonial Period to the Age of Terrorism*. Princeton: Princeton University Press, 2009.

Kim, Caleb Chil-Soo. "Considering Ordinariness in Studying Muslim Culture and Discipleship." In *Discipleship in the 21st Century Mission*, edited by Timothy Park and Steven Tom, 177–192. Kyunggi, Korea: East West Center for MRD, 2014.

———. *Islam among the Swahili in East Africa*. 2nd ed. Nairobi: Acton, 2016.

Kinzer, M. *Jerusalem Crucified, Jerusalem Risen: The Resurrected Messiah, the Jewish People and the Land of Promise*. Eugene: Wipf & Stock; Cascade Books, 2018.

Kisiara, Richard. "Some Sociopolitical Aspects of Luo Funerals." *Anthropos* 93, no. 1/3 (1998): 127–136.

Klauck, Hans-Josef. *Magic and Paganism in Early Christianity: The World of the Acts of the Apostles*. Minneapolis: Fortress, 2003.

Klepper, Deeana. "Historicizing Allegory: The Jew as Hagar in Medieval Christian Text and Image." *Church History* 82, no. 2 (2015): 308–344.

Koloska, Hannelies. "The Sign of Jonah: Transformations and Interpretation of the Jonah Story in the Qur'an." In *Qur'anic Studies Today*, edited by Angelika Neuwirth and Michael A. Sells, ch. 3. London; New York: Routledge, 2016.

Kraft, Charles H. *Anthropology for Christian Witness*. Maryknoll: Orbis, 1996.

———. *Issues in Contextualization*. Pasadena: William Carey Library, 2016.

———. *Worldview for Christian Witness*. Pasadena: William Carey Library, 2008.

Kravtsev, Andrei. "Aspects of Theology of Religion in the Insider Movements Debate." Unpublished Paper, 2015.

Kristal, Efraín. "Art and Literature in the Liquid Modern Age." In *A Companion to Comparative Literature*, edited by Ali Behdad and Dominic Thomas, 108–119. Chichester: Wiley-Blackwell, 2011.

Lamb, Christopher. *The Call to Retrieval: Kenneth Cragg's Christian Vocation to Islam*. London: Grey Seal, 1997.

Larson, Warren. "Ordinary Muslims in Pakistan and the Gospel." In *Margins of Islam: Ministry in Diverse Muslim Contexts*, edited by Gene Daniels and Warrick Farah, ch. 8. Littleton: William Carey Library, 2018.

———. "The Spirit World of Islam." Online course syllabus. Columbia International University. n.d. http://www.ciu.edu/sites/default/files/academics/S14%20-%20ICS%206013%20-%20Larson.pdf.

Lausanne Movement, The. *The Cape Town Commitment: A Confession of Faith and a Call to Action*. Peabody: Hendrickson, 2011.

Leveen, Adrianne. "Reading the Seams." *Journal for the Study of the Old Testament* 29, no. 3 (2005): 259–87.

Lindstedt, Ilkka. "Pre-Islamic Arabia and Early Islam." In *Routledge Handbook on Early Islam*, edited by Herbert Berg, 159–161. Abingdon: Routledge, 2018.

Lingel, Joshua. *Islam's Issues, Agendas, and the Great Commission*. Garden Grove: i2 Ministries, 2016.

Lingel, Joshua, Jeff Morton, and Bill Nikides, eds. *Chrislam: How Missionaries Are Promoting an Islamized Gospel*. Revised edition. Garden Grove: i2 Ministries, 2012.

Lingenfelter, Sherwood. *Transforming Culture: A Challenge for Christian Mission*. 2nd edition. Grand Rapids: Baker, 1998.

Lipka, Michael. "Muslims and Islam: Key Findings in the U.S. and around the World." Pew Research Center, FactTank, 9 August 2017. www.pewresearch.org/fact-tank/2017/08/09/muslims-and-islam-key-findings-in-the-u-s-and-around-the-world/.

Lodahl, Michael. *Claiming Abraham: Reading the Bible and the Qur'an Side by Side*. Grand Rapids: Brazos, 2010.

Love, Rick. *Glocal: Following Jesus in the 21st Century*. Eugene: Cascade, 2017.

———. *Muslims, Magic and the Kingdom of God: Church Planting Among Folk Muslims*. Pasadena: William Carey Library, 2000.

Lucey, Michael. "A Literary Object's Contextual Life." In *A Companion to Comparative Literature*, edited by Ali Behdad and Dominic Thomas, 120–135. Chichester: Wiley-Blackwell, 2011.

Lugira, Aloysius Muzzanganda. *African Traditional Religion*. 3rd edition. New York: Chelsea House, 2009.

Luther, Martin. "Comm. Gen. 21:15–16 (WA 43.164; LW 4.40–41)." Cited in John L. Thompson, "Hagar, Victim or Villain?: Three Sixteenth-Century Views." *Catholic Biblical Quarterly* 59 (1997): 213–233.

Lyons, William J. "Hope for a Troubled Discipline? Contributions to New Testament Studies from Reception History." *Journal for the Study of the New Testament* 33, no. 2 (2010): 207–220.
Maimela, S. "Salvation in African Traditional Religions." *Missionalia* 13, no. 2 (1985): 63–77.
Malbon, Elizabeth. *In the Company of Jesus: Characters in Mark*. Louisville: Westminster John Knox, 2000.
Manahan, Ronald E. "A Theology of Pseudoprophets: A Study in Jeremiah." *Grace Theological Journal* 1, no. 1 (1980): 77–96.
Markusse-Overduin, Gabrielle. "Salvation in Mark: The Death of Jesus and the Path of Discipleship." PhD dissertation, University of Manchester, 2013.
Marshall, Howard. *Acts*. Tyndale New Testament Commentaries. Leicester: Inter-Varsity Press; Grand Rapids: Eerdmans, 1980.
Marshall, Tim. *Divided: Why We're Living in an Age of Walls*. London: Elliot & Thompson, 2018.
Martin, Craig. *A Critical Introduction to the Study of Religion*. New York: Routledge, 2014.
Marty, Martin, and Scott Appleby, eds. *The Fundamentalism Project*. Chicago: University of Chicago Press, 1995.
Masalha, Nur. *The Palestine Nakba: Decolonising History, Narrating the Subaltern, Reclaiming Memory*. London: Zed, 2012.
Matobo, T. A., M. Makatsa, and E. E. Obioha. "Continuity in the Traditional Initiation Practice of Boys and Girls in Contemporary Southern Africa Society." *Studies of Tribes and Tribals* 7, no. 2 (2009): 105–113.
Mazrui, Ali A. "African Islam and Competitive Religion: Between Revivalism and Expansion." *Third World Quarterly* 10, no. 2 (1988): 499–518.
Mbiti, John S. *African Religions and Philosophy*. New York: Praeger, 1969.
———. "African Theology." In *Initiation into Theology: The Rich Variety of Theology and Hermeneutics*, edited by S. Maimela and A. König, 141–158. Pretoria: Van Schaik, 1998.
———. "Challenges of Language, Culture, and Interpretation in Translating the Greek New Testament." *Swedish Missiological Themes* 97, no. 2 (2004): 141–164.
———. "Christianity and African Culture." *Journal of Theology for Southern Africa* 20 (1977): 26–40.
———. *The Crisis of Mission in Africa*. Mukono: Uganda Church Press, 1971.
———. "The Encounter of Christian Faith and African Religion." *Christian Century* 97, no. 27 (1980): 817–820.
———. *Introduction to African Religion*. 2nd revised edition. Portsmouth: Heinemann, 1991.
———. *The Prayers of African Religion*. Maryknoll: Orbis, 1975.
McAuliffe, Jane Damen. *Qurʾānic Christians: An Analysis of Classical and Modern Exegesis*. Cambridge: Cambridge University Press, 1991.

Meeks, Wayne A. *The First Urban Christians: The Social World of the Apostle Paul*. New Haven: Yale University Press, 2003.

Meiring, Arno. "As Below, So Above: A Perspective on African Theology." *Hervormde Teologiese Studies* 63, no. 2 (2008): 733–750.

Melchert, Christopher. "The Early History of Islamic Law." In *Method and Theory in the Study of Islamic Origins*, edited by Herbert Berg, 293–324. Leiden: Brill, 2003.

Micklethwait, John, and Adrian Wooldridge. *God Is Back*. London: Penguin, 2009.

Mohammed, Khaleel. *David in the Muslim Tradition: Bathsheba Affair*. London: Lexington, 2015.

Möller, Karl. "Prophecy and Prophets in the OT." In *Dictionary for Theological Interpretation of the Bible*, edited by Kevin J. Vanhoozer, 626–628. Grand Rapids: Baker Academic, 2005.

Moloney, Francis J. *Mark: Storyteller, Interpreter, Evangelist*. Peabody: Hendrickson, 2004.

Moreau, Scott. *Contextualization in World Missions: Mapping and Assessing Evangelical Models*. Grand Rapids: Kregel, 2012.

Morris, Benny. "Revisiting the Palestinian Exodus of 1948." In *The War for Palestine: Rewriting the History of 1948*, edited by Eugene L. Rogan and Avi Shlaim, 37–59. Cambridge: Cambridge University Press, 2001.

Morton, Jeff. "IM: Inappropriate Missiology?" In *Chrislam: How Missionaries Are Promoting an Islamized Gospel*, edited by Joshua Lingel, Jeff Morton, and Bill Nikides, ch. 3.5. Garden Grove: i2 Ministries, 2011.

———. *Insider Movements: Biblically Incredible or Incredibly Brilliant?* Eugene: Wipf & Stock, 2012.

Muasher, Marwan. *The Second Arab Awakening*. London: Yale University Press, 2014.

Muck, Terry. *Why Study Religion? Understanding Humanity's Pursuit of the Divine*. Grand Rapids: Baker Academic, 2016.

Muck, Terry, and Frances S. Adeney. *Christianity Encountering World Religions: The Practice of Mission in the Twenty-First Century*. Grand Rapids: Baker Academic, 2009.

Muir, Diana. "A Land without a People for a People without a Land." *Middle East Quarterly* 15.2 (Spring 2008): 55–62.

Mumo, Peter Mutuku. "Western Christian Interpretation of African Traditional Medicine: A Case Study of Akamba Herbal Medicine." *Ilorin Journal of Religious Studies* 8, no. 1 (2018): 41–50.

Musk, Bill. *Touching the Soul of Islam: Sharing the Gospel with Muslim Cultures*. Crowborough: MARC, 1995.

———. *The Unseen Face of Islam*. E. Sussex: MARC, 2009.

———. *The Unseen Face of Islam: Sharing the Gospel with Ordinary Muslims at Street Level*. Oxford: Monarch Books, 2004.

Nagel, Tilman. *Allahs Liebling: Ursprung und Erscheinungsformen des Mohammedglaubens*. Munich: Oldenbourg, 2008.

Ndungane, N. *A World with a Human Face: A Voice from Africa*. London: SPCK, 2003.
Netland, Harold. "Evangelical Missiology and Theology of Religions: An Agenda for the Future." *IJFM* 29, no. 1 (2012): 5–12.
———. "On Worshiping the Same God: What Exactly Is the Question?" *Missiology* 45, no. 4 (2017): 441–456.
Netland, Harold, and Craig Ott. *Globalizing Theology: Belief and Practice in an Era of World Christianity*. Grand Rapids: Baker Academic, 2006.
Neusner, Jacob, and Tamara Sonn. *Comparing Religions through Law: Judaism and Christianity*. London: Routledge, 1999.
Neuwirth, Angelika. "Qur'an and History – a Disputed Relationship: Some Reflections on Qur'anic History and History in the Qur'an." *Journal of Qur'anic Studies* 5, no. 1 (2003): 1–18.
Newbigin, Lesslie. *Foolishness to the Greeks: The Gospel and Western Culture*. Grand Rapids: Eerdmans, 1986.
———. *The Gospel in a Pluralist Society*. Grand Rapids: Eerdmans, 1989.
Nguvugher, C. D. "Conflicting Christologies in a Context of Conflicts: Jesus, the Īsāwā, and Christian-Muslim Relations in Nigeria." PhD dissertation, Universität Rostock, 2010.
Niebuhr, Richard. *Christ and Culture*. New York: Harper and Brothers, 1951.
Nikides, Bill. "One-Ist Missiology: Insider Movements and Theology of Religions." (2011). http://www.pefministry.org/Nikides_files/One-ist%20Missiology%20 and%20Insider%20movements%20copy.pdf.
Nishioka, Yoshiyuki B. "Worldview Methodology in Mission Theology: A Comparison between Kraft's and Hiebert's Approaches." *Missiology* 26, no. 4 (1998): 456–476.
Nongbri, Brent. *Before Religion: A History of a Modern Concept*. New Haven: Yale University Press, 2013.
Ntombana, L. "The Trajectories of Christianity and African Ritual Practices: The Public Silence and the Dilemma of Mainline or Mission Churches." *Acta Theologica* 35, no. 2 (2015): 104–119.
Nwafor, Mathew Ekechukwu. "Integrating African Values with Christianity: A Requirement for Dialogue between Christian Religion and African Culture." *Mgbakoigba: Journal of African Studies* 6, no. 1 (2016).
Nwaigbo, Ferdinand. "Faith in the One God in Christian and African Traditional Religions: A Theological Appraisal." *OGIRISI: A New Journal of African Studies* 7 (2010): 56–68. https://www.ajol.info/index.php/og/article/view/57922.
Oduyoye, Mercy Amba. *Hearing and Knowing: Theological Reflections on Christianity in Africa*. Eugene: Wipf & Stock, 1986.
Ogot, Bethwell A. *History of the Southern Luo*. Nairobi: East African Publishing House, 1967.
Olupona, Jacob K. "Major Issues in the Study of African Traditional Religion." In *African Traditional Religions in Contemporary Society*, edited by Jacob K. Olupona, 25–34. St. Paul: Paragon, 1991.

Omoregbe, J. I. *Philosophy of Religion*. Lagos: Joja, 1993.

Ong, J. Walter. *Orality and Literacy: The Technologizing of the Word*. London: Routledge, 1982.

Ongong'a, Jude J. *Life and Death: A Christian-Luo Dialogue*. Eldoret, Kenya: Gaba, 1983.

Onyeka-Joe, Amaegwu. *Globalization vs African Cultural Values*. Enugu: n.p., 2013.

Osborne, Grant R. *The Hermeneutical Spiral: A Comprehensive Introduction to Biblical Interpretation*. Downers Grove: IVP, 1991.

Oseje, Lawrence. *African Traditions Meeting Islam: A Case of Luo-Muslim Funerals in Kendu Bay, Kenya*. Carlisle Monographs: Langham Monographs, 2018.

Pappe, Ilan. *The Ethnic Cleansing of Palestine*. London: Oneworld, 2007.

Parshall, Philip L. *Bridges to Islam: A Christian Perspective on Folk Islam*. Grand Rapids: Baker, 1983.

———. "Danger! New Directions in Contextualization." *Evangelical Mission Quarterly* 34, no. 4 (1998): 404–406; 409–410.

Pauw, B. A. *Christianity and Xhosa Tradition: Belief and Ritual among Xhosa-Speaking Christians*. New York: Oxford University Press, 1975.

Penn, Michael Philip. *Envisioning Islam: Syriac Christians and the Early Muslim World*. Philadelphia: University of Pennsylvania Press, 2015.

———. *When Christians First Met Muslims: A Sourcebook of the Earliest Syriac Writings on Islam*. Oakland: University of California Press, 2015.

Pennington, Perry. "From Prophethood to the Gospel: Talking to Folk Muslims about Jesus." *IJFM* 31, no. 4 (2014): 195–203.

Presner, Todd. "Comparative Literature in the Age of Digital Humanities: On Possible Futures for a Discipline." In *A Companion to Comparative Literature*, edited by Ali Behdad and Dominic Thomas, 193–207. Chichester: Wiley-Blackwell, 2011.

Prince, Ruth. "Christian Salvation and Luo Tradition: Arguments of Faith in a Time of Death in Western Kenya." In *AIDS and Religious Practice in Africa*, edited by Felicitas Beeker and P. Wenzel Geissler, 49–88. Leiden: Brill, 2009.

Rabbah. *Midrash Rabbah, Vol. 3: Exodus*. London; New York: Soncino, 1983.

Ramban, Rabbi Moses ben Nahman. *Shemos: The Torah with Ramban's Commentary*. Translated by Artscroll Mesorah (2007). www.sefaria.org/Ramban_on_Exodus.3.15?lang=bi.

Rashi. *Pentateuch with Targum Onkelos, Haphtoroth and Prayers for Sabbath and Rashi's Commentary*. Edited and translated by M. Rosenbaum and A. M. Silbermann. London: Shapiro, Vallentine, 1946.

Reisacher, Evelyne. *Joyful Witness in the Muslim World: Sharing the Gospel in Everyday Encounters*. Grand Rapids: Baker Academic, 2016.

———. "Who Represents Islam?" In *Margins of Islam: Ministry in Diverse Muslim Contexts*, edited by Gene Daniels and Warrick Farah, 1–12. Littleton: William Carey Library, 2018.

Reynolds, Gabriel Said. *The Emergence of Islam: Classical Traditions in Contemporary Perspective.* Minneapolis: Fortress, 2012.

———. "The Muslim Jesus: Dead or Alive?" *Bulletin of SOAS* 72, no. 2 (2009): 237–258.

———. *The Qur'an and Its Biblical Subtext.* New York: Routledge, 2010.

Rhoads, David, and Donald Michie. *Mark as Story: An Introduction to the Narrative of a Gospel.* Philadelphia: Fortress, 1982; repr. 1984.

Richard, H. L. "Religious Syncretism as a Syncretistic Concept: The Inadequacy of the 'World Religions' Paradigm in Cross-Cultural Encounter." *IJFM* 31, no. 4 (2014): 209–215.

Rippin, Andrew. "Muhammad in the Qur'an: Reading Scripture in the 21st Century." In *The Biography of Muhammad: The Issue of the Sources*, edited by Harald Motzki, 298–309. Leiden: Brill, 2000.

Roberts, Jonathan. "Introduction." In *The Oxford Handbook of the Reception History of the Bible*, edited by Michael Lieb, Emma Mason, and Jonathan Roberts, 1–8. Oxford: Oxford University Press, 2011.

Robinson, Martin. *Planting Mission-Shaped Churches Today.* Oxford: Monarch, 2006.

Rodinson, Maxime. *Mahomet.* 2nd edition. Paris: Éditions du Seuils, 1968.

Roper, Geoffrey, ed. *World Survey of Islamic Manuscripts.* Vol. 3. London: Al-Furqan Islamic Heritage Foundation, 1992.

Rosner, Brian S. "The Concept of Idolatry." *Themelios* 24, no. 3 (1999): 21–30.

Rothschild, Fritz A., ed. *Between God and Man: An Interpretation of Judaism from the Writings of Abraham Heschel.* New York: Free Press Paperbacks, 1959.

Rowe, C. Kavin. *World Upside Down: Reading Acts in the Graeco-Roman Age.* Oxford: Oxford University Press, 2009.

Rubin, Uri. "Ḥanīfiyya and Ka'aba: An Inquiry into the Arabian Pre-Islamic Background of Dīn Ibrāhīm." *Jerusalem Studies in Arabic and Islam* 13 (1990): 85–112.

Ruthven, Malise. *Islam in the World.* 3rd edition. Oxford: Oxford University Press, 2006.

Rynkiewich, Michael. "A New Heaven and a New Earth? The Future of Missiological Anthropology." In *Paradigm Shifts in Christian Witness*, edited by Charles Van Engen, Darrell Whiteman, and Dudley Woodberry, 33–45. Maryknoll: Orbis, 2008.

Sabo, Theodore. *From Monophysitism to Nestorianism: AD 431–681.* Cambridge: Cambridge Scholars, 2018.

Sadeghi, Behnam, and Uwe Bergmann. "The Codex of a Companion of the Prophet and the Qur'an of the Prophet." *Arabica* 57 (2010): 343–436.

Safa, Reza. *Inside Islam: Exposing and Reaching the World of Islam.* Orlando: Creation House, 1996.

Sahin, Abdullah. "Islam, Secularity and the Culture of Critical Openness: A Muslim Theological Reflection." In *British Secularism and Religion: Islam, Society and the State*, edited by Yahya Birt, Dilwar Hussain, and Ataullah Siddiqui, chapter 1. Markfield: Kube, 2011.

Samir, Samir Khalil. "The Prophet Muhammad as Seen by Timothy I and Some Other Arab Christian Authors." In *Syrian Christians under Islam: The First Thousand Years*, edited by David R. Thomas, 77–81. Leiden: Brill, 2001.

Sangari, Kumkum. "Aesthetics of Circulation: Thinking Between Regions." *Jadavpur Journal of Comparative Literature* 50 (2013–2014): 9–38.

Saritoprak, Zeki. *Islam's Jesus*. Gainesville: University Press of Florida, 2014.

Schacht, Joseph. *The Origins of Muhammadan Jurisprudence*. Oxford: Clarendon, 1950.

Schimmel, Annemarie. *Deciphering the Signs of God: A Phenomenological Approach to Islam*. Albany: State University of New York, 1994.

Schnabel, Eckhard J. *Early Christian Mission – Vol. 2: Paul and the Early Church*. Leicester: Apollos; Downers Grove: IVP, 2004.

Schwartz, Nancy. "Active Dead or Alive: Some Kenyan Views about the Agency of Luo and Luyia Women Pre- and Post-Mortem." *Journal of Religion in Africa* 30, no. 4 (2000): 433–467.

Segal, Judah B. "Arabs in Syriac Literature before the Rise of Islam." *Jerusalem Studies in Arabic and Islam* 4 (1984): 89–124.

Setiloane, G. M. *African Theology*. Cape Town: Lux Verbi, 2000.

Shah, Zulfiqar Ali. *Anthropomorphic Depictions of God: The Concept of God in Judaic, Christian and Islamic Traditions: Representing the Unrepresentable*. Herndon: International Institute of Islamic Thought, 2010.

Shehadeh, I. N. *God With Us and Without Us: Oneness in Trinity Versus Absolute Oneness*, vol. 1. Carlisle: Langham Global Library, 2018.

Shiino, Wakana. "Death and Rituals among the Luo in South Nyanza." *African Study Monographs* 18, no. 3/4 (1997): 213–228.

Shipton, Parker MacDonald. *Mortgaging the Ancestors: Ideologies of Attachment in Africa*. New Haven: Yale University Press, 2009.

Siddiqui, Mona. *Christians, Muslims, and Jesus*. New Haven: Yale University Press, 2014.

Sinai, Nicolai. *The Qur'an: A Historical-Critical Introduction*. Edinburgh: Edinburgh University Press, 2017.

Sizer, Stephen. *Christian Zionism: Road-map to Armageddon?* Leicester: Inter-Varsity Press, 2004.

———. *Zion's Christian Soldiers? The Bible, Israel and the Church*. Leicester: Inter-Varsity Press, 2007.

Smith, Jay. "The Case for Polemics." In *Between Naivety and Hostility: Uncovering the Best Christian Responses to Islam in Britain*, edited by Steve Bell and Colin Chapman, 241–247. Milton Keynes: Authentic, 2011.

Smith, Wilfred Cantwell. "Comparative Religion: Whither and Why?" In *The History of Religions: Essays in Methodology* 34, edited by Mircea Eliade and

Joseph M. Kitagawa. Chicago: University of Chicago Press, 1959. https://www.religion-online.org/book-chapter/comparative-religion-whither-and-why-by-wilfred-cantwell-smith/.

Sozomen. *The Ecclesiastical History of Sozomen: Comprising a History of the Church from AD 324 to AD 440*. Translated by E. Walford. London: Henry G. Bohn, 1855.

Span, John. "Are Bible Translators Trying to Bring Christianity and Islam Closer Together?" *Biblical Missiology*, 24 February 2020. https://biblicalmissiology.org/2020/02/24/are-bible-translators-trying-to-bring-christianity-and-islam-closer-together/.

Spitzer, Toba. "'Where Do You Come From, and Where Are You Going?': Hagar and Sarah Encounter God." *Reconstructionist* 8 (1998): 8–18.

Stacey, Vivienne. *Christ Supreme over Satan: Spiritual Warfare, Folk Religion and the Occult*. Lahore: Masihi Isha'at Khana, 1986.

Stamp, Patricia. "Burying Otieno: The Politics of Gender and Ethnicity in Kenya." *Signs: Journal of Women in Culture and Society* 16, no. 4 (1991): 808–845.

Stein, Robert H. *Mark*. Baker Exegetical Commentary on the New Testament. Grand Rapids: Baker Academic, 2008.

Sternberg, Meir. *The Poetics of Biblical Narrative: Ideological Literature and the Drama of Reading*. Bloomington: Indiana University Press, 1985.

Stichele, Caroline Vander. "The Head of John and Its Reception or How to Conceptualize Reception History." In *Reception History and Biblical Studies: Theology and Practice*, edited by Emma England and William J. Lyons, 79–94. London: Bloomsbury T&T Clark, 2015.

Stokl, J. "Ancient Near Eastern Prophecy." In *Dictionary of the Old Testament: Prophets*, edited by Mark J. Boda and J. G. McConville. Downers Grove: IVP Academic, 2012.

Stott, John. *The Message of Acts: To the Ends of the Earth*. The Bible Speaks Today. Leicester; Downers Grove: IVP, 1990.

Strange, Daniel. *Their Rock Is Not Like Our Rock: A Theology of Religions*. Grand Rapids: Zondervan, 2014.

Strong, James. *A Concise Dictionary of the Words in the Greek Testament and The Hebrew Bible*. Bellingham: Logos Bible Software, 2009.

Stroope, Michael W. *Transcending Mission: The Eclipse of a Modern Tradition*. Downers Grove: IVP, 2017.

Stroumsa, Sarah. "The Signs of Prophecy: The Emergence and Early Development of a Theme in Arabic Theological Literature." *The Harvard Theological Review* 78, no. 1/2 (Jan–Apr 1985): 101–14.

Swanson, Herb. "Said's Orientalism and the Study of Christian Missions." *International Bulletin of Missionary Research* 28, no. 3 (2004): 107–112.

Sweetman, J. Windrow. *Islam and Christian Theology: A Study of the Interpretation of Theological Ideas in the Two Religions*. 4 vols. London: Lutterworth, 1967.

Taha, Mahmoud Mohammed. *The Second Message of Islam*. Translated by Abdullahi Ahmed An-Naʻim. Syracuse: Syracuse University Press, 1987.

Talman, Harley. "Is Muhammad also among the Prophets?" *IJFM* 31, no. 4 (2014): 169–190.

Talman, Harley, and John J. Travis, eds. *Understanding Insider Movements: Disciples of Jesus within Diverse Religious Communities*. Pasadena: William Carey Library, 2015.

Tennent, Timothy. "Followers of Jesus (Isa) in Islamic Mosques: A Closer Examination of C-5 'high Spectrum' Contextualization." *IJFM* 23, no. 3 (2006): 101–115.

———. *Invitation to World Missions: A Trinitarian Missiology for the Twenty-First Century*. Grand Rapids: Kregel, 2010.

Theron, Pieter François. *African Traditional Cultures and the Church*. Pretoria: ISWEN, 1990.

Thomas, David R., and Barbara H. Roggema, eds. *Christian-Muslim Relations: A Bibliographical History, Vol. 1 (600–900)*. Leiden; Boston: Brill, 2009.

Tottoli, Roberto. *Biblical Prophets in the Qur'an and Muslim Literature*. New York: Routledge, 2002.

Towner, Philip H. *The Letters to Timothy and Titus*. New International Commentary on the New Testament. Grand Rapids: Eerdmans, 2006.

Travis, John Jay. "The C1–C6 Spectrum after Fifteen Years." *Evangelical Missions Quarterly* 51, no. 4 (2015): 358–365.

———. "The C1 to C6 Spectrum: A Practical Tool for Defining Six Types of 'Christ-centered Communities' ('C') Found in the Muslim Context." *Evangelical Mission Quarterly* 34, no. 4 (1998): 407–408.

———. "Messianic Muslim Followers of Isa: A Closer Look at C5 Believers and Congregations." *IJFM* 17, no. 1 (2000): 53–59.

———. "Must All Muslims Leave 'Islam' to Follow Jesus?" *Evangelical Mission Quarterly* 34, no. 4 (1998): 411–415.

Trigg, Roger, and Justin L. Barrett. *The Roots of Religion*. Farnham: Ashgate, 2014.

Trimingham, J. Spencer. *Christianity among the Arabs in Pre-Islamic Times*. London: Longman, 1979.

Tsevat, Matitiahu. *The Meaning of the Book of Job and Other Biblical Studies: Essays on the Literature and Religion of the Hebrew Bible*. New York: Ktav, 1980.

Tutu, D. M. *No Future without Forgiveness*. London: Rider, 1999.

Tylor, Edward. *Primitive Culture*. Cambridge: Cambridge University Press, 2010 [original 1871].

van Doren, John W. "Death African Style: The Case of S. M. Otieno." *American Journal of Comparative Law* 36, no. 2 (1988): 329–350.

Van Rheenen, Gailyn. "A Theology of Culture: Desecularizing Anthropology." *IJFM* 14, no. 1 (1997): 33–38.

Vanhoozer, Kevin J. *The Drama of Doctrine: A Canonical-Linguistic Approach to Christian Theology*. Louisville: Westminster John Knox, 2005.

Volf, Miroslav, Prince Ghazi bin Muhammad bin Talal, and Melissa Yarrington, eds. *A Common Word: Muslims and Christians on Loving God and Neighbor*. Grand Rapids: Eerdmans, 2009.

Voll, John O. and Kazuo Ohtsuka. "Sufism." In *The Oxford Encyclopedia of the Islamic World*, Oxford Islamic Studies Online, edited by John L. Esposito. Oxford: Oxford University Press, 2009. http://www.oxfordislamicstudies.com/article/opr/t236/e0759.

Waldman, Marilyn. "New Approaches to 'Biblical' Materials in the Qur'an." *Muslim World* 75 (1985): 1–13.

Walker, Allen, et al. *The New International Webster's Comprehensive Dictionary of the English Language*. Naples, FL: Trident Press International, 2004.

Wallace, Daniel B. "Greek Grammar and the Personality of the Holy Spirit." *Bulletin for Biblical Research* 13, no. 1 (2003): 97–125.

Walls, Andrew. *The Missionary Movement in Christian History: Studies in the Transmission of the Faith*. Maryknoll: Orbis, 1996.

Wansbrough, John. *Qur'anic Studies: Sources and Methods of Scriptural Interpretation*. Oxford: Oxford University Press, 1977.

———. *The Sectarian Milieu*. Oxford: Oxford University Press, 1978.

Watson, Francis. *Paul and the Hermeneutics of Faith*. London: T&T Clark, 2004.

Watt, Montgomery. *Muhammad at Mecca*. Oxford: Clarendon, 1953.

———. *Muhammad at Medina*. Oxford: Clarendon, 1956.

Weber, Max. *The Sociology of Religion*. London: Methuen, 1965.

Welch, A. T. "al-is Argument." In *Encyclopaedia of Islam*, 2nd ed., edited by P. Bearman, T. Bianquis, C. E. Bosworth, E. van Donzel, and W. P. Heinrichs. Leiden: Brill, 1960.

Wenham, Gordon. *Genesis 1–15*. Word Biblical Commentaries. Nashville: Thomas Nelson, 1995.

———. *Rethinking Genesis 1–11: Gateway to the Bible*. Oregon: Cascade, 2015.

Wensinck, A. J. *The Muslim Creed: Its Genesis and Historical Development*. Cambridge: Cambridge University Press, 1932.

White, Ben. *Israeli Apartheid: A Beginner's Guide*. London: Pluto, 2014.

Whittingham, M. *A History of Muslim Views of the Bible: The Bible and Muslim Identity Formation*, Vol. 1. Berlin: De Gruyter, forthcoming.

Wilde, Clare. "The Qur'ān: Kalām Allāh or Words of Man? A Case of Tafsīr Transcending Muslim-Christian Communal Borders." *Parole de l'Orient* 32 (2007): 1–17.

Witherington III, Ben. *The Acts of the Apostles: A Socio-Rhetorical Commentary*. Grand Rapids: Eerdmans, 1998.

Wood, Nicholas J. *Faiths and Faithfulness: Pluralism, Dialogue, and Mission in the Work of Kenneth Cragg and Lesslie Newbigin*. Eugene: Wipf & Stock, 2009.

Woodberry, J. Dudley. "Contextualization Among Muslims: Reusing Common Pillars." In *The Word among Us: Contextualizing Theology for Mission Today*, edited by

Dean S. Gilliland, 282–312. Dallas: Word, 1989. (Reprinted with more complete footnotes in *International Journal of Frontier Missions* 13, no. 4 [Oct–Dec 1996]: 171–186. www.ijfm.org/PDFs_IJFM/13_4_PDFs/03_Woodberry.pdf.)

———, ed. *From Seed to Fruit: Global Trends, Fruitful Practices, and Emerging Issues among Muslims*. Revised edition. Pasadena: William Carey Library, 2011.

Wright, Christopher J. H. "The Christian and Other Religions: The Biblical Evidence." *Themelios* 9, no. 2 (1984): 4–15.

———. *The Mission of God: Unlocking the Bible's Grand Narrative*. Downers Grove: IVP Academic, 2006.

Wright, N. T. *Jesus and the Victory of God. Vol. 2, Christian Origins and the Question of God*. London: SPCK, 1996.

———. *Mark for Everyone*. The New Testament for Everyone. London: SPCK, 2001.

Yip, George. "The Contour of a Post-Postmodern Missiology." *Missiology* 42, no. 4 (2014): 399–411.

Zakovitch, Yair. *"And You Shall Tell Your Son . . .": The Concept of the Exodus in the Bible*. Jerusalem: Magnes, 1991.

Zuhayli, Wahbah. *Concise Interpretation of the Grand Qur'an with the Causes of Descent and Rules of Reciting*. Damascus: Dar Al Fikr, 1994.

Zwemer, Samuel. *The Influence of Animism on Islam: An Account of Popular Superstitions*. New York: Macmillan, 1920.

———. *Studies in Popular Islam: A Collection of Papers Dealing with the Superstitions and Beliefs of the Common People*. London: Sheldon; New York: Macmillan, 1939.

List of Contributors

Martin Accad serves as the Chief Academic Officer of Arab Baptist Theological Seminary (ABTS) in Beirut, Lebanon. He is also Associate Professor of Islamic Studies at ABTS and Fuller Theological Seminary in Pasadena, California, as well as Director of ABTS's Institute of Middle East Studies. In addition, he is Director of Programs, Middle East, for the Centre on Religion and Global Affairs (www.crga.org.uk). He is the author of *Sacred Misinterpretation: Reaching across the Muslim-Christian Divide* in addition to numerous articles and book chapters. Having a rich multicultural background in his own family, he is very involved in faith-based peacebuilding and bridging Arab-Western cultural divides. He earned his PhD from the University of Oxford, defending his dissertation on "The Interpretation of the Gospels by Muslims of the 8th to the 14th Centuries" on 11 September 2001.

Muhammad Al-Arabi is Egyptian and was raised in a Sunni Muslim family. Beside his daily business work, he is involved in mentoring others in their journey with Christ as well as peace building initiatives.

Rose Mary Amenga-Etego is Associate Professor of Religious Studies and Head of the Department for the Study of Religions, University of Ghana, Legon. She is also a Research Fellow at the Research Institute for Theology and Religion (RITR), University of South Africa, South Africa. Her research interests include topical issues in African Indigenous Religions, gender issues in religion and African culture, and methodological concerns of indigenous African scholars. Recent publications include: "The Practice of Traditional Medicine and Bioethical Challenges," in *Bioethics in African: Theories and Praxis* (2018) and "Crossing Research Boundaries: 'Our Nankani Daughter' in Academia," AASR *E-Journal* 4, no. 1 (2018). She is also the author of *Mending the Broken Pieces: Indigenous Religion and Sustainable Rural Development in Northern Ghana* (2011).

Jonathan Andrews is British and lives in the UK. He has been researching and writing on the Middle East since 2003. He is the author of two books on the Middle East and the editor to two more (see bibliography) prior to co-editing this work.

Susan Azzam is from the Shouf area of Lebanon. She is from a Druze background and became a believer in 2004 when she and her family started attending church where she became engaged in ministry. She is currently leading her own ministry in Allay.

Shirin Bahrami is an Iranian and French citizen. She is a committed counselor with ten years' experience providing professional counselling services. She is a member of the British Association of Counselling and Psychotherapy (BACP). She has worked with clients who deal with trauma, abuse, depression, addictions, marital difficulties, anger, anxiety, grief, self-harm and relational conflicts. Working in both France and the UK, she has developed the ability to work with different nationalities and backgrounds. She graduated with a Computer Science and Linguistics degree from Sorbonne Nouvelle Paris III and received her Counselling degree from Nottingham University, UK. She is the owner of Healing 4 Living ministry whose purpose is to bring inner healing for men and women who are abused or marginalized in Muslim societies, and to help them to explore their God-given purpose, which empowers them to work toward positive change in the world around them.

George Bristow is an American who is based in Turkey. He earned his PhD from the Vrije Universiteit Amsterdam. Having lived in Istanbul since 1987, he has served since 2009 as coordinator of a theological training network working with churches in Turkey. He is a research fellow with the Institute for the Study of Religion in the Middle East and is the author of *Sharing Abraham?: Narrative Worldview, Biblical and Qur'anic Interpretation and Comparative Theology in Turkey* and *The Promise of God: God's Unchangeable Purpose through Human History.* He is also the author of *Sürgün Ve Ötesi: Kutsal Kitaptaki Daniel, Hagay, Zekeriya Ve Malaki Bölümleri Üzerine Yorum*, a commentary on Daniel, Haggai, Zechariah and Malachi.

Daniel (Dan) Brown is an American based in Istanbul, Turkey. He directs the Institute for the Study of Religion in the Middle East (ISRME). The focus of ISRME is on the multi-disciplinary study of religious phenomena including religious texts, ideas and belief systems, and also the rituals, histories and social structures of religious communities. In addition, he is the author of *Rethinking Tradition in Modern Islamic Thought* (Cambridge) and *A New Introduction to Islam* (Wiley-Blackwell). He was awarded a doctorate in Islamic Studies from the University of Chicago and has taught at Mount Holyoke College and Smith College and has been a visiting scholar at the Islamic University in Islamabad, the Institute of Islamic Culture in Lahore,

Cairo University and Oxford University. His interests include modern Muslim intellectual history, Hadith studies and Muslim-Christian relations.

Emad Botros is from Egypt. He is a Global Field Staff member with Canadian Baptist Ministries, teaching in the area of Old Testament at the Arab Baptist Theological Seminary (ABTS). Emad's research focuses above all on the intersection of the biblical text and the Qur'an. He completed an MA in Christian Studies at McMaster Divinity College (2013), where his past research focused on the intersection of the book of Exodus and the Qur'an, with a particular interest in the Golden Calf narrative in the book of Exodus and the Qur'an. He is currently in a doctoral program at the same college, where his current research focuses on the intersection of the Minor Prophets Corpus and the Qur'an, particularly the book of Jonah and the Prophet Yunus.

Anton Deik is a Palestinian Christian from Bethlehem. He is a Lecturer in Biblical Studies at Bethlehem Bible College (online) and works as an e-learning consultant for theological colleges in Palestine and Bolivia. Anton is currently a PhD candidate in New Testament Studies at the University of Aberdeen and Trinity College, Bristol, and is also a networking team member of the International Fellowship of Mission as Transformation. Previously, Anton worked as the Director of Online Education at Bethlehem Bible College, and he served with Operation Mobilization on board MV *Logos Hope*. He also has several years of experience working on computer science research projects with Birzeit University and the Palestinian government. Anton holds an MA (with merit) in Biblical Studies from London School of Theology and a bachelor's degree in computer systems engineering from Birzeit University.

Havilah Dharamraj is Academic Dean and Professor of the Old Testament at the South Asia Institute of Advanced Christian Studies in Bangalore, India. Her academic degrees include an MS in biochemistry, an MA in Christianity, and a PhD from the University of Durham, UK. She is author of various articles and books including *Altogether Lovely: A Thematic and Intertextual Reading of the Song of Songs* (Fortress, 2018). She was one of the editors of the *South Asia Bible Commentary: A One-Volume Commentary on the Whole Bible* (Zondervan, 2015). Dr Dharamraj serves on the peer review team for Priscilla Papers.

Issa Diab is Lebanese. He is Professor of Semitic and Interfaith Studies (Judaism, Christianity and Islam) and Global Translation Adviser at the United Bible Societies. Further, he is a Bible interpreter and translation consultant for the United Bible Societies and regular lecturer throughout Lebanon and the Middle East, having taught at Saint Joseph University, the Near East School of Theology (NEST), Hagazian University, Middle East University and Arab Baptist Theological Seminary among others. He holds a total of four doctorates in the following fields: New Testament Studies, Ancient Near Eastern Civilizations, Islamic Culture and Society, and Old Testament Studies. He is a prolific author of articles and books.

Senem Ekener was born and raised in the Asia Minor of the Bible. She graduated from Istanbul University with a BA in philosophy. After working in the secular media industry, Senem completed an extension program in media at the University of California, Los Angeles. She became a follower of Christ in 2002 after a strong encounter with the Holy Spirit. She is a member of Pera Resurrection Church, where she serves on the council and is part of the worship and preaching team. Senem has been serving as the country director of the Ravi Zacharias International Ministries (RZIM) Turkey office since 2007, also as a speaker and teacher. Senem has produced many television and radio programs and is a regular program producer and host for SAT-7 Turk, a Christian satellite television channel. Her burden is to share the good news of Jesus with the Turkish-speaking audiences and defend the uniqueness of Christ through the fields of academics, media, arts, society and the church. Senem also regularly teaches seminars with Hasat (Harvest) Ministries in Turkey.

Warrick Farah holds a doctorate in Missiology from Fuller Theological Seminary. He serves as a missiologist and theological educator in the Middle East with One Collective (onecollective.org). His research on conversion, theological paradigms of witness, and "insiderness" has been published in journals such as *Evangelical Missions Quarterly*, *International Journal of Frontier Missiology* and *Global Missiology*. He is co-editor of the book *Margins of Islam: Ministry in Diverse Muslim Contexts*.

Amal Gendi was born in Egypt and lives in Canada. He has much experience serving the people of the Middle East and North African region. He holds a doctorate in Ministry from Tyndale University College and Seminary focused on identifying and addressing barriers to discipleship in the Middle East. He also holds a Master of Theological Studies from the same institution. Dr Gendi currently serves as Missionary Theologian and Muslim Ministries Coordinator with Pioneers Canada as well as Dean of Bachelor's Studies and Ministry Training with Pioneers International. He is the former Executive Director of Arab World Ministries and currently serves as adjunct professor with Heritage

Baptist College and Theological Seminary and visiting professor with Tyndale University College and Seminary.

Ida Glaser is the International Academic Coordinator and Founding Fellow at the Oxford Centre for Muslim Christian Studies, where she oversees a number of international projects. She previously taught in the areas of Qur'an and Bible, and the history of Muslim-Christian dialogue at the University of Edinburgh, and her personal research interests focus on reading the Bible in the context of Islam. She is an associate staff member at Wycliffe Hall, Oxford. Ida has taught physics in Islamic contexts and done church-based outreach in multi-racial, inner-city Britain. She has worked among people of other faiths for Crosslinks, the Anglican Mission Agency, and is a past director of Faith to Faith, a Christian consultancy about other faiths. Her doctorate examined Genesis 1–11 in the context of parallel qur'anic material. She has taught Muslim-Christian relations at the post-graduate level in Jamaica, Nigeria, the Philippines and the UK.

Nabil Habiby is a youth pastor who also works as a Dean of Students at the Nazarene School in Beirut. He is a lecturer in the New Testament at the Arab Nazarene Bible College and an adjunct faculty member and lecturer in the New Testament at Arab Baptist Theological Seminary (ABTS). He is also a part-time doctoral student at the Nazarene Theological College in Manchester, UK, where he is researching the relationship between impurity and demonic spirits and doing a conceptual study on the relationship of the two in the Ancient Near East, the Hebrew Bible and Second Temple Judaism. He is also conducting a narrative-spatial reading of the mentions of "impure spirits" in Mark. He holds a Master's degree from Nazarene Theological College, Manchester.

Hiba al-Haddad and her husband, Rafed, are currently finishing their final year toward a Bachelor of Theology at the Arab Baptist Theology Seminary (ABTS). They have a daughter called Milia and a son called Shadi. Both Rafed, Hiba and their two children fled their hometown in Syria early in the war, leaving their destroyed house behind, and they came to Lebanon four years later. Hiba currently leads Bible studies with refugee women at the Oasis Ministry Center run by the Free Evangelical Church of Beirut. They intend to start a home group ministry when they return to Syria.

Hanane is a Moroccan follower of Christ. She holds a Bachelor's of Divinity from the Arab Baptist Theological Seminary (ABTS) and a Bachelor's degree in English Literature from Ibn Zohr University. She currently teaches English literature and is an online tutor at ABTS.

Chaden Hani was born and raised in a Druze community in the Lebanese mountain area. She received her BA in Computer Science from Beirut University College before travelling to Europe where she became a follower of Christ in the year 2000. She had a conviction that God wanted her and her family to serve him in the Druze community. Back in Lebanon she and her family joined a local church for ten years during which she obtained her Bachelor's degree in Theology from the Arabic Baptist Theological Seminary (ABTS) and her Master's degree in Religion from the Institute of Middle East Studies (IMES) which is based at ABTS. She currently works as a Peacebuilding Initiatives Coordinator at IMES and co-pastors a local church of believers from a Druze background together with her husband.

Alexander (Alex) Massad is in the final stages of a PhD in Intercultural Studies from Fuller Theological Seminary and currently serves as an adjunct professor at California Lutheran University. His research focuses on how religious identities are formed through historically contextualizing theological dialogue between Muslims and Christians. In addition, he is interested in religion and politics, international relations, religious studies and pedagogy. He holds a Master of Theology and Religious Studies from Georgetown University and a Master of Middle Eastern and South Asia Languages and Cultures from the University of Virginia.

Michel and Janane Mattar are longstanding ministers in Lebanon. They lead a church and an organization that serves displaced Syrians and Iraqis as well as disadvantaged Lebanese people. As part of Triumphant Mercy Ministries Lebanon, they operate a community center, facilitate schools for refugee children and youth, organize day camps, run vocational assistance trainings, assist with medical emergencies, and facilitate spiritual activities such as Bible studies and praise.

Richard McCallum is a Senior Fellow at the Oxford Centre for Muslim-Christian Studies (OCMCS) and Lead Faculty for MENA Cultures in the MREL Program at Arab Baptist Theology Seminary (ABTS). He first travelled to North Africa in 1984 while studying for a BSc in Physics at Imperial College, London, and later lived in Tunis from 1992 to 2002 where he taught English and Linguistics at the Université de Tunis, having received an MA in Applied Linguistics. In 2011, Richard completed a PhD in Sociology at the

University of Exeter looking at Christian responses to Islam in Britain and taught Sociology of Religion. In 2012, Richard moved to Oxford to work as a freelance researcher for both the Centre for Muslim-Christian Studies at Oxford and for the Cambridge Interfaith Program, particularly looking at the impact of recent interfaith initiatives and the teaching of Islam to Christian students. In November 2013, Richard joined the staff of OCMCS as a research fellow. He has also taught on various aspects of Islam and worked with Muslims at several colleges in the UK. Richard occasionally works as a freelance cross-cultural trainer and delivers intercultural workshops particularly for companies working in the Arab world.

Lawrence Oseje is a Langham Scholar and earned his PhD in Interreligious Studies from Africa International University (AIU). He is an ordained minister of the gospel and has served as a pastor for twelve years in one of the largest cities in Kenya. He pioneered a department in Islam for Missions and Ministry in Uganda Christian University (UCU). Currently he is a lecturer and adjunct faculty in Missions and Interreligious Studies at a number of other universities and seminaries across Africa, including Africa International University, Nairobi, Kenya; Africa College of Theology, Kigali, Rwanda; and Regent University in the USA. Lawrence is married to Dorcas, and together they are blessed with three children, Jael, Emmanuel and Rosebell.

Grant Porter serves as the Program Director for Middle East, North Africa and Central Asia for Cornerstone Trust. Originally from Australia, Grant and his wife, Laura, until recently lived and served in Lebanon focusing on mobilization, evangelism, church planting and ministry partnering. They have three children and three grandkids and live in Michigan, USA. Grant earned his PhD from Vrije Universiteit, Amsterdam, focused on church-planting practices in the Middle East.

Teresa Sfeir graduated from the Lebanese University with a Masters degree in English Literature in 2018. She worked as an English Language Teaching (ELT) textbook editor at Educational Research Center (Librairie du Liban Publishers) from 2011 to 2016. Since 2016, she has been working at the Arab Baptist Theological Seminary as a Communication and Editing Officer.

Karen Shaw lived in the Middle East from 1990–2019 and was Associate Professor of Cross-Cultural Ministry at the Arab Baptist Theological Seminary (ABTS) from 2008–2019. She also shepherded the International Community Church in Beirut, Lebanon. Karen and her husband now live in Sydney, Australia. She is the author of *Wealth & Piety: Middle Eastern Perspectives* *for Expat Workers*, as well as numerous articles, book chapters and presentations. She holds a doctorate in Cross-Cultural Ministry from Gordon-Conwell Theological Seminary, and a Masters from Princeton Theological Seminary. Karen enjoys poetry and nature photography.

Anna Turner is a poet and playwright from the UK, now living in the Middle East. She loves exploring how creativity can help us to reflect the Creator God and draw us closer to him and to one another.

Yasser is a current Arabic Baptist Theology Seminary (ABTS) student finishing his second year toward a Bachelor of Theology. He is from Kalamoun, Syria, but he and his family fled to Lebanon in 2012 because of the war. He currently lives in Mansourieh and serves God with his local church in Airn Zhalta. He oversees the progress of a recently planted church in Nabaa and works with Syrian people coming to Christ.

Ashoor Yousif is an Assyrian-Iraqi Christian who is fluent in Arabic and Assyrian in addition to his knowledge of Aramaic, Hebrew and Syriac. His teaching portfolio includes multiple universities and seminaries in Canada and the Middle East, including Tyndale University, University of Toronto, and the Arabic Baptist Theological Seminary (ABTS) in Lebanon. His doctoral thesis "Allah's Deputy and Christ's Apostle: The Early Abbasid Ruler in Syriac and Syro-Arabic Sources" examines the interaction of Muslim rulers and Christian clergies, and the religious and political impact of Islam on the presence and status of Christian communities within the caliphate. He has taught and lectured on various topics including the history of Middle Eastern and North African Christianity, the history of Christian-Muslim relations, Middle Eastern religions and cultures, and Islam.

Gamal Zaki is Egyptian and was raised in a Sunni Muslim family. He is very active in training youth across the country in the areas of peace building and Christian-Muslim dialogue.

Abed Zieneldien is a Lecturer in Pastoral Ministries at the Arabic Baptist Theology Seminary (ABTS). He is a DMin candidate at Nazarene Theological Seminary in Kansas City, Missouri. Abed has written a few publications.

Subject Index

9/11 22, 430
   significance of 24
ʿAbd al-Malik b. Marwān, caliph 175
ʿAbduh, Muhammad 347
   reformist movement 346
ʿUmar Ibn al-Khaṭṭāb 222
ʿUthmān b. ʿAffān, caliph 177,
     223–226
   Muṣḥaf of 220, 223–227, 229, 240

A
Abbasid 178
Abdallah b. al-Zubayr 226
Abel 70, 72, 73
   in Qurʾan 70
abjection 44
Abraham 21, 4–45, 47–51, 64, 81, 82,
     85, 86, 99, 136, 151–153, 172,
     242, 247, 250, 260, 261, 266,
     285, 306, 309, 320, 323, 327,
     378, 385, 444, 451
   Abrahamic family 81
   Bible-Qurʾan commonality 326, 377
   blessing is for all 85, 447
   expels Hagar 46
   family 44
   in Qurʾan 82, 152, 325, 311, 333,
     447
   linked to Muhammad 332
   link to Kaʿba 327, 328, 332
   NT refers 269, 320, 372
   self-identity 47
   start of salvation story 446
abrogation 258, 297, 299, 300
Abu Bakr, caliph 167, 22–226
Abū Lahab (Muhammad's uncle) 218
Accad, Martin 20, 22, 28, 112, 124,
     189, 203, 285, 444, 449, 457
ad-dunyā 345

akedah (Abraham, Isaac & sacrifice)
   327
Akhtar, Shabbir 94, 96, 268–272
al-Ahbar, Kaʿb 168
al-ākhira 345
Al Arabi, Muhammad 28
al Azhar 384
al-Baqara 167
al-Faruqi 310
al-Furqān 167
al-Ghazālī, Abū Ḥāmid 349
al-Haddad, Hiba 336, 460
Ali b. Abī Ṭālib 223
   caliph 167
   legitimacy of decendents 180
   Muṣḥaf of 223, 226
   Ṣanʿāʾ Manuscripts 229
al-Jassās, Abu Bakr 298
al-Mahdi, Caliph 162
al-yawm al-ākhir 345
al-ʿāmm wa al-khāṣṣ 297
Amenga-Etego, Rose Mary 31, 96,
     450
Ammonites 45, 379
   line of Messiah 378
Andrews, Jonathan 106
an-nāsikh wa al-mansūkh 219, 297,
     300
anomie 91
Anṣār 225
anthropology 67, 89, 109, 110, 112,
     116, 184, 196, 198, 206
   biblical 69
   cultural 110, 113, 191
   postmodern 111
   secular 189
   theological 110
archaeology 68, 176
   none in Mecca, Medina 175
asbāb an-nuzūl 218, 220, 288, 300

as-sā'a 345
assurance, doctrine of 339, 340
　none in Islam 340
Ateek, Naim 78
atheism, rising in Arab world 274
Atwood, Margaret 100
āyat as-sayf 296
Āzar 260
Azzam, Susan 20, 30
a'māl 368

B
Babel 70–72, 85
　fusion of religion & empire 379
Babylon 68, 69, 71, 73
　exile in 68
Badr, Battle of 219
Baghdad 379
Bahira, Sergius, monk 162–164, 168, 169, 172
Bahrami, Shirin 338, 395, 461, 463
Bailey, Kenneth 34
Bal, Mieke 401, 405, 410
Barth, Karl 34, 191
basmala 168
Bauckham, Richard 320
Bavinck, J. H. 321, 436
belonging 43, 44, 86, 91, 110, 177, 202, 306, 316, 419, 421
　chosen 45
　dual 192
　heritage 323, 368
　in Christ 66
　Muhammad 302
　stranger 47
Berger, Peter 91, 92
Birmingham Manuscript 227
Birmingham Qur'an Manuscript 227
Botros, Emad 11, 215, 240, 384, 455
Bristow, George 242, 308, 444, 458
Brown, Daniel (Dan) 173, 286, 324, 355, 444, 453, 456
Bukhārī, Hadith collection 179, 222, 225

Byzantine 143, 144, 146–149, 157, 160, 294
Byzantine-Sassanian wars 144

C
Cain 70, 72–74
　in Qur'an 70
Calder, Norman 260
Casanova, José 93
Chaitanya, Satya 102
Chapman, Colin 75, 85, 135
Christian Zionism. *See* Zionism
circumcision 44, 64, 170, 199, 378
　Arabs 328, 332
　covenant of 44
　of heart 373–375
classics 268, 278, 456
Coleman, Doug 322
colonialism 95, 99, 109, 192, 379, 445
　Arab, Islamic 17
　endorsed by God? 78
　neo 110, 379
　postcolonial 110, 112, 116, 127, 202
common reader 99–105
Common Word 128, 129
comparative literary approaches 242
comparative literature 99, 101
comparative theology 242, 308
converts 277
　community 92, 356
　group belonging 91
　Islamic practices 357
　not extracted 21
　obedience to scripture 360
　remain in community 306, 307, 357
　telling family 275, 339, 360
　to Islam 425
Cook, Michael 182, 183, 289
Cornelius 79, 80, 321
　conversion of 79
covenants 64, 74, 261, 310, 326, 329, 330, 332, 333, 368, 371, 373, 375, 377, 380, 381, 383, 444, 458
　Abrahamic 152, 325, 327, 330

basis for religious law? 371
Davidic 313, 326
in Qur'an 325, 458
Mosaic 372
rainbow 74, 323, 451
Cragg, Kenneth 137, 272
Crone, Patricia 182, 183
Cumming, Joseph 272
Curry, Bishop Michael 41

D

Daesh. *See* ISIS
Damascus 63, 379
Daniel 390, 463
four beasts 147, 149
David 327, 404–406, 409
house of 408
in Qur'an 325
da'wa 16, 348
Deedat, Ahmed 272
defense mechanisms 340
dehumanize 83, 84, 195, 385
Deik, Anton 52, 74
demonic(?) 202, 214, 216, 304, 398, 423, 430–433, 435, 436, 447, 463, 464, 466
oppression 437
demonization 5, 22, 134, 217, 385, 430, 446, 447, 450
Dharamraj, Havilah 42, 98
dhimmitude 22
Diab, Issa 217, 455
dialogue 27, 30, 98, 132, 196, 201, 209, 216, 259, 276, 363, 367
artifical dichotomy with evangelism 128
Christian-Muslim 125, 128–130, 206, 242, 305, 331, 333
Christian–Muslim 24, 27
dialogical spectrum 26, 27
legitimacy of 24
dīn 177, 347
discipleship xv, 3, 93, 115, 206, 217, 241, 278, 290, 307, 364, 366, 432

complexities of 202, 277, 388
essence of 197
ministry of 192, 194, 206, 257, 286, 305, 307, 458
primacy of 455
Dozeman, B. Thomas 44
Druze 20–22, 31, 63, 69, 356, 367
Durkheim, Émile 90, 91
Dyrness, William 199

E

ecclesiology 19, 36, 446
practical outworking 356
Ekener, Senem 273, 282, 456, 457
Elijah 107, 330, 378, 408
in Qur'an 247
Elisha 40–42, 321, 330
empire 17, 379, 441
fusion with religion 26, 379
enemy 133, 361, 362, 379
attitude toward 40
blessing of 38, 378, 450
love of xv, 66, 361, 362, 367, 385, 462
who is? 34
Enlightenment 111, 115, 192, 420
epistemology 198
Esau 49, 378
eschatology 147, 382, 383, 389, 402, 403
Islamic 319
ethnocentrism 80, 428
ethnography 89, 431, 433
Eusebius 151
exclusivism 343
exegesis 288, 320, 429
actual v public meaning 103
classical Muslim 288, 296, 297, 300, 305
NT of OT 320
of Qur'an 245, 288, 297, 301
Exum, Cheryl 44, 45, 47

F

familial terms. *See* translation

Farah, Warrick 108, 189, 430, 444, 454, 466
Fedeli, Alba 227
fiṭra 346, 350–352, 354, 446
  definition 346
forgiveness 106, 254, 283, 284, 336, 337, 361, 362, 369, 381, 398, 404
  need for 345
  of sins 315
  seeking from Jesus 336
Francis, Saint 399
Frymer-Kensky, Tikvah 50
Fung, Ronald Y. K. 261, 262
furqān 163, 218

G

Gadamer, Hans Georg 244
Gandhi, Mahatma 95
Gendi, Amal 215
Ghana 31, 32, 96, 97
Glaser, Ida 66, 243, 323, 367, 444, 459, 462
Gnosticism 209
golden calf 106, 326
Goldziher, Ignaz 173, 180, 181, 183
Görke, Andreas 182
Green, Tim 91
Guercino 45

H

Habiby, Nabil 400, 464
Haddad, Elie 397
Hadith 25, 110, 174, 178, 179, 182, 194, 196, 221, 222, 225, 286, 288, 289, 304, 382, 434
  collections of 179
  confidence of 180
  definition of 179
  development of 182
  Islamic critique 205
  isnād-matn system 179
  polemic use 331
  scholarship 183
  source for 181
  study of 181
  transmission of 179
  use of 183
Ḥafṣa 223, 226
  Muṣḥaf of 223, 224
Hagar 42–45, 47–51, 77, 100–103, 105, 151, 152, 270, 327, 450
  allegorical 152, 261, 266, 269, 271
  in Qur'an 101
  sons of 151
haggadah 368–373, 375, 376, 380–383
  northern Kingdom 329
  rewritten in Islam 378
hajj 204, 337
halakhah 368–377, 379–381
  much retained in Islam 378
Haleem, Muhammad Abdel 243, 246, 260
Handmaid's Tale, The 100
Hani, Chaden 338
ḥanīf 153
Hashemi, Nader 95
hermeneutics 184, 199, 244, 255, 259, 263, 266, 268, 271, 300, 355, 431
  behind, of, in front 67, 243
  classical Muslim 288, 297
  gospel centered 322
  leap 342, 347, 351, 352
  missional 114
  Muhammad 265
  practicalities 272
  Qur'an 241, 256, 299
  Qur'an by the Qur'an 246
  religion and culture 199, 365
Herzl, Theodor 83
Hick, John 259
Hiebert, Paul 197, 198, 363, 427
Hijaz 175, 178, 285, 320
  script of 228, 229
hijra 228, 286, 299–301
historical-critical scholarship 184, 265, 299
historiography 101, 187

Holton, Kyle 192
hybridity 192, 417, 450

I
Ibn Abbas 298
Ibn al-Ḥajjāj 221
Ibn Hishām (d. 808) 178
Ibn Isḥāq 178, 179
Ibn Kathīr 226
Ibn Masʿūd 224–226
  Muṣḥaf of 224
Ibrahim, Ayman 308
idealization 5, 23, 186, 447, 450
  of Muhammad 311, 458
identity 14, 33, 44, 47, 91, 96, 97, 113, 151, 177, 344, 345, 364, 385, 420, 421, 424, 450
  assigned 100
  a Turk is a Muslim 273
  converts 190, 307
  group 91
  Islamic 371
  Israel 45, 47
  Muslim 344, 353, 431
  Muslim–Christian duality 31
  religious 21, 29, 91, 114, 160, 202, 273, 302, 342, 343, 345, 357, 359, 383
idolatry 58, 61, 65, 114–116, 193, 199, 200, 209
  challenging 311
  forms of 115, 436
  golden calf 106, 326
  humans as participants 435
  led into 314
  spiritual impurity 441
  topic of engagement 114, 437
  wrath of God toward 59
Imāmiyya, Shiʿite 223
īmān 154, 346, 368
imperialism. *See* colonialism
inclusivism 343
India 98
inimitability, doctrine of 265
Insider Movement 23, 125, 126, 130

inspiration 264
Isaac 44, 45, 48–51, 99, 136, 152, 325–328, 378
Ishmael 44–46, 48–51, 151, 152, 172, 250, 252, 270, 325, 326, 332, 378, 386, 444
  Arabs as descendants 327
  identified with Kaʿba 328
  in Qur'an 152, 332
  linkage to Arabs 332
  visited by Abraham in Arabia 327
Ishmaelites 45, 47, 50, 149, 151
ISIS 14, 22
Islam
  Abraham 81
  abrogative 297
  best version of Jesus's message 23
  derived from Judaism and Christianity 207
  developed alongside Judaism 380
  diversity of 5, 297, 340, 436
  examples of occult practices 434
  five pillars of 433
  folk 433
  meaning making 202
  Meccan 298, 299
  parallels with Samaria 329
  seen as a form of Judaism 170, 205
  shaped by Muslims 435
  view of 29
Islamicists 132, 196
isnād 179–182
isnād-matn. *See* Hadith
Israel 44, 46, 47, 50, 67, 152, 161, 199, 312–314, 326, 377–379, 383
  defined against neighbors 45
  God of 318
  God's dealings with 147
  in Qur'an 106, 291, 333
  reprises Hagar 50
  state of 15, 397
  State of 75, 78, 84
  universalize 325, 332
Isrāʾīliyyāt 219

J

Jauss, Hans Robert 244
Jeffery, Arthur 227
Jeffrey, Arthur 225
Jeroboam 138, 329, 330, 378
Jerusalem 34, 137, 145, 175, 197, 286, 317, 326, 380, 444
  Davidic covenant 326
  destruction in AD 70 19, 379, 381
  East 75
  fight over 171, 379, 380
  Islamic conquest 379
  Jesus in 212, 316, 404, 409
  site of akedah 327
  site of Jesus's exodus 107
jihad, reaction to the word 439
jinn 420, 426, 434
jizya 22
Johns, A. H. 249, 250
John the Baptist 309, 315, 318, 319, 322, 398
  in Qur'an 311, 315, 319
  last prophet 162
Jonah 11, 12, 22, 241, 244, 245, 276, 278, 312, 450
  in Qur'an 245, 247–255
  in Qurкn 246
  model for Muhammad 251
  response to mercy 133
Jonah Syndrome xvii, 13, 36
Josephus 327
Judaism 51, 69, 81, 106, 166, 169, 170, 383, 388
  contrast with Islam 156, 323, 326, 376, 378, 382
  how viewed by Christians 261
  influence on Jewish Christians 79
  influence on Muhammad 324
  Islam's view of replacing it 301
  Jerusalem 380
  Muhammad's view of 290
  place of law keeping 34
  post destruction of the temple 372, 379
  rabbinic 369–371, 380
  reaction to Jesus 282
  within Christian worldview 368
Judeo-Christian 69, 152, 172, 286
  in Qur'an 289, 291, 293, 331, 333
  Muhammad 290, 302–304, 331

K

Kaemingk, Matthew 18
Kairos Palestine document 79
Kaltner, John 242
Kaskas, Safi 293, 298, 299
Ka'ba 152, 157, 327, 328, 332, 433, 444
  built by Abraham 327
Kenya 414, 416, 419
kerygmatic approach 1–3, 5, 24, 29, 286, 304, 333, 430, 449
  avoids 303
  definition of 25
  in dialogue 305
  in practice 27, 445
Khalil, Mohammad Hassan 345
Koloska, Hannelies 249, 253
Kraft, Charles 191, 197, 198
kufr 346

L

Lausanne Covenant 257
Lebanese civil war 35, 397
Lewis, C. S. 282
liminality 43, 46, 192
Lingel, Joshua 194, 200
Lingenfelter, Sherwood 190
Lodahl, Michael 242
Luther, Martin 46

M

Marduk, temple to 71
Marx, Karl 90
Mary 277
  in Qur'an 311
Massad, Alexander (Alex) 341, 373, 444, 461
matn 179. *See also* Hadith
Mattar, Michel and Janane 397, 464

Mbiti, John 97, 427
McCallum, Richard 13, 87
Mecca 152, 175, 197, 220, 248, 285,
    286, 288, 379
  flight from 152
  home of Ishmael and Hagar 327
  pilgrimage to 433
  replacing Jerusalem 326–328, 332
Mecca-Medina schema 218, 289, 297,
    299–301, 328
  Meccan universalism 297
  Medinan temporality 297
  not assumed 288
  unnecessary 303
Medina 175, 220, 225, 288, 298, 327,
    379
  Constitution of 177
  Muhammad's flight to 152
  originally Yathrib 285
Meeks, Wayne 359
Melchert, Christopher 183
Midrash 302
missiology 19, 108, 117, 130, 184–
    186, 199, 206, 308, 445
Moabites 45, 379
  line of Messiah 378
Mormons 308
Morocco 203–205
Morton, Jeff 190, 193
Moses 107, 118, 136, 137, 162, 256,
    285, 314, 315, 326, 327, 374,
    378, 390
  cf. Muhammad 306
  in Qur'an 82, 107, 247, 252, 253,
    291, 325, 326, 347
  Jesus greater than 372
  law of 62, 317
  succeeded by Jesus 137
Motzki, Harald 182
mufassirūn 245
Muhammad 152, 155, 162, 187, 202,
    217, 240, 248, 250, 252, 289,
    296, 301, 309, 346, 348, 349
  Apostle of Islam 223
  archaeological silence 176

  biographical 178, 179, 182, 183
  cf. biblical prophets 162
  cf. Elijah 107
  cf. Jeroboam 378
  cf. Jonah 248, 249, 251, 252
  cf. Moses 107, 306
  Christian influence on 163, 164, 168
  companion Ibn Abbas 298
  companion Ibn Masʿūd 224
  companions of 159, 179, 180, 218,
    219, 221, 226, 228
  companion ʿUmar Ibn al-Khaṭṭāb
    222
  early life 159, 160, 163
  exclusive truth claims 295
  faith community belonged to 302
  Hadith 179, 183
  hijra 286, 300
  identity 286, 300, 303
  in Qur'an 177
  intention 290, 291, 301, 324, 325,
    329
  Jewish followers 169
  Jewish influence of 171
  Jews and Christians 292–296
  Judeo-Christian 302, 304
  key to Islam 194
  living Qur'an 265
  miracles 166
  no biography 178
  of faith 285, 286, 290, 304, 305,
    370, 457
  of history 184, 286–290, 299,
    303–305, 457
  origin of Qur'an 217, 218, 220, 221,
    228, 240, 265
  OT prophecy 259
  outside of covenant history 329
  prophethood 153, 162, 164, 309–
    311, 317, 319, 321, 322, 328,
    371
  prophet of Islam 220, 308
  rejection of 252, 311
  relating with Jews 177
  religious teaching 160

reviver of Abrahamic monotheism 164
salvation 115
seal of the Prophets 259
social reformer 328, 385
traditional Islamic 305
traditions attributed to 181
view of 26, 143, 158, 160, 161, 165, 170, 172, 173, 187, 206, 240, 306–308, 322, 324, 329–331, 376, 379, 444, 463
Muir, William 180
Muṣḥaf 217, 224
Muslim Brotherhood 28, 384

N

Naaman, the Syrian 37–42, 86, 133, 321, 450
Nakba 75, 78
Naksa 75, 78
narrative criticism 400
naskh 258, 299
neocolonialism. *See* colonialism
Neuwirth, Angelika 255
Newbigin, Lesslie 365, 426
Nicene Creed 131
Nicodemus 138, 212, 213, 386, 390, 454, 463
Niebuhr, Richard 189, 201
Nigeria 425
Nikides, Bill 193
Noah 70, 72–74, 85, 451
in Qur'an 247, 250, 252, 253
Nöldeke 227

O

Okullu, Henry, Bishop 421
orthopathic responses 119, 452
Oseje, Lawrence 414, 465

P

paganism 146, 154
neopaganism 429
Pappe, Ilan 75

peacebuilding 19, 27, 97, 98, 290, 305, 307, 449, 450
Pennington, Perry 322
people, power and land 71, 380, 444
Persia 143, 147, 149, 152, 228, 260
Persian-Byzantine war 146
Pew Forum 15, 94
Pharisee 107, 136, 283, 336
phenomenology 184–188
place of worship 56, 68, 136, 139, 444
in Jerusalem 157
Islam 332
Jeroboam 329
Jesus 137
Jews 136
pluralism 343
polemics 290, 291, 303, 304, 307, 450
in Qur'an 293, 294, 296
moratorium on 305
why unscientific 287, 305, 331, 457
Porter, Grant 273, 356, 462, 463, 465
prophethood 161–163, 165, 166, 250, 254, 259, 301, 308, 309, 318, 329
biblical and quar'anic views 317, 322
covenantal integrity 313
in Islam 132
Israel as locus of 326
prophetology 115, 437
prophets 89, 136, 147, 161, 162, 177, 219, 240, 245, 246, 248, 252, 256, 259, 264, 285, 289, 303, 309, 312, 314, 315, 317, 323, 325, 326, 329, 330
in Qur'an 241, 247, 248, 250, 253, 254, 310, 311, 321, 328
Jesus 137, 138
miracles 282
NT 316
psychology 46, 89, 98, 119

Q

qibla 137, 156, 286, 327, 328
definition of 170

Jewish 286
Qur'an 164, 196, 217, 241, 244, 246, 253, 266, 267, 271, 286, 287, 306, 342
  abrogation 219
  claims for itself 240, 263, 310
  composition of 163, 263
  consists of 218
  contents 219, 289, 309, 326, 345, 370, 381, 434
  direction of influence 99
  doctrinal differences 168
  duality 288, 291, 294, 296, 297, 299, 301, 303
  history 227, 228, 240
  human condition 446
  Jesus 382
  Jews and Christians 293, 294, 296
  meaning of term 218
  Meccan message 297
  methods 246
  Muhammad 286, 288, 289, 300, 302, 324
  Muhammad's miracle 166
  origin 174, 177, 178, 187, 217, 219–226, 257, 265, 304, 433
  polemics 294
  prophets 241, 253, 254, 256, 289, 308, 309, 311, 320, 328
  role of 194
  salvation 353
  textual criticism 227
  theology of 455
  Torah, *Injil* 258
  use of 216
  view of 26, 143, 154, 165–167, 169, 170, 172, 173, 206, 240, 241, 259, 266, 272, 276, 278, 305–307, 323, 331, 444, 447
  war only in self-defense 296

R
Ramayana 101–104
Rāshidīn Caliphs 224, 240
reception history 244, 245

Reisacher, Evelyne 439
Restorationism 85
Reynolds 319
Riḍā, Rashīd 342, 346–355, 461
Rightly-Guided Caliphs. *See* Rāshidīn Caliphs
Robinson, Martin 426
Royal Aal al-Bayt Institute, Amman, Jordan 128
Ruth 359, 379, 420
Ruth Syndrome 420

S
Sabean 294
Sahin, Abdullah 93
Said, Edward 109
Salam, Abdallah b. 168
ṣalāt 196, 432, 433
salvation 339, 369, 377, 382, 383
  assurance 339
  biblical history 310
  definition 389
  God dwelling with his people 326
  God's priority 74
  in Judaism 34
  in multi faiths 294
  in Shi'a Islam 340
  key human need addressed 446
  of Samaritans 137
  seeking 337
  universal need 380
Samaritans 135, 137, 312, 378
  parallels with Muslims 329
  the Good Samaritan 35, 424, 450
  woman at the well 135, 452
Ṣanʿāʾ Manuscript 227
Ṣanʿāʾ Manuscripts 229, 240
Sarah 42–45, 47, 50, 51, 78, 152
  allegorical 152, 261, 266, 269, 271
Sassanian Empire 144
Schacht, Joseph 181, 182
Schoeler, Gregor 182
secularism 69, 88, 94
SEKAP spectrum. *See* kerygmatic approach

shahāda 433, 460
Shah, Zulfiqar Ali 318
Sharīʿa 18, 91, 298, 371, 377, 379, 381
  commonality & difference with Judaism 371
Shaw, Karen 37, 61, 117, 134, 452
shekinah 106–108
  missing in Qur'an 326
Siddiqui, Mona 341, 344
ṣidq al-īmān 347
Sinai, Nicolai 299
Sira 174, 178, 183, 288, 304
Smith, Joseph 308
sociology 13, 89–92
  of religions 112
  socio-cultural 31, 33, 96–98, 288, 414
  socio-economic 17
  socio-political 96, 158, 194, 290, 327, 328, 368, 379, 418, 426
  socio-religious 190, 202, 254, 435
Sophronios, Chalcedonian Patriarch of Jerusalem 145
soteriology 19, 36, 132, 342, 380, 446
  exclusivism 343, 380
  inclusivism 343, 380
  Islamic 342, 345, 346, 347, 352–354
  Riḍā's 342
Sozomen, Greek historian 151, 328
Span, John 127
spiritual oppression, dual causation 437
spirit world 418
Sprenger, Aloys 180
Stott, John 58, 59
Sufism 297, 434
sumasum 97
sword verse 296
syncretism 116, 192, 198, 303, 422, 429
  why inadequate 287
systematics 259

T
tabernacle 106, 326, 372
  Qur'an omits 106, 326
tafsīr 260, 263, 269, 272, 288, 347, 349
Taha, Mahmoud Mohammed 297, 299
taḥrīf 136, 137
takbeer 281
Talman, Harley 308, 309, 313, 317, 319, 321, 459
tawhid 318
Tennent, Timothy 190, 191
textual criticism 227, 240, 264
Theology of Religions 67
transcendence 333
transfiguration 107
translation 3
  Bible 24, 126–128, 203
  Muslim-friendly Bible 23, 125, 130
  Qur'an 220, 260, 266, 293, 298
  Smith-Van Dyck-Boustani 126
  True Meaning Bible 126
Turkey 15, 92, 273–275, 308
  becoming more Islamic 92
typology 241, 255, 256, 269

U
Ubayy b. Kaʿb 225
  Muṣḥaf of 225
Uganda 425
Umar I, mosque of 157, 159, 171
Umayyad 178
umma 91, 110, 225, 286, 370, 378, 420
  including Jews 177
  righteous and God fearing 177
unreached
  by Islam 349

V
Vanhoozer, Kevin 312
Verstehen movement 90
Volf, Miroslav 129

W

waḥī (inspiration) 220
  scribes 221
Waldman, Marilyn 242
Wali, Dr 228
Wallace, Daniel B. 405
Walls, Andrew 113
Wansbrough, John 174
Waraqa b. Nawfal 153, 220
Watson, Francis 320
Weber, Max 90
West Bank 75
Wright, Christopher 435

Y

Yahya. *See* John the Baptist
Yamama, battle of 221, 222
Yathrib. *See* Medina
yawm al-ḥisāb 345
yawm al-qiyāma 345
Yip, George 111
Yousif, Ashoor 143, 378, 444, 453
Yūnus. *See* Jonah

Z

Zabūr 258
Zacchaeus 356
Zacharia, Ravi 273
Zaki, Gamal 384, 463
Zayd b. Thābit 222, 226
Zieneldien, Abed 34
Zionism 75, 77, 83, 84, 451
  Christian 74, 76–80, 84, 85, 380

Bible Index

OLD TESTAMENT

Genesis
1–11 67
1:26–27 118
1:28 71
1:29 71
2:18 420
2:23 118
3:1–12:3 85
4:7 73
6:6 391
11:1–9 70
12:1–3 85
12:10–20 51
16 42
16:10–12 378
17:20–26 378
17:23–26 44
19:30–38 45
21 43
21:9–21 152
21:13 378
22 327
22:8 316
25:1 51
27 378
30:1 43
30:3 100
30:14 43
31:19 82
33:9 378
41:45 82

Exodus
2:23–25 106
3:14 376
19:16 106
20:17 136
34:33–35 118

40:34–38 106

Leveticus
11 34
19:2 377
19:3–37 377
19:18 377
20:7–26 377

Numbers
6:25 118
12:10 38
24:2 314
31:8 314

Deuteronomy
2:4–5 378
2:9 379
2:19 379
18:18 .... 137, 162
23:7–8 378
23:3–6 379
29:18–28 375
30:1 375
30:11–14 .... 374, 375

Joshua
5:13–14 82

Judges
8:24 50

Ruth
1:16–17 420
4:21–22 379

1 Samuel
1:1–10 43

10:10–13 313
19:20–24 314

1 Kings
14:31 379
18:16–45 133
18:19 .... 313, 330
21:1–16 133

2 Kings
5:1–4 321
5:1–29 37
13:23 330
14:27 330
17:26 137

1 Chronicles
1–9 71
1:28 51
25:1–3 312

2 Chronicles
7:1 107
12:13 379
26:20 38
29:25–30 317
36:15–16 317

Ezra
6:16 107

Psalms
1:5 371
33:16 395
51:4 283
83:6 50
118:26 316
147:10 395

Ecclesiastes
3:11 89

Isaiah
6 313
11:1–9 316
21:7 162
40:1–11 315
40:31 396
42:1–9 316
44:3 402
45:22 118
53:6–7 316
59:20–21 316
61:1–11 316
62:4–5 316

Jeremiah
23:22 313
23:26 313
23:30–32 313
27:9 313

Ezekiel
1 313
10:18 107
39:29 402

Hosea 330
6:6 35

Joel
2:25 396
2:28 402

2:30 316

Amos
3:2 312

Jonah
1:9 12
4 11
4:2 12
4:6–11 12
4:11 12

Micah
5:2 316

Malachi
3:1 .... 315, 316
4:1–3 316

NEW TESTAMENT

Matthew
1:1–17 71
1:5–6 379
3:7–9 79
3:7–12 319
5:9 305
5:17–20 373
7:5 109
7:12 202
11:9–13 315
16:18 20
16:23 134
17:1–13 107
21:33–46 316
22:41–46 320
23:34 316
28:20 137

Mark
1:7–8 402
1:9–11 402
1:10 405
1:12–13 403
1:22 408

1:23–26 408
1:37 409
2:1–12 282
2:4 409
2:13–14 409
3:20–35 404
3:29 404
4:11–12 409
5:4 408
5:40 409
6:7–13 407
7:17–30 409
7:24–30 409
8:33 134
8:34–38 409
9:2–13 107
9:14–29 407
9:17 408
9:24–28 409
9:26 409
10:21 409
10:46–52 409
10:48 409
11:1–25 409

11:18 404
12:36 404
13:9–13 404
13:11 413
15:9–13 409

Luke
2:13–14 98
3:16 316
3:17 316
4:20–29 40
5:17–26 282
7:36–50 336
9:28–36 107
10:25–37 34
10:37 34
19:9 356
24:25 316
24:25–49 322

John
1:15 316
1:29 316
1:32 316

2:23–24 212	**Romans**	2:2 116
3:29 316	1:1–4 321	3:16–17 317
3:30 398	1:5 373	9:19–23 116
4:4–42 135	1:16–17 372	9:21 317
4:22 312	1:18–23 353	9:22 ....62, 66
6:1–15 395	1:18–23 354	12:3 316
8:36 441	1:18–32 ....114, 436	13:5 59
8:56–58 320	1:20 ....64, 321	13:12 xvi
11:44–52...........................314	2:1 62	15:22 63
14:2 386	2:11....................................62	
16:7 162	2:12–14 373	**2 Corinthians**
18:36 379	2:14–15 64	2:11....................................448
19:38–39 213	2:17–20 62	3:13 118
	2:21–27 62	3:18–4:1 118
Acts	3:1–2, 9 64	4:4 61
1:3 322	3:2 312	4:6–7 119
1:8 117	3:9–10 62	4:7 66
2:1–36 314	3:18–20 62	6:14–17 438
3:24 316	3:22 ....62, 63	6:14–18 116
5:38–39 428	3:22–23 114	11:23–27............................62
6:8–7:60 54	3:23 62	12:9 66
10.......................................79	3:31 373	
10:28 80	5:10 61	**Galatians**
10:34–35 ....80, 81	5:16–17 63	1:6–9 63
11:14.................................321	8:1–13 374	2:11–21 82
12:1–4 52	8:38–39 373	3:2 108
12:21–22 52	9:1–3 62	3:26–28 108
14:15–17 316	9:12–13 378	3:28 62
14:16–17 441	10:4 374	4..261
14:17 ....64, 321	10:4–5 64	4:21–31 ....152, 269
15.......................................201	10:5–10 374	6:10 66
17:6–9 52	10:12 ....62, 65	6:13–14 64
17:7 96	11..370	
17:16–34 52	11:17–18............................64	**Ephesians**
17:23 322	11:28.............................61, 62	2:1 ....61, 63
17:24–31 316	11:30..................................61	2:1–3 436
17:26 432	11:32............................62, 65	2:2 61
17:27–29 65	12:17–21 66	2:3 ....61, 63
17:28 64	13:1–7 66	2:8–9 64
17:30 ....61, 317	15:18 373	2:12 61
18:25–26 317	16:26 373	2:19–22 317
19:1–10 317		2:20–22 315
19:37 62	**1 Corinthians**	3:4–10 316
21:27–22:21 54	1:19–20 61	4:11....................................315
24:1–23 54	1:28–29 64	6:10–18 398

6:12 12

Philippians
3:7–8 63

Colossians
2:8 61
2:9 139
2:18 61
3:11 62
4:6 66

1 Thessalonians
2:7 62
2:14–16 62

1 Timothy
1:4 320
1:13, 15 63
2:4–6 65
4:1–3 315
4:7 320

2 Timothy
3:16 245
4:16 1

Titus
1:12 314
1:14 320
2:11 65
3:1–2 66
3:3 61

Hebrews
1:1–2 .... 312, 316
1:1–3 245
2:3–4 312
4:1–10 372
7–8 381
7:11–22 372
10:19–11:40 372
11:17–19 48
12:1–2 372
13:14 379

1 Peter
1:10–12 .... 312, 316
3:15 28

2 Peter
2:1 315
2:1, 16 314
3:1–2 315
3:2 312
3:9 354

1 John
4:1–6 315

Jude
3 315

Revelation
19:10 321
21:9–22:5 317
22:4 118

Qur'an Index

al-Baqara
2:23 166
2:48 319
2:61 347
2:62 .... 294, 347, 349
2:67–71 326
2:107 299
2:111 169
2:113 295
2:120 293
2:124 325
2:185 310
2:190 296
2:190–193 298
2:193 296

Āl-ʿImrān
3:3–4 291
3:19 347
3:39 311
3:49 382
3:67 153
3:161 226

an-Nisā
4:48 311
4:115 .... 347, 350, 351
4:116 311
4:155–159 382
4:157 319
4:171 .... 164, 320, 382

al-Māʾida
5:18 295
5:27–31 70
5:47 293
5:51 294
5:66 293
5:68 292
5:69 .... 294, 347
5:72–75 320
5:82 292
5:83 292

al-Anʿām
6:10 311
6:74 260
6:78–84 311
6:84–86 311
6:109 162
6:161 311
6:164 319

al-Aʿrāf
7:143 107
7:148–154 326
7:157–158 166

al-Anfāl
8:1 .... 218, 328

at-Tawba
9:29 .... 296, 473
9:29–30 298
9:30 297

Yūnus
10:47 310
10:98 .... 245, 252

Hūd
11:120 256

Yūsuf
12:111 256

Ibrāhīm
14:39 152

al-Ḥijr
15:9 240

an-Naḥl
16:36 310
16:103 263

al-Isrā
17:15 319
17:59 162
17:88 166
17:107–109 293

Maryam
19:12–14 311

Ṭā Hā
20:85–97 326

al-Anbiyāʾ
21:87–88 .... 245, 249

al-Ḥajj
22:17 296

ash-Shuʿarāʾ
26:192–197 291
26:195 263

al-ʿAnkabūt
29:46 295

Luqmān
31:13 311

al-Aḥzāb
33:40 310

Sabà
34:22 311

aṣ-Ṣāffāt
37:12–17 246
37:139–148 245–247
37:144 251

az-Zumar
39:65 311
39:69 310

al-Aḥqāf
46:12 291

al-Ḥadīd
57:27 382

al-Ḥashr
59:21 166

al-Jumuʿa
62:5 293

al-Qalam
68:43–52 248
68:48 251
68:48–50 245

al-Insān
76:23 218

al-Masad
111:1–5 218

Langham

Langham Literature and its imprints are a ministry of Langham Partnership.

Langham Partnership is a global fellowship working in pursuit of the vision God entrusted to its founder John Stott –

to facilitate the growth of the church in maturity and Christ-likeness through raising the standards of biblical preaching and teaching.

Our vision is to see churches in the Majority World equipped for mission and growing to maturity in Christ through the ministry of pastors and leaders who believe, teach and live by the word of God.

Our mission is to strengthen the ministry of the word of God through:
- nurturing national movements for biblical preaching
- fostering the creation and distribution of evangelical literature
- enhancing evangelical theological education

especially in countries where churches are under-resourced.

Our ministry

Langham Preaching partners with national leaders to nurture indigenous biblical preaching movements for pastors and lay preachers all around the world. With the support of a team of trainers from many countries, a multi-level programme of seminars provides practical training, and is followed by a programme for training local facilitators. Local preachers' groups and national and regional networks ensure continuity and ongoing development, seeking to build vigorous movements committed to Bible exposition.

Langham Literature provides Majority World preachers, scholars and seminary libraries with evangelical books and electronic resources through publishing and distribution, grants and discounts. The programme also fosters the creation of indigenous evangelical books in many languages, through writer's grants, strengthening local evangelical publishing houses, and investment in major regional literature projects, such as one volume Bible commentaries like *The Africa Bible Commentary* and *The South Asia Bible Commentary*.

Langham Scholars provides financial support for evangelical doctoral students from the Majority World so that, when they return home, they may train pastors and other Christian leaders with sound, biblical and theological teaching. This programme equips those who equip others. Langham Scholars also works in partnership with Majority World seminaries in strengthening evangelical theological education. A growing number of Langham Scholars study in high quality doctoral programmes in the Majority World itself. As well as teaching the next generation of pastors, graduated Langham Scholars exercise significant influence through their writing and leadership.

To learn more about Langham Partnership and the work we do visit **langham.org**